# The Best
# of
# Online
# Shopping

# The Best of Online Shopping

## The Prices' Guide to Fast and Easy Shopping on the Web

Lisa and Jonathan Price

Ballantine Books • New York

A Ballantine Book
Published by The Ballantine Publishing Group

www.randomhouse.com/BB/

Library of Congress Cataloging-in-Publication Data

Price, Lisa, 1952-
The best of online shopping: the Prices' guide to fast and easy shopping on the Web / by Lisa Price and Jonathan Price. —1st ed.
p. cm.
Includes index.
ISBN: 0-345-43681-4 (trade: alk. paper)
1. Teleshopping Guidebooks. 2. Shopping—Computer network resources Guidebooks. 3. Consumer education Guidebooks. I. Price, Jonathan, 1941- II. Title.
TX335.P72 1999
381.1'0285467—dc21   99-32180

Cover design by Barbara Leff

Manufactured in the United States of America

First Edition: October 1999
10 9 8 7 6 5 4 3 2 1

# Contents

# Acknowledgments

We've wanted to write this book for a long time. We saw the benefits of online shopping, we enjoyed it, and we wanted to share our experiences with others. That's where our first two thanks come in. One is to our wonderful agent, Al Zuckerman of Writer's House, who, even though he rarely explores the Web, saw the value of our book at once and quickly went about placing it with a good publishing house. Our other mega-thanks goes to our fabulous editor at Ballantine, Susan Randol. Susan "got it" at once and shared our vision of writing a book that would help busy folks find what they want fast, at reputable stores on the Web. Her professionalism, open-mindedness and cheerfulness were a constant source of encouragement to us, especially as our deadline was looming on the horizon.

Being on the Web literally for ten to twelve hours at a stretch, researching this book required a lot of technical expertise. We'd like to thank our dear friend, Joyce Daza, of Advanced Technology Consulting (LLC) in Albuquerque, for redesigning our phone system. She thought of solutions that even our local phone company was at a loss to devise.

We'd also like to thank Gateway Computer. We knew we needed a new computer to handle this job. We ordered a Gateway, which unfortunately arrived without a zip drive. Gateway sent a REAL LIVE PERSON to our home the next day to install the drive. Between Joyce Daza and Gateway, we were able to proceed quickly and efficiently.

And, speaking about efficiency, we'd like to send a big thank-you to Fay Greenfield of Writer's House. Fay believed in the book from the moment she read the proposal. She spent hours making sure it was delivered into the right hands and even went the extra mile of talking the book up to people who might be interested in it. Fay is another one of those wonderfully enthusiastic, lively people we kept coming in contact with as we developed this book.

To help our perspective, we asked some experts what they thought about online shopping. You'll read their comments in the book, but we'd like to say right here that we appreciate the time they took to look at the appropriate chapters. So, thanks Stevanne Auerbach, Ann Douglas, and Leah Ingram.

On a very personal note, we want to thank, with hugs and kisses, our two precious sons, Ben and Noah. Having one's parents chained to their computers for three months isn't exactly a lot of fun (except for all the fast-food dinners). Ben and Noah handled it beautifully. Both of them helped us at various times, checking URLs, critiquing stores aimed at teenagers, and doing research for us. They even insisted that we go "on a date" one night. They "forced" us to eat out and go to a movie. When we arrived home from eating sushi and watching *Shakespeare in Love*, we found that not only had Ben and Noah devoured a whole box of pizza that we'd had delivered, but they had also totally cleaned the house. We love you guys. (And, no, these kids are not for sale online.)

—Lisa and Jonathan Price

# Welcome

# Attention, Online Shoppers!

**Welcome!**

Web stores are transforming the way we shop. Online sales seem poised to bring about as big a transformation to the retail business as mail-order catalogs and department stores did, because of the rapid growth of Web sales. A Harvard historian, Nancy Koehn, expects that Web stores will outsell mail-order catalogs within three years.

**Why folks like to shop online**

Why do people shop the Web?  Recent surveys show we're all getting cozy with the concept.  Consider that:

- You can shop after-hours.  A lot of people do.  The latest figures from America Online, for instance, reveal that 40% of electronic shopping takes place between 10 P.M. and 10 A.M., when most physical stores are closed.

- You don't have to venture out of your cocoon to buy.

- You save time.  You can browse a half-dozen virtual stores in less time than it takes to park at a busy mall on a weekend.

- You save headaches and foot pain.  No sweat. You can shop in your pajamas, and you don't have to carry any packages down the miles of mall corridors, and across the hundred-acre parking lot. Services like FedEx and UPS bring your goodies to your door within a day or two.

- Your neighbors are doing it, too.  Forty-eight million of us use the Web regularly now according to New CommerceNet/Nielsen Media Research, which claims that repeat Web shoppers have reached a critical mass, at which they begin to influence each other.

- Even grandparents are getting into the habit, when shopping for their grandchildren (10% of grandparents who browse for toys and kids' software make a purchase—a phenomenal percentage for a group normally thought to be averse to computers).

- Books, flowers, clothing, beverages, travel, and autos are the categories pulling people beyond the original focus, which was computer equipment and software. The mix of shopping is beginning to approximate the discretionary spending patterns of the population as a whole.

- You also save money, because you can shop around and settle on the best deal without getting waylaid by salespeople or crowds. Forty-five percent of Web shoppers said they were saving money by going online, according to a survey by Ernst & Young for the National Retail Federation. How is this possible? Because electronic stores do not need to pay rent for showrooms, hire salesclerks, or, in some cases, run a warehouse, they can keep their costs 20% to 45% lower than a physical store, while increasing revenue by 10% to 20%, according to Andersen Consulting.

- You get what you want, because in many stores all sizes are available, and more products appear online than on the shelves of an average department store. For combination products like computer hardware, you can put together your own configuration, rather than having to accept the version on the store shelf.

## The trend is up!

People are pouring into the online stores. Eighty-one percent of Web users plan to shop online during 1999, and, given the amounts they intend to spend, Intelliquest estimates that annual revenues will triple for these stores. By 2003, consumers may be spending $108 billion shopping online, while businesses will be shelling out $1.3 trillion, according to estimates by Forrester Research.

Certainly a booming U.S. economy has accelerated this trend, as have secure online transaction safeguards and endless publicity. But the biggest change is that consumers are starting to feel safe about shopping online, and are coming to regard it as a convenience, like salad bars and delis in supermarkets, or 24-hour ATMs.

## More people are shopping online than ever before

Here are some details on the growth of online shopping:

- Online shopping in 1998 more than doubled from a year before, according to Jupiter Communications, Boston Consulting Group, and Forrester Research.

- More than half of online shoppers are women, according to Media Matrix.

- 77% of buyers go online with a specific purchase in mind, and 79% visit several different shops before making a purchase, according to Cyber Dialogue.

- Revenues **just for holiday shopping** in 1998 soared to $3.14 billion, according to Jupiter.

*Fortune* calculates that the online stores' revenues rose during 1998 by huge percentages:

- 150% in clothing

- 210% in household goods

- 230% in computer hardware and software

- 250% in travel

- 290% in books and music

- 310% in toys

- 340% in gifts.

Stunning increases like these brought the total of consumer sales online in 1998 to more than $13 billion, by conservative estimates (from the Boston Consulting Group). To put that figure in perspective, though, it represents about 1% of total retail sales in the U.S., although, in certain periods, the percentage spiked to 4% (in the spring), and 10% (right after Thanksgiving), according to Marketing Corporation of America.

In addition to purchasing online, people are doing research on the Web, then going to a physical store to buy. Automakers estimate that in the first half of 1998, they sold $10 billion in cars to consumers who chose a dealer on the Web.

**But people still have some trouble shopping online.**

Unhappiness has grown. In mid-1998, only about 12% of online shoppers said they felt dissatisfied. But during the 1998 holiday season, that figure rose to 26% of all online shoppers, according to a survey by Jupiter and NFO Interactive. Asked why, Nicole Vanderbilt, an analyst at Jupiter, said, "They quantified what we suspected, which is that with the unbelievable and, in many ways, unexpected growth in the amount of business online, quality suffered as a result of quantity." Echoing that opinion, a survey of 33,000 online shoppers by BizRate showed that the most unhappy customers were those who ordered between December 4 and December 22, because they experienced delays in delivery from stores that had not anticipated the sudden volume of traffic.

There are a lot of online stores out there, but only a few are well run. The majority are inconvenient for most consumers , because the owners have not put enough effort into informing visitors, helping them around, and making shopping easy. An Internet market analyst, Shelley Taylor, recently surveyed 50 online stores in a cross-section of industries, and came away convinced that many stores make it hard to find products, hard to move from one department to another, hard to find out how to order. About a third of her sample told the consumer almost nothing about the products. Her report at http://www.infofarm.com confirms our own analysis of almost 8,000 sites, most of which we rejected as subpar, or downright annoying. (Our book picks out the best stores, so you can skip the mediocre and crummy sites.)

The biggest hassle for consumers is threading their way through the giant search mechanisms, which yield so many hits that the average person gives up after trying only the first ten or twenty. We remedy this situation by culling out the businesses that we think you will really want to visit. Using our book will help you get over the Alta Vista blues, avoiding 9,999 dud hits and zipping to the right address right away.

But once you reach an average or worse-than-average online store, you still face a lot of challenges:

- The store may not offer a search mechanism to its products.

- There may be no information, or almost none, about how to order, what shipping rates might be, or what the return and privacy policies are.

- There may be skimpy or no information about the products.

- The screen may be hard to read, the pictures are blurry and small, or the pages may take forever to load.

- You can't easily order.

- You can't order at all, because the site turns out to be a catalog or brochure but not a Web store. (Just come on down to our store at the mall in downtown Norfolk.)

- You can order, but the store does not offer secure online ordering.

- You can't tell what the shipping charges are going to be until you have filled out a long order form.

- You don't get a confirmation of your order.

- There is no easy way to contact the store for customer support or order tracking.

The other leading constraint on online shopping is nervousness about using a credit card online. Only 52% of the current shoppers felt completely confident about that, according to a recent Ernst & Young study. We devote some of our Answers to Frequently Asked Questions to security, to show where the problems could lie, to highlight efforts that online merchants have made to secure transactions and to point out that statistically, shopping in a local small business puts you at far greater risk than shopping on the Web.

## Our book guides you to the best stores

No more duds. No more brochures pretending to be stores. No more sleazo discounters. We have gone to **more than 8,000** sites, and rejected most of them. We have picked the best stores, using a tough set of criteria. We favor a store if it offers most of these services:

- The store offers a secure area for ordering, to protect your personal and credit information.

- The store guarantees that it will not pass along your personal information to any other company. Period.

- The site offers a fast and accurate search system.

- The site lets you find products by looking through categories, without having to plunge down, down, down through a lot of levels.

- The store actually sells the items it says it does, and they're easy to locate on the site.

- The product descriptions are rich, with components such as good photos (small and large), lists of features and benefits, pricing, shipping information, manufacturer's name and warranty, samples, suggestions for add-on products, and reviews by critics and customers.

- Prices are easy to determine.

- Prices are low to mid-range, and if the store does not offer serious discounts, there is a reasonable explanation or compensating value on the site (extra information, super service, free shipping).

- The store offers extensive instruction on how to order, how to pick shipping, how to return products.

- The store posts its customer service phone number and email prominently, so you know how to get in touch with them.

- The ordering system is easy to find and use.

- Shipping choices are visible early, on the product description or in the shopping cart before you order.

- Orders are immediately confirmed with a detailed page or email, or both.

- You can opt out of receiving email announcing their sales.

- Return policies are clear and reasonable.

- The layout looks good.

- Navigation is easy.

Of course, not every site in our book manages to do all these things well, but to qualify for our book, a site has to be outstanding in many of these areas.

So, welcome to our book! We hope we can help you find great products online, explore some fascinating sites, discover amazing bargains, and get what you want, fast. Oh, and one other thing: With these stores, we think you're going to have a heck of a lot of fun!

# How to Get the Most Out of This Book

Please make this book your own. Scribble in the margins, highlight favorites, circle stores you might want to visit. We wrote this book for *your* convenience—so you can quickly find an online store that sells just what you want, for less. So here's how to get the most out of this book when you feel like taking an online shopping trip.

## How to find a particular store

You can locate a store three ways:

- If you have no idea what store to shop in, go to the Contents, look up the category that seems like the best fit, and browse through that chapter. You'll find descriptions of the best stores in that category, and the stores' Web addresses.

- If you want to zip right to a particular store, look it up in our list of store addresses in the appendix at the back of the book, get the store's URL (Web address), type that in your browser, and go.

- If you know the name of the Web store, or have a particular product category in mind, look that up in the index, and you'll find out which pages explore stores carrying that kind of product.

## How to pick the best store for you in a chapter

Each chapter offers our picks of the best stores in a particular product category, such as pet supplies or consumer electronics. Here's how to browse a chapter for the store that's right for you:

- If you wonder what a store feels like, or what kind of products it focuses on, start with our **description**. You'll get a sense of the store's atmosphere, size, emphasis, pricing, and shipping.

- Want to window-shop, to see some examples of the products sold at a store?  Skim the list of **sample products** right after the description.

- If you want help finding a product within a big collection, look at **Search** to see if the store offers a way of looking products up with a search mechanism.

- Need to get a picture of the products? Check **Photos**, to see if the store shows you what the products look like.

- Want to know if you can order in different ways? Check **Ordering** to see how to order, whether that's online, or by phone, fax, or email.

- Need a gift pronto?  Check **Gift Wrap** to see if the store will wrap your purchase for you.

- Want to know how fast you can expect to get your purchases? Check **Delivery** to see what shipping options a store offers.

You may very well find several stores that look promising. Just put a check mark next to each name, circle it (remember—it's YOUR book), or, if you don't want to mark up the book yet, just put a yellow sticky next to the description. Then, when you're ready, go online and use the **Web address** (at the top of the description) to browse through the stores you thought most promising.

## How to find a particular service fast

We know that sometimes you need to find something in a hurry and you don't want to do a lot of reading. Maybe you're looking for a store that can send out an item, gift-wrapped and delivered the next day. That's what those little categories are for at the end of each store description. You can skim through every store in the chapter, just checking Delivery, say, or Gift Wrapping, to find which store offers the services you need—and then read the descriptions.

## What those categories at the end of each store description mean

We added these summaries so that you can skim through a chapter looking for a particular service, one that may mean all the difference in the world. For example, if you positively have to have it overnight, you can just look at the Delivery line for every store, to see which stores offer Overnight shipping.

Here are explanations of the services we cover in these summaries.

- **Search:** Most of the good stores have some kind of search mechanism to make locating a product easier and faster. With some stores, a good search is essential, because they carry such a big inventory. With others, it doesn't matter much. But we thought this could be something you might be concerned with, especially if you want to find something fast at a particular store. "Yes" means it does have a search. "No" means it doesn't.

- **Photos:** Personally, we like photos. Seeing a picture of the product helps us make up our minds to buy or skip on by. But sometimes you have already made up your mind exactly what brand and model you want, so you don't care so much about the picture; or you have a slow connection and prefer sites that are mostly text. So we've listed which stores have photos of their inventory and which do not. With a few stores, you'll see that we've written in "Some," meaning that they've put up pictures of some of their products but not all.

- **Ordering:** We thought you'd like to know what your options are. We prefer online ordering. Secure online ordering is the safest method. With a click of the mouse you can select which products you want sent to your home. You don't need to print anything out or use another phone line to call in your order while you look at what's available on the computer screen. (In fact, any store that doesn't offer secure online ordering was eliminated from consideration.) But there may be times when online ordering is inconvenient, or you just don't feel comfortable with it.

1. **Online**—Order immediately, using your credit card.

2. **Phone**—Call in your order using the number the store gives you on its Web site.

3. **Fax**—Print out the order form, fill it in, and then fax it to the store.

4. **Email**—Write out your order and then email the order to the store.

- **Gift Wrap:** If you want to send a gift to someone, this category is very important. That's why we've broken this category down into three answers. This is what they mean:

  1. **No**—The store offers no wrapping services whatsoever.

  2. **Yes**—Your gift will either be wrapped with paper or placed in a gift box with a bow and a card. If wrapping is critical for you, consider the shops that specialize in Gifts or Gift Baskets.

  3. **Card**—The store does not offer gift wrapping, but your present will be sent with a card if you wish. Usually the order form has a space where you can type your personal message for the card. Sometimes, when stores offer this service, they also put a bow on the gift.

- **Delivery**: When you need something ordered and delivered pronto, look for a store that offers Overnight delivery. But be aware that Overnight doesn't always mean overnight. Some stores will tell you up front how long it takes for a product to leave their store (sometimes the product is shipped within an hour or so, but sometimes the store may take two to three days to process your order). So Overnight means that your purchase will be delivered overnight—once it leaves the store. But still, Overnight is the fastest (and most expensive). If you're not in a hurry, save yourself some money and select a slower method. This is what the different shipping options mean:

  1. **Ground**—This is the slowest and cheapest method. It usually (but not always) means UPS Ground service. Figure about a week from the time your order leaves the store. When a store says that they offer free shipping, well, this is the kind of shipping they are talking about.

  2. **3rd Day**—This is often U.S. Priority Mail or a more inexpensive service from one of delivery services, such as DHL or UPS. Your order will arrive three days after it leaves the store.

  3. **2nd Day**—This is a reasonably fast service, when you do not have an urgent need for speed. This is a good option to choose when you don't need delivery yesterday because it will save you considerable money over the Overnight option. Your package will arrive two days after it leaves the store.

  4. **Overnight**—Look for this option when you need something fast. Many stores will be able to accommodate your overnight order if you order before 12 noon. However, this cutoff time does vary from store to store. If you really need something overnight, make sure you check the store's shipping policy, usually located behind a button such as

Frequently Asked Questions (FAQ), Help, How to Order, or Shipping. Some stores offer two forms of Overnight delivery: one the next morning, and the other, well, sometime during the next day.

# Frequently
# Asked
# Questions

# Frequently Asked Questions

Here are the answers to the questions people often ask us when we are chatting about online shopping. We've answered the questions in this order:

- Why Shop Online?

- What Do I Need to Shop Online?

- What Kind of Stores Are on the Web?

- How Can I Find a Good Store?

- How Can I Find a Product in the Online Shop?

- Why Does the Store Want Me to Register and Log In?

- How Can I Get Help with the Site Itself?

- How Do I Order and Pay?

- How Fast Will I Get Delivery?

- What About Returning a Product?

- Where Can I Find Out More About Problems I May Face as an Online Consumer?

- How Did You Decide Which Stores to Include or Reject?

# Why Shop Online?

**Can I save time shopping online?**

You'll save *tons* of time when you shop online.

- You do not have to drive to the mall, park, hike inland for a mile or so, buy stuff, hike back, and drive home.

- You can shop whenever you want. These stores are always open. If you get an urge to book a trip at 2 A.M., you can work out all the details, and have tickets coming your way even though all real travel agents are asleep.

- The minute you enter an online store, you can find what you want a lot faster than you can going from department to department in a big mall store.

- Purchases that involve purely electronic transactions can be completed in a few seconds (or minutes, on a very busy day). For instance, several online stockbrokers promise that trades will be completed within ten seconds. If you reserve a car, flight, or hotel via the Web, you get confirmation in less than a minute.

You'll save even more time if you use our book. We steer you past the biggest time-wasters for Web shoppers, such as:

- Web sites that pretend to be stores but are just brochures advertising a retail store or mail-order company. These sites may offer online catalogs, but they force you to call their offices to buy anything, or, worse, urge you to come on down to the mall outside a city 2,000 miles from your home.

- Web sites that look like stores but are actually just the owner's opinions. For instance, if you go to a site that sounds as if it might sell CDs, you may discover what someone thinks of a new band, period.

- Web sites that are lists of other Web sites. Most of these lists include every site that has anything to do with the topic, including university courses, personal pages, magazines, newsgroups, and, oh, some stores. Depending on the dedication of the list maker, these links may be 5% to 20% broken. The best-maintained lists include a wide range of sites, from information hoards to online stores, without extensive evaluation of the real worth of the sites, and with descriptions that are often a bit vague, leaving one unsure whether or not a particular site actually sells stuff.

- Graphics-heavy sites that take forever to download.

- Amateur and back-alley sites that try to sell you their products without using a secure connection.

## Well, what *does* take time when I shop online?

Starting your computer, getting connected to the Web, and deciding where to go to shop: these take more time than they should, particularly if you are using an older computer and regular phone lines. Other ways you might spend more time than you expected:

- You may get distracted by all the neat products. If you are browsing rather than looking for one particular item, you can enjoy yourself for quite a while, learning about a product category, considering various products, comparing prices. Oddly, most people do not notice time passing when they are doing this kind of research, so you may easily pass half an hour or more at a giant store, amusing yourself, downloading free software, playing this or that tune. Strictly speaking, this takes time. But because it's fun (and informative), most people don't object.

- Filling in a store's registration or order form for the first time may involve typing your name and address into little slots, which can take a few minutes if you are a hunt-and-peck keyboarder.

- When you buy a physical item such as a book, CD, or computer, you do have to wait a day or two for delivery, or a week if you decide to save money on shipping. But for many people, getting a book or CD within a day or two is good enough, and not having to take an hour or so to go to a physical store is the real time-saver.

## Can I save money when I shop on the Web?

Yes, even though you pay for shipping, you can generally save a lot online, compared to what you might have to spend in a retail store built out of steel, glass, and concrete blocks. Every online store can offer better prices than their physical cousins, because each online sale carries less overhead. Even if the company has retail outlets, an online sale does not carry the burden of expenses that must be charged to retail sales. An online store has:

- No rent, air-conditioning, heating, or janitorial services for a retail showroom

- No salesclerks out on the floor

- No paper catalog, no postage

In fact, some online stores have no warehouses, either. Of course, like a retail operation, an online store has to pay someone to maintain a database with their current inventory. And unlike their physical counterparts, the online store has to hire programmers to enable credit card verification and purchases over the Web, Web designers to make the site easy to visit, and content experts to post descriptions of all the products. Those hires cost major bucks, but if the store reaches a certain volume, a small profit margin can cover all those Web-related expenses.

A few stores don't even make a profit on each sale. They offer huge discounts, basically selling at whatever they paid for a product, hoping to make money on banner ads or links to partner sites. Are these store owners crazy? In Silicon Valley, they're considered brilliant pioneers.

For some kinds of products, such as CDs and books, you'll find a few stores competing primarily on price, so discounts drop even more, and in the shops that get the biggest discounts (because they buy the most), you may even end up paying less than small retail shop owners usually pay their wholesalers.

## Can I find neat stuff online?

You betcha. In fact, if your experience is like ours, you will be amazed how many strange and wonderful products other people have been buying for years. Suddenly you see how incredibly specialized some products have become, and how many twists and turns there are in customization and service, because the Web merchants are trying to outdo each other.

## Can I learn enough about the product I want to buy?

The amount of information you get on each product varies enormously from site to site, but if you go to stores we recommend for their product descriptions, you will learn a lot, probably more than you could pick up walking around and talking with salespeople in a regular store. Instead of dealing with a clerk who hardly knows what products lie under the glass countertop, you get a product description that often includes a list of specific features and benefits, system requirements, optional add-on products, and possibly reviews by critics and other customers. Not every online store piles on the info like this, but the best ones do.

And the rest of the Web acts as a giant clearinghouse for reviews, surveys, gossip, and research, so if you are new to a product arena, you can learn from the stores and these other Web sites what kind of products are available, what differentiates the good from the mediocre, and what features you might really want. Online shoppers, in general, are better informed than their mail-order cousins or mall denizens.

After you buy a product, you may be able to get a little (only a little) phone support from the store, mostly about assembling or installing. But for real technical support you have to call the manufacturer.

## Can I avoid human contact?

Some people tell us that anonymity is a major attraction of shopping online. They don't have to push past slowpokes in the crowded aisles; they don't have to wait for a salesclerk to finish slurping a soda; they don't have to suffer embarrassment as they buy intimate apparel or health products.

On the other hand, people build these sites, and you can definitely tell which site-builders are friendly and which ones just don't care what you think. Even though you are looking at the store through the screen of a computer, you get a feeling for these people behind the site. And naturally, you're going to gravitate toward the sites that seem to understand what you want to do, how you feel, and what questions you might ask. You don't have to wait while they change the cash register tape, or finish planning dinner on the phone; but you still get a sense of their attitudes, which range from "We always put our own convenience first," to "We have worked like heck to make this site easy for you."

## Is some stuff free?

Yes, but the amount and quality vary from one product category to another. If you are shopping for a CD, for instance, you can often download parts of songs and listen to them for free. (Even after you leave the site, you can listen to the snippets or tracks again, because they are sitting on your hard disk.) Ditto for clips of video. Also, you can download freeware (software and fonts you don't have to pay for), shareware (software you can try out, but should pay for if you decide to use it on a regular basis), and demo programs. For a vast collection of shareware and freeware, see Ziff-Davis's library, at http://www.hotfiles.com or http://www.zdnet.com/swlib/

Also free, or almost so, are tons of information you used to have to pay for. For instance, in the past if you wanted to get a stock quote, you phoned your broker, who charged you an annual fee for your account, plus a commission on each trade. Now you can get 20-minutes-old quotes free from any online broker, and many also offer real-time quotes for free. Similarly, the information that brokerages developed (and charged high rates for) is now available in part for free, and in part for a few bucks per report. In the past you could also get rates and fares directly from individual airlines, hotel chains, and car rental companies, but you had to go to a travel agent to get detailed comparisons of the offerings of all the companies. Now you get those comparisons for free online, and the online agencies will make your reservations pronto, also for free, or for a small "membership" fee.

## Can I just research products online, and then go to a local store?

Sure. In fact, more people use the Web for research than for purchases. There are some real benefits to buying locally. You have a person you can talk to if you have a complaint; you can touch and feel and smell the merchandise; you can have a café latte while you are resting after carrying your purchases down the escalator.

One downside to learning about products on the Web, then going to your local retailer or mall, is that, even though you have discovered the perfect product online, your local store may not carry that particular item, manufacturer, or type of product. The store may have something that is a little better and a little more expensive, and several that are cheaper or worse.

Instead of using the Web to locate the "perfect" product, use the online information to develop a set of criteria that really matter to you. "My new cell phone must be 900 MHz, but I don't care about any calling area outside of my city, and I do not need voice mail, just a phone number to call back, and . . ." That way you can see if your local store's product (whatever the vendor, whatever other features it has) actually meets your criteria.

We praise certain stores because they provide plenty of good product descriptions and good surveys of what's available. You might want to start your research in these stores, then go to one of the Web search engines that arrange their links by category. Use the categories rather than a search, to avoid coping with thousands of hits. For our favorite category lists, see page 34.

# How private is the information I provide to an online store?

Your credit card information is safer online, within a secure shopping area, than it is when you give your card to a waiter at a restaurant or a clerk at a gas station. Far more credit card fraud stems from stolen paper receipts than from hackers intercepting transmissions to and from a secure shopping site.

But the real question is: What will the store do with your email address and street address? Will the store sell that to other companies, so you end up getting junk email and paper catalogs?

Recently, the Federal Trade Commission at http://www.ftc.gov/ found that 86% of online stores provided no information about how they would use this kind of demographic data. Reasonably enough, many customers at these stores have refused to provide such information at one time or another, and 40% have occasionally provided fake information, which often results in the credit card companies rejecting the request to charge a purchase. Eighty percent of Web users said they wouldn't object if the stores would just issue a statement promising not to resell the personal data.

Many of the stores we like do provide what they call a Privacy Statement inside their Customer Service area, the Frequently Asked Questions, or Help. Most of these statements say that they will only use the information in the aggregate, to spot trends, and they will only send you email about specials if you click a button indicating that you would like to receive these messages (permission email). And most swear they will not pass along the data to another company.

But you may not see these policies, because you have to poke around a bit to find them. Best is when a store puts their promise not to divulge the information on the very form in which they are asking for the data.

We think the situation is improving, particularly in the best stores. But if you have any qualms, look for that privacy statement, and if you don't find it, or you find it and don't like it, just exit. There are plenty of stores that really care about privacy, so you don't have to settle for one that seems indifferent to your concerns.

# What Do I Need to Shop Online?

**Do I have to have a particular computer or Web browser?**

No, you just need a computer with a modem, Web browser software (such as Internet Explorer, Netscape Navigator, or America Online's browser), and a phone number that connects you to the Internet. If you subscribe to America Online, you go through their local phone number; if you have another service, or a local Internet Service Provider, you go through theirs.

Older browsers may have trouble with some aspects of some sites, as we detail in the answer to the next question, but the most sophisticated sites have been designed to be easy to use, even if you haven't upgraded your browser in years. Older computers have less memory, less oomph, and therefore creak a little as they surf. If you have an older computer (we call them "mature"), the whole experience will be slower for you than for your neighbor who has the SuperPowerWhizBang, but if you are used to the pace, you may not mind. You just know that when you start to collect a large file from a Web site, you can go boil some water, make a pot of tea, pour a cup, and blow the steam off the top before coming back to the computer to see if the download is complete.

**What problems will I face shopping online with my old browser or old computer?**

The biggest problem is speed. If you happen to go to a site that uses a lot of large graphics, the pages will take quite a while to download. If a download seems to be taking a long, long time, you might want to click your browser's Stop button and go to another store.

If the store's designers are so unfriendly as to use something called frames, you will be at a disadvantage. Frames are independent files that get pasted together by your browser to produce what looks like a single page. One frame may present a list of departments, while a second frame presents the content itself. So the second frame may keep changing while the first one stays put. Of course, even if your browser lets you look at frames, you may find them confusing. For instance, if you try to save or print the page, you may end up with the text of one frame but not the other. Also, people frequently get confused when both frames change. The experience resembles rowing with oars of different lengths while heavy waves roll you left and right, forward and back. Occasionally, designers offer you the choice of viewing their sites "with frames" or "without frames." That choice is just an admission of guilt, but with older software you should click the No Frames button. In fact, "No Frames!" should be a bumper sticker.

Similarly, a few sites offer you the opportunity to view the site as "Text Only," which is nice if you are using a really ancient browser on a slow connection. But most stores are so proud of their images that they do not offer this possibility. On the other hand, you may be able to set your own browser to ignore graphics and just display text. The text may look a bit odd because it was written and laid out assuming art would surround it, but you can probably navigate OK using text only.

If your monitor or computer can handle only a few colors at low resolutions, photographic images will probably look a bit lurid or splotchy. The minimum setting you need, to see pictures that look somewhat realistic, is 800 pixels by 600 pixels (800 x 600) with 256 colors. Pixels are picture elements, and the more you crowd into a square inch of screen space, the better, because each pixel can show you a tiny detail, and when an image has millions of these little details in every square inch, you get the impression of terrific clarity. The more colors you display, the more the pixels can differentiate shadings, so the image becomes more realistic. Two hundred fifty-six colors on screen mean you can tell what the picture is about. With millions of colors and tons of pixels, you get a very clear impression of what the product itself looks like.

## Do I have to use a credit card?

No, but you do need to use one if you want delivery within a week or so. You get the fastest delivery if you use the credit card on the Web store, in its secure shopping area, or phone the store directly. Second best is to find the product and fax the store with your information (although this method is less safe than ordering on a secure area on the Web). Least recommended: emailing your request with credit card information, which is not cool because email sometimes goes to the wrong recipient. Also dangerous: using a debit card, because the money is transferred immediately to the merchant, so you do not have the opportunity to cancel payment, as you do with a credit card.

If you don't have a credit card, you can usually place an order and just say that you will send them a check or money order, which takes a few days, and then they will want to clear the check, which takes as much as two weeks, and then they will start processing the order. Slow boat, but secure.

## What about digital cash?

Digital cash is a fad whose time has not yet come. Basically, you deposit money into an account, then use an electronic version of a debit card, deducting purchases from your balance until you need to replenish it. A few investment research companies sell their reports for $5 each, using digital cash. The dream is that you might use digital cash for a series of small purchases, such as articles from the archives of a magazine, at something like a buck or two apiece. But so far very few stores have decided to accept digital cash.

If you're curious, here's how it works:

1. You set up a bank account with a bank that offers digital cash accounts.

2. You download software that lets you transfer money to the digital cash account.

3. You use the software to transfer money from your regular account to your digital cash account.

4. You find a store that accepts digital cash (and not many do).

5. For each item, you pay from your digital cash account.

# What Kind of Stores Are on the Web?

**Is there only one kind of Web store?**

Actually, there are lots of different business models for these stores. You'll find all of the following types of stores, and then some.

- Individual or mom-and-pop enterprises, the Web equivalent of the corner deli

- Retailers who branch out onto the Web, while continuing to do their main business at the physical stores

- Mail-order catalogs who go online to expand their business, such as L.L. Bean at http://www.llbean.com/ or Lands' End at http: //www.landsend.com/

- Stores that have been created from scratch to sell on the Web, saving money that other companies spend on retail showrooms, paper catalogs, and, sometimes, warehousing. Some of these stores focus on one product, such as music CDs, books, or travel. Others are more like traditional department stores, with hundreds of thousands of products.

- Manufacturers who choose to sell for a very high list price, so that their dealers can look good by offering specials, discounts, and bargains. Example: Compaq Computer, at http://www.compaq.com/

- Manufacturers who deal directly with you as a consumer (without distributing through dealers or resellers), and therefore give you the wholesale price, which is often lower than anything advertised by dealers or retailers. Examples: Dell Computer, at http://www.dell.com/ and Gateway at http://www.gateway.com/

- Anyone with a huge real-time transaction database, such as airline reservation companies and stockbrokers, because these electronic systems allow you to enter a transaction and get confirmation within a few seconds.

- Online malls, which are essentially lists of dozens or hundreds of other online stores, both large and small, gathered together for strength, and sometimes sharing a common ordering system. Example: The Internet Mall at http://www.shopnow.com/ has links to 15,000 stores.

- Auction sites, which come in two flavors: 1) a company lets you bid on overstocks, leftovers, end-of-the-line, or demo products, or 2) a company that acts as a host for individuals offering items for public auction, somewhat like a classified ad section in which you have to make a competitive bid to win the right to buy the item.

- Partners with the major online services, such as America Online, CompuServe (now run by AOL, but a different service), Microsoft Network. Each service has a few partner stores in every major area that you might want to shop in. If you subscribe to AOL, you get to browse from store to store within AOL, adding items to the same shopping cart, whereas out on the Web, each store has its own shopping cart. The result: At AOL we tend to buy too much. Also, AOL itself guarantees your money back, even if the merchant balks. Your credit card company will reimburse you for all but $50 of any credit card fraud, but AOL will pay the remaining $50 if you have trouble at one of their partner stores. Many of the AOL partners also have storefronts on the Web, so even if you are not a subscriber, you can come in through the front door. The only problem with these partnership arrangements is that, to guarantee good income to each partner, the service tends to limit the number of stores in any one area, such as computers, and as a result, you really don't get a wide range of products or prices.

# What makes online stores possible?

Several technologies came together in the 1990s to make Web stores possible:

- The Web, new in the '90s, making it possible to publish pages full of graphics with links to other pages, an electronic catalog open to the public.

- The credit card network, already in place, allowing any merchant to transmit your credit card number and the purchase amount to the credit card folks, and get their approval back within a few seconds (or quite a few seconds on a slow day), all electronically.

- A special computer for handling credit card information, called a secure server, which is just a variation on the kind of computer that has been hosting networks for many years. And the software that makes the computer secure derives from existing programs.

- Rapid delivery systems like Airborne Express, DHL, FedEx, and UPS, because these can deliver products to the stores overnight, and then, when you order a product, zip it from the store to your door in a day or two, rather than making you wait a week or two, as in the old days of snail mail; and some Web stores skip warehousing altogether, relaying your order to a manufacturer or wholesaler who packs and ships the product directly to you, using these services.

- The inventory database, already in place for most existing companies, storing and reporting information about every product, such as pictures, specs, and prices.

- Programming languages, old and new, that allow the Web site to look a product up in the inventory database and report back to you, on whatever Web page you are looking at, within a few seconds.

- Electronic mail, which the store uses to send you a confirmation of your order, and which you can use to ask questions, complain, or send your reviews of products.

Most of these technologies were already mature when the Web was born, so Web site builders do not have to guess how they work. The hard part of creating an online store involves hooking all these pieces together so that they work efficiently without too many errors.

Once the pieces are smoothly stitched together, the next problem is success: as new customers pour into the company's site, the site's computer may bog down, and network connections may clog up. Result: You can't get in, or you experience delays.

At that point, the happy owners have to add more servers and more bandwidth (enlarging the network pipeline so more transactions can come through at the same time).

## What are the signs that an online store is reliable?

Most online stores hope for repeat business, and work hard to persuade you to come back again. Obviously, even the best make mistakes, but we have found that you can feel increasingly confident when a store offers a lot of the following features, most of which should be visible on the welcome page:

- A professional layout, with clearly separated areas for menus and product information

- A search box on every page

- A list of major product categories on the first page, and every page thereafter, so you can jump from one area to another without climbing back up to the home page

- Prominently placed information about how to order, shipping possibilities, and frequently asked questions; best to have these as buttons on a menu that appears on every page, second best to lump them all under a button for Customer Service or Ordering Information

- Little photographs (for fast downloading) that you can click to enlarge (but only if you really want to)

- Detailed descriptions of the products, with features and benefits, specs, requirements, samples, reviews

- Icons toward the bottom of the home page from organizations that certify the reliability of the site, such as the Better Business Bureau Online at http://www.bbbonline.org/

- Secure ordering, so you can safely provide personal and credit card information to the store's electronic systems (not a salesclerk or other human being) without worrying that some hacker can pick it up

- Awards by magazines or sites that review Web sites

- A prominently placed, very visible 800 number for questions, not just purchases

- A very visible way to email their customer support team, such as a Contact Us button on every page

- A snail mail address, possibly in a section called About Us, so you can write them, or call the president

- A fairly detailed history of the store in a section called something like About Us, with acknowledgment of key partnerships (like they use Yahoo to take credit cards) or ownership, so you have some idea who you are dealing with

When the store owners incorporate these features in the site, you get a sense of their openness and generosity.

And, on the other hand, people who withhold information, force you to jump around to look stuff up, hide from contact, and present an ugly, hard-to-read page, can hardly be called welcoming or businesslike.

## What makes an online store easy to use?

Goodwill. The attitude that the Web team takes toward you shows up in their interface: the buttons, menus, forms, and page layouts you use to get around, look up products, and order them.

Here are ten signs that the team cares about your experience on their site:

1. There is a main menu on every page, at the top or on the side, offering links to every major department, including some form of help, and the order form, so you can go anywhere from anywhere, without leaning on the Back button.

2. On every page you can get advice and information, whether it is called Customer Service, Frequently Asked Questions, Help, or Order Information.

3. No matter where you are, you can look at the contents of your shopping cart to see what you have tentatively ordered so far.

4. Each page has some titles telling you where you are: for instance, what department you are in, and, within that, what category of products you are looking at, and finally what the name of this particular product is, so you know where you are in the overall structure of the site.

5. You can always see how to buy a product (for instance, there is a giant red Buy button next to the product description).

6. You can get extra information about a product, if you want.

7. Whenever you click a link, you know where it will take you.

8. You can read the text. (The staff has not put up white or blue text on a black background, to be cool.)

9. Images start as thumbnails, and you have the option to make them larger or not, so you do not get stuck with endless download times if you are on a slow connection.

10. The searches result in a manageable set of hits: not too many, and not too few.

These common courtesies help you move around the site with confidence, avoiding dead ends, wrong turns, detours, and pitfalls.

**Tip**: Stores that don't offer most of these features will certainly be hard to navigate, and may turn out to be inconsiderate in other ways.

# How Can I Find a Good Store?

**When I ask my search engine for sites that deal with a particular type of product, I get thousands of hits, and most are junk. What to do?**

That's one reason we put this book together. We went through these enormous site lists, seeking out the best stores, so that you won't have to waste your time clicking, going, backing up, and so on through a dozen sites, just to find one that is actually a first-rate store.

Search mechanisms are still extremely crude. If a site mentions the topic, bang, there it is on the list of results. You have no easy way to distinguish the good from the bad, the stores from the personal sites, the high school class pages from the Australian community council pages. Result: You may waste a ton of time going to sites that turn out to be absolute duds.

Even using the so-called advanced searches, you get piles of junk. For instance, if the search mechanism lets you specify a word that must NOT appear on the page, as a way of filtering out crummy sites, you have to imagine all the words that bad sites will use but good sites will omit. And when you try to figure out words that must ALSO be on the page, along with the product name, you can try *secure* (on the theory that only a real store will mention its secure server), but you can't be sure of *order, purchase,* or even *shipping,* because those all appear on sites that are nothing but online catalogs. The bad news is that even advanced searches cannot pinpoint your product's Web stores, and nothing but.

**I've used your chapter on the products I want to buy, and now I want to check out some more stores, even if they aren't "the best."**

Fine. In this book we have tried to save you time by picking the best shops and ignoring the not-so-hot ones. But sometimes you are after a very specific item that these shops don't carry, or you just want to do some more comparison shopping.

Then, if you still haven't quite found the shop you want, try the shopping lists at major portals (look under Shopping). The portal staff have selected their own favorites, or, in some cases, their partners. But remember, these sites are not necessarily the best, or even the most popular, stores. They may actually be a) ones that have paid to be listed or b) ones that have come up highest on the search results, a dubious distinction. Remember that these long lists are just links to stores; the list servers themselves offer nothing for sale. If you have stamina, though, try any of the following lists:

- About.com (formerly The Mining Company) at http://www.about.com

- All Internet Shopping Directory at http://www.all-internet.com/

- Buyer's Index at http://www.buyersindex.com/

- Excite Shopping at http://www.excite.com/shopping/

- Go To at http://www.goto.com/

- HotBot Shopping Directory at http://www.hotbot.com/shop/

- Lycos Shopping at http://www.lycos.com/

- Shopfind at http://www.shopfind.com

- Snap at http://www.snap.com/

- Yahoo Shopping at http://shopping.yahoo.com/

## Is there a Better Business Bureau for online stores?

Yes. You can get BBB information two ways. If you can locate the home address of the company, go to the BBB Web site, at http://www.bbb.com, and look up a bureau near the company (see Locate a BBB). You can contact the local office to get a free report about the company, telling you how long it has been in business, whether the BBB has fielded any complaints about the company, and whether or not the FTC or a state Attorney General has moved against the company during the last three years.

The BBB has an online division, called BBBOnline at http://www.bbbonline.com/ They have set up some criteria a company must meet before it can put up the Better Business Bureau seal on their site. The company must have been in business for a year, have a plan for resolving complaints fast, correct or withdraw misleading Internet advertising, and post the company's phone number and email on the site, along with the name of at least one company official. When a company meets these standards and earns a "satisfactory" rating, it can put up the BBB seal. The BBB Online folks run periodic surprise checks to make sure the company is still following the rules. If you click the seal, you get a Reliability Report on the company, direct from the Better Business Bureau; that report will show whether or not there have been any complaints.

## Where can I find the store with the lowest prices for my particular product?

First, please read our chapter on that kind of product. We point out the low-price leaders. In any product category, there are usually three or four stores contending for the crown of Bargain Basement. We have discovered that no one store has all the lowest prices. For one product, one store wins; for another product, another store wins. But the difference between the low-price leaders is usually less than a buck, up to $20, and less than $5 on items costing between $20 and $75. Then there is usually a cluster of stores offering good discounts but not the best. You may want to shop at these stores for reasons other than price: they often offer more information, better service, better shipping, more guarantees, whatever. And finally there are a few stores that show no interest in giving you a good deal: we have usually dropped these places, unless they have items no one else offers.

There are a number of services with robots that go out on the Web and look for lowest prices. Most of these services do not actually look at every shop on the Web, but instead scan a few dozen sites, all of which are known to offer good deals. You type in a product, and they respond with a list of all the stores (in their group) that sell the item, with the current prices. You'll find quite a range of prices, even though all are lower than retail. For instance, a music CD may be quoted as $11 from the least expensive store, and $18 by the most expensive in such a table. If price is all you care about, though, you can find today's lowest price at these sites:

- Bottom Dollar at http://www.bottomdollar.com

- Compare Net at http://comparenet.com/

- Killer App at http://www.killerapp.com/

- My Simon at http://www.mysimon.com/

- Price Scan at http://www.pricescan.com/

- Price Search at http://pricesearch.net/

- Price Watch at http://www.pricewatch.com/

- The View at http://www.the-view.com/shopper.html

Also, About.com's guides list stores they like, in their subject-matter area, which often covers a lot more than your particular product. Some guides even comment on the prices, too, telling you which stores offer the best and worst deals, at http://www.about.com/

# How Can I Find a Product in the Online Shop?

## Why are some brands available at a store, but not others?

Most likely, the store has negotiated to be an authorized reseller only for certain manufacturers. Or the store has an arrangement with a wholesaler who supplies products only from those manufacturers, at least in that product category.

How come? Perhaps the store is concentrating on some other product category, and just puts up products with these brand names, as a gesture, to suggest that the store has a wider range of products than it really does. Or maybe the owner believes that these brands offer the best products for customers, considering quality, availability, or price.

If you want a particular brand, you could go directly to the manufacturer's site. But, depending on what products they sell, you may find that the manufacturer's prices are far above those in the stores (to make their dealers look good), or the manufacturer may just refuse to sell on the Web, in order not to undermine relationships with dealers and resellers. Best to go to another store in the product category, and try there. (In our chapter about the product category, skim the list of sample products to see if you spot the brand you want.)

## Why doesn't this store offer a paper catalog?

Sometimes a store does offer a paper catalog. But companies who created their stores just for the Internet may never have published a catalog, and they may refuse to print one because a) it is so expensive and b) it is really a different business and c) they like trees, and resolutely limit their use of paper.

Companies that began life as mail-order catalogs still offer you a chance to get on their mailing list. And so do some retail stores who have sent out catalogs for years. And a few companies put the equivalent of a paper catalog up on their site, so you can download it and read or print it using Adobe Acrobat or Microsoft Word. Interesting ploy: they shift the printing cost to you.

## Why does the store offer all these lists of product categories, anyway?

The lists should help you find a product by category when you don't have a particular product name, brand, or phrase to enter in a search box. These lists resemble a table of contents in a book, where you turn to a chapter that seems to cover what you want, then look at the headings to find one that seems most relevant. Searches are more like using the index.

Most sites offer a list of product categories on the welcome page. You click a category, such as *telephones*, and get a list of subcategories, such as 2.4 GHz cell phones, 900 MHz cell phones, 25-channel cell phones, old-fashioned analog phones, pagers, beepers, and phones for the hearing impaired. When you spot a subcategory you like, you click that and get, perhaps, a list of brands. You are drilling down, down, down into the store's inventory. Eventually, when you click a sub-, sub-, sub-category, you get to a list of actual products, and when you click one of those, you arrive, at last, at a description of a particular product.

This hierarchy may be well designed or not. Bad designs force you to click, click, click, going down as many as ten levels to get to a particular product. Good designs put a lot of choices right at the top, so you don't have to go down so many staircases. Crummy designers think of their approach as logical, because they start with only one or two categories, and divide those up gradually, the way we were supposed to do outlining in school. The result is just as tedious as making an outline. Their hierarchy starts out very narrow and gets much, much deeper. Good design, on the other hand, starts with a wide horizon at the top, with dozens or even a hundred categories spread out across the page, with shallow information under each category. That's faster, because you don't have to dig as deep.

Looking through categories in this way is sometimes called browsing, to distinguish the process from looking something up in the database directly, which is called searching.

## What lies behind the store's search mechanism?

A database with a record for each product usually lies behind the search. In the database, each record has a bunch of fields, like the columns in a table, for information such as the product name, price, manufacturer, description, and image. Like a shoe box full of index cards, the database keeps track of all the information on the store's inventory, but because the database is electronic, it can look through all those records very quickly and come back to you with an onscreen report showing all the records that contain whatever word you typed into the search box.

Most people couldn't care less what lies behind the search box. But if you personally are curious about the way these work, consider three kinds of database, which run the vast majority of these searches.

- The small sites may have what's called **a flat-file database**, which is like your address book. Every record has the same slots to fill in, like a form. There is only one file, and, usually, that file does not contain many records.

- Bigger sites use a **relational database**, which has different tables for different information. So there's a table for product descriptions, and another for the manufacturers' addresses. The information from each table is put together on the fly and served up to you on the screen as a single page, or part of a page. The advantage to the company is that they have to update information such as the company address only once, because it lives in only one table. (By contrast, in a flat file, you have to put the company address on every record that refers to one of their products, meaning that if you want to update that information everywhere, you have to go to every relevant record, erase the old address, and type in the new one, or something like that.) The relational advantage is that with a lot of products you get quick responses.

- Fanciest of these databases are **transaction systems**, created to accept, record, and report on transactions—actual purchases—so quickly that the data is recorded almost instantaneously (laughingly called "real time"). Examples include airline reservation systems and online stockbroker systems. When you say where you want to go, on what day and time, the airline system paws through hundreds of thousands of flights to come up with the closest matches, usually in less than a minute. Try doing that with index cards in a shoe box!

## How can I search for a product if I don't know a brand name?

Use a unique *keyword*. Keywords are very important words—that is, words that most people would associate with this particular product. These words act as keys to the database, opening it up to show you a particular product, or a set of products, all of which are associated with that idea. You can type in a keyword you think describes the product you are looking for, and the database comes back with a bunch of products that the store staff has described with that word. For instance, for a frying pan, the store folks might decide that keywords include *pan, frying, cooking, fry, fries, stovetop, cast iron*, the manufacturer's name, *steak, hash browns, omelets, scrambled eggs, pancakes,* and *griddle cakes.* That way, if you type in *pancakes*, you get a list of products, one of which is the frying pan, because in the Keyword field on its record, the word *pancakes* appears.

To limit the number of products you turn up, think of a keyword that applies to your kind of product but no other. For instance, *pancakes* will bring up frying pans, skillets, and warmers, but not steamer baskets, microwave ovens, and ice-cream makers. Not too bad, in a big database. Of course, you may think of a word that is so unusual that the store staff didn't think of it either when they entered keywords for the product. Time to back off, and enter a more general term, such as *pan.*

## So what kind of searches do stores offer?

The sophistication of searches varies from store to store.

- Simple stores offer simple searches by keywords such as the product name, the manufacturer, or, least helpful, their own number for the product (as if you had any idea what that might be). You type in one word or one phrase, and you get whatever products have that text in their descriptions.

- Bigger stores have so many products that they let you ignore whole bunches of them, narrowing your search down. Instead of asking the system to search through every field on every record for "ball," you can use the advanced search, and point out that this word should show up only in the title of a book, and that this word is not an author or publisher. Or, in a CD store, you can specify the type of music, and specify that the word you type in is part of a title, not the name of an artist, a group, or a label. Tips like these help the database ignore the other fields, and just look in the Title field, which speeds up the search enormously. Advanced searches let you specify what field to look in, and whether or not a word or phrase MUST appear there, while another word or phrase CANNOT appear, and so on. From the designer's point of view, these constraints let the system filter out irrelevant information, resulting in a faster search and a more focused report. In a variation of this advanced search, you go to a department and, once there, you can search for items within that department. Good aspect: Because no other department's records are examined, the search goes faster. Downside: You won't discover a product that happens to belong to a different department. For instance, if you go to the Electronics department looking for a hair dryer, the search may come up empty, because the store figures that a hair dryer belongs in the Personal Care department.

The best databases offer many different ways you can limit your search, telling the database what field to look in, what text to insist on, and what to ignore. Of course, creating a database that has all those fields takes more work than a simple product list. But, when shopping online, you can judge a store by its search.

## I got too many results. How can I narrow down my search?

First look for an advanced search. The best stores advertise their more sophisticated search mechanisms, but mediocre stores, for some reason, hide this functionality or don't even offer it. Advanced searches let you say things like "Find me books about Washington, but not the president, the county, or the state" or "The book I am after must have the word *Architecture* in the title, and Addison-Wesley as the publisher, and publication date after 1997."

No advanced search? Then get more specific. The challenge you face is that each store's database acts a little differently, so what forces one database to be more precise may result in another database widening its arms to include 20,000 records or more.

In general, try to get more specific. For instance, if you tried just one word from the CD title, type in the whole title of the CD, or the entire name of the product. If the database is the kind that imagines an *and* between each word you type, it interprets what you type as "To qualify, a record must have this word AND that word AND the next word, all of them." If the database thinks this way, you will get records only for that particular CD.

Unfortunately, this approach may simply get you more results than before, if the database interprets your criteria as meaning, "Find me any products whose records include any of these words." That's OR-ing. In other words, the database imagines you have put the word *or* between every word you typed, and it has surfaced any products whose records include this word OR that word OR the other.

OK, if that seems to have happened, you must get tough. Put quotes around your whole phrase. Some databases understand that to mean that the whole phrase must appear in a record before it qualifies to appear in the report you see on the screen.

And finally, if that fails, go back to a single word. But make that word the most unusual, the most relevant to the product. Non-technical note: to improve database performance, consider prayer.

**I got no results from my search, but I am sure they have this product. How can I have better luck locating it?**

If the database comes back to you with some lame expression like "No matches were found," you may be tempted to say that you weren't looking for a box of matches. But the database is just being stupid. To help it find a record you are positive is there, try the following:

- If you are entering the name of a singer, author, or artist, try the complete name forward and backward: *Jonathan Price*, or *Price, Jonathan*, with and then without a middle name. (Some databases drop middle names, others know about them; some databases think of last name, first name, while others expect the name to be complete, and in order, a combination of first-name-and-last-name-all-in-one.)

- To cast a wider net, use a more general term. If you tried *Hunan* for a cookbook, try *Chinese* instead.

- Remember that some human being had to look at the product and come up with keywords describing it. Think of a busy person who doesn't care very much about this product. Think of someone who puts in only the most obvious terms. Then try one of those terms.

**What if I completely fail to discover the product using the search?**

Well, maybe the store just doesn't have it! (This is the most common situation.) Stores often look as if they carry a wide range of products but turn out to focus on 10 categories, or a hundred. Inevitably, they ignore something. You may have stumbled on that something.

If you think they really have the product somewhere, or might carry it soon, email them. Many stores are set up to call their wholesalers to see if a product is available.

They should get back to you within 24 hours with the news that they can supply it, if they can. Otherwise, you should get a letter thanking you warmly for your interest and support, and admitting sheepishly that they don't carry the product.

## Once I find a product at a store, how much will I be able to learn about the product?

Product descriptions vary enormously from store to store. Sometimes you get no more than the product name, their code number, and the price. (Generally, this spartan approach is adopted only by stores that distinguish themselves from other stores by price alone.)

Ideally, a product description should include all of the following:

- An overview of the product, in brief

- Photos, small and large

- Features and benefits

- Requirements, such as what operating system and how much memory you need to run a piece of software; also, compatibility issues ("This plug will not work in Europe.")

- Customer reviews

- Samples, such as a chapter from a book, or partial tracks from a music CD, to play on your computer

- Suggestions of similar products that other customers have bought

- Constraints, such as the limitations on discount air tickets (can be used only on Tuesday, and so on)

- Warranty (yes, the complete warranty for this particular product)

- Shipping costs for delivery of this product in a week, a few days, overnight

**Tip:** If you are interested in a fairly common item, like a hair dryer or CD system, and you want to get some unbiased advice about these products, go to the *Consumer Reports* site, at http://www.consumerreports.org/ for detailed reports on their testing. They give you tables comparing products. Unfortunately, you have to pay for some articles, but particularly if you're going to pay big bucks for a product, their fee is probably worth paying, to be sure you get what you really need.

## How can the store offer these discounts?

Depending on the industry, the wholesale price of a brand-new item is 20% to 55% off the retail price, so virtual stores can easily offer you 15% to 50% off retail, and still make a slight profit on each sale. But you may wonder: How can they manage to offer discounts that go way below those offered by physical stores?

Stores that live entirely online, with no retail showrooms, no paper catalogs, and (in some cases) no warehouses can offer major discounts because their overhead is less than anyone else's. The lightest virtual stores accept orders electronically, relay those orders electronically to a supplier, and the supplier ships the products out, for a small fee. A few stores charge you exactly what they pay, making not even one used dime on each transaction, because they hope to sell advertising on their sites, on the theory that extremely low prices will bring people through, exposing them to the banner ads as they buy other products. Next up the scale are stores that must have a physical warehouse. For instance, Amazon.com and eToys have found they can ship more efficiently if they handle warehousing themselves, rather than counting on a big wholesaler. But suddenly these companies discover they must hire workers to run the forklifts, pour Styrofoam pellets into boxes, label the packages, and hand them over to the delivery services. So the discounts at these stores, while dramatic, are a little less than at the rock-bottom locations. And so it goes.

When a store supports retail storefronts and paper catalogs, as well as their online operation, the amount they can discount goes way down. But you should still get products for a little less than you would if you walked into the showrooms. Most of these stores also feature overstocks, discontinued items, and remainders, at even deeper discounts.

You will almost always get a product for a lower price online than you could in a retail store, so that, even including your shipping charges, you are ahead of the game. But remember that the amount you save is only part of the incentive for shopping online. When you take into account the convenience, time-saving, and information available online, you may well find yourself ordering products even when you are only saving a buck or two over retail.

# Why Does the Store Want Me to Register and Log In?

**Is registration, or membership, primarily a convenience for the store, or for me?**

Often, when you reach a store you are invited to "log in," meaning identify yourself, and if you do not already have a user name and password, the store may nudge you, subtly or not, to register, or "become a member." On these sites, you see buttons taking you to areas with names like My Account, Registration, My Profile. So what's in it for you?

You do get some benefits from registering:

- Once you register, you have given them your billing and shipping address, and perhaps even your credit card information, so when you come to purchase something, you may not have to retype all that. Nice.

- If you start shopping and leave the site before making a purchase, and then come back, the items will probably still be in your shopping cart, because the store recognizes you and saves your shopping cart hoping you will continue. Non-members lose whatever they put in their carts.

- You may be offered a chance to do what Amazon calls 1-Click Shopping. You click a button and the system applies all your membership information, including your shipping address and credit card, so that you do not have to do anything more than click to make the purchase. Dangerously tempting!

Of course, the stores suggest or demand registration because it is helpful for them, too.

- Having your registration information already on file helps them fill out your order form for you, lessening the chance of typos fouling up the process.

- Because they have all this information on file, they can locate your order faster, for order tracking.

- The answers to the "optional" questions about your tastes, age, sex, other products you own, and so on, help build a demographic profile of their audience, which is very valuable for the marketing department.

- If you allow them to send you email, your profile may allow the store to tailor alerts, news bulletins, and specials so they describe products similar to what you have already bought, or in line with your profile.

For all these reasons, registration may be required before you get past the welcome page. Often, such stores offer a guest pass allowing you to taste the benefits of membership for a few weeks, figuring you will be hooked, and sign up at the close of the free sample period. We always try the free trial. But watch out for "automatic conversion," where you innocently agree to let the site turn your free pass into an annual fee, which just shows up on your credit card statement, without your making another move. This approach stinks. Look for a guarantee that you will have to make a positive statement that you want to become a member at the end of the trial period, or a promise not to "convert" you.

Other sites offer substantial incentives for becoming a member, without absolutely requiring that you sign up: members get lower prices, some kind of annual dividend like that offered by a cooperative supermarket, extra research, faster information (such as real-time quotes from the stock market), a newsletter, or email notification of products that you might be interested in. (This is a benefit?)

## If I register or become a member, will I be deluged with junk email?

Probably not. But look for a promise of privacy. At the bottom of the registration form, watch for a little button that says something like, "From time to time we like to let our members know about special bargains. Is this OK? Yes, No."

Even if you let them send you email (this is called permission email), you probably won't get more than one notice a month.

Just to be safe, look carefully at the first email that arrives, to see how you can cancel. If the store is decent, they will tell you how to cancel the email, right there at the top of the message. If the store is run by weasels, and they don't give you an easy way to cancel, then go to the site and start emailing the president until they give up and go away.

## Why does the store want to know about my tastes, interests, age, and marital status?

Just because they're curious. No, really it's because they can tailor marketing pitches more precisely, using this demographic data. For instance, if you are 30 and play video games, they have a hunch you'll be interested in the next Sega game console, whereas if you are 75, and interested in golf and square dancing, they won't send you an email about the Sega, but you might hear about that great new release, *Square Dancing in Old Virginia.*

But isn't this close to invading your privacy? Yes, it is. Decent sites allow you to skip these slots in their form. (Often the required information, which has to do with billing and shipping, has red asterisks next to it, or a little hand pointing to it. And the extra info is marked "Optional.") Feel free to opt out. If they insist on knowing stuff you don't want to reveal, leave their site and never go back. You have plenty of other places to shop on the Web. If a site insists on getting this kind of personal information without letting you opt out, you can figure they will be rude in other ways, as well.

Also, check to see if the site advertises that it follows the rules of a privacy watchdog like TRUSTe, a nonprofit group that sets standards, and polices the site to make sure they follow those. For information, see http://www.truste.org

## Why do I have to create a user name and password?

Because their programmers are so lazy. Well, sort of. You see, to keep your records separate from everyone else's, they need a way to distinguish you from the other customers. Unfortunately, many people have similar names, or the same names, so the names aren't enough to tell one customer from another. Also, people move so often that the address isn't a reliable piece of evidence. Now, an energetic programmer could simply identify you as your Name AND your Phone Number AND your Email Address AND your ZIP Code. No one else would have that combination. But, you guessed it, that is hard to program.

So the programmers fall back on a technique they learned when they used UNIX networks back in school. Just to sign on to the network, you have to give a make-believe handle (a user name) and a password, and if those are on the list, you get access to the network. Same here. The programmers just make sure that the user name and password combination is unique. (You may have to try several times to get a unique user name.) So far so good. Wouldn't it be great if you could use the same user name and password everywhere? You bet.

Unfortunately, many sites require slightly different variations, so you cannot use the same password and user name everywhere. Different sites require:

- A different number of characters, minimum and maximum. For instance, at one site your user name can be 6 characters long, but at another, it must be at least 15 characters long.

- Various capitalization schemes: some uppercase letters and some lowercase letters allowed, or no uppercase allowed. (And some sites let you type with upper- and lowercase letters, then rewrite your user name entirely in lowercase letters, without warning you, and later refuse to let you enter the site if you happen to use the uppercase letters again.)

- Various combinations of text and numbers, such as at least one number and one letter in the password, no punctuation allowed.

- A user name that no one else has chosen.

As a result, trying to meet different requirements, you may end up with half a dozen user names, and as many different passwords. Who can remember all this stuff? We have to write the different user names and passwords down, or else we cannot get back into the sites. (Doing this book, we developed a list of more than 50 different name-and-password combinations, because the sites made such inconsistent demands.)

**Caution**: Do not make up a password based on your birth year, pet names, or middle name, because if you do draw the attention of a hacker, these are too easy to guess.

Most of us forget these weird combinations after a week or so. The best sites offer a way of getting a hint (like your user name). You enter a question they can ask you when you need a hint, and you give them the correct answer. Usually the hint should be something you really can remember, like your mother's maiden name or your email address. But even the hint doesn't give you both halves of the security apparatus: the user name and the password. That's why we recommend writing the combination down on a yellow sticky, or in a file created just to keep track of all these codes.

## Why are they sending me cookies?

Wouldn't it be great if every store sent you chocolate-chip cookies just for visiting? Alas, the cookies you receive from some stores are just a bunch of electrons. A cookie is a small file that the store sends to your browser after you register. The cookie contains the store's name and a code identifying you, something like your Customer Identification Number.

Next time you visit the site, the site's software asks your browser: "Do you have a cookie with our name on it?" The browser looks on your hard disk, in the directory for temporary Internet files, and when it finds a cookie with the store's name on it, sends that back to the store. The store digests the cookie and discovers your Customer Identification Number (or whatever they call it). In a few seconds, the store pulls up all your information. You can tell that this has happened if you see a message such as "Welcome Lisa Price" at the top of the welcome page.

The store has recognized you, thanks to the cookie exchange. From now on, if you press the Buy button, the order form comes up with almost every line filled in, because the store has drawn that from your customer record on their database. So you give up a little hard disk space, sacrifice a little privacy, in order to avoid retyping all that stuff. And from the store's point of view, the cookie is reassuring evidence that you are who you say you are and, in fact, you are a repeat customer, the best kind.

Shopping.com calls the cookie "a visitor's badge that lets you move from page to page within password-protected areas of the site." (Those are the pages that deal with ordering, and they live on the secure shopping server.) They urge you not to "deactivate" their cookie. "Doing so means that your visitor's badge cannot be read, and this will prevent you from using the site. You cannot, for instance, make any purchases without your cookie." You can see that from a store's point of view an empty shopping cart is devastating.

If you don't like the idea of some stranger plopping a little file onto your hard disk, you can set your browser to refuse cookies. If you do this, you will not be able to shop at some sites. If that's OK with you, here's how to keep crumbs off your hard disk:

- In Internet Explorer 4.0 or later, click View, then Internet Options, and click the Advanced tab. In the Cookie area, choose Disable All Cookie Use. If you just want to be notified when someone sends you a cookie, choose Prompt Before Accepting Cookies. That way you can judge the reliability of a site before accepting the cookies.

- In Netscape Navigator 4.0 or later, click Edit and Preferences, then choose Advanced, and set the options for cookies.

## What if I forget my user name or password?

What? You didn't write it down? Bad user! (Just kidding).

The worst offender in this area is a site that asks you to type in a 16-digit number to identify yourself. They act as if you should remember this code, but I doubt that anyone can, except maybe Millie the Magnificent Memorizer.

So what can you do if you have tried, say, half a dozen variations of your user name and password, and been rejected every time?

- You may be able to have the store email you with your password and user name, sometimes in two different messages, for security. But that means waiting for a few minutes, or a few hours, to get the secret codes. Meanwhile, you may be locked out, if it is a membership site.

- If the site offers a hint based on some secret you passed along to them during registration, like your mother's maiden name, take the hint and get your user name. At least that's a start. Now, what the heck was the password?

- Open a new account. But, of course, because there is already an account for someone with your name and address, the store may not accept your application, deeming you a fraud, or interloper, pretending to be you. And opening a new account means typing in all that information all over again. Tedious.

## Can I change my account information?

Yes, there is usually some way to do this. You have to enter your user name and password, and then choose something like Edit Information, or Change User Name or Password. You make the changes, and press a button such as Save or Submit.

## What is this log-in stuff?

In organizations with heavy security, like the Central Intelligence Agency, there is a sign-in book at the door of every building and every floor, with a guard who asks you for identification; you are leaving a record of your travels through the spook house. When programmers created the first networks, they borrowed the idea of logging in from these logbooks. Each user had to log in, identifying himself or herself to the system, getting permission to use the network.

As far as the store is concerned, you are an unknown user arriving over the Internet. By making you log in, they force you to identify yourself. Why do they care?

Well, if you have already registered, they can bring up your customer record and pour its information into the order form as soon as you click Buy. Similarly, they can tell whether you gave them any problems on your last order, like canceling or refusing to pay.

From the store's point of view, logging in as soon as you arrive also means that they can locate your customer information, even if you have deleted (or refused) their cookie, the little file they sent to your hard disk way back when you first registered.

Of course, if a store urges you in big letters to log in on the welcome page, they may have organized everything in two tiers: the free information, available to anyone who visits the site, and the good stuff, for which you have to register and log in. Some of the investment information services adopt this model. They tempt you with lots of market data, but force you to sign up (for a fee, or for free) to get real-time quotes or research. In cases like this, logging in is a way of making sure you pay at the gate.

# How Can I Get Help with the Site Itself?

## Where is helpful information hidden on the site?

Hidden is right, on some sites. They hate to tell you how much shipping is going to be until you have filled out the whole order form. Then they surprise you with those charges. Similarly, unfriendly sites assume you know how to order online, how to find products, how to get customer support if you have a problem. So they just don't tell you. To get answers from these sites, you have to be psychic.

Even good sites vary in the way they give you information about using the site. Look for any of the following buttons to take you to instructions:

- FAQ (Frequently Asked Questions)

- Help

- How to Order

- Customer Service

- Customer Support

- Order Information

- Shipping

Also, scrounge around the About Us or Contact Us to find out what number to call to talk to a live human being. Best hours to call are outside of business hours.

## Can I send email to the people at the store?

Most sites include an email address somewhere, like at the bottom of every page or inside the Contact Us area. The best sites offer specific email addresses for different issues, such as billing, cancellations, international questions, order status, product questions, returns, and Webmaster. You just click a button, and your browser calls up your email software, ready to send a message to the right address.

Remember that many sites get more than a thousand emails a day. You are not alone. The person reading your message does not know your order number, your preferences, your suffering.

So put every key detail into the email, so the staff person at the other end can look up your order and find out what went wrong. At a minimum, put in your full name, full address, order number, the products you tried to purchase, the date on which you ordered, and any confirmation number that they came back with. Do not put your credit card number into the email, because email is not as secure as the computer on which you placed your order.

# How Do I Order and Pay?

**Are there different ways to pay?**

Most stores offer several ways to order, but only the larger, more professional stores offer four or five methods.

If you prefer the familiar, you can still pay using the old-fashioned ways:

- Calling an 800 number and placing an order, using your credit card over the phone (just as fast as it has always been, with shipments going out within a day or two, usually)

- Taking the information about the product, writing a letter, slipping a check or money order into the envelope, and sending it to the store's snail mail address (delaying the date of shipment by a week or two)

- Cutting a purchase order and sending it in by mail (again, causing a delay of a few weeks as they verify credit and set up a formal account)

If you want to order electronically, there are several ways to do that:

- Going to a secure server, filling out the form with your credit card info, and submitting it

- Printing out the form, filling it in, and faxing it to the store (causing a slight delay, perhaps a day or so, as they verify the credit card by phone)

- Emailing the form to the store with your credit card information (the least secure method, and not recommended)

Of all these methods, we recommend ordering online, as long as you are dealing with a reputable store that has a secure server. The very worst is email. By mistake, you can send your credit card information to your department list at work, or the people on that newsgroup you've been following. Uh-oh!

## What exactly does the Buy button commit me to?

Nothing. So far. Clicking a button like Buy, Order, or Place in Shopping Cart just starts the purchase, placing an item in your imaginary shopping cart. Glitch: Sometimes you have to enter a quantity into the slot next to the Buy button, or else you get rejected because the stupid system thinks you have not asked to buy anything, because you did not select the zero under Quantity and change it to one. (Why do programmers set the quantity to zero? Do they really think someone will eagerly order zero units of the product?)

Generally, you wait a moment, and then you see information about the product you are proposing to buy. Often, this information is displayed in what is known as your shopping cart, or shopping bag, which contains everything you have thought you might buy so far. The shopping cart just lets you make a pile of items you might buy, without ordering any of them yet. You just get to see your order so far, with information like this about each item:

- The product name

- The product number

- The price

- The quantity

- The extended price (price times quantity)

- Perhaps the shipping costs for this item

You have not committed to anything yet. You are just staring at your cart full of items as you rest in the aisle of the online store.

## What is this shopping cart thing?

The shopping cart (or shopping bag, or whatnot) is the mechanism by which the store keeps track of your order, as if you were putting items into a cart at the supermarket. The idea is that you don't have to actually pay when you drop items into the cart, and you can remove them, change quantities, and so on before you go to checkout. In some stores you can edit the order directly, and in other stores, you have to click a button named Modify Cart, or something like that. To remove an item, just revise the quantity to read zero.

In some stores, you can choose shipping methods at this time. Other stores just ship by ground, so you don't get a choice.

In a well-designed site, you can view your order or shopping cart at any time. In a lousy site you have to pretend to buy something to see what you already have in the cart.

## What is checkout?

As in a real store, when you have finally decided what you want to buy, you wheel your cart by the checkout counter.

In many stores, this is the time you have to enter your credit card info, or confirm the info you gave when you registered, which now shows up again (except for your password). For instance, your billing and shipping addresses appear all filled in, but you can change them now, although many stores insist that your shipping and billing addresses match the address to which the credit card company sends its bills. You also get one last chance to edit quantities and remove products. Pay particular attention to the shipping method to make sure that is really what you want. (In some systems, you must wait until checkout to pick a shipping method, and find out how much it will cost only during checkout. Ugh.)

When everything is the way you like it, click Submit or Order to send your order in. In a well-designed site, you should immediately get a page confirming the order details and asking you, one more time, to confirm that this is really, really what you want. One more OK, and the order is really, really sent in. (Poorly designed or greedy sites just accept your order the first time, not giving you a moment to reconsider.)

In a few minutes an email should go out from the site confirming the purchase. (You may get the confirmation in a quarter hour, or a few hours, depending in part on the traffic on the Internet and the speed with which your email is delivered.) Be sure to save this confirming email, in case anything goes wrong with the order. You might even consider setting up a folder to save mail from stores so you can find it quickly.

## What is this express checkout or 1-Click purchase?

This is a neat way to buy with one click of your mouse. You have to sign up for this privilege, giving your address, preferred shipping method, and credit card number ahead of time. Because the store has all that information on file, and you agree that they should use it whenever you click the Express or 1-Click button, you can now go browsing away, and whenever you feel the impulse, click that button. That's all you have to do. They confirm that you have ordered such and such, and in a few days it arrives.

Of course, this method is so easy that you may find you order unnecessary or impulse items. We certainly do.

## Why do I need a billing address?

This helps the credit card company confirm that you are who you say you are. Most stores will reject your order if the credit card number is wrong, or if your address does not match the address the credit card sends its bills to. So at most stores you must enter a billing address, and for many that must also be the shipping address, so they can be sure you are not a criminal who has stolen a card and wants stuff sent direct to a motel room.

Sites specifically set up for gifts do allow you to have the present sent directly to the recipient, but that is unusual.

## How safe is my credit card information with an online store?

Your credit card information is safer online than at your local gas station, convenience store, or restaurant—at least if the online store uses a secure server for your order. A secure server is a computer that uses software that protects your personal and credit card information.

Just make sure that you have gone to a secure site before you hand over credit card info. How can you tell? Well, every time you leave a "nonsecure" area and go to the "secure" site, you are notified with a little pop-up window, saying, "You are about to view pages over a secure connection" (unless you have told your browser to stop showing you this little message). Although this alert sounds like a warning, it is actually a reassuring signal that your transaction will, in fact, be private. Other good signs: the address line changes from *http* to *https*, meaning you are using a secure site. Also, in Internet Explorer you see an icon of a lock in the status bar at the bottom of the screen; or in Netscape Navigator, you get a bright yellow key on a blue background at the bottom of the screen. You may also see the letters SSL, which stand for Secure Sockets Layer (a set of standards for plugging in to the secure server), or SET, which stands for Secured Electronic Transaction. You should also see the address change from http to https, for secure, and an icon of a key or lock appears in your status bar.

Techie note: The Secure Sockets Layer, developed by Netscape, authenticates you to the store, and vice versa, and scrambles your messages back and forth so anyone who tapped into them could not figure them out. This encoding is called *encryption*, like what governments use to hide their messages from prying eyes. Good encryption means that it would take a team of programmers months or years, using a supercomputer, to figure out that you were ordering a hair dryer.

## What exactly is encryption?

The purpose of encryption is simply to keep messages private and whole, so they cannot be read by outsiders and cannot be tampered with en route.

Encryption takes your order and turns it into a secret code so that only the intended recipient (you or the store) can read it after mutual authentication—that is, confirmation that the store is who they say they are, and that you are who you say you are.

How does encryption work? That computer, the secure server, has two secret codes, called keys. One is a public key: a big complicated number sent to you, which is embedded in your messages back to the site, which is itself coded, or "encrypted," which is just a fancy word for "made secret by turning it into code." The other is the private key, for you alone, which is what the site uses to match up with the public key, to authenticate that this message comes from you. When the keys match, the system can unlock the code to translate your scrambled information.

Techie note: The private key is the prime factors of the public key. Thus, if the public key were 45, the private key would be 5 and 9, the factors that multiplied together make 45.

Once all these keys match up, the server translates your order and sends it to the accounting or ordering system. No human gets to read your credit card number during this, and there are no paper receipts lying around for vicious jerks to steal. That's why this process is, ultimately, a lot safer for you than giving your card to the clerk down at the dry-cleaning store.

## Which credit cards do stores take?

Almost every online store takes both MasterCard and Visa. Many also take American Express and Discover.

## What does this mean, submit?

At the end of checkout, you are asked whether you want to submit the order or clear the form. Submitting the order just means sending the order in officially, committing yourself to the purchase.

Generally, the system digests the order, checks with your credit card company, checks product availability, then comes back with a confirmation showing what you ordered, where it will be sent, and oh yes, what the order ID or confirmation number is. Save this number. If possible, print this confirmation page or save it on your hard disk, because this number is what you need to use to track your order or cancel.

## How long after I submit my order is it acted upon?

If you buy or sell stocks, your transaction should be completed in 10 to 60 seconds. Ninety seconds is considered slow, because by then the market may have moved, and the prices bid and offered have changed from what you thought was available.

Reservations for airfare, hotel, and rental cars are usually completed within a minute.

If you have ordered something tangible, like a book, your order goes right into the store's computer system and enters the queue of products to be shipped. After that, the stores vary quite a bit in the speed with which they actually ship. The product itself may be "picked" from a warehouse shelf in anywhere from a few hours to a few days if the item is in stock, in two to four weeks if it is out of stock or back-ordered, and in six to eight weeks if you asked for engraving, customization, or hand crafting.

## Why do I have to verify some information after ordering?

If you asked for an academic discount on software, you have to fax in your student or faculty identification, a course schedule, or school bill, to prove you are really in academia. (This is a requirement by the software companies who extend this discount.)

Software upgrades are similar: You have to prove you own the original software to qualify for the discounted rate. You may have to fax them a page from the original manual, or the original serial number.

## Why was my credit card refused?

Who knows? The Web shop does not know why the card was turned down. Only the credit card company knows for sure. Common causes include:

• You can easily have made a typo in that long string of numbers. Recheck. (If you entered spaces between those blocks of numbers, try again without any spaces.)

• Perhaps you typed in a version of your name that does not match the name on the card or on the billing.

• Maybe you typed in a billing address that is different from the one the credit card recognizes.

• Perhaps you typed or selected the wrong expiration date.

Any one of these mistakes will result in a turndown. We find it helps to have the card right in front of us when we re-enter the information. And if you get bumped two or three times, well, try a different card. Then call the original card company and find out if you have reached your limit.

## How do I get a record of my order?

Do your part by printing out the form before you submit it, and then printing and saving the confirmation that should come up directly after you submit the order.

Good stores confirm a) on the screen, right after you send the order in, or b) by email, or c) both ways.

Once you see the confirmation, the order has been placed and you cannot easily change it. If you see a terrible mistake, look for a customer service number or email, and call or send a message right away. The faster you intervene, the more likely you can head off disaster.

The confirmation may be called a purchase verification, and you are sometimes asked, one more time, to confirm that you really, really want to place this order.

## What if I don't get a confirmation of my order?

If you do not receive a confirmation by email within 24 hours, in addition to a confirming message on screen, you should call customer service, to make sure all is well. You have to be concerned that:

- The order has not been received by their system.

- The order was mysteriously rejected, and they have not told you.

- You typed in a wrong email address, and someone who has an address very like yours is wondering, right now, why this company has charged them for your purchase.

## How do I cancel an order with an online store?

You need to act quickly, because these places ship quickly, and once the product has been shipped you cannot completely cancel. You may be able to plan for a return, but you will often be dinged for shipping costs.

- Phone Customer Service, so you can talk with a real human.

- If no one answers for half an hour or so, send email to the Customer Service people, using the Contact Us email address.

You'll be in luck if you ordered a product that is not in stock, because then the store has not shipped it and canceling is easy.

## Is there any limit to the hours when I can order from an online store?

Most sites that use secure servers are set up to take orders 24 hours a day, seven days a week. But if delivery times are crucial, order very early in the day, to be sure that the product can go out that day, or at slower stores, the next day. Wonder when their cutoff time is for shipments? Look on the Frequently Asked Questions (FAQ) list, under shipping, to see when they process orders, or when the cutoff time is, after which your order goes out the next day.

A few sites want to call you back to confirm the details of a messy or complex order, such as a two-week adventure in Mongolia. Some online stockbrokers are so suspicious that they insist on calling you just to make sure you are the one trying to set up the account. In these cases, your order is not really processed until a clerk calls you for confirmation during business hours.

## Is there a problem ordering from outside the U.S.?

Many American stores refuse to accept orders where the credit card billing address is outside the U.S. Some stores are more international than others; for instance, music stores seem to be better prepared to ship anywhere in the world than other stores are. Most stores that ship internationally specifically disclaim responsibility for customs difficulties. And they absolutely won't ship to countries we are currently bombing, or terrorist and outlaw regimes. Plus, some fancy computers and advanced software cannot be shipped to countries that might use it for military advantage (read Iraq, North Korea, and Serbia, these days).

If the store is in Europe or Australia, they are more likely to be set up to accept international orders. (They tend to ship by air to the U.S.)

## What if the product is not in stock?

Some companies tell you, in every product description, exactly how many copies they have in stock, so you know in advance if something is currently available, out of stock, or back-ordered.

But many stores do not tell you ahead of time whether the product is really available. This failure, often due to laziness or poor systems integration, can be a real nuisance, because these are the very stores that wait a week or so before grudgingly acknowledging that the product is not in stock. You have a legal right to cancel the order at that time, whether or not the store tells you so.

Even worse, disreputable companies just put your order on hold without telling you, and you have to call in or use order tracking to find out why it didn't arrive. (This casual habit is against the law and the regulations of the Federal Trade Commission, a fact you might point out to any store that pulls this trick.)

A responsible company will keep notifying you if the date of shipping keeps getting pushed out, perhaps because a manufacturer is slow, or the product is not yet released (like a CD you have requested ahead of its publication date, or a video game for which the orders have overwhelmed the manufacturer).

## When is my credit card charged for the order?

The timing varies. We think you should not be charged until the product ships.

But some sites run the charge through as soon as they receive the order. Technically, this is not quite legal, but you often do not discover this trick until you receive your credit card statement.

A few sites have to charge you right away for reservations of airfare, car rentals, or hotel space, in order to lock in the discounts you want. Once you have paid for the reservation, you get that discount rate. If you were to wait to pay, the discount could evaporate.

Most stores, though, charge only when they ship.

## Do I have to pay sales tax?

Yes, if you are in the same state as the offices of the company. For instance, if you live in New York, New Jersey, or Virginia, you have to pay sales tax to Barnes and Noble, which has offices in each of those states.

So if you want to avoid sales tax, be alert to any indication that you live in the same state as the store's main office. If you think you might be stuck with sales tax but aren't sure, look in the Customer Service area, Help, or Frequently Asked Questions to find out. Of course, the other way to find out is to place your order, which always involves mentioning what state you live in as part of your billing and shipping addresses. Bingo! As soon as they find out, the sales tax goes on.

A few places actually collect sales taxes for a dozen states that have been extremely assertive about their right to taxes on any goods shipped into their borders, and stores that go along with this demand often tax the shipping and handling fees as well.

Eventually, you can figure that all the governors of all the states will march on Washington and insist that online stores impose your local sales tax on anything you buy, and transmit the proceeds to the state treasury electronically, so that the states can put a straw in this fountain of cash. This could reduce the discounts you enjoy online by a quarter to a half. So get ready to send protest email to your congressperson and senators.

## How do I take advantage of a manufacturer's coupon or rebate?

Usually you have to deal directly with the manufacturer to get the extra discount or money back. To be sure you can apply the coupon or rebate, though, take these steps:

- Make sure the site advertises the rebate, and if it does not, email them asking whether you can get the rebate if you buy the product through them.

- Make sure you get a rebate form in the package when it arrives.

- Send the rebate form or filled-out coupon to the original manufacturer right away. (And wait a few months.)

# How Fast Will I Get Delivery?

**How fast will the store get around to shipping my product?**

That depends on the way you pay the store, and on their routine for picking and packing orders. If you send your order in electronically from the Web site, or phone with your credit card info, you get the shipping process started right away. The clock ticks from that moment. But if you send the order by fax or email, a human has to read it, call up the credit card company, and get the OK before anything else happens; a day or so may go by before the clerk gets around to verifying the card. Slowest of all is sending your order in by mail, because that adds another two to five days to the delay.

Once the store's computer system receives the fully confirmed order, the staff has to read the order, pick the products off the shelf, pack them, and pile them up for a delivery service to collect. In some stores, if you get an order into their system by a certain time (from early morning until right after lunch, their time), your order is shipped that day or the next morning. For instance, most orders for flowers go out the same day if ordered before lunchtime.

Most stores take 24 to 48 hours before they actually hand the package over to the delivery service. Stores run by individuals or families may take three days to ship.

And all of these figures assume that the product is in stock. If it's not available, you may have to wait a few weeks (you should receive an email warning you of the delay and offering to let you cancel the order). And if you have asked for special engraving, or customization, you may have to wait a month and a half or more before the personalized product is ready to be shipped.

If delivery times are critical, you should check the store's policy on shipping. The best stores have a button called Shipping, taking you to this kind of information. Others put the info under Customer Service, FAQ, or Help. In some cases, you have to start ordering in order to find out when they ship.

## How reliable are the company's promises about when they will get the product out the door?

Pretty good, in our experience, as long as the items are in stock. With items that come from some other company, though, the store has less control, and you may have to wait as long as a month for "back-ordered" items. The Federal Trade Commission has a Mail Order Rule that applies here: 1) The company has to ship whenever they say they will. 2) If they encounter a delay, they must tell you about it, and get your agreement to that delay. You have the right to cancel the order at that time.

## What shipping options do I have?

Some stores ship only by ground or via the mail. But most offer a variety of methods, with delivery coming the next day, or two or three days after the product leaves the store. (Remember, the store may take a while to pack your order, which adds significantly to the total time until delivery.) Here are typical options offered by stores using delivery services:

- Overnight, in the morning or during the day

- 2nd Day

- 3rd Day

- Ground, which means about a week of business days

- Saturday (not offered very often)

And then there are the various services offered by the U.S. Postal Service, at http://www.usps.gov/

- International air

- Priority Mail, which may take two or three days for delivery. For a fee you can also get package tracking, insurance, and confirmation of delivery, making this almost as expensive as the services' Ground delivery, but not quite as reliable.

- Express Mail, which generally gets to you overnight, with the added plus of being insured and having a tracking number, so you can locate the package if it gets lost (expensive)

- Parcel Post or Book Rate, which may take a few weeks

Very few stores are willing to ship for Cash on Delivery (COD), and if they do ship this way, they insist on receiving a cashier's check or money order.

## Why won't they ship to a post office box?

Two reasons:

- Delivery services like Airborne Express, DHL, FedEx, and UPS are not allowed into post offices.

- Credit card companies take a dim view of a P.O. box as a billing address, and prefer that the store ship only to the same address as the billing address on the credit card.

## On a military base, what kind of shipping can I get?

You'll have to rely on the government, that is, the U.S. Post Office, for delivery, because the brass do not like delivery services wandering around the base trying to deliver a package directly to your barracks or house.

## How much does shipping cost?

Good question, because some sites refuse to tell you how much the shipping charges will be until you give them credit card info, billing address, and shipping address, all of which could take a few minutes, so you get committed to the order. Only then will they let you know. Bad practice. The best sites tell you, right in the product description, how much each kind of shipping will cost you for that product, so you can estimate your total cost, not just the price of the product.

Here are some of the ways sites disclose shipping costs:

- Some stores charge a standard amount, and just drop that figure into the order without telling you what you get for the money—that is, how long it will take to deliver, given that fee.

- Others let you pick different shipping services and delivery times, but do not tell you how much they cost until you submit the order.

- Better stores offer you the complete table of choices, and let you pick before you decide whether to submit the order.

- The absolute best stores tell you how much each delivery type will cost you, and how soon you can expect delivery that way, on the product description page, so you can factor that information into your decision to buy.

Increasingly, stores compete with each other on shipping costs, which is good, because this pressure will drive them all to advertise what a good deal they offer. The best deal, apparently, is free shipping.

But how long does that take? Usually a week, because the store is talking about shipping by ground, or at the cheapest postal rates. You always pay more for faster delivery. Charges for shipping go up when:

- You ask for faster delivery. (The cost of delivery of a CD overnight in the morning may be more than $25, whereas if you could wait a week, you might pay less than $4.)

- You order more products than are covered by their standard or flat fee. (For instance, some music stores will ship four CDs for a set fee, but start charging you a bit more if you order more than that.)

- You order a heavy product, or one that weighs more than a certain threshold amount.

- The store charges you by the item, whereas other stores charge by the whole order, which is usually cheaper.

- You ask to have your multiple-item order shipped as items become available, rather than waiting for all of them to be sent in a single shipment. (You may have to pay a separate charge for each shipment.)

So, if you can stand waiting, you can save quite a bit of money by accepting the slowest delivery, which usually takes about a week.

Also, if you get the chance, take the option that says, "Only ship when all the products are ready," because then you pay only one shipping charge, not several.

## How do I check on my order, while I'm waiting for it to arrive?

If your order was shipped with a delivery service such as FedEx or UPS, the store can tell you the package number, so you can go to the delivery service's Web site and check on the package's progress. (You may have to wait 24 hours after the order is actually shipped to see your package on the Web site.)

Or, if you registered or became a member at the store, you may be able to log in with that name and password, go to an order tracking area on the site itself, use your confirmation code (from the store), and plug into the delivery service's tracking systems from there.

## Do I have to sign for the package?

In many cases, the store likes to have you sign a receipt to confirm that the package really reached you. The delivery services obey these requests.

But if you must go out, you can put up a note authorizing the driver to leave the package (print your name and sign it).

Or, if you get a lot of packages but you are often out, you can get a small form from the delivery service to glue to your door, authorizing them to leave packages even if you are not home. We've found that this little sticker often encourages drivers to ignore the requirement for a signature, so we come home to find a package on the doorstep. (Our front door is hidden from the street by a gate and an adobe wall.)

## What should I do the moment I receive my product?

Try it out quickly, so you can get credit if it fails. If you wait more than 10 days, some stores refuse to accept returns. (Other stores extend the grace period to 30 days.)

Save everything, in case you have to return the product: manuals, cards, warranty, packing slip, original box, foam pellets. Don't fill out the registration form until you know the product works.

## Does the product have a warranty?

Well, we can't say for sure, but most products that cost more than $20 have some kind of warranty, however feeble. The warranty is issued by the original manufacturer, though, not the store.

If the product has a warranty, that will come with the product, as long as you are buying a new item. (Once a product has been used, or bought in auction from the original user, the warranty may no longer apply.)

Some stores mention that there is a warranty, but only an excellent few actually show you the warranty online.

## What is guaranteed by the online store, if anything?

If the store promises to ship your package out within a certain time, the Federal Trade Commission considers that a guarantee. Ditto for any statements such as "Lowest prices guaranteed." Usually any store that actually uses the word *guarantee* has a long legalistic explanation of what is included and what is excluded, but we have found that the sheer effort their lawyers have expended on this description indicates that the store takes the guarantee seriously. (These stores usually do have extremely low prices.)

Money-back guarantees are heavily advertised, if they exist, and usually require that you complain about the product within 10 to 30 days after receipt. Many stores charge a 10% restocking fee if you wait for 15 days to complain. If you dawdle for more than 30 days, you may find the store refuses to accept a return, or accepts a return only in exchange for another copy of the same product, and then only if the product turns out to be defective and is still covered by its warranty. You can see that if you have a problem with a product, you'd better call or email immediately. (Remember: Even if the product is an OOBF, that is, an Out-of-Box Failure, you probably will not get your shipping costs back.)

# What About Returning a Product?

**How can I return a product?**

Basically, you must contact the store and get their OK before you send the product back, for whatever reason, and you should do this quickly, to make sure you are within the time frame they have established for returns.

**How can I discover a store's policy on returns?**

A good store posts its policy on returns in an area called something like Customer Service, FAQ, Help, or Returns.

The Azazz store at http://www.azazz.com/ has a policy we like: "We want your business over the long term, not just today. If your order is damaged or defective, return it. If it is the wrong color or size, return it. If you simply made a mistake in purchasing a product, return it. Your satisfaction is our number one goal." OK!

You might want to print out the returns policy during your visit, if you anticipate you might ever have to return an item. The return policies we've studied are all over the ballpark. Some are generous, some incredibly nasty.

The FTC says that if the store uses a phrase like "money-back guarantee," that means they have to give you a full refund without asking nosy questions or forcing you to jump through hoops. But the stores have developed several variations you ought to look for if you are concerned about being able to return the product. Questions you might want to explore:

- Can you return a product just because you don't like it? (You should be able to, if you are quick to ask.)

- Can you return a product if you opened the box? The question for the store is: Can we resell this item? In many cases, all you have to do is slip the gizmo back in the original package, and as long as you haven't ripped and torn the packaging or the product, the store will accept the return. On the other hand, some products, such as lingerie, swimming suits, and food cannot be returned after opening, for health reasons. And software vendors will not allow stores to resell an opened box, because you could easily have loaded the software on your hard disk, then asked to get your money back.

- If the product is defective, can you get your money back, or do you have to settle for another product of the same kind? (Usually your credit card company will back you up if you insist on a complete refund, no matter what the official store policy is.)

- When do you have to ask to return the product? You are often given between 10 and 30 days, no more.

- Is there a restocking fee (usually 10% to 15% of the purchase price) for returning a product just because you don't like it? (Lousy requirement, suggesting that the store may be receiving too many returns by unhappy customers,)

## What's the usual method of returning a product to an online store?

Usually you have to email or phone the store, telling them your order number and the complete product name (both are on the confirmation page that you printed out when ordering, and the email you received confirming your order, which, of course, you saved).

Then you have to tell the store your reason for wanting to return the product, your name, daytime phone, and email and shipping addresses. All of this information helps them locate your order in their system.

You must get their OK for the return, and that usually means they will send you something like a Return Merchandise Authorization (RMA) with a special number. You place that RMA and number in the original package with the product and send it to the special address they give you. (The return location is often different from the warehouse that shipped you the product in the first place.) The RMA number is good only for returning this particular product. If the number doesn't match the one the store sent, you will have great problems getting a refund or exchange. To make sure your return does not get lost, use a service that allows order tracking, such as FedEx or UPS, or the Post Office's Priority or Express Mail.

If the product breaks at some time after the store will accept a return, you have to turn to the original manufacturer, using the warranty.

## Why was my return rejected?

A store may refuse to accept a return if:

- You waited too long to complain (like more than 30 days after receipt).

- You just sent the darn thing back to the warehouse, without getting an OK for a return, and without enough information for them to recognize that you are the person sending the package.

- You sent it to the warehouse, not the returns location.

- You forgot to send back all the items the manufacturer included, such as the manual, the warranty, the registration card, and, oh yes, the product.

- You forgot to send the RMA number.

## When do I get the credit?

If you can return a product for credit, the credit shows up about three weeks after the product reaches the vendor. Most of that delay is due to the credit card companies slow accounting processes, not the store.

# Where Can I Find Out More About Problems I May Face as an Online Consumer?

**Does the federal government have any information about online shopping?**

Yes, the Consumer Information Center, in Pueblo, Colorado, has a bunch of pamphlets that cost money if you buy the paper versions but cost nothing if you pick them up from their Web site, at http://www.pueblo.gsa.gov/

And for links to government agencies that deal with scams, warnings about unsafe products and consumer recalls, and health alerts, go to the U.S. Consumer Gateway at http://www.consumer.gov/

**Are there any non-profit organizations offering consumer advice on the Web?**

Consumer Action gives you Chinese, English, and Spanish advice and research on all kinds of shopping, not just online shopping. They provide free paper publications in eight languages and Braille. Plus, they offer links to a passel of consumer sites at http://www.consumer-action.org/

Consumer World offers links to government agencies, consumer organizations, bargain sites, and news about shopping on the Web. They also have a robot who gets prices from discount stores, for comparison shopping, at http://www.consumerworld.org/

**What can I do to avoid scams and fraud online?**

Use the same common sense you use when shopping in a store. If the deal seems too good to be true, it is. If you get a queasy feeling, walk out.

We have carefully studied every store we recommend in this book, and we believe these stores are all reliable. But even these stores might change their spots. And once you venture out to the motley collection of stores across the rest of the Web, you can easily wander into a dubious site.

There are some signs to watch out for in the online world. The National Fraud Information Center at http://www.fraud.org/ publishes warnings about scams on the Internet, most of which take place through email (fake work-at-home offers, credit repair, offshore trusts, pyramid schemes). But a few scams may appear in online stores. Here are some of the NFIC suggestions for caution dealing with an online store:

- Make sure that the store posts a phone number and mailing address, as well as a convincingly detailed description of themselves, including some real history, not just marketing claims.

- Make sure you have entered a genuinely secure shopping area. You should see an alert that you are entering a secure area, your address line should begin with https (not just http), and you should see an icon of a key (in Netscape) or a lock (in Internet Explorer). If you have any doubts about security, leave.

- Never deal with a site whose phone number begins with 809. That's a number outside of the U.S., so the vendor is out of reach of the U.S. justice system. Also, the vendor may make money every minute you are on hold, often at outrageous charges per minute.

- Never redial into the Internet using a vendor's software. If a store urges you to download some software, log off your own Internet service provider, and then use the software to reconnect to the Internet, you may be dialing long-distance to a site in Russia, or Singapore, without knowing it. You could end up with high per-minute charges on your phone bill.

- Be cautious about free trials. Most are OK, but make sure you are dealing with a company you recognize, one you can get in touch with directly, if you have a complaint. Make sure that the store does not convert your free trial into a surprise subscription, with charges on your credit card bill.

- Don't buy stocks or bonds based on a flurry of excitement on a discussion board or chat session. Those forums can easily be manipulated by scam artists. Always research a stock thoroughly on real investment research sites like those we describe in this book.

- Watch out for auction items offered by individuals who want you to send cash. Online auctions result in two-thirds of the reports of fraud on the Web, and almost all of these complaints deal with individuals pretending to offer items for auction. The host often takes no responsibility for these classified auctions. Worse, if you send cash or a money order, you have no legal recourse, because the seller can so easily say the cash never arrived. Look for an escrow service, to hold your payment until the product arrives; or insist on paying by credit card, so you can back out of the sale if it goes south.

- Never use debit cards online. They are not protected against fraud. Your credit card is, so that no matter how much you are taken for, you pay only $50.

- Never give out your Social Security number. No legitimate business needs this.

- Never give out your bank account numbers. Again, no legitimate business asks for these over the Internet.

- Never respond to junk email. Anyone who sends you unsolicited offers is violating Netiquette, the unwritten rules of courtesy on the Internet. How did they get your email address? Did they ever ask you for permission to send this junk? If not, just get rid of the message. When investigated, many of these offers turn out to be pure bunk; a few are genuinely sinister, trying to con you out of your financial information or passwords to your Internet Service Provider (so they can cruise at your expense). When in doubt, delete.

- Get full information about the product, and save or print that out before you order: product description, total price, delivery date, return policy, and any guarantees.

In general, act on your suspicions. If you begin to have doubts about the reliability of a site, get out of there. You can, of course, check with the Better Business Bureau at http://www.bbbonline.org/, CPA Web Trust at http://www.aicpa.org, or NetCheck at http://www.netcheck.com, but if a store is truly fly-by-night, they may disappear before organizations like this receive complaints. If you don't like a store, go to another.

## What can I do if I am the victim of fraud?

Gather all the information you saved or printed when you were ordering, and call the store's customer service department. Try to straighten things out directly.

If the store refuses to consider your complaints, or temporizes, or just plain doesn't answer the phone, you'd better talk to your credit card company right away. Give them the full details, and ask for the charge to be removed.

If you sent a check, call your bank to stop payment. (If you used a debit card, you are out the money, and may have a heck of a time recovering it.)

If you decide that the store really indulged in fraud, as opposed to being incompetent, report the case in full detail to the Federal Trade Commission at http://www.ftc.gov/ or 202-FTC-HELP (382-4357), the National Fraud Information Center at http://www.fraud.org/ or 1-800-876-7060, the Better Business Bureau online at http://www.bbbonline.com/, or your state attorney general. You may not get your money back, but you are helping shut the scam artists down.

# How Did You Decide Which Stores to Include or Reject?

## What criteria did you use to reject a store?

We're a tough filter. We rejected most of the sites we visited, so you won't have to.

Here are some of the specific reasons we omitted a site:

- It doesn't really sell online. You have to call their 800 number or visit the store. The site is just a catalog.

- The store delivers only in its local area.

- The store does not offer secure ordering, or uses "special software" to order. (No thanks!)

- The products are copycat, me-too, or boring.

- The store only sells one thing, or a few, and the products are just like what a hundred other stores offer.

- The interface or layout stinks (illegible text on black backgrounds, no menus, crazy wallpaper behind everything, ugly layouts).

- We couldn't find some of the items they claimed to sell.

- We couldn't order items they claimed to sell.

- Their main focus is selling to businesses, at large volumes.

- Their prices are too high, when similar stores seem to be able to offer discounts.

- The store is really a brochure for the manufacturer, and a) does not sell anything, or b) sells only at the manufacturer's suggested retail price, which is way above realistic street prices.

- The search mechanism does not work well.

- The store does not give detailed information about its history, mission, or partners.

- The store seems to work hard to hide prices, shipping rates, or delivery times.

- The store refuses to provide enough product information for a reasonable consumer to decide what it is, and how it compares with similar products.

- The store makes it hard or impossible to get in touch with them, hiding or refusing to publish a customer service number, contact email address, snail mail address, or order-tracking system.

- The store's relationship with independent shops under its umbrella seems unclear; we could not figure out whom we were really dealing with. (Whom would we complain to, in this pyramid of hosts, mall-like sites, and boutiques?)

Basically, we turned against a site if it seemed unfriendly, unusable, or ugly.

On occasion we did give a site the benefit of the doubt on some of these criteria, if:

- It's clearly a small, not-super-professional mom-and-pop site, but it offers unique, hard-to-find, or beautiful products.

- It's a one-product site, but the product is fantastic.

- The prices are mid-range, but the site offers you the ability to search for every conceivable product in a particular product category (such as computer-aided design) all in one place, for easier comparison, and faster access to what you want, without distractions.

## So what prompted you to include a site in the book?

In each category, we have tried to include several different kinds of stores:

- Gigantic, we-sell-everything, we-discount-like-crazy warehouses (great if you know exactly what you want).

- Smaller stores that add value by giving you detailed information about products, comparison tables, and reader reports, so you can learn about the range of products before you choose.

- Sites devoted to an interesting niche, particularly if it's a product category that the bigger stores overlook or dismiss.

- Sites that are such a joy to visit that we think if you're at all interested in the chapter's products, you'll want to go there again and again.

We favor a store if it offers most of these features:

- A secure area for ordering, to protect your personal and credit information.

- A guarantee that it will not pass along your personal information to any other company. Period.

- A fast and accurate search system.

- Browsable lists of products so you can look through categories without having to plunge down, down, down through a lot of levels.

- Availability of the items the store says it sells.

- Rich product descriptions, with components such as good photos (small and large), lists of features and benefits, pricing, shipping information, manufacturer's name and warranty, samples, suggestions for add-on products, reviews by critics and customers.

- Prices that are easy to determine.

- Prices that are low to mid-range, and if the store does not offer serious discounts, there is a reasonable explanation, or compensating value on the site (extra information, super service, free shipping).

- Extensive instructions on how to order, how to pick shipping, how to return products.

- A prominently posted customer service phone number and email, so you can get in touch with the store.

- An ordering system that is easy to find and use.

- Shipping choices that are visible early on, before you order.

- Immediate confirmation of orders with a detailed page or email, or both.

- Opportunity to opt out of receiving email announcing their sales.

- Return policies that are clear and reasonable.

- A layout that looks good.

- Navigation that is easy.

Of course, not every site manages to do all these things well, but to qualify, a site had to be outstanding in many of these areas.

## What if I hate a store you recommend?

Gosh, we'd be disappointed. But we certainly want to hear about it. Sometimes stores go downhill fast, or change owner-ship.

If you think a store stinks, check our Web site at http://www.theprices.com to see if we have issued an alert about that store, and if not, please let us know at theprices@swcp.com. We will go back to the site, and ax it from the next edition if the store has really gone off the deep end.

## What if I find a store has changed or disappeared?

Yes, just like on Main Street or out at the mall, some online stores do change ownership, switch addresses, go out of business, or transform themselves. We've double- and triple-checked all the sites described in this book, but sites change, and despite the many pluses of the book as a medium, such as fast and random access, portability, and stability, we can't update the paper pages. So if a store has changed or died, or if we made a mistake in our description, please let us know at theprices@swcp.com. We'll make a note for the next edition, and post important change notices on our Web site, at http://www.theprices.com

## What if I discover a store you might like?

Please let us know if you discover a great store. Email us at theprices@swcp.com. We'll go take a look.

We post recent discoveries on our Web site, so visit us at http://www.theprices.com

# The Best
# Online
# Shops

# Animal & Pet Supplies

This was one of our favorite chapters to research and write. First, you have to understand that we have a special fondness for a sweet, chow-loving beagle named Summer. And an incredibly smart but stubborn Welsh corgi named Toby. They both excel at sleeping and chasing birds out of our backyard. We also have an alien goldfish named Joe Montana. We know that Joe is an alien because our son won him at the State Fair by throwing a Ping-Pong ball into his teeny bowl . . . 10 years ago. (Don't worry, Joe's bowl is lots larger now.) Along the way, we've also been the home for some lizards, tropical fish, parakeets, and an Amazon parrot. So it was with sheer delight that we found all the neat stores on the Web that cater to pets and animals. We found places that will personalize a number of items for you or your pet. Some shops even sell natural pet food, medicine, and flea controls. And we even discovered a pet deli and a store that offers designer kitty litter boxes. So have fun reading this chapter. We suspect you'll have a good laugh and find some critter accessories you must have.

## Aardvark Pet

http://www.aardvarkpet.com

Cute store where you can pick up lots of pet supplies, toys, gifts, and training aids. Despite the name of the store, most of the items for sale are for dogs, cats, and their owners. They really do a good job of offering very practical and useful products. Samples:

- Bedding for dogs
- Car-seat covers
- Collars and leads
- Elevated feeder for big dogs
- Grooming supplies
- Hiking boots for dogs
- Kitty drinking fountain
- Kitty window perch
- Nylon pet bowl for backpacks
- Puppy housebreaking kit
- Self-cleaning litter box
- Self-filling water bowls
- Treats and toys

**Search:** Some
**Photos:** Yes
**Ordering:** Online, Phone
**Gift Wrap:** Card
**Delivery:** Ground

## Arcata Pet Online

http://www.arcatapet-online.com

This is a huge pet store that caters to many different kinds of household guests, from the more common ones like dogs and cats, to the more challenging reptiles, fish, birds, and ferrets. It's easy to find what you're looking for. Each animal has its own search mechanism. Shipping is a flat $5. Samples:

- Aquarium systems
- Cat window perch
- Dog-training supplies
- Ferret-deodorizing shampoo and spray
- Flea and tick products
- Hummingbird feeders
- Medications and vitamins
- Pet doors
- Reptile heating systems
- Treats and toys

**Search:** Yes
**Photos:** Yes
**Ordering:** Online, Phone
**Gift Wrap:** No
**Delivery:** Ground

# Bone to Be Wild

`http://www.io.com/life/pets`

We don't know about you, but we think that dogs and cats that wear scarves look real cool. We don't know how they feel about it, though. We do know that one Halloween we put a Superman cape on our Welsh corgi, who then chased our beagle around the backyard for about a hundred times. Well, this place doesn't sell canine Superman capes, but it does sell lots and lots of different scarves tailor-made for your dog or cat. Sample scarves:

- Classic bandanna
- Crazy cat
- Fourth of July stars and stripes
- Picnic time
- Victorian cat

**Search:** No
**Photos:** Yes
**Ordering:** Online, Phone, Fax
**Gift Wrap:** No
**Delivery:** Ground

# Care-a-lot Pet Supply Warehouse

`http://www.carealot.org`

This is an absolutely huge store that sells supplies for dogs, cats, birds, fish, horses, reptiles, pigs, rabbits, donkeys, frogs, ferrets, goats, spiders, llamas, snakes and . . . well, you get the idea. You can join in on one of their animal chat rooms or post a query on their message board. You can search by animal or by product. Samples:

- Bathing supplies
- Beds
- Cages
- Grooming products
- Housebreaking aids
- Litter boxes
- Nail clippers
- No-dig sprays

- Pet doors
- Skin and eye products
- Toys and treats
- Vitamins and supplements
- Wormers and medications

**Search:** Yes
**Photos:** Yes
**Ordering:** Online, Phone, Fax
**Gift Wrap:** No
**Delivery:** Ground

# Cranberry Lane

`http://www.cranberrylane.com`

It's always nice when, browsing through several online stores, you find one that seems to have fun with the assortment of items it offers for sale. One such store is Cranberry Lane. Their products are all natural, 100% biodegradable, using no preservatives. If you want your pet to enjoy the same natural products you prefer, sneak a peek at this store. Samples:

- Carpet shake
- Formulas to make natural products
- Gentle soap to clean and repel fleas
- Massage oil

**Search:** Yes
**Photos:** Some
**Ordering:** Online
**Gift Wrap:** No
**Delivery:** Ground, 2nd Day, Overnight

# Dr. Goodpet

`http://www.goodpet.com`

For over 10 years this company has been making high-quality (with lots of awards to prove it) dog food, grooming products, homeopathic medicines, and more. If your dog is scratching or his coat is looking a little dull, you might want to try some. Samples:

- Arthritis relief
- Natural medicine

- Non-toxic flea control solutions
- *Pet Allergies: Remedies for an Epidemic*
- Pure shampoo
- Stain-control garments for dogs
- Vitamins and mineral supplements

**Search:** Yes
**Photos:** Some
**Ordering:** Online
**Gift Wrap:** No
**Delivery:** Ground, 3<sup>rd</sup> Day, 2<sup>nd</sup> Day, Overnight

## Doggie Diamonds

http://www.doggiediamonds.com

Hey, you dog lovers. Take a stroll over to this Web store designed just for you. There's a lot of custom and pre-made stuff here, including over 400 pieces of dog artwork and doggie clothing. You can browse through the entire store or do a search by entering the breed you're most fond of. As a crazy extra, they also deliver fresh-cut flowers. Go figure! Sample items that you can have your favorite breed painted or embroidered on:

- Baseball shirts
- Birth announcements
- Bumper stickers
- Checkbook covers
- Decorator pillows
- Fanny packs
- Holiday cards
- Ladies' and men's denim shirts
- Luggage tags
- Stuffed animals
- Sweatshirts
- T-shirts
- Velour hand towels

**Search:** Yes
**Photos:** No
**Ordering:** Online, Phone, Fax
**Gift Wrap:** No
**Delivery:** Ground

## Dogtoys.com

http://www.dogtoys.com

At this store, there are over 400 toys that your pooch can play with. You can search for toys that are especially good for certain breeds, or look for items by dog size or product category. And, just in case your cats are feeling left out, this store sells some toys for them, too. Samples:

- Balls
- Bones
- Cat toys
- Dental-health toys
- Fleece and plush toys
- Funny cards and gifts
- Treat dispensers

**Search:** Yes
**Photos:** Yes
**Ordering:** Online, Phone, Fax
**Gift Wrap:** No
**Delivery:** Ground

## The Domino Video Company

http://www.dvcnet.com

The American Kennel Club (AKC) produces a series of videos explaining the history of many breeds of dogs. Their videos also showcase various prime pedigrees for breeding. If you are thinking about formally showing your dog, watching all of the various dog shows will be quite instructional. You can order the tapes by breed. Sample videotapes:

- American Maltese Association
- Beddington Terrier Club of America
- Bichon Frise Club of America
- National Beagle Club of America
- Pembroke Welsh Corgi Club of America
- Puli Club of America

**Search:** Yes
**Photos:** No
**Ordering:** Online
**Gift Wrap:** No
**Delivery:** Ground

## Good Eats

http://www.goodeats.com

You'll find a large assortment of natural foods for you and your dog or cat at this store with the fun name. Food for your pals comes either canned or dry. There's also a good selection of organic Kosher foods (for you, silly). Minimum orders are $20. Samples:

- Canned-beef cat food
- Canned D'Lite dog and cat food
- Canned turkey-and-brown-rice dog food
- Dog biscuits
- Hardy dinner cat food
- Mackerel cat food
- Puppy food
- Tuna-and-chicken cat food

**Search:** Yes
**Photos:** No
**Ordering:** Online, Phone, Fax
**Gift Wrap:** Card
Delivery: Ground, 3rd Day, 2nd Day, Overnight

## Lafeber's Critter Products

http://www.lafeber.com

Lest you think we've given an unequal amount of space to the dog and cat owners, be patient, your wait is over. This store sells premium-quality food and treats for birds, rabbits, guinea pigs, hamsters, and gerbils. Samples:

- Avicakes for all birds
- Baby-bird food
- Bird vitamins
- Critter berries
- Critter cakes
- Critter crunch
- Jungle-joy parrot toy
- Nutriberries for parakeets, cockatiels, parrots, macaws, or cockatoos
- Nuts 'n Nuggets parrot, macaw, or cockatoo food
- Pelleted food for finches, canaries, parakeets, cockatiels, parrots, and macaws

**Search:** No

**Photos:** Some
**Ordering:** Online, Phone
**Gift Wrap:** No
**Delivery:** Ground

## Merrick Pet Delicatessen

http://www.merrick-deli.com

Nothing's too good for your pet. And by shopping at this deli, you're proving it. After you finish browsing and buying, you might want to fill out the dog birthday card, and Merrick will mail your chow hound a treat on his birthday. If one treat won't do, you should check out the Fun Treat Pack. All of the pet food has no added salt, sugar, or preservatives. There is a $15 minimum. Samples:

- Bully sticks
- Cat and ferret treats
- Lamb-and-potato chips
- Pig ears
- Treat baskets
- Treats for older dogs
- Venison-and-potato chips

**Search:** Yes
**Photos:** Yes
**Ordering:** Online, Phone, Fax
**Gift Wrap:** No
**Delivery:** Ground

## Nature's Pet Marketplace

http://www.naturespet.com

Only natural products for your pet are for sale at this store. Consider it a health food store for animals. Samples:

- 100% natural cat and kitten litter
- All-natural dog and cat food
- Conditioning shampoos and dips for dogs and cats
- Nontoxic bug spray
- Nontoxic flea controls
- Puppy food

- Vitamins and herbal supplements
- Yeast and garlic bits

**Search:** Yes
**Photos:** Yes
**Ordering:** Online, Fax
**Gift Wrap:** Card
**Delivery:** Ground

# Noah's Pet Supplies

http://noahspets.com

Great assortment of products for dogs, cats, birds, ferrets, fish, guinea pigs, mice, hamsters, gerbils, and small reptiles. There are the everyday essentials and items that make you ask, "Who'd ever thought they'd have something like this?" And with over 10,000 quality supplies for sale, you're sure to find exactly what you're looking for. Have a question? Just ask one of their professionals online. Samples:

- Anti-barking devices
- Aquarium supplies
- Bark and moss
- Cage cleaners and deodorizers
- Cat scratchers
- Collars, leads, and harnesses
- Dog and cat doors
- Flea and tick control for dogs and puppies
- Hairball remedies
- Hamster and gerbil racing car
- Kennels
- Nesting supplies
- Plants and vines for reptile cages
- Science Diet dog food
- Treats and toys

**Search:** Yes
**Photos:** Yes
**Ordering:** Online, Phone, Fax
**Gift Wrap:** No
**Delivery:** Ground

# Pet Expo

http://www.pet-expo.com

A large warehouse store that sells thousands of items for your animal friends. The wide variety of products, including some hard-to-find things, makes it almost certain that you'll be able to locate whatever supply you need. Samples:

- Bag balm
- Cat-scratching posts
- De-matting combs
- Engraved pet tags
- Exercise pens
- Ferret vitamins
- Flea shampoos
- Rabbit and guinea pig cages
- Rawhide and edible toys
- Small, medium, and large dog car seats
- Toys and treats
- Training items

**Search:** Some
**Photos:** Yes
**Ordering:** Online, Phone, Fax
**Gift Wrap:** No
**Delivery:** Ground, 3rd Day, 2nd Day, Overnight

# PetHouse, Inc.

http://www.netusa.com/
pethouse.html

Who says this book isn't terrific? You might be wondering why we ask that question. But where else can you find out about a place that sells (for a mere $25 each) designer cat boxes on the Web? This is the real stuff. Each "box" comes complete with a washable waterproof plastic litter tray. These cat boxes would be perfect for people who, in everyday conversation, call a toilet a commode. Sample styles:

- Black or white pyramid complete with gold hieroglyphics
- Red barn with removable sliding doors and a granite print roof

- Wooden outhouse with a crescent moon, removable sliding door, and skylight roof

**Search:** No
**Photos:** Yes
**Ordering:** Online, Phone, Email
**Gift Wrap:** No
**Delivery:** Ground

## PetPro

http://www.petpro.com

Animal lovers . . . this is the place for you! You'll find little trinkets for your critter as well as lots of neat items for you. This is also a great place to shop if you want to send a gift to an animal-loving friend. Many similar stores just specialize in dogs or cats, but this store has a wide selection of merchandise for various animals, including horses, birds, reptiles, insects, dolphins, whales, and, of course, dogs and cats. (In fact, they have products for over 150 different breeds of dogs!) You can also custom-order an automobile license plate frame with an animal-friendly slogan. They also provide you with lots of links, especially to organizations that help endangered species. Samples:

- Amazon parrot "crossing signs"
- Animal calendars (lots of varieties)
- Cat notepaper
- Dog jewelry
- Flamingo magnets
- Hand-painted puffin figurines
- Horse T-shirts

**Search:** Yes
**Photos:** Some
**Ordering:** Online, Fax, Email
**Gift Wrap:** Card
**Delivery:** Ground

## Pets.com

http://www2.pets.com

What we really liked about this animal-warehouse store is all the wonderful resources available for pet owners. For instance, they have a searchable database of hotels and motels that welcome pets, and you can even search for an emergency veterinarian clinic if you need one while traveling. They also dispense info on dog desserts, dogstrology, and, but of course, pets in politics. Our favorite section is the Photo of the Day. Pets.com carries supplies for just about every pet you can think of. The search at this store is excellent. Samples:

- Aquarium kits
- Bird feeders and waterers
- Bunny bedding and cages
- Dog cologne
- Ferret shampoo
- Flea and tick controls
- Hamster and gerbil brush
- Odor disposers
- Pet doors
- Pet food and health aids
- Small reptile heaters

**Search:** Yes
**Photos:** Yes
**Ordering:** Online
**Gift Wrap:** No
**Delivery:** Ground

## R.C. Steele Co.

http://www.rcsteele.com

For 40 years, this company has been selling pet supplies at substantial discounts. Their Web store is the same. You'll find health-care supplies, treats, toys, beds and training equipment for your pet. As if the great prices weren't enough, they also send a free gift with every order. Samples:

- Aquarium supplies
- Bird cages and accessories
- Cat and dog beds
- Crates and travel houses
- Housebreaking supplies
- Pet apparel

- Reptile vitamins and supplements
- Stain and odor removal items
- Wheat-grass bird supplement

**Search:** Yes
**Photos:** Yes
**Ordering:** Online
**Gift Wrap:** No
**Delivery:** Ground

## Radio Fence

http://www.radiofence.com

Pet containment (that is, how to keep your pet in your yard and not bother the neighbors, or how to keep your pet off your $2,000 sofa) is the specialty of this store. They sell indoor and outdoor containment systems, including some less-extensive and less-expensive training products. Samples:

- Bark-control collars
- Citronella spray
- Indoor-containment devices
- Outdoor-fence kits and accessories
- Professional installation service
- Remote-training devices

**Search:** Some
**Photos:** No
**Ordering:** Online, Phone, Fax
**Gift Wrap:** No
**Delivery:** Ground, 3rd Day, 2nd Day, Overnight

## Sherpa Products

http://www.sherpapet.com

This store will be an enlightening experience if you take your pet with you when you travel. Several years ago, Gayle Metz had to fly with her Lhasa Apso dog, named Sherpa. She couldn't find a travel carrier that was conformable and that the airlines allowed, so she created one . . . and then another . . . and then another. Today, there are numerous soft-sided bags available for your pet. You carry your pet, in these bags, with you on the following airlines: Air Canada, AirWest, Alaska, American, Continental, Delta, Northwest, Pan Am, TWA, United, and US Airways. The Humane Society, the ASPCA, and many veterinarians recommend all of these bags. The bags come in various sizes and colors. Samples:

- Nylon-mesh bags
- Original portable pet den with wheels
- Roll-up bag with shoulder strap
- Tote bags (not for in-flight use)

**Search:** Some
**Photos:** Yes
**Ordering:** Online, Phone, Fax
**Gift Wrap:** No
**Delivery:** Ground, 2nd Day, Overnight

## State Line Tack

http://www.statelinetack.com

Horse owners will love the selection of items for sale here. There are close to 3,000 products for them and their horses. Click on the English or Western buttons to begin your search. Equestrian clothing is also available. And, in case you have one of those cute herding dogs around, this store also sells some supplies for your dog, too. Samples:

- Bandages and wraps
- Blankets
- Boots
- Coolers
- Fleece-lined horse boots
- Instructional books and videos
- Leg wraps
- Mane tamers
- Riding clothes for men, women, and kids
- Tack and accessories
- Turnout rugs

**Search:** Yes
**Photos:** Yes
**Ordering:** Online
**Gift Wrap:** No
**Delivery:** Ground

# Top Drawer

`http://www.k9design.com`

This is the place for personalized products for you and your dog. Think it's silly? Well, we have two dogs, and they have water bowls and food bowls with their names on them. Do they eat and drink exclusively from the right bowls? Of course not, they're dogs. But we love it. Samples:

- Personalized embroidered scarves for dogs
- Cuddle dogs
- Personalized knit shirts and denim shirts with your favorite breed
- Sweatshirts (up to size 2XL) with your dog's likeness embroidered on them
- Virtual postcards

**Search:** No
**Photos:** Yes
**Ordering:** Online, Phone, Fax
**Gift Wrap:** No
**Delivery:** Ground

# Traveling with your pet?

Get some great advice from Air Animal at http://www.airanimal.com. You'll also get some practical advice and facts. Did you know, for example, that your pet's moving expenses are tax deductible?

# Looking for a dog breeder?

Go to http://www.cyberpet.com/cyberdog/breed for a list of reputable breeders in your area. You can search by breeds. Photos available.

# Auctions

You might get an aluminum suitcase for a dollar, or you might never see your money again—such uncertainties give an edgy excitement to the flea markets and more formal auctions available on the Web.

To avoid frenzy, plan ahead: know what you want to get, set a budget, and make sure you know who's offering the product for bid. Safest sites are those that auction off manufacturers' overstocks, or appraised lots in traditional auction houses, but the classifieds and garage sales—sites that let individuals offer (mostly used) items for best offer—astonish with their variety (who would have thought you could buy beat-up fishing poles on the Web?).

If you are dealing with an individual, the Better Business Bureau suggests getting (and confirming) a street address, phone number, insurance on the shipment, and a clearly stated return policy. Never pay in cash; consider using an online escrow service to hold your money until you receive the goods. Also, check the feedback areas to make sure the seller isn't being blackballed. For a way to search hundreds of auction sites at once, go to http://www.BidFind.com/

## AuctionGate

http://www.auctiongate.com

If you are interested in hot, high-end computer gear, this site offers good bargains, some from individuals, some from original manufacturers, and some from AuctionGate itself, when they buy manufacturers' overstocks. You can watch the bids go up through special software, even if you are not bidding; you can also tell their server your maximum, and it will keep topping other folks' bids until it reaches your limit (bidding while you sleep). Or you can have them email you the second your bid is topped, so you can get right back into the fray. Samples:

- Ethernet adapters (5-pack)
- Intel network router
- 150-foot roll of bubble wrap for shipping motherboards

**Search:** Yes
**Photos:** Some
**Ordering:** Online bidding
**Gift Wrap:** No
**Delivery:** Ground, 2nd Day, or by arrangement with the seller

## AuctionMax

http://www.auctionmax.com

They advertise themselves as a warehouse outlet for new computer stuff. A banner shows the screen names of the latest high bidders, while a flag waves under the sign, Latest Winners. Live auctions, with many starting at $1. You can set up your own personal account manager, which shows your current bid status, a history of bids that have won, and current shipping status. Bid Alert sends email to let you know when your bid has been topped. BidMax keeps bidding for you when you are offline, placing the lowest bid possible to keep your bid alive, up to a maximum you set. Samples:

- CD Recordable drive with software
- Corel PhotoPaint
- 56K modem
- Full-duplex sound card
- Pentium II AGP Motherboard with 3-D sound, 450 MHz

**Search:** No
**Photos:** Yes
**Ordering:** Online bidding
**Gift Wrap:** No
**Delivery:** 1 to 3 weeks

# Auction Universe

http://
www.auctionuniverse.com

A well-designed person-to-person site, with auctions of
varying time periods. Each area alerts you to auctions
ending today. You get plenty of info about most items,
which range from practical to cultural (Ansel Adams
photographs, with starting bids in the range of $1,500
to $15,000). You can use their robot bidder to keep
topping someone else's bid, up to some limit you set.
They guarantee buyer and seller some safety through
their BidSafe intermediary. After you register and make
a bid, they notify you if you have been outbid.
Samples:

- Automatic wire-stripper
- Portable trade show display with lights
- 50 blank white greeting cards with envelopes
- A Kenyan 10-shilling coin from 1991
- Insulated wine tote

**Search:** Yes
**Photos:** For some items
**Ordering:** One-time bids, robotic bids
**Gift Wrap:** No
**Delivery:** Depends on seller

# eBay

http://www.ebay.com

The most crowded site, with tons of junk and jewels,
many people bidding, in more than 1,000 categories.
But size hasn't made this popular auction site hard to
navigate. Look at the information about a seller; good
and bad comments from previous users show up. Link
to additional comments about the people making the
comments, to check their biases. For most excitement,
visit the auctions about to close at Going, Going,
Gone. Samples:

- The Talking GI Joe
- Laser pointer with 24 different heads
- 10-CD set of rock classics
- Vintage paper tablecloth with donkeys
- Old Japanese kaleidoscope
- Matchbox Caterpillar tractor

- Antique Disney tin windup toy

**Search:** Yes
**Photos:** Occasionally
**Ordering:** Bid, and if you win, contact the seller
directly
**Gift Wrap:** No
**Delivery:** Varies with seller

# Encore Auction

http://www.encoreauction.com

A popular site for computer products, office and
consumer electronics. Many good descriptions, and
specifications for products. Bids seem to top out well
below retail prices. Some items go to the highest bidder;
others to anyone who exceeds the minimum bid; and still
others are just sold at a given price (which tends to go
down if nobody buys). Samples:

- 1,300-watt vacuum
- Digital video camera with 3-inch color LCD
  screen
- Fax, color printer, copier, and scanner all in one

**Search:** No
**Photos:** Some
**Ordering:** Online, Fax (may be delayed)
**Gift Wrap:** No
**Delivery:** Ground

# Excite Classifieds and Auctions

http://www.excite.com/col-
lectibles/

What a yard sale! A sprawling mix of classified ads and
auctions of collectible items such as Beanie Babies,
comic books, trading cards, and autographs. Read
comments about the seller to see what others think. If
you do a search and can't find what you want, choose
Cool Notify, and get email alerts when that item comes
up for sale. An online escrow service can hold your
money for you until you get the product, then hand
the money over to the seller. Sample wares:

- 83rd Fighter Interceptor patch
- 85-piece Pez collection

- Dukes of Hazzard thermos bottle
- Small Soldiers metal lunchbox
- Model of a schooner, fully assembled

**Search:** Yes
**Photos:** Sometimes
**Ordering:** Online bid, Email
**Gift Wrap:** No
**Delivery:** Varies, depends on what you work out with seller

## FirstAuction

http://www.firstauction.com

A house auction site with department store items (some reconditioned). You deal directly with the site, not another individual. Focus is on home products, such as jewelry, lingerie, and health and beauty products, with some consumer electronics. Some Flash auctions offer great bargains, because they're over in half an hour, and many potential bidders miss them. Products go to shipping within 10 days after bids are accepted. Sample opportunities:

- 74-piece flatware set
- Black stretch lace body suit
- NFL San Francisco 49ers watch
- Cordless phone
- Satin corset bustier in red and black
- Washable silk shirt (extra large)
- Wireless outdoor pet fence

**Search:** Yes
**Photos:** Yes
**Ordering:** Bid
**Gift Wrap:** No
**Delivery:** Ground

## Golf Club Exchange

http://
www.golfclubexchange.com

Just golf. But if you want a particular club, or would like to sell a bag full, come here. You can bid on used clubs, or just buy new stuff, and you get two days to try out the clubs before you are committed. They offer

a blue book of prices based on sales over the last four months, so you can see what's normal. Their search lets you be specific about shaft type, shaft flex, year, manufacturer, gender, and handedness. Oh, and they do sell golf books, too. Sample products:

- Used Arnold Palmer putter
- Used left-handed ladies' 4-iron from Hogan, 1994 - 1995, with bubble shaft, and ladies' flex
- Used 4-wood, gripless stiff shaft, right-handed men's club from 1997
- Ben Hogan practice tee collection
- USGA Rules of Golf video

**Search:** Yes
**Photos:** Some
**Ordering:** Online, Fax
**Gift Wrap:** No
**Delivery:** Ground, 3$^{rd}$ Day, 2$^{nd}$ Day, Overnight

## Infinite Auction

http://www.sweetdeal.com

If you know what hardware works with your computer, you can pick up bargains among the overstocks auctioned off here. Auctions get extended if there are active bidders at the end, so you can counter any bids that come in at the last moment. Products are shipped by the manufacturer, not the site. Delivery may take 10 to 15 days after the bidding closes. Samples:

- Joystick from Logitech
- 600 dpi scanner
- Intel Pentium II 350 MHz chip

**Search:** No
**Photos:** Yes
**Ordering:** Online bid
**Gift Wrap:** No
**Delivery:** Ground

## Onsale at Auction

http://www.onsale.com

Real-time fun during the day, if you like bargains and auctions. Along with low-priced computers, peripherals, and software, Onsale offers one-hour auctions on lots of refurbished or close-out high-tech gear for the home office. If your bid is accepted, you may get a big savings off the suggested retail price. Brands are well-known. Most items are available for immediate shipping, but some are in short supply (that's why they are on sale), and if you want a computer built to your specs, that may take three to five days. Sample products:

- Combination printer, fax, copier
- Digital cameras
- Digital color copier
- Drawing tablet with pressure pen
- Electric bench grinder
- Joysticks

**Search:** Yes
**Photos:** Yes
**Ordering:** Online
**Gift Wrap:** No
**Delivery:** Ground, 2nd Day, Overnight (but not Saturdays)

# Up4Sale

http://up4sale.com

With free sign-up and auctions closing fast, this site pulls in lots of people with classified ad items. If you win the bidding, you get an email at 3:30 A.M. the next morning; if you post an item for sale, you'll see it on the site within about half an hour. Bonus: homey tips like how to soften honey that has crystallized. (Bids may not be promptly displayed if you are using the AOL browser.) Sample items:

- Candy dish held by Nubian, from 1950s
- Copper Buddhas found in grandfather's barn
- Joe DiMaggio Baseball Hall of Fame pins
- Original, unopened box of Barbie and Ken as Dana Scully and Fox Mulder of *The X-Files*, from Mattel (with miniature badges)

**Search:** Yes
**Photos:** Yes
**Ordering:** Online bidding
**Gift Wrap:** No
**Delivery:** Negotiated with seller

# Vegas Today

http://www.vegastoday.com

Bidding is always a gamble, and Vegas Today makes this classified-ads-style auction exciting, with items from antiques and autographs to weird and western items. They explicitly ban guns and adult products. Participation is free, but you have to register, and accept their user agreement. You are encouraged to query sellers by email; if your bid is topped, you get an email alerting you, so you can return to raise your bid. They make sure that sellers don't surreptitiously make bids on their own stuff to drive the prices up. Samples:

- Alien T-shirt
- Benton arrowhead found along Wolf Creek in Tennessee
- Brand-new gargoyle modeled on Victorian garden art
- Egyptian scarab from 1700 B.C. with certificate of authenticity
- Old wall clock with two weights
- Savings bank in shape of old-fashioned toilet, complete with pull chain and movable seat

**Search:** No
**Photos:** Some
**Ordering:** Online bidding
**Gift Wrap:** No
**Delivery:** Up to you and the seller

# Webauction

http://webauction.com

Hosted by MicroWarehouse, a major catalog vendor of computers, this site branches out into auctions on jewelry, home electronics, vacation packages, sporting goods and collectibles, as well as computer gear. They offer new and "refurbished" stuff, with a reserve price (starting bid), or let you start at $1 and go up. Hourly Madness auctions keep the drama going. You may be pondering whether to bid, and find the auction closing right in front of you. But auctions get extended so that you have five minutes to respond to a bid that has topped your own. If you're disappointed, you can always settle for buying a similar item on a clearance deal. Shipping on the next business day after the auction closes (to give them time to check your credit). Sample products:

- 150-watt subwoofers
- Canon portable color printer
- Handheld global navigation receivers
- Panasonic Palm Theater Portable DVD and CD player with 5.8-inch liquid crystal display (LCD)
- Ricoh digital camera with two-inch LCD
- Swiss army officer's watch with two time zones

**Search:** No
**Photos:** Yes
**Ordering:** Bidding online
**Gift Wrap:** No
**Delivery:** Ground, 2ⁿᵈ Day, Overnight

## Yahoo! Auctions

http://auctions.yahoo.com

Lots of folks sell here because they don't have to pay a fee to post an item. When your bid beats others, you get email telling you that you are the current winner, but someone else may still outbid you. If you end up as the final winner, you have to contact the seller to work out shipping. You can use an online escrow service to hold payment until delivery is made. Premium auctions involve appraised jewelry, antiques, memorabilia, and rare or unique collectibles offered by the auction house of Butterfield and Butterfield. If you have Real Audio and a Java-enabled browser, you can watch a real auction going on, and, if you register, bid. (Difficult with AOL.) Samples:

- 1862 $3 gold coin, U.S.
- First edition (1961), John Cage's *Silence*
- Hewlett-Packard 9000 Series 700 Workstation
- Lee Roy Parnell Signed Cherry Red Fender Stratocaster

**Search:** Yes
**Photos:** Some
**Ordering:** Bidding online
**Gift Wrap:** No
**Delivery:** Varies with seller

## Caution

Online auctions, particularly those involving individuals offering items for bid, generate two-thirds of the complaints about Web shopping, according to the National Fraud Information Center, at http://www.fraud.org/

To protect yourself, steer clear of individuals who want you to send cash or a money order. Always check the host's policy about disputes. If possible, use an escrow service, which acts as a go-between, holding your money until the product is actually delivered. Or use a credit card, which gives you some time to cancel the purchase if the product is not delivered, or if it arrives but turns out to be nothing like what the seller claimed it would be.

# Baby Stuff

We recently got a call from dear friends, who live 2,000 miles away, saying that they were now the proud parents of a baby boy, their first child. We wanted to send them a gift to celebrate this joyous occasion, so naturally we went to the Web. Boy, we had no idea how many baby-related stores had popped up just in the last few months. It took us a while to find what we wanted, but it doesn't have to take you very long, whether you're looking for a gift or something for your baby. You can just browse through the descriptions listed in this chapter. We also thought to add stores that sell baby shower items as well as places where you can order birth announcements. Even though many of the stores listed in this chapter sell baby toys, you might also want to read the chapter on Toys to get a wider assortment of toy stores.

## Appointments

http://www.appointments.com

This is a good place to shop when you are looking for that special baby gift, because you can personalize many items. If you can't decide what to buy, check out the gift boxes that contain several different products. You can search by the child's sex or by price. Free gift wrapping on all purchases. They also offer free shipping on some items. Samples:
- Baby gifts from $20
- Brahms Lullaby music box
- Monogrammed silver cups
- Personalized birth plates
- Silver-plated rattles
- Staffordshire enamel children's boxes
- Sterling silver hair-cut box
- Tower of toys

**Search:** Yes

**Photos:** Yes
**Ordering:** Online
**Gift Wrap:** Yes
**Delivery:** Ground

## Babies 'N Bells

http://www.babiesnbells.com

If you're expecting, take this advice: Once your baby arrives, the last thing you'll feel like doing is schlepping to the store to pick out birth announcements and thank-you cards. This online store lets you "pre-order" your announcements. You might be wondering how it works if you don't know the vital statistics or the name. Simple, you just pick out some of the wording and select a boy and girl card. When your baby arrives, just let them know the name, weight, height, etc., and the announcements will be sent to you within 48 hours. Sample themes:
- African-American babies
- Baby boy
- Baby girl
- Noah's Ark
- Sports
- Western

**Search:** Yes
**Photos:** Yes
**Ordering:** Online
**Gift Wrap:** No
**Delivery:** Ground, 2nd Day, Overnight

## Baby Bag Boutique

http://www.babybag.com

Hard-to-find baby things that the stork forgot to deliver. They also carry high-quality items at discounted prices. Pregnant women can also find some comfortable items for themselves. Like so many other baby stores, this one serves as a community for parents. Besides an ample amount of newborn and parent-to-parent information, there is also a bulletin board where you can submit your birth announcements. Fun place. Samples:
- Baby-food cookbook

- Breast-feeding CD-ROM
- Inflatable and portable booster seat
- Lead-detection kits
- Maternity jeans
- Product reviews
- Rocking chair/cradle combo
- Swim diapers and goggles

**Search:** Yes
**Photos:** Yes
**Ordering:** Online, Phone, Fax
**Gift Wrap:** No
**Delivery:** Ground

## Baby Best Buy

http://www.babybestbuy.com

A whole range of baby items are available at tremendously discounted prices. This store gets these discounts (sometimes as much as 70% off retail) by buying end-of-the-line products direct from the manufacturers. Everything they have is in limited supplies, so the inventory changes often. If you want to stay up-to-date on the latest discounted shipments, sign up for their free biweekly newsletter. Samples:

- Cotton-terry fitted changing-table covers
- Hooded bath towels
- Layette sets
- Outback stroller
- Prefolded diapers
- Swimsuit diapers
- Washable nursing pads

**Search:** Yes
**Photos:** Yes
**Ordering:** Online, Phone, Fax
**Gift Wrap:** Yes
**Delivery:** Ground, 2nd Day

## Baby Connect

http://www.babyconnect.com

Looking for a super original present? How about giving the new parents a birth announcement that can be viewed by their friends or family members on the Web?

The service is confidential (they'll give out the Web address only to the people you specify). It works this way: You send them three photos of the little bundle of joy, give some info such as height, weight, parents' names, and so on, and a special message. Baby Connect will take all of this and create a virtual birth announcement. Samples:

- Underwater themes
- Mountain themes
- New ones are developed

**Search:** No
**Photos:** Yes
**Ordering:** Online
**Gift Wrap:** Card
**Delivery:** N/A

## Baby Cyberstore

http://
www.babycyberstore.com

Tons of baby furniture and equipment are offered at this store. Once you enter, you'll find that this shop doesn't waste your time. Products and prices are listed right up front: no shillyshallying around here. The furniture is a blend of contemporary, traditional, and some really cute and original pieces. We particularly like the wood cradles, modeled on Colonial-era pieces, and the beds for toddlers. The prices are excellent and most of the inventory is shipped for free and arrives about three to four weeks after you place your order. Samples:

- 18th century Arch crib
- 3-in-1 convertible crib, changer, and cradle
- Animal rocking chairs
- Early American custom cradles
- Heirloom toddler bed
- Runabout bike trailer-stroller
- Upholstered toy chest

**Search:** Yes
**Photos:** Yes
**Ordering:** Online, Phone Fax
**Gift Wrap:** No
**Delivery:** Ground

## Baby Grams

http://www.babygrams.com

Simply put, this store sells personalized birth announcements wrapped around chocolate candy bars. Minimum order is only 36, so go have some fun and surprise your friends. Samples:

- Chocolate cigars (It's a boy or girl!)
- Sibling "cigars"
- Baby-shower bars
- Christening chocolate bars
- Triplet candy

**Search:** Some
**Photos:** Yes
**Ordering:** Online, Phone, Fax
**Gift Wrap:** Card
**Delivery:** Ground, 2nd Day

## The Baby Lane

http://thebabylane.com

How perfect! A baby store owned and operated by mothers! There's loving detail in the store as well as a selection of warm and cuddly stuff for Mom and her baby. Lots of environmentally friendly products. One of the sweetest stores on the Web. No high-power sales here. You might also want to join one of their Web rings to come in contact with other women. Refer a friend to this store and get $5 off your next order. Samples:

- Baby slings
- Bi-O-Kleen laundry supplies
- Botanical bath supplies for baby
- Fir doll cradles
- Flannel diapers
- Healthy Times teething biscuits
- Playstands
- Sheepskin rugs
- Wooden toys

**Search:** Yes
**Photos:** Yes
**Ordering:** Online, Phone
**Gift Wrap:** Card
**Delivery:** Ground, 3rd Day, 2nd Day

## BK Puff and Stuff

http://bkpuffnstuff.com/baby.htm

Fun gifts for a new baby or for a baby shower, and then some, at this capricious store. Search for that perfect gift in such whimsical categories as Cool Baby, Precious Baby, Noah's Ark, and the more traditional ones, Christening, Nursery, and Baby Shower. Samples:

- "Diaper Dad" kit
- Antiqued pewter-and-gold picture frame
- Baby's first curl box
- Bunny hats
- Lamb boo-boo ice-pack covers
- Lullaby cassette player
- Noah's Ark night-light
- Pewter tooth fairy box

**Search:** Yes
**Photos:** Yes
**Ordering:** Online
**Gift Wrap:** No
**Delivery:** Ground

## Chocolate Arts

http://www2.cybernex.net/~mhourin/

If you're hosting a baby shower, or would like to create really original and personal birth announcements, this store offers some interesting nuggets. They can create almost anything chocolate from scratch by making a mold and then pouring melted chocolate into it. Great for personalized gifts for baby showers or weddings. They ship most items within two weeks, but favors take six weeks. They use cold packs in hot weather or for hot climates. Samples:

- Chocolate baby bottles
- Chocolate flower pots with roses, daisies, or tulips
- Chocolate messages
- Chocolate pretzels (milk, dark, white, or with jimmies)
- Chocolate swans

**Search:** None
**Photos:** Yes

**Ordering:** Online, Email, Fax, Phone
**Gift Wrap:** Card
**Delivery:** Overnight

## Dawn Software

`http://www.dawnsoft.com`

Whether you are pregnant or trying to get pregnant, the software and other products offered here are for you. Their pregnancy software comes with a customizable pregnancy calendar, pregnancy adviser, and journal where you can keep track of your doctor's appointments and the results of any tests. If you're not pregnant yet, you might be interested in the Fertility Friend, which is an online service. (Free trial is available.) The software is very inexpensive. You order it and then they email you a code that you use to download the software. Samples:

- Baby-name software
- Baby-name trivia game
- Baby screensavers
- Fertility quiz

**Search:** Yes
**Photos:** No
**Ordering:** Online, Phone, Fax
**Gift Wrap:** No
**Delivery:** Download from the Web

## Ecobaby

`http://www.ecobaby.com`

Organic and environmental products for your sweet baby. If you want only the purest and most natural materials touching his or her skin, this is the place to shop. Samples:

- Homeopathic medicines
- Natural and organic toddler snacks
- Natural chemical-free disposable diapers
- Natural-fiber clothing
- Organic bedding and diapers
- Organic cotton towels
- Organic futons
- Organic mattresses
- Wood toys and furniture

**Search:** Yes
**Photos:** Some
**Ordering:** Online, Phone, Fax
**Gift Wrap:** No
**Delivery:** Ground, 3rd Day, 2nd Day, Overnight

## Especially for You

`http://kids-store.com`

Hand-picked items for your baby. The range of baby stuff is wide. The owners seem to have picked just a few quality items in each category. You might think this translates into "expensive," but it doesn't. The prices are very reasonable. Send them a picture of your newborn and they'll create a picture birth announcement online. Samples:

- Feeding dish with suction cup base
- Flannel receiving blankets
- Fleece crib blanket
- Infant mittens
- Infant sleepers
- Safety latches
- Training pants

**Search:** Yes
**Photos:** Yes
**Ordering:** Online, Phone, Fax
**Gift Wrap:** Yes
**Delivery:** Ground, 2nd Day, Overnight

## Everything But The Baby

`http://www.everythingbutthebaby.com`

We knew this store had the right attitude when we read its motto: "The best thing to happen to new parents since sleep." If you don't get the point, you've never been the parent of a newborn. This store lives up to its motto by having just about everything you would desire or need that first year. The owners wisely realized that you don't want to spend a lot of time shopping, so the site is light on heavy graphics (which sometimes take eons to download) and the search is intuitive. Now go take a nap. Samples:

- Baby registry
- Cloth booties
- Humidifiers
- Kiddie Cruisers
- Ottomans
- Silver-plated rattle
- Swivel bath seat

**Search:** Yes
**Photos:** Yes
**Ordering:** Online, Phone, Fax
**Gift Wrap:** No
**Delivery:** Ground, 2$^{nd}$ Day, Overnight

## Go Babies

`http://www.gobabies.com`

In the old days, babies stayed at home, and when they ventured out "for some air," they were bundled up and placed in huge perambulators (prams) where you could hardly see them. Today babies go everywhere. Evidence the fact that nary a department store rest room is complete without a changing table. This store carries all those great products that make traveling with the tiny tot easier. Samples:

- Diaperware swimsuits
- Disposable bibs
- Gift sets
- Paper baby bag and supplies
- Travel diaper-changing kits

**Search:** Yes
**Photos:** Yes
**Ordering:** Online, Phone
**Gift Wrap:** Card
**Delivery:** Ground

## iBaby.com

`http://www4.ibaby.com`

This is one big baby store. It bills itself as "the store for all your baby needs." Maybe it's right. There are over 20,000 products from over 200 brands. But iBaby.com doesn't sell only to new parents. It is also a resource with listings of product recalls, a baby-name finder, new

parent checklist, and even a pregnancy calendar. Baby gifts are sorted by age and price range. Don't forget to check out their Best Buy section for closeout sales. Samples:

- 3-D activity gym
- Bath toys
- Bed rails
- Car seats
- Crib accessories
- Diaper bags
- Monitors
- Strollers

**Search:** Yes
**Photos:** Yes
**Ordering:** Online, Phone
**Gift Wrap:** No
**Delivery:** Ground, 2$^{nd}$ Day

## Kamyra in Print

`http://www.partyinvitations.com`

This Web printing store has thought of everything. There are lots of personal extras you can order on your birth announcements or baby shower invitations, such as a detachable bow, plus they'll send you the envelopes ahead of time (at no extra charge), so you can address them before you are suffering from acute sleep deprivation. Reasonable prices and high-quality stationery, plus free envelopes and shipping, make this store a keeper. Sample announcements:

- A star is born
- Baseball
- Create your own
- Noah's Ark
- Teddies and toys
- Twins

**Search:** Yes
**Photos:** Yes
**Ordering:** Online
**Gift Wrap:** No
**Delivery:** 3$^{rd}$ Day, Overnight

## Little Prince and Princess

`http://www.royalbaby.com`

Lots of neat little outfits, toys, furniture, and other necessities for your bundle of joy are found at this pretty store. Like some other places, it also serves as a resource for new parents by alerting you to product recalls and offering links to many other child-related sites. Before you do any serious shopping, make sure you check out their Clearance Department for some good buys. From time to time, they also provide free gifts for orders over $50. Samples:

- Hand-painted furniture
- Infant-carrier musical-toy bar
- Leopard print cotton Teddy Toes
- Newborn washable booties
- Nursing pillows
- Stroller activity center
- Yellow bear sensory teether

**Search:** Yes
**Photos:** Yes
**Ordering:** Online, Phone, Fax
**Gift Wrap:** No
**Delivery:** Ground, 2$^{nd}$ Day

## National Parenting Center

`http://www.tnpc.com`

Founded as parenting information service 10 years ago, this organization has grown steadily to give advice to parents about all sorts of products for children from newborns to elementary-school-age kids. All of their products are reviewed by other parents. If you see it for sale, you'll know the item received a "thumbs-up!" They have a nice selection of products for babies and toddlers. Samples:

- Audiotapes
- Books
- Car booster seats
- Changing table
- Cribs
- Cuddle Hearts
- Lamb's wool rug
- Stuffed animals

- Waterproof sheet protectors

**Search:** Some
**Photos:** Yes
**Ordering:** Online, Mail
**Gift Wrap:** No
**Delivery:** Ground

## Parenting Concepts

`http://parentingconcepts.com`

This place is like the funky, little out-of-the-way store with a hard-working friendly staff that you just happen to stumble upon. The store is definitely a small cottage industry: parents working in their homes make many of the products. Samples:

- Arm's reach bedside co-sleeper
- Cuddle cap and snuggle booties
- Flannel and satin "security" blankets
- Flushable biodegradable diaper liners
- Homeopathic medical kits
- Lullaby tapes
- Sheepskin stroller/car seat liner
- Sling-Ezee infant carrier

**Search:** Yes
**Photos:** Yes
**Ordering:** Online, Phone, Fax
**Gift Wrap:** No
**Delivery:** Ground

## RainBee

`http://www.rainbee.com`

The first thing we liked about this store was that it didn't have the word "Baby" in its name. (It probably has something to do with the fact that the founder's daughter is named Monsoon.) What it does have is a huge supply of pretty specialties (actually some of them are quite ritzy) for your baby and toddler. Some items can be custom designed. When we visited RainBee they were offering free shipping on orders over $500. Samples:

- Canopied wicker and rattan bassinet
- Chenille nursery blanket

- Gift sets
- Hand-embroidered (in Madeira) christening gowns
- Jersey crib sheets with thick bumpers
- Old-fashioned music boxes
- Silver-plated comb and brush sets
- Velvet layette gift sets

**Search:** Yes
**Photos:** Yes
**Ordering:** Online, Phone, Fax
**Gift Wrap:** Yes
**Delivery:** Ground

## Looking to get those baby shoes bronzed???

Dip over then to the Bron Shoe Company at http://www.bronshoe.com. They've been preserving those first shoes for over 60 years. (You can also call them at 614-252-0967.)

## Good advice from Ann Douglas

Ann Douglas, co-author of *The Unofficial Guide to Having a Baby* (Macmillan), says, "A simple trip to the mall can become an all-day event when you've got a young baby in tow. Is it any wonder that the newest generation of parents is choosing to shop online instead?"

# Baseball & Softball

Baseball is still our national pastime, and with good reason. It can be played almost anywhere by anyone. A good bat is good, but a sturdy stick will do. Little Leagues are all over the place. And, thanks to the wonderful accomplishments of Mark McGwire and Sammy Sosa, it looks like baseball and its cousin, softball, are making a comeback.

## Athletic Team Uniforms Direct

http://
www.ateamuniformsdirect.com

One-stop shopping for all your team uniforms. This place specializes in outfitting your team or your whole league. There's a $50 minimum-order requirement. All colors are available. Sizes come in small to XXL for adults; small to extra large for youth sizes. The more you buy, the greater your discount. Shipping is $10 on orders under $200 and $15 on orders over $200. Samples:

- Adult and youth elastic belts
- Belted pin-striped pants for adults and youths
- Major League replica caps
- Solid-color and two-tone caps
- Stirrup socks
- Twill pin-striped cap
- Two-button and full-button jerseys
- Youth and adult pull-on pants
- Youth and adult belted pants in colors or white

**Search:** Some
**Photos:** Yes
**Ordering:** Online, Phone, Fax
**Gift Wrap:** No
**Delivery:** Ground

## Baseball Express

http://www.baseballexp.com

Whether you like to play a lazy game of catch occasionally or you get up early every Saturday, oiled glove in hand, and drive to the local baseball field, this store has something for you. Just about any kind of equipment for baseball and software is available. The clothes often go up to size XXL. If you are a softball or baseball coach, check out the Team Sales department, where you'll find unique equipment, clothes and accessories, plus uniform packages. (There are discounts available for large orders.) One ding, though: the search mechanism needs a little help. You have to know what you are looking for, because there is no way to browse except for the front page of each category. Samples:

- Bike nylon V-neck pullover
- Corkball bat
- Rawlings McGwire first base mitt
- Strength shoes
- Team sales and accessories
- Ultrajoc sliding shorts
- Wilson Pro Pudge catcher's mitt

**Search:** Yes
**Photos:** Yes
**Ordering:** Online, Mail
**Gift Wrap:** No
**Delivery:** 2nd Day, Overnight

## Batter's Choice

http://www.batterschoice.com

You want bats? This place's got bats . . . plenty of 'em. All sizes. Eastons, Worths, you name it. They also carry lots of other baseball necessities. Samples:

- Adult aluminum, graphite, and wood bats
- Baseball and softball bat sleeves
- Batting gloves
- Equipment bags
- Fielders' gloves
- Pitcher's training kit
- Senior-league bats
- Softball bats with extender knobs

- T-ball bats
- Youth baseball bats

**Search:** Yes
**Photos:** Yes
**Ordering:** Online, Phone
**Gift Wrap:** No
**Delivery:** 5th Day, 2nd Day

## Better Batter

http://www.betterbatter.com

The "Better Batter" is a simple training aid that looks a little like a riding crop. It helps coaches train their players on the right way to swing at a ball. There's an adult version and a kid's version. There are also a few other batting practice devices for sale. Samples:

- Better Batter training aids
- StatTrak Baseball/Softball software
- Swing 'N Slam

**Search:** No
**Photos:** Yes
**Ordering:** Online, Phone, Mail
**Gift Wrap:** No
**Delivery:** Ground

## Capsized

http://www.capsized.com

Ever wonder where those custom-made baseball caps come from? You know the ones . . . those that say something really cool? Well, we don't know where they were bought, but we do know where you can have them made on the Web. Click on the Customized button and you'll be brought to a page full of choices (font, color, and so on). Fun for teams, family, or class reunions, or anything else you can think of. Oh, did we forget something? You can also get every cap imaginable by any major sport team. Samples:

- Cap cleaner and deodorizer
- Cartoon caps
- Designer caps
- Major and Minor League baseball caps

**Search:** Yes

**Photos:** Yes
**Ordering:** Online, Fax
**Gift Wrap:** Card
**Delivery:** 3rd Day

## Direct Sports

http://www.directsports.com

Lots of equipment and accessories (with a few clothing items) for baseball and softball players. You'll find a lot of information on their bats, and if you aren't sure what size to order, go to their FAQ (Frequently Asked Questions) section, where they'll explain how to figure stuff out. Samples:

- Cordless radar gun
- Dudley Heat softballs
- Instructional videos
- Pitching machines
- Rawlings fielding gloves
- Redline Z-Core bats
- Slow-pitch softball bats

**Search:** Yes
**Photos:** Yes
**Ordering:** Online, Phone
**Gift Wrap:** No
**Delivery:** Ground

## Fogdog Sports

http://www.fogdog.com

What kind of a name is this for a sporting goods store? We asked and found out that one definition of fog dog is the "arc or ray of light sometimes seen burning through the fog." Well, baseball players will surely see the light after shopping here. This Web store is huge; it covers every sport. But it does have a special baseball store that carries all sorts of clothing and equipment. If, after all this, you still can't find what you're looking for, contact the Fogdog Search Squad and they'll personally find it and buy it for you. Samples:

- Aluminum, fungo, warm-up, and wood bats
- Bat bags
- Batting gloves

- Coaching shoes
- Field accessories
- Game jerseys
- Leather gloves
- Protective equipment
- Sport bottles
- Stopwatches
- Team gear and equipment
- Umpire equipment
- Various types of cleat shoes

**Search:** Yes
**Photos:** Yes
**Ordering:** Online, Phone
**Gift Wrap:** No
**Delivery:** Ground

## Smith Sports

http://www.netsportstore.com

Want to shop for baseball gear for your son or daughter? Stop by this store, then. You'll find a good selection of equipment specifically made for kids. They also have an excellent selection for women. You'll get a lot of descriptions and a lot of sizes. They also have a very good supply of adult-sized bats. Samples:

- Dudley Fusion bats
- Equipment and bat bags
- Fielding gloves for left and right hands
- Pitching machines
- Slo-pitch softball bats
- Youth League bats by Easton, Louisville Slugger, Worth, and Wilson

**Search:** Yes
**Photos:** Yes
**Ordering:** Online, Fax
**Gift Wrap:** No
**Delivery:** 3rd Day

## Psst!

Wanna get all caught up on the latest scores and news on your favorite players and teams? Go to Major League Baseball's Web site at http://www.majorleaguebaseball.com.

## If you like other sports, slide into these chapters:

- Basketball
- Bicycles
- Boating & Sailing
- Bowling
- Golf
- Skating
- Tennis

# Basketball

OK, so Michael Jordan retired . . . we guess it's time to get over it. His Airness was a treat to watch on the court and on TV commercials, but if the thought of a Bull-less championship has put you in a funk, get ready for March Madness and keep your eye peeled for the next great one. He or she is probably shooting some hoops right now. If you like to shoot some hoops, travel (oops, we mean dribble) over to these stores for some gear. You can outfit your team or yourself, pick up logo items from professional or college teams, and get all those accessories for time on the bench, and practices. Of course, if what you really want is to watch on TV, perhaps you should take a look at the chapters on Furniture and TV & Video Gear.

## Athletic Team Uniforms Direct

`http://`
`www.ateamuniformsdirect.com`

One-stop shopping for all your team uniforms. This place specializes in outfitting your team or your whole league. You have to order $100, minimum. All colors are available. Sizes come in small to XXL for adults (special orders for up to XXXXL sizes); small to large youth sizes. The more you buy, the greater your discount.  Shipping is $10 on orders under $200 and $15 on orders over $200. Samples:
- Dazzle basketball shorts and jerseys with and without trim
- Double-ply shorts with drawstring elastic waist
- Ladies' basketball jerseys and shorts
- Ladies' shooter shirts
- Matching jerseys and shorts
- Reversible solid, color jerseys
- Tearaway/breakaway pants

**Search:** Some

**Photos:** Yes
**Ordering:** Online, Phone, Fax
**Gift Wrap:** No
**Delivery:** Ground

## Gear.com

`http://www.gear.com`

This is a big sporting goods store that just happens to have a good basketball section. Go to their main page and then click on Basketball. You'll find basketballs from $9 to $45. Everything in this store is heavily discounted. Samples:
- Official-sized leather basketball
- Texas Longhorns basketball
- UCLA Bruins basketball
- Water bottles

**Search:** Yes
**Photos:** Yes
**Ordering:** Online, Phone, Fax
**Gift Wrap:** No
**Delivery:** Ground, 2nd Day

## National Basketball Association Store

`http://store.nba.com`

The name pretty much says it all. NBA authentic gear, from clothes to equipment. Click a button and you'll even get to sample the stuff from the WNBA (Women's National . . . oh, you know!). Kids' sizes available on a lot of the clothes. Samples:
- 23-karat gold-foil rookie card set
- Adult authentic jerseys and shorts
- Basketball trading cards
- Card games
- Desk diary
- NBA Barbies(???!!!)
- Team music CDs
- Watches
- Youth practice and shooting shirts
- Youth replica jerseys and practice shorts

**Search:** Yes

**Photos:** Yes
**Ordering:** Online, Fax
**Gift Wrap:** No
**Delivery:** Ground

# Sports Fan

http://www.sports-fans.com

It's all here. Whether your favorite team is the Bulls, the Knicks, or the Pistons, you'll find all of the officially licensed products for the NBA. They also have terrific selection of products from NCAA colleges. Familiar brand names, like Champion, Russell, and Starter, are sprinkled throughout this store. Many of the items can be personalized for an extra fee. Once you've finished shopping, go to their links and get caught up on the latest news from your favorite teams. Samples:

- Bulls' 1998 championship T-shirts, caps
- Sport leather jackets
- Team hats
- Jerseys
- Watches
- Sweatshirts
- Gift certificates

**Search:** Yes
**Photos:** Yes
**Ordering:** Online, Phone, Fax
**Gift Wrap:** No
**Delivery:** Ground, 2nd Day

# If you like other sports, set a pick for these chapters:

- Baseball
- Bicycles
- Boating & Sailing
- Bowling
- Golf
- Skating
- Tennis

# Bath

The story goes that when Napoleon was returning from one of his lengthy military campaigns, he sent a note to Josephine and said, "I am coming back, do not bathe." Maybe that's why the French are so famous for their perfumes. In any case, taking a nice leisurely bath, filled with scented bubble bath or oil, is one of life's pleasures. To Napoleon we say, "Go eat some cake." Oops, maybe that's the wrong French monarch. Oh well, we'll take a bath and contemplate that one.

## Abby's Herb Company

http://www.abbysherbs.com/index.html

This store offers a unique selection of handmade herbal creams and lotions, herb baths, tub teas, insect repellents, herbal supplies, and a lot more. All of the products are made from Abby's own formula. A nice touch is the custom service offered where Abby will blend a formula for you, or possibly as a very personal gift. She uses quality ingredients that are all natural. Her unique tub "teas" are just what you think they are: herbs wrapped in tea bags that you steep in a hot bath. Some of the tub teas are formulated to help with:

- Aching joints
- Colds and fevers
- Detoxification process
- Energy
- Weight loss
- Yeast infections

**Search:** Yes
**Photos:** Yes
**Ordering:** Online, Fax, Mail
**Gift Wrap:** Yes
**Delivery:** Priority Mail

## Acadian Rain

http://www.acadianrain.com/index.html

Sheila LeBlanc started her herbal soap store by creating 17 different handmade natural soaps. The soaps are made with a blend of palm, olive, and coconut oil, plus a dash of sodium hydroxide. What separates the various soaps are their distinctive fragrances.

- After-work gritty bar
- Cajun wake-up bar
- Herbal shampoo bar
- Lavender bath salts
- Rosemary massage oil
- White magnolia bar

**Search:** Yes
**Photos:** Yes
**Ordering:** Online, Fax
**Gift Wrap:** Yes
**Delivery:** Ground

## Beauty Boutique

http://www.beautenaturel.com

Large assortment of hard-to-find beauty and bath products from around the world. Nice touch: They offer free samples with each purchase. They also have occasional Blowout Sales. Samples:

- Aromatherapy products from Australia
- Bath fizzies
- Bath oils from Germany
- Green Goddess bath salts
- Scented soaps from France

**Search:** Yes
**Photos:** Yes
**Ordering:** Online, Phone
**Gift Wrap:** Yes
**Delivery:** Ground, 2nd Day, Overnight

## bioDERM

http://www.bioderm.com

First determine your particular skin type (sensitive, acneic, mature, and so on) and then use the bioDERM product selection guide and discover the all-natural products that are right for you. These creams, lotions, and bath items aren't cheap, but a good way to shop is to check out their gift baskets, and they also offer monthly specials. Samples:

- Cellufirm body cream
- Energizing mineral bath salts
- Exfoliation sponge
- Greaseless massage crème
- Home spa kit
- Moisturizing shower gel
- Stress-relieving bath treatment

**Search:** Yes
**Photos:** Yes
**Ordering:** Online, Phone, Fax
**Gift Wrap:** Yes
**Delivery:** Ground, 2nd Day, 3rd Day, Overnight

## Clean Kids Naturally

http://www.kidprices.com

This simple site is actually written for kids. In clear, easy-to-understand language, they describe their cleaning products (with a pitch to tell Mom and Dad or Grandma and Grandpa). The products are all natural and guaranteed not to burn the eyes or skin. Samples:

- Animal-shaped sponges
- Banana Smoothie Detangler
- Germ-Busting Hand Soap
- Tiny Bubbles Foaming Bath
- Tropical Orange Burst Shampoo

**Search:** No
**Photos:** Some
**Ordering:** Online, Fax, Phone
**Gift Wrap:** No
**Delivery:** Ground

## Cloud Nine

http://www.cloudninehi.com

From the shores of Kailua and Kona floats this store filled with all-natural, biodegradable products filled with Hawaiian botanicals. Most of the bath products are available with custom scents such as almond, Hawaiian rain, pikaki, and coconut, to name just a few. They also carry a full line of skin-care products. Samples:

- Aromatherapy spa line
- Double bubbles
- Foaming bath gel
- Hawaiian-dream bath salts
- Products for men and babies
- Seaweed loofah body buffer
- Therapy crystals
- Tropical spa salts

**Search:** Yes
**Photos:** No
**Ordering:** Online
**Gift Wrap:** No
**Delivery:** Ground

## Crabtree and Evelyn, Ltd.

http://www.crabtree-evelyn.com

One of the best-smelling brick-and-mortar stores is now selling big time online. One of the first companies to commercially use herbs and other natural ingredients in its products, this company is famous for its goat-milk baths, English lavender soaps, and patchouli cologne. But lest you think this store is selling only its tried-and-true varieties, you may want to take a peek at its comestibles section, too. Samples:

- Bath brushes, mitts, sponges, and loofahs
- Breakfast china
- Bridal registry
- Gardener's salad bowls and seeds
- Gift certificates and collections
- Hungary Water (men's cologne originally created for Hungarian royalty)

- Natural food and teas
- Scented votive candles
- Skin and fragrance products for men and women

**Search:** Yes
**Photos:** Yes
**Ordering:** Online, Fax
**Gift Wrap:** Yes
**Delivery:** Ground, 2nd Day, Overnight

# Dionis

http://dionissoap.com

Based in Charlottesville, Virginia, this store specializes in skin-care items made from traditional, fresh goat's milk recipes. Why base a whole Web store on goat's milk products? Simple; the stuff smells great and it moisturizes your skin in a natural and gentle way. (Warning: one of the writers absolutely loves this stuff, so the reporting here might be a tad biased.) OK, so let's just stick to the facts: The pictures of baby goats are irresistible. (We tried!) Samples:

- Body lotion
- Foaming milk bath
- Gift baskets
- Liquid and bar soaps
- Perfumes
- Shampoo
- Soap sachets

**Search:** Some
**Photos:** Yes
**Ordering:** Online, Phone
**Gift Wrap:** No
**Delivery:** Ground, 2nd Day

# Emelauren's

http://www.emelauren.com

Handcrafted, environmentally friendly herbal bath and skin-care products are what you'll find in this store. They offer a lot of products, but the specialty of this Pennsylvania family-owned business is herbal soaps. (Emelauren is a blend of their daughters' names.)

Samples:
- Almond-coffee kitchen scrub
- Baby soap with shea butter
- Basil foot scrub
- Bug spray and soap
- Herbal bath bags
- Herbal foot-bath bags
- Lemongrass soap
- Men's products
- Poison-ivy soap
- Soaps for oily skin
- Spa bar

**Search:** Minimal
**Photos:** Some
**Ordering:** Online
**Gift Wrap:** No
**Delivery:** Ground

# Garden Botanika

http://
www.gardenbotanika.com

Their online store is an extension of their 300 wood-and-glass shops. All of their fragrances, skin-care products, and cosmetics contain natural botanical ingredients. They are adamant about not using animal by-products and do not conduct animal testing. These environmentally friendly cosmetics sell for a fraction of department store prices. Samples:

- Custom-blended bath oil
- Fragrant bubble bath
- Fruit and floral aromatics
- Glycerin soaps
- Moisturizing body mists
- Products for men
- Scented oils, candles, and body lotions
- Spa Botanika

**Search:** Yes
**Photos:** Yes
**Ordering:** Online, Phone
**Gift Wrap:** Yes
**Delivery:** Ground, Overnight

# Me Body and Bath

http://www.mebodyandbath.com

Bathe with these high-quality soaps, creams, oils, and
lotions. They specialize in gentle products, many using
pure vegetable emollients and purified water. A fun,
friendly online store, complete with rubber ducks.
Samples:
- All-over body shampoo
- Aloe-vera bubble bath
- Custom-scented shower gel
- Loofahs
- Skin-care products
- Sponges

**Search:** Minimal
**Photos:** Some
**Ordering:** Online, Phone
**Gift Wrap:** No
**Delivery:** Ground

# The Natural Body Bar

http://www.bodybar.com

One of the largest online selections of natural beauty
products. This well-designed site carries just about
every kind of hair, skin, body, bath, and foot products.
It even supplies a line of all-natural children's products.
Samples:
- Chocolate mint kiss glycerin soap
- Gift baskets
- Hair and skin products
- Loofah cleansing disks
- Polishing bathing gloves
- Soothing baby and bath oil
- Strawberry-love bathing beads

**Search:** Yes
**Photos:** Some
**Ordering:** Online, Phone, Fax
**Gift Wrap:** Yes
**Delivery:** Ground, Overnight

# Batteries

When the lights go out during a summer storm, we fumble around for a flashlight, and we usually discover that someone has left every single flashlight on, in the drawer, or out in the tent in the backyard. We click the button, but no light comes out. So then we start feeling around in the kitchen cabinet for replacement batteries. We have an alphabet soup of sizes there, but we rarely have enough of the right size to brighten up the room. That's when we reach for the candles. Now, where are those matches?

If you have gadgets that eat batteries, or anticipate giving a bunch of presents that have those innocuous labels "No Batteries Included," then you might want to stock up the easy way, using the Web stores that are devoted to the battery, in all sizes, shapes, brands, and voltages.

## Aardvark Batteries

http://aardvarkbat.com

An enormous selection of factory-direct batteries and accessories for camcorder and cell phones. They boast that you can find a battery for any camcorder or cell phone in existence. They also carry Zero-Memory™ batteries that let you recharge without first discharging. Free shipping on U.S. orders! Samples:
- CCB-104 for Sears 5372 Camcorder
- CCD-112C battery for Curtis Mathes model MV800

**Search:** Yes
**Photos:** No
**Ordering:** Online
**Gift Wrap:** No
**Delivery:** Ground

## Access Batteries

http://www.accessbattery.com

If you need more than just another battery for the portable power tools, check out this major supplier of batteries for cell phones, defibrillators, flashlights, laptops, pagers, and two-way radios. Information on recycling batteries. Samples:
- 12-volt, 2-amp Yuasa sealed-lead acid battery
- Access Battery defibrillator battery
- Ritron RT 156 Battery, 7.2-volt, for radio

**Search:** Yes
**Photos:** No
**Ordering:** Online
**Gift Wrap:** No
**Delivery:** 3rd Day, 2nd Day, Overnight

## Battery Outlet

http://www.batteryoutlet.com

They offer batteries for cellular phones from Motorola, Nokia, and Sprint. You often get your choice of original or after-market batteries, which are cheaper. Shipping is included in the price. Samples:
- Nickel-cadmium extra-capacity battery for flip and pocket phones
- Extra-capacity nickel-cadmium battery for original Motorola cell phone

**Search:** Yes
**Photos:** No
**Ordering:** Online, Phone
**Gift Wrap:** No
**Delivery:** 2nd Day

## Battery Terminal at Wholesale Advantage

http://
www.wholesaleadvantage.com/
battery_index.htm

Wide selection of batteries in this shop within the gigantic Wholesale Advantage. Top brand names with batteries for calculators, camcorders, cameras, car alarms, cell phones, computers, cordless phones, hearing aids, and watches. The ordering system is antique; you have to write down the product number on a yellow sticky, then enter that in the order form. Samples:

- 7.2-volt battery with charger for radio-control model cars
- Battery for insulin pump
- Lithium-coin battery

**Search:** Yes
**Photos:** No
**Ordering:** Online, Phone, Fax
**Gift Wrap:** No
**Delivery:** Ground

## E-Battery

http://e-battery.com

Batteries for camcorders, cellular phones, laptop computers, medical devices, and two-way radios. E-Battery emphasizes that its prices beat the average retail price; in fact, we found that its prices are often about a third below retail. Shipments go out within 24 hours. Samples:

- 10-amp sealed-lead battery
- Battery pack for Harvard Urometer

**Search:** Yes, in some departments
**Photos:** No
**Ordering:** Online, Phone, Fax
**Gift Wrap:** No
**Delivery:** Ground, 2nd Day, Overnight

## House of Batteries

http://houseofbatteries.com

Right away you see a few hundred batteries laid out for a photograph. This no-nonsense old-line battery supplier sells alkaline, lithium, lithium-ion, nickel cadmium, nickel metal hydride, sealed-lead acid, silver oxide, and zinc air batteries, plus battery assemblers, chargers, and holders from more than two dozen

vendors. Oh, and they do offer flashlights, too! You should know the exact number and type of battery you want *before* you arrive. And you have to order at least $50 worth of batteries before they agree to ship you anything. Samples:

- Float charger for optimum life of batteries used in standby applications, with continuous charging (burglar and fire alarm, memory protection, or UPS systems)
- Yorklite battery for emergency lights
- Zinc air hearing aid battery from Duracell

**Search:** No
**Photos:** A few small ones
**Ordering:** Phone, Fax
**Gift Wrap:** No
**Delivery:** Ground

## Laptop-Battery

http://www.laptop-battery.com

New, original, and rebuilt batteries for laptop computers from Acer to Zeos, including older models. A storefront for Access Micro, focused just on batteries, this site lets you pick the product without the blur of other computer-related stuff. Purchasing, though, takes place on the Access Micro site (which has thousands of other computer products). They ship the day they receive your order. Samples:

- Battery Biz battery for Apple StyleWriter printer
- Battery for Zenith MasterSport 386SL laptop computer

**Search:** Yes
**Photos:** No
**Ordering:** Online, Phone, Fax
**Gift Wrap:** No
**Delivery:** Ground, 3rd Day, 2nd Day, Overnight, Saturday

## Personal Solar

http://www.yessolar.com

Look, no extension cord! Convert the sun's energy into a new charge for your battery, or just absorb that energy in a power unit, and run a small appliance directly from the unit. Sample items:

- Laptop 15-watt solar charger
- Portable solar-power unit, with 60-watt panel, 36 amp per hour, battery pack, able to power a 21" TV for 7 hours without sunlight (after 8 hours of sunlight)
- Solar-panel experimental kits, any voltage or amperage configuration

**Search:** No
**Photos:** Yes, very helpful
**Ordering:** Online, Phone, Fax
**Gift Wrap:** No
**Delivery:** USPS First Class, Overnight

# Photofilm

http://www.photofilm.com

Just batteries and film, in a very clean site built around their database. No information about the products, no pictures; you just pick an item and when you see the speed and price appear, you can set the quantity you want, and add the purchase to your order. They stock almost the entire line of Duracell, Panasonic, and camera batteries. Samples:

- Duracell USA AAA batteries, 4-pack
- Panasonic 9-volt battery
- Photographic and Electronic Batteries CD 1225

**Search:** Yes
**Photos:** No
**Ordering:** Online
**Gift Wrap:** No
**Delivery:** Ground

# PowerPalace

http://www.powerpalace.com

Hearing-aid batteries and accessories, medical batteries. A site mostly for seniors, with links to resources for them. Shipping is included in the price. Samples:

- Earwax-removal system
- Size J medical battery

**Search:** No

**Photos:** No
**Ordering:** Online, Phone, Fax
**Gift Wrap:** No
**Delivery:** Ground

# ZZZap

http://www.zzzap.com

With physical stores in the United States and Canada, this site offers uninterruptible power supplies, voltage and line conditioning, surge and lightning protection, power inverters, standby generator sets, converters, battery chargers, and solar- or wind-powered generators. Sample items:

- AA Battery solar-powered charger for up to 4 AA Nicad batteries in 12 hours of sunlight
- 17.1-volt solar-panel electricity generator, 120 watts

**Search:** No
**Photos:** A few
**Ordering:** Online
**Gift Wrap:** No
**Delivery:** Ground, 2nd Day, Overnight

# Beauty & Cosmetics

If you've ever driven 20 miles to the mall to pick up a tube of mascara, you'll delight in the ease of some of these Web stores. Making yourself feel and look great doesn't have to take a lot of time.

By the way: in the next chapter, we've described some online shops that specialize in cosmetics and beauty products made of all-natural ingredients.

## Avon

http://www.avon.com

The Avon lady no longer has to physically come to your door. She's taken all of those wonderful little cosmetics that she used to carry in those big leather bags and posted them on the Internet. Miss that personal attention she gave you? No need to. If you answer the questions posed by the Virtual Beauty Adviser, you'll find just right products and shades especially for you. Samples:

- 12-hour makeup items
- Contests
- Free gifts
- Glitter-wear for body, face, and hair
- Press-on nails
- Skin problem-solving tips
- Styling "tool" kits
- Weekly specials

**Search:** Yes
**Photos:** Yes
**Ordering:** Online
**Gift Wrap:** No
**Delivery:** Ground, Overnight

## Clinique

http://www.clinique.com

This is the cosmetic firm that made it fashionable to cleanse one's face with soap again. It also was one of the first to "scientifically" type your skin and recommend products based on the findings. If you've browsed the cosmetic counters in the department stores, you're familiar with Clinique's low-tech computer, the box with the pink, yellow, light-green, and powder-puff blue little sliding categories. You can use this on their online site, also, to find out which skin-care items are designed for you. When we visited the site, it was only accepting orders shipped to the U.S. Samples:

- Email their experts with your specific questions
- Face creams
- Fragrance
- Gift sets
- Makeup customized around your lipstick shade
- Nail polish
- Products for men
- Service that remembers your favorite products

**Search:** Yes
**Photos:** Yes
**Ordering:** Online
**Gift Wrap:** Yes
**Delivery:** Ground, 2nd Day, Overnight

## Cosmetic Mall

http://www.cosmeticmall.com

Entering this site is like walking into your local drugstore. It has a little of everything. It mostly carries the lesser-known (inexpensive) brands. You might also want to check out their Frequently Asked Questions (FAQ) and their links to other beauty resources. A nice plus is that you can check out the list of ingredients for many of their products. Samples:

- Alpha-hydroxy skin creams
- Grooming kits
- Hair-loss products
- Men's grooming items

- Moodmatcher lipstick
- Nail files
- Nail polish
- Tweezers
- Weekly specials

**Search:** Some
**Photos:** Some
**Ordering:** Online
**Gift Wrap:** No
**Delivery:** Ground

# Cosmetics Counter

http://
www.cosmeticscounter.com

Entering this online store is a bit like walking into the first floor of most department stores. You have to walk through aisles of cosmetic counters full of special deals, packaged sales, and all the "regular" stuff. You'll find well-known brand names such as Clinique, Estée Lauder, Elizabeth Arden, and Lancôme—and some newer brands like Zirh, de Chine, and California North. This site doesn't offer everything these companies manufacture, but it comes close. Prices are about what you'd pay in a department store. Samples:

- Aromatherapy products
- Atomizers
- Bath oils
- Cuticle and hand conditioners
- Lipsticks, eye makeup, foundation
- Travel-size mirrors
- Vitamin-enriched face creams

**Search:** Yes
**Photos:** Yes
**Ordering:** Online, Phone
**Gift Wrap:** No
**Delivery:** Ground, 2nd Day

# CRH International, Inc.

http://www.aloealoe.com

The juice of the aloe-vera plant has long been a folk remedy for soothing the skin of burns and relieving minor arthritis pain. Now science is proving what many have known for a long time, that aloe vera heals. This store specializes in products made from this succulent. If you have a little time, you can even get some custom-blended products. Samples:

- After-sun lotion
- Anti-wrinkle cream
- Arthritic body rub
- Facial mask
- Medicated gel
- Pure aloe-vera juice
- Whole-leaf aloe-vera capsules

**Search:** No
**Photos:** No
**Ordering:** Online, Phone
**Gift Wrap:** No
**Delivery:** Ground, 2nd Day, 3rd Day, Overnight

# Fragrance Net

http://www.fragrancenet.com

This store bills itself as the "World's Largest Discount Fragrance Center." While we can't be certain of its claim, we can attest to the buckets of low-priced, name-brand (and some lesser known) perfumes sold at this site. These perfumes are the real McCoy, not some ne'er-do-scents. Besides the perfume, they offer gift certificates and a gift-reminder service. They also say they'll beat any competitor's price by 5%. This site makes things easy for the online buyer. Samples:

- Aramis
- Chanel
- Chloé
- Gift sets
- Jean Naté
- Michael Jordan
- Miniature fragrances
- Perry Ellis

**Search:** Yes
**Photos:** Yes
**Ordering:** Online, Phone, Fax
**Gift Wrap:** Yes
**Delivery:** Ground

## Hard Candy Cosmetics

http://www.hardcandy.com

This is not your mother's cosmetic counter. In fact, it might not even be for you. But your daughter will love it. The makeup here is made in cosmic colors with names like Trailer Trash, Fetish, Luscious, Gold Digger, and Scam. According to this site, they introduced the current fad of blue, green, and anything-but-red nail polish. In fact, nail polish is the reigning item on this site. Oh, don't let all the Japanese characters fool you. Hard Candy is strictly a California outfit. Samples:

- Candy Man masculine nail polish
- Dork nail polish
- Glitter eye pencil
- Hippie-chick lip pencil
- Pyro lipstick
- Techno eye shadow

**Search:** Yes
**Photos:** Yes
**Ordering:** Online, Phone
**Gift Wrap:** No
**Delivery:** Ground

## Harmon Discount

http://www.harmondiscount.com

Low prices (20% to 65% off on the manufacturers' suggested retail prices) on name brands, such as Almay, Revlon, Max Factor, and Maybelline, and lesser-known cosmetics and perfumes. This site offers terrific discounts. Does not ship outside of the U.S. Samples:

- Aftershave and cologne for men
- Makeup
- Nail polish
- Roll-on glitter lipstick
- Vitamins

**Search:** Yes
**Photos:** No
**Ordering:** Online
**Gift Wrap:** No
**Delivery:** Ground, 2nd Day

## Madison Avenue Salons

http://madison-avenue.com

The owners of two New Jersey salons (one in Madison, New Jersey; hence the name) have put their unusual hair and skin-care products online. The selection is unique. Browse if you are looking for something different. Samples:

- Altoona Enzymetherapy
- Aromatherapy gift baskets
- Color-effect hair and mascara highlights
- Rusk hair care
- Skin creams and bath oils
- Thinning-hair products

**Search:** Some
**Photos:** Some
**Ordering:** Online, Fax, Phone
**Gift Wrap:** Yes
**Delivery:** Ground

## My Basics.com

http://www.mybasics.com

Sometimes online superstores are just a mess. Kinda like walking around a bargain basement the day after a big sale, when everything is chaos and it's impossible to find anything. This online store is refreshingly different. It's a drug superstore, with a lot of everything. The search is first rate and the store is not only well designed, but pretty to look at, too. Go ahead and try it. Your first order is shipped free. Samples:

- Batteries
- Body, ear, eye, dental products
- Diapers
- Feminine products
- First-aid supplies
- Hosiery
- Over-the-counter drug products
- Paper goods
- Razor blades
- Travel-size merchandise
- Vitamins

**Search:** Yes

**Photos:** Yes
**Ordering:** Online
**Gift Wrap:** No
**Delivery:** Ground

# Oleda

http://www.oleda.com

Oleda Baker started her professional life as a beautician and, after a trip to New York, she started modeling for the Wilhelmina Agency. Her desire to help people look their best took her on a long path of experimentation into skin-care products. Today, her online store is devoted to selling products that help you look and feel younger. Samples:

- Aloe-vera products
- Aromatherapy
- Biotaniplex
- Fat burners
- Gift certificates
- Moisturizing mist
- Mudd masque
- Shampoos and conditioners
- Sunscreen
- Wrinkle-smooth night cream

**Search:** Minimal
**Photos:** Some
**Ordering:** Online, Fax
**Gift Wrap:** No
**Delivery:** Ground, 2$^{nd}$ Day, Overnight

# Urban Decay

http://www/urbandecay.com

Even though these cosmetics are said to be the very latest, they remind us of '60s high fashion. The colors are inspired by the urban landscape. The makeup colors are industrial chic and all the rage. If you think this store was founded by some bored Gen Xers, think again. CEO Sandy Lerner was a co-founder of Cisco Systems, the hot Silicon Valley computer network company. Samples:

- Acid Rain lipstick
- Graffiti lip gunk
- Litter nail polish
- Smog body haze
- Westside Highway eye shadow

**Search:** Yes
**Photos:** Some
**Ordering:** Online, Fax
**Gift Wrap:** No
**Delivery:** Ground, 2$^{nd}$ Day, Overnight

# Beauty & Cosmetics— Going Natural

You probably started to indulge in all-natural, nonpreservative beauty supplies as a kid. We know someone, very well in fact, who as a teenager wanted to look drop-dead gorgeous for a dance. She cut up a cucumber and placed the slices on her "baggy" eyes and rested for 15 minutes. OK, so far. But she had heard that mayonnaise made an excellent hair conditioner. So she glopped on the stuff, rubbed it in for a while and then lightly rinsed it out. Today, her hair would have looked right in style; then it was a disaster. But you don't have to worry about disasters with these companies, who have experimented with natural recipes, fine-tuned them, and now can deliver them straight to your door.

## AFE Cosmetics and Skincare

http://www.cosmetics.com

This 12-year-old company specializes in quality cosmetics and skin-care products. Visit the Skincare Salon and answer the questionnaire to find the products just right for your skin. This store not only sells products, but it gives lots of instructions (complete cleaning information for teens, for example) and tips. If you're not sure, this site offers something unique: individual mini "testers." How can you go wrong? Samples:
- Cosmetic brushes and sponges
- Custom-blended makeup

- Lash thickeners
- Lip fixers
- Nail polish
- Skincare for men

**Search:** Yes
**Photos:** No
**Ordering:** Online, Phone, Fax
**Gift Wrap:** No
**Delivery:** Ground, 2nd Day, Overnight

## African Formula Cosmetics

http://africanformula.com

A large selection of natural products for your hair, body and skin. Check out the special discounts offered on bulk orders. Don't have that much to order? Call some of your friends! Samples:
- Acne creams
- Bath oils
- Dental care
- Hair products
- Protective botanical protein moisture fluid
- Rejuvenating treatment
- Therapeutic botanical skin wash

**Search:** Yes
**Photos:** Yes
**Ordering:** Online, Phone
**Gift Wrap:** No
**Delivery:** Ground

## Arbonne International

http://
www.personalskincare.com

These products are formulated in Switzerland and available through a U.S. distributor. They are all pH correct, made from a blend of herbs and botanicals, 99% allergen-free, with natural fragrances. They DO NOT contain alcohol, artificial colors, petroleum products, or harmful chemicals or preservatives. Take the brief online skin quiz to find out your skin type.

Sample products:

- After-sun lotions
- Exfoliants
- Eye creams
- Facial scrubs
- Herbal foot care
- Masques
- Night serums and creams
- Skin conditioning oils

**Search:** Limited
**Photos:** A few
**Ordering:** Online, Phone
**Gift Wrap:** No
**Delivery:** Ground, 3rd Day

# Beauty Boutique

http://www.beautenaturel.com

Large assortment of hard-to-find beauty products from around the world. Bonus: they offer free samples with purchases. Keep an eye out for their occasional Blow-Out Sales. Samples:

- Aromatherapy products from Australia
- Bath oils from Germany
- Citrus facial scrubs
- Diet aids and supplements
- Eyelid masks
- Farmers Market skin care
- Natural skin products
- Pure natural jojoba vitamin E creams

**Search:** Yes
**Photos:** Yes
**Ordering:** Online, Phone
**Gift Wrap:** Yes
**Delivery:** Ground, 2nd Day, Overnight

# The Beauty Cafe

http://www.beautycafe.com

This online component of the regular retail shop offers a lot of unique products plus some well-known natural manufacturers, such as Bauelaire, Bursts Bees, Absolute Soap, and Bath Bloomers. Looking for a special gift? Try out their personal shopper or send a gift certificate. This friendly shop has also set up a community where you can talk to others who like natural products and care about our environment. Depending on the size of your order, you may get free shipping. Samples:

- Aloe-vera moisturizers
- Aromatherapy
- Baby products
- Products for men
- Sea-mud soap
- Tea-tree solutions

**Search:** Yes
**Photos:** Yes
**Ordering:** Online, Phone
**Gift Wrap:** Yes
**Delivery:** Ground, 2nd Day, Overnight

# Beauty Naturally

http://
www.beautynatually.com

This 20-year-old company's philosophy is that "as human beings, we should live in harmony with nature and immerse ourselves in the beauty that surrounds us in life." Their skin and hair-care products strive to bring one's skin up to its youthful potential by healing it and then keeping it healthy using all-natural ingredients. Samples:

- Alpha/beta-hydroxy acid creams
- Anti-aging cosmetics and creams
- Exfoliants
- Green papaya powder
- Jojoba bead scrubs
- Natural deodorants
- Phlorogine treatments for acne
- Pore cleansers

**Search:** Some
**Photos:** No
**Ordering:** Online, Phone, Fax
**Gift Wrap:** No
**Delivery:** Ground, 2nd Day, 3rd Day

# Beehive Botanicals

http://www.beehive-
botanicals.com

All of the products offered here contain some of the "gifts of the honeybee," such as pollen, royal jelly, propolis, or honey. Besides carrying a dizzying array of "bee" products, this store also offers links to sites of interest to bee lovers. Sample products:

- Bath oils
- Dietary supplements
- Facial cleansers
- Lip balm
- Organic food
- Pollen and honey shampoo and conditioners
- Propolis tincture
- Toothpaste

**Search:** Yes
**Photos:** Some
**Ordering:** Online, Phone, Fax
**Gift Wrap:** No
**Delivery:** Ground, 2nd Day, Overnight

# Better Botanicals

http://
www.betterbotanicals.com

This store offers a range of skin, hair, body, and bath products based on the ancient Indian healing system known as Ayurveda, which means "knowledge of life." According to the Ayurveda tradition, health is maintained when the three body energies (Kapha, Pitta, and Vata) are in balance. The products sold at this store are all made from various food-grade herbs and plant oils. They DO NOT contain synthetic color or fragrance. Products are blended to suit your individual constitution. You can fill out the online questionnaire to find out your type, to determine which products are best suited for you. Samples:

- Amla Shine shampoo
- Aromatherapy
- Baby products

- Clarifying facial scrub
- Dead Sea bath-salt therapy
- Neem care shampoo
- Pure gloss conditioner
- Rose and tulsi toners
- Sandalwood moisturizer

**Search:** Yes
**Photos:** Yes
**Ordering:** Online, Phone, Fax
**Gift Wrap:** Yes
**Delivery:** Ground

# bioDERM

http://www.bioderm.com

Your skin is the number-one priority at this store. First determine your particular skin type (sensitive, acneic, mature, and so on) and then use the bioDERM product selection guide to discover the appropriate all-natural products for you. These creams, lotions, and bath items aren't cheap, but a good way to shop is to check out the gift baskets. They also offer monthly specials. Samples:

- Calendula oil-free moisturizer
- Exfoliation sponge
- Glycolic treatment crème
- Men's skin care
- Plant-essence toner
- Vegetable mud masque

**Search:** Yes
**Photos:** Yes
**Ordering:** Online, Phone, Fax
**Delivery:** Ground, 2nd Day, 3rd Day, Overnight

# Body Maintenance

http://
www.bodymaintenance.com

Started a decade ago, this upscale Miami-based company has become well-known for providing the highest-quality products. They rely on fresh vegetable, plant, and fruit extracts for all their products. Their motto says it best: "Keep it simple. Keep it natural." You won't find any animal by-products in any of these products and, of course, none of their merchandise is tested on the little furry creatures. You might think that their merchandise is pricey, but nice surprise here: Everything is very reasonably priced. Samples:

- 100% cotton plush terry bathrobes
- Aloe-based cleanser
- Exfoliants
- Grapefruit toner
- Hair care products
- Humectant gel moisturizer
- Natural fragrance

**Search:** Some
**Photos:** Yes
**Ordering:** Online, Phone, Fax
**Gift Wrap:** Yes
**Delivery:** 2nd Day

## Botanics of California

http://
www.botanicscalifornia.com

Joan Griswold noticed big changes in her hair and skin after age 30. Finding some of the traditional remedies her grandmother used, Griswold started her own organic garden and raised the plants, herbs, and flowers needed. Several years later, she refined these "recipes" and started her own company. You won't find any fillers, additives, or chemicals in these reasonably priced skin, hair, and body products. Samples:

- Grapefruit body lotions
- Great list of herbs and their benefits
- Mallow massage lotion
- Meadowsweet clay masks
- Mint exfoliants
- Rose-geranium cleansers
- Rosemary toner
- Sampler kits

**Search:** No
Photos: Some
Ordering: Online, Phone

Gift Wrap: No
Delivery: Ground

## Cranberry Lane

http://www.cranberrylane.com

These folks seem to have fun with the assortment of items they offer for sale. Their products are all-natural, 100% biodegradable, using no preservatives. Just check out the eclectic inventory of this place! Samples:

- Alpha-hydroxy-acid cleansers and lotions
- Bubbling bath-softener kit
- Herbs
- Natural beauty kits
- Nonchemical sunscreen
- Oils
- Pet-care products
- Soap-making supplies

**Search:** Yes
**Photos:** Some
**Ordering:** Online
**Gift Wrap:** No
**Delivery:** Ground, 2nd Day, Overnight

## Garden Botanika

http://www.gardenbotanika.com

This company was started eight years ago in the Northwest and has grown to almost 300 stores nationwide. Their online store is an extension of their physical shops. All of their fragrances, skin-care products, and cosmetics contain natural botanical ingredients. They are adamant about not using animal by-products and they do not conduct animal testing. These environmentally friendly cosmetics are also wallet friendly. They sell for a fraction of the department-store prices. Samples:

- Custom fragrances
- Fruit and floral aromatics
- Natural-color cosmetics
- Products for men
- Scented oils, candles, and body lotions

- Skin-care kits for five different skin types
- Spa Botanika

**Search:** Yes
**Photos:** Yes
**Ordering:** Online, Phone
**Gift Wrap:** Yes
**Delivery:** Ground, Overnight

## Lite Cosmetics

http://www.litecosmetics.com

This cosmetic company specializes in anti-aging creams with a twist. All are especially made for sensitive, allergic, dry, or damaged skin. Their products are free of perfume, lanolin, talc, and dyes. This site also offers skin-care tips in 12 categories—arranged, for example, by age group, for smokers or drinkers, and men's skin care. Sample products:

- Antioxidant day cream
- Eye-wrinkle cream
- Hand-made glycerin face soap
- Sunscreen lotion with SPF-27
- Wrinkle removers

**Search:** No
**Photos:** Some
**Ordering:** Online, Fax, Phone
**Gift Wrap:** No
**Delivery:** Ground

## Me Body and Bath

http://www.mebodyandbath.com

This store specializes in gentle products such as soaps, creams, oils, and lotions, many using pure vegetable emollients and purified water. Although the site looks like it is reaching for Gen Xers, anyone will appreciate their attempt at a fun, friendly online store. The rubber ducky is a nice touch. Samples:

- Alpha-hydroxy moisture cream
- Bath products
- Coral grain cleanser

- Face brush
- Sensitive skin eye cream
- Vitamin E moisture cream

**Search:** Minimal
**Photos:** Some
**Ordering:** Online, Phone
**Gift Wrap:** No
**Delivery:** Ground

## The Natural Body Bar

http://www.bodybar.com

One of the largest online selections of natural beauty products, this well-designed site carries just about everything in hair, skin, body, bath, and foot products. It even supplies a line of all-natural children's goods. Sample products:

- Bath oil
- Cleansing nail brush
- Cucumber eye gel
- Foot polishers
- Gift baskets
- Hair products for men and women
- Lobster after-sun lotion
- Sea-foam facial wash

**Search:** Some
**Photos:** Some
**Ordering:** Online, Phone, Fax
**Gift Wrap:** Yes
**Delivery:** Ground, Overnight

## Skin Life Products

http://www.skinlife.com

Dermatologist Jon Morgan has formulated cosmetics and facial creams that are hypoallergenic, oil-free, and mostly nonfragrant. They also do not have unnecessary additives and are not tested on animals. Samples:

- Anti-aging creams
- Cleansers

- Hair care products
- Moisturizers
- Sunscreens
- Toners

**Search:** Yes
**Photos:** No
**Ordering:** Online
**Gift Wrap:** No
**Delivery:** Ground, 2nd Day

## No, Really???

Back in the 18th and 19th centuries wealthy women used something called ceruse to make their faces look fashionably pale. Not a good idea, because ceruse was made mostly of white lead. If you want to find out more about the products you put on your face, go to the Consumer's Guide to Cosmetic Safety at http://www.cosmeticmall.com/cm/html/cg/CG_cosm_safety.html

# Beer & Wine Equipment

We must admit that we are pretty clueless when it comes to making wine and beer, having been mostly watchers and tasters, while our neighbors mashed their grape crops. However, we do know a good online store when we see one, and we found a few stout shops. Most of these places sell equipment and supplies for making both wine and beer. Some even sell stuff for making soda. Sometimes it's hard to tell by the name of the store what kind of fermentation they specialize in, so we've put that into the store description.

## Beer, Beer and More Beer

http://www.morebeer.com

This place, with the name reminiscent of that song we all sang for hours on the bus coming home from a long field trip, sells more than brewing materials. They offer their expertise, meaning you'll get some fine service. Free shipping to the U.S. on orders over $35. Orders under that will be charged a flat $4 for shipping. Samples:

- Beer kit of the month
- Bottles
- Brewing sculpture systems
- Carboy drainers
- Gift certificates
- Glass carboys
- Grain
- Starter kits

**Search:** Some
**Photos:** Some
**Ordering:** Online, Phone
**Gift Wrap:** No
**Delivery:** Ground

## Beer- and Wine-making Supplies

http://
www.aardvarkbrewing.com

Twenty-five years ago, the owners of this shop started with wine-making supplies, and started offering the same for beer in 1979. Check out their Recipe of the Month, for some inspiration. Samples:

- Beer kits
- Caps, cappers, and gaskets
- Carboy brushes
- Fermenters
- Glass bottles
- Hydrometer
- Soda kits
- Starter kids
- Used Coke or Pepsi kegs
- Wine kits
- Wort chiller

**Search:** No
**Photos:** Some
**Ordering:** Online, Phone
**Gift Wrap:** No
**Delivery:** Ground

## Brew Your Own Beverages

http://www.onlinesu.com/byob

This store makes BYOB mean something more than just buying a bottle—it means *making* a bottle. They'll sell you everything you need to brew some beer or start your own winery. Something different for this type of store is that it also offers you the ingredients to make several flavors of soda, too. Samples:

- All-natural flavor extracts
- Beer- and wine-making kits
- Bottle-washing equipment
- Champagne stoppers
- Complete keg systems
- Corkers
- Glassware
- Gum stoppers

- Soda extracts
- Straining equipment
- Wine concentrates
- Wine-making equipment

**Search:** Some
**Photos:** Some
**Ordering:** Online, Phone
**Gift Wrap:** Card
**Delivery:** Ground

## Gourmet Trader

http://www.gourmettrader.com

The emphasis at this store is on hot and spicy gourmet food. So, imagine our surprise to find out that it also carries a supply of beer-making (excuse us, brewing) supplies. Samples:

- Customizable ingredient kits
- Mason Deluxe Homebrewing system (with all the fixin's)
- Nut-brown ale
- Pale ale
- Red ale
- Stout
- Wheat beer

**Search:** Some
**Photos:** No
**Ordering:** Online, Phone, Fax
**Gift Wrap:** No
**Delivery:** Ground

## Hatfields and McCoys Home Brew Supplies

http://www.hatfields-mccoys.com

Despite the name, this store is a friendly place to shop. They sell all of the beer and wine-making supplies you can think of (over 600 products), plus they offer a place where you can post your favorite recipes and print out theirs. They have one of the best searches of any of the stores in this chapter. They also have some extracts for making soda. Samples:

- Beer and wine books
- Beer- and wine-making kits
- Cleaners and sterilizers
- Fermenters
- Fruit bases
- Grains, yeast, hops, and malts
- Malt mill
- Soft drink extracts
- Test equipment
- Wine additives
- Wort chiller

**Search:** Yes
**Photos:** Yes
**Ordering:** Online, Phone, Fax
**Gift Wrap:** No
**Delivery:** Ground

## The Homebrew Experience

http://www.brewguys.com

This store sells all of the equipment you'll need, and it offers lots of recipes and links to other sites that you may find helpful pursuing your hobby. If you're new at this, you'll find their lengthy explanations helpful. How about taking the guesswork out of your brewing? This place sells brewing software, including a recipe-brewing log, a recipe-calculator program, and more. Samples:

- Airlocks
- Beer and wine books
- Beer and wine labels
- Bottling equipment
- Complete brewing kits
- Fermenting containers and accessories
- Fruit purees and concentrates
- Hops, yeast, grains, and malt extracts
- Kegs and accessories
- Mash equipment
- Siphons and tubing
- Spoons, paddles, and funnels
- Temperature controller
- Thermometers and test equipment

- Wine-making equipment

**Search:** Yes
**Photos:** No
**Ordering:** Online
**Gift Wrap:** No
**Delivery:** Ground

## You may also want to sample these chapters:

- Food—Gourmet
- Wine

# Bicycles

We guess bikes are so popular because they're the first vehicle we were able to use that made us go fast. Around and around the house we went, past the lilacs and back, making that brick walk into the Indianapolis Speedway, including occasional spills, tip-overs, and scraped knees. Of course, those were the three-wheel variety of cycle, and the ones we explore in this chapter are strictly two-wheelers. And we didn't have gears on those old trikes, and we certainly didn't need special clothes or equipment. But now that we're all grown up, we like to dress up and wear the right clothes and strap on the right accessories so we can go fast and look good. Some things never change.

## Bike Nashbar

http://www.bikenashbar.com

On the day we browsed through this store they had almost 9,000 different cycling products for sale. They sell bicycles, yes, but this is the place to come for all those special bike parts that make cycling so pleasurable. You'll be able to find almost anything you need or want at this store. Samples:

- Cable hangers
- Chain rings
- Cycling clothes and shoes
- Hydration systems
- Hyperends
- Inflators
- Lizard-skin bar end covers
- Titanium axles

**Search:** Yes
**Photos:** Some
**Ordering:** Online, Phone
**Gift Wrap:** Card
**Delivery:** Ground, 2nd Day, Overnight

## Brauns

http://www.brauns.com

Gordon and Grace Braun started repairing bikes in their little Canadian shop seventy-five years ago. Four generations later, their little repair shop has grown into a bicycle superstore in Ontario. They sell just about any bike-related product you could think of. Samples:

- Baby trailers and strollers
- Car racks
- Clothing
- Cycling computers
- Kid's bikes and scooters
- Locks, horns, and bells
- Repair tools and parts
- Sports jewelry
- Unicycles

**Search:** Yes
**Photos:** Yes
**Ordering:** Online
**Gift Wrap:** No
**Delivery:** Ground

## Colorado Cyclist

http://www.coloradocyclist.com

This place is for serious cyclists. The store carries a lot of the top-of-the-line, state-of-the-art bikes and accessories. They also sell cycling clothing and have one of the best selections for women of all the online stores.

Samples:

- Cranks
- Cycling software, books, and videos
- Derailleurs
- Footwear
- Indoor training accessories
- Men's and women's clothing
- Mountain and road bikes
- Nutritional products
- Reflective wear
- Tour de France posters

**Search:** Yes
**Photos:** Yes

**Ordering:** Online, Phone
**Gift Wrap:** No
**Delivery:** Ground, 2nd Day

## Kelly Bike.com

`http://www.kellybike.com`

Remember when you were a kid and you'd go to your local car dealer and watch your parents pick out the model they wanted, then select the paint job, interior color, and accessories or options? Kelly's is like that, only you're buying a bicycle, not a car. Oh, not that you can't buy ready-made ones, too. They carry plenty of those, but if you want to select a custom road frame and even a custom color, this is the place for you.

Samples:
- Custom-made bikes
- Custom stems
- Cyclo-cross frames
- Energy food
- Knobby cross frames
- Mountain frames
- Road and track frames
- Some apparel

**Search:** Yes
**Photos:** Yes
**Ordering:** Online
**Gift Wrap:** No
**Delivery:** Ground

## LBIC

`http://www.lbic.com`

This is one of the largest manufacturers of cross-country and mountain bikes for adults, and they also make bikes for kids, as well as selling lots of components. They've been making fully assembled bikes for over 25 years in their factory in China, then bringing them over to sell in the U.S. and Europe. If you've watched video of commuters in the cities of China, you've seen how experienced these folks are, using bikes every morning, noon, and night. These bikes look a lot better than the ones we've seen folks riding on TV in Beijing. The prices are excellent. Many of the bikes are hand painted.

Samples:
- Beach cruisers
- Kids' mountain bikes
- Scorpio, Monza, and Delta bikes
- Specially designed bikes for women
- Ultralight aluminum accessories

**Search:** Some
**Photos:** Yes
**Ordering:** Online, Phone, Fax
**Gift Wrap:** No
**Delivery:** Ground

## O'Neil's

`http://www.oneils.com`

This is like walking into a store that sells a little of everything. (No wonder—their online store is fashioned after their building in Massachusetts.)  They have an excellent supply of cycling clothes by Assos, Giordana, Sugoi, and others (sizes run from small to XXL). You can have your bike custom made. They carry some biking accessories that we didn't find in any other stores. If you get tired of browsing the merchandise you can click on the Flex and Floyd cartoon show for some laughs. Before you shop, we suggest you click the Cheap button for a large supply of sale items. Free shipping for online orders.

Samples:
- Chamois cream
- Knee-warmers
- Limar helmets
- Road shoes
- T-Bib knickers
- Team uniforms
- Thermo tights and jackets

**Search:** Yes
**Photos:** Yes
**Ordering:** Online, Phone, Fax
**Gift Wrap:** No
**Delivery:** Ground

# PricePoint

`http://www.pricepoint.com`

PricePoint says they offer the lowest prices of all the Internet stores (50% below retail). In fact, if you can find a better price after you buy from them, they will refund you the difference. They offer a lot on this Web store and offer even more from their catalog, which you can order from this site. They sell frames, clothes, parts, and a huge supply of various accessories. If you're new to this, or just unsure what to buy, read their product reviews, helpfully sorted into categories such as clothing, frames, parts, pedals, and more. Don't forget to look at their Blow-Out Special section for some even better savings. Samples:

- Accelerator shoes
- Component package kits
- Disc brakes
- Heart monitors
- Helmets
- Pro clipless pedals
- Rock Shox Indy XC
- Videotapes
- Wheelsets

**Search:** Yes
**Photos:** Yes
**Ordering:** Online, Phone, Fax, Email
**Gift Wrap:** No
**Delivery:** 2nd Day

# Santa Cruz Bicycles

`http://www.santacruzmtb.com`

This bike company doesn't sell its bikes online (you can get a list of dealers from this site, though). What you can buy from the online store is their Santa Cruz clothing and some accessories. There isn't a lot for sale here, but if you like things with the Santa Cruz name on it, this is the place. Samples:

- Ball caps
- Bike posters
- Decals
- Hooded sweatshirts
- Jerseys
- T-shirts

**Search:** Yes
**Photos:** Yes
**Ordering:** Online
**Gift Wrap:** No
**Delivery:** Ground

# Schwinn

`http://www.schwinn.com`

This bike company has been around for a long time. You might have even owned a Schwinn as a kid. Click the Cyberstore tab to enter their store. Unfortunately, their Web store doesn't sell outdoor bikes, although it does sell a lot of other things, including fitness clothing (great selection of women's clothing and wild jerseys for men and women) and accessories. Samples:

- BMX T-shirts, caps, and clothing
- Headbands
- Sleeveless jerseys
- Spinning workout video
- Team jerseys
- Wool jackets

**Search:** Yes
**Photos:** Yes
**Ordering:** Online
**Gift Wrap:** No
**Delivery:** Ground, 3rd Day

# Totally Outdoors

`http://www.totallyoutdoors.com`

After finding so many stores that sold only clothes for men, it was a pleasure to find one devoted to women. There's lots of equipment designed for the female of the species and clothing ranging in sizes from XS to XXL. Besides every item of clothing you could need for cycling, you'll also find a great selection of clothes for other sporting activities and some equipment specifically designed for women. Samples:

- Arm and leg warmers
- Cardigan jackets

- Dirt socks
- Instructional books
- Lycra shorts
- Ponytail headbands
- Precision gloves
- Rain gear
- Saddles
- Sleeveless jerseys
- Sports bras
- Supplex fitness shorts
- Waterproof/breathable socks

**Search**: Yes
**Photos**: Yes
**Ordering**: Online
**Gift Wrap**: No
**Delivery**: Ground, 3rd Day, Overnight

# If you're interested in other active endeavors, pedal on over to this chapter:

- Sporting Goods

# Boating & Sailing

From canoeing on the little stream that turns into the Mississippi River, boating on inland lakes, and sailing the ocean off Maine on a three-masted schooner, we learned a healthy respect for barnacles, teak, and water, so we don't even try boating on the Rio Grande, our local river. (Actually, it's often more of a stream through quicksand, mud, and sand-bars.) OK, so you won't be able to buy a motor launch or sailboat online. We guess the manufacturers are still a little shy about letting you put $12,000 to $1,200,000 on your credit card. But what you can buy at these Web stores is a massive amount of sailing and boating gear, including navigational equipment (electronic and other), clothing (including some just for women), custom-made sails, winches, and flotation systems. And if you haul your boat to the marina or lake, we even found a place that sells elec-tronic black boxes that let you know if there's something amiss with your towing system while you're on the road.

## Bart's Water Sports

http://bartswatersports.com

Like water sports? You'll love this place. It has tons of sports equipment, gear, clothes, accessories, gifts . . . you name it. Offers 3rd Day shipping for Ground prices.
Samples:
- Barefoot skis, ropes and handles
- Combo skis
- Dry suits
- Gear bags
- Goggles
- Hydrofoils
- Jump skis

- Kneeboards
- Sunglasses

**Search:** Yes
**Photos:** Yes
**Ordering:** Online, Phone, Fax
**Gift Wrap:** Card
**Delivery:** 3rd Day

## Bearing Alert

http://www.bearingalert.com

If you are fortunate enough to be able to dock your boat permanently at a marina, skip this store. But if you haul your boat with you every time you go to the lake or ocean, this store makes products that allow you to tow your boat safely. It works like this: "The Bearing Alert System is a small microproccessor which attaches to the wheel hub of your trailer and allows you to monitor the temperature of your wheel bearings. When the wheel bearings begin to overheat (a sign indicating that failure is getting ready to happen) the system will activate a warning light on your dash board, alerting you to the problem." Sound expensive? Systems cost less than two hundred bucks, which is probably a lot less than you paid for your boat.
Samples:
- Double-axle unit
- Single-axle unit
- Triple-axle unit

**Search:** No
**Photos:** Some
**Ordering:** Online, Fax, Mail
**Gift Wrap:** No
**Delivery:** Ground

## The Cap'n

http://www.thecapn.com

Getting lost at sea is no laughing matter. If you have a laptop computer on board you'll be able to take advantage of some navigational software for sale at this store. (If you already own an older title of The Cap'n software, you can purchase upgrades here, too.) We

noticed that a lot of the boating sites link to this one.
Samples:
- 3D Sea
- Coastal directions
- Electronic charting systems
- Light lists
- Planning charts
- Route plans
- Tides and currents
- Visual-passage planner

**Search:** Some
**Photos:** No
**Ordering:** Online, Phone
**Gift Wrap:** No
**Delivery:** Ground, Overnight

# Celestaire

http://www.celestaire.com

This company makes a line of marine and air navigation instruments. These are the instruments you use as a backup to your GPS when you are experiencing electronic or battery failure. They also sell a big line of electronic navigational equipment. The number of tools offered here is amazing. Plan to spend a lot of time browsing through this store. Samples:
- Binoculars
- Books
- Compasses
- Computer software
- Depth-sounder/Speedlog
- Electronic charts
- Marine sextants
- Navigation computers
- Night vision for the sextant
- Plotting tools
- Starfinding aids
- Videos
- World band radio

**Search:** Yes
**Photos:** Yes
**Ordering:** Online, Phone, Fax
**Gift Wrap:** No
**Delivery:** Ground, 2nd Day, Overnight

# Hern Marine

http://www.hernmarine.com

You'll find a huge inventory of boating supplies. This really has to be called a boating superstore. We didn't see anything else like it on the Web. You name it, they carry it, from the mundane but necessary cleaning supplies to the more glamorous stuff, like water sports gear. You'll also find a lot of fishing and sporting goods here. Samples:
- Anchors
- Books
- Cleaning supplies
- Clothing
- Covers and canvas
- Electrical and lighting equipment
- Engines and controls
- Fiberglass accessories
- Flotation systems
- Ladders and platforms
- Marine sanitation supplies
- Paint and caulk
- Pumps
- Seating and other furniture
- Signal and safety equipment

**Search:** Yes
**Photos:** Yes
**Ordering:** Online, Phone, Fax
**Gift Wrap:** No
**Delivery:** Ground, 2nd Day, Overnight

# Marine Scene

http://
www.marinescenemall.com

This minimall gives you a good selection of marine electronics, software, and other products. This is another one of the supersites, but the emphasis here is on high-tech stuff, although they also sell everyday items, such as cup holders. The search mechanism is good, but a little hard to use. It's best if you really know what you're looking for. Samples:
- Electronic chart plotters
- Electronic fish finders

- Eyewear
- Handheld VHS radios
- Motor accessories
- Radar equipment
- Software
- Swingback chair
- Underwater cameras

**Search:** Yes
**Photos:** Some
**Ordering:** Online, Phone, Fax
**Gift Wrap:** No
**Delivery:** Ground

## Maritech Marine Electronics

http://www.maritech.com

This Connecticut-based store is a full-service marine electronics company. Their online store carries lots of navigational aids. It also has lots of other information for sailors, such as news and links to other helpful sites. Once you're ready to order, you'll be brought to a page on Yahoo for ordering. Samples:

- Flat-screen displays
- GPS and charting systems
- Icom PCR-1000
- Navigation software
- NMEA Serial Multiplexer

**Search:** Some
**Photos:** Yes
**Ordering:** Online
**Gift Wrap:** No
**Delivery:** Ground, 3rd Day, 2nd Day, Overnight

## Meissner Winches

http://www.meissner-winches.com

Without some good winches, you won't be sailing anywhere, no matter what the weather. This store specializes in winches, and winches only. You'll find many different sizes (fractional or metric). Samples:

- Classic and custom-made winches
- Electric winches

- Grinder winches
- Handles
- Hydraulic winches
- Mega winches
- Mooring winches
- Self-tailing winches
- Service kits
- Standard winches

**Search:** Yes
**Photos:** Yes
**Ordering:** Online, Phone, Fax
**Gift Wrap:** No
**Delivery:** Ground

## North Sails One Design

http://northsailsod.com

Want a sail delivered to your home, or, better yet, your boat? It's easy at this Web store. Just fill in the information describing the sail you want, including your color preference for the sail number and country letters, spinnaker colors, and any other special requests. North Sails also has a lot of guides to help you sail faster, plus a new column and information about adult and junior sailing classes. Sample sails:

- Folded
- Genoa
- Jib
- Mainsail
- Rolled
- Spinnaker

**Search:** No
**Photos:** Yes
**Ordering:** Online, Phone, Fax, Email
**Gift Wrap:** No
**Delivery:** Ground, 3rd Day, 2nd Day

## Sailor's Choice

http://www.sailorschoice.com

This place is a lot more than a store. Maybe you'd call this a ship's chandlery, or a place where you buy stuff that your boat really needs. There are many varied and fun stores under one umbrella. You can also find out about boat financing, fishing charters, marine insurance, boating associations, travel accommodations, and so much more. You'll locate just about any neat doodad or useful piece of equipment here. Samples:

- Coastal navigation tool
- Decorative ships
- Dinghy lifts
- Dry storage systems
- Fine sheepskin boots and footwear
- Galley/Safety belts
- Jacklines and tethers
- Lefton historic American lighthouse collection
- Mast Mate climbing system
- Motor toes
- Sail snaps
- Sea steps
- Towing bridle

**Search:** Yes (depending on store)
**Photos:** Yes
**Ordering:** Online (varies a bit by store)
**Gift Wrap:** Varies
**Delivery:** Varies

## She Sails

http://www.aztec.com/
shesails

For some reason, the name of this store reminded us of the children's tongue twister that starts, "Sally sells seashells by the seashore." We don't know if there's a Sally at this shop, but there's a lot for sale. All of the merchandise is especially created for the woman sailor. Most of the clothing, if it's not a Small, Medium, and Large thing, comes in sizes 6 to 16; most shoes come in sizes 5 to 12. Samples:

- Foul-weather gear
- Lifejacket with harness
- Nautical jewelry
- Sailing gloves
- Stainless steel hand tools
- Sun-protection gear
- Training software
- Water Dogs

**Search:** Yes

**Photos:** Yes
**Ordering:** Online, Phone, Fax, Mail
**Gift Wrap:** No
**Delivery:** Ground

## ShipStore.com

http://www.shipstore.com

This is a fun place to shop, especially excellent if you're looking for a present (just about the only Web boating store that offers gift wrapping!). Their assortment is fun, practical, and a little frivolous in some cases. Perfect for the yachtsman or woman who has everything. Samples:

- Antiqued porthole frames and mirrors
- Authentic *Titanic* collectibles
- Bilge pump controller
- Helmsman clocks
- Message in a bottle (yes, with paper and pen included)
- Nautical bar accessories
- Ship's bell
- Shipwreck treasures
- Slot machines

**Search:** Yes
**Photos:** Yes
**Ordering:** Online, Phone, Fax
**Gift Wrap:** Yes
**Delivery:** Ground, 3rd Day, 2nd Day

## Yacht Saver

http://www.yachtsaver.com

This store sells one of the best pieces of safety equipment you can have on your boat. With it, you can stay on your ailing ship (with your food, navigational equipment, and radio) instead of abandoning ship. It works like this: Compressed gases from an onboard cylinder inflate flotation bags around your boat, which keeps it aloft until help comes. This company sells a lot of different varieties, depending upon what kind of boat you own. Samples:

- Rescue pack for boats less than 3,000 lbs.
- Various sizes of marine flotation systems

**Search:** Some
**Photos:** Yes
**Ordering:** Online
**Gift Wrap:** No
**Delivery:** Ground

## Can't get to the Boat Show? No problem.

You can catch it on the Web at http://www.boatshow.com/

## If you camp out after you sail all day, or just like hiking, climbing, and sports in general, take a tack toward these chapters:

- Camping & Hiking
- Sporting Goods
- Travel Adventures

# Books

Browsing for books is one of the great luxuries of buying on the Web. From superstores with millions of titles, to smaller, specialty shops and author sites, the Web has tens of millions of books, in print or out of print, and, within a day or so, the package comes to your door. No shuffling through the shelves at the megastore at the mall, and, unlike the cozy neighborhood bookstore, no out-of-stocks— or fewer. Some stores even let you set up a profile describing the authors or subjects you like, so you get email alerts about new volumes that might interest you. It's like having your own personal shopper. The only thing missing is the cappuccino.

## ABS—the Alternative Book Shop

http://Web-star.com/
alternative/books.html

You won't find John Grisham's latest, or Tom Clancy's either. What you will find is a unique selection of hard-to-find books from small and self-publishers. The store has somehow retained that tiny, off-the-main-drag feeling. All of the books are reviewed. Sample titles:

- *Cold Noses at the Pearly Gates*
- *Cornerstones of Sobriety and Sanity*
- *Da Sweetman Iz Comin*
- *Glans of Tarunan*
- *How to Inspect Your Home and Understand Inspection Reports*

**Search:** Yes
**Photos:** No
**Ordering:** Online, Phone, Fax
**Gift Wrap:** No
**Delivery:** Ground

## Amazon.com

http://www.amazon.com

This wasn't the first online bookstore, but it certainly was the first one to embrace the new technology and use it in a constructive way. Instead of putting a brick-and-mortar bookstore online, it *started* its venture online. Everything in this store is designed to help the customer, from a fantastic search to an easy checkout system. The selection is huge. Our favorite feature is that you can go to a particular book page and find out what other books were bought by customers who ordered the book you have highlighted. When you are researching a topic or have an avid interest, this one feature alone is invaluable. You'll also be able to participate in auctions, buy music, and link to a drugstore. Soon, Amazon will be known as a department store on the Web, but we'll always have a fond place in our heart for its bookstore. Samples:

- Audiobooks
- Book and toy sets
- Calendars
- Customer review
- Email recommendations
- Extensive computer-related section
- Moodmatchers
- Reading group guides
- Videos and DVDs

**Search:** Yes
**Photos:** Yes
**Ordering:** Online
**Gift Wrap:** Yes
**Delivery:** Ground, 2nd Day, Overnight

## Barnes and Noble

http://www.barnesandnoble.com

This online version of the bookstore giant is about what you'd expect it to be. It is big. Of course, you can buy just about any book that's ever been printed in the recent era. (No fooling, they have terrific out-of-print lists that come up when you search for an author and a rare-book section.) You can also read reviews from outside sources, such as *The New York Times, Publishers Weekly*, and *Kirkus Reviews*. If you usually stop by the large magazine rack on your way out of the store, you'll appreciate the large selection of magazines available for subscription from this online store. Don't forget to check out their bargain book section, which sometimes offers discounts up to 90% off the original. Samples:

- Address books
- Audio books
- Baby and preschooler gifts
- Collector's editions
- Gift certificates
- Magazine matcher
- Software
- Videos

**Search:** Yes
**Photos:** Yes
**Ordering:** Online, Phone
**Gift Wrap:** Yes
**Delivery:** Ground, 2nd Day, Overnight

## Books.com

http://www.books.com

The first thing you notice when you go to this shop is the white space. They obviously believe that less is more, at least on the home page. It's very easy on the eyes. All of the best-sellers are 40% off the cover price and they have a button you can click to compare prices at some other online bookstore. One negative about this friendly shop is the extremely slow speed at which the pages download. Hopefully that's changed by the time this book is published. Samples:

- Book forums
- Conference area for teachers
- Cook's nook
- Hall of mystery
- Parenting chat area
- Soul talk

**Search:** Yes
**Photos:** Yes
**Ordering:** Online
**Gift Wrap:** Yes
**Delivery:** Ground, 3rd Day

## Borders

http://www.borders.com

It has always seemed to us that the Borders store you enter from the street is a massive bookstore whose owners are trying very hard to keep that small-bookstore feel. From the coffee shop with lots of sweets, to the huge inventory of audio CDs and cassettes, Borders is a nice place to hang out. Their online store is very similar (without the coffee, of course). You can call or email your book questions to their Info Desk Staff (even if all you remember is what the cover looks like). Samples:

- Audio CDs
- Chat at Talk City
- Discount books
- Discussion boards
- Gift certificates
- Ideas for educators
- Large children's section
- Videos

**Search:** Yes
**Photos:** Yes
**Ordering:** Online, Phone, Fax
**Gift Wrap:** Yes
**Delivery:** Ground, 2nd Day, Overnight

## Business and Computer Bookstore

http://www.bcb.com

Over 15,000 titles line the virtual shelves of this store. Many of the books come with a 25% to 50% discount, and there are discounts for big orders. The store also offers a good search mechanism: You can look up a book by author, title, or category. Sample categories:

- Communications
- General computing
- Internet
- Linux
- Mac and DOS-only books
- Programming

**Search:** Yes
**Photos:** No
**Ordering:** Online
**Gift Wrap:** No
**Delivery:** Ground

# Chronicle Books

`http://www.chronbooks.com`

At this chic bookstore with a San Francisco Bay flare, the emphasis is on art and architecture books. Lots of beautiful photographs and attention to detail. There's a kids' section, complete with dates of author tours and a fun house where kids can play with mazes. Samples:

- Calendars
- Generous book excerpts
- Journals
- Kids' games
- Stationery
- Teaching guides

**Search:** Yes
**Photos:** Fantastic
**Ordering:** Online, Phone
**Gift Wrap:** No
**Delivery:** Ground

# Computerliteracy.com

`http://www.clbooks.com/home.html`

This place is a techie's delight. Like the shelf-and-cash-register stores in California, the online store is so rich in computer-related books that we often find ourselves picking out half a dozen books in a casual visit. The site has the same advantage of clear focus. Easy to navigate (unlike many of the computer programs they use day in and day out) and easy to search, the site is a real pleasure to browse. All titles are discounted at least 10% from the manufacturer's suggested price. If you are researching a subject, you'll find their related-items section a big plus. You might also want to look for the red

ball, which is their seal of approval. They also sell a small amount of computer- and business-related software. Sample categories:

- Business and culture
- Certification
- Database
- Games
- Java
- Networking
- UNIX
- Y2K Bug

**Search:** Yes
**Photos:** Yes
**Ordering:** Online
**Gift Wrap:** No
**Delivery:** Ground, 2nd Day, Overnight

# Drum and Spear

`http://www.drumandspear.com`

This complete African-American bookstore offers books and a whole lot more, from mysteries to romances to best-sellers and children's books. There are links to African-American resources and even recipes from Gigi, who we suspect is one of the owners who moonlights with her own special catering service. Discounts are offered. Samples:

- Author events
- Autographed copies of books
- Bookmarks
- Calendars
- Computer training software and videos
- Online chats
- Posters

**Search:** Some
**Photos:** No
**Ordering:** Online, Phone
**Gift Wrap:** No
**Delivery:** Ground

# ERIC Clearinghouse on Assessment and Evaluation

`http://ericae.net/bstore`

If you are a teacher or a parent, you've probably heard of ERIC. For years it has served as a resource for educational research. Many of the books offered here are technical in nature, although some are commercial and popular. All of them are fully described. The best part of the site is the wonderful Site Plan that serves as an easy-to-use guide to the appropriate subject, without any techno-babble. Once you've selected your books, you are linked to Amazon.com. Is that cheating? Not really. Our bet is that Amazon.com helped them design their site and that's why it's so bright and friendly. It's worth the extra click. Sample topics:

- Grading
- Learning styles
- Program evaluation
- Statistics
- Strategies
- Study skills
- Teacher testing
- Test construction

**Search:** Yes
**Photos:** Yes
**Ordering:** Online
**Gift Wrap:** Yes
**Delivery:** Ground, 2nd Day, Overnight

# Future Fantasy Bookstore

`http://futfan.com/home.html`

Well-done science fiction makes you forget the reality that you live in right now. It creates a world, some intriguing characters, and if it's really good, it suggests a whole new set of assumptions and beliefs, and maybe even alters your consciousness. Sound interesting? Then beam up to this bookstore and take advantage of their wide range of titles within the categories of science fiction and fantasy, as well as mysteries, offering both books and games, and a lot of neat extras. For instance, a thoughtful touch is the feature letting you automatically order the next book in a series. Want the next Star Wars paperback? (For the uninitiated, there are only four Star Wars movies but dozens of novels.) You can have it delivered to your door as soon as it's published. This is more of a club than a simple store. Samples:

- Author-signed copies
- Games
- Horror, mystery, and fantasy books
- Hugo Award winners
- Links to sites of interest
- T-shirts

**Search:** Some
**Photos:** No
**Ordering:** Online
**Gift Wrap:** No
**Delivery:** Ground

# NC Buy Book Store

`http://www.ncbuy.com/books`

This store sells all of the best-sellers, and you can find all of the popular books that appear on most of the other mega-bookstore sites. However, this one is definitely set up to appeal to young adults. There's a generous computer section, and it even offers subscriptions (with full details) of several magazines, such as *Teen People, Maxim,* and *Sports Illustrated.* Check out the links to free stuff. Besides books, you'll find:

- Career center
- Cartoons
- Horoscope
- Online games
- Personals
- Poems
- Screensavers
- Software

**Search:** Yes
**Photos:** Yes
**Ordering:** Online
**Gift Wrap:** No
**Delivery:** Ground

## Powell's Books

http://powells.com

This store carries new books, but what it excels at is used and out-of-print books. There's a terrific search in which you hunt for books by typing in the basics, like the title, keyword, or author. But if that's not enough, there are seven other search categories as well. The descriptions of the books are a bit skimpy, but many come with biographical info on the authors. Samples:

- Contests
- Gift certificates
- Newsletters
- Rare books
- Sales on out-of-print books
- Staff picks
- T-shirts, coffee mugs, and book bags

**Search:** Yes
**Photos:** No
**Ordering:** Online
**Gift Wrap:** No
**Delivery:** Ground, 2nd Day, Overnight

## The Storyteller Audio Book-store

http://audio-books.com/
index.html

Our family loves to take long car trips in the summer. We load up the van with the kids, the cooler, and lots of books on tape. One year we learned about the art of baseball from author Tony La Russa, but we HEARD about it from Bob Costas. Another year, we followed the trials and tribulations of Paris, Agamemnon, and Achilles. Audiotapes don't take the place of books; they can actually enhance the experience. If you're unsure what to order, you can email the owners, Vicky or Mildred, to receive a personal recommendation. This audio bookstore carries the very latest releases and the classics. Other categories:

- Business
- Children's stories

- Fiction
- Inspiration
- Nonfiction
- Self-help

**Search:** Yes
**Photos:** No
**Ordering:** Online
**Gift Wrap:** No
**Delivery:** Ground

## Varsity Books

http://varsitybooks.com

Tuition is only the beginning of the enormous expenses one incurs while attending college. The cost of books can be astronomical. This store brings those prices down to earth by offering around 40% off new textbooks! And the best part is that you don't have to stand on line to purchase them. With one semester's worth of books costing around $600 (unless you're a science major—then be prepared to shell out about $1,000), this store will save you hundreds of dollars. They also sell popular books and best-sellers. Sample courses:

- Anatomy and neurobiology
- Animal and plant biology
- Business management
- Cell and molecular biology
- History
- Journalism
- Natural sciences
- Occupational therapy

**Search:** Yes
**Photos:** Yes
**Ordering:** Online
**Gift Wrap:** No
**Delivery:** Ground, 2nd Day, Overnight

## Ready to write the next best-seller? Flip the pages to:

- Writing Tools

# Bowling

We think of bowling as a birthday party event, because so many kids can crowd around the lanes, competing without getting upset, and gorging on hot dogs and sodas while gabbing with each other between turns. What is it about bowling that makes it so much fun? Is it the party atmosphere, where you can bring your soda and nachos right up to your lane? Is it the fact that a bunch of you can all play together? Maybe it's that you can bowl for an hour or two without spending a fortune, or maybe it's the combination of luck and skill that comes together when you score a strike. Who knows? We just know that our family loves to bowl, and we bet you do, too.

## Beach Bowl Pro Shop

http:// www.beachbowlproshop.com

Big selection, good quality, fair prices. This shop is like the pro shop you peek into at the bowling alley, only their prices are a lot better. When we shopped here they were offering free finger inserts with any ball purchase. Don't forget to check for their Factory Seconds, Bonanzas, and Close-Outs for even better bargains. Free shipping in the U.S. Samples:

- 2-speed ball spinner with removable bucket
- Bowling balls
- Men's and ladies' bowling shoes with replaceable, contoured insoles
- Single and double-ball bags in many colors

**Search:** Some
**Photos:** Some
**Ordering:** Online, Phone
**Gift Wrap:** No
**Delivery:** Ground

## BigBowling.com

http://www.bigbowling.com

We always like a store that offers you something you don't expect. At this place, they offer a mini travel agency for hotel reservations in Las Vegas. Free shipping to orders in the U.S. $20 minimum for online orders. Samples:

- Bowling balls
- Double- and single-ball bags
- Men's and ladies' bowling shoes
- Instructional bowling videos and books
- Ball polishers and cleaners

**Search:** Some
**Photos:** No
**Ordering:** Online, Phone
**Gift Wrap:** No
**Delivery:** Ground

## Bowl USA

http://bowlusa.com

This is a good store to get the very latest bowling equipment, even before you can find it in most other stores. They sell bowling shirts in sizes up to XXX. This would be a good place to shop if you're looking for gifts for a bowler friend. They charge $5.00 per item for shipping heavy items. Samples:

- Ball banks
- Bowler earrings
- Bowling balls and bags
- Bowling doormat
- Bowling pin clocks
- Instructional books, tapes, and videos
- Ladies' and men's bowling shoes
- Men's 100% cotton bowling shirts
- Pin banks
- Bowling towels

**Search:** Some
**Photos:** Some
**Ordering:** Online, Phone
**Gift Wrap:** No
**Delivery:** Ground

## Bowlers Depot

http://www.bowlersdepot.com

If you can't find the bowling ball you want after shopping at this store, we really think it doesn't exist. This place has a huge selection from all the main brand names, like Columbia, Brunswick, AMF, and Ebonite, to name a few, in many different weights, covers, and colors, many deeply discounted. In fact, the price of everything at this store is heavily reduced from retail. You'll love the selection. Samples:

- Ball cleaners and polishers
- Ball spinners
- Bowling balls and bags
- Ladies' and men's bowling shoes
- Men's shirts
- Wrist supports and tape

**Search:** Some
**Photos:** No
**Ordering:** Online, Phone, Fax
**Gift Wrap:** No
**Delivery:** Ground, 3rd Day, 2nd Day

## Want to learn how to bowl better?

Go to the Professional Bowling Instruction site at http://www.pbiin.com for information on bowling instruction workshops around the country for adults. They also have information about youth bowling camps.

## If you like other sports, consider these chapters:

- Baseball & Softball
- Basketball
- Fishing
- Fitness
- Golf
- Skating
- Sporting Goods
- Tennis

# Camping & Hiking

We once went on a camping trip and brought everything we needed . . . except a can opener. If you've ever been camping, you know that this could have been a catastrophe of biblical proportions. Luckily, we had enough chips and crackers, while "roughing it" in the wilds of the Jemez Mountains.

Frankly, we were surprised at all of the first-rate camping and hiking stores taking up residence on the Web. We found old standbys and new friends. Bonus: We even found some stores that specialize in products for the child going to summer camp. The amount of gear for sale at these stores is immense . . . although we didn't find any that sold can openers.

## Action Direct

http://www.action-direct.com

This is a large camping and hunting store with an emphasis on the hunting. (You won't find tents or that sort of large camping gear.) The prices are always good, and sometimes they're terrific (such as a teardrop backpack for $5). We found a lot of unusual yet useful items, such as a rolling duffel bag on wheels. Great selection of useful camping tools. They carry a small supply of clothes. Samples:
- Flex lamp
- Folding knives and fixed blades
- Leatherman super tool and wave tool
- Waterproof boots with removable liner
- Wet/dry gear bag

**Search:** Yes
**Photos:** Yes
**Ordering:** Online, Phone, Fax
**Gift Wrap:** No
**Delivery:** Ground, 2nd Day

## Adventure Gear

http://www.ewalker.com

Lots and lots of camping equipment of every sort, with a special emphasis on climbing gear and survival equipment, in this sporting goods store. There's a good section about maximum emergency preparedness in the event of a natural disaster. Ground shipping to the U.S. is free. Samples:
- Camping furniture
- Cast-iron and enamel cookware
- Climbing rope
- Climbing shoes
- Dog packs (small to extra-large sizes)
- Double-wide hammock
- First-aid kits
- Ice tools and snow-protection gear
- Lightweight ovens
- Paddle-sport equipment and waterproof clothing
- Portable toilets
- Stainless-steel coffee percolators
- Tent totes
- Travel packs

**Search:** Yes
**Photos:** Yes
**Ordering:** Online, Fax
**Gift Wrap:** No
**Delivery:** Ground, 3rd Day, 2nd Day, Overnight

## A Happy Camper

http://www.ahappycamper.com

Just as the name of this store announces, they strive to make your camping experience a pleasant one by offering all of the essentials and fun things you'll need for your next camping trip. If you're worried about forgetting something, print out their camping checklist *before* you leave. Samples:
- Alaska knives
- Backpacks
- Camp ovens
- Outdoor cooking stoves
- Rolltop table
- Roll-a-cot
- Sleeping bags

- Tents
- Three-ply seat
- Water-purification system
- Waterproof, fire-resistant covers

**Search:** Some
**Photos:** Some
**Ordering:** Online, Phone, Fax
**Gift Wrap:** No
**Delivery:** Ground, 2nd Day, Overnight

## Backcountry Store

http://www.bcstore.com

This store really stands behind what they sell, because they test everything in the Wasatch Mountains in Utah before putting it up for sale to you. Those mountains are sometimes so steep that the mountain sheep have trouble climbing, from what we could tell through the binoculars. That should be a good enough endorsement for anyone, but just in case, everything in their store is guaranteed unconditionally. The emphasis here is on gear for climbing and camping in cold and snowy conditions. You can also check their site for maps and avalanche advisories. They also print reviews of some of the items for sale. Free shipping in the continental United States. Samples:

- Avalanche beacons
- Fleece vests and jackets
- Kids' and adult-sized snowshoes
- Lightweight and heavy-duty child carriers
- Lightweight shovels
- Petzl duo headlamp
- Ski pole/avalanche probe
- Skis
- Snowboards
- Towing sleds
- Watch altimeter/compass/barometer

**Search:** Yes
**Photos:** Yes
**Ordering:** Online, Phone, Fax
**Gift Wrap:** No
**Delivery:** Ground, 3rd Day, 2nd Day

## Camping World Online

http://www.campingworld.com

Calling all RV owners! This is your store. It has literally everything you'll need to keep your RV in tip-top shape, and other things that'll make your life on the road more enjoyable. This store has a HUGE inventory. No item is too little (porta-clothesline) or too big (generators). If you have a laptop computer on board while traveling, use this site to place your order and have it shipped to your next destination. If you think you might be shopping here often, you should think about joining their Buyers Club, which entitles you to a 10% discount on all orders, group rates on excursions, $100 off RV insurance (in many states) and occasional special sale notices. Yearly membership cost is $19.95. Samples:

- Air conditioners
- Awnings
- CB radios
- Cleaners
- Fans and vents
- Furnishings
- Mini vacuum cleaners
- Portable shower
- Refrigerators and freezers
- Satellite TVs
- Solar-battery chargers
- Surge suppressor
- Turbo-jet swivel-faucet aerator

**Search:** Yes
**Photos:** Yes
**Ordering:** Online, Phone, Fax, Email
**Gift Wrap:** No
**Delivery:** Ground, 2nd Day

## Camp Store

http://www.shopforcamp.com

If your kids are going to sleep-away camp this summer, or if you're going to be a camp counselor, you'll definitely want to bookmark this store. Every camp sends home a list of equipment and supplies that are mandatory for the camper to bring and a bunch of other items that are handy to have. Take those lists and shop at this store in one easy visit. You can type in exactly what you're looking for or use their directory for a list of vendors that sell that particular item. It's like a mini-camp mall. Camp owners will also find this store useful for its business directory of services, camp equipment suppliers, and food service vendors. If you think you'd like a job at camp (great for teachers and teenagers), click on their Job Opportunities button, where you can search their classifieds or post up your own résumé. Samples:

- Backpacks
- Clothing
- Cooking gear
- First-aid kits
- Lanterns and flashlights
- Sleeping bags
- Tents

**Search:** Yes
**Photos:** Yes
**Ordering:** Online
**Gift Wrap:** No
**Delivery:** Varies

## Denali

http://www.denali1.com

That's Denali with a number 1 after it, in the address. There's lots of stuff for the serious camper here, especially for those of you brave enough to camp where the temperature dips into the single digits. They have the largest selection of snowshoes of any online store. Our impression is that they offer only equipment that expert campers choose. This is the good stuff. Free shipping in the lower 48 on orders over $100. Samples:

- Custom ground covers
- Dog accessories
- Hydration systems
- Kid carriers
- Mapping tools
- Men's and women's backpacks
- Single- and double-wall tents
- Snowshoes
- Trekking poles
- White gas, auto gas, and kerosene stoves

**Search:** Some
**Photos:** Yes
**Ordering:** Online

**Gift Wrap:** No
**Delivery:** Ground

## Expedition Leader

http://www.expedition-leader.com

This Canadian manufacturer offers you direct savings (40% to 50% off retail). All of their products are hand-made, using excellent materials. We figured that their equipment would be terrific for an extra-cold camping spot, but what we were surprised by was the selection of goods perfect for camping in humid areas, too. They sell a fair variety of things, but you really should check out their high-tech camping mattresses. Samples:

- Canoe packs
- Cordura briefcases for portaging
- Down sleeping bags (good to -40°F)
- Fanny packs
- Rescue belts
- Seat bags and thwart bags
- Ultimate camping mattress (requires no inflation)

**Search:** Some
**Photos:** Yes
**Ordering:** Online, Phone, Fax
**Gift Wrap:** No
**Delivery:** Ground, 3rd Day

## Fogdog Sports

http://www.fogdog.com

This Web sporting goods store is huge; it has it all. If you can't find what you're looking for, contact the Fogdog Search Squad and they'll personally find it and buy it for you. Samples:

- Adult sport clothing and shoes
- Camping equipment
- Children's shoes
- Fitness equipment

**Search:** Yes
**Photos:** Yes
**Ordering:** Online, Phone
**Gift Wrap:** No
**Delivery:** Ground

## The Hiking Shack

`http://www.hikingshack.com`

Love to take hikes in the woods? Climb the face of a red-rock cliff? Good! But before you start out on your trek, browse through this store and make sure you have everything you need for a safe and enjoyable hike. Samples:

- All-terrain hiking boots
- Back-mounted hydration systems
- Backpacks
- Climbing gear
- First-aid kits
- Freeze-dried foods
- Lightweight camping stoves
- Rock shoes
- Sleeping bags
- Tents
- Water-purification filters

**Search:** Some
**Photos:** Yes
**Ordering:** Online
**Gift Wrap:** No
**Delivery:** Ground, 3rd Day

## JC Wunderlich and Co.

`http://www.jcwunderlich.com`

All of the many, many items for sale at this camping company have been personally tested by their camping-loving staff. It's fun browsing. Samples:

- Animal-warning device
- Biodegradable cleaners
- Clothing
- Compact tripods
- First-aid kits
- Fluorescent lantern
- Mink oil
- Packing accessories
- Percolators and espresso makers
- Pocket spotting scopes
- Sleeping bags
- Stainless-steel cook set
- Tents
- Tools

- Triangle chair
- Waterproof match box

**Search:** Yes
**Photos:** Yes
**Ordering:** Online, Phone
**Gift Wrap:** No
**Delivery:** Ground

## Kids' Camps

`http://kidscamps.com`

This is another great mall for summer campers, parents, and staff. You'll be able to order all of those little necessities (like iron-on name labels, laundry bags, and stationery) and big items (like tents, backpacks, and sleeping bags). This "mall" sends you to other stores that have just what you're looking for. What we really liked about this place is that it seems to have thought of everything. For instance, you can find a store that will send toiletries directly to your child at camp and another place that will actually personalize, with your child's name, many of the items needed at camp, such as their flashlight, sleeping bag, wash kits, duffel bags, and towels. They also provide an excellent summer camp directory divided into categories such as sport camps, special needs, day camps, and art camps. Samples:

- Clothes
- Flashlights
- Personalized items
- Sleeping bags
- Sporting equipment
- Tents

**Search:** Yes
**Photos:** Some
**Ordering:** Depends on the store
**Gift Wrap:** No
**Delivery:** Varies

## Loon Lake Outfitters

`http://www.loonlake.com`

Outdoor gear at low prices is the calling card of this store. They don't offer a wide variety of items. What they do offer, however, is an extensive collection of tents, backpacks and stoves. Samples:

- 4-season tents
- Backpacking tents
- Backpacks
- Breezeway screen houses
- Family tents (up to 12 people)
- Self-pressurized stoves
- White gas, kerosene, and alcohol stoves

**Search:** Some
**Photos:** Yes
**Ordering:** Online, Phone, Fax
**Gift Wrap:** No
**Delivery:** Ground

# Mountain Gear
`http://www.mgear.com`

Here's a camping store that gives you excellent prices on high-quality gear. The emphasis here is on climbing and snow sports. Free shipping on orders over $50. Samples:

- Backpacks
- Clothes for men and women
- Rock-climbing, mountaineering, and big-wall equipment
- Ski apparel
- Skis, poles, bindings, and boots
- Snowboards
- Snowshoes and boots

**Search:** Yes
**Photos:** Yes
**Ordering:** Online
**Gift Wrap:** No
**Delivery:** Ground, 3rd Day, 2nd Day, Overnight

# The Outdoor.com
`http://www.theoutdoor.com`

Backpacking, camping, even boating supplies are found at this Web store. The prices are good and the selection is ample. They also offer many outdoor-related links and guides to help you accomplish many tasks, such as how to waterproof your gear and how to make the best use of the space in your backpack.

Samples:

- Backpacks
- Bike, luggage, and ski car mounts
- Camping tools
- Climbing gear
- Gift certificates
- Life jackets for men and women
- Men's and women's clothing
- Sleeping bags
- Stove/cook sets
- Tents
- Water paddles

**Search:** Yes
**Photos:** Yes
**Ordering:** Online, Phone, Fax
**Gift Wrap:** Card
**Delivery:** Ground, 3rd Day, Overnight

# REI
`http://www.rei.com`

When our kids were tiny tots, their favorite activity was to go to our local REI store with us and "sample" all of the tents. Our kids have good taste. Now REI is also on the Web, so you can shop here anytime, no matter where you live. This is a terrific store, especially if you are looking for camping gear, but they have a fine selection of equipment for snow sports, cycling, and hiking, too. All of their products are first rate.

Samples:

- Child carriers
- Climbing gear
- External-frame packs
- Family camping bags
- Hydration packs
- Self-inflating pads
- Snow sports gear and clothes
- Survival gear
- Thermal underwear for kids and adults
- Winter/mountaineering tents

**Search:** Yes
**Photos:** Yes

**Ordering**: Online, Phone, Mail
**Gift Wrap**: No
**Delivery**: Ground, 3rd Day, Overnight

## Totally Outdoors

http://
www.totallyoutdoors.com

After finding so many camping stores that sold only clothes for men, it was a pleasure to find one devoted to the woman camper. There's lots of equipment designed for the female of the species, and clothing ranging in sizes from XS to XXL. Samples:

- Berber vests
- Bicycling clothes
- Expedition shirts
- Full-featured travel packs and fanny packs
- Outdoor instructional books
- Ski apparel
- Sleeping bags
- Supplex fitness shorts
- Waterproof/breathable socks
- Windstopper jackets

**Search**: Yes
**Photos**: Yes
**Ordering**: Online
**Gift Wrap**: No
**Delivery**: Ground, 3rd Day, Overnight

## For fun at your campsite, consider the chapter on:

- Sporting Goods

# Cars

This is what we know about buying cars: Several years ago, when our kids were very small, we went into a car dealer to buy a specific car. We had a certain amount to spend, period. We let the salesman show us this and that, and when it came time to bargain, we let our kids loose on the show-room floor. As they "drove" each car, the price kept going lower and lower. We finally got the price we wanted because the poor salesman was not about to lose a sale after putting up with the hassle. Nowadays, you can buy your car on the Web. There aren't a lot of virtual car dealers, but we did round up the best. What you will find on the Web is LOTS of information about buying a car. Before you start your journey to a new car, we suggest you think about your price range and what kind of car you really want. Being clear about those issues will make your search a lot easier. Many sites offer a calculator that lets you deter-mine how much your monthly payments will be, based on your down payment, if you decide to finance your car.

You should also know that car sites are a little different from other Web stores because instead of actually buying online, you have to fill out some information and then the site has a broker or dealer near your location email you with an invitation and, perhaps, a tempt-ing price.

Also, since you really aren't buying a car online, we won't go into all of the services available. We will, however, point to a few of the high-octane sites.

## Autobytel

http://www.autobytel.com

This place makes getting a quote easy and fast. You probably want to do your research before coming here. You let them know which type of vehicle you want, then Autobytel shows you, with photos, the cars (with their base prices) in your area. Then you go to a page that lists all of the car's accessories. If you like what you see, you let them know and a dealer calls you within 24 hours. If you're looking for a used car—oh, excuse us—a pre-owned car—you can find out about that, too. Samples:

- Articles and consumer reviews
- Loan vs. lease comparisons
- Online application for leases or car loans
- Online, no obligation, insurance quotes
- Used-car photos

**Search:** Yes
**Photos:** Yes
**Ordering:** Varies
**Delivery:** Varies

## AutoConnect

http://www.autoconnect.com

This is a good place to shop if you're in the market for a used vehicle, because that's all they "sell." Basically, you type in some general information about the kind of car you're looking for. The AutoConnect searches its 600,000-plus used-car listings for a match. A nice plus to the search answers is that they'll tell you how far away from you the place is where the used car is for sale. If there's more than one car available meeting your criteria, you can click on the Compare button for a side-by-side look. Samples:

- Free insurance quotes
- Loan calculators
- Reviews
- Side-by-side comparisons

**Search:** Yes
**Photos:** Some
**Ordering:** Via dealer
**Delivery:** Varies

# Autoweb.com

http://www.autoweb.com

Go to their new car "showroom" to get the facts about the car(s) you want to buy. You'll see a large photo, plus the MSRP price and the dealer invoice price. Want the gas mileage? You'll get that info, too. Once you know which car you want, you fill out a questionnaire. This questionnaire is the most complete we have seen. Besides the usual info, they also ask you about a trade-in, how much you want to put down on the car, how you intend to pay for it. This is a no-nonsense deal. They make it very clear that they will get you a good price, but are only interested in dealing with you if you are buying, not just kicking tires. Samples:

- Auto forums
- Car reviews
- Free insurance quotes from State Farm
- Kelley Blue Book info
- Loan calculator
- Recalls and service bulletins

**Search:** Yes
**Photos:** Yes
**Ordering:** Via dealer
**Delivery:** Varies

# Car Point

http://www.carpoint.msn.com

This store has Microsoft as its parent. It gives the Microsoft slogan, "Where do you want to go today?" new meaning. But this is a terrific site for helping you gather as much information about your planned purchase as possible and helping you locate a dealer who will give you the lowest price. In fact, if you want to spend the time, Car Point gives you the flexibility to create your own personal auto page. When looking for a new car, you first fill out a purchase inquiry form. Then a "sales consultant" contacts you within two days. If you like the price, Car Point sends you a lot of the paperwork so you can fill it out ahead of time, and don't have to spend a lot of time at the dealership. You'll be also be able to find a used car through this site. If you find the car of your dreams, you can have

your car financed online through People First Finance or get general financing information. Samples:

- Finance and insurance advice
- Kelley Blue Book quotes
- New car reviews
- Payment calculators
- Reliability ratings

**Search:** Yes
**Photos:** Some
**Ordering:** Via dealer
**Delivery:** Varies

# Cars.com

http://www.cars.com

One thing real car lovers will appreciate at this site is their "Auto News" section, right on the front page. On the day we shopped, we were intrigued by an article about a factory that was recycling plastic bumpers. We decided that this new kind of bumper will be stronger than the metal ones we have now, which seem designed to crumple at five miles per hour. The way you find a new car from this site is to type in what kind of car you want, and Cars.com gives you a list of affiliated dealers in your area. As best as we could tell from this site, you can get a quote from some of the dealers listed, but the dealers in New Mexico (our state) evidently do not participate. If they do, the fact was buried. But even if you don't discover some dealers near you at this site, you will get lots of information. We really like the section with reviews and model reports on all the new cars. There was another helpful section describing which options add value to your car. Samples:

- Advice
- Car talk
- Model reports

**Search:** Yes
**Photos:** Some
**Ordering:** Via dealer
**Delivery:** Varies

## DealerNet

`http://www.dealernet.com`

You can locate both new and used cars through this store. They offer two ways to "buy" a car from them. In one, you give them some information and they search for a dealer that meets your qualifications. The other way, you give them some information and they have one or more dealers call you within 24 hours with their best quotes. The only drawback to this site is that if you live in an area without any DealerNet affiliates, you're out in the cold. We live in a thriving New Mexico town, and DealerNet said there weren't any subscribing dealers in our area. Because they "sell" used cars, they have an excellent section helping you find the most accurate trade-in value for your present car. They also have a Free Lemon Check, where you can discover if the "previously owned" vehicle you want has seen more than its share of auto repair shops. Samples:

- Information about rebates
- Lemon checker for used cars
- Research resources for leasing and insurance
- Side-by-side model comparisons

**Search:** Yes
**Photos:** Yes
**Ordering:** Via dealer
**Delivery:** Varies

## What's your car worth?

Find out at the Kelley Blue Book site at http://www.kbb.com. Answer a few questions to discover the trade-in value of your current car.

# Chocolate

If you tend to get dreamy and romantic about chocolate; if you know just where the last piece of chocolate is in your house; or if you pinpoint chocolate stores as landmarks when you drive around town, you may want to expand your perspective by going online. You'll discover that stores all over the world have been busy dreaming up new ways of molding, filling, glazing, carving, softening, and shaping an amazing array of recipes based on the cocoa bean. Here are the top shops for bars, blocks, truffles, and molds, plus chocolate poured over just about anything you can eat.

## 3 Friends in Kona

http://www.aloha.net/~chee/ 3friends.html

Aloha! This shop has the friendly spirit of the shops near the beaches of the Big Island, Hawaii. Alongside the koa wood bowls, Kona coffee, and "dis 'n dat," we found luscious chocolate-covered macadamia nuts, and fresh candies that have gotten raves from *Chocolatier* and *Bon Appetit* magazines. Samples:

- Dark chocolate honu (turtles) of macadamia nuts and chocolate
- Golden Ginger Macadamia Nut Clusters with white chocolate
- Guava Rum Tropical Truffles
- Konaroca (toffee and macadamia nut candy with chocolate)
- Lilikoi Coconut Tropical Truffles (passion fruit and chocolate)
- Mauna Kea snowballs (white chocolate and coconut, for folks who can't have chocolate or nuts, but love them both)
- Chocolate gift baskets

**Search:** No

**Photos:** Some
**Ordering:** Online, Phone, Fax, Email
**Gift Wrap:** Yes
**Delivery:** Ground

## Ann Hemyng Candy's Chocolate Factory

http://www.mmink.com/mmink/ dossiers/choco.html

In the Pennsylvania hill country, where farmhouses are still made out of fieldstone, this company crafts a wide range of chocolates, putting them together into towers, tins, and gift baskets. In hot weather they ship with gel ice packs. Samples:

- 2.5 pounds of chocolates in a velvet heart
- Chocolate fish in a tin
- Chocolate rosebuds
- Chocolate tool set
- Chocolate-dipped Pennsylvania Dutch bow pretzels
- Copper mold with Bucks County Classic Assorted Chocolates
- Fresh fruit dipped in chocolate (in season)
- Solid chocolate computer and mouse
- Solid flat bar of chocolate with line drawing based on your photo or art
- Wedding favors

**Search:** No
**Photos:** No
**Ordering:** Online, Phone, Fax, Email
**Gift Wrap:** Yes
**Delivery:** Ground, 3rd Day, 2nd Day, Overnight

## Belgian Chocolate Online

http://chocolat.com

(Note that the address does not contain the usual three w's.) The pictures make these chocolates look like Belgian sushi. You see the candy whole, then cut in half. No preservatives or chemical flavorings, just original recipes from Belgium, cooked up in Philadelphia. Samples:

- Apricot truffle
- Cappuccino truffle
- Chantilly
- European brands of chocolate, such as Callebaut, Droste, Lindt, Perugina, and Toblerone
- Florentino bar
- Kirsch squares
- Zebra bar

**Search:** Yes
**Photos:** Gorgeous
**Ordering:** Online, Phone, Fax, Email
**Gift Wrap:** Gold ballotin (box) with your message
**Delivery:** Ground, 2nd Day

## Belgian Chocolate Shop

http://www.giftex.com/belgian

Part of a giant gift site, this shop makes up orders daily, using Belgian chocolate to stock tins, theme boxes, and cups with different assortments, shapes, and variations. Based in Canada, they ship around the world. We particularly liked the combination of Winnie the Pooh, a heart made out of porcelain, and a chocolate heart inside. Samples:

- Chocolate cigars
- Chocolate teddy bears
- Miniature chocolate elephants, cats, rabbits, ducks, or bears in bulk
- Sugarless chocolates
- White chocolate golf balls
- White chocolate snowman with dark chocolate hat
- Winnie the Pooh porcelain heart with chocolate heart inside

**Search:** No
**Photos:** Plentiful
**Ordering:** Online, Phone, Email
**Gift Wrap:** But of course. Also, cards.
**Delivery:** Ground, 2nd Day, Overnight

## Brigittine Monks Gourmet Confections

http://greatbend.com/brentw/fudge.htm

Based in the Willamette Valley of Oregon, the Brigittine monks have been making five divine fudge flavors and ten kinds of heavenly truffles for sale through this site. Mixed in silence and contemplation, these chocolates feature fresh butter, cream, and nuts, all with no preservatives, and recipes no one can talk about. Samples:

- Monks Fudge Amaretto
- Monks Fudge Royal with or without nuts
- Monks Truffles

**Search:** No
**Photos:** A few
**Ordering:** Online, Phone, Email
**Gift Wrap:** Boxes
**Delivery:** Ground

## Casa de Fruta

http://www.casadefruta.com

Starting as a roadside fruit stand in the lush farming valley of central California, Casa de Fruta has put together tins, boxes, and wood gift-crates of chocolate-dipped fruits, beans, and nuts for online sale. All that's missing is the wonderful mix of smells inside the store. Order in English or Spanish. They ship within 48 hours of your order. Samples:

- Cappuccino almonds
- Chocolate Bing cherries in a tin
- Chocolate blueberries
- Chocolate macadamia nuts
- Chocolate-dipped apricots
- Truffle cherries
- Tuxedo coffee beans

**Search:** No
**Photos:** Yes
**Ordering:** Online, Phone, Email
**Gift Wrap:** Boxes, crates, tins
**Delivery:** Ground

## Chin Chin

http://www.chinchin.com

An online Chinese restaurant whose dim sum and shredded chicken salad will get your chopsticks clicking, they also offer giant fortune cookies coated in chocolate, weighing in at 12–14 ounces; each is about 5 inches high. You can add your own special message. Samples:

- Dark chocolate-dipped Giant Fortune Cookie
- Half-and-half (double-dipped) Giant Fortune Cookie
- White chocolate Giant Fortune Cookie

**Search:** No
**Photos:** Yes
**Ordering:** Online, Phone, Email
**Gift Wrap:** Yes
**Delivery:** Ground, 2nd Day, Overnight

## Chocoholic

http://www.chocoholic.com

A very high-tech site jammed with lore, trivia, games, and recipes, a chocolate-of-the-month club, and a reminder service. (Have you had your chocolate today? Isn't it time to send yourself a birthday surprise?) You can shop by looking through dozens of products, or search by type of chocolate. Orders go out the next day, with 2nd Day or Overnight delivery in warm areas, 3rd Day delivery for colder climes. Samples:

- Five-pound chocolate bar from Ghiradelli
- Blue Moon chocolates
- Boehm's chocolates
- Chocolate basket from Ghiradelli
- Lindt chocolate bars
- Lou Retta's custom chocolates
- Marich Confections
- Peppermint chocolate cookie from Grand Avenue
- Toblerone bars

**Search:** Yes
**Photos:** Plentiful
**Ordering:** Online, Phone, Fax
**Gift Wrap:** Various
**Delivery:** 3rd Day, 2nd Day, Overnight

## Chocolate Arts

http://www2.cybernext.net/
~mhourin

You name it, they can probably make it using a mold or creating something from scratch. Great for personalized gifts for baby showers or weddings. They ship within two weeks of your orders, but favors take six weeks. They use a cold pack in hot weathers or for warm climates. Samples:

- Chocolate bottles
- Chocolate flower pots with roses, daisies, or tulips
- Chocolate pretzels (milk, dark, white, or with jimmies)
- Chocolate swans
- Golf tools made out of chocolate

**Search:** No
**Photos:** Yes
**Ordering:** Online, Phone, Fax, Email
**Gift Wrap:** Card enclosed
**Delivery:** Overnight

## Chocolates, Etc.

http://www.leisurelan.com/
connections/shops/chocetc

The U.S. source for Natalie's Belgian Chocolates, imported direct from Europe, as well as boxes of chocolate creams, nougats, chewies, and caramels. Samples:

- Assorted creams
- Natalie's Belgian Chocolates (the entire line)
- Nuts and chews

**Search:** No
**Photos:** Yes
**Ordering:** Online, Phone
**Gift Wrap:** Fancy boxes
**Delivery:** Ground

## Chocolate Rampage

http://www.fishnet.net/
~chocolate/

It's a jungle out there in San Buenaventura, California, where four different critters have left behind chocolate paw prints:

- Dinosaur Pawws
- Panther Pawws
- Polar Bear Pawws
- Tiger Pawws

**Search:** No
**Photos:** Yes
**Ordering:** Online, Phone, Fax, Email
**Gift Wrap:** No
**Delivery:** Ground

## Daskalides Chocolatier

http://www.daskalides.com

Started in 1931 in Ghent, Belgium, this family pastry and confection shop soon opened a series of tea rooms and chocolate shops, and has focused on making pralines, and molded and coated chocolates for the foreign market. They recently won the French Laurier d'Or de la Qualité. They pack chocolates in polyfoam, and ship on Monday, Tuesday, or Wednesday by air for 2$^{nd}$ Day or Overnight delivery; they charge extra to send out a shipment on Friday or Saturday. (We guess they take Thursday off.) Samples:

- Amandines (roasted almonds covered with chocolate)
- Cerisettes (each with a Kirsch-soaked cherry inside)
- Fines (Cognac-flavored butter creams)
- Noix Crème Beurres (Hazelnut creams)
- Pistachio-filled Chocolate Tulip (orange creams)
- Venus (Pistachio cream)

**Search:** No
**Photos:** Gorgeous close-ups
**Ordering:** Online, Phone, Email
**Gift Wrap:** Yes
**Delivery:** 2$^{nd}$ Day, Overnight

## Godiva Chocolatier

http://www.godiva.com

Their gold-plated stores on Fifth Avenue, in New York, and other upper-crust shopping spots are always jammed with people edging up to check out a sample. A full catalog appears online, so no matter what obscure combination you have become addicted to, you can find it here. (For instance, they have five single-spaced pages of Kosher chocolates alone.) They ship within 24 hours to continental U.S. only. Samples:

- Coconut Truffles
- Golf Ball Set
- Hazelnut Praline Truffles
- Key Lime Truffles
- Kosher Grande Mints
- Mandarin Orange Truffles
- Mint Twigs
- Pecan Caramel Truffles
- Raspberry Truffles

**Search:** No
**Photos:** Yes
**Ordering:** Online, Phone, Fax, Email
**Gift Wrap:** Gold boxes
**Delivery:** Ground, Overnight

## Mendocino Chocolate

http://www.mendocino-
chocolate.com

Among the woods and grassy slopes running down to the Pacific from Northern California into Oregon, this company's stores offer chocolates that seem to have been inspired by the sea air. They ship by UPS Ground for free; but if you are in a warm climate, or suffering really hot weather, they recommend a cold pack shipped 2$^{nd}$ Day. Samples:

- Aunt Phyllis' Gift Box
- Chocolate-covered coffee beans (Kona or Espresso)
- Convent Fudge
- Edible Sea Shells
- Irish Beach Cream Fudge Sauce

- Mendocino Breakers (caramel rolled in almonds, with dark and white chocolate covering)

**Search:** No
**Photos:** Yes
**Ordering:** Online
**Gift Wrap:** Card
**Delivery:** Ground, 3rd Day, 2nd Day

## La Patisserie

http://www.patisserie.com

A French pastry shop with chocolate cookies and Belgian-style truffles sold individually or in gift baskets. Samples:

- Chocolate Walnut Chunk Cookies
- Double-Chocolate Truffles
- Hazelnut Truffles
- Miniature Eclairs
- Miniature Chocolate-Butter-Cream Cake
- Raspberry Mousse Tart
- White Chocolate Almond-Chunk Cookies

**Search:** No
**Photos:** Yes, lots
**Ordering:** Online, Phone, Email
**Gift Wrap:** Boxes and baskets, with cards
**Delivery:** Ground

## Sarris Candies

http://www.nb.net/~bsarris/
index.html

Celebrate a sweet arrival with pure milk chocolate or white chocolate, accented in pink or blue, for baby showers and birth announcements. The store also has a great assortment for Mother's Day. This place has the most unique chocolate gifts around.

- Baby Booties Chocolates
- Baby Carriage Chocolates
- Baby Chocolate
- Chocolate long-stemmed roses
- Chocolate Wedding Favors
- Diaper Pins Chocolates
- Rattle Chocolates

**Search:** No
**Photos:** Yes
**Ordering:** Online, Phone, Email
**Gift Wrap:** Yes, with card
**Delivery:** Ground, 2nd Day, Overnight

## Teuscher Chocolate

http://www.2nite.com

From a retail store on one of Boston's classiest shopping streets, this company has won awards for the best chocolate in Boston, with products such as:

- Assorted Truffles
- Champagne Truffles
- Pralines, Marzipan, and Truffles Assortment

**Search:** No
**Photos:** Some
**Ordering:** Online, Phone, Fax
**Gift Wrap:** Yes
**Delivery:** Ground

## West Point Market

http://www.westpoint-
market.com

No, not that West Point. This shop is in Akron, Ohio, and features a Chocolate Shop, headed by Andrea Garcea, whose favorites are "Godiva, Joseph Schmidt, and Leonidas chocolates." They carry the Austrian Mozart chocolates, wrapped in a gold picture of the composer, but they also give you the do-it-yourself recipe for coating rose leaves with chocolate. Samples:

- Chocolate-Dipped Marzipan Strawberries
- Godiva Boxed Truffles
- Joseph Schmidt Mini Truffles
- Leonidas Belgian Chocolates
- Moonstruck Chocolate Cone Truffles
- Mozart Chocolates

**Search:** No
**Photos:** Yes
**Ordering:** Online, Phone, Email
**Gift Wrap:** Yes
**Delivery:** Ground

# Cigars

Tasting a truly fine, premium cigar is getting harder and harder to do. Neighborhood smoke shops are closing right and left. But there is a continuing and easy source for cigars and cigar accessories: your friendly neighborhood Web store. Many of these virtual smoke shops take great care in the manufacture and delivery of their cigars, because they know the pleasure you take in smoking one. And if you thought an exquisite Havana was out of reach, stretch out that arm and grab a lighter, because we've found some stores on the Web that'll sell them to you.

## Cigar International

http://www.cigarintl.com

Despite the name, the tobacco for these cigars is grown mostly in one area: Costa Rica, the Dominican Republic, Honduras, and Nicaragua. Once the tobacco is properly aged, the cigars are hand rolled. You'll find that each cigar is described in great detail, including what type of wrapper, binder, and filler is used. Cigars are sold by the box. A box of 25 will run you about $125. Samples:

- Cruzado
- La Hoja Rica
- Leyenda
- Soleares

**Search:** Some
**Photos:** Yes
**Ordering:** Online, Phone, Fax, Mail
**Gift Wrap:** No
**Delivery:** Ground

## Connoisseurs Cigar Company

http://www.ccigar.com/order-ing/index.html

Premium personalized cigars, good for a special occasion, for fun or for your business. Use one of their many preprinted labels to wrap the cigars you order, or create your own. Rush orders OK. Sample labels for:

- Alumni reunions
- Anniversaries
- Bachelor parties
- Birthdays
- Fraternity parties
- Holidays
- Weddings

**Search:** Some
**Photos:** Yes
**Ordering:** Online, Phone, Fax
**Gift Wrap:** Yes
**Delivery:** Ground (rush orders available)

## GourmetMarket.com

http://www.gourmetmarket.com

Besides carrying epicurean morsels from around the world, this store also stocks a huge supply of imported cigars by brand names, such as La Gloria Cubana, Olivero, Dunhill, Fonseca, and Hoyo de Monterrey, plus a good variety of accessories. Samples:

- Antique laser lighter
- Cubano Sterling cutter
- Double-bladed cigar cutter
- Humidors with locks
- Portable cigar cases

**Search:** Yes
**Photos:** Some
**Ordering:** Online, Phone, Fax
**Gift Wrap:** No
**Delivery:** 3rd Day

## Limbo Bros. Cigar Club

http://www.cigar98.com

Join the club (memberships cost either $20 per month for four cigars or $37 per month for eight) and each month you'll receive a collection of hand-selected, premium cigars sent fresh from a humidor straight to your home or office. Gift memberships are also available. Samples:

- Cigar connoisseur deluxe box
- Discounts on some cigar accessories

- Hand-rolled cigars from the Dominican Republic, Honduras, Philippines, and Jamaica
- Sampler gift box

**Search:** No
**Photos:** Some
**Ordering:** Online, Phone, Fax
**Gift Wrap:** Card
**Delivery:** First Class Mail

## Madazz Enterprises, Ltd.

http://madazz.co.nz

This New Zealand store specializes in selling the Majestic humidors. But they also sell a large supply of Cuban cigars. Last time we checked, they said they were gearing up for online auctions of boxed Cuban cigars. They list the prices in New Zealand and U.S. dollars. Boxes start at $60 and go up to about $400. Shipping to the U.S. is about $35 per box. Samples:

- Bolivars
- Cohibas
- Diplomaticos #2
- Distilled water for your humidity regulator
- Humidors that can store up to 200 cigars
- Regenerating solution for your humidor
- Trinidads
- Upmanns

**Search:** Yes
**Photos:** Yes
**Ordering:** Online, Phone, Fax
**Gift Wrap:** Yes
**Delivery:** 3rd Day

## Northend Cigars

http://www.necigars.com

Over 125 different cigars are available here. But this is more than just a cigar store. It also sells all those nice things that make smoking a first-class cigar so worthwhile. You'll find most of your favorites at this store, so we'll list the other sample accessories. Free shipping on orders over $200. Samples:

- Cigar favors

- Double-bladed cigar cutter
- Humidor regulator
- Laser micro-torch lighters
- Solid wood (oak, mahogany, cherry) humidors
- Travel humidors

**Search:** Yes
**Photos:** Yes
**Ordering:** Online
**Gift Wrap:** No
**Delivery:** Ground, 2nd Day, Overnight

## Ricardo's Cigar Shop

http://ricardoscigar.com

Flavored cigars make this shop unique. Most of them are grown from Cuban seed and are hand rolled. Variety is not a problem, either. There are over 60 brands and 40 flavors available. You'll also be able to purchase "dipped" cigars, which are about the size of cigarettes. Light up for an aromatic smoke. There's no minimum order required. Samples:

- Al Capone Sweets Cognac
- Don Albero Classico Espresso
- El Incomparable Malt Whiskey
- Hula Girl Kona Coffee
- Lucky Lady Cherry and Vanilla
- Rum Raider
- West Indies Vanilla

**Search:** Yes
**Photos:** Some
**Ordering:** Online, Phone, Fax
**Gift Wrap:** No
**Delivery:** Ground

## Smokey's Cigar Shop

http://www.smokeyscigars.com

Here's a quaint mom-and-pop store from Ardsley, New York, that took their reduced-priced cigars and put them on the Web. They offer a lot: over 600 cigars, most of them substantially discounted. How do they do it? They buy cigar "seconds"; these are cigars that were slightly damaged in some very small way or not rolled entirely correctly. Samples:

- Astral
- Butera Royal Vintage
- Crown Achievement
- Cubita
- La Gloria Cubana
- Macanudo
- Sampler packs
- Te-Amo

**Search:** Some
**Photos:** Some
**Ordering:** Online, Phone
**Gift Wrap:** No
**Delivery:** Ground

## Smoking Place

http://w3.sistelcom.com/smoking-place

Cigars from all over the place, including Cuba, are offered from this Spanish store. The cigars are sold by the box. They must have a good-size American clientele, because they also list the prices in U.S. dollars, as well as Spanish pesetas. Delivery costs run about $20 per box. But that's nothing compared to the price of a box of Cohiba Lanceros, which goes for a whopping $800. Samples:

- Canarios
- Cohiba
- Dunhill
- Fonseca
- Habana Gold
- Monte Cristo
- Sancho Panza

**Search:** Some
**Photos:** No
**Ordering:** Online
**Gift Wrap:** No
**Delivery:** Private courier

## Stoie's Stogies

http://www.astogie4u.com

Aged cigars are at a premium at this store. Two-, three-, four-, and even five-year-old vintage collections are available. (The cigars are rolled by Cuban masters and aged in Spanish cedar chests.) If that's a little too aged for your taste, try the premium and flavored varieties (yes, that's right . . . *flavored* cigars!). Depending on the cigar, you buy by the box or by the cigar. Some cigar accessories are also for sale. Samples:

- Black alligator cigar cases
- Compass torch
- Custom-pack assortments
- Guillotine self-sharpening double-blade cutter
- John Waynes (aged four years)
- Mini torch lighters
- Rum-, vanilla-, and chocolate-flavored cigars
- Storm-proof lighters
- Torpedo (aged five years)

**Search:** Some
**Photos:** Yes
**Ordering:** Online
**Gift Wrap:** Yes
**Delivery:** Ground

## TNT Cigars

http://tntcigars.com

The name of this place invokes a Marx Brothers movie. (OK, so now we're in real trouble.) Actually, you won't find exploding cigars here, just ones with dynamite taste. While many of the stores listed in this chapter will sell only by the box, TNT makes their cigars available in small quantities, even in singles, if you like. Samples:

- Bauza Casa Grande
- Churchill mix box special
- Classic Robusto six-pack special
- Hoyo de Monterrey Excalibur
- La Gloria Cubana Pyramide
- Palio cigar cutter
- Partagas No. 1
- Volcano Magma Series Torch

**Search:** Some
**Photos:** Yes
**Ordering:** Online
**Gift Wrap:** Card
**Delivery:** Ground

## Tomtom Cigars

http://www.tomtom.co.uk/

If you live in the U.S. or Canada, you might be wondering why anyone would want to order cigars from a London, England, establishment. Simple...they sell Cuban cigars. You know, the ones that are like gold to devoted cigar smokers. TomTom also carries other brands, but the Cubans are definitely the big-ticket item. For some reason, they make Americans actually phone in their orders of Cubans (they can order all of the rest online). All of the prices are listed in Pound Sterling (We guess they haven't heard of the Euro yet!). Samples:

- Cohiba
- Cuaba
- El Rey de Mundo
- H Upmann
- Havanas
- Ramon Allones
- Romeo y Julietta

**Search:** Some
**Photos:** Yes
**Ordering:** Online, Phone
**Gift Wrap:** No
**Delivery:** Royal Mail, Courier

## Track Town Smoke Shop

http://
www.tracktownsmokeshop.com

With over 100 brands of premium cigars, you're sure to find one you like from this New Jersey store. They even carry a house brand, named Public Enemy. But cigars aren't the only fine product sold; you'll also find a lot of accessories to make that first puff a luxurious one. Free shipping is available on most orders. You can also save money by joining their Frequent Smoker Program. Samples:

- Cigar "catering" service
- Davidoff White Label
- Don Diego
- Hand-carved wooden Indian statue
- La Tradition
- Monte Cristo

- Playboy

**Search:** Some
**Photos:** Some
**Ordering:** Online, Phone, Fax
**Gift Wrap:** No
**Delivery:** Ground

## Uptown Cigar Company

http://www.uptowncigar.com

Wow! A cigar store owned by a woman—cool! Michelle Tuchman prides herself on having "the largest, finest, and most meticulously kept walk-in humidor in the Hudson Valley of New York." This is a real family operation, with Michelle's kids also helping out. You'll find some favorites, some hard-to-find cigars, as well some neat accessories. Samples:

- Cigar ashtray that fits in the beverage holder in your car
- La Veija
- Padron Aniversarios
- Perolo crystal ashtrays
- Pocket ashtray
- Prometheus lighters
- Red Dot Dominican Cohiba

**Search:** Some
**Photos:** Yes
**Ordering:** Online, Phone, Fax, Email
**Gift Wrap:** No
**Delivery:** Ground

## Wholy Smokes

http://www.wholysmokes.com

Great name for a cigar store. Started by a lover of the tobacco leaf for some extra money, this online venture has blossomed into a full-fledged store, thanks to customers who want to smoke an occasional hard-to-find stogie. Prices go all over the place. Samples:

- Bahia
- Don Tomas
- El Rey del Mundo
- Fuego Cubano

- Gilverto Olivero
- La Tradicion

**Search:** No
**Photos:** No
**Ordering:** Online, Phone, Fax
**Gift Wrap:** No
**Delivery:** 2nd Day, Overnight

## Wide West Imports

http://www.big-mountain.com/widewestimports

This Durango-based store specializes in the exquisite taste of Gallardo cigars, which are hand rolled monthly in small quantities and then shipped out the day they are made at Wide West, where they are stored in a walk-in humidor. A bit of the sale of each of the Gallardos goes to the aid of a tree farm in Honduras that is organically preserving mahogany, Spanish cedar, and teak trees. Boxes run about $55–$100. Samples:
- Aged wrappers from Ecuador
- Gallardo and Agua D'T Sampler Pack
- Long-leaf filler and binders from Danli Region

**Search:** No
**Photos:** Yes
**Ordering:** Online, Phone, Fax
**Gift Wrap:** No
**Delivery:** Ground

## World Class Cigars

http://www.wccigars.com

This place bills itself as the world's largest cigar store on the Internet. We don't know if that's true, but we do know that they sell lots of cigars and provide the consumer with lots of information and advice. Don't know which cigar to order? You can email them your question and one of their cigar experts will promptly answer. Special prices are available for commercial clients. They deliver worldwide. A box of 25 will cost anywhere from $85 to $220. Samples:
- 898 collection
- Al Capone

- Don Lino
- El Paraiso
- Felipe Gregorio
- Havana Sunrise
- Macanudo
- Papayo
- Tatou
- Zino

**Search:** Some
**Photos:** No
**Ordering:** Online, Phone
**Gift Wrap:** No
**Delivery:** Ground

## Cigars in History!

Did you know that Columbus was the first European to smoke a cigar? When he landed in Cuba in 1492 the natives handed him a "cohiba," the ancestor of the finest cigars in the world.

## Watch Out!

Don't store that first-class cigar in the refrigerator: you'll be sure to dry it out. If you don't have a humidor, the next best place is . . . Tupperware—really! Especially if you also put a damp paper towel in the container.

## To go with that cigar . . . see

- Chocolate
- Coffee & Tea
- Food—Gourmet
- Wine

# Clothes—All

Here's our own virtual clothing mall. You'll find clothing and accessories for men and women. We've given you a good sampling of stores, from the expensive to the discount stores, and also thrown in a few specialty shops. What these stores all have in common is that they offer clothing for both men and women. Some even have clothes for kids. If you'd like more-focused stores, read the chapters Clothes—Men, and Clothes—Women. And don't forget the entries on Extended Sizes for Men and for Women, where you'll find a great assortment of clothes for the petite and large figures.

## America Offprice

http://www.amoffprice.com

Discount clothes from American designers are found on the racks of this new Web store. Every item is discounted 25% to 75% off of manufacturers' suggested retail prices. America Offprice wants to make sure you get the very lowest price, so they've made a guarantee that if you find the same thing at a lower price on another Web store, America Offprice will beat that price by 10%. Don't forget to take a peek at the Weekly Specials. Sample designers and brands:

- Brooks Brothers
- DKNY
- Lacoste
- Nautica
- Ralph Lauren
- The Gap
- Tommy Hilfiger

**Search:** Yes
**Photos:** Yes
**Ordering:** Online
**Gift Wrap:** No
**Delivery:** Ground, Airmail

## Birkenstocks

http://www.birkenstockexpress.com

In 1908, Konrad Birkenstock created the first flexible arch support. Today, Birkenstocks are known for their unusual shape (very wide toe space) and their comfortable fit. They used to come in only a few funky styles, but now they've expanded with a big assortment of shoes. Birkenstocks come in many colors and a wide range of sizes and widths, allowing almost anyone to order them. There are some styles available for children. Samples:

- Betulas
- Birki clogs
- Birki Kids
- Birki sport sandals
- Classic
- Leather free
- Professional styles

**Search:** Yes
**Photos:** Yes
**Ordering:** Online, Phone
**Gift Wrap:** No
**Delivery:** Ground, 3rd Day, Overnight

## Bloomingdale's

http://www.bloomingdales.com

Bloomie's has become so famous as the chic department store that it's hard to believe that it has concrete-and-carpet stores in only eight states. If you don't live in one of those states, or you want to grab something quick without schlepping to an actual store, @ Your Service, their Web store, is the place for you. We did find it a bit annoying, though, that we had to create a "B profile" before we could actually go shopping, although once we answered all of the many questions, a personal dressing room was created based on our preferences. Samples:

- Anne Klein gabardine skirt
- Calvin Klein underwear
- Dana Buchman printed velvet T-shirts
- DKNY long-sleeved beaded cardigan

- Millennium shop
- Ralph Lauren robes

**Search:** Yes
**Photos:** Yes
**Ordering:** Online, Fax
**Gift Wrap:** Yes
**Delivery:** Ground

## CashmereClub.com

http://
www.millioncashmere.com

Just as this store's name implies, cashmere garments for men and women are what's on hand. Beautiful 100% Scottish cashmere apparel at very reasonable prices. But if you want to save even more, make sure you check back from time to time and see what the latest cashmere special is. You can also find some items in their new 100% pure lightweight cashmere fabric. They also offer custom orders from men for sizes 58 to 70. Samples:

- Blankets and throws
- Cashmere cape
- Classic 2-ply cardigan
- Round-neck pullover
- Short-sleeve jewel-neck pullover
- Socks, scarves, gloves, and shawls

**Search:** Yes
**Photos:** Yes
**Ordering:** Online, Phone, Fax
**Gift Wrap:** No
**Delivery:** Priority

## Denim Blues

http://21stcenturyplaza.com/
blues/jeans.html

Levi's, Levi's, and more Levi's. All shapes (from a 28 to 40 length), all sizes (from a 28 to a 40 waist). The prices are about the same as you'd pay in a brick-and-mortar store. Samples:

- Classic 501 Blues
- Colored jeans

- Zip-fly jeans

**Search:** Yes
**Photos:** Yes
**Ordering:** Online
**Gift Wrap:** No
**Delivery:** Ground

## Designer Deals

http://www.designerdeals.com

This store buys big quantities of designer labels of men's, women's, and children's clothing and then sells them to you at a discount. Some of the brands they sell are Brooks Brothers, Calvin Klein, Elizabeth, Gold's Gym, Perry Ellis, Izod, and Reebok. Their inventory changes frequently, so you'll probably want to stop by every so often. Samples:

- Cargo pants
- Ministriped gauze top and drawstring bottom
- Nature vest
- Short sets

**Search:** Yes
**Photos:** Yes
**Ordering:** Online
**Gift Wrap:** No
**Delivery:** Ground, 2nd Day, Overnight

## Eddie Bauer

http://www.eddiebauer.com/
home/home.html

Yes, there really was an Eddie Bauer, and he started his store, Eddie Bauer's Sport Shop, in downtown Seattle 79 years ago. Eddie developed the first-ever goose-down-insulated garment, known as the Skyliner jacket, in 1936. These jackets were used by aviators in the U.S. Army Air Corps, during World War II (a version of these jackets is still available for sale from this store). Today, there are over 500 stores worldwide. The clothes and accessories for men and women are classic, well-made casuals. Go to their virtual dressing room, where you can mix and match different items together to see how they look. Samples:

- Argyle cardigans
- Cotton-canvas jackets
- Microfiber jackets
- Pleated-front relaxed-fit khakis
- Scarves, jewelry, and belts
- Silk-shirt dresses
- Suede sneakers

**Search:** Yes
**Photos:** Yes
**Ordering:** Online, Phone, Fax
**Gift Wrap:** Yes
**Delivery:** Ground, 2nd Day, Overnight

## Fashion Mall

http://www.fashionmall.com

Just like the name says, this is a mall, on the Web. Clothes for kids, teens, men, women, and brides, as well as lots of accessories, are sold here. You'll find fashions by well-known designers sprinkled throughout the mall. There's also an "outlet" store where you can sometimes find good values. As with any virtual mall, you get a large selection, but you must make many clicks to make a purchase. Sample stores:

- Aldo Shoes
- Fortunoff
- French Toast
- Georgio Armani
- Gucci
- Mondani
- Sunglasses International

**Search:** Yes
**Photos:** Yes
**Ordering:** Online (some by Phone and Fax)
**Gift Wrap:** Depends on the store
**Delivery:** Depends on the store

## The Gap

http://gap.com/onlinestore/gap

Baby boomers flocked to this store when it first opened up because of the huge selection of jeans (the uniform of the day). Through the years, they slowly added higher-quality and higher-priced casual clothes to their store. Today, the store is shopped mainly by teens who have Mom's credit card. The nostalgia for this store is so great, though, that they have wisely added a BabyGap and GapKids as part of the Gap empire. Samples:

- Denim shirts, jackets, and pants
- Gift certificates available
- Knit drawstring pants
- Jackets
- Men's zip-front suede jacket
- Oxford-cloth pajama sets
- Slim, classic, and loose-fit khakis
- Women's suede wrap skirt

**Search:** Yes
**Photos:** Yes
**Ordering:** Online
**Gift Wrap:** Yes
**Delivery:** Ground, Overnight

## Honeycomb Mittens

http://www.altnews.com.au/mittens

Are you sick of the phrase "warm hands, cold heart"? We know about cold hands, which is why this store was such a find. Originally designed for astronauts driving NASA's space vehicles (translation: space is cold), these gloves are perfect for really cold weather, like when you are skiing down the slopes, because they do not trap moisture and, even when damp, they retain warmth. The gloves are curved to fit your hands. Basically, you'll enjoy the warmth of mittens with the dexterity of gloves due to a free index finger hybrid design. These gloves cost $140. Main products:

- Honeycomb mittens for men
- Honeycomb mittens for women

**Search:** None needed
**Photos:** Yes
**Ordering:** Online, Phone
**Gift Wrap:** No
**Delivery:** Ground

## J. Crew

`http://www.jcrew.com/cgi-bin/index.cgi`

Go-anywhere, well-made casual clothes are the hallmark of J. Crew. You know if you're the type who likes to shop here, because you're sporty, probably like to go camping, and play a good game of backyard baseball. None of the clothes you buy here will go out of style. Click on their Fun Stuff spot for some neat screensavers. You should also check the Clearance and Weekly Sale areas for good discounts. Samples:

- Cashmere V-neck sweater
- Espadrilles
- Golf windshirt
- Lightweight barn jacket
- Pigment-dyed T-shirts
- Stretch and cotton voile dresses
- Swimwear

**Search:** Yes
**Photos:** Yes
**Ordering:** Online
**Gift Wrap:** Yes
**Delivery:** Ground, 3rd Day, Overnight

## Kerrits

`http://www.kerrits.com`

If you want to look superb while chasing the hounds, or just taking a ride around the back 40, you'll love the equestrian collection of clothes sold here for men, women, and kids. Samples:

- Baby-fleece printed vests
- Baby tights
- Duo-fleece zip turtlenecks and pants
- Kids Duo-fleece shirts and pants
- Kids sculptured horse hats and headbands
- Classic fleece vest
- Milano Lycra pants
- Outback hat
- Reversible Microfibre coats
- Water-resistant pants

**Search:** Yes
**Photos:** Yes

**Ordering:** Online, Phone, Fax
**Gift Wrap:** No
**Delivery:** Ground

## Lands' End

`http://www.landsend.com`

This place started as a catalog-only clothing store for men and women. Over the years, they've branched out to include clothing for kids, and added luggage, towels, sheets, and many accessories. They've built a base of tremendous customer loyalty by being big on service and quality and keeping their prices as low as possible. Their online store is consistently winning awards as one of the easiest stores for shopping on the Web. We've shopped here for years and can attest to the quality of their clothes. And if you want to return something, no problem: Lands' End makes that easy, too. Don't forget to check their Overstocks section for terrific bargains on discontinued stock. Sample apparel:

- Chino-twill skort
- Newborn and kids' clothing
- Ottoman slim skirt
- Peruvian pima-cotton Interlochen polo shirts
- Pinpoint cotton Oxford-cloth shirts
- Polartec shirts, jackets, hats and coats
- Thermal-knit 100% cotton Henley shirts
- Waterproof boots

**Search:** Yes
**Photos:** Yes
**Ordering:** Online, Phone, Fax
**Gift Wrap:** Yes
**Delivery:** Ground, 2nd Day

## Macy's

`http://www.macys.com`

One of the original, huge New York department stores, Macy's has made the transition into the 21st century by offering a slew of products online at fairly reasonable prices. You'll find clothes for every member of your family here, with lots of categories (you can even search by designer name if there is a brand that you're partial to), which makes your searching a little less time-consuming. Samples:

- Calvin Klein dress shirts
- Clothes for infants, kids, and teens
- Fleece crewneck pullovers
- INC gray one-button jacket
- Large and petite sizes
- Liz Claiborne seasonless crepe jacket
- Sleepwear and robes
- Twill cargo pants

**Search:** Yes
**Photos:** Yes
**Ordering:** Online, Phone, Fax
**Gift Wrap:** Yes
**Delivery:** Ground, 2$^{nd}$ Day, Overnight

# Nordstrom

`http://www.nordstrom.com`

We've heard more people talk about service at these stores than that at any other major department store; perhaps good service is so rare that people feel they have to tell you about it, or maybe Nordstrom goes beyond the perfunctory, to make people feel recognized as individuals. For whatever reasons, this high-end department store made its reputation by offering personal service in a busy world. The Web shop is the same. It's the best of the department stores. You can browse and buy online, or leave a message to have one of their personal shoppers contact you and help you with your purchases. Samples:

- Extended sizes for men and women
- Flannel pajamas
- Lambskin bomber jacket
- Sheer rayon-mesh T-shirts
- Soft-tailored pumps
- Wrinkle-free cotton chinos

**Search:** Yes
**Photos:** Yes (in 3 sizes!)
**Ordering:** Online
**Gift Wrap:** Yes
**Delivery:** Ground, 2$^{nd}$ Day, Overnight

# NPC Activeware

`http://npcwear.com`

NPC is short for National Physique Committee of the USA, Inc. They sell an adequate supply of fitness clothes for men and women. Shipping by ground is free, but costs more for express mailing. Samples:

- 2-tone polar fleece pullover
- Black and white karate tops
- Embroidered velour shirts
- Mesh tank tops
- Oversized T-shirts
- Sport bras
- Unisex silk body top
- USA muscle ribbed long-sleeve tops
- Zipper plaid shirt

**Search:** Yes
**Photos:** Yes
**Ordering:** Online, Phone, Fax
**Gift Wrap:** No
**Delivery:** Ground, 2$^{nd}$ Day, Overnight

# The Territory Ahead

`http://www.territoryahead.com`

This store offers one of the most unique collections of all the online clothing stores for women and men. According to their site, their clothes are made from "special fabrics, distinguishing details and easy, wearable designs." Most of the merchandise is handmade from their own designs. These designs are given names of exotic destinations to evoke a feeling of adventure. Custom service is also available. Give them your in-seam measurements and let them know if you want your pants cuffed or not, and they'll hem the pants to the correct length for you. Sizes run from 2 to 16 for women; 34 to 48 for men. The clothing is surprisingly affordable. Samples:

- Après-stress French terry zip-front jacket
- Bahia coyote Henley shirt
- Baja Shangri-La dress
- Enlightened skivvies
- Seagrass seashore sun hat
- Spanish sun sandals

- Silk T-shirts

**Search:** Yes
**Photos:** Yes
**Ordering:** Online, Phone
**Gift Wrap:** No
**Delivery:** Ground, 3rd Day, 2nd Day, Overnight

# If you'd like stores that focus on a particular type of clothes, try some of these on:

- Clothes—Kids
- Clothes—Maternity
- Clothes—Men
- Clothes—Men's Extended Sizes
- Clothes—Women
- Clothes—Women's Extended Sizes

# Clothes—Kids

One of our kids (we won't mention any names) so disliked shopping for clothes that he would sometimes just sit down in the dressing room, fold his legs, and refuse to try on any more garments. If we had to go out and get another size, forget it. When we got back to the dressing room, he was all dressed again and ready to leave. When the first children's clothing catalog arrived in our mailbox one day, we rejoiced. From that day on, we never entered a dressing room with him again. Clothes shopping for kids can be a challenge, to put it nicely. Today our choices (and yours, too) are limitless because of the big variety of kids, clothing stores on the Web. If you have a baby or toddler at home, please turn to the chapter on Baby Stuff.

## April Cornell

http://www.aprilcornell.com

This store is a cross between a department store and a boutique. There are lots of really nice items, from mother and daughter dresses to table linens. All of the clothing designed for girls is just simply beautiful. Lots of pretty floral prints and designs. You won't find these dresses in any other place. When you enter the store, depending upon what you're looking for, click on either Mommy and Me or the Cornelloki section to find clothing for sophisticated and sweet little ladies. Samples:

- Coral cotton-pique dress with embroidery
- Flower-girl dresses
- Long-sleeve cotton T-shirts
- Matching seaside dress and hat
- Pin-tucked yoke dresses
- Sister dresses

**Search:** Yes
**Photos:** Yes

**Ordering:** Yes
**Gift Wrap:** No
**Delivery:** Ground

## Children's Wear Digest

http://xoom.freeshop.com/
pg00523.htm

You might be familiar with their catalog. Now you can shop quickly and easily on their Web site. They have a fabulous assortment of styles for boys and girls. Most of their clothes are made of cotton. We really liked the brother-and-sister area for shopping, but that's from an adult point of view. This store outfits toddlers to teens. Keep an eye out for their online bargains. Some of the brands they carry are Big Ball, Flapdoodles, Sara's Prints, Speedo, and Sweet Potatoes. Samples:

- Baby-doll dresses
- Baseball T-shirts
- Gone fishing T-shirts and shorts
- Mother-and-daughter outfits
- Ribbed long johns
- Soccer shorts
- Swimsuits
- Toddler rompers

**Search:** Yes
**Photos:** Yes
**Ordering:** Online, Phone
**Gift Wrap:** No
**Delivery:** Ground, 3rd Day, Overnight

## Classy Kids

http://www.classykids.com/
home.htm

This is the place to shop for those special occasions, such as weddings, christenings, or any other event when only the fanciest clothes will do. Samples:

- Black or white boy's tuxedo
- Brocade, satin, and lace dress with adjustable pearl collar
- Flower-girl dresses
- Knickers and satin vest set

- Rose-lace long dress with matching purse
- White satin shorts-and-vest set

**Search:** Yes
**Photos:** Yes
**Ordering:** Online, Phone
**Gift Wrap:** No
**Delivery:** Ground

## Cute as a Bug

http://www.cuteasabug.com

Here's a great selection of casual clothes for toddlers and kids (up to size 7). All of the clothes are very reasonably priced. You'll receive 10% off your next order if you join their free mailing list. Today, you can get bargains by shopping their Clearance department. Samples:

- Le Top racing shirts
- Polo shirts
- Printed T-shirts
- Shorts for toddlers and kids
- Swim diapers
- Toddler dresses

**Search:** Yes
**Photos:** Yes
**Ordering:** Online, Phone
**Gift Wrap:** Yes
**Delivery:** 3rd Day, 2nd Day

## GapKids and BabyGap

http://gap.com/onlinestore/gap

Parents who once shopped at The Gap as teenagers for denim jeans love shopping for their kids at these two Gap stores. The baby line is cute, very in stuff. Gap Kids is really a mini-version of the adult store, with a few modifications. The prices are steep. We found a leather jacket for toddlers costing $168. Samples:

- Denim shorts
- Girls fringed suede jacket
- Mesh basketball pants
- Nylon drawstring skirt
- Stone-washed sweatshirts

- Toddler leather jackets
- Toile dresses

**Search:** Yes
**Photos:** Yes
**Ordering:** Online
**Gift Wrap:** Yes
**Delivery:** Ground, Overnight

## Gymboree

http://www.gymboree.com

You might have first come in contact with this company when you brought your toddler or young child to one of their playtimes. We did. And we fondly remember the huge "parachute" that gently wafted down on the kids at the end of the session. The same type of playful fun is evident in their clothes and accessories, too. Bright colors and merry patterns predominate the line. Sizes range from baby to about size 7 for girls and boys. Samples:

- Bike shorts
- Floral bouquet jumpers
- Hooded fleece sweatshirt
- Matching T-shirts, leggings, and cardigans
- Nylon pullover windbreaker
- Polo shirts with matching cargo pants
- Rugby shirts
- Socks and tights

**Search:** Yes
**Photos:** Yes
**Ordering:** Online
**Gift Wrap:** Yes
**Delivery:** 2nd Day

## Hanna Andersson

http://www.hannaandersson.com

Twenty years ago, when Hanna Andersson had her first child, she visited her homeland in Sweden and bought some clothes for her new son. On her return to the U.S., many of her friends marveled at the clothes and asked her how they could buy some, too. That gave her the idea to start her own clothing business, and she did, starting with catalog sales and branching out to the

Web. All of the clothes are 100% cotton. They are very pretty—with bright colors and patterns—and all of the fabrics feel soft against tender young skins. Samples:

- "Survival" jackets
- Cotton jersey cottage-garden dress
- Denim jumpers
- Double knee sweat pants
- Long johns
- School uniforms
- Swimwear
- Twill sport shorts

**Search:** Yes
**Photos:** Yes
**Ordering:** Online
**Gift Wrap:** Yes
**Delivery:** Ground, 3rd Day, 2nd Day, Overnight

# Heirloom Shoppe

`http://www.spinneret.com/`
`heirloom`

Halloween has always been our kids' favorite holiday. They start planning what they'll be for Halloween on November 1. This store has a fantastic collection of beautiful costumes. Not the junky wear-it-once-and-it's-ripped kind, but beautiful costumes that will be used over and over again for younger siblings or for dress-up. Most of the costumes are fully washable and fit sizes 2 to 8. Your kids will LOVE browsing through this store. Samples:

- Dorothy
- Fairy Godmother
- Festival Knight
- King
- Pirate
- Snow White
- Swan Princess

**Search:** Yes
**Photos:** Yes
**Ordering:** Online, Fax
**Gift Wrap:** No
**Delivery:** Ground

# Kid's Clothing Outlet

`http://www.kidclothing.com`

School uniforms are being adopted in many towns across the country. For the most part, parents love them, but kids don't. Nevertheless, they are a way of life for thousands of children. This store sells most of the styles, colors, and sizes (up to size 20). The store is strictly no-frills (don't let the funky home page turn you off), and that approach shows in the fantastically low, low prices. Samples:

- Adjustable cross tie
- Long-sleeve wrinkle-free Oxford shirt
- Pleated skirts
- Short- and long-sleeve, wrinkle-free Peter Pan blouses
- Short-sleeve dress shirt
- Short-sleeve knit polo shirt
- V-neck cardigan sweater
- V-neck jumpers
- Wrinkle-free twill shorts
- Wrinkle-free, double-knee pleated pants

**Search:** Yes
**Photos:** Yes
**Ordering:** Online
**Gift Wrap:** No
**Delivery:** Ground

# Lands' End

`http://www.landsend.com`

If you have active kids, zoom over to this store. The clothes are "cool" enough for the most popular kid in the class and durable enough so you feel you've gotten your money's worth out of the short time they actually wear them. If your kids grow slowly, then maybe you'll be able to keep these clothes awhile; we never had that luxury. But we can say that these clothes are so well made that they amply wend their way through the hand-me-down chain. How do we know this? We've been buying their clothes for our kids for years. Their unconditional guarantee on all of their merchandise takes the worry out of ordering. They have many clothing items for newborns, toddlers, kids, and teens. And take the time to explore their large Overstocks section for terrific bargains on discontinued stock. Samples:

- Chafe-free 100% combed cotton sundresses
- Corduroy skirts
- Denim jeans
- Flannel PJs and footed PJs
- Fleece sweats
- Polartec hats, coats, gloves, and earbands
- School uniforms
- Silk or cotton long underwear
- Waterproof boots

**Search:** Yes
**Photos:** Yes
**Ordering:** Online, Phone, Fax
**Gift Wrap:** Yes
**Delivery:** Ground, 3nd Day, 2nd Day, Overnight

many a night reading one of his classics to your kids. We know we have. This store has a few fun items that kids will love to wear. (Shh! There are some nifty items for Mom and Dad, too.) There isn't a lot available here, and if it was any other place, we wouldn't include it, but, after all, it *is* Dr. Seuss. Now go finish your green eggs and ham! Samples:

- Cat-in-the-Hat slippers
- Cat-in-the-Hat stovepipe hat
- Fishbowl gel watch
- One Fish, Two Fish, color-on T-shirt
- Sam-I-Am color-on T-shirts

**Search:** Yes
**Photos:** Yes
**Ordering:** Online, Phone, Fax
**Gift Wrap:** No
**Delivery:** Ground, 3rd Day, Overnight

# L-Bow Mittens

http://www.lbow.com

In the winter, our kids like to go sledding and ice-skating until dark. Their hands and toes are often in the pre-frostbite stage when they arrive home. If this scenario sounds familiar, then you'll love this store, which guarantees no more frozen fingers. L-Bow's revolutionary design extends the mittens all the way up to the elbow, so the mittens stay on and wrists stay dry. These mittens are waterproof and lined with Thinsulate. Sizes are available for toddlers up to teens. They cost $17 per pair. Samples:

- 9 different colors of mittens
- Gloves
- Long-neck head sock

**Search:** Yes
**Photos:** Yes
**Ordering:** Online, Fax
**Gift Wrap:** No
**Delivery:** Ground

# Seuss Wear

http://www.seusswear.com

Who hasn't loved the lovable characters created by the wonderful Dr. Seuss? Most of you have probably spent

# Clothes— Maternity

This is such a special time in your life. You're nurturing a new soul during its journey. How wonderful. We remember all the hilarious times we had trying to come up with names. Of course, with the last name of Price, we had lots of fun trying out first names like, Low-Low, Discount, and Rock Bottom. So much for great moments in the Price Family history. Now you're starting (or continuing) a family. You may be tired at times, but you always want to look your best. We found stores that cater to every facet of your life, from eating ice cream on the sofa in front of the TV, to giving a presentation at work. We also found some shops that offer maternity clothes for extended sizes. If you're entering your third trimester, you might want to read the Babies chapter, too. We've found lots of great baby gear and clothing stores, including places where you can order birth announcements.

## Anna Cris Maternity

http://www.annacris.com

You'll look great through all three trimesters if you shop from this store. They offer you high-quality, very fashionable clothes for the weekend, the office, or for working out. They carry some of the well-known maternity brands, such as Japanese Weekend, and offer the Pregnancy Survival Kit from Belly Basics. Most of the fashions run from size 4 to 18. If your purse is a little thin because of all the "baby stuff" you're buying, browse the On Sale area. Samples:

- Bike short unitards
- Career suits
- Cotton jumpsuit
- Cotton/Lycra long slim skirts
- Denim tops
- Maternity hosiery
- Satin slinky tops
- Soft cotton sweater with boot-leg pant
- Twill shorts

**Search:** Yes
**Photos:** Yes
**Ordering:** Online
**Gift Wrap:** Card
**Delivery:** 3rd Day, 2nd Day, Overnight

## Baby Becoming

http://www.babybecoming.com

Maternity fashions for the full-figured, pregnant mom-to-be are what make this shop so special. They were just getting their Web store together when we browsed, and didn't have a lot for sale via the Web (everything in the sample list below *is* for sale on the Web, though), but they do have LOTS of clothes available, if you wish to phone or fax in your order. Samples:

- Maternity sleep pillows
- Nursing pillows for fuller bodies
- Silken blouses in many colors
- Straight-leg blue jeans

**Search:** Yes
**Photos:** Yes
**Ordering:** Online, Phone, Fax
**Gift Wrap:** No
**Delivery:** Ground, 3rd Day, Overnight

## Dan Howard Maternity Factory Outlet

http://www.momshop.com

For over 40 years, Dan Howard has been designing high-quality maternity fashions. This store not only offers a fabulous collection of clothes, but offers them at great prices, too. You'll find a thorough collection of outfits for the office and for home. Some designs come in extended sizes, also. Samples:

- Bootleg pants
- Corduroy overall dress
- Denim jeans
- Interlock turtleneck
- Jumpsuits
- Matching vest and trousers
- Nursing crew-neck diki
- Rib leggings

**Search:** No
**Photos:** Yes
**Ordering:** Online
**Gift Wrap:** No
**Delivery:** Ground

## Hot Mamas

http://www.hot-mamas.com

Great name for a store, huh? No, it's not what you're thinking. This store specializes in nursing clothing and accessories for women who live in hot climates. (They're also great for women whose hormones make them just *feel* like they are living near the equator.) All of the fashions are very reasonably priced. You'll also find some helpful links to breast-feeding organizations. Samples:

- Green-and-blue tropical short nursing dress
- Matching hair scrunchies
- Plum batik nursing dress with matching baby jumpsuit

**Search:** No
**Photos:** Yes
**Ordering:** Online, Mail
**Gift Wrap:** No
**Delivery:** Priority

## Jaggar Maternity

http://www.maternityclothes.com

Having a hard time finding a pair of jeans that fit you during your pregnancy? Your hard time is over.

Jaggar's specializes in the "Maternity Vintage Jean," meaning that their jeans are not the flimsy ones you see in most maternity stores. And they have that well-worn look of your favorite pre-pregnancy pair. Their jeans are available in a lot of sizes and in various "fades." A nice touch is that every pair of pants is made with a girdle-like material in the back for support. Samples:

- "Pouchless" straight legs
- Black "recycled"
- Cutoff shorts
- Relaxed fit
- Straight legs

**Search:** No
**Photos:** Yes
**Ordering:** Online
**Gift Wrap:** No
**Delivery:** Ground

## Japanese Weekend

http://www.japaneseweekend.com

This line has developed over the years to include just about every article of clothing a pregnant woman could want. From lingerie to sophisticated career clothing to nursing garments, you'll find well-tailored clothes that will make you *feel* good while you *look* good. The inventory on the store is updated often, so make sure you keep checking back to their Sale Page for recent bargains. They offer many of their styles in Petite sizes. Samples:

- Knit top and pants
- Linen overalls
- Long linen dress with mandarin collar
- Long nursing gowns
- Microfiber tights
- Nursing bras and tops
- Rayon acetate beige suit
- Workout clothes

**Search:** Yes
**Photos:** Yes
**Ordering:** Online, Phone, Fax
**Gift Wrap:** No
**Delivery:** 3rd Day, 2nd Day, Overnight

# Little Koala

`http://littlekoala.com`

This is a friendly store that goes out of its way to make your shopping experience a pleasant one. They offer lots of clothes, as well as some items you'll want to have on hand as soon as your baby is born, like nursing bras, diaper bags, and a breast-milk storage container. They also have a small line of nursing clothing. Sizes range (depending on the garment) from extra small to extra large. Samples:

- Batik shirt and matching skirt
- Collared sleeveless top
- Cotton maternity/nursing blouses
- Cotton/Lycra long-sleeve jumpsuit
- Crop jacket
- Exercisewear
- Long-sleeve cotton jersey nightgown
- Short-sleeve T-shirts
- Tank tops
- Tie-front midcalf-length nursing dress
- V-neck contemporary nursing top with matching vest

**Search:** No
**Photos:** Some
**Ordering:** Online, Phone, Fax
**Gift Wrap:** No
**Delivery:** Ground

# MaternityMall. com

`http://www.maternitymall.com`

This is a minimall, of sorts. There are clothing stores for you and your new baby. You'll also find some informational sites, such as La Leche League, and even a place where you can play around with a free interactive baby name search. Sample stores:

- Baby Songs
- eToys
- Gymboree
- Mimi Maternity

- Motherhood Nursing Wear and Maternity
- Pea in the Pod
- Stork Avenue

**Search:** Yes
**Photos:** Yes
**Ordering:** Depends on the individual store
**Gift Wrap:** Depends on the individual store
**Delivery:** Depends on the individual store

# Nordstrom

`http://www.nordstrom.com`

One of the best online department stores also carries a line of upscale maternity fashions. This high-end store made its reputation by offering personal service in a busy world. The Web shop is the same. Samples:

- Fitted leggings
- Stretch wrinkle-resistant slacks
- Stretch Faille knit top
- Swingy cotton dress

**Search:** Yes
**Photos:** Yes (in 3 sizes!)
**Ordering:** Online
**Gift Wrap:** Yes
**Delivery:** Ground, 2nd Day, Overnight

# If you'd like stores that focus on another type of clothes, please slip into some of these chapters:

- Clothes—All
- Clothes—Kids
- Clothes—Men
- Clothes—Men's Extended Sizes
- Clothes—Women
- Clothes—Women's Extended Sizes

# Clothes—Men

For many men, nothing could be more boring than shopping for clothes. The physical layout of the department stores is confusing, the sales help patronizing, and who wants to spend hours trying stuff on, taking it off, struggling in and out of pants and shirts and jackets just to see if "they go together"? Why can't you just pick the right stuff out, like a hammer, and be on your way? Little wonder most guys really hate to take the time out of a weekend to find a parking spot, then browse through the mall, fighting the crowds. If this sounds like you, you are the quintessential Web shopper. We've done our best to find a wide selection of different stores so you can shop efficiently for clothes while staying at home. If you have trouble finding your size in this chapter, you might want to read the next chapter, on men's clothing in extended sizes.

## Arnold's Men's Online Store

http://arnoldsmensstore.com

It's hard to believe that the Web offers the carefully tailored pants that are usually only available at exclusive men's shops, but here is an online tailor. Select their Sansabelt brand slacks from wool blends, polyesters, cotton, mirofiber polyester, and denim fabrics. Then give them your waist and exact length, and select the style (pleated front, plain front, and so on). At that point, Arnold's will go to work. Slacks take about two weeks to ship from date of order. All of their slacks are completely washable or dry cleanable. Samples:
- Double-reverse pleated 1/8 pocket pants
- No-shrink polyester and pima cotton slacks
- Prewashed stretch denim pants

**Search:** Some
**Photos:** No

**Ordering:** Online, Phone, Fax
**Gift Wrap:** No
**Delivery:** Ground

## Bill's Khakis

http://www.billskhakis.com

If you're one of those guys who lives in his khaki pants, you'll never have to go shopping again, because that is all this store sells. There are four basic patterns, with slightly different accessories, and lots of sizes (from 30 to 46). Just in case you don't know how to take care of your khakis, there's a maintenance section. Samples:
- "Blue Label" distressed
- Flannel-lined
- Fuller cut, plain front with huge pockets
- Lightweight preshrunk poplin
- Plain front with reverse pleat
- Vintage khaki twill shirt

**Search:** Yes
**Photos:** Yes
**Ordering:** Online
**Gift Wrap:** No
**Delivery:** Ground, 3rd Day, 2nd Day, Overnight

## Brooks Brothers

http://www.brooksbrothers.com

Shortly after the colonies won their independence from Great Britain, Henry Brooks opened his clothing business in New York City. His motto was "to make and deal only in merchandise of the finest quality." Generations later, the store is still doing that. The current fads of fashion never make a dent in the clothing offered at Brooks Brothers, as far as we can tell, having shopped there since college. They pride themselves on offering classic tailoring, using only the finest materials. If you tell them your measurements, such as in-seam, waist, and length, they'll alter the trousers for free. They also guarantee free shipping to anywhere in the continental U.S. If you've ever shopped at Brooks Brothers, you know that their merchandise isn't cheap, but it does last forever. Samples:
- Canvas and leather penny loafers

- Heathered button-front vest
- High-roll 3-button navy stripe suit
- Old Irish Hound enamel cuff links
- Pique stripe knit polo shirts
- Poplin suit, 2-button jacket with plain-front trousers
- V-neck tennis sweater

**Search:** Yes
**Photos:** Yes
**Ordering:** Online, Phone, Fax
**Gift Wrap:** Yes
**Delivery:** 3rd Day, Overnight

## Corsair Ties

http://www.couchpotato.net/
~corsair

For 40 years men could shop in any one of Corsair's three shops in New Orleans, skimming through their unique collection of ties. The doors are closed now, but the shops have been reincarnated on the Internet. Today anyone can buy these ties with just a few clicks of a mouse. Samples:

- Classic ties
- Fun, novelty, and logo ties
- Religious ties
- Scarves and belts
- School and uniform ties
- Tiger silk boxers
- Wrinkle-free, polyester ties
- Write-on ties

**Search:** Yes
**Photos:** Some
**Ordering:** Online, Phone, Fax
**Gift Wrap:** No
**Delivery:** Ground, 2nd Day

## Crooks Clothing

http://www.crooksclothing.com

This clothing store hasn't changed its Pennsylvania location in nearly a century—until recently, that is, when it opened up a store on the Web. They carry

mostly higher-end casual clothes from designers such as Tommy Hilfiger, Nautica, Timberland, and Polo Jeans. Don't forget to check their sale page section for savings of up to 60%. Samples:

- 33 Degrees acrylic-knit sweaters
- Doc Martin nylon coats
- Tommy Hilfiger Surf Co. T-shirt
- Unionbay sweater vests
- Woolrich Polartec fleece vests

**Search:** Yes
**Photos:** Yes
**Ordering:** Online, Phone, Fax
**Gift Wrap:** No
**Delivery:** Ground, 2nd Day, Overnight

## eTuxedo

http://www.etuxedo.com

If you're thinking of buying a tux instead of renting one, check this store out. They have great prices on quality tuxedos and accessories. (Tuxedos start at less than $200.) You'll find many different styles and sizes (36R to 50L, with extra-large sizes available) to choose from. If you're still not sure, they offer a full refund on any unaltered garment returned within 30 days. Samples:

- Classic 100% pure worsted wool cutaway
- Double-breasted wool tuxedos
- One-button, shawl-collar white dinner jacket
- Pure cotton and cotton-blend wing-tip formal shirts
- Single-breasted tailcoat
- Tuxedo separates
- White double-breasted tailcoat

**Search:** Yes
**Photos:** Yes
**Ordering:** Online, Phone, Fax
**Gift Wrap:** No
**Delivery:** Ground, 2nd Day, Overnight

## Gary's Island

`http://www.garysisland.com`

Grab a pi a colada, a straw hat, some sandals, and then go and find the perfect Hawaiian print shirt to go with everything. Gary's has a lot of bold prints, colorful florals, and surfing designs. Shirts run anywhere from $50 to $80. Samples:

- 100% cotton parrot shirt
- 100% rayon rain forest shirt
- 100% silk Bahama shirt
- Rayon, cotton, linen paradise shirt

**Search:** No
**Photos:** Yes
**Ordering:** Online, Phone
**Gift Wrap:** No
**Delivery:** Ground

## Giftopia

`http://giftopia.com`

Now we've heard of everything: a silk tie MALL! Only on the Web! The ties are all handmade in Korea and the silk used comes exclusively from Italy. Ties cost about $10 each, with the price going down when you order in bulk. There are no photos, but very detailed drawings of the designs. You should definitely shop this store if you're feeling lucky: they give away a free silk tie to every tenth customer. Samples:

- 100% silk bow ties
- Casual ties
- Colorful ties
- Novelty ties

**Search:** Some
**Photos:** No
**Ordering:** Online, Phone, Fax
**Gift Wrap:** Yes
**Delivery:** Ground, Airmail

## Harold's

`http://harolds.net`

Compared to some of the other men's clothing stores, this one is a just a newbie. For over 50 years Harrolds has been making and selling fine men's clothing, including silk ties. They've updated their stores and added an online one, too. They offer women's clothing and an outlet section, but good men's clothes are still the forte of this shop. Samples:

- Black-and-cream windowpane sportshirt
- Herringbone-knit polo shirt
- Navy linen blazer
- Silk glen-plaid sport coat
- Tan microfiber jacket
- Women's clothing

**Search:** Yes
**Photos:** Yes
**Ordering:** Online, phone
**Gift Wrap:** Yes
**Delivery:** Ground

## HugeStore.com

`http://www.hugestore.com`

The name of this store says it all. There is a fantastic amount of clothing available here. You'll find the biggest selection in shirts, and, boy, do they have shirts! You name it . . . dress shirts, T-shirts, golf shirts, casual shirts, shirts you've never heard of. What makes this store stand apart is the way you order. You enter in your requirements, like the collar style, cuff type, fabric type, and shirt size, and then they give you a list of all of the possible shirts, providing large virtual clothing swatches for you to inspect. The prices are excellent, considering the quality. Samples:

- Boxers
- Casual and dress pants
- Jeans
- Shirts, shirts, and more shirts
- Sport coats
- Suits
- Ties

**Search:** Yes
**Photos:** Yes

**Ordering:** Online, Phone
**Gift Wrap:** Yes
**Delivery:** Ground, 2nd Day, Overnight

## Premier Formal Wear

http://www.magibox.net/~premier

Simply put, this store sells name-brand formalwear at low prices. After seeing their prices (from $189 to $260), you'll probably never rent a tux again. They also carry a good supply of formal accessories to help you get it all together for that special occasion. Samples:
- 100% cotton wing collar shirt
- 5-button full-back vest
- Cuff links, studs, and button covers
- Full-dress 100% tropical wool tuxedo
- Fumagalli 3-button notch-lapel tuxedo
- Poly/cotton band-collar shirt
- Shawl-lapel 100% tropical wool tuxedo
- Silk bow tie and cummerbund
- White or ivory dinner jackets

**Search:** Yes
**Photos:** Yes
**Ordering:** Online, Phone, Mail
**Gift Wrap:** No
**Delivery:** Ground, 3rd Day, Overnight

## Rubber Neckties

http://www.rubber-neckties.com

The thing about ties is that they're so fragile. One little spot of pesto sauce and the tie is done for. How would you like a tie with a 500-year guarantee? No, this isn't a dream. It's an eco-tie store. Maybe the first in the nation. The ties are actually made from recycled rubber. You're laughing now, right? But think about it. A tie for life. No more looking past trays and trays of ties until they all look alike. And after all, you gotta love a tie that's dishwasher safe and springs back to life after a light dusting of Armour All. Samples:
- Blackwall ties

- Custom lettering
- Personalized ties
- White raised-lettered ties
- Whitewall ties

**Search:** No
**Photos:** No
**Ordering:** Online, Phone, Fax
**Gift Wrap:** Card
**Delivery:** Ground

## Sports Fan

http://www.sports-fans.com

This is the place to gorge yourself on officially licensed clothes, hats and other gear from the MLB, NBA, NFL, and NHL. You'll also be able to find a large section of sports-related college gear. They carry adult and youth sizes. The only drawback is that often the items from the more popular teams are sold out. Some of the clothes can be personalized. Sizes, depending on the item, go up to XXL. Samples:
- Bulls' championship clothes
- College mini football helmets
- Iron Man 100% cotton T-shirt
- Jerseys from every team imaginable
- NFL team flags
- Wrestling shirts

**Search:** Yes
**Photos:** Yes
**Ordering:** Online, Phone, Fax
**Gift Wrap:** No
**Delivery:** Ground, 2nd Day, Overnight

## Suit Source

http://www.suitsource.com

Every once in a while, it's gratifying to find a store like this. Gorgeous, quality suits at slightly above-factory cost. You'll find custom-made suits for as low as $164. They also carry tuxedos. You'll be asked a ton of measurement questions, so that the fit is just right. They also offer portly, athletic, and standard fits. (Sizes often run from 35 to 60.) But even if after all that you're not satisfied with your suit, they'll refund your money. After all, at a store like this, you'd expect that your satisfaction is guaranteed. (Psst: They also pay the shipping to anywhere in the continental U.S.) Samples:

- Black-and-white houndstooth check
- Black-and-white glen plaid
- Cambridge gray with chocolate pinstripes
- Dark charcoal with blue and burgundy pinstripes
- Navy with light-gray pinstripe
- Olive with gray and cocoa pinstripes
- Poly/worsted wool wrinkle-resistant suits

**Search:** No
**Photos:** Some
**Ordering:** Online, Phone, Fax
**Gift Wrap:** No
**Delivery:** Ground

## The Territory Ahead

http://
www.territoryahead.com

This store offers a unique collection among all the online clothing stores for men. According to the site, their clothes are made from "special fabrics, distinguishing details and easy, wearable designs." Most of the merchandise is handmade from their own designs. These designs are given names of exotic destinations to evoke a feeling of adventure, travel, and getting away from it all. Custom service is also available. Give them your in-seam measurements and let them know if you want your pants cuffed or not and they'll hem the pants to the correct length for you. Sizes run from 34 to 48. The clothing is surprisingly affordable. Samples:

- El Rey Sol shirt
- Go Native boxers
- Good sport suede pullover
- Play It soft chinos
- Portofino sport shirt
- Seagrass seashore sun hat
- Surf City plaid shirt

**Search:** Yes
**Photos:** Yes
**Ordering:** Online, Phone
**Gift Wrap:** No
**Delivery:** Ground, 3rd Day, 2nd Day, Overnight

# If you'd like stores that focus on another type of clothes, try some of these on:

- Clothes—All
- Clothes—Kids
- Clothes—Maternity
- Clothes—Men's Extended Sizes
- Clothes—Women
- Clothes—Women's Extended Sizes

# Clothes—Men's Extended Sizes

If your body size isn't "average," you know what a challenge it can be to find clothes and shoes that fit well and, just as important, that you like to wear. Surprisingly, there are many stores on the Web that cater to you. We found stores that sell designer fashions for the man 5' 8" and under, as well as shops that cater to the big and tall man. We've also included some shoe stores that carry a wide range of sizes and widths. You might want to glance through the chapter Clothes—Men, as well, because several of those stores carry a few items in extended sizes.

## BigMen, TallMen, StoutMen's Shop

http://www.bigmen.com

This is the big Kahuna of all big and tall shops for men. Clothing, shoes, socks, belts, you name it, and you'll find it here. For men with large feet, you'll be relieved to know they stock shoes from sizes 6 to 20 with widths from AAA to EEEEEE. There's a flat rate of $6.00 for shipping. Samples:

- Classic trench coat
- Executive-quality all-wool blazer
- Extra-wide medical sock
- Hunting clothes
- Izod swimwear
- Reversible dress belt
- Ski clothes
- Summer cotton suit

**Search:** Yes
**Photos:** Yes
**Ordering:** Online, Phone, Fax

**Gift Wrap:** No
**Delivery:** Ground, 3rd Day, 2nd Day, Overnight

## Epic Menswear

http://www.epicmenswear.com

Quality clothes at affordable prices are the hallmark of Epic. Most of the clothes are sold straight from their inventory, but they do offer a customized shirt in a variety of fabrics, colors, and prints. All in all, they have a good selection of merchandise that will add a little sparkle to your closet. Sizes, depending on the garment, go up to 8X. Samples:

- Blue cable-knit sweater
- Brushed leather belt
- Cotton briefs and boxers
- Fleece pullover
- Golf herringbone shirt
- Oxford shirts
- Wrinkle-free khakis

**Search:** Yes
**Photos:** Yes
**Ordering:** Online
**Gift Wrap:** No
**Delivery:** Ground

## Hanover Clothing Co.

http://www.bigandtall.com

The name of the store comes from the Pennsylvania town that Harry Blumenthal settled in during the late 1800s. He originally started selling men's clothing to factory and farm workers, before changing to dress the man of any size today. Sizes range from small to portly regular and small to portly short. Samples:

- Arrow straight-collar shirts
- Beltless plain-front pants
- Cuffed, uncuffed, or unfinished trousers
- Gabardine twill slacks
- Poly/worsted wool hopsack-weave blazer

**Search:** Yes
**Photos:** Yes
**Ordering:** Online, Phone, Fax

**Gift Wrap:** Yes
**Delivery:** Ground

## Hitchcock Shoes

http://www.wideshoes.com

Hitchcock has been selling only men's wide shoes for several decades. They carry over 160 different styles, so finding the perfect ones for you shouldn't be too hard. You'll find shoe sizes from 5 to 13 and widths starting at EEE and going up to EEEEEE. Samples:

- Curved-sole Hush Puppies
- Dress socks
- Glossy leather loafers
- Madison Oxfords
- New Balance running, walking, and hiking shoes
- Rubber-bottom waterproof boots
- Smooth-leather deck shoes
- Steel-toe work boots
- Straight-tip oxfords

**Search:** Yes
**Photos:** Yes
**Ordering:** Online, Mail
**Gift Wrap:** No
**Delivery:** Ground

## JC Penney

http://www.jcpenney.com

This store has morphed over the years into a giant retailer seen in most of the malls across America. They wisely decided to set up shop on the Web and have done a good job of it. You can find most of the same merchandise that's available at their glass-and-concrete stores, including a wonderful assortment of clothes from their Big and Tall Shop. Samples:

- Bomber jacket
- Cardigan sweaters
- Haggar gabardine trousers
- Hooded rain parka
- Loose-fit and relaxed-fit cotton jeans
- Silk boxers
- Single-breasted trench coat

- Striped kimono
- 3-button, single-breasted sport coat
- Tricot solid long-sleeve pajamas

**Search:** Yes
**Photos:** Yes
**Ordering:** Online
**Gift Wrap:** No
**Delivery:** Ground

## Lands' End

http://www.landsend.com

You'll find good, classic, casual, and some office clothes and accessories at this easy-to-use Web shop. They've built a base of tremendous customer loyalty by being big on service and quality and keeping their prices as low as possible. Their online store is consistently mentioned as one of the easiest stores for shopping on the Web. Don't forget to check their Overstocks section for terrific bargains on discontinued items. Samples:

- Double-breasted gabardine jackets
- Fleece sweats
- Pima-cotton Oxford shirts
- Polo mesh shirts
- Shrink-resistant V-neck T-shirts

**Search:** Yes
**Photos:** Yes
**Ordering:** Online, Phone, Fax
**Gift Wrap:** Yes
**Delivery:** Ground, 3rd Day, 2nd Day, Overnight

## Nordstrom

http://www.nordstrom.com

This high-end department store made its reputation by offering personal service in a busy world. The Web shop is the same. It's the best of the department stores. You can browse and buy online, or leave a message to have one of their personal shoppers contact you and help with your purchases. Go to the Men's section and click on the Extended Sizes icon for a wonderful selection of well-made clothes. Samples:

- Cotton-velour robes
- French blue cotton dress shirt
- Merino-wool mock turtlenecks
- Wrinkle-free cotton chinos

**Search:** Yes
**Photos:** Yes (in 3 sizes!)
**Ordering:** Online
**Gift Wrap:** Yes
**Delivery:** Ground, 2nd Day, Overnight

## Short Sizes, Inc.

http://www.shortsizesinc.com

Fashionable, distinctive clothes for men who are 5'8" or under. This store sells just about everything, from activewear to overcoats. The prices are high and so is the quality. Shop here if you want the good stuff. Samples:

- 100% wool flannel slacks
- Crew neck wool/acrylic sweaters
- Henley knit top
- Leather bomber jacket
- Pure camel-hair sportcoat
- Velour jogging suits
- Yves Saint Laurent classic dress shirts

**Search:** Yes
**Photos:** Yes
**Ordering:** Online, Phone, Fax
**Gift Wrap:** No
**Delivery:** Ground

## Suit Source

http://www.suitsource.com

Every once in a while, it's gratifying to find a store like this. Gorgeous, quality suits at slightly above factory cost. You'll find custom-made suits for as low as $164. You'll be asked a ton of measurement questions, to ensure that the fit is just right. They also offer portly, athletic, and standard fits. (Sizes often run from 35 to 60.) But even if after all that you're not satisfied with your suit, they'll refund your money. After all, at a store like this, you'd expect that your satisfaction is guaranteed. (They also pay the shipping to anywhere in

the continental U.S.) Samples:

- Black-and-white houndstooth check
- Black-and-white glen plaid
- Cambridge gray with chocolate pinstripes
- Dark charcoal with blue and burgundy pinstripes
- Navy with light gray pinstripe
- Olive with gray and cocoa pinstripes
- Poly/worsted wood wrinkle resistant suits

**Search:** No
**Photos:** Some
**Ordering:** Online, Phone, Fax
**Gift Wrap:** No
**Delivery:** Ground

## Like wearing a tie? Hate it?

You can either blame or praise the Roman Legionnaires, who seem to be the first men to have worn them, or Louis the XIV, who resurrected them. (We guess ties just died out during the Middle Ages.) Louis so admired the ties worn by the Croatian soldiers who were helping him in an endless series of wars with Germany that he had a whole bunch of "cravats" (a word that derives from the French word for Croatians) made up for him and his court.

## If you'd like stores that focus on another type of clothes, change to some of these nearby chapters:

- Clothes—All
- Clothes—Kids
- Clothes—Maternity
- Clothes—Men
- Clothes—Women
- Clothes—Women's Extended Sizes

# Clothes—Women

Nothing will ever take the place of peeking at the racks in an exclusive dress shop or getting a terrific bargain at your favorite store. But what about all those times you want something fast, or you're looking for something unique or unusual?

That's when these Web stores can be your best friend. We've rounded up our own minimall of stores for women. You'll find fashions for teenagers and adults. If your body doesn't easily snuggle into the average size, check the next chapter, which focuses on extended sizes for apparel geared to petites, tall women, and full-figured women.

## Avalon Intimates

http://www.emporium.net/avalon

Soft exotic fabrics are used for this feminine lingerie line. You'll find garments for all your basic needs, as well as cute, fun, and slightly outrageous creations. They also carry a good selection of figure-enhancing items. Samples:

- Embossed shimmer and tulip-lace camisole
- Lace-trimmed sheer robe with belt
- Stretch fishnet bras
- Rayon-fringe bras
- Tummy-tucking body slip
- Velvety boucle-knit gown

**Search:** Yes
**Photos:** Yes
**Ordering:** Online, Fax
**Gift Wrap:** No
**Delivery:** Ground

## Bloomingdale's

http://www.bloomingdales.com

Bloomie's has ceiling-and-floor stores in only eight states. If you don't live in one of those states, or if you want to grab something quick without schlepping to an actual store, @ your service, their Web store, is the place for you. You have to create a "B profile" before you can actually go shopping, but once you answer all of the many questions, a personal dressing room is created based on your preferences. Samples:

- Anne Klein gabardine jacket
- Dana Buchman printed velvet T-shirt
- DKNY long-sleeved beaded cardigan
- Ferragamo calfskin pumps
- Ralph Lauren lamb's-wool sweater

**Search:** Yes
**Photos:** Yes
**Ordering:** Online, Fax
**Gift Wrap:** Yes
**Delivery:** Ground

## Carushka

http://www.caruska.com

Good-looking body- and sportswear, just for women. No unisex anything. Everything has been carefully designed for a woman's figure. So go ahead and sweat: you never looked so good. Prices are reasonable, but you should also check their Sale Rack. Sometimes they offer free shipping. Samples:

- Activa bras
- Ankle tights
- Logo top
- New York stretch velvet pants
- Sprinter shorts with drawstring waistband
- Tencel/Lycra performance pants
- Washable nylon/Lycra camisoles
- Workout hat

**Search:** Yes
**Photos:** Yes
**Ordering:** Online
**Gift Wrap:** No
**Delivery:** Ground

## Chic Paris

`http://www.inetbiz.com/chic`

The owners of this San Francisco–based shop fly to Paris every two or three months and load up on the latest fashions. (We should all have this job!) They look for three things when they are traipsing through the Parisian fashion houses: style, quality, and reasonable prices. Samples:

- Black polyester crepe skirt
- Chiffon skirt with elastic waist
- Embroidered bodysuit
- Velvet-collar blouse
- Wrinkle-free printed skirt

**Search:** No
**Photos:** Yes
**Ordering:** Online, Phone
**Gift Wrap:** No
**Delivery:** Ground

## Delia's Clothing

`http://www.delias.com`

Absolutely cool fashions for teenage girls are the exclusive domain of this Web store. The site is fresh and easy to navigate. If you don't know what to buy your teenage daughter, niece, or friend for her next birthday, steer her to Delia's Wish List section, where she can let you know what she *really* wants. Samples:

- Denim Butterfly shorts
- Hooded nylon parkas
- Jellyfish sandals
- Logo T-shirts
- Strappy cotton seersucker dress
- Strawberry cotton tank top
- Swimwear

**Search:** Yes
**Photos:** Yes
**Ordering:** Online, Phone
**Gift Wrap:** No
**Delivery:** Ground, 2nd Day

## Fair Trade Naturals

`http://www.algomaya.com`

Only organically grown cotton is used in these stylish clothes. FTN tells us that "one billion pounds of herbicides and another billion pounds of fertilizer are used on U.S. cotton production per year." If you shop here, your clothes will be free of pesticide and fertilizer, and they will be colored using natural dyes. Sizes range from Small to XXL. Samples:

- Bolero jacket with matching dress
- Cape, poncho style
- Classic button-down dress
- Handmade appliquéd vest
- Short-sleeved striped blouse
- Soft natural-colored cotton shorts
- Two-piece short jacket with wrap skirt

**Search:** Yes
**Photos:** Yes
**Ordering:** Online
**Gift Wrap:** No
**Delivery:** Priority Mail

## GirlShop

`http://girlshop.com`

Size two? Young? Sexy? Want New York designs at slightly less than New York prices? Shop here for an good selection of happening clothes . . . (OK, you don't have to be a size 2; some of the fashions go up all the way to size 8.) If you live in Manhattan, you can get delivery by messenger. Samples:

- Amy Chan quilted bucket tote
- Carrie Rosten Cie Katrina shirt
- Cynthia Rowley Miro curve sunglasses
- Paxton head scarf
- Wang A-line cargo skirt

**Search:** Yes
**Photos:** Yes
**Ordering:** Online
**Gift Wrap:** Yes
**Delivery:** Ground

# IC London

`http://www.iclondon.com`

Beautiful, elegant, shimmering, tasteful lingerie and loungewear is available from this North Carolina store. This is the good stuff. You'll find everything from the basics to the fancy. Want to feel like a movie star tonight?  Slip into one of the silk gowns. Prices are very reasonable. Sizes, depending upon the style, range from petite to extra large. Samples:

- 100% cotton bath wraps and spa robes
- Backless body briefer
- Buttercup lace T-shirt
- Lace-mesh body suit
- Satin seamless bustier
- Seamless mesh bras
- Silk camisole and tap pants
- Silk kimonos
- Wide-strap, anticling cami

**Search:** Yes
**Photos:** Yes
**Ordering:** Online
**Gift Wrap:** No
**Delivery:** Ground, 3rd Day, 2nd Day, Overnight

# Lands' End

`http://www.landsend.com`

Probably the biggest drawback to buying clothes online is that you can't try them on first. Lands' End realized this and has done something about it by creating a Personal Model that actually tries on the clothes for you. You enter your hair color, height, and some approximate measurements and your "model" is created for you, and she goes about "trying on" the clothes. You'll also be brought to a section of their store that has suggestions for clothes that will flatter your figure. There is a wide selection of good, classic, casual, and office-type clothes and accessories, including shoes. They've built a base of tremendous customer loyalty by being big on service and quality and keeping their prices as low as possible. Their online store is consistently mentioned as one of the easiest stores for shopping on the Web. Don't forget to check their Overstocks section for terrific bargains on discontinued

stock. Samples:

- Double-breasted gabardine jackets
- Fine-gauge jewel-neck cardigans
- Fleece sweats
- Plain-front corduroy skirt
- Print twill skort
- Shrink-resistant V-neck T-shirts
- Silk georgette crepe sweater
- Waterproof boots

**Search:** Yes
**Photos:** Yes
**Ordering:** Online, Phone, Fax
**Gift Wrap:** Yes
**Delivery:** Ground, 3rd Day, 2nd Day, Overnight

# Melrose Place Fashion

`http://www.ibcnet.com/dir/`
`fashion/melrose`

The name of this store says it all. If your idol is Heather Locklear, or just want to dress like her, grab your credit card and start shopping here. You'll find tight, revealing, and loud blouses, as well as super-slinkies, and a few (very few) practical items.  This is a store for glitz, romance, and drama, though not outfits for pulling weeds or tossing hay. The search categories (tight pants, sheer pants, and so on) say it all. These fashions aren't cheap, but if you check their Specials department, you might just find a bargain. Samples:

- Lycra stretch pants
- Open-lace-back short dresses
- Rayon lace-up shirt
- Soft Lycra lace body shirt
- Soft Lycra strip top
- Zip-fitted soft lambskin jacket

**Search:** Yes
**Photos:** Yes
**Ordering:** Online, Phone, Fax
**Gift Wrap:** No
**Delivery:** Ground

## Nordstrom

`http://www.nordstrom.com`

This high-end department store made its reputation by offering personal service in a busy world. The Web shop is the same. It's the best of the department stores. You can browse and buy online, or leave a message to have one of their personal shoppers contact you and help you with your purchases. Samples:

- Flannel pajamas
- Matte crepe knit dress with lace bodice
- Packable raincoat with travel pouch
- Rayon-blend mesh cardigan set
- Sequined pucker jumpsuit
- Sheer rayon mesh T-shirts
- Suede coat

**Search:** Yes
**Photos:** Yes (in three sizes!)
**Ordering:** Online
**Gift Wrap:** Yes
**Delivery:** Ground, 2nd Day, Overnight

## The Outdoor Woman

`http://www.theoutdoorwoman.com`

Everything for the sporting woman. No, we're not talking tennis here, we're talking big-game hunting, fishing, and sport shooting. Accessories are also for sale. Sizes range from XS to XXL. There are also clothes for young girls from size 2–4 to 18–20. Don't forget to check their specials. Free shipping on orders over $100. Samples:

- Chamois blouse and pants
- Hardwood fly-rod case
- Lady Nomad waterproof laced boots
- Mountain jackets
- Rain jacket and pants
- Saddle ponchos
- Shooters pouch with embroidery
- Stowaway hearing protectors
- Wading shoes
- Waterproof waders with removable pouch

**Search:** Yes
**Photos:** Yes
**Ordering:** Online, Phone, Fax
**Gift Wrap:** No
**Delivery:** Ground, 3rd Day, 2nd Day, Overnight

## The Territory Ahead

`http://www.territoryahead.com`

This store offers one of the most unusual collections of all the online clothing stores for women. According to their description, their clothes are made from "special fabrics, distinguishing details and easy, wearable designs." Most of the merchandise is handmade from their own designs. These designs are given names of exotic destinations to evoke a feeling for the styles. Custom service is also available. Give them your in-seam measurements and let them know if you want your pants cuffed or not, and they'll hem the pants to the correct length for you. Sizes run from 2 to 16. Samples:

- Après-stress French terry-cloth zip-front jacket
- Bahia linen jacket
- Baja Shangri-La dress
- Buena Suerta knit dress
- Seagrass seashore sun hat
- Spanish sun sandals
- Sun-splash swimsuit

**Search:** Yes
**Photos:** Yes
**Ordering:** Online, Phone
**Gift Wrap:** No
**Delivery:** Ground, 3rd Day, 2nd Day, Overnight

## Totally Outdoors

`http://www.totallyoutdoors.com`

We found a lot of camping stores that sold only outdoor sporting clothes for men. So it was a pleasure to find one devoted to women. This store not only carries camping, climbing, and bicycling clothes, it also sells a

number of sporting gear designed for the female of the species and clothing ranging in sizes from XS to XXL.
Samples:

- Berber vests
- Bicycling shorts
- Expedition shirts
- Sport bras
- Ski apparel
- Sleeping bags
- Supplex fitness shorts
- Waterproof/breathable socks
- Sleeveless jerseys

**Search:** Yes
**Photos:** Yes
**Ordering:** Online
**Gift Wrap:** No
**Delivery:** Ground, 3$^{rd}$ Day, Overnight

# If you'd like stores that focus on another type of clothes, try slipping into one of these chapters:

- Clothes—All
- Clothes—Kids
- Clothes—Maternity
- Clothes—Men
- Clothes—Men's Extended Sizes
- Clothes—Women's Extended Sizes

# Clothes— Women's Extended Sizes

Browsing through some stores, trying to find the clothes that fit, can be difficult if your body size doesn't conform to what is supposed to be "average." Shopping on the Web is different. We discovered some great stores, just for you. And just what did we find? Petite fashions, full-figured clothes, tall sizes, even a maternity shop. We also found a lot of specialty stores with extended sizes, such as fashions for women over 30 and organic clothing. We've also included a few department stores that have a good selection of extended sizes, too. Now go pick out something that makes you look like a million bucks.

## Audradella's

http://www.audradella.com

Wonderful selection of full-figured, elegant clothes, especially tasteful for women over 30. From blouses to formal dresses, this store sells it all. You'll find pretty outfits perfect for wearing to the office or to the movies. The pages take a little long to download, but we've included this store because of its marvelous selection. Free shipping on orders over $200. Samples:

- Sequined evening wear
- Silk blouses
- Soft-leather skirt suits
- Stylish brown lace pantsuit
- Swimwear

**Search:** Yes
**Photos:** Yes

**Ordering:** Online, Fax
**Gift Wrap:** No
**Delivery:** Ground

## Avalon Intimates

http://www.emporium.net/ avalon

Soft, exotic fabrics are used in this feminine lingerie. While not having a particularly big selection for full figures, they do offer some cute, sexy outfits that are hard to find in the stores. Sizes range from 1X to 4X. Samples:

- 2-piece leather-and-lace teddiette set
- Black stretch lace baby dolls
- Lace teddies with adjustable straps
- Peek-a-boo French net baby dolls
- Short, sheer, lace-trimmed robe with tie belt

**Search:** Yes
**Photos:** Yes
**Ordering:** Online, Fax
**Gift Wrap:** No
**Delivery:** Ground

## Baby Becoming

http://www.babybecoming.com

Maternity fashions for the full-figured, pregnant mom-to-be make this shop special. They were just getting their Web store together when we browsed, and didn't have a lot for sale via the Web (everything in the sample list below is for sale on the Web), but they do have LOTS of clothes available, if you wish to phone or fax in your order. Samples:

- Maternity sleep pillow
- Nursing pillows for fuller bodies
- Silken blouses in many colors
- Straight-leg blue jeans

**Search:** Yes
**Photos:** Yes
**Ordering:** Online, Phone, Fax
**Gift Wrap:** No
**Delivery:** Ground, 3rd Day, Overnight

## Discount Lingerie Rack

http://www.lingerierack.com

There are discounts of up to 50% off retail and then there are even greater savings in their Queen clearance section. Most of the lingerie comes in many pretty colors. Sizes range from 1X to 4X. Samples:

- Frosted Lycra bustier with shiny print overlay
- Halter-neck stretch-fishnet thong teddy
- Lace and Lycra bikini panties
- Lace garter belts
- Lace robes
- Long peignoir with lace bodice
- Rose-bud embellished teddiettes
- Stretch-lace and velour dresses
- Stretch-lace baby dolls with full skirt

**Search:** Yes
**Photos:** Yes
**Ordering:** Online, Phone, Fax
**Gift Wrap:** No
**Delivery:** Ground

## Extreme Lengths

http://www.extremelengths.com

If you are a tall lady, then you know how frustrating it can be shopping for stylish clothing. That's where this store comes in. They don't have a very big selection yet. But what they do offer is great. They usually have their 50% off section up and running, which offers you terrific savings on beautiful clothes. Samples:

- A-line scroll full-length skirt
- Crinkle-cotton pantsuit
- Rayon cascade dress
- Relaxed drawstring-waist pants
- Sleeveless mock turtlenecks
- Slimming knit empire dress

**Search:** Some
**Photos:** Yes
**Ordering:** Online, Phone, Fax
**Gift Wrap:** Yes
**Delivery:** Ground, 3rd Day, 2nd Day

## JC Penney

http://www.jcpenney.com

This store has morphed over the years into a giant retailer seen in most of the malls across America. A while ago, they wisely decided to set up shop on the Web, and they have done a good job of it. You can find most of the same merchandise available at their physical stores. They have an excellent supply of petite and tall sizes, and for sizes 16-plus there's the JCP Woman department. Samples:

- Career suits
- Full-figured bras
- Jeans
- Lace-up tunics
- No-iron cotton twill shorts
- Robes
- Slips
- Wrinkle-free side elastic waist shorts

**Search:** Yes
**Photos:** Yes
**Ordering:** Online
**Gift Wrap:** No
**Delivery:** Ground

## Lands' End

http://www.landsend.com

Probably the biggest drawback to buying clothes online is that you can't try them on first. Lands' End realized this and has done something about it by creating a Personal Model who actually tries on the clothes for you. You enter your hair color, height and some approximate measurements and your "model" is created for you, who "tries on" the clothes you select. You are also offered suggestions for clothes that will flatter your figure. Lands' End carries a good selection of petites and full-figured sizes, including tall sizes for women. You'll find good, classic, casual, and office clothes and accessories, including shoes. They've built a base of tremendous customer loyalty by being big on service and quality and keeping their prices as low as possible. Their online store is consistently mentioned as one of the easiest stores for shopping on the Web. Don't forget to check their Overstocks section for terrific bargains on discontinued

items. Samples:
- Fine-gauge jewel-neck cardigans
- Fleece sweats
- Night shirts
- Print twill skort
- Shrink-resistant V-neck T-shirts
- Silk georgette crepe sweater

**Search:** Yes
**Photos:** Yes
**Ordering:** Online, Phone, Fax
**Gift Wrap:** Yes
**Delivery:** Ground, 3rd Day, 2nd Day, Overnight

# Macy's

http://www.macys.com

Like their massive mall stores, Macys.com. offers a big selection of clothes in petite and plus sizes for women. And they haven't skimped on the search for these items, either. You can search by category and type (such as career, casual, active, social) or by designer name, which is helpful if you've found just the right brand for you. Samples:
- Anne Klein slim-fit pants
- Black matte jersey long dress
- INC petite knee-length skirts
- Linen pull-on pants
- Liz Claiborne seasonless crepe jacket
- Stretch denim jeans
- Wrinkle-free cotton twill pants

**Search:** Yes
**Photos:** Yes
**Ordering:** Online, Phone, Fax
**Gift Wrap:** Yes
**Delivery:** Ground, 2nd Day, Overnight

# Making It Big

http://www.bigwomen.com

What a find! All-natural fiber clothes for full-figured ladies. The fabrics are not bleached, and any coloring comes from natural dyes. The ordering part is a little funky (they download their entire inventory on an order

form for you to check), but since this is such a unique store, we just have to include it. Samples:
- Blue seas swimsuit
- Calico shirt
- Leggings
- Panty hose
- Raglan T-shirts
- Tank tops
- Tapered gauze pants
- Tuscany tunic

**Search:** Yes
**Photos:** Yes
**Ordering:** Online, Phone, Fax
**Gift Wrap:** Yes
**Delivery:** Ground

# Nordstrom

http://www.nordstrom.com

One of our favorites, partly because of the merchandise, and partly because the atmosphere is friendly. This high-end department store made its reputation by offering personal service in a busy world. The Web shop is the same. It's the best of the department stores. You can browse and buy online, or leave a message to have one of their personal shoppers contact you and help with your purchases. Go to the Women's section and click on the Extended Sizes icon for a wonderful selection of well-made clothes (petites, talls, pluses). Samples:
- Cotton velour robes
- Floral dresses
- French blue cotton dress shirt
- Linen two-piece suits
- Merino wool mock turtlenecks
- Silk blouses
- Wrinkle-free cotton chinos

**Search:** Yes
**Photos:** Yes (in 3 sizes!)
**Ordering:** Online
**Gift Wrap:** Yes
**Delivery:** Ground, 2nd Day, Overnight

# The Outdoor Woman

`http://`
`www.theoutdoorwoman.com`

Everything for the sporting women. No, we're not talking tennis here, we're talking big game hunting, fishing, and sport shooting. Accessories are also for sale. Sizes range from XS to XXL. There are also clothes for young girls from size 2–4 to 18–20. Free shipping on orders over $100. Don't forget to periodically check their specials. Samples:

- Chamois blouse and pants
- Hardwood fly-rod case
- Lady Nomad waterproof laced boots
- Mountain jackets
- Rain jacket and pants
- Saddle ponchos
- Shooters pouch with embroidery
- Stowaway hearing protectors
- Wading shoes
- Waterproof waders with removable pouch

**Search:** Yes
**Photos:** Yes
**Ordering:** Online, Phone, Fax
**Gift Wrap:** No
**Delivery:** Ground, 3rd Day, 2nd Day, Overnight

# Totally Outdoors

`http://`
`www.totallyoutdoors.com`

This store also caters to the sportswoman, but offers clothes for camping, climbing, and bicycling. You'll also find some sporting gear designed just for females (such as backpacks and sleeping bags). Clothes range in sizes from XS to XXL. Samples:

- Berber vests
- Bicycling shorts
- Expedition shirts
- Sport bras
- Ski apparel
- Sleeping bags
- Supplex fitness shorts

- Waterproof/breathable socks
- Sleeveless jerseys

**Search:** Yes
**Photos:** Yes
**Ordering:** Online
**Gift Wrap:** No
**Delivery:** Ground, 3rd Day, Overnight

# Ulla Popken

`http://www.ullapopken.com`

So often women whose dress size isn't in the average range have to pay through the nose for decent fashions. This store has changed all that by creating their own fashions. A pretty, friendly place to shop that does everything but serve you a cup of coffee while you make up your mind what to buy. They've also taken the guesswork out of figuring out your sizes. Just follow their three steps and you'll get a garment that fits perfectly. Don't forget to browse their Clearance center. Sizes range from 12 to 30. Samples:

- Crepe blazers
- Elegant dresses
- Fluid dresses
- Lace shirts
- Rugged bluejeans
- Soft pique knits
- Stylish garden dresses

**Search:** Yes
**Photos:** Yes
**Ordering:** Online, Phone, Fax
**Gift Wrap:** No
**Delivery:** Ground, 3rd Day, 2nd Day

# If you'd like stores that focus on another type of clothes, try some of these chapters:

- Clothes—Kids
- Clothes—Maternity
- Clothes—Men
- Clothes—Men's Extended Sizes
- Clothes—Women

# Coffee & Tea

When we drink green tea, or skim the foam off a cappuccino, we find ourselves reflecting that these beverages have been quenching the thirst of human beings for millennia. Tea plants may have been cultivated before coffee bushes, but both plants seem to have won humans' attention because they offer the drinker a lift, and, depending on the variety, good health, as well. Today it seems as if coffee and tea houses have sprung up on every block, and our taste buds have matured to include many different brews. With so many stores offering to mail you vacuum-packed bags and tins of the stuff, you need never run out at your house.

## Appybean

http://www.appybean.com

Coffee with an attitude. This unusual coffee store has a small but uncommon selection of gifts such as an antique glass canning jar filled with coffee beans. If you order three or more bags, you get 5% off your order. Samples:

- Chocolate cinnamon hazelnut
- Juan Valdez Colombian Supremo
- Jamaican Blue Mountain Ultra
- Schiz-Espresso
- Tiramisu Dream

**Search:** No
**Photos:** No
**Ordering:** Online
**Gift Wrap:** No
**Delivery:** Ground

## Aroma Borealis

http://www.tgx.com/coffee

First of all, let's tip our hats to whoever thought up the name of this store. Conjures up lots of exotic images, doesn't it? They carry coffee and tea from the slopes of Mount Kilimanjaro in Tanzania to Colombia's Bucaramaga. You can also find organic, herbal, and caffeine-free varieties. The tea is available in loose leaves or bags. Samples:

- Bella Coola herbal tea
- Brazil Bourbon Santos coffee
- Chocolate Raspberry Cream coffee
- Darjeeling Mim
- Mexico Pluma Altura
- Special Saigon Style

**Search:** Yes
**Photos:** No
**Ordering:** Online, Phone
**Gift Wrap:** No
**Delivery:** Ground

## Balducci's

http://www.balducci.com

Over 75 years ago Louis Balducci set up a fruit-and-vegetable stand on a corner in New York City. Just after World War II he moved into a storefront in Greenwich Village and started importing delicacies from around the world. How wonderful it was to live just up the avenue, and to pass this tempting store going to work and coming home. There was always some fantastic new jam, pasta, or deli item in the crowded aisles. Today Balducci goes online to sell delicacies from all over the world, including coffee. And, to go with your coffee, you can also order some chocolate confections. Samples:

- Balducci House Blend
- Café la Semeuse regular and decaf
- Chocolate-covered espresso beans
- Cool-brew cappuccino Viennese
- Handmade chocolate truffles
- Melita coffee grinder
- Nina's PM and AM Brew

**Search:** Yes
**Photos:** Yes
**Ordering:** Online
**Gift Wrap:** Card
**Delivery:** Ground

## Caesar's Palate

`http://www.caesarspalate.com`

Coffee wasn't around during Caesar's time (not in Italy, anyway). But if it was, Caesar would definitely have ordered it served at his table. Tea was available, but somehow we doubt if Caesar drank tea. The selection at this Web store is incredible. It has an interesting assortment of Oriental teas. If you want to have a taste of the good life (or are entertaining and want to make an indelible impression on your guests), shop here. The beverages and food aren't cheap, but you won't feel cheated, either. Samples:

- Chocolates and candies
- Colombian Supremo coffee
- Dragon Well tea
- Gourmet food
- Green Sea Anemone tea
- Japanese Sencha tea
- Tian Mu Quin Ding tea
- Wuyi green tea

**Search:** Yes
**Photos:** Yes
**Ordering:** Online
**Gift Wrap:** Card
**Delivery:** 2nd Day, Overnight

## Cook's Nook

`http://www.cooksnook.com`

Unusual coffees and Asian teas. Also, cooking appliances, cookware, and accessories that will make your gourmet cooking experience a real treat. Samples:

- Bridgetown coffee
- Cinnamon Hazelnut Praline coffee
- Green ginger tea
- Khatsa Tibetan teas
- Moonstruck chocolates
- Oregon Chai liquid concentrates in 3 flavors
- Panache gourmet coffees
- Snow Ghost coffee
- Tazo tea bags
- Xanadu teas

**Search:** Yes
**Photos:** Yes

**Ordering:** Online, Phone, Fax
**Gift Wrap:** No
**Delivery:** Ground, 2nd Day, Overnight

## Dean and Deluca

`http://www.dean-deluca.com`

A fixture in New York's SoHo (south of Houston Street) for a quarter century, D-and-D's was hip before SoHo was. (We used to shop there when they opened their doors next door to our loft.) The owners, Joel Dean and Giorgio DeLuca, expanded their deli as New Yorkers discovered this epicurean mecca. For those of us who don't live in New York, or remember when, we can salivate at the wonderful coffees, teas, and gourmet food online. The decaf coffees are made using the chemical-free Swiss water process. Samples:

- Chinese red and green teas
- Chocolate truffles
- Coffee urns
- Espresso
- Gourmet food
- House-blend coffee
- Mariage Frères tea
- Senbiki teakettle
- SoHo-blend coffee
- St. Helena coffee
- Yixing earthenware teapot

**Search:** Yes
**Photos:** Yes
**Ordering:** Online
**Gift Wrap:** Card only
**Delivery:** Ground, 2nd Day, Overnight

## Everybody's Store

`http://www.nas.com/~goodbuy`

Not everything that comes out of the state of Washington these days has to do with computers. Near the Canadian border, this general store has a little of everything, from organic food and beverages to brightly colored clothing. Samples:

- Breathe-deep tea

- Male vitality tea
- De-Tox tea
- Beef jerky
- Alaska wild teas

**Search:** Some
**Photos:** Some
**Ordering:** Online, Phone, Fax
**Gift Wrap:** No
**Delivery:** Ground

# GourmetMarket.com

`http://www.gourmetmarket.com`

Besides carrying all of the delicate morsels from around the world, this store also offers flavored coffees and cigars. It has a large selection of decaf coffees. Even though this is a gourmet "general store," we did notice a strong emphasis on chocolate. Samples:

- Copper teakettle
- Decaf Colombian Supremo
- Decaf Irish crème coffee
- Espresso
- Kona macadamia blend
- Organic coffee
- Sumatra Mandehling

**Search:** Yes
**Photos:** Some
**Ordering:** Online, Phone, Fax
**Gift Wrap:** No
**Delivery:** 3rd Day

# International Coffee House

`http://`
`www.21stcenturyplaza.com/`
`stor101/stor101.htm`

The coffee sold at this shop is micro-roasted, which means the beans are roasted in small batches (under 30 pounds) so you won't get any green or partially roasted beans in your bag. Nice selection of decaf and flavored coffees. Samples:

- Decaf Ethiopian
- Kahlua

- Kona Fancy
- Vanilla nut
- Zephyr blend

**Search:** Yes
**Photos:** No
**Ordering:** Online
**Gift Wrap:** No
**Delivery:** Ground

# International Gourmet

`http://www.intlgourmet.com`

As the name of the store implies, you can order gourmet food, coffee, and tea from many lands. They have an extensive tea collection at very reasonable prices. Samples:

- Armenian coffee
- Caykur aromatic tea
- Ciciban herb tea from Croatia
- Efendi coffee
- Ginseng Royal Jelly tea
- Venizelos coffee
- Wild Strawberry tea

**Search:** Yes
**Photos:** Some
**Ordering:** Online
**Gift Wrap:** No
**Delivery:** Ground, 2nd Day

# Istanbul Express

`http://`
`www.istanbulexpress.com`

Started as coffee hangout for the students at UC Berkeley, this store has gone online, keeping its small, university flavor. They now also offer teas from around the world. Check out the Hot Tips section for some do's and don'ts on brewing a super cup o' joe. Buy in bulk and save a lot. Samples:

- Apricot decaf tea
- Jasmine Fancy tea
- Java Estate coffee
- Keemum Confou tea
- Lapsang Souchong tea
- Russian caravan tea

- Vienna Roast coffee

**Search:** Some
**Photos:** No
**Ordering:** Online, Phone, Fax
**Gift Wrap:** No
**Delivery:** Ground

# Maui Coffee Store

`http://www.maui.net/~jstark/`
`mauicofe.html`

Coffee and a few other items from the Hawaiian Islands are the specialty of this store. Most folks are only used to the traditional Kona blend. But as you'll find when you visit, there are many more varieties available. If you have someone in the house who prefers non-Hawaiian blends, you'll be able to find those here, too. Samples:

- Chocolate Macadamia Nut
- Haleakala Sunrise Blend
- Hawaiian Hazelnut
- Kaanapali Maui
- Macadamia Nut

**Search:** Some
**Photos:** No
**Ordering:** Online
**Gift Wrap:** No
**Delivery:** Ground

# OnlyGourmet.com

`http://www.onlygourmet.com`

You might know Only Gourmet as the webzine of good taste, and you'd be right. It also puts its money where its mouth is, so to speak, by selling many scrumptious delicacies, as well as a wide assortment of coffee. Join the Coffee Club and you can have coffee delivered on a prearranged schedule. Samples:

- Beal's coffee
- Decaf Hazelnut coffee
- Distant Lands coffee
- Ethiopian Yrgacheffe
- Oren's Daily Roast
- Swiss water decaf blends
- Vanilla coffee

**Search:** Yes
**Photos:** Yes
**Ordering:** Online, Phone
**Gift Wrap:** No
**Delivery:** Ground

# Peet's Coffee and Tea

`http://www.peets.com`

Once upon a time there was a young mother with a toddler who reveled in waking up at 4:45 A.M. every day. At midmorning, this mom would bundle up her child in a stroller and trek the two-and-a-half miles to Peet's, buy a cup of coffee (no cappuccino machines back then), and sit on one of the wooden benches thoughtfully provided in a sunny area just outside of the store. This was Peet's. Anyone who has ever sampled any of their deep-roasted coffees or delicate teas will understand the joy this same mother felt when she moved 1,500 miles away and discovered she could have those precious beans shipped to her house. Samples:

- Aged Ethiopian
- French Roast
- Gaia Organic Blend
- Garuda Blend
- Green teas
- India Black teas
- Maduro
- Major Dickason's
- Oolong teas
- Viennese

**Search:** Yes
**Photos:** No
**Ordering:** Online, Phone, Fax
**Gift Wrap:** Card
**Delivery:** Ground

# Starbucks

`http://www.starbucks.com`

They might not have started the current coffee craze, but Starbucks certainly has cashed in on it. You can find them in almost any neighborhood, but just in case you really live in the middle of nowhere and would like to order online, you'll find a lively, café-style Web store.

Samples:
- Arabian Mocha Sanani
- Caffe Verona
- Coffee travel kits
- Colombia Narino Supremo
- Decaf Guatemala Antigua
- Espresso Roast
- LightNote Blend
- Serenade Blend

**Search:** Yes
**Photos:** Some
**Ordering:** Online
**Gift Wrap:** No
**Delivery:** Ground, 2nd Day, Overnight

# Great Moments in Coffee History . . .

Legend has it that a goat herder in Africa noticed that his goats became more playful after they munched on the red cherrylike beans growing from some shrubs. After another boring day, he tasted the "cherries" himself and felt a slight lift. He brought the "cherries" to the elders, who fooled around with them for a few centuries until a version of the coffee we now know came into being.

# And to go with that . . . perhaps you would like to consider these chapters:

- Cigars
- Food—Gourmet

# Computers & Computer Gear

If you're not sure what computer is best for you, we suggest you read the most recent issues of the computer magazines, to learn what features are hot and why you should care. For news of the latest releases, you might also visit the sites of the manufacturers who got top ratings. Then, for comparisons, visit the multiproduct Web stores we describe here, because they offer better prices on a ton of stuff, but not a lot of background, particularly not information an ordinary consumer can understand. Some stores, for instance, condense everything into numbers and acronyms, so they can display all the key facts about one computer on one line. Once you have used magazines or books to pick up the meaning of these awful TLAs (Three-Letter Acronyms), you can comparison-shop.

Remember that the lowest prices for individual components often show up in stores that cater to experienced users, hackers, and engineers, all of whom feel at ease with strings of alphanumeric characters.

Oddly, original manufacturers who distribute rather than selling everything themselves tend to charge more than the stores who resell their hardware, perhaps so that they can make the resellers look good. Here, then, are our favorite sites for computer gear.

## 2BuyPC

http://www.2buypc.com/shop/

With a good selection of brand-name hardware, from computers to networks, this site claims to offer wholesale prices, a term that's a bit vague in the computer business. Some items strike us as real bargains, well worth snapping up, while others carry price tags close to those of mail-order catalogs, which, of course, are still a lot better than the amounts charged by physical stores in high-traffic locations. One limit on this service is that they do not sell every single major brand, and even within some major brands they may not carry the whole line. Also, although the site offers a jargon-filled summary of the functionality of each piece of equipment, you should go elsewhere if you aren't sure which product to buy, because the information here is not sufficient to help you make an informed comparison. Samples:

- 101 Dalmatians printed mouse with mouse pad from Delta Millenium
- Hewlett-Packard 720C DeskJet printer, 600 dpi, 8 pages per minute black, 4 pages per minute color
- ISDN interface module for the 3COM router
- Parallel-port LoopB test plug from Sun

**Search:** Yes
**Photos:** No
**Ordering:** Online
**Gift Wrap:** No
**Delivery:** Ground

## Anything PC

http://www.anythingpc.com

Well, almost anything. They claim to provide more than 170,000 products, which is certainly a lot, but even with that many items, they have to select a limited number of vendors. This is a good place to come if you don't care too much who makes the product. They offer some brand names and some no-names in each category. Information about the gear is slender. Samples:

- 10-pack of ZIP 100 MB cartridges for PC
- 64 MB memory upgrade for TNT 2000

- License for Adsmconn Agent for Lotus Notes (no media, no documentation, just the license)

**Search:** Yes
**Photos:** No
**Ordering:** Online
**Gift Wrap:** No
**Delivery:** Ground, 2nd Day, Overnight

## Backpack Computing

http://www.shopbuilder.com/
backpack

A boutique offering selected notebook computers from major manufacturers, with plenty of RAM, hard disk space, and bright displays. And, yes, they offer backpacks to carry your laptop in. Shipping takes place within one or two business days of your order, if the item is in stock. Sample items:

- Hewlett-Packard OmniBook 2100, with 233 MMX, 32 MB RAM, 3 GB hard drive, 24X CD-ROM, 12.1" dual scan SVGA display
- Kensington Notebook Backpack, with water-resistant coating, double-zipper closure, and padded straps
- Xircom CreditCard 56K modem

**Search:** No
**Photos:** Yes
**Ordering:** Online, Phone
**Gift Wrap:** No
**Delivery:** Ground, 2nd day, overnight

## Buycomp

http://www.buy.com/

Lowest prices guaranteed at this site. If you find a lower price within seven days of your invoice date, from an authorized reseller, Buycomp refunds the difference, and gives you a dollar. This computer store is one of a series of BuyThis and BuyThat online shops, featuring software, books, videos, and games. Here you can have computer products listed by manufacturer, you can work by categories, or you can

use the fast search. Tables let you make comparisons between similar equipment from different vendors. Special deals appear at the top of categories, and prices, in general, are very low. Plus, you can lease as well as buy. They offer 24-hour order tracking. Samples:

- 100 MB ZIP drive without cartridge, but with power cable, with CD-ROM with software
- Hewlett-Packard DesignJet 3500 CP with 600 dpi photo-quality color on 54-inch paper
- Kodak DC240 Digital Camera, with 1.3 megapixels

**Search:** Good
**Photos:** A few
**Ordering:** Online Purchase and Lease, Phone
**Gift Wrap:** No
**Delivery:** Ground, 2nd Day, Overnight

## CDW

http://www.cdw.com

With 80,000 computer-related products, CDW tries to be a complete one-stop shop. In fact, they claim to be the top seller of brands such as Compaq, IBM, Microsoft, and Toshiba. CDW provides a list of similar computers (like all the 400 MHz computers in the store), you click a few, and CDW shows a detailed table comparing those, so you can decide which one will work best for you. Plus, CDW shows you reviews from Ziff-Davis publications such as *PC Magazine* so you can see what the critics think. If there's a rebate or coupon offered by the manufacturer, you can find out about that, too. Before rebate, the prices here are low, although not rock bottom. If you register, you can get buyer's alerts on products whose prices you want to track. Most orders are shipped the day they are placed (up to 9:00 p.m. Central Time). Samples:

- 3Com SuperStack II Switch 2000 Token Ring switch
- Hewlett-Packard PhotoSmart Photo Printer, with extended cable, and color and black cartridges
- Ms Actimates Interactive Barney
- Sharp Electronics handheld Mobilon personal computer with 16MB of memory, high-contrast color screen, and 33.6K modem

**Search:** Yes

Photos: Yes
Ordering: Online
Gift Wrap: No
Delivery: Ground

# CompUSA Direct

http://www.compusa.com

We've bought one computer through the retail CompUSA store, and it's a great machine. We also bought the extended service plan, which promises repairs at your home or office. But when the floppy drive flopped, they lost the repair order, forgot to order the parts, and, uh, well, didn't exactly rush to let us know when they might be coming out to the house. (When we complained, the local store brought us a temporary replacement, which was nice, while we waited for parts from the original manufacturer.) Still, they have a good online store, particularly if you're buying products that won't need servicing. They have hardware, software (in boxes and downloads), and accessories, with special clearance sections, an Apple Store (and showcases for other manufacturers, if you want to shop by brand), and a section just for IBM employees. Samples:

- 500 MHz computer, 128 MB RAM, 13.5 GB hard drive, DVD-ROM
- Apple Studio 17-inch monitor in blue translucent enclosure
- Dragon Naturally Speaking Preferred speech recognition software
- Laser printer with full-color photorealistic quality, network ready, 16 pages per minute in black and white, 5 pages per minute color
- Sony VAIO computer, with video ports in front and back, ZIP drive

Search: Yes
Photos: Yes
Ordering: Online, Phone
Gift Wrap: No
Delivery: Ground

# Computers4Sure

http://
www.computers4sure.com

A good range of products (40,000 when we visited) at good prices. Tabs take you to categories such as modems, scanners, and storage. They offer order tracking through UPS and FedEx. Samples:

- Princeton 17-inch Ultra 72 monitor, with .27mm dot pitch
- Sony Mavica MVC-FD81 digital camera for stills, video, and audio with 3X optical zoom, 1024 x 768 resolution
- Toshiba Satellite notebook, 45 MB RAM, 56K modem, 24X CD ROM

Search: Yes
Photos: Only for specials
Ordering: Online
Gift Wrap: No
Delivery: 2nd Day, Overnight

# Dell

http://www.dell.com

The biggest, most profitable maker of personal computers offers a well-organized site at which you can buy computers for small business, school, home, and home office, as well as giant corporations. They even sell reconditioned Dell products, with guarantees. We have bought two computers through their site, but one arrived with the inside cables unattached. Someone had forgotten to connect them to the hard drive, the CD-ROM drive, and the ZIP drive. We found technical support abysmal. But plenty of other folks swear by Dell. Our hunch: They make their money by turning capital over faster than anyone else, and we think that the very speed with which they work may occasionally get them into trouble. On the other hand, when their products work, they are inexpensive (often the cheapest in the category) and slick. The site itself is fun. For instance, in the home section, they show a computer system, and as you hover over different areas of the image, you can click to find out about the components. The software that lets you put together a customized computer is simple and easy to use. Next door, a little boutique sells DellGear such as mugs, teddy bears, mouse pads, and totes with the Dell logo. Ship date depends on how many components you've asked to be added to the standard computer. Samples:

- Dell Dimension mini-tower computer with power game pack
- Dell Inspiron notebook computer, 366 MHz, 14.1-inch Active Matrix display, with 10GB hard drive, 1.5-inches thin

**Search:** Yes
**Photos:** Small
**Ordering:** Online Purchase and Leasing
**Gift Wrap:** No
**Delivery:** Ground, 2nd Day, Overnight

## Gateway

http://www.gw2k.com

Yes, these are the folks with the boxes that look like Holstein cows. We've bought two Gateways through their site, and we've found the service friendly, reliable, and fast. Tech support has been outstanding. Their prices are competitive (the lowest, or almost the lowest) even when compared with other less-well-known brands. They help you customize your own special computer (which may take a little longer to build), and they even offer "remanufactured PCs," which look like bargains, and plenty of peripherals. If you want, you can get Internet access bundled with some personal computers, or you can have them preset a combined Yahoo and Gateway site as your Web start page. You can download drivers for your peripheral equipment, tech information, and support plans. Payment plans include "easy pay," credit card, and the Gateway 2000 Moola MasterCard. Sample items:

- Beanie the Cow, a velour doll available from the Spot Shop
- Laptop with 14.1-inch active matrix TFT color display, Pentium II, 366 MHz, 10 GB removable hard drive
- Remanufactured portable PC with 13.3-inch active matrix display, Intel Pentium II at 233 MHz, with 64 MB of RAM, CD-ROM drive, and floppy drive

**Search:** Yes
**Photos:** Yes
**Ordering:** Online, Phone
**Gift Wrap:** No
**Delivery:** Ground

## Gigabuys

http://gigabuys.us.dell.com

Run by the computer manufacturer Dell, this site sells Dell's and other folks' accessories, such as keyboards, mice, joysticks, as well as hard drives, printers, and even computers. If you own a Dell machine, the site will tell you the name of every Gigabuy product that's compatible with it (mostly from Dell), but you can shop here even if you aren't a Dell-o-phile. The site also lists the other manufacturers' phone numbers and Web addresses, so you can go there for more info or to make actual purchases. Ship date is within two days of order. Samples:

- Canon BJC-5000 Color Bubble Jet Printer
- Hewlett-Packard PhotoSmart glossy photographic paper
- Iomega ZIP drive for 100 MB removable disks

**Search:** Yes
**Photos:** Not many
**Ordering:** Online
**Gift Wrap:** No
**Delivery:** Ground, 2nd Day, Overnight

## Inksite

http://www.inksite.com

A small but very friendly shop, Inksite focuses on "consumable" ink-jet products from a few vendors. Inksite offers almost half off what you would pay for original-brand cartridges in a local store. They have bulk inks for experienced and continual recyclers (in pints, gallons, and drums), individual refill ink systems, and inexpensive paper. Because they spend all day thinking about ink-jet printing, they have interesting information about the various vendors and their marketing efforts, paper stiffness, and ease of use. They are surveying visitors to find out how they feed their printers, and, on our visit, more people refilled their own cartridges than bought cartridges from their printer's manufacturer. Sample products:

- Konica photo quality ink-jet paper, 15 sheets to a pack
- Repeat-O-Type bulk black ink in gallon bottle, for Hewlett-Packard DeskJet 500 series

**Search:** No
**Photos:** Some
**Ordering:** Online
**Gift Wrap:** No
**Delivery:** Ground, 3rd Day, 2nd Day, Overnight

# Mac Mall, PC Mall

http://www.cc-inc.com

Several stores in one: a small business shop, a home computing shop, clearance center, education area, and a government shop. You can visit additional "stores" for almost two dozen vendors. Prices are good, but not super bargains. An interesting range of products. Samples:

- 500 MHz computer, 128 MB RAM, 19 GB hard drive, 4X DVD, from Hewlett-Packard
- Kensington WebRacer controller with preset buttons to go directly to particular sites, or jump to email, four-way menu button to speed use of bookmarks or favorite lists, buttons for commands such as Back, Print
- Polaroid photo printer
- Sierra's *Half Life*, action game
- Wacom ArtZ II 6" x 8" graphics tablet, factory refurbished, limit 5 to a customer, no dealers

**Search:** Yes
**Photos:** Yes
**Ordering:** Online, Phone
**Gift Wrap:** No
**Delivery:** Ground, Overnight

# MacWorks

http://www.macworks.com

A good Mac site with cartoons, specials, and reconditioned Apple equipment, from computers to cards. Samples:

- Apple 24X CD-ROM drive
- Refurbished LaserWriter 8500, 600 dpi, 20 pages per minute, 11" x 17" pages, with Ethernet, LocalTalk, and Parallel connections

**Search:** No
**Photos:** Yes
**Ordering:** Phone, Fax, Email
**Gift Wrap:** No
**Delivery:** 3rd Day, 2nd Day, Overnight

# Microwarehouse

http://www.warehouse.com

You've probably gotten their paper catalogs, with blurbs for same-day shipping for overnight delivery (not always available everywhere). We've bought software from them, and found them fast and reliable. This site offers major-brand computers, drives, memory, modems, printers, and software. You get a pretty good range of preassembled machines, but you can't mix and match, configuring your own special system. For many products, they suggest extras or accessories you might want to add, such as paper and cartridges for a printer. Most orders shipped same day. Samples:

- 256 MB PC, 100 DIMM SDRAM, 100 MHz 8 nanoseconds
- Clearance sale on Epson Stylus color printer, refurbished
- Microtek Scanmaker, flatbed scanner at 600 x 1200 dpi

**Search:** Yes
**Photos:** Some
**Ordering:** Online, Phone
**Gift Wrap:** No
**Delivery:** Ground, Overnight, Saturday

# NECX

http://necxdirect.necx.com

Started as a global swap site for more than 200 million electronic, computer, and network products, NECX has branched into an online store focusing on office and personal high-tech. Last year's revenues topped $420 million. The site sells complete computers, chips, peripherals, and software. They even help you decide which memory chip is right for your upgrade, through the Memory Configurator. They also offer side-by-side comparisons, rebates and coupons, and specs on many products. For end-of-life, open-box, and demo equipment (mostly add-on or insertable gizmos like disk drives, memory, and modems), see their Outlet Center. Products are shipped from one of 34 warehouses around the country. For Saturday delivery, call on Friday. Samples:

- 8X/20X speed CD-Recorder with SCSI connections
- Compaq Deskpro EP Celeron 400 MHz, 64 MB RAM, 6.4 GB hard drive, 32X CD-ROM drive, with chassis that converts from desktop to tower
- Video capture card and color camera for video conferencing

**Search:** Yes
**Photos:** Small
**Ordering:** Online, Phone
**Gift Wrap:** No
**Delivery:** Ground, 2nd Day, Overnight, Saturday

# Notebook Superstore

http://
www.notebooksuperstore.com

Narrow focus, limited number of models from each vendor, and same-day shipping add up to speed, if you spot the model you want. If you have already done some homework, come here to see if the model you want is being sold. Samples:

- Toshiba laptop, 300 MHz, 64 MB RAM, 6.4 GB hard drive, floppy disk drive, 24X CD-ROM drive, 13.3" diagonal active matrix display
- Digital HiNote VP 745 laptop, 266 MHz, 48 MB

RAM, 4 GB hard drive, 20X CD-ROM drive, 13.3" diagonal active-matrix display

**Search:** No
**Photos:** Some
**Ordering:** Online, Phone, Fax
**Gift Wrap:** No
**Delivery:** 3rd Day, 2nd Day, Overnight

# PC Connection

http://www.pcconnection.com

An award-winning mail-order company goes online. When you arrive, you can flip a switch to see only Mac products, or only PC, or everything. They let you focus on small business, education, corporate, or government products, set up a small-business account, bid on auctions, and get help from a wizard called Smart Selector. Prices are reasonably low. After the sale, they offer order tracking, and more tech info than most sites. If you want overnight delivery be sure to order before 2:45 A.M. Eastern Time. Samples:

- Cisco Catalyst 2924 XL Switch with 24 autosensing ports at 10 or 100 Mps speeds
- ClarisWorks for Kids with Free Lunchbag
- Macintosh Workgroup Server G3, 400 MHz, twin 9 GB drives, 256 MB DRAM, 4 PCI slots, 10/100 BASE T Ethernet connector, with preinstalled AppleShare software

**Search:** Yes
**Photos:** Some
**Ordering:** Online, Phone, Fax
**Gift Wrap:** No
**Delivery:** Overnight, 2nd Day

# PriceSCAN

http://www.pricescan.com

Great idea! These folks don't sell anything themselves, but they read magazine ads and run their bots through sites that sell computer gear, to find which vendor offers the best deal on almost any product. We have found they located the best deals on specific configurations of computers, often spotting a best price a few hundred dollars lower than bargain sites we'd visited. If price alone is your main concern, come here first. You may discover some dealers you never heard of. Clicking the dealer name takes you to the site. Remember, though, that prices way below the average (shown in a graph for each product) raise questions of credibility. PriceSCAN lets you see whether your favorite site is coming close to the lowest price. If you see that a familiar dealer is charging only a few bucks more, you may decide to buy there anyway, because you know you can count on friendly service and good support. How much is reliability worth to you? PriceSCAN claims it takes no money from the vendors mentioned; instead, it makes money off banner ads, and, to maintain independence, removes vendors who do not honor advertised prices. Sample info:

- Graph of the high, average, and low prices over the last six months for the Hewlett-Packard DeskJet 720C printer
- List of computer vendors
- List of price quotes for the DeskJet 720C, collected over the last month, most in the last few days, with vendor name, price, link, and, sometimes, the vendor's 800 number

**Search:** Yes
**Photos:** No
**Ordering:** Via Vendor
**Gift Wrap:** No
**Delivery:** No

# RJTech

http://www.rjtech.com

Feeling brave? Want to build a computer yourself? RJ will help you find the components you need, if they are fairly standard. Or you can pick what you want, and they will assemble the computer for you, for less than most name brands. RJ has a limited number of suppliers, not many exotic items; and, when we visited, absolutely no printers. They offer techies good background on subjects like parity, removing old SIMMS, and, "What's the difference between EDO and regular FPM memory?" Sample items:

- Intel Pentium II 500 MHz central processing unit (CPU)

- V. 90 Lucent Voice Internal PCI Modem, 56 Kps

**Search:** Yes
**Photos:** No
**Ordering:** Online, Phone, Fax
**Gift Wrap:** No
**Delivery:** Ground, 3rd Day, 2nd Day, Overnight, Saturday

# Shopping.com

http://www.shopping.com

Good prices, and good info on a wide range of computer hardware, without a lot of items in each category. Computers are just one of their many lines (from patio furniture to books and back), but if you need something generic, and don't care exactly which manufacturer it comes from, you may get it inexpensively at this mall. Samples:

- Graphics Blaster Riva TNT with 16MB AGP, true color, with fast refresh, for 2-D and 3-D games
- Office Connect ADSL Router with 4 ports, and 10Base-T hub from 3COM
- Palm IIIx Connected Organizer

**Search:** Yes
**Photos:** Yes
**Ordering:** Online, Phone
**Gift Wrap:** No
**Delivery:** Ground

# TigerDirect

http://www.tigerdirect.com

Whole computers, components, and "refurbished" (previously owned) computers. They offer a few suggested systems at excellent prices, and let you put together one you like, within the range of the most commonly requested functions for home and office. Their "value line" offers especially good deals. With some systems, they will come and install at your home. We've used their software store with pleasure. Orders placed by 9:30 p.m. EST on a weekday are shipped that day, overnight for in-stock items up to five pounds, or 2nd Day for heavier orders. Samples:

- Dual Pentium II server
- Home computer system with 300 MHz chip, 64 MB of RAM, 4.3 GB hard disk, and 56.6K modem

**Search:** Yes
**Photos:** Not many
**Ordering:** Online
**Gift Wrap:** No
**Delivery:** Overnight, 2nd Day

## Voltex

http://
www.voltexcomputers.com

Voltex focuses on sales items, special offers, and exclusive deals. They sell parts, not whole computers. You may not find exactly the CPU, hard drive, motherboard, or scanner that you want, but if you are willing to settle for something close, you can save a lot of money. Samples:

- 42X CD-ROM
- Pentium II motherboard with sound

**Search:** No
**Photos:** A few, small
**Ordering:** Online
**Gift Wrap:** No
**Delivery:** Ground, 3rd Day, 2nd Day, Overnight

## WebShopper

http://www.webshopper.com

Drawing on the 290 magazines, 170 Web sites, and 41 market research centers of the International Data Group (IDG), this site offers you tons of info about hardware and software, plus the ability to order the products through other companies, known as resellers. Each reseller has a special toll-free customer service number for folks buying through WebShopper, with specially trained representatives. WebShopper positions itself as "an objective consumer advocate." The site does not endorse any particular product or reseller, and claims not to alter the reviews, award lists, buying advice, and product roundups from their contributing

publications. With popular products, you get to choose between the resellers, who compete on price and service. Welcome addition to the product info: a glossary of terms, and how-to tips on common problems and upgrades. One caution: When you get email confirmation of your order from the reseller, make sure the price is what you expected, because the resellers may have changed it before WebShopper got the news. Samples:

- Eizo Nanao flat-panel LCD monitor, 18" viewing area, less than 8" deep, for mounting "like a painting on the wall," or on a swing arm
- Kodak inkjet snapshot 4" x 6" paper, 36 sheets
- Sony Mavica photo printer with its own floppy disk drive, video in and video out connections to grab TV images

**Search:** Yes
**Photos:** Some
**Ordering:** Online, Phone
**Gift Wrap:** No
**Delivery:** Overnight

## Wholesell.com

http://www.wholesell.com

Some of the lowest prices for computer gear appear on this site. How do they do it? They negotiate with the actual vendors of computers and components to get volume discounts, then charge you 3% to 7% above that, as a "price negotiating fee," built into the price they offer to you. If you have a problem or need support, you must go to the original manufacturer. You can order a complete computer, have them put one together following your specs, or just buy parts. There are, naturally, more no-name vendors than brand names in the mix, and some items come without much information. But then, how much information do you want about a hard drive? Samples:

- CD Dupe-It! Stand Alone 2X/6X CD Copier
- Hewlett-Packard Officejet PRO 1175CXI 600 x 600 dpi color printer-copier-scanner
- Nimble 100 MB ZIP drive

**Search:** No
**Photos:** Yes
**Ordering:** Online

**Gift Wrap:** No
**Delivery:** Ground, 2nd Day, Overnight

## Zones.com

`http://www.zones.com`

Another team of mail-order folks who have gone
online, these zones are based on the catalogs you may
know as PC Zone, MacZone, AuctionZone, or U-
name-it Zone. The online zones offer selected computer and peripherals, plus downloadable software.
They seem to have a rather short list of manufacturers,
focused on the most popular items. If you've already
had a good experience with their mail-order operation,
as we have, you may feel at home here. Good product
info. If you order on a weekday, they ship the same
day. If you want a Saturday delivery, you have to call
them to make sure it's feasible. Samples:

- Connectix Virtual Game Station so two people
  can play Sony PlayStation® games on your factory
  original G3 Mac (no upgrade cards!) and OS 8 or
  later
- Downloadable version of Symantec Norton
  Utilities (new or upgrade)
- Auction of Apple Lime iMac

**Search:** Yes
**Photos:** Yes
**Ordering:** Online Purchase. Bid, or Lease, Phone
**Gift Wrap:** No
**Delivery:** Ground, 3rd Day, Overnight, Saturday

## Ready for more? Try these chapters:

- Consumer Electronics
- Software
- Software for Kids

# Consumer Electronics

Some famous electronics stores have not yet moved to Web sales. Led on by blurbs such as "convenient online ordering," you might go to their sites, only to find that although they have put their catalogs on the Web, you can't really order anything over the Internet. To buy something you may have to make a phone call, print out a form and fax it in, or get in the car and go to a local store. But we have found some real Web stores, many with thousands of electronic products, others with just a few very special ones. Here, then, are the wonderful, quirky, personal, and fascinating Web stores dealing in consumer electronics.

## 800.com

http://www.800.com

Here's a site that understands why some of us love the Internet experience. They do a lot more than sell products; they host discussions, post classified ads, and offer a lot of information about most products, focusing on home theater, audio, and portable electronics, plus plenty of movies and music to load into the gear. Their slogan is "High performance gear for the couch potato." We identified right away. The site invites email, and, if you want, emails their detailed product descriptions to you or a friend. Product descriptions often include articles and advice about the item, and customer reviews (if any). You can get a comparison chart on any products you select within a category, so you can figure out which product fits your needs best. There's also an active discussion area with several threads, where customers talk to each other about the products and their experience on the site. Shipping varies with availability of product

(advertised in listing). Most electronics under 30 pounds go 3rd Day, after that. Heavier gear goes by Ground. Some free shipping. Sample items:

- Aiwa Home Theater System with Dolby Pro Logic® Surround System, 3-disc changer
- One-touch remote from Harman Kardon
- Sharp MD-MS 702 Portable MiniDisc Player

**Search:** Yes
**Photos:** Yes
**Ordering:** Online
**Gift Wrap:** No
**Delivery:** Ground, 3rd Day

## Advance Recording Products

http://www.tapeweb.com

If you care about the quality of your audio or video, listen up! This place is full of tape: magnetic media for recording audio and video, from major manufacturers like BASF, Fuji, Maxell, Sony, TDK. They carry analog reel-to-reel tapes, digital audiotapes, professional videotape. They also duplicate audiotapes and print your label right on the cassettes. Samples:

- Empty advance reel, 5" clear plastic, with small hub, carton of 180
- Maxell digital audiotape (DAT), 124 minutes, carton of 10
- Professional broadcast cartridge, audio, FM Station, 10 seconds, carton of 24

**Search:** No
**Photos:** No
**Ordering:** Online, Phone, Fax
**Gift Wrap:** No
**Delivery:** Ground

## American Digital

http://www.am-dig.com

Wholesale digital recording equipment and media! You should probably know what you are doing before you venture into this techie site, but if you do, you can earn digital dollars redeemable for products or prizes. Sample products:

- Maxell 180-minute digital audiotape, minimum of 5 tapes
- Philips CDR765 dual-well CD recording deck
- Sony Home Mini Disc Deck

**Search:** No
**Photos:** A few
**Ordering:** Online, Phone
**Gift Wrap:** No
**Delivery:** Ground, 2nd Day, Overnight

# Calculated Industries

http://www.calculated.com

These folks offer calculators tailored for particular jobs, such as concrete pouring, plotting your position at sea, estimating painting jobs, remodeling your patio. These neat specialty calculators are built from scratch for individual jobs, so every button is relevant. Some even exchange data with a personal computer. Most come with battery-saving automatic shut-off, vinyl case, and a Lithium battery. Samples:

- NautiCalc Plus for boaters calculating speed, time, distance, course triangulation, fuel range, efficiency, capacity, and conversion from nautical miles and fathoms
- Pocket Handyman IV® for do-it-yourselfers and woodworkers, calculates circumference, circle area, arc length, weight per volume, material costs, conversions of square and cubic formats
- Real Estate Master IIx® for solving financing problems, taxes, insurance, amortization schedules, rent-vs.-buy calculations

**Search:** No
**Photos:** Yes
**Ordering:** Online, Phone, Fax, Email
**Gift Wrap:** No
**Delivery:** Ground

# Cassette House

http://www.tape.com

If you want something to record onto, such as digital audiotape, blank cassettes, blank CDs, or minidiscs,

visit the little red cassette house, and opt for the online store. Prices are good on bulk items. Information is minimal. They ship products on the next business day, Ground. Call for 3rd Day, 2nd Day, or Overnight deliveries. Samples:

- 100-pack, C-45 BASF chrome cassettes
- 50-pack, bulk Kodak VHS videotapes, 10 minutes each

**Search:** Yes, in online store
**Photos:** No
**Ordering:** Online, Phone, Fax
**Gift Wrap:** No
**Delivery:** Ground, 3rd Day, 2nd Day, Overnight

# Electronic Marketplace

http://www.emrkt.com

Within a large marketplace, going down Electric Avenue takes you to Ben's House of Electronics and several other specialty shops, all tied in to the same ordering system. Together, these shops offer some fascinating gadgets, as well as regular electronic stuff and "practical" items such as radar detectors. With some products, they provide magazine-style articles explaining what the gizmo does and how it works.

- Alpan Solar Pathway Light, with solar cell to collect enough energy to power a fluorescent light at night, without wires, on a post you can place in the ground next to a walkway
- CatScram infrared motion detector with ultrasonic speaker to deter cats from surfaces

**Search:** No
**Photos:** Yes
**Ordering:** Online, Phone, Fax, Mail
**Gift Wrap:** No
**Delivery:** Ground

# Electronics.Net

http://electronics.net

"The biggest electronics store everywhere!" We're not sure how they measure big, but this site, one of the Cybershop fleet, is dedicated to electronics, including auto equipment, cameras, camcorders, home audio, home office stuff, personal care items, telephones, TV, and video. In each of about 60 categories, they offer a handful of products (from two or three to a dozen) from a few manufacturers, at substantial discounts from retail. "We will not be undersold!" Within 10 days of purchase, they will beat a lower price from a listed competitor by 10%, match another competitor's price, or refund your money. Some categories that we expected, such as DVD players, were not represented when we visited. For each product, they offer a photo (or two), a table of features (not always completely filled in), and specs. For orders placed by 3 P.M., New Jersey time, you can get 2nd Day delivery, or Overnight Standard or Priority (except for large, bulky items, on which the delivery varies). Samples:

- Conair 1875-watt hairdryer with 3 heat settings, 2 speeds, removable air filter, 8' cord
- RCA digital satellite system, with 8-event scheduler, 32-bit processor, digital-optical output
- Sharp 3 Viewcam, 64X zoom, stabilized, with 3" color LCD screen, 100 minutes continuous recording
- Water Pik Personal Dental Center, with conical plaque remover

**Search:** Excellent
**Photos:** Small and big
**Ordering:** Online, Phone
**Gift Wrap:** No
**Delivery:** Ground, 2nd Day, Overnight

# ElectroWeb

http://electroweb.com

We love the accuracy and resolution of DVD, but we haven't taken the next step, to record in that format. If you are already recording in digital format, and need to buy tape or disks in volume, this store is a good source for blank media for recording in DVD, CDR, and other digital formats. If you know what you want, come here. If you are hovering, you won't learn enough here to decide between competing products. Elsewhere on this site are cordless phones, regular phones, portable audio, and radar detectors, from a very limited number of vendors, but with neat special items

such as Rolodex™'s information manager (with docking station). Samples:

- DVD rewritable disk, 5.2 GB
- Ricoh 10-pack recordable CDs, 74 minutes or 650 MB blank in jewel boxes
- Timex Data Link Model 150 Watch, with software to transfer scheduling info from a PC

**Search:** Yes
**Photos:** A few
**Ordering:** Online, Phone, Fax
**Gift Wrap:** No
**Delivery:** Ground, 3rd Day, 2nd Day

# Global Mart

http://www.globe-mart.com

If you have a hard time getting out of a hardware store without buying a few impulse items, Global Mart may be tempting. Lots of small images (with labels) form the menus that take you through this visually attractive site offering neat power tools, communications devices, audio and video. Samples:

- Cordless 3/8" adjustable clutch drill/driver kit
- Freeplay® solar-powered AM/FM radio
- Magellan Color Trak Global Positioning System
- Portable solar-power panel with alligator clips to trickle-charge 12-volt marine, automotive, or RV batteries
- Color-graphing scientific calculator

**Search:** No
**Photos:** Yes
**Ordering:** Online, Phone
**Gift Wrap:** No
**Delivery:** Ground, 2nd Day, Overnight

# Navstation

http://www.maritech.com

When we sailed in the waters off Portland, Maine, we loved matching the islands to the charts, but we never had to use the stars to figure out where we were. Here's an electronic way to navigate your boat by satellite, using electronic charting systems for sailors. This is a

Yahoo store, so your shopping basket shows any other outstanding purchases from Yahoo stores. Samples:

- VDO Logic Chart Plotter Map 8, with high-definition 8" display, 500 way-points, interface with a Global Positioning System (GPS) sensor via 10-meter cable
- Visual Navigation Suite from Nobeltec, including features of their GPS Planner, Tides, and Visual Navigator programs, with animated current arrows and tide bars, using NOAA/BSB charts

**Search:** Yes
**Photos:** Small
**Ordering:** Online
**Gift Wrap:** No
**Delivery:** Ground, 3rd Day, 2nd Day, Overnight

# Smart Home

http://www.smarthome.com

Our walls are made out of thick adobe bricks, and we have to use a cement drill just to slide a phone line through, so we haven't moved up to total house automation. But if you're interested in trying to hook every electronic device together, to get better control over heating, air-conditioning, alarm system, door, and even music and TV, browse this shop. They offer gizmos and programs to control electronic devices throughout your house. They provide pictures or screenshots, and a few bulleted items about each product. Samples:

- Home-theater system to control most audio or video components and devices through a single touch-screen
- Motorized drape system, using remote
- Low-voltage electrified door hinges to work with wireless remote on your key chain
- Wireless weather sensor in weather-resistant shelter, solar panel, regulator, and rechargeable battery
- IBM Mousehouse 2.0 and Home Director Kit for the Mac, to control home devices realtime, or via timed schedules

**Search:** Yes
**Photos:** Yes
**Ordering:** Online, Phone

**Gift Wrap:** No
**Delivery:** Ground

# Speak To Me!

http://www.clickshop.com/speak

"Give the gift that says something!" Indeed, everything they sell talks. And they sure have a lot of talkative objects, such as clocks, games, key chains, lighthouses, magnets, mugs, music boxes, pens, and Star Trek items. Visit this site just to see what people have come up with. Sample devices:

- Budweiser Cooler musical bank (well, at least it makes the sound of a beer tab popping, and a beer pouring into a glass, when you insert a coin)
- Musical Hummingbird Fountain (as you walk past the sensor, water starts flowing, and the fountain plays one of six love songs)
- Voice-It personal note recorders

**Search:** No
**Photos:** Yes
**Ordering:** Online, Phone, Fax
**Gift Wrap:** No
**Delivery:** Ground

# Spider Gear

http://www.spidergear.com

No, they don't sell electronics that spiders can use. But their site must appeal to the electronic spiders who go out on the Web and discover the most interesting sites. The background of their home page is gray with the names of all the electronics manufacturers who make their home audio and video, car audio, headphones, and musical instruments. The partners have set this site up as a co-op, so that the membership numbers can give the site some clout when negotiating with vendors. You don't have to join up, but if you do, you get emails alerting you to new shipments, so you can buy before the public. Also, you get a 1% rebate on whatever you spend during a year, to be applied to a purchase in the next year. Most orders are shipped within two days. Sample products:

- *Boomerang 2* with speech recognition, from Dictaphone
- KLH Model 146 Refurbished 40-watt, 3-way surround-sound speakers for indoor or outdoor use
- *Lace Electric Guitar with Sensor Gold Pick-up,* candy-apple red

**Search:** No
**Photos:** Yes
**Ordering:** Online, Phone, Fax
**Gift Wrap:** No
**Delivery:** Ground

## SutterTel

http://www.suttertel.com

Rick Sutter looks for appealing electronics items that most stores make a big margin on. He slashes that margin, so you can buy these items at or near wholesale prices. Then he throws in free shipping, too. As a result, his site offers great bargains on a few hundred items that are normally expensive, or at least mid-range in price. We found the write-ups and illustrations useful. He also provides a neat service, by which you can jump directly to technical support from a manufacturer, if you want. Meanwhile, Sutter stresses that his phone lines are answered by real human beings, and fast. (We can testify to that. When we emailed him a question, he called us back within ten minutes).

- 900 MHz wireless stereo headphones, transmit through walls and floors
- DISH network satellite system with one-year contract for programming for America's Top 100 package
- Uniden 2-line dual keypad 900 MHz cordless phone with speakerphone, 20-number speed dial

**Search:** No
**Photos:** Nice and big, but you have to ask for them
**Ordering:** Online, Phone
**Gift Wrap:** No
**Delivery:** Ground

## Tek Discount Warehouse

http://www.tekgallery.com

In Maine, we like the small-town general stores, with the potbelly stove and barrels of dog biscuits; this store reminds us of those warm, crowded shelves, but with a difference. This is a Yahoo store with amps, camcorders, cassette decks, equalizers, headphones, keyboards, radar detectors, and TVs. They have a reassuring variety of major brands, with pretty good prices. Samples:

- Gemini CDJ-1200 Single CD Player with digital output for first-generation transfer to DAT, CD-R, and samplers, with precision frame search, extra-large jog wheel, pitch lock
- Koss JR/900 Cordless Headphones, with 5-channel stereo, to listen to music anywhere in the house
- Teac-A-H500 Integrated Amplifier, 80 watts per channel, toroidal power transformer

**Search:** Yes
**Photos:** Yes
**Ordering:** Online, Phone
**Gift Wrap:** No
**Delivery:** Ground

## Total Mart

http://www.totalmart.com

A bright, cheerful site, with low prices on car audio, DVDs, home audio, microwaves, phones, TVs, video tape recorders, video cameras. In each category, they have several different name-brand manufacturers' goods, at different price points, so you have some real choices. Good list of features for most products. Also, a nice tutorial on how to shop. Samples:

- Panasonic full-size white microwave oven, 1,100-watt, with auto cooking, auto reheat, auto defrost, and popcorn key
- JVC Dolby Digital Receiver
- JVC Personal CD Player, with triple shock protection, 10-second shock-proof memory, high-speed pickup servo, dynamic suspension system, 13-hour playback

**Search:** Yes
**Photos:** Yes

**Ordering:** Online
**Gift Wrap:** No
**Delivery:** Ground

# Some batteries required? Need some other electric or electronic stuff?  Plug into these chapters:

- Batteries
- Home Office Supplies
- Photography
- Surveillance Gear
- TV & Video Gear
- Video & Computer Games

# Craft & Art Supplies

Like kids running into the art room at school, we kept being tempted to try out a little of this and a lot of that on these sites. These stores supply the raw materials, manufactured goo, and special tools for handworking baskets, making paper, grinding paints, sculpting, and just generally playing around. The vast majority of sites dealing with crafts are simply informational—a brochure or catalog, with the address of the physical store, or a phone number. We've culled the stores you can really order from over the Web.

## Art and Woodcrafter Supply

http://www.artwoodcrafter.com

Like a great old-fashioned hardware store, this site has items you never knew you needed. We remember Vermont barn sales like this place, except here the items are new. Shipping is free on orders over $75. Samples:

- Fancy finial with 3/8" tenon
- One-sided sanding pads
- Quartz bezel fit-ups
- Scroll-saw blades
- Spandrell balls
- Spoked wheels
- Sponge brushes
- Wire-curling tool

**Search:** Yes
**Photos:** Yes
**Ordering:** Online, Fax, Phone
**Gift Wrap:** No
**Delivery:** Ground, 3rd Day, 2nd Day, Overnight

## BasketPatterns

http://www.basketpatterns.com

A home business created by folks who couldn't find a nearby store with basket patterns. They pack up and ship orders, oh, two or three times a week, but they monitor the Web site day and night, and respond to email personally. They offer patterns in many designs and weaving levels. These baskets are fantastic, creative, artistic, colorful, and (mostly) practical. These very inexpensive patterns are arranged by author, and as you browse, you soon spot individual styles varying from cute to classic. Samples:

- Appalachian herb basket
- Cattail earth basket
- Fretwork carryall basket
- Humped-bottom potbelly
- Little catchall
- Noah's basket

**Search:** No
**Photos:** Yes
**Ordering:** Online
**Gift Wrap:** No
**Delivery:** First Class, Priority Mail

## Big Horn Quilts

http://www.bighornquilts.com

Quilts and quilting fabric imitating old designs. You can click to see a larger image of each fabric. Samples:

- Azul Bali elephants on batik by Princess Mirah, of Bali
- Diamond-dot pattern on hunter-green fabric from Springs
- Light-blue fronds on dark-blue background, batik
- Peach wallpaper fabric, with little naked cherubs
- Pink batik

**Search:** Yes
**Photos:** Thumbnail and large
**Ordering:** Online
**Gift Wrap:** Yes
**Delivery:** Airmail

# Charm Woven Labels

`http://www.charmwoven.com`

If you make clothes for friends or customers, or work in a sewing guild, you might want to consider adding the finishing touch, a personal label, made up here. You have to order a minimum of 20 labels in any one style, and they only do wording (not logos or art), but they have a variety of prepared art (needles, skeins, portraits, teddy bears, and borders) that you can choose to surround your text. You just pick the style. Samples:

- Labels with white border with one of 18 colors for the text
- Printed care-instruction labels
- Woven content labels
- Woven size tabs

**Search:** No
**Photos:** Yes
**Ordering:** Online, Phone, Fax, Email
**Gift Wrap:** No
**Delivery:** Express and Airmail

# Cherry Tree Hill Yarn

`http://www.cherryyarn.com`

Cheryl Potter runs this shop from a hill in Vermont, overlooking the Onion River Valley. "We derive inspiration from our panoramic view of the Green Mountains, but we don't kid ourselves: It's cold here in the winter." All of the yarns are processed by hand at the studio. Samples:

- A hank of 100% preshrunk chenille ribbon with put-up of 8 ounces in 130 yards, gauge of two stitches to the inch on size 17 needles, handpainted
- A close-fitting sweater knit with draped neckline and hem with three-quarter-length sleeves, in Champlain Sunset color
- A hank of 50/50 alpaca wool worsted-weight with a gauge of 5.5 stitches and 7.25 rows to the inch on size 4 needles, handpainted

**Search:** No

**Photos:** Yes
**Ordering:** Online, Phone
**Gift Wrap:** No, but they offer gift certificates
**Delivery:** Ground

# Cross Stitches

`http://www.xstitches.com`

Focused on needlepoint, crewel, and cross-stitch items, this site offers a vast array of kits, instructions, and supplies. For instance, their beads come in many forms: antiques, seeds, petites, and bugles. Their fabric ranges from 14 to 32 count. They host a classified ads auction. Good discounts on orders over $10. Shipments go out within 7 business days of order. Shipping is free on orders over $50 after discount. Samples:

- Alphabet afghan design
- Apple Harvest trivet kit with foam insert, styrene base, pushpins, and cardboard template
- Perforated papers
- Place mat how-to leaflets for herb designs
- Q-snap frames

**Search:** Yes
**Photos:** Yes
**Ordering:** Online
**Gift Wrap:** No
**Delivery:** Ground

# Diane's Design

`http://host.fptoday.com/
dianes`

Diane offers a wide variety of stitching supplies, along with a free chart of the month (ready to print out from the Web site). Samples:

- 45mm rotary cutter
- 5mm, 8mm, and Picot lace
- Magnifying light for close work
- Small pumpkin-shaped pincushion
- Stretcher bars to hold your needlepoint or rug hooking stable
- Victorian Potpourri fabric pack

- Wrist ball holder for tatting

**Search:** No
**Photos:** Yes
**Ordering:** Online or call Diane directly
**Gift Wrap:** No
**Delivery:** Ground

## Discount Art Supplies

http://www.discountart.com

You might not expect an art supply store in the White Mountains, but this site puts fall foliage on its home page, and shows a frightening view of Tuckerman Ravine covered with snow, on the page "about us." It's tax free, and they really do discount steeply. They carry major brands of art supplies, such as Grumbacher, Holbein, and Academy, as well as pens, markers, canvas, and art tools. Shipping is free on orders over $100. Samples:

- Acrylic primed medium-texture cotton duck canvas
- Air brush with internal mixing, self-lubricating Teflon needle, for left- or right-handed use, nonslip trigger
- Berol Prismacolor 120-color pencil set
- Environmentally safe, nontoxic brush and hand cleaners

**Search:** No
**Photos:** Yes
**Ordering:** Online, Phone
**Gift Wrap:** Yes
**Delivery:** Ground

## Fascinating Folds

http://www.fascinating-folds.com

This is the land of origami and paper arts. If you cut, make, or mold paper, fold it, pop it up, or marble it, come here. For box-making, collages, decoupage, and origami, this site can keep your hands busy for months. Shipping

is free on orders over $100. Samples:

- 30 sheets of wazome and unryu washi papers, in three sizes
- Book-binding tape, thread, and book cloth
- Kit for making geometric shapes with paper
- Lightweight vellum, slightly translucent, for making paper boxes
- Mold-release mist, to free handcast cotton paper from a terra cotta mold
- Opaline glitter to add when making paper

**Search:** No
**Photos:** Yes
**Ordering:** Online
**Gift Wrap:** No
**Delivery:** Ground

## Frame U.S.A.

http://www.frameusa.com

If you need a bunch of frames for your prints or posters, in standard sizes, come here. They also create custom orders with back-loaded molding or U-channel molding in wood or metal, turning out about 500 pieces in a week. Samples:

- 12 frame shells (without glass)
- 12 green marble mat paper background, on 1/8" foamcore in 24"x 36" frame
- 12 wood frames with real glass, 12" x 8"
- Collage mats 16" x 20", 12 to carton

**Search:** No
**Photos:** A few
**Ordering:** Online
**Gift Wrap:** No
**Delivery:** Ground

## Fruit of the Hands

http://www.fruit-of-the-hands.com

Papier-mâché heaven. You can get kits for making ornaments, boxes, and other papier-mâché paraphernalia, as well as finished papier-mâché products. Samples:

- House models made out of paper-mâché (set of three)
- Papier-mâché kid's pack for making Christmas ornaments with wood cutouts, hearts, stars, jute, paint, paintbrush, and instructions
- Star-shaped gift box made out of paper-mâché, ready for decorating (with ribbon, bells)

**Search:** No
**Photos:** Some color, some black-and-white
**Ordering:** Online, Fax, Phone
**Gift Wrap:** No
**Delivery:** Ground

## Green Drop Ink

http://206.216.201.175

If you do intaglio, monotype, waterless, lithography, relief, or screen printmaking, and can't stand the fumes and harsh solvents, you might want to try out these water-based inks. Naresh Sampat, the founder of the company, claims these are professional grade, and highly permanent, so universities are adopting them because they are nontoxic and ecologically sound.
Samples:

- Pthalo green ink for etching, intaglio
- Universal printmaking ink system, with inks you can modify for waterless lithography, monotype, intaglio, relief, and screen printing
- Water-based ink sampler

**Search:** Yes
**Photos:** No
**Ordering:** Online, Fax, Phone
**Gift Wrap:** No
**Delivery:** Ground

## Hobby Builders Supply

http://www.miniatures.com

A fun supplier of dollhouse kits and miniature-making tools and materials. Typical slogan: "Stick with us for your glues!" Samples:

- 1 jar of dollhouse stucco to give your miniature

Tudor or Southwestern home an authentic look
- 2.8 fluid ounces of fast-drying glue for attaching siding, flooring, to your dollhouse
- 4-piece tweezer set with case
- German doll of handyman with pail and toilet plunger, flexible in many directions
- Ready-to-play firehouse, fully assembled or as a kit, made out of wood trim with a lithographic print of bricks on the outside; large enough to hold one fire truck (no tools required)

**Search:** Yes
**Photos:** A few
**Ordering:** Online
**Gift Wrap:** No
**Delivery:** Ground, 2nd Day

## Nautilus Arts and Crafts

http://www.nautilus-crafts.com

Founded by a Canadian aviator, this shop started by selling shells like the chambered nautilus to craft people. Boy, how they have expanded since those days! They sell tools for polishing stones, carving stone and wood, making clocks, creating jewelry, sawing rock, making stained glass, working with parchment.
Samples:

- Beads of semiprecious stone
- Chiming pendulum for clock assembly
- Combination saw and grinder/polisher with rock vise and slash guard
- Diamond band saw for making curved cuts in glass, thin slabs of stone or tile
- Half-inch fishtail chisel with tapered blade sides
- Parchment perforating tool diamond
- Woodburner with writing tip to sign carvings

**Search:** Gem search
**Photos:** Yes
**Ordering:** Online, Fax, Phone
**Gift Wrap:** No
**Delivery:** Ground

## On the Fringe

`http://www.onthefringe.com`

"If I don't knit, I get cranky," says the T-shirt sold in this small Southwestern yarn center for inexpensive knitting and Navajo Churro roving. Samples:

- 110-yard ball of Hayfield's cotton-blend yarn with vest pattern in chambray
- Kit and pattern to make miniature sheep
- Stitch holder for currently inactive stitches

**Search:** No
**Photos:** A few
**Ordering:** Online, Phone
**Gift Wrap:** No
**Delivery:** Ground

## Pacific Pedestal

`http://www.carmelnet/`
`PacificPedestal`

Show off your small sculptures on a pedestal: that's the message from Carmel, California. This manufacturer produces stands for sculpture, customizing color and lighting if you wish. Samples:

- 50-inch-high circular pedestal in almond
- Square, open column pedestal in matte black with motorized swivel
- Two-tiered square pedestal with lighting

**Search:** No
**Photos:** Yes
**Ordering:** Online
**Gift Wrap:** No
**Delivery:** Ground

## Patchworks

`http://`
`reproductionfabrics.com`

Fabric for quilters—but what fabrics! These cottons reproduce designs from 1775 to 1950, as well as natural indigo-dyed prints. You learn a lot about the history of fabric just browsing. (Did you know that folks made buttons out of metal, horn, bone, and fabric before the English started shipping pressed china buttons in the 19th century?) Typical advice: the indigos may be heavily sized, but soften with one washing, to a delicate feel. "For a more faded look, wash in regular detergent until you get the desired color, then set by washing with Color Shield." Samples:

- 36-inch-wide South African indigo design based on English paisley from the 19th century
- 58-inch-wide cotton with German pink design from 1860–1880
- Calico buttons for undergarments or work dresses
- *Dating Fabrics: A Color Guide, 1800–1960*, 208-page book
- Quilt patterns based on samples in the Daughters of the American Revolution collection of Virginia Tidewater fabrics

**Search:** No
**Photos:** Lush
**Ordering:** Online, Phone, Email
**Gift Wrap:** No
**Delivery:** Ground

## Rex Art

`http://www.rexart.com`

A colorful, efficient site. You can "pick an aisle," or category, search, or browse the gallery. Shipping is free on an individual order of more than $100. Samples:

- Archival box in black
- Children's disposable aprons (100 pack)
- Double-action airbrush kit with acrylic paints, frisket sheets, illustration board
- Gesso brush
- Wooden brush rack with 16 hooks

**Search:** Yes
**Photos:** Yes
**Ordering:** Online
**Gift Wrap:** No
**Delivery:** Ground, 2nd Day

## Scrapbooks 'n More

http://
www.scrapbooksnmore.com

If you work with kids and stickers, albums, or paper punches, this site offers specialized tools for you, items that aren't so easy to find at a stationery store or office-supply place. Samples:

- 2-way glue dispenser with chisel tip
- Memories Forever Leather Premier 12" x 12" black photo album
- Pop-up die cut in two pieces
- Tape squares and corners

**Search:** Yes
**Photos:** Yes
**Ordering:** Online
**Gift Wrap:** No
**Delivery:** Ground

## Sculpture.Org

http://www.sculptor.org

A wonderful site for sculptors, with job listings, links to dozens of sculptors, and an enormous set of links to foundries, machine replication services, and computer-aided sculpture sites. The founder, Richard Collins, makes a little money selling books via Amazon. Samples:

- *How to Carve Wood: A Book of Projects and Techniques*, by Richard Butz
- *The Big Book of Whittling and Woodcarving*, by Elmer Tangerman

**Search:** No
**Photos:** No
**Ordering:** Online link to Amazon.com
**Gift Wrap:** From Amazon
**Delivery:** Ground, 2nd Day

## Sierra Enterprises

http://www.sierra-
enterprises.com

These folks must have a fascinating warehouse. Their site offers plenty of ideas for paper play, fabric crafts, and small finger gear ranging from rubber stamps to iridescent liquid colors. Samples:

- Celtic rooster rubber stamp
- Pinking shears for paper edging
- Gold embossing powder
- Samurai rubber stamp
- Translucent vellum paper for making gift boxes
- Waterproof, acid-free dye-based ink pad in crimson

**Search:** No
**Photos:** Yes
**Ordering:** Online
**Gift Wrap:** No
**Delivery:** Ground

## Sinopia

http://www.sinopia.com

If you like grinding your own colors or creating materials from scratch, this store will supply you with the right stuff for artists, decorators, luthiers, and gilders. Samples:

- 100-gram glass jar with English raw sienna (clay containing iron oxide)
- German cold-pressed linseed oil
- One-quart acrylic glazing liquid (covers 150 to 300 square feet, with extended drying time)
- Poppy oil for use in zinc white (does not yellow)
- Porcelain mortar and pestle faced with rough surfaces for grinding (5-inch diameter bowl)
- Resinous dragon's blood powder for dying

**Search:** No
**Photos:** Few
**Ordering:** Online, Phone, Fax, Email
**Gift Wrap:** No
**Delivery:** Ground, 3rd Day, 2nd Day, Overnight

## Utrecht

`http://www.utrechtart.com`

A manufacturer's site, with painting, printmaking, and graphic supplies. We've used their products extensively, and like them. The online store carries plenty of other folks' products, too, so this site acts as a general art-supply store. Samples:

- 4 Arches watercolor paper rolls, neutral pH, 100% rag, 140 pound, 44.5-inch x 10 yards
- Faber-Castell™ PITT Graphite set, with graphite pencils, crayons, erasers, sharpeners, and sandpaper
- Lightweight, portable easel, folds flat, with metal-lined tray, for canvases up to 32 inches wide
- Mayline™ 5-drawer flat-file cabinet made out of heavy steel, stackable, in sand beige (tan), interior drawer 43" x 32 ¾"
- Utrecht Professional Artist's Charcoal, extra-soft stick

**Search:** Yes
**Photos:** Yes
**Ordering:** Online
**Gift Wrap:** No
**Delivery:** Ground

## Wood N Crafts

`http://www.wood-n-crafts.com`

Mostly, this site lists tons of other craft sites and resources, so if you can't find an unusual product, you might browse through these lists. They sell some wood and craft stuff on their own, too. Sour note: Piano, organ, and harpsichord music springs to life whenever you arrive at a new page. Shipping is free for orders over $70. Samples:

- Plywood rabbit cutout
- Tiny plywood cow
- Varnished wooden beads

**Search:** Yes
**Photos:** Yes
**Ordering:** Online, Phone, Fax, Email
**Gift Wrap:** No, but gift certificates
**Delivery:** Ground

## Feeling inspired? Take a look at these other chapters for more creativity:

- Party Supplies
- Photography
- Sculpture & Art

# Department Stores

Most department stores have not joined the online store revolution. But we have found a few forward-thinking stores where you can browse through a variety of sections for a little bit of everything. A growing trend, we found, was Web bridal registries and wish lists, where you sign up for those items you'd love someone else to buy for you. (If you want to find out more about stores that cater to those couples planning to get married, see the Weddings chapter.)  Gift certificates, the mainstay of many of these stores, are available at most of them.

## Bloomingdale's

http://www.bloomingdales.com

Bloomie's has become so famous as the chic department store that it's hard to believe that it has stores in only eight states. If you don't live in one of those states, or you want to grab something quick without schlepping to an actual store, @ Your Service, their Web store, is the place for you. We did find it a bit annoying, though, that we had to create a "B profile" before we could actually go shopping, although once we answered all of the many questions, a personal dressing room was created based on our preferences. Samples:

- Braun shavers
- Bridal registry
- Electronic gift cards
- Godiva chocolate
- Millennium shop
- Ralph Lauren robes

**Search:** Yes
**Photos:** Yes

**Ordering:** Online, Fax
**Gift Wrap:** Yes
**Delivery:** Ground

## Gottschalks

http://gotts.com

Even though this is a publicly traded company, Gottschalks is still run by one of the family, a grand-nephew of ole Emil Gottschalk. You'll find clothes and home items, plus a nice selection of "stress solutions." Samples:

- Chenille throws
- Fat-monitor scale
- Gift certificates
- Goose-down comforters
- Hot/cold knee wrap
- Izod polo shirts
- Russell Athletic apparel

**Search:** Yes
**Photos:** Yes
**Ordering:** Online
**Gift Wrap:** No
**Delivery:** Ground

## iQVC Network

http://www.iqvc.com

You've probably watched at least a little bit of their TV shopping network, waiting for just the right thing. Now you can take advantage of their bargains without the wait. Always check the Last Click department for fantastically discounted merchandise. If you're looking for jewelry, go to their Gems and Jewels site at www.gemsandjewels.com/  Samples:

- Cameras
- Clocks
- Dolls
- Electronics
- Figurines
- Home furniture

- Major appliances
- Office supplies
- Outdoor patio furniture
- Toys
- Video Games

**Search:** Yes
**Photos:** Yes
**Ordering:** Online, Phone
**Gift-Wrap:** Yes
**Delivery:** Ground, 3rd Day, 2nd Day, Overnight

## JC Penney

http://www.jcpenney.com

This store has grown over the years into a giant retailer seen in most of the malls across America. They recently decided to set up shop on the Web, and they have done a good job of it. You can find most of the merchandise that's at their brick-and-mortar stores. Samples:

- Arizona Jean Co. jeans
- Bridal accessories and gifts
- Camcorders, VCRs, and TVs
- Drums and keyboards
- Fax machines
- Gift certificates
- Home-office furniture
- Jewelry
- Maternity shop
- Men's, women's, and kids' clothing
- Outdoor patio furniture
- Telephones
- Telescopes
- Towels and shower curtains

**Search:** Yes
**Photos:** Yes
**Ordering:** Online
**Gift Wrap:** No
**Delivery:** Ground

## Macy's

http://www.macys.com

The original is a neighbor of the Empire State Building, and this huge New York department store has put a slew of products online at fairly reasonable prices. You can find just about everything, but their Santa doesn't make house calls. Samples:

- Babies' and kid-size clothes
- Brand-name cosmetics
- Gift and bridal registries
- Handbags
- Jewelry
- Large and petite sizes
- Sunglasses

**Search:** Yes
**Photos:** Yes
**Ordering:** Online, Phone, Fax
**Gift Wrap:** Yes
**Delivery:** Ground, 2nd Day, Overnight

## Nordstrom

http://www.nordstrom.com

This high-end department store made its reputation by offering personal service in a busy world. The Web shop is the same. It's the best of the department stores. You can browse and buy online, or leave a message to have one of their personal shoppers contact you and help you with your purchases. Samples:

- Cultured pearl earrings
- Extended sizes for men and women
- Flannel pajamas
- Lambskin bomber jacket
- Sheer rayon mesh T-shirts
- Soft-tailored pumps
- Wrinkle-free cotton chinos

**Search:** Yes
**Photos:** Yes (in 3 sizes!)
**Ordering:** Online
**Gift Wrap:** Yes
**Delivery:** Ground, 2nd Day, Overnight

## Sears

`http://www.sears.com`

Even though Sears wasn't the original mail order catalog sales store (that honor goes to Montgomery Ward), they sure did make their name shipping everything a family in the middle of nowhere could want. Today, they've taken that concept and rethought it so now they offer everything a suburban family could want. (Well, that's a stretch, but you know what we mean!) Samples:

- Craftsman tools
- Furniture
- Sporting equipment
- Toys and dolls
- Wet/dry vacuum
- Women's jewelry

**Search**: Yes
**Photos**: Yes
**Ordering**: Online
**Gift Wrap**: No
**Delivery**: Ground

- Software
- Stereos
- Toys
- Videos

**Search**: Yes
**Photos**: Yes
**Ordering**: Online, Phone
**Gift Wrap**: No
**Delivery**: Ground

## For another set of stores with almost as wide a range of items for sale, consider these chapters:

- Auctions
- Clothes—All

## Wal-Mart

`http://www.wal-mart.com`

There's probably one in your area, so we bet you know what they carry. But, in case you've been marooned on Jupiter for the last decade, we can tell you that Wal-Mart is one of the biggest, the best, and the cheapest department stores in the U.S., and now on the Web. Samples:

- Appliances
- Baby products
- Books
- Camcorders
- Cameras
- Camping equipment
- Fax machines
- Golf clubs
- Jewelry
- Music tapes
- Office and school supplies
- Portable basketball system
- Prescription and over-the-counter drugs

# Fishing

A few years ago, we drove to Lakeside, Arizona, and stayed in a cabin near some well-stocked lakes. We rented a boat and some fishing equipment and took off for a leisurely day of fun. We spent a lot of time in the boat that day. We tried this lure and that lure; this type of bait and no bait. While people all around us were reeling trout in, we sat and waited. As the sun set around that gorgeous area, we headed back up to our cabin, past all the wonderful smells emanating from that day's grilled catch. We walked quickly to our picnic table and ate takeout pizza. We tell you this story so you know that we're definitely not experts at fishing. However, we are experts at online shopping—and these stores will not disappoint you.

## Angler's Express

http://www.anglers-express.com/index.htm

You gotta have a good lure to, well, lure the fish to hook, and this store has lures aplenty. A good line is also important when you're reeling in the big one, and you'll find a top-notch selection here, too. They primarily sell Yo-Zuri lures and Seaguar fluorocarbon fishing lines, which they say are perfect for ice fishing. Samples:

- Original, Riverge, Carbon Pro, and Carbon Ice Fluorocarbon series lines
- Yo-Zuri Bass Arms series lures
- Yo-Zuri Mag Minnow and Max Action series

**Search:** No
**Photos:** Yes
**Ordering:** Online
**Gift Wrap:** No
**Delivery:** Ground

## Bass Pro Shops

http://www.basspro-shops.com

Goin' fishin'? Goin' huntin'? Come here first. This store has just about everything you'll need for your time in the woods or on the lake. From equipment to clothes and food, we can't think of anything you'll need that this store doesn't sell, except maybe fair weather. Samples:

- Baitcast, spinning, and spin cast reels
- Boating accessories
- Camping equipment
- Casting, spinning, trigger, and big-game rods
- Fly-fishing equipment
- Hard, soft, and wire baits
- Molded plastic fold-down boat seat
- Rod-and-reel combos
- Tackle
- Uncle Buck's cooking mixes
- Waterproof waders

**Search:** Yes
**Photos:** Yes
**Ordering:** Online
**Gift Wrap:** No
**Delivery:** Ground, 2<sup>nd</sup> Day, Overnight

## Cat Tracker

http://www.cattracker.com

If you don't live in Florida, you might not know what this store is all about. No, we didn't make a mistake and put this place in the wrong chapter. This is a shop devoted to catfish fishermen. If you're scratching your head, you must be living north of the Mason-Dixon line. Cat Tracker has been testing baits and other equipment for over 20 years, so they really know this type of fishing cold. Free shipping on orders over $100. Samples:

- "Bite Me! I'm a Cat Tracker" T-shirt
- Boat anchor
- Dip baits
- Fishing line
- Hooks, lines, and sinkers
- Junnie's Cat Tracker coating mix
- Magic blood additive (bait thickener)

- Plastic egg worms
- Proskinner tool

**Search:** Some
**Photos:** Yes
**Ordering:** Online
**Gift Wrap:** No
**Delivery:** Ground

# Cotton Cordell

http://www.cottoncordell.com

You might know the name because of the lures he designed for decades. Looking for new horizons, Cotton Cordell turned his attention to fishing rods. He now manufactures fine graphite rods. But quality fishing rods aren't the only lure (we couldn't help it). Cordell has passed on his 50 years of fishing experience in the Tips, Tricks and Question section. He's also amassed a great set of fishing links. Free shipping in the continental U.S. Samples:

- Camouflage caps and shirts
- Casting and spinning rods
- Fish key chains
- Instructional fishing videos and books

**Search:** No
**Photos:** Yes
**Ordering:** Online, Fax
**Gift Wrap:** No
**Delivery:** Ground

# Fishing Mall

http://www.fishingmall.com

After visiting this mall, we knew more about fishing than we ever thought possible. Who (except you avid anglers) would have known that there's such a thing as a fishing consultant? But now we know and you do, too. Like all malls, you have a variety of stores, most of them specializing in something such as rods and reels, boats and motors, clothing, even charters. Now, since this is a mall, some of the stores in it meet our basic requirement that they offer secure online ordering, but some of them don't. But because there's so much here, we just had to include this mall. Samples:

- Binoculars
- Fishing travel consultants
- Instructional fishing books
- Marine electronic products
- Rods and reels
- Tackle
- Taxidermists
- Video equipment
- Waterproof clothing and boots

**Search:** Some
**Photos:** Some
**Ordering:** Varies by individual store
**Gift Wrap:** No
**Delivery:** Varies by individual store

# Gear.com

http://www.gear.com

This is one big sporting goods store. They have a section for just about every sport you can think of. One of their better departments is fishing. Everything in this store is heavily discounted. Samples:

- Assorted flies
- Deep-sea fishing accessories
- Fishing vests
- Fly-fishing tying kit
- Frame kits
- Graphite fly-rod
- Saltwater pliers
- Super forceps
- Traditional fly-fishing outfit

**Search:** Yes
**Photos:** Yes
**Ordering:** Online, Phone, Fax
**Gift Wrap:** No
**Delivery:** Ground, 2nd Day

# Orvis

http://www.orvis.com

Orvis has been around for more than a century. Their staying power is due to the quality of merchandise they sell and the service they give their customers. Their specialty is, and has always been, fishing. People who love to do fly fishing will find the selection especially reward-ing. If you're looking for a gift for a fly fisherman, look no further. The pictures introducing each section are spectacular. Samples:

- Bamboo fly rods
- Battenkill rod bags
- Children's animal games
- Fishing luggage
- Fleece fly vest for men
- Fly-tying kits
- Graphite spin rods
- Men's snakeproof boots (in widths up to EE)
- Women's outdoor-type clothing

**Search:** Yes
**Photos:** Yes
**Ordering:** Online, Phone
**Gift Wrap:** Yes
**Delivery:** Ground, 3rd Day, Overnight

## Tackle Outlet, Inc.

http://
www.hooklineandsinker.com

This store is dedicated to the sport fisherman who demands "quality gear and a large selection at discount prices." Usually, a slogan like that means low service and low prices. However, at this store, they pride themselves on their service. In fact, if after looking at the lures they carry you still don't find the right one, you can email them, telling them the details you are after, and they'll find one for you. They also offer a lot of information, such as clear step-by-step drawings of how to tie various line knots. Not bad. Samples:

- Crab pots and traps
- Digital scales
- Downriggers
- Fish/depth finders
- Float tubes
- Folding and fillet knives
- GPS systems
- Nets
- Rods and reels
- Tackle boxes
- Trolling motors
- Waders

**Search:** Some
**Photos:** Some
**Ordering:** Online, Fax
**Gift Wrap:** No
**Delivery:** 3rd Day

## Wolff Fishing Products

http://www.wolfffishing.com

Lots and lots of fishing gear is available at this store. They say they have over 1,000 pages of products online. Quite frankly, we didn't browse through all 1,000 to make sure that's accurate, but we can tell you that there is a plethora of fishing equipment, clothing, tools, accessories, and even marine products. Luckily, with such a large inventory, they also give you a number of different ways to search or browse. Shipping on orders over $75 is free. Samples:

- Boat pumps and switches
- Casting nets
- Downriggers
- Fishing gloves
- Fishing vests
- Fly rods
- Fresh- and saltwater flies
- Gift certificates
- Harnesses and belts
- Hook removers
- Knife sharpeners
- Sinkers
- Stainless-steel pliers with cordura sheath
- Vests and safety equipment

**Search:** Yes
**Photos:** Yes
**Ordering:** Online, Phone, Fax
**Gift Wrap:** No
**Delivery:** Ground, 2nd Day

# Fitness

If your idea of fitness is crossing and un-crossing your legs while you watch TV, you probably ought to skip this chapter. What we did find here were some very well-laid-out stores that carry a lot of the latest fitness and bodybuilding equipment and accessories. Many of them also offer informative articles and other information relevant to keeping yourself healthy.

Some of these stores also sell nutritional products, but if you would like a complete list of stores that sell vitamins and other supplements, please turn to the chapter Vitamins & Supplements. If you like a particular sport, look it up in the table of contents or index and see if we have a chapter for it. If not, read the Sporting Goods chapter for some all-purpose equipment.

## Body Trends

http://www.bodytrends.com

You'll feel better and stronger just by browsing the quality exercise equipment and other fitness accessories available at this store. This is not some Johnny-come-lately shop. They've been around for 17 years. You'll also find some products that were previously sold on TV. They offer discounts for large orders. In fact, if your order is really large, you can apply for financing. Samples:
- Anatomical charts on CD-ROM
- Balance boards
- Elliptical cross-trainers
- Exercise mats
- Fat scale
- Gravity boots
- Gymnastic and medicine balls
- Heart rate monitors

- Home gyms
- Rowing machines
- Spas and saunas
- Steps and slides
- The torso track
- Treadmills

**Search:** Yes
**Photos:** Yes
**Ordering:** Online, Phone, Fax, Email
**Gift Wrap:** No
**Delivery:** Ground

## BuyItOnTheWeb.com

http://www.buyitontheweb.com

Here's a neat idea. Round up all those items sold on the TV infomercials and put them for sale on the Web. Offer a 100% money-back guarantee on everything, and for kicks (as in having a good time, not kick boxing or kick aerobics), offer a monthly contest with incredible prizes. The exercise equipment for sale is manufactured by Guthy-Renker. Samples:
- Buns and thigh exerciser
- Cross-climber
- Elliptical power train
- Exercise videos and music
- Perfect-form exercise machine
- Ruth Prodan burner machine
- Skincare by Victoria Principal, Judith Light, Connie Sellecca, and Victoria Jackson
- Slice buster
- Target heart rate monitor
- Vita Power nutritional formulas

**Search:** Yes
**Photos:** Yes
**Ordering:** Online
**Gift Wrap:** Card
**Delivery:** Ground

## Fitness Zone

http://www.fitnesszone.com

As the name of this store implies, you'll find lots of fitness equipment, supplies, and accessories for sale. They also have a decent supply of workout clothes. If you're looking for a good gym in your area, or one for when you're one the road, check out their gym locator feature. Samples:

- Belts and gloves
- Cooling equipment
- Elliptical trainers
- Exercise bikes
- Exercise videos and music
- Heart-rate monitors
- Inversion equipment
- Racks and caddies
- Stairclimbers
- Steam and saunas
- Steps
- Tanning supplies
- Treadmills
- Versaclimbers

**Search:** Yes
**Photos:** Yes
**Ordering:** Online
**Gift Wrap:** No
**Delivery:** Ground

# Fit-Net Health Clubs

http://www.fit-net.com

Most places spend the precious space on their front page (the first page you see) by selling you something. Then they bury the informative stuff (reviews, articles) in subsequent pages. The first thing you see here is a lot of information and, buried on the bottom of the front page, is a place where you can click to go to their mall, where they sell a small number of products. This site has so much information, you'll want to plan to spend a lot of time here. Sample products:

- Bodybuilding posters
- Exercise bands
- Golf gym
- Instructional videos and books
- Tina Jo Bagne trading cards

**Search:** Yes
**Photos:** Yes
**Ordering:** Online
**Gift Wrap:** No
**Delivery:** Ground

# HealthCheck Systems, Inc.

http://
www.healthchecksystems.com

There's a lot to browse through at this store. They take a very scientific approach to keeping fit and healthy. Read their fitness info section to find out the facts about free radicals and antioxidants, cholesterol, glycemia, how to calculate your body fat, get low-fat cooking tips, and learn where to shop for healthier fast foods. Samples:

- Body-fat monitors
- Diet/cooking scales
- DietMate weight-control program
- Heart-rate calculator
- Professional body-composition analyzers
- Smoking-cessation program

**Search:** Yes
**Photos:** Yes
**Ordering:** Online, Phone, Fax, Email
**Gift Wrap:** No
**Delivery:** Ground

# The Iron Viking

http://www.ironviking.com

No, this isn't a site devoted to Randy Moss, but you will find lots of powerlifting equipment, apparel, and nutritional supplements. This Canadian company has thoughtfully listed their prices in both Canadian and American currency. Shipping prices are determined by weight and distance. Samples:

- Chalk
- Creatine citrite
- Double or single pronged powerlifting belts (up to XXXXL)
- Hightop safeshoes (up to size 15)
- IPF singlets (up to XXXXL)
- Wrist and knee wraps

**Search:** No
**Photos:** Yes
**Ordering:** Online, Phone, Email
**Gift Wrap:** No
**Delivery:** Ground

## Wholesale Fitness Products

`http://www.shoptsite.com/whfp`

The majority of items for sale here are supplements to help you with your bodybuilding or fitness regime, with a few other items thrown in. Ground shipping within the continental U.S. is free when you order $125 or more. Samples:

- Androstene
- Chocolate whey protein
- DHEA caps
- Glutamine complex
- Leather skull caps
- Low-carbohydrate protein supplements
- Mocha-blast protein bar
- Thermadrene

**Search:** No
**Photos:** Some
**Ordering:** Online
**Gift Wrap:** No
**Delivery:** Ground

## Now that you're in superb shape, how about bench-pressing some other chapters?

- Camping & Hiking
- Sporting Goods

# Flowers

Sending bouquets from a Web florist is incredibly easy. What we like the best is that you can actually see a color picture of whatever you are thinking of ordering. In the past, you had to rely on a description from the phone operator that might or might not resemble what was eventually delivered. No more. And many of these stores have sorted out their arrangements by category and price. You can look for an arrangement that says, "Congratulations" or "Thanks" for a price under $30. You can easily find what you're looking for in a jiffy.

Basically, online florists fall into two categories. One is the megastores buying their flowers from growers and then sending them out. These stores usually have the largest variety and the most services available but they cost a bit more. The other type of online flower store is run by a grower. The same people grow and ship their own flowers. You save by eliminating the middleman. Often their selection is somewhat smaller, but it is always ample. If a store is a grower, we'll let you know.

If you're looking for a gift to send to someone and you're not sure if you want to send flowers or something else, you might want to read the Gift Baskets chapter for some other ideas. If you are looking for seeds or trowels to grow your own flowers, please read the Gardening chapter.

## 1 800 Flowers

http://www.1800flowers.com

Yes, they sell flowers, but their best sellers include live plants, vases, bouquets, balloons, and baskets of goodies. They help you look up floral arrangements and gift baskets by season, occasion, flower type, or arrangement. If you place your order before 2 P.M. in the recipient's time zone, they can deliver that day, but later orders go out the next day. If you plan ahead, you can specify a later date for delivery. Samples:

- 18 roses, in arrangement or boxed
- Beauty-and-beast bouquet
- Café bouquet
- Flower birthday cake
- Hibiscus in a cache pot (live plant)
- Holiday centerpieces
- Mini-blooming plant in a teapot
- Pastel bulb garden in a basket
- Rustic wildflowers

**Search**: Yes
**Photos**: Yes
**Ordering**: Online
**Gift Wrap**: Card
**Delivery**: 2nd Day, Overnight, Same Day

## 1st in Flowers

http://www.1stinflowers.com

A third generation of florists have taken the family business on the Web in a big way. As an FTD florist, they will easily be able to deliver your order anywhere in the U.S., Canada, or anyplace else. They have a wide selection of fresh-cut flowers and living plants. They will also send food gift baskets. Order before 12 noon in the delivery time zone for same-day delivery. Before you make a decision on which arrangement to send, make sure you click their Best Values button for some good bargains. Samples:

- Balloon bouquet
- Birthday-surprise bouquet
- Chinese evergreen plant with fresh flowers
- Fresh-flower dish garden
- Joyful occasion basket
- New arrival bouquet
- Schefflera plant
- Single rose in a bud vase

- Spathiphyllum plant
- Treasure-Always basket with teddy bear

**Search:** Yes
**Photos:** Yes
**Ordering:** Online
**Gift Wrap:** Card
**Delivery:** 2nd Day, Overnight, Same Day

## 888 Live Flowers

`http://www.liveflowers.com`

This is a grower-direct floral shop. With no middle-man, your flowers are shipped directly from the source. These folks make up cut floral bouquets, as well as living flower arrangements. They do not deliver on Mondays or Tuesdays. But they do have a large assortment of arrangements to choose from. Samples:

- Autumn mist arrangement
- Basket of buds
- Blue irises
- Holiday centerpiece
- Indian summer arrangement
- Rain forest (bromeliad) basket arrangement
- Rhapsody in Bloom
- Roses with water tubes
- Sweetheart roses

**Search:** Some
**Photos:** Yes
**Ordering:** Online, Phone
**Gift Wrap:** Card
**Delivery:** 2nd Day, Overnight

## Buy Flowers.net

`http://www.buyflowers.net`

You'll be rewarded with some very unique arrangements here. Just tell them what your price range is, occasion (anniversary, new baby, birthday, get well, and more), and type of gift (such as flower type or color, bouquet, or basket). Then your order is sent to a local florist, who can call you if you would like, or just process your order. The prices are lower here because they don't use a wire service (which adds 7% to your bill). Samples:

- Balloon bouquets
- Fresh-cut flower arrangements
- Gift baskets

**Search:** No
**Photos:** No
**Ordering:** Online
**Gift Wrap:** Card
**Delivery:** 2nd Day

## Click for Flowers

`http://www.clickforflowers.com`

Here's something a bit different. How about a floral store that can make many different arrangements, ship them anywhere in the world, and, on the Web, offer a live floral chat area? Well, we found one. The store does everything the more well-known ones do, but it does so in a fun, hip style. If you're not sure what to order, or you have questions about the care of your flowers, you can ask Akinyi, their online florist. You can also add helium balloons to almost any arrangement. Orders received before 2 P.M. in the recipient's time zone will be delivered that day. International orders take three business days. Some weekend deliveries, but not everywhere. Samples:

- Birthday balloon-and-flower arrangement
- Floral wreaths
- Flowers in a ceramic baby bear
- Heliconia (Bird of Paradise) arrangement
- Holiday centerpieces
- Roses in a basket, vase, or in a box
- Sympathy carnations
- Toddler rocking chair with flowers
- White calla lilies and orchids

**Search:** Yes
**Photos:** Yes
**Ordering:** Online
**Gift Wrap:** Card
**Delivery:** 2nd Day, Overnight, Same Day

## Farmacopia

http://www.farmacopia.com

Here's a farmer's market online! This store offers all of those beautiful dried flowers you often see at your local farmer's market. All flowers are freeze dried. Samples:
- Antique silk swag
- Country winter swag
- Fall harvest wreath
- Geraniums in clay pot
- Peonies in a ceramic vase
- Soft pink wall garland
- Spring floral wreath
- Wild roses and ivy hanging plants

**Search:** Some
**Photos:** Some
**Ordering:** Online, Phone, Fax
**Gift Wrap:** No
**Delivery:** Ground, 2nd Day

## Fleurs Per Mail

http://www.fleurspermail.com

How about sending some flowers that will last months, even years? No, we're not talking plastic here. We're talking silk. These beautiful creations will keep your memory fresh with the recipient for a long time. The funny thing is that after looking at the prices, we noticed very little difference from their "fresh" counterparts. All domestic shipping costs are $5, international are $20. Sample silks:
- Bridal bouquets
- Calla lily sympathy arrangements
- Corsages
- Holiday arrangements
- Plants
- Roses
- Wedding packages

**Search:** Yes
**Photos:** Yes
**Ordering:** Online, Phone
**Gift Wrap:** Card
**Delivery:** Ground

## Florist.com

http://www.florist.com

This floral shop has an international flare. If your recipient is in one of 14 foreign countries, the site will automatically change all of its information to reflect the costs and other information, pertaining to delivery in that country. They also give you the option of filling out any order with a balloon (happy birthday, get well, anniversary, congratulations) for $4, or a cute teddy bear for $15. Orders received by 2 P.M. in the recipient's time zone (within the U.S.) will be delivered the same day. Samples:
- Azalea bushes
- Cyclamen in a basket
- Fragrant bouquets
- Gourmet baskets
- Planter baskets
- Roses in a vase or in a box
- Tropical bouquets

**Search:** Yes
**Photos:** Yes
**Ordering:** Online, Phone
**Gift Wrap:** Card
**Delivery:** 2nd Day, Overnight, Same Day

## Flowernet

http://www.flowernet.com

This store grows its flowers in its own exclusive gardens located in many different countries. These are the flowers that fill your local florist's vases, but now you can buy direct, to get fresher blooms. And you pay less this way. Flowernet ships your flowers no more than 48 hours after they've been cut. Same-day delivery is available if you place your order before 3 P.M. in the recipient's time zone. Samples:
- Birthday bouquets
- Bouquet of rose and baby's breath
- Bridal bouquets
- Candy-cane surprise
- Chinese carnations
- Freesia bouquet

- Holiday celebration arrangemeria
- Long-stemmed alstroemeria

**Search**: Yes
**Photos**: Yes
**Ordering**: Online, Phone, Fax
**Gift Wrap**: Card
**Delivery**: 2nd Day, Overnight, Same Day

## Flowers Direct

http://www.flowersdirect.com

Lots of different floral arrangements are online for you to view from this floral megastore. Don't want to send flowers? Send a candy-and-fruit basket instead. If your friend is nutritionally challenged, send the Junk Food Lover basket. But flowers are the real stars here. You'll love the variety. They have a reminder service and a great selection of flowers for kids. Same-day service for orders (in the U.S.) placed before noon in the recipient's time zone. Samples:

- Champagne-dream corsage
- European garden basket
- Exotic arrangements
- Festive balloon and floral arrangements
- Free digital postcards
- Holiday centerpieces
- Peter Rabbit garden bouquet
- Pooh-and-friends arrangement
- Puzzle-fun bouquet
- Small and large indoor plants

**Search**: Yes
**Photos**: Yes
**Ordering**: Online, Phone
**Gift Wrap**: Card
**Delivery**: 2nd Day, Overnight, Same Day

## FTD

http://www.ftd.com

This was the first service to use florists all around the country for sending flowers fast. They now offer their services online as well as by phone. They are equipped for large orders, and will be happy to take on business accounts. They publish a few articles about flowers. But, besides having a huge selection of floral arrangements, they also send teddy bears, fruit baskets, and balloons. You can add a stuffed animal to any order for $10 and a balloon for $5. If you're a United Frequent Flyer, you will earn miles by shopping here. Orders received by 1 P.M. in the recipient's time zone (U.S.) will be delivered that day. Samples:

- Candle-and-flowers centerpiece
- Dieffenbachia in a wicker basket
- Exotic tropical bouquets
- Floral arrangements with M&M's
- Giant Winnie the Pooh
- Holiday bouquets
- Long-stemmed roses
- NFL Game Day gift basket
- Sweet Dreams bouquet in baby blue basket

**Search**: Yes
**Photos**: Yes
**Ordering**: Online, Phone
**Gift Wrap**: Card
**Delivery**: 2nd Day, Overnight, Same Day

## Great Flowers

http://www.greatflowers.com

Flowers delivered fresh from the growers will ensure days and days of enjoyment. As with most grower-direct stores, the prices are a little lower than the rest. You can open up a corporate account from this store and they'll also set up a reminder service for you. The variety isn't as big as some of the megasites, but you'll love the prices. (One dozen long-stemmed roses — in several colors—for $38!!!) Orders received before 4 P.M. Eastern Time can be shipped the same day for next-day delivery. Samples:

- Bunches of mums
- Floral extravaganza
- Roses in vases sent in one to five dozen
- Seasonal bouquets
- Tiger lily bouquets

**Search**: Yes

**Photos**: Yes
**Ordering**: Online
**Gift Wrap**: Card
**Delivery**: 2$^{nd}$ Day, Overnight

## Greenhouse Express

http://
www.greenhouseexpress.com

Flowers sent from this store are shipped directly from their own fields, saving you money and making sure that the flowers are extremely fresh when delivered. (They even *guarantee* that their flowers will stay fresh for at least seven days!) If you think you'll want to use this store a lot, you should sign up for their free reminder service. They don't have the variety of arrangements that bigger floral stores do, but their prices are extremely low. Samples:
- Classic rose bouquet
- Holiday arrangements
- Seasonal mixed arrangements
- Stargazer lilies
- Tropical bouquets

**Search**: Yes
**Photos**: Yes
**Ordering**: Online, Phone
**Gift Wrap**: Card
**Delivery**: 2$^{nd}$ Day, Overnight

## PC Flowers and Gifts

http://www.pcflowers.com

First, you should know that the PC in the name of this store stands for *Personal Computer*, not *Politically Correct*, which is good because a lot of their arrangements come with chocolate, which has loads of sugar in it (banned in Berkeley). Actually, this store was started from the ground up as an Internet store—and it shows. It has a dynamite search, the best we've seen. You can search by a key word, such as a favorite flower; by a category, by price, or by occasion. Their prices are

about the same as the mega flower stores, but they always have about six or seven arrangements on sale right on the front page. Something different for sale here, besides the food gift baskets, is the jewelry. Order by midnight Pacific Time for next-day delivery.
Samples:
- Asiatic lily bouquet
- Boxed roses
- Floral arrangements with stuffed animals
- Flowers, truffles and a vase
- Garden baskets with live green and floral plants
- Jelly-bean bonanza
- Party bouquet
- Rose-petal chocolates
- Sterling-silver I Love You bracelet
- Winnie the Pooh ceramic vase with assorted flowers

**Search**: Yes
**Photos**: Yes
**Ordering**: Online, Phone
**Gift Wrap**: Card
**Delivery**: 2$^{nd}$ Day, Overnight

## ProFlowers

http://www.proflowers.com

This shop ships directly from the growers to save you some money. They have a good selection and also run monthly contests, if you're feeling lucky. If you like this store, sign up for their reminder service. Orders placed by 12 noon Pacific Time can be delivered the same day.
Samples:
- Blue iris arrangement
- Carnival of Color
- Classic bouquets
- Exotic arrangements
- Heather bouquet
- Ivy Topiary
- Monthly bouquets
- Oriental lilies
- Potted pink roses
- Rainbow freesia bouquet
- Roses
- Small evergreen plants

- Wildflower arrangements

**Search:** Yes
**Photos:** Yes
**Ordering:** Online
**Gift Wrap:** Card
**Delivery:** 2nd Day, Overnight, Same Day

Thinking of tossing a bouquet?
Gather some more rosebuds,
floral gifts, or at least some
seeds at these chapters:

- Gardening
- Gift Baskets
- Weddings

# Food—Gourmet

This is one area that we bet you're very familiar with if you have had to supply goodies to family members scattered around the country, or if you yourself crave some of the delicacies that can be found only in true gourmet-food stores. Many of these stores have been selling their stuff for years by catalog, so taking their stores online was just a natural extension of their business. But other stores have sprung up just on the Web. Warning: If you are hungry, rip up your credit cards. You won't believe the mouthwatering morsels that can be delivered to your door. You may never order pizza again.

## Balducci's

http://www.balducci.com

Over 75 years ago, Louis Balducci set up a fruit-and-vegetable stand on a corner in New York City. Just after World War II he moved into a storefront in Greenwich Village and started importing delicacies from around the world. Usually a store like this specializes in something like desserts or meat. But we can personally attest (from our days living in Greenwich Village) that this store seems to carry everything, and just about everything there is absolutely luscious. As Pop Balducci would have said, "Buon Appetito." Samples:

- Cassis essence
- Chocolate-covered blueberries
- Farro-e-Fagioli soup
- Freula Sarda pasta
- Risotto with tomatoes and black olives
- Spanish goat cheese in olive oil
- White truffles

**Search:** Yes
**Photos:** Yes

**Ordering:** Online
**Gift Wrap:** Card only
**Delivery:** Ground

## Caesar's Palate

http://www.caesarspalate.com/

The selection at this store is incredible. If you want to have a taste of the good life (or are entertaining and want to make an indelible impression on your guests), shop here. The food isn't cheap, but you won't feel cheated, either. Samples:

- Gift baskets
- Goose foie gras with truffles
- Gourmet fruit mixes
- Russian Beluga caviar
- Smoked sliced turbot
- Wild-boar tenderloin

**Search:** Yes
**Photos:** Yes
**Ordering:** Online
**Gift Wrap:** Card
**Delivery:** 2nd Day, Overnight

## CIBO's

http://www.greatfood.com

Natural pesto sauces, cheese, and herb butters are the specialties of this shop. Some of their cheeses are good enough to make a meal by themselves. Or you may want to combine the butters, cheeses, and sauces with other food for a festive night. Samples:

- Basil-roasted herb butter
- Basil-roasted walnut cheese
- Classic basil pesto
- Creamy goat cheese with fresh herbs
- Garlic sun-dried tomato cheese
- Roasted-garlic herb butter
- Smoked jalapeno cheese
- Sun-dried tomato pesto

**Search:** Some
**Photos:** Some

**Ordering:** Online, Phone, Fax
**Gift Wrap:** No
**Delivery:** 2nd Day, Overnight

## Cook's Nook

http://www.cooksnook.com

You'll find a good assortment of gourmet food here, but what this store specializes in is cooking appliances, cookware, and accessories to make your gourmet cooking experience a real treat. Unsure what to get? Let their staff custom-design a gift basket just for you. Samples:

- Asian teas
- Brass Turkish pepper mill
- Candles
- Chinook roasting planks
- Cookbooks
- Endurance cocktail shaker
- Fat free Kiwi-fruit vinaigrette salad dressing
- Gourmet salt crystals
- Microwave hot plate
- Scanpan line of cookware

**Search:** Yes
**Photos:** Yes
**Ordering:** Online, Phone, Fax
**Gift Wrap:** No
**Delivery:** Ground, 2nd Day, Overnight

## Dean and Deluca

http://www.dean-deluca.com

A fixture in New York's SoHo (south of Houston Street) for a quarter century, D and D's was hip even before SoHo was. The owners, Joel Dean and Giorgio DeLuca, expanded their deli as New Yorkers discovered this epicurean mecca. We used to live next door, and watched the place fill up every Saturday. Those of us who no longer live in New York (or never even visited the place) can salivate at the wonderful offerings online. Samples:

- Black-and-white truffle paste
- French cooper cookware and kitchen gadgets
- French foie gras
- Jamon Serrano ham
- La Cigale Tarte de Saint Tropez
- Passion-fruit crème chocolate truffles
- Sevruga caviar
- Toscano salami
- Wine

**Search:** Yes
**Photos:** Yes
**Ordering:** Online
**Gift Wrap:** Card
**Delivery:** Ground, 2nd Day, Overnight

## Earthly Delights

http://www.earthy.com

Originally offering its delectables only to professional chefs, this place has expanded, and now the home chef can take advantage of its eclectic tidbits at very reasonable prices. Samples:

- 30-year-old Balsamic vinegar
- Chanterelles
- Cherry-honey spread
- Chestnut confections
- Dried fruits
- Fiddleheads
- Genoa pesto sauce
- Gift Baskets
- Spelt pasta
- Truffle oil

**Search:** Yes
**Photos:** No
**Ordering:** Online, Fax, Phone
**Delivery:** Ground

## Fancy Foods Gourmet Club

http://www.ffgc.com/

Don't let the word "Club" scare you off from this store. You can belong to this shopping club for free. If you do join, you'll be notified of their upcoming sales. The large selection is just scrumptious. Samples:

- Applewood-smoked chicken breasts
- Caviar sampler
- Chesapeake Bay crab cakes
- Laderach truffles
- Lobster Thermidor
- Norwegian salmon
- Shrimp Louisiane

**Search:** Some
**Photos:** Yes
**Ordering:** Online
**Gift Wrap:** Yes
**Delivery:** Ground, 2nd Day, Overnight

## Farmacopia

http://www.farmacopia.com

Here's a farmer's market online! The emphasis is on *fresh*. A nice assortment of specialty and low-fat foods and some other items that you'd find at your local farmer's market. You probably think the food is expensive: guess again. Samples:

- Athenian Dalmata olive tapenade
- California baby artichokes
- Freeze-dried flower arrangements
- Gourmet canned albacore tuna and oysters
- Lowfat and nonfat breads, muffins, and cookies
- Potted herbs
- Roasted red bell mousse sauce

**Search:** Some
**Photos:** Some
**Ordering:** Online, Phone, Fax
**Gift Wrap:** No
**Delivery:** Ground, 2nd Day

## GourmetMarket.com

http://www.gourmetmarket.com/

Besides carrying epicurean morsels from around the world, this store also supplies tons of articles about food and health, free CD-ROMs, recipes, wine

reviews, and more. Even though this is a gourmet "general store," we did notice a strong emphasis on chocolate. Samples:

- Cigars
- Escargots de Bourgogne
- Fig jam
- French chocolates
- Golden gourmet caviar
- Goose, sausage, and bean casserole
- Pumpkin cheesecake
- White Amaretto almond fudge

**Search:** Yes
**Photos:** Some
**Ordering:** Online, Phone, Fax
**Gift Wrap:** No
**Delivery:** 3rd Day

## Gourmet Trader

http://www.gourmettrader.com

Love hot and spicy food? You know who you are! Those of us who love the stuff secretly realize this is an addiction. (Have you ever heard anyone say, "I need my chili fix?" We have, often.) So may we suggest you either make a reservation at a chili detox center, or you rush over to this store and fill up the pantry. (Oh, yes, this store has a lot of the other gourmet food stuff, too.) Samples:

- Anasazi beans
- Chili-pepper heat chart
- Chili gift baskets
- Crushed red chili
- Diablo-red chili powder
- Endorphin Rush hot sauce
- Green chili dip mix
- Mad Coyote salsa
- Painted-desert chili mix
- Pasilla Negro
- Whole Ancho peppers

**Search:** Some
**Photos:** No
**Ordering:** Online, Phone, Fax
**Gift Wrap:** No
**Delivery:** Ground

# GreatFood.com

http://www.greatfood.com

Unique and hard-to-find gourmet food items are what's on the menu at this online store. Besides posting recipes, an online forum, and gift finder, this store has the best search of any gourmet shop in this chapter. For example, you can find food ideas for pregame buffets, beach parties, holiday dinner, even back-packing! It also has one of the largest assortments of any store. Samples:

- Bourbon-pecan tart
- Corporate gifts
- Green-tomato relish
- Kosher turkeys
- Lemon-peppered smoked turkey breast
- Mocha-almond-fudge cheesecake
- Pasta salads with bruschetta
- Sun-dried tomato cheese sticks

**Search:** Fantastic
**Photos:** Yes
**Ordering:** Online, Phone
**Gift Wrap:** No
**Delivery:** Ground, 2nd Day, Overnight

# Harry and David

http://www.harryanddavid.com

Known for decades as the premier creator of quality fruit and nut gift baskets, Harry and David have gone online in a big way. Samples:

- Baklava
- Chilean Andes peaches
- Chocolate truffles
- Flowering plants
- Fruit-of-the-Month Club
- Hand-painted fresh fruit basket
- Royal Riviera pears

**Search:** Yes
**Photos:** Yes
**Ordering:** Online, Phone, Fax
**Gift Wrap:** Yes
**Delivery:** Ground, 2nd Day, Overnight

# International Gourmet

http://www.intlgourmet.com

As the name of the store implies, you can order gourmet food from places as diverse as the Middle East, Russia, France, and even the good ol' USA. Samples:

- Kataif Dough
- Kosher smoked salmon
- Middle-Eastern coffee and teas
- Snail casserole
- Truffle peelings
- Tyropites Greek appetizers
- Wasabi caviar

**Search:** Yes
**Photos:** Some
**Ordering:** Online
**Gift Wrap:** No
**Delivery:** Ground, 2nd Day

# Omaha Steaks

http://omahasteaks.com

Juicy photos are a plus of this online gourmet butcher. If you like meat (chicken, pork, lamb, beef, or veal), your mouth will water as you browse the aisles of this store. You'll also be able to enter contests for free steaks, print recipes, and even learn some interesting facts about the food for sale. They also sell fish, but as their name implies, meat is the main attraction here. Samples:

- Basil-chicken chili
- Boneless chicken breasts
- Boneless pork chops
- Filet mignons
- Gourmet burgers
- Pork Chateaubriand
- Rack of lamb

**Search:** Yes
**Photos:** Yes
**Ordering:** Online
**Gift Wrap:** Card
**Delivery:** Ground, 2nd Day, 3rd Day, Overnight

## OnlyGourmet.com

http://www.onlygourmet.com.

You might know Only Gourmet as the Webzine of good taste, and you'd be right. It also puts its money where its mouth is, so to speak, by selling many of the scrumptious delicacies it talks about in its articles. Some items have minimum-purchase requirements. Samples:

- Capers in sea salt
- Chocolate truffles
- Duck prosciutto
- Lemon-curd scones
- Rustichella d'Abruzzo penne pasta
- Terrine of foie gras with sauternes
- Wild Yukon salmon pack

**Search**: Yes
**Photos**: Yes
**Ordering**: Online, Phone
**Gift Wrap**: No
**Delivery**: Ground, 2nd Day, Overnight

## Vis Seafood

http://www.visseafoods.com

This family has been fishing for generations. The current crop of fishermen are located in Alaska. Their entire "inventory" consists of wild Alaskan, Grade #1 seafood. All of their products are either fresh-frozen, canned, or hot-smoked. Samples:

- Fish-of-the-Month Club
- Garlic-pepper hot-smoked salmon
- Osetra caviar
- Pacific medium shrimp
- Smoked salmon spreads
- Willapa Bay smoked oysters

**Search**: Some
**Photos**: No
**Ordering**: Online, Phone
**Gift Wrap**: Card
**Delivery**: Ground, 2nd Day

## To round out your gourmet picnic, perhaps you'd like a taste of these chapters:

- Coffee & Tea
- Food—Organic & Special Diets
- Food—Supermarket
- Wine

# Food—Organic & Special Diets

Whether you're on a special diet or you just want to eat natural, organic food that hasn't had every beneficial nutrient processed out it, you'll find what you're looking for in these stores. From organic shiitake-and-sesame vinaigrette to Kosher dairy-free shakes, we've rounded up a wonderful assortment of stores dedicated to your health (and your taste buds).

If you are looking for health-related equipment and supplies, please also read the Health Products chapter. And, while many of the stores listed here sell vitamins, we found many stores focused on vitamins, and they are described in the Vitamins & Supplements chapter.

## Beehive Botanicals

http://www.beehive-botanicals.com

All of the products offered contain some of the "gifts of the honeybee," such as honey, pollen, propolis, or royal jelly. Besides carrying a dizzying array of "bee" products, this store also offer links to sites of interest to bee lovers. Samples:

- Chewing gum
- Dietary supplements
- Gourmet honey
- Honeybear candy
- Honeystix
- Pollen granules
- Royal jelly liquid
- Toothpaste

**Search:** Yes
**Photos:** Some

**Ordering:** Online, Phone, Fax
**Gift Wrap:** No
**Delivery:** Ground, 2nd Day, Overnight

## Christina Shops

http://www.christinaschoice.com.market.html

You might have seen Christina on TV cooking up a batch of healthy food. Her online store sells a lot of the items she uses on her show. Many are organic and all are clearly labeled. Samples:

- Basmati rice
- Eden genmai-cha tea
- Macrobiotic food
- Sea vegetables
- Soy and rice drinks
- Umeboshi plums
- Yellow corn grits

**Search:** Yes
**Photos:** No
**Ordering:** Online
**Gift Wrap:** No
**Delivery:** Ground

## Crusoe Island

http://www.crusoeisland.com

Fresh-milled organic flours, grains, beans, seeds, and baking supplies are just some of the items available here. All of the food items have been grown free of any trace of agricultural chemicals or pesticides. Even the containers and bags they come in are processed and packaged with no chemical additives or preservatives. The prices are extremely reasonable. Samples:

- 50-pound sack of dry active baking yeast
- 7-grain cereal
- Dairy-free beverages
- Honey Gone Nuts granola
- Raspberry hot mustard
- Sea vegetables

- Shiitake-and-sesame vinaigrette
- Soy products
- Sweetened corn flakes

**Search:** Yes
**Photos:** No
**Ordering:** Online, Fax, Phone
**Gift Wrap:** No
**Delivery:** Ground, 3rd Day, 2nd Day, Overnight

## Dixie Diner Club

http://dixiediner.com

We've heard soy-based food referred to as a "beef alternative." We think that maybe the person who said that has it backward. Either way, you'll find a slew of soy products here, as well as some other healthy treats. Many of the products are also free of gluten, dairy, and sugar. If you are new to soy foods, you may want to read the recipe section. Samples:

- Egg substitutes
- Kosher dairy-free shakes
- Lentil soups
- Milk-free yogurt
- Organic green tea
- Soy sausage
- Soybean coffee

**Search:** Yes
**Photos:** Some
**Ordering:** Online
**Gift Wrap:** No
**Delivery:** Ground, 2nd Day

## Everybody's Store

http://www.nas.com/~goodbuy/

Not everything that comes out of the state of Washington these days has to do with computers. Near the Canadian border, this general store has a little of everything, from organic food to brightly colored clothing. Samples:

- Alaska wild teas

- Beef jerky
- Italian salami
- Raw-milk cheeses
- Wine-cured Italian sausages

**Search:** Some
**Photos:** Yes
**Ordering:** Online, Phone, Fax
**Gift Wrap:** No
**Delivery:** Ground

## Good Eats

http://www.goodeats.com/

You'll find a large assortment of natural foods at this store with the fun name. There's a solid selection of organic kosher foods, and Good Eats hasn't forgotten your four-legged pals, either. Minimum orders are $20. Samples:

- Baby food and products
- Baking supplies
- Breakfast cereals
- Chili
- Coffee substitutes
- Cotton clothing
- Gift certificates
- Macrobiotic
- Nondairy beverages
- Pet food

**Search:** Yes
**Photos:** No
**Ordering:** Online, Phone, Fax
**Gift Wrap:** Card
**Delivery:** Ground, 3rd Day, 2nd Day, Overnight

## The Healthy Trader

http://www.healthytrader.com

Judy Jones wanted to take the good, healthy food she knew as a child and make it available to people everywhere. The result is The Healthy Trader. People with food allergies or others who just want to avoid certain ingredients will find the 13 symbols listed next to each item very helpful. Among the symbols are icons indicating that a product has no caffeine, milk, refined sugars, or white flour. Their motto, "Eating well is the best revenge," says it all. Samples:

- Fat-free fudge topping
- Flax spices
- Instant stuffed potatoes
- Organic canned kid's meals
- Radiatore with sun-dried tomato and basil
- Tortilla soup

**Search:** Yes
**Photos:** Yes
**Ordering:** Online, Phone, Fax
**Gift Wrap:** Yes
**Delivery:** Ground

## Kinnikinnick Foods

http://www.kinnikinnick.com/
kinnik/welcome.vs

If you or a family member has Celiac Disease, you know how difficult it is just to go out to dinner. People with Celiac's cannot eat any food with gluten in it. Read the labels at your grocery store sometime and see just how much food has gluten in it. All of the items for sale here are gluten-free and wheat-free. If you are allergic to corn, dairy, egg, or some other food, you'll find some products that won't offend your allergy. Samples:

- Bagels
- Cakes
- Cereal
- Chocolate-covered cookies
- Corn bread
- Dairy-free tapioca-rice hot dog buns
- Soups
- Waffles
- White-rice bread

**Search:** Yes
**Photos:** No
**Ordering:** Online, Fax
**Gift Wrap:** No
**Delivery:** Ground, Overnight

## Mori Nu Tofu

http://www.morinu.com

This California-based company specializes in selling low-fat tofu. All of their tofu products come packed in hermetically sealed containers for freshness. Not sure how to cook with tofu? Check out their recipes and sandwich ideas. Shipping is free. Samples:

- Eggless "egg" salad
- Extra firm tofu
- Lemon crème pudding and pie mix
- Silken tofu
- Strawberry banana shake

**Search:** Some
**Photos:** Some
**Ordering:** Online, Phone, Fax
**Gift Wrap:** No
**Delivery:** Ground

## The Natural Place

http://www.naturalplace.com

The store has the feel of a local health food store. They sell the usual assortment of healthy food, plus there are bulletin boards with articles about organic gardening, natural foods, and even a message exchange. Samples:

- Black mission figs
- Delicate olive oil
- Gift baskets for new babies
- Hot-and-spicy turkey jerky
- Italian balsamic vinegar
- Teriyaki ahi jerky

**Search:** Some
**Photos:** Yes
**Ordering:** Online
**Gift Wrap:** Card
**Delivery:** Ground

## Whole Foods

`http://www.wholefoods.com`

Brand new to the Web, Whole Foods has taken their very successful chain of health food grocery stores and designed a beautiful online store. Shopping is easy and everything looks terrific. You shop by browsing the "aisles" or by doing a quick search for the items you want. We liked the fact that they offer a lot of information in the form of articles from their *Whole Living* magazine and recipes from their kitchen. And if you think they're interested in just feeding your body, think again. They've put up some moving poetry by the 14th century spiritual master Rumi. Ground shipping is free on orders over $70. Samples:

- Baked cheese curls
- Broccoli-and-cheddar mashed-potato cup
- Brunch 'n Munch gift box
- Decaf aged Sumatra coffee
- Fat-free chili beans
- Green tea in tins
- Herbal moisturizing lotions
- Herbal tinctures for kids
- Homeopathic gels
- Organic energy bars
- Organic Semolina pastas

**Search:** Yes
**Photos:** Yes
**Ordering:** Online
**Gift Wrap:** No
**Delivery:** Ground, 2nd Day, Overnight

information about healthy living. Samples:

- Condiments
- Food supplements
- Gifts
- Gluten-free foods
- Healthy snacks
- Holistic practitioner search
- Organic juices
- Soy and rice drinks
- Sweets
- Vitamins

**Search:** Yes
**Photos:** Some
**Ordering:** Online
**Gift Wrap:** Yes
**Delivery:** Ground, 2nd Day, Overnight

## To round out your healthy meal, perhaps you'd like a taste of these chapters:

- Food—Gourmet
- Food—Supermarket
- Health Products
- Herbs
- Vitamins & Supplements

## Wild Oats

`http://www.wildoats.com`

Started a decade ago by the husband-and-wife team of Mike Gilliland and Libby Cook as a small vegetarian health food shop in Boulder, Colorado, Wild Oats has grown to supermarket status in 18 states and Canada. In fact, it's now the second-largest natural food chain in North America. Its online store carries just about everything and offers lots of online resources and

# Food—Supermarket

OK, let's get serious here. Who actually *likes* to go grocery shopping, especially after working nine hours at the office? All of you who raised your hands can skip this chapter. For the rest of you, this chapter will be an "enlightening" experience, and we don't use that word lightly. Depending on the store, you can browse their aisles—virtually, of course, and then submit your order. Their professional shoppers will do the footwork for you and deliver your groceries. All of the supermarkets listed here have a wide service area, but no store delivers everywhere, so check what states it works in BEFORE you shop.

## American Foods

http://www.americanfoods.com/

If you're lucky enough to have a large freezer, you know how easy life can be at dinnertime, or when your teenage son's football team decides to visit "for a snack." How does this work? Well, for starters, you have to live in one of the 15 states this company services. Then you order on the Web, and your frozen stuff is delivered in a refrigerated truck. The truck driver will even load your frozen food in your freezer. Samples:
- Bone-in strip steaks
- Cream-cheese cake
- Filet mignon
- London broil
- Porterhouse steak
- Steak samplers

**Search:** Some
**Photos:** Yes

**Ordering:** Online, Phone
**Gift Wrap:** No
**Delivery:** By freezer truck

## Dinner Direct

http://www.dinnerdirect.com

This is THE site for those of us who don't have the time to cook every night but are getting tired of the fast-food avenue. The entrees all come frozen: you either put them in the oven, or if you order the pouches, you just plop them in boiling water. Dinner Direct makes good meals possible every night of the week. Order any three items and the shipping's free! Samples:
- Beef Wellington
- Stuffed chicken breast
- Turkey en croûte
- Beef Stroganoff
- Beef Teriyaki
- Thai chicken
- Sesame chicken

**Search:** Yes
**Photos:** Yes
**Ordering:** Online
**Gift Wrap:** No
**Delivery:** 3rd Day

## HomeRuns

http://www.homeruns.com

Place your order by midnight and you can have a week's worth of groceries delivered right to your door. Everything you can get at your local grocery store is available. The way this store works is that they have their own warehouse filled with the same groceries you'll find at your local market. Fill out the Web shopping list with as much detail as you like and HomeRuns' trained shoppers will fill your order. They even accept coupons. Use the ZIP code finder to determine if they're in your area. Shipping on orders over $60 is free! (Delivery for smaller orders is $10 and there is a minimum or $30 per order.) Samples:

- Aged meats
- Fresh produce
- Healthy Choice dinners
- Kellogg's cereal
- Low-fat foods
- Paper products
- Tropicana orange juice

**Search:** Yes
**Photos:** Yes
**Ordering:** Online
**Gift Wrap:** No
**Delivery:** Same or next day

## Net Grocer

http://www.netgrocer.com

This is one of the few supermarkets on the Web that services everywhere in the U.S. It has just about everything you'd find in any huge grocery store, except there are no perishables, no parking lot, no checkout line to stand in, and no shopping carts to return. Samples:

- Baby products
- Cleaning supplies
- Coffee
- Coupons
- Diapers
- Over-the-counter drugs
- Pet food
- Prepared and international foods
- Specialty foods

**Search:** Yes
**Photos:** Yes
**Ordering:** Online
**Gift Wrap:** No
**Delivery:** 2–4 Days

## Peapod

http://www.peapod.com

Freshness is the key to Peapod. The way this supermarket service works is that it trains professional shoppers to go into your local supermarket and shop for you. So you can order anything that your local grocery store carries, including fresh meat and produce. Your order is processed quickly (although you might want to think twice about ordering a gallon of ice cream). This service is available in many major metropolitan areas. Hint: You can always shop from work, but don't tell the boss. Samples:

- Baby products
- Bakery
- Deli
- General grocery food
- Health and beauty items
- Liquor
- Meat, poultry, and seafood
- Pet food
- Produce

**Search:** Yes
**Photos:** Some
**Ordering:** Online
**Gift Wrap:** No
**Delivery:** Same day

## To round out your super dinner, perhaps you'd like a taste of these delectable chapters:

- Coffee & Tea
- Food—Gourmet
- Food—Organic & Special Diets
- Wine

# Furnishings for Home & Office

"Buying furniture on the Web . . . are you crazy?" you ask. No, we're not crazy. First of all, you don't have to schlep to the store and you don't have to pay tax, which is an important consideration when making big-dollar purchases. Many online stores do charge shipping, but you'd have to pay a delivery charge to the brick-and-mortar store, so that's a wash. And we did find some stores that don't charge for shipping, making your purchase on the Web even more of a bargain. We found stores that sell furniture for your home and others that offer it for your home office. Some sell furniture for both. We'll let you know which is which in the descriptions.

Some of the stores mentioned in the Office Supplies chapter also sell office furniture, so if you're looking for furniture for your home office, you may want to read that chapter, too.

## 101 Furniture

http:/www.101furniture.com

This place is like those huge unfinished-furniture stores you go into where everything looks good. Most of the furniture is made from pine or poplar. All of it is manufactured in their plant in North Carolina. Samples:

- Corner shelf
- Drop-leaf end table
- Grocery-bag trash bin
- Jam and jelly cupboard
- Magazine rack
- Old-fashioned sleighs
- Scalloped benches
- Three-tier quilt rack
- Washstand

**Search:** Yes
**Photos:** Yes
**Ordering:** Online
**Gift Wrap:** No
**Delivery:** Ground

## All Seasons Spas and Accessories

http://www.allseasonsspas.com

Home spas, accessories, and supplies at a 25% discount in this Colorado-based store. The spas are from Jacuzzi, Nordic, and Softub. Shipping runs 10% of the checkout price. Samples:

- Chlorine
- Enzymes
- Foam fighters
- Indoor and outdoor spas
- pH adjusters
- Spa cleaners and polishers
- Spa fragrances
- Start-up chemical kits
- Thermometers
- Vacuums, pumps, and skimmers
- Vinyl and cover protectors
- Water clarifiers

**Search:** No
**Photos:** Yes
**Ordering:** Online, Phone
**Gift Wrap:** No
**Delivery:** Ground

## Beanie Furniture

http://
www.beaniefurniture.com

Beanie Babies have become such a phenomenon that it's no wonder they have their own online furniture store. All of the products are made of either pine or poplar, and they are kits, meaning that you have to put them together. But the assembly looks easy. Sample:

- Small and large Beanie Baby display stands

**Search:** No

**Photos:** Yes

**Ordering:** Online

**Gift Wrap:** No

**Delivery:** Ground

# BedandBath.com

http://www.bedandbath.com

Depending on where you live, you may already be familiar with the type of things this store sells. Besides the products that you'd associate with a store called BedandBath.com, they also sell a fair supply of kitchen furniture, curtains, and rugs. They also have a 60-day return policy that is great for those of you who have a hard time making up your mind. Free shipping on orders over $250. Samples:

- Bath rugs
- Bed ruffles
- Comforters and comforter set
- Kitchen and bath towels
- Kitchen curtains
- Mattress pads and covers
- Place mats
- Shower curtains
- Sports sheets
- Wedding registry
- Window hardware

**Search:** Yes

**Photos:** Yes

**Ordering:** Online, Phone

**Gift Wrap:** No

**Delivery:** Ground, 2nd Day, Overnight

# ChairNet

http://www.chairnet.com

Let's face it. The chair you sit on for eight-plus hours a day is a very important piece of furniture. This store specializes in office chairs. You'll find all kinds for your home or small office. Select the chair or chairs you want, then go to the fabric section and choose from 15 different weaves and colors. (They also give you a selection of heavy-duty Scotchguard fabrics for an additional $10.) Frames come in black or gray. Shipping is included in the price of the chair. Sample chairs:

- Conference
- Ergonomic
- Executive side
- Pneumatic with lumbar support
- Reception
- Steno
- Swivel-tilt

**Search:** No

**Photos:** Yes

**Ordering:** Online

**Gift Wrap:** No

**Delivery:** Ground

# CosmopolitanHome.com

http://www.cosmopolitanhome.com

Contemporary furniture (like what you see in the chic magazines) at affordable prices. And they carry the big stuff, such as complete bedroom sets, along with the small accessories, such as candles and mirrors. Most of the upholstered furniture comes in a variety of colors and fabrics. They have a nice search that feels as if you were looking through a paper catalog. First you search by category (chairs, dining room, vases) and then a small group of photos appears. Click the photos that look like possibles and they are enlarged for you to examine more closely. Free ground shipping within the continental U.S. Samples:

- Big-boy loveseat
- Cube magazine rack
- Diamond-back chair
- Glow wall clock
- Halogen table lamp
- Metal canopy bed
- Moon Shadow five-piece dining set
- Parisian bar stool
- Pewter ashtray

- Slipcover chair
- Steam towel bar

**Search:** Yes
**Photos:** Yes
**Ordering:** Online
**Gift Wrap:** No
**Delivery:** Ground, 2nd Day, Overnight

# Desperate.com

http://www.desperate.com

On a road trip have you ever stopped at one of the local general stores or antique shops and ended up marveling at all of the neat old stuff? This place has taken those wonderful nostalgic items and reproduced them. They don't sell any furniture, but they do sell lots of accessories for your house. The best selection is their tin-sign collection. They have just about every design ever made. They also sell a few original items, but of course these cost more. Samples:

- Alexander (the man who knows) original sign
- Cadillac neon sign
- Chevy neon clock
- Cretor's original popcorn box
- Farm-equipment switch plates
- Ferry Seed notepads
- Gasoline tin signs
- Ivory Soap notepads
- Original Coca-Cola ink blotter
- Original Pinex laxative tin boxes
- Seed catalog tin signs
- Various icebox magnets

**Search:** Yes
**Photos:** Yes
**Ordering:** Online, Phone, Fax
**Gift Wrap:** No
**Delivery:** Ground

# EZ Shop.com

http://www.ezshop.com

Besides finding lots of furniture and accessories for your home at this store, you'll also spot some appli-ances, electronics, and hardware. You'll recognize many brand names such as Hamilton Beach, Sharp, Somerville, and Vaughn-Bassett. The prices are excellent. Ground shipping to the continental U.S. is free. Samples:

- Antique-style chairs and ottomans
- Baby and toddler furniture
- Bedroom furniture
- Bistro-style kitchen dining sets
- Glider rocking chairs
- Greek statues
- Jewelry armoires
- Lighting
- Outdoor furniture
- Picture frames
- Recliners
- Rugs
- Sheets and towels
- Sofa ensembles
- TV stands
- Vases
- Wall art

**Search:** Yes
**Photos:** Yes
**Ordering:** Online, Phone
**Gift Wrap:** No
**Delivery:** Ground

# Furniture.com

http://www.furniture.com

There are over 50,000 individual items for sale at this store. In other words, selection is no problem. They offer discounts on everything. (Some items are marked down as much as 40%.) They haven't skimped on service, either. You can have the services of a Personal Shopper. They also offer a glossary of furniture terms (in case you're wondering about a description), and informative articles on topics such as veneers, construc-tion features, and home offices. You can browse through a category, such as Casual Dining, or you can do a detailed search where you select a piece, style, finish, and price range. How you shop is up to you. Delivery is free. When we browsed, Furniture.com was offering a free BBQ with orders over $100. Samples:

- Accent pieces
- Bedroom sets
- Contemporary dining sets
- Entertainment units
- Home office furniture
- Kids' furniture
- Leather chairs
- Lighting
- Mattresses
- Rugs
- Sofas
- Wicker outdoor dining groups

**Search:** Yes
**Photos:** Yes
**Ordering:** Online, Phone
**Gift Wrap:** No
**Delivery:** Ground

## FurnitureFind.com

http://www.furniturefind.com

This is your furniture superstore on the Web. You'll find well-known brands such as Vaughn-Bassett, Sealy, and Berkline, as well as lesser-known, and brand-new companies. The prices are really good—so good, in fact, that they'll double the difference if you find a better bargain. There is usually a 30% to 50% discount off retail here. Also, the shipping is free on orders over $600. Samples:

- Bedroom, living room, and dining room groups
- Daybeds and futons
- Entertainment centers
- Mattresses
- Office furniture
- Recliners
- Relax-R chairs
- Rustic-style furniture (pine with iron handles)
- Sleeper sofas
- Top-grain leather four-piece living room set

**Search:** Yes
**Photos:** Yes
**Ordering:** Online, Phone, Email
**Gift Wrap:** No
**Delivery:** Ground

## FurnitureOnline.com

http://
www.furnitureonline.com

Started four years ago by two business executives who saw the Internet as a natural place to shop for furniture for one's office, this store has grown to carry a whopping number of desks, chairs, workcenters, and accessories. It now also sells some furniture that is strictly for your home. If you need modular office systems installed, you should call their 800 number for free space planning. Samples:

- Bedroom furniture
- Bookcases
- Corner and L-shaped desks
- Country-style furniture for the home
- Entertainment centers
- Executive leather chairs
- Glider rocking chairs
- Jewelry armoires
- Lamps
- Office systems with panels
- Paintings
- Pneumatic drafting chairs

**Search:** Yes
**Photos:** Yes
**Ordering:** Online, Phone, Fax
**Gift Wrap:** No
**Delivery:** Ground

## Golf Furniture

http://www.golffurniture.com

You've really got to love golf to appreciate the items for sale here (and you really have to go to the store and look at the pictures). The selection is very small, but tailored to folks who just love getting up at the crack of dawn on the weekends to beat the crowd at the first hole. Samples:

- Cherry (or walnut or hunter-green) pottery-top golf table, complete with a little flag
- Fish pottery-top table with a glazed finish
- Golf pottery-top table with glazed finish and lipped rim

**Search**: No
**Photos**: Yes
**Ordering**: Online
**Gift Wrap**: No
**Delivery**: Ground

## Home Office Direct

http://
www.homeofficedirect.com/

This is a good place to shop for a home office or small office. We found high-quality desks and chairs at reasonable costs. They've been in business for 25 years and know their business. Most of the furniture will require assembly when it is delivered.  Samples:

- Computer credenza
- Computer desk with hutch
- Computer hide-away armoire
- Copy holders
- Corner computer desk with file cabinets
- Drafting chair
- Ergonomic task chairs
- Footrests
- Glare filters
- Keyboard drawers
- Laptop drawers
- Lateral wood file drawers
- Leather executive chair
- Monitor arms
- Small, medium, and large computer carts
- Swivel tilt chairs with arms

**Search**: Yes
**Photos**: Yes
**Ordering**: Online, Phone, Fax
**Gift Wrap**: No
**Delivery**: Ground

## Lamp Fashions

http://www.lamp-fashions.com

Decorative lighting for your home or your office. They have an excellent selection of museum-quality reproductions of Tiffany lamps. If you're into cartoon characters, check out their selection of stained-glass lamps and night-lights inspired by Disney and Warner Brothers cartoons. If you're not sure which fixture would offer the lighting effect you're going for, consult with their free decorating service. Samples:

- Crystal chandeliers
- Desk-lighting fixtures
- Halogen floor lamps
- Piano lamps
- Torchiere floor lamp
- Wildflower Tiffany-style hanging lamp
- Wisteria Tiffany-style table lamp with cast metal base
- Wrought-iron table lamps

**Search**: No
**Photos**: Yes
**Ordering**: Online, Phone, Email
**Gift Wrap**: No
**Delivery**: Ground

## The Natural Luxury Home Style Store

http://www.widerview.com

No plastic or similarly "unnatural" materials are in the furniture and accessories sold at this store. The designer bedding collections are all made from natural materials. And many items are made from hand-forged ironwork. Samples:

- Damask duvet covers
- Decorative pillows
- Iron-canopy bed frames
- Iron fixtures for the bathroom and fireplace
- Tasseled matelasse throws
- Velvet and chenille bedspreads

**Search**: No
**Photos**: Yes
**Ordering**: Online
**Gift Wrap**: Card
**Delivery**: Ground

## Office Furniture Concepts

`http://www.ofconcepts.com/`

This is a good place to shop for a home office or small office. You get a good selection and expert service, because office furniture is the only thing this store sells. They have very good pictures with virtual material swatches, when applicable. Their prices are good, but the items in their Clearance Center offer great bargains. Make sure to check there first. Furniture is shipped within three working days. And the best part—shipping and handling are free! Samples:

- Bookcases
- Conference tables
- Full-room sets of office furniture
- Halogen desk lamp
- High-rise computer workstation with monitor tilt
- High-back swivel chair
- Malaga ergonomic chair
- Pedestal file cabinets
- Storage solution

**Search:** Yes
**Photos:** Yes
**Ordering:** Online, Phone
**Gift Wrap:** No
**Delivery:** Ground

## O'Sullivan

`http://www.furnituredirect.com`

This is a great place to shop if you're setting up (or want to spiff up) your home office or small office. They have lots of different desk arrangements. Most of these have been designed with your computer in mind. We were very impressed with all of the little extras they put in their desks, such as tilting worksurfaces and footrests. You'll be able to find huge desks that can accommodate all your machines and smaller ones (great for a computer and a few other odds and ends) that can fit in a small place in the den or bedroom. With a wide assortment of designs, you can choose from oak, alder, pine, and nonwood materials. They also carry a small assortment of kitchen cabinets and other household furniture, but the real selection is for your office. The prices are extremely reasonable. Samples:

- Bookcases
- Corner desk with CD rack and vertical organizers
- L-shaped spacious alder desk with filing cabinets
- Oak executive workcenter with lighted hutch
- Storage units
- Straight desk with revolving storage tray
- TV/VCR cabinets

**Search:** Some
**Photos:** Yes
**Ordering:** Online, Phone
**Gift Wrap:** No
**Delivery:** Ground

## Pennsylvania Avenue Mall

`http://www.amishfurniture.com`

This is an Amish furniture store. All of the items are crafted out of solid oak. Your furniture is made from scratch as soon as they receive your order, so sometimes it takes as long as 10 to 12 weeks for it to be delivered. Samples:

- Bedroom furniture
- Chairs, benches, barstools
- China cabinets
- Desks
- Dining room sets
- Dry sinks
- Filing cabinets
- Jelly cupboards
- Pie safes

**Search:** No
**Photos:** Yes
**Ordering:** Online, Phone
**Gift Wrap:** No
**Delivery:** Ground

## "R" Dreams

`http://www.rdreams.com`

The "R" stands for the last name of the store's owner, Michael Reese. For 20 years he was an interior designer. Now he puts his talents into designing children's furniture. These designs aren't just scaled-down editions of adult furniture; they've been planned from the ground up just for the bodies and imaginations of our little ones. The furniture is colorful and smooth, without any sharp edges to hurt a whirling dervish—er, four-year-old. Samples:

- Boomerang stool
- Boomerang-style chair and table set
- Cherry, red, yellow, or blue rockers and side tables
- Natural very light cherry clover-leaf table and chair with strawberry or blueberry disks
- Yellow and blue table and chairs

**Search:** No
**Photos:** Yes
**Ordering:** Online
**Gift Wrap:** Card
**Delivery:** Ground

## Southwest Shopping Mall

`http://www.swshopmall.com`

A few years ago, Southwestern decor was all the rage. We don't know what's in today, but we do know that two things happened due to that craze. One is that it raised the prices on any Southwestern accessory, and two, it created an awareness of many of the beautiful things made by Native Americans. Most of the items for sale here were made on the many pueblos dotting New Mexico and Arizona. This is the real stuff. Samples:

- Dreamcatchers
- Drums
- Flutes
- Kachinas
- Masks
- Pottery
- Sandstone coasters

**Search:** Some

**Photos:** Yes
**Ordering:** Online, Phone, Fax
**Gift Wrap:** No
**Delivery:** Ground

## Sunland Imports

`http://www.sunlandimports.com`

You'll find a lot of Southwestern accessories and some furniture for your house. They also carry a lot of items from Mexico. Samples:

- Desert steer skulls
- Genuine cowhide pillows
- Hand-woven Baja shirts
- Lizard mailbox flags (a must!)
- Longhorn and cowhide furniture
- Pine log ladders
- Southwestern-style switchplates
- Tin mirrors with brass accents
- Wool blankets and bedspreads
- Wrought-iron sun wall hangings

**Search:** No
**Photos:** Yes
**Ordering:** Online
**Gift Wrap:** No
**Delivery:** Ground, 3rd Day

## To round out your furnishings, you might move on over to these chapters, too:

- Home Office Supplies
- Kitchenware & Cooking Equipment

# Gardening

Whether you are working on your garden almost every day or just starting to develop a green thumb, you'll find the stores listed in this chapter a real delight. From fragrant roses to heirloom seeds; from redwood garden furniture to slug bars (no kidding) . . . absolutely everything can be found at these Web stores. Sometimes shipping can be expensive when you order a lot of heavy items, especially garden tools and furniture, so we've noted which stores offer free shipping or substantial discounts on big orders.

## Ambrose Gardens

http://www.ambrosegardens.com

If you live in the north (Growing Zones 3 and 4) your garden has special requirements, like a short growing season and extremely cold winters. All of the plants sold from Ambrose have been nurtured to withstand winters in Minnesota and other cold climates. Don't forget to read their excellent gardening tips and also look at their "garden baskets" specifically designed for problem areas, such as the driveway or a shady corner. Samples:
- Blue Cadet hostas
- Carrara peonies
- Gift certificates
- Oriental lilies
- Purple Moor grass
- Siberian irises
- Spring bulbs

**Search:** Yes
**Photos:** Yes
**Ordering:** Online, Fax
**Gift Wrap:** Card
**Delivery:** Ground

## Avalon Garden.com

http://www.avalongarden.com

Unusual and decorative gardening supplies are available at this unique gardening store. All of the Avalon Garden products are made from a material named "MarLette," which is a mixture of Georgia marble and some secret additives that are supposed to give the item a much longer life outside. They also offer a lot of personalized items. Free shipping for orders over $75, so go ahead and order that two-ton marble birdbath. Samples:
- Animal statues
- Boot brushes
- Cherub wall fountain
- Decorative and personalized garden rocks
- Golf thermometer and clock
- Personalized signs
- St. Francis bird feeder
- Sunflower planter

**Search:** Some
**Photos:** Yes
**Ordering:** Online, Phone
**Gift Wrap:** No
**Delivery:** Ground

## Burpee

http://www.burpee.com

If your favorite day in January is the day the first seed catalog arrives, then this is the store for you. Burpee's has been refining and cultivating their seed crop for generations. They've also developed many of their own varieties. Like many seed nurseries, they've expanded to include bulbs and many gardening supplies, but we can tell you from personal experience, their flower and vegetable seeds are the main attraction. Samples:
- Herb plants
- Monet-style garden furniture
- Seed starting kits
- Slug bars
- Spring bulbs
- Vegetable and flower seeds

- Wall o' water

**Search:** Yes
**Photos:** Yes
**Ordering:** Online, Fax, Phone
**Gift Wrap:** No
**Delivery:** Ground

# Canterbury Farms

http://www.spiritone.com/
~canfarms/

Want to have your own culinary and medicinal herb arsenal growing in your own backyard? It's easy to do when you go shopping here. For about a penny a seed you can protect yourself by using your homegrown herbs for many uses, such as keeping those nasty flies away on a sunny afternoon or sipping a cup of tea to relieve some bloating. Samples:

- Capillary mat
- Compost activator
- Copper slug-barrier tape
- Germinating mixes
- Newspaper pot maker
- Plastic pots
- Seed starting system
- Soil block maker
- Soil thermometer

**Search:** Yes
**Photos:** Some
**Ordering:** Online
**Gift Wrap:** No
**Delivery:** Ground

# Carpenters Lace, Inc.

http://www.carpenterslace.com

What's a backyard without a lot of birds? Our feathered friends not only look pretty, they benefit our gardens by eating menacing insects. (OK, so sometimes they nibble on our veggies, too, but they are so cute!) This place specializes in making your garden or patio

area a haven for birds by creating beautiful and unusual cedar houses for them. Sample styles are:

- Church
- Dove cote
- Lantern
- Lighthouse
- Slat house
- Victorian

**Search:** Some
**Photos:** Yes
**Ordering:** Online, Phone
**Gift Wrap:** No
**Delivery:** Ground

# Dan's Garden Shop

http://dansgardenshop.com

Dan's is like the small neighborhood nursery on the corner. It's small, but ample, with all your favorites in stock. This store is pretty and easy to navigate. Besides seeds and supplies, Dan supplies links to useful gardening sites. Samples:

- Gardening-related books
- Indoor growing equipment
- Season extenders
- Soil-moisture additives
- Soil-warming equipment
- Vegetable, herb, and flower seeds

**Search:** Yes
**Photos:** Yes
**Ordering:** Online, Phone
**Gift Wrap:** No
**Delivery:** Ground

# Edmund's Roses

http://www.edmundsroses.com

It must be a nice job running a rose nursery. So many of them have been at it for a long time! This one is going on 50 years and seems to be growing nicely. You'll find many of the more popular floribundas and tea roses, but what Edmund's offers is a good selection of hard-to-find unique and unusual roses. Check out the new roses for Y2000 (guaranteed not to ruin your computer!). Discounts of 5% offered on rose orders over $175. Samples:

- Climbers
- Fragrance collection (these go very early)
- Gardening tools
- Grandifloras
- Shrubs

**Search:** Some
**Photos:** Yes
**Ordering:** Online, Phone
**Gift Wrap:** Card
**Delivery:** Ground, 2nd Day

## Garden.com

http://www.garden.com

A huge online nursery with barrels full of flowers, shrubs, trees, vegetables, and just about anything else you can grow in your garden (except maybe weeds). Not sure what plants to get for your particular garden? Use the Plant Finder, answer some questions, and you'll be rewarded with a slide show of possibles. Samples:

- David Austin roses
- Fragrant garden plants
- Fruit trees
- Garden designs
- Gardening gloves
- Herbs
- Planner tutorials
- Shrubs
- Vegetable seeds
- Weed killers

**Search:** Yes
**Photos:** Yes
**Ordering:** Online, Phone
**Gift Wrap:** No
**Delivery:** Ground, Overnight

## Garden Talk

http://gardentalk.com

This family-owned store has been around for a long time, and with good reason. They specialize in selling useful and high-quality gardening tools from around the world. It's not all work here, though. You can read some amusing and informative gardening articles, too. Samples:

- Classic rose arches
- English hand-forged steel digging tools
- Felco pruners
- Galvanized metal watering cans
- Gooseneck hoes
- Stainless steel botanical labels

**Search:** Yes
**Photos:** Yes
**Ordering:** Online
**Gift Wrap:** No
**Delivery:** Ground

## Gardener's Supply Company

http://www.gardeners.com

If you can't go to your local gardening center, this is the next-best thing. The company is owned by a bunch of avid gardeners, so you know you'll get the good stuff here. Besides carrying much of what you'll need, from seeds to fertilizers, this store also gives you tons of advice. So, whether you're a novice or a master gardener, you'll find everything you need. Don't forget to check out their Clearance Department. Samples:

- Climbing roses
- Copper support markets
- Garden furniture
- Goatskin gloves
- Natural weed killer
- Pots and planters

**Search:** Yes
**Photos:** Yes
**Ordering:** Online, Fax
**Gift Wrap:** No
**Delivery:** Ground

# Home Harvest Garden Supply

http://www.homeharvest.com

You know the health food store that carries all those environmentally safe and good items that are so hard to find in the regular grocery stores? Well, think of this place as a gardening health store. These earth-friendly products are not easy to find elsewhere. Perfect for the organic gardener. Great selection of hydroponic supplies, too. Samples:
- Beneficial insects
- Cloning gels
- Fluorescent plant grow tubes
- Grow light accessories
- Hydroponic systems
- Natural pest controls
- Nonchemical disease and fungus controls
- Organic fertilizers
- Peat pots

**Search**: Yes
**Photos**: Some
**Ordering**: Online, Phone, Fax
**Gift Wrap**: No
**Delivery**: Ground

# Jackson and Perkins

http://
www.jacksonandperkins.com

You'll be able to find hanging baskets, perennials, annuals, and gardening tools here, but the real stars of this store are the roses. J and P have been in this field for over a century and they know their stuff. Wondering just which rose or roses would be good for you? Use the Rose Search and discover which roses have the color, fragrance, or type you're looking for. Have no idea what you want? Just look at the lovely pictures. Make sure you look at the Net Savings department for discounts. Samples:
- Climbing roses
- Hedge roses
- Hybrid tea roses
- Miniature roses
- Rose collections (saves you $$$)
- Rose trees

**Search**: Yes
**Photos**: Yes
**Ordering**: Online, Phone, Fax
**Gift Wrap**: Card
**Delivery**: Ground, 2nd Day, Overnight

# Landscape USA

http://www.landscapeusa.com

A nice selection of gardening supplies and live plants. With reasonable prices, the emphasis is on helping you design and maintain your landscaping. You'll find a huge selection of irrigation supplies, such as underground sprinklers and night lighting, arches, arbors, even putting greens. Samples:
- Bonsai trees
- Bulbs
- Gardening tools
- Greenhouses and cold frames
- Organic emendments
- Pond supplies
- Resource center
- Seed starting mix
- Wind chimes

**Search**: Yes
**Photos**: Yes
**Ordering**: Online, Phone
**Gift Wrap**: No
**Delivery**: Ground, 2nd Day, Overnight

# Niche Gardens

http://www.nichegdn.com

The niche of this store is nursery-propagated wildflowers, native perennials, and plants for xeriscaping. Samples:
- Groundcovers
- Herbaceous plants
- Low-water plants
- Native plants

- Ornamental grasses
- Unique seeds

**Search:** Some
**Photos:** Some
**Ordering:** Online, Phone, Fax
**Gift Wrap:** No
**Delivery:** Ground

## Pearsall's Garden Center

http://www.pearsalls.com

Starting in a local grocery store, Oscar Pearsall decided to offer some fertilizer to accommodate the local farmers. Guess which part of his business thrived and grew? Today, a century later, this family-owned business prides itself on providing great customer service, in the tradition of Oscar. Besides all of the usual items you'd expect to find at an all-purpose garden-supply store, you can find a large assortment of bird-watching and bird-feeding stuff. Samples:

- Birdhouses and bird feeders
- Garden clogs
- Left-handed Felco pruners
- Organic fishmeal fertilizer
- Personalized accent garden rocks
- Sundials
- Topiary forms (ready for you to design)

**Search:** Yes
**Photos:** Yes
**Ordering:** Online
**Gift Wrap:** No
**Delivery:** Ground

## Shepherd's Garden Seeds

http://www.shepherdseeds.com

Unusual and old-variety seeds and bulbs. There are over 500 seed varieties to choose from. Once you select your seeds, browse through their Reference Library and Growing Guides and receive some expert advice. Samples:

- Biogarten sprouter

- Harvesting tips
- Heirloom seeds
- Herb, flower, and vegetable seeds
- Jersey Knight asparagus plants
- Natural insecticide
- Saffron crocus

**Search:** Yes
**Photos:** Some (mostly drawings)
**Ordering:** Online, Phone
**Gift Wrap:** No
**Delivery:** Ground

If you'd like flowers without the effort of growing them yourself, you might dig into the stores in the chapter on Flowers.

# Gifts

If you have run out of time, or you're drawing a blank when you struggle to come up with ideas for a present, these stores may strike a match to your imagination, suggesting gorgeous and silly, preposterous and luxurious items. Because most of these stores wrap and ship direct to a recipient, you can pick and go, leaving the hard work to their staff. You can even have some stores add engraving or a personal message to the product itself. In a few days, your gift arrives at the door of the person you wanted to surprise. You get the thanks, without the hassles of parking at the mall, wrapping, boxing, and lugging the package to the post office or delivery service. We love it.

When Stuart and Janice's baby Willem was born, we found tot toys pronto online, and when we were caught off guard by a relative's upcoming anniversary, we were able to get the crystal vase delivered on time, thanks to an online gift store.

These stores specialize in gifts, not just general merchandise; some even give you suggestions for particular occasions, ages, or interests. Sure, you could find a product elsewhere, have it shipped to your house, wrap it up, and then ship it out yourself. But these stores focus on products that make good gifts, and they ship direct to the recipient, which saves you time and effort. That's a gift to yourself.

## 1 800 Birthday

http://www.1800birthday.com

A site just for birthday presents, with a reminder service, and more than 100 interesting gifts, including cigars, flowers, gags, and personal electronics. Best service: Get an accurate reproduction of an original newspaper from the day someone was born. The Historic Newspaper Archive provides the whole paper, not just the front page, for newspapers from any major American city, from 1880 to 1997. Newspapers are folded in half and inserted into a protective folder. You get to specify a date on which you want products shipped. Samples:

- 20 balloons with the theme Congratulations!
- Historic Newspaper Edition with Personalized Deluxe Gold Leaf Case
- Premium cigar sampler
- Teddy bear with sweater carrying your personal message

**Search:** No
**Photos:** Yes
**Ordering:** Online
**Gift Wrap:** Message only
**Delivery:** Overnight

## 911 Gifts

http://www.911gifts.com

Uh-oh. It's an emergency. You have to get the right gift, right away. This site understands. It's built to help you find the right present for an anniversary, apology, birthday, bridal shower, engagement, graduation, housewarming, illness, new baby, retirement, romance, thank-you, upcoming holiday, or wedding. When you are wondering what would be right for a particular person, they offer a list of more than two dozen types (niece under 18, grandfather, client), so you can get gift ideas that have been targeted at that age, gender, and relationship. You can also look up presents by price. For your inspiration, they list birth flowers, birth stones, astrological stones, and the right stuff for each anniversary year. Neat: Next to some products they show you what shipping method to choose, depending on when you want the gift to arrive. Samples:

- Computer vacuum for the new graduate
- Flashlight screwdriver

- Kama Sutra Weekend Kit, with Original Oil of Love, Pleasure Balm, bathing gels, and Honey Dust with feather applicator
- Root Beer Gift Tin, bucket with nonalcoholic Henry Weinhard's Root Beer, black bean and corn salsa, butter toffee pretzels, tortilla chips, roasted almonds, and chocolate chip cookies

**Search:** Yes
**Photos:** Yes
**Ordering:** Online
**Gift Wrap:** Yes, with messages
**Delivery:** Ground, 3rd Day, 2nd Day, Overnight

## As Seen on TV

http://www.asontv.com

Amazing! All those products sold at 2 A.M. have come back together, on the shelves of this virtual store. If you forgot to write down the 800 number, now you have a second chance to get the AB Exerciser, Dough Magic, Handy Shredder, or Smart Wrench. Two hundred fifty products appear in categories such as automotive, beauty, electronics, health, housewares, sports, tools, and video. These novelty items may be just the gift to amuse, or solve a problem. For each product you get a picture, list of benefits, and the pricing (showing how much of a discount you are getting). You can have product descriptions translated into French, German, Italian, Portuguese, or Spanish. Some products come with free shipping. Order more than $100, and you get free gifts. Samples:

- Peel-A-Magic (peels, cores, and slices all at once)
- Space Bag Organizer (shrinks storage up to 75%, works with any household vacuum cleaner for airtight, waterproof protection against bugs, odors, moisture)
- Weazel Ball ("It moves as if it's alive!")

**Search:** Yes
**Photos:** Yes
**Ordering:** Online, Phone, Fax
**Gift Wrap:** No
**Delivery:** Ground, Overnight

## Azazz

http://www.azazz.com

With 12,000 classy products, this store works hard to make it a snap for you to find a gift you'll feel proud to give, in departments such as accessories, apparel, baby and kids, games and toys, gourmet, health and beauty, hobbies, home, jewelry, office, outdoors, pro shop, sports, and travel. In each department, you can search for individual products, or shop by brand. Top brands only, and stiff prices (discounted if you apply for their free membership), but if you want to find a gift you can count on, no matter what the cost, this store will probably have something that appeals to you. You can get the assistance of a personal shopper during business hours. Odd: no gift wrapping. Samples:

- Celestron Beginning Bird-Watching Kit
- Fred Couples Autographed Golf Ball on wooden stand
- Olympus Zoom Digital Camera
- Swiss Army Brand Travel Alarm

**Search:** Yes
**Photos:** Yes
**Ordering:** Online, Phone
**Gift Wrap:** Message only
**Delivery:** 3rd Day

## Banker's Collection

http://www.bankers-collection.com

Yes, if you love a banker, this is the place to get financially sound gifts, with an investment-grade flare. You don't have to pay until the goods arrive and you approve. (Basically, they bill you.) Delivery takes about two weeks. Samples:

- Euro-currency gold watch, 14-karat solid gold, with the SWIFT abbreviations for the older national currencies around the dial, and your own country symbol extra polished
- Gold Bull-and-Bear cuff links, handmade, 18-karat solid gold
- Triple A Choker, 14-karat solid gold, with symbol of the top credit rating

**Search:** No
**Photos:** Yes
**Ordering:** Online
**Gift Wrap:** No
**Delivery:** Ground

## Barrington

http://www.barrington-ltd.com

They bill themselves as an executive gift collection of pens and leather goods, and most of these little gifts are elegant, if you don't mind paying executive rates. (The owner seems to be hoping for corporate orders, because he offers engraving of logos, names, and initials, as well as custom boxes.) Samples:

- Green Marble Grand Rollerball pen
- Masters Black Money Clip
- Masters British Tan Portfolio in leather

**Search:** No
**Photos:** Yes
**Ordering:** Online, Phone
**Gift Wrap:** Custom boxes
**Delivery:** Ground

## Best by Mail

http://www.bestbymail.com

Based on a mail-order business, this site helps you pick an interesting, offbeat, and often beautiful gift by type (office, home, outdoors, collectibles), occasion (baby shower, birthday, graduation, wedding, housewarming, anniversary), or recipient. Good descriptions, big pictures, and nice extras (for instance, you can listen to the sound of the wind chimes). Most orders go out within 48 hours, and if there is going to be a delay, they let you know by email. They ship directly to the recipient, if you wish. Samples:

- Hand-tuned wind chimes
- Indian Cliff indoor water fountain made of earth-toned slate, with pump
- Picnic backpack set, with oak cutting board, cotton napkins, cheese knife, acrylic wineglasses, combined corkscrew, bottle opener, and knife,

dinner plates, steel flatware, and detachable insulated wine duffel, four-person model

**Search:** Yes
**Photos:** Yes
**Ordering:** Online, Phone, Fax, Email
**Gift Wrap:** Card
**Delivery:** Ground

## Bowl USA

http://bowlusa.com

Love a bowler? This is a good store to get the very latest bowling equipment, even before you can find it in most other stores. They sell bowling shirts in sizes up to XXX. They charge a low, flat fee per item (for heavy items) for shipping. Samples:

- Ball banks
- Bowler earrings
- Bowling balls and bags
- Bowling doormat
- Bowling-pin clocks
- Instructional books, tapes, and videos
- Ladies' and men's bowling shoes
- Men's 100% cotton bowling shirts
- Pin banks

**Search:** Some
**Photos:** Some
**Ordering:** Online, Phone
**Gift Wrap:** No
**Delivery:** Ground

## Disney Store

http://store.disney.go.com/
shopping/

Disney offers hundreds of games, toys, collectibles, music CDs, videos, and software, all designed to remind you of their movies. The site helps you look for a present for an infant, a kid, or an adult. Wonderful: You can pick a Disney character, write a greeting, and have the image and text placed on a mouse pad, mug, baby blanket, or whatchmacallit, using their Design Online system (but the personalization may take a month or so before they can ship the finished product). Bright, fun, and full of must-have items, this online site is as attention-grabbing as their shop at the local mall. Samples:

- *Beauty and the Beast* authentic 35mm film cel, in frame, with backlighting at the touch of a button
- Dancing Flik, the ant who dances in time as you clap or sing
- Eeyore Business Card Holder
- Mickey and Minnie Wedding Plate, with bride-and-groom names engraved, along with the wedding date
- Pooh Curio Cabinet Clock with your family name on the door

**Search:** Yes
**Photos:** Yes, with great close-ups
**Ordering:** Online
**Gift Wrap:** Gift box available on some items
**Delivery:** Ground, 4th Day

# Dixie's Gifts

http://www.dixiesgifts.com

Toys that move, shake, sing, and make noise. Yo-yos. And a lot of magic, or really, practical joke items. These items will appeal to kids and teenagers, and grown-ups who just can't resist. Some gizmos are certain to make parents gag. The store usually ships within 48 hours, with a fixed rate for two pounds or less. Samples:

- Bubba Teeth, made out of acrylic denture material, to look like terribly rotten teeth
- Dancing Ga-Ga Gorilla, moves feet, arm, heads whenever you play music nearby
- Electronic Whoopie Machine
- Fart Bomb Bags

**Search:** No
**Photos:** Yes
**Ordering:** Online, Phone, Fax, Email
**Gift Wrap:** No
**Delivery:** Ground, 3rd Day, Overnight

# EarthDream

http://www.earthdream.com

Green gifts, including alternative medicine, aromatherapy scents, coffee, puppets, puzzles, umbrellas, and veggie fare. Samples:

- Aloe-and-Chamomile Baby Bar
- Honeysuckle Baby Bath
- *Peaceful Cook Vegetarian Cookbook*
- Sunflower Baby Bar

**Search:** Yes
**Photos:** No
**Ordering:** Online, Phone, Fax
**Gift Wrap:** Baskets, Certificates
**Delivery:** Ground

# eGift

http://egift.com

Well, the gifts themselves are solid, not just a bunch of electrons. But this subsidiary of CyberShop is a well-thought-out electronic store, with a gift finder, gift reminder, gift expert, and suggestions based on relationships, categories of gifts, favorites, and occasions. They emphasize the discounts they offer, which are often excellent. In fact, they swear that if you find a better price at a "reputable retailer," they will match the price or refund the difference (except with Furbys). For next-day delivery of flowers, order by 1 P.M. Eastern Time. Orders for gourmet food and candy must be placed before 9 A.M., Monday through Wednesday, for delivery through Friday. Everything else, if you order by 9 P.M., will be shipped the next day. Samples:

- Ahava Body Spa Kit, with hand cream, foot cream, body lotion, shower gel
- Baby's Time Capsule
- Casio Portable Sports TV
- Chocolate truffles in a box shaped like a kite
- Emerald-and-diamond pendant in 14-karat gold
- Waterford round votive vase from Vatican Library Collection

**Search:** Yes
**Photos:** Yes

**Ordering:** Online, Phone
**Gift Wrap:** Certificates only
**Delivery:** 2nd Day, Overnight

# Foodstuffs

http://www.foodstuffs.com

For foodies, this store offers stuff that looks like food, smells like food, or reminds you of cooking, noshing, sniffing, tasting, and chewing with gusto. The joke is you can't eat these items. Candles that look like pears, a bird feeder in the shape of an eggplant, soap that has the scent of chocolate, these are the gifts for chefs, gardeners, and people who really don't need another t-shirt. Some products must be made to your wishes, and that could take 6 to 8 weeks. If you're in a hurry, call them directly to make sure the product is immediately available. Order by 3 P.M., Eastern Time, for next-day shipping. Samples:

- Chili Pen, with two refills
- Cook's bracelet with miniature skillet, cleaver, pepper mill, and wine opener in pewter
- Kitchen Sink Fountain, with handmade terra-cotta dishes and real water cycling through, pumped by an electric motor
- Velvet pillows in the shape of olives, grapes, eggplants, or artichokes, sewn to order

**Search:** No
**Photos:** Yes
**Ordering:** Online, Phone
**Gift Wrap:** No
**Delivery:** Ground, 2nd Day, Overnight

# GiftTree

http://www.gifttree.com

Gifts that are ready to go. GiftTree offers balloons, baskets, flowers, funny items, plants, roses, and virtual gifts (for electronic delivery). If you need a gift for a particular situation, GiftTree gives you suggestions for a new baby, get-well, romance, thank-you, or sympathy gift. If you want a very specific set of products in a gift basket, you can request those, and get back several bids from local vendors near the recipient, so you can decide which seems best. To get flowers or fruit to someone by 6 P.M., order by 1 P.M. in the recipient's time zone; after that, the package arrives the next business day (no deliveries on Sunday or holidays). Gift baskets go by air or ground. Samples:

- Bonsai tree
- Bouquet of half-dozen latex balloons
- Loving Memories, floral arrangement, small, medium, or premium size
- Virtual card with color picture of a river

**Search:** Yes
**Photos:** Yes
**Ordering:** Online
**Gift Wrap:** Yes
**Delivery:** Ground, 3rd Day, 2nd Day, Overnight, Email

# Hammacher Schlemmer

http://www.hammacher.com

A wonderful gadget store from 19th century New York, Hammacher Schlemmer has grown through mail order to Web sales, still specializing in the unusual (sometimes only one of a kind) and the unexpected. The Hammacher Schlemmer Institute puts some of these products through testing, to pick the best. (We've found several of their products incredibly tough and durable.) They ship within 24 hours. Samples:

- Aerial-photography model Cessna airplane with camera controlled by radio transmitter, for taking pictures in midair
- 7-foot-diameter vinyl bubbles for kids to roll around from the inside, on lawn or carpet
- 8-foot arched redwood landscaping bridge, weather-and-insect-resistant, assembly required
- Best Nose Hair Trimmer, rust-resistant blades
- 10-piece maze kids can crawl inside, with house, ball pit with 25 colored balls, blocks, and tunnels

**Search:** No
**Photos:** Yes
**Ordering:** Online, Phone
**Gift Wrap:** No
**Delivery:** Ground, 2nd Day, Overnight

## Harry and David

http://www.harryanddavid.com

This store started when these two brothers ran into trouble during the Depression. To save their orchard, they dreamed up the idea of selling pears by mail. In our youth, these wonderful boxes of grapefruit, pears, and apples started arriving after Thanksgiving, and supplied us with dessert through January. Lush, perfect fruit, in a soft nest, that's what we liked. This beautiful site lets you pick quickly, using their Gift Finder. Each product description shows a picture to make you drool, describes the package, gives its weight, and tells you when it is available. Delivery takes about two weeks, unless you pay extra for speed. Samples:

- Fruit-of-the-Month Club®
- Oil-and-vinegar decanter
- Pearsnapples and Cheeses, 5 pounds

**Search:** Yes
**Photos:** Yes, yes, yes
**Ordering:** Online, Phone, Fax
**Gift Wrap:** Yes
**Delivery:** Ground, 2nd Day, Overnight

## Indian River Gift Fruit

http://www.giftfruit.com

Sliced oranges drip on the welcome page of this Florida store offering grapefruit, oranges, and tangelos, with gift boxes, baskets, and other edible presents such as ham and turkey. Because in many cases we are talking about real fruit, availability depends on the season. Free delivery in the U.S, but they do not ship to Hawaii or Alaska. Samples:

- 12 long-stemmed red roses
- Honey-basted ham
- Indian River Fruit Club, 7 months
- Ruby red grapefruit
- Smoked turkey

**Search:** No
**Photos:** Yes
**Ordering:** Online, Phone
**Gift Wrap:** Yes, with message
**Delivery:** Ground

## InterCenter

http://www.InterCenter.com

Modestly priced items you might choose as a gift. Products range from the handy to the impressive, in departments such as automotive, cameras, electronics, hardware, lawn and garden, pet supplies, toys, travel, and sporting goods. Samples:

- Hedge Shears
- Remington Garment/Fabric Steamer
- Westclox Arcadia Quartz Wall Clock
- Zojirushi Tuff Road Commuter Mug, stainless steel

**Search:** Yes
**Photos:** Yes
**Ordering:** Online
**Gift Wrap:** No
**Delivery:** Ground

## Internet Kitchen

http://www.your-kitchen.com

Great source for quality brand-name kitchen gifts at good prices. Which brands are we talking about? Logos like Cuisinart, Farberware, Fiskars, KitchenAid, and Krups. This store offers individual items and cooking sets, plus some china sets. You'll also find those little items that are necessary in any kitchen, such as aprons, towels, and hot pads. Don't forget to check for open-stock specials. Gift wrapping is free. Samples:

- Chef's blue or white jacket
- Compact coffeemakers
- Electric-cooking products
- Espresso makers
- Food processors
- Hand blenders
- Hand-anodized nonstick cookware sets
- Hardwood cutting tables
- Ice-cream makers
- Nonstick stainless-steel cookware sets
- Rice cookers
- Steamers
- Strainers and colanders
- Toasters

- Waffle-makers

**Search**: Yes
**Photos**: Yes
**Ordering**: Online, Phone, Fax
**Gift Wrap**: Yes
**Delivery**: Ground

# Island Gifts Direct

http://oldhawaii.com/igd

Like one of the stores in Waikiki, this site offers gift coconuts, coffee, and ukuleles, as well as items that will bring back memories of your Hawaiian vacation. But if you go in the back, you'll find items that folks who live in Hawaii really use, so if you are trying to find a present for a displaced kamaaina, this Kaunakakai store can provide care packages of mochi crunch and dried plums, as well as real leis. You can pick out a bunch of items, and have the store plop them into a raffia basket as a gift. And, for fun, you can have the staff write a message on a coconut and mail that off, too. They are accustomed to shipping internationally, particularly to Japan. If you want delivery faster than a week, you have to email them to find out how much more they will charge. Samples:

- Chant of Aloha Gift Basket, with Kona coffee, chocolate truffles, notecards, photo album with 120 views, Tapa photo frame, mugs, and chocolate-covered Kona coffee beans
- *How to Hula*, video and book set
- Li Hing Mui Red snacks
- Smoked Cuttlefish Legs
- Wasabi Norimaki
- Yellow and white plumeria lei

**Search**: No
**Photos**: Yes
**Ordering**: Online, Phone, Fax, Email
**Gift Wrap**: Yes
**Delivery**: Ground, 3rd Day

# JewelryWeb.com

http://www.jewelryweb.com

Need something pretty, wrapped in a gift box, and delivered in two days? Look no further. At this store you'll not only find the perfect gift but you'll also be able to purchase it at a 40%–60% savings off retail. The photos show good detail, so you can see what you're getting. The store also lets you substitute various gemstones, so if the ring you see in the picture has a ruby in it, you may be able to switch it to a topaz. Multipay, no-interest payment plan available. Samples:

- 14-karat Brazilian amethysts and diamond ring
- Diamond pendant-and-earring set
- Platinum demi-hoop earrings
- Tri-color stackable burnished rings
- 2-tone diamond ring
- White-gold cubit zirconia rings

**Search**: Yes
**Photos**: Yes
**Ordering**: Online, Phone, Fax
**Gift Wrap**: Yes
**Delivery**: Ground, 2nd Day

# Latin American Nexus

http://www.lanexus.com

Beautiful pots, posters, books, and clothing from Latin America, South America, and the Caribbean. They have cultural artifacts and newly made crafts from many countries. The site is well-organized, and offers lots of help when you want to move around. Each product gets a brief description, and pictures, small and large. Orders go out within two business days. Free shipping on orders over $65. Samples:

- Diego Rivera, *Flower Seller, 1926*, on 4 notecards with envelopes, 5" x 7"
- Douglas Rodriguez, *Nuevo Latino: Recipes that Celebrate the New Latin American Cuisine*
- Mayan 3-Generations Mask, 7" x 11"
- Nicaraguan Swan Vase, 3" x 5.5"
- Poster of Frida Kahlo's *Self Portrait as a Tehuana*, 39" x 26"
- Poster of Nivia Gonzalez's *Rose to the Deer*
- Zapotec Corn God Urn, 12" x 10"

**Search**: Yes
**Photos**: Yes

**Ordering:** Online
**Gift Wrap:** Yes
**Delivery:** Ground, 2nd Day, Overnight

## Museum Shop

http://www.museumshop.com

A partnership of stores at a few dozen museums, ranging from the posh Yale University Art Gallery, in New Haven, to the erudite Academy of Natural Sciences, in Philadelphia, and the arty Los Angeles County Museum, this shop is specifically set up to help you locate the right gift. The Gift Finder helps you navigate through books, clothing, food, games, home furnishings, jewelry, posters, prints, sculpture, and stationery, most of which is elegant, although not always chic. They will remind you when gifts are due, if you want, and you can put together a gift list, if you can't buy everything all at once. Samples:

- Deluxe Fire Fighter Hat and Vest Set, Cincinnati Fire Museum
- Fabergé egg tins, Hillwood Museum and Gardens
- Mount Everest "Reliorama" from Museum of Science, Boston
- Picasso plates, microwavable, dishwasher safe
- Van Gogh, *Wheatfield with Crows*, poster, 31" x 49.5", L. A. County Museum of Art

**Search:** No
**Photos:** Yes
**Ordering:** Online
**Gift Wrap:** No
**Delivery:** Ground, 2nd Day

## Netropolitan Plaza

http://
www.netropolitanplaza.com

If you want to find something really unusual, try this minimall of tiny little shops, each with a few products, most of which you couldn't find anywhere else. Each boutique seems to be run by an individual craftsperson. Samples:

- Floral arrangement made by coiling, shaping, and assembling narrow strips of paper in a process known as quilling
- Giant pencil with your 30-character message
- Hand-carved, wood-burned gourds
- Hand-stitched baby bonnet made out of handkerchief, with lace
- Your favorite Bible verses hand-written and mounted on a plaque

**Search:** No
**Photos:** Yes
**Ordering:** Online
**Gift Wrap:** No
**Delivery:** Ground

## Orvis

http://www.orvis.com

Figuring out how to satisfy shoppers as the dawn of the new century rises shouldn't be hard for Orvis, because they already did that at the beginning of the last century. Yes, Orvis has been around that long. Their staying power is due to the quality of merchandise they sell and the service they give their customers. Their specialty is, and has always been, fishing. People who love to do fly fishing will especially find the selection rewarding. If you're looking for a gift for a fly fisherman, Orvis has a good selection of gifts. The pictures introducing each section are spectacular. Samples:

- Bamboo fly rods
- Battenkill rod bags
- Children's animal games
- Fishing luggage
- Fleece fly vest for men
- Fly-tying kits
- Graphite spin rods
- Men's snake-proof boots (in widths up to EE)
- Women's outdoor-type clothing

**Search:** Yes
**Photos:** Yes
**Ordering:** Online, Phone
**Gift Wrap:** Yes
**Delivery:** Ground, 3rd Day, Overnight

# Paper Paradise

http://www.khs.com

Kitty Hawk software brings you a paper folder's paradise, with rubber-band-launch paper jets, print-and-build western buildings, and Origami animals and flowers. They ship within 24 hours. Samples:
- *Fun Flyers: Jets*, software for customizing airplane designs, with 10 precut paper airplanes to assemble and fly, Windows or Mac
- *Paper Airforce*, software for creating paper airplanes on Windows or Mac
- *Print and Build Western Buildings*, software with 20 buildings for model railroads and dioramas

**Search:** No
**Photos:** Yes
**Ordering:** Online, Phone
**Gift Wrap:** No
**Delivery:** Ground

# Paper Studio

http://www.paperstudio.com

You order their nicely designed paper, download free designs, and put the paper and images together, using your computer and printer, to turn out greeting cards and party projects. You can choose traditional rectangular paper, squares, or curving shapes such as circles and hearts. Designs are colorful. They give away the fonts that they use in the designs, too. Order paper by 3 P.M. Central Time on business days to have product shipped same day. No Saturday deliveries. Samples:
- Greeting card and party sampler, with 14 sample sheets, for edge-to-edge printing, with scoring down center
- Standard greeting card paper, matte, rectangular, for edge-to-edge printing on both sides, scored to fold down the center, 15 cards with envelopes

**Search:** No
**Photos:** Yes
**Ordering:** Online, Phone, Email
**Gift Wrap:** No
**Delivery:** 3rd Day, 2nd Day, Overnight

# Perfect Present Picker

http://presentpicker.com/ppp

The whole reason for this site is an elaborate search mechanism, which is far and away the most sophisticated available on sites devoted to gifts. You can search for presents by the recipient's interests (with more than 50 topics), by occasion (more than three dozen possibilities), or personality traits (four dozen). The site offers six kinds of top-12 lists (choice, expensive, inexpensive, outrageous, popular, and sleepers). They also provide a calendar, and info about anniversaries and birthstones. Unfortunately, you have to jump to some other vendor's site to purchase each product, and some of those vendors do not sell online. Samples:
- Panama straw hat, "museum quality"
- Small angel wings for child up to 3' 5", with extra feathers for replacements

**Search:** Yes
**Photos:** Yes
**Ordering:** Online, Phone, Fax, Email
**Gift Wrap:** Some
**Delivery:** Ground

# Rabid Home

http://www.rabidhome.com

We don't know why this store chose such a, well, crazy name, but their beautiful site offers designer gifts for the bath, table, and desk. Nice extra: Stylegirl records her design discoveries in photos taken at flea markets and other locations, showing products that are stylish, even though the site doesn't offer them for sale. If you live in Manhattan, you can have items delivered within hours by messenger if you order by 10 A.M. Samples:
- Three spiral notebooks with bright yellow pages (small size), red pages (medium size), and lime-green pages (large), inside black covers
- Boxed bamboo chopsticks, 10 pairs
- Cedar sake cups, set of 5
- Glazed ceramic cup with rim shaped like a petal, set of 4

**Search:** No
**Photos:** Yes

**Ordering:** Online
**Gift Wrap:** No
**Delivery:** Ground, 2nd Day, Overnight

## Scent Warehouse

http://www.scentwarehouse.com

You can almost smell these fragrances through your computer. In fact, the site reminds us of a spice warehouse we used to live near, where we could smell the cinnamon and ginger from a block away. This store sells designer scents at discount. No imitations, no knock-offs. Shipping is $3 per order anywhere in the U.S.; they ship within two days. Samples:
- Curve for Woman by Liz Claiborne
- Hugo for Woman by Hugo Boss
- Opium pour Homme by Yves Saint-Laurent
- Polo Sport Woman by Ralph Lauren

**Search:** Yes
**Photos:** Yes
**Ordering:** Online
**Gift Wrap:** No
**Delivery:** Ground

## Serenity Shop

http://www.serenityshop.com

Inspirational gifts addressing addiction and recovery, with products for participants in the Anonymous groups devoted to alcoholism, cocaine, co-dependency, gambling, marijuana, overeating, sex, and smoking. Products include cuddly bears, self-help books, bumper stickers with slogans, notecards, jewelry, medallions, runes, and audio or videotapes. Samples:
- 60 Angel-Power Cards
- Al-Anon pendant, 14K gold
- Anne Katherine, *Boundaries, Where You End and I Begin*
- Deepak Chopra, *Boundless Energy*, audio tape
- *My Daily Moral Inventory* wallet card

**Search:** Yes
**Photos:** A few
**Ordering:** Online

**Gift Wrap:** No
**Delivery:** Ground

## Service Merchandise

http://
www.servicemerchandise.com

Pretty presents, starting with the jewelry that formed the core of this store when it began, with diamonds, gold chains, silver, even wedding bands. They've sorted other gifts into categories such as electronics, health, home, kids, kitchen, and seasonal. You can register and list products you'd like for your wedding, in the gift registry. Samples:
- 5-quart electric ice-cream freezer
- Homedics Therma Pro™ Extendible Heat Massager
- LEGO Celestial Stinger kit
- Tabletop fountain with marble-ball design

**Search:** Yes
**Photos:** Yes
**Ordering:** Online, Phone
**Gift Wrap:** Cards
**Delivery:** Ground, 2nd Day

## Sharper Image

http://www.sharperimage.com

The slickest, classiest, and often most expensive gifts come from this image-is-everything gadget store. Neat twist: good descriptions, with 3-D pictures of the product and its use. You can see some products in 3-D animation, too: You drag the object around, zoom in, and, absolutely the best effect, you click the power button to turn the product on. They give you a discount of a few bucks on every online order. They ship within 48 hours, unless the product is very heavy, or comes from a far-off factory. Samples:
- Executive massage chair
- Ionic Bath Pet Brush, to remove pet odors
- Mini Scooter Rollerboard, with in-line skate wheels, rear friction brake
- Model of a Hum Vee (High Mobility Multi-

Purpose Wheeled Vehicle) or Hummer, hard top, with tan interior, authentic details
- Sonic Mole Chaser, 300 Hz, pet safe, sends out sonic pulse for 1,300 square yards, to drive away moles, gophers, ground squirrels, pocket mice, shrews, and voles

**Search:** Yes
**Photos:** Yes
**Ordering:** Online, Phone, Fax
**Gift Wrap:** Yes, and message
**Delivery:** 2nd Day, Overnight, Saturday

# ShipStore.com

http://www.shipstore.com

This is a fun place to browse. Especially excellent if you're looking for a present (just about the only Web boating store that offers gift wrapping!). Their assortment is fun, practical, and a little frivolous in some cases. Perfect for the yachtsman or woman who has everything. Samples:
- Antiqued porthole frames and mirrors
- Authentic *Titanic* collectibles
- Bilge-pump controller (always amusing!)
- Helmsman clocks
- Message in a bottle (complete with paper and pen)
- Nautical-bar accessories
- Ship's bell
- Shipwreck treasures
- Slot machines

**Search:** Yes
**Photos:** Yes
**Ordering:** Online, Phone, Fax
**Gift Wrap:** Yes
**Delivery:** Ground, 3rd Day, 2nd Day

# Shopping.com

http://www.shopping.com

A department in the giant store suggests gifts such as candles, dinnerware, figurines, frames, home decor, jewelry boxes, and silver-plated stuff. Each product description emphasizes how much you are saving

compared to list prices. Because many of these items are, well, unusual, you may not be able to find them anywhere else, for price comparisons. Basically, if you like what they sell, you'll have a great time exploring, because there are so many different products. For instance, they have the following categories of figurines: angels, aquatic, bears, bells, birds, bookends, carousels, children, clowns, country, domestic animals, fantastical/magical, farm animals, flowers, horses, houses, nostalgia, seasonal, Orient, and unique wood carving. When these folks explore a product category, they go whole hog. Samples:
- Hand-carved, hand-painted wooden figurine of banana tree with ripe fruit
- Model of three-masted clipper ship, 28" x 25", fully assembled
- Nikko Summer Glade fine China, 20-piece dinnerware set
- Poly resin figurine of the Virgin Mary holding Jesus Christ as little Cupids watch, 10.75" high on wooden base

**Search:** Yes
**Photos:** Yes
**Ordering:** Online
**Gift Wrap:** Certificates
**Delivery:** Ground

# South Eastern Gifts

http://www.southeasterngifts.com

Gifts with a Southern touch, plus luggage and kitchenware from all over. Nice touch: a link to a list of speed traps that tourists ought to watch out for, as they cruise through the area. Sample products:
- 18th Century Moravian Butterfly Wall Sconce
- Cape Hatteras Afghan, with image of Cape Hatteras Lighthouse
- Tar Heel sweater, for fans of University of North Carolina

**Search:** No
**Photos:** Yes
**Ordering:** Online, Phone
**Gift Wrap:** No
**Delivery:** Ground

## Stones and Bones

`http://www.stonesbones.com`

If you know someone who's into rocks and fossils, this could be the place to find an intriguing gift, such as amber with embedded insects, ammonites, fossil fish, fossil plants, mineral specimens, and the teeth of ancient sharks. You can get a display case for your gift, too, and add a label engraved in brass. Each specimen has a photo and a short description. Neat feature: You can trade in an old fossil for a better model to improve your collection. They ship within three business days. Samples:

- Columbian amber with many flying insects, large ant, large leafhopper, 3.25"
- Dominican amber with complete pseudo-scorpion inside
- Fossilized dinosaur dung (coprolite) Cretaceous Age, from Utah, 1.5 pounds
- Large Cave Bear foot, *Ursus spelaeus*, from Ural Mountains, Russia, Pleistocene period, 12"
- *Pseudofarrella garatei*, Jurassic period ammonite, from Peru, 4.75 pounds

**Search:** No
**Photos:** Yes
**Ordering:** Online, Phone, Fax, Email
**Gift Wrap:** No
**Delivery:** Ground

## Tennis Menace

`http://www.tennismenace.com`

From the state of Georgia comes this Internet pro shop. You'll find all the tennis-pro equipment and clothes here, but you'll also find a terrific assortment of gifts for your tennis-loving friend at great prices. Samples:

- 14-karat gold and sterling silver jewelry
- Christmas cards
- Cocktail napkins
- Coffee mugs
- Doormats
- Gold-plated and brass jewelry
- Greeting cards

- Invitations
- Sneaker-and-ball key rings
- Stationery
- Tennis-racquet-shaped pasta

**Search:** Some
**Photos:** Some
**Ordering:** Online, Phone, Fax
**Gift Wrap:** No
**Delivery:** Ground, 3rd Day, Overnight

## The Gift

`http://www.thegift.com`

A friendly, well-designed site built around gift-giving. Here's our favorite twist on the traditional search mechanism: Their Gift-O-Matic™ robot helps you pick a product type, manufacturer, and price range, to get a list of "perfect" gifts. For fine china, flatware, stemware, or dishes, you can look up your favorite pattern. Find bakeware and cookware by item (such as pan) or manufacturer. Or shop by occasion (more than a dozen possibilities). They swear they will not be undersold by any authorized retailer, within a month of sale. They take this vow so seriously that they post a detailed low-price guarantee. If you're about to get married, you can register your preferences here, and point guests to the site. Samples:

- Bon Voyage basket
- Bouquets Direct Spring Mix, small
- Evenflo Snugli front-and-back pack for baby, with padded shoulder harness, removable bib and strap for pacifier
- Gorham Aspen flatware, 5-piece place setting
- Noritake Paris champagne flute glasses in boxed sets

**Search:** Yes
**Photos:** Yes
**Ordering:** Online, Phone, Fax
**Gift Wrap:** Yes, or message
**Delivery:** Ground, Overnight

# Toe Picks to Toe Shoes

http://www.www.aiminc.com/
eoi/eoimain.htm

This store is a nice combination of ballet and figure-skating supplies, clothes, jewelry, and accessories for girls and women. Many items are delicate and pretty, just right for your young ballerina or hardworking figure skater. If you're a little leery of buying ice skates on the Web, go to their Custom Boot Fitting room for step-by-step instructions on how to order the correct size. You can also order size 13 and up for an additional $30. This is a nice place to come when you're looking for a gift for your favorite skater or ballet dancer.

Samples:
- Ballet hair accessories
- Ballet jewelry
- Figure-skating paper dolls
- Gift certificates
- Pewter skating earrings
- Rhinestone skating pendants
- Sequined competition dresses
- Skate guards
- Skating necklace
- Stuffed animals on skates
- Travel bags

**Search**: Some
**Photos**: Some
**Ordering**: Online, Phone
**Gift Wrap**: Yes
**Delivery**: Ground, Overnight

# Tropic Traders

http://www.tropicgifts.com

If you want to surprise a Jimmy Buffett fan or anyone who loves the Caribbean, this store has Caribbean Soul. With Corona apparel and Conch Republic cigars, steel-drum music, and tropical lights, you can outfit a whole party. They ship within three days of your order "barring hurricanes or pirate attacks."

Samples:
- Caribbean Catch Lights, 10 lights that look like fish, 12-foot string
- Cheeseburger hat
- Corona ball cap
- Key-Lime Cooler cookies
- Tropical Shores Pot Pourri Sachet

**Search**: No
**Photos**: Yes
**Ordering**: Online, Phone
**Gift Wrap**: Baskets
**Delivery**: Ground, 3rd Day

# Universal Studios

http://
store.universalstudios.com

We remember the tedium of this studio's town square, where our tour got stalled for a few hours, while we stared at the sets, at the other tourists, at the roof, at the sets. So we'd rather visit the virtual store than the real thing. If you want a fun present for a movie buff, or a fan of Xena, this Hollywood backlot store can supply you with clothing, collectibles, DVDs, music, software, stuffed animals, theme park tickets, toys, and videos based on Universal's properties. They generally ship within 48 hours.

Samples:
- 1-Day Adult Ticket to Universal Studios, Hollywood
- *Back to the Future* "Outatime" license plate
- *Battlestar Galactica* Cold-Cast Statue
- Beethoven (the dog) lunchbox
- *Crash Bandicoot 2: Cortex Strikes Back*, game for Sony PlayStation
- Curious George Banana Bank
- *Hercules: The Legendary Journeys: The Gauntlet*, video

**Search**: Yes
**Photos**: Yes
**Ordering**: Online, Phone, Fax, Email
**Gift Wrap**: No
**Delivery**: Ground, 2nd Day

# Need some other ideas for gifts? Flip ahead to chapters such as:

- Food—Gourmet
- Gift Baskets
- Sculpture & Art
- Wine

# Gift Baskets

These stores specialize in bundles of goodies, often including fresh food or flowers. Unlike stores focusing on individual products that would make good gifts, the gift-basket folks think of the whole effect, fitting half a dozen items together to look like an impressive cornucopia, like a Christmas stocking or birthday bonanza. The wrapping, then, is part of the effect. Some stores even let you pick a little of this and a little of that, to go together in the basket.

Of course, these stories may offer excellent individual gifts as well as baskets. But we've pulled together the shops that seem to put their heart into the gift baskets, with a little extra flare, or a lot more offerings than regular gift shops. After you visit these places, you may decide you want a basket for yourself!

## 1 800 Flowers

http://www.1800flowers.com

Yes, they sell flowers, but their best sellers include live plants, vases, bouquets, balloons, and baskets of goodies. They help you look up floral arrangements and gift baskets by season, occasion, flower type, or arrangement. If you place your order before 2 P.M. in the recipient's time zone, they can deliver that day, as long as it is not during a holiday season; later orders go out the next day. Or you can specify a later date for delivery on someone's birthday or annivesary. Samples:
- 18 roses, in arrangement
- 6 balloons in the Happy Birthday Air-Rangement
- Fruit and Gourmet Basket, with fresh fruit, cheese, cookies, in a wicker basket
- Hibiscus in a cache pot (live plant)

- Pail of Plenty, with candy bars, cookies, chips, and soda

**Search:** Yes
**Photos:** Yes
**Ordering:** Online
**Gift Wrap:** Card with message
**Delivery:** Overnight, 2nd Day

## EarthDream

http://www.earthdream.com

Green gift baskets. Samples:
- Baby Gift Basket, with Honeysuckle Baby Bath, Sunflower Baby Bar, Aloe and Chamomile Baby Bar, lotions, shampoos, and conditioners
- Vegetarian Gift Basket, oval basket with meatless taco filling, bacon-less bits, and the *Peaceful Cook Vegetarian Cookbook*

**Search:** Yes
**Photos:** No
**Ordering:** Online, Phone, Fax
**Gift Wrap:** Baskets, certificates
**Delivery:** Ground

## GiftTree

http://www.gifttree.com

For gift baskets that are ready to go, GiftTree offers combinations of balloons, flowers, funny items, and plants. If you want a very specific set of products in a gift basket, you can request those, and get back several bids from local vendors near the recipient, so you can decide which seems best. Samples:
- Deluxe Fruit Basket with cheese, crackers, fruit, sausage
- Hat box filled with special gifts for everyone in the family

**Search:** Yes
**Photos:** Yes
**Ordering:** Online
**Gift Wrap:** Yes
**Delivery:** Ground, 3rd Day, 2nd Day, Overnight

## Harry and David

http://www.harryanddavid.com

This store sells not baskets but boxes of plump, hand-chosen fruit, in a soft bed. Each product description shows a well-lit picture, describes the package, gives its weight, and tells you when it is available. Delivery takes about two weeks, unless you pay extra for speed. Samples:

- Cherimoyas, the Inca fruit, 3.5 pounds
- Pearsnapples and Cheeses, 5 pounds

**Search:** Yes
**Photos:** Yes, yes, yes
**Ordering:** Online, Phone, Fax
**Gift Wrap:** Yes
**Delivery:** Ground, 2nd Day, Overnight

## Indian River Gift Fruit

http://www.giftfruit.com

This Florida store offers gift boxes and baskets of grapefruit, oranges, and tangelos, and other edible presents. They make up special baskets for new babies, Mother's Day, Father's Day, graduations, weddings, housewarmings, birthdays, anniversaries, bar/bat mitzvahs, bereavement, retirements, and just plain thank-yous. Because we're talking real fruit, availability depends on the season. Free delivery in U.S., but they do not ship to Hawaii or Alaska. Samples:

- Imperial Delights box of oranges, grapefruit, pecans, orange blossom honey, tea, pineapple-macadamia cake, and fruit candies
- Indian River Fruit Club, 3 months
- Minneola Honeybell Tangelos
- Ruby red grapefruit

**Search:** No
**Photos:** Yes
**Ordering:** Online, Phone
**Gift Wrap:** Yes, with message
**Delivery:** Ground

## Tropic Traders

http://www.tropicgifts.com

If you want to surprise a Jimmy Buffett fan or anyone who loves the Caribbean, this store has Caribbean Soul baskets, as well as other tourist gear. They ship within three days of your order "barring hurricanes or pirate attacks." Sample:

- Caribbean Soul Basket, with baseball cap, key ring, license plate, music tape, Lizard Logo decal, Key-Lime Cooler cookies, and Tropical Shores Pot Pourri Sachet

**Search:** No
**Photos:** Yes
**Ordering:** Online, Phone
**Gift Wrap:** Baskets
**Delivery:** Ground, 3rd Day

## Uptown Baskets

http://giftsforyou.com

Baskets, and nothing but baskets, and they will even put together a special basket at your email request. They deliver within hours by messenger, if the recipient lives within the boroughs of New York. Samples:

- Hollywood Basket, with popcorn, director's clapboard, silver-screen ribbon, candy, soda
- Red Hot Lover Basket, Rated R

**Search:** Yes
**Photos:** Yes
**Ordering:** Online, Phone
**Gift Wrap:** Message only
**Delivery:** Ground, 3rd Day, 2nd Day, Overnight

## Wild Alaska Smoked Salmon

http://www.smoked-fish.com

Run by a real fisherman, this beautiful site offers gift baskets built around smoked salmon, with no artificial ingredients or preservatives. You don't have to refrigerate the product until you open it. Jamie Fagan also posts recipes (smoked salmon burgers, for instance), testimonials to the healthiness of eating salmon (it's the Omega-3), and praise from customers. He likes to make up custom gift baskets (just call). Samples:

- Kodiak Canoe, with reindeer jerky, wild teas, teriyaki sticks, hot honey mustard, sweet honey mustard, reindeer salami, Terra chips, Gouda cheese roll, port wine cheese wedge, Havarti cheese, Brie, onion cheese wedge, chocolate maple leaves, water crackers, salmon in 3-, 8-, and 16-ounce packages
- Kodiak Gift Box, with reindeer jerky, wild teas, teriyaki sticks, hot honey mustard, sweet honey mustard, Terra chips, Gouda cheese, port wine cheese wedge, chocolate maple leaves, wheat wafers, and Wild Alaska Smoked Salmon
- Sockeye Salmon, 16 ounces

**Search:** No
**Photos:** Yes
**Ordering:** Online, Phone
**Gift Wrap:** Yes, with card
**Delivery:** Ground, 3rd Day

# Wondering about other items you might offer as gifts? Unwrap these chapters:

- Food—Gourmet
- Gifts
- Wine

# Golf

For us, a fondness for golf may have started when we caddied for 18 holes for big tips, or maybe it was all those fun rounds of mini-golf. Did you become enthralled when an adult took you along on a round or two, and let you tap a few in on the putting green? Possibly, you just liked watching the pros, with names like Palmer or Nicklaus, make it all look so easy on TV. Or maybe you like watching the new stars, like Woods and Singh. Regardless of how you got started, if you're reading this chapter, we bet golfing is one of your passions. Many of the stores listed here obviously share your interest, because they offer a lot more than some wedges and irons. Golfing used to be a pretty expensive sport to engage in, but we've found a lot of stores on the Web that specialize in high-quality clubs at discount prices.

## A-1 Cheap Golf

http://www.cartserver.com

These folks say that they have the "lowest-priced golf equipment on the planet." No little boast. But they live up to it by providing exceptionally low prices on their golf clubs. Lots of well-known brand-name club manufacturers, such as Taylor Made, Titleist, Armour, Spaulding, Cobra, Mizuno, and Odyssey. They also carry some clothes (in sizes up to XXL) and accessories. All of the clubs, clothes, and shoes are for men. Samples:

- Black-and-white saddle waterproof golf shoes
- Copper wristbands
- Crew windshirts
- Golf bags
- Three Stooges club head covers
- Wedges, putters, irons, and woods

**Search:** No
**Photos:** No

**Ordering:** Online, Fax, Email
**Gift Wrap:** Card
**Delivery:** Ground

## AAA Spectra Discount Golf

http://www.discount-golf.com

Maybe this store and A-1 Cheap Golf, listed above, ought to duke it out for the title of the lowest golf prices on the Internet. This store says, "Nobody beats our prices." So which one is cheaper? It's like comparing apples to oranges or putters to woods. AAA Spectra sells high-quality golf equipment without the name brands, somewhat like the generic drugs you get at the discount drugstore. This is how it works: You go to the order form and pick the general kind of club you want, let's say an iron. Then the form gives you some options to choose from, such as model type, iron type, flex type, shaft material and length, grip type and length, and so on. The site grinds for a while and comes up with a product that fits the criteria, and a price. With all of the other merchandise, you just select what you want. Samples:

- Golf bags
- Golf shoes
- Hats and visors
- Junior clubs
- Woods, irons, putters

**Search:** No
**Photos:** Some
**Ordering:** Online, Phone, Fax
**Gift Wrap:** No
**Delivery:** Ground

## Advanced Custom Golf

http://www.tylan.com

Custom-made golf clubs at reasonable prices are offered at this shop. You pick the head, shaft, grip, swing weight, length, lie and loft, and they do the rest. Many of the golf stores offers only clubs for men, but this store carries clubs specifically designed for ladies, too. They also carry some clubs for kids. Samples:

- Club sets for kids
- Graphite and titanium woods
- Stainless/nickel/alloy, forged or titanium irons
- Wedges and putters

**Search:** No
**Photos:** Some
**Ordering:** Online, Phone
**Gift Wrap:** No
**Delivery:** Ground

## Advantage Products

http://
www.advantageproducts.com

This Las Vegas golf store mainly stocks clubs for its online visitors. If you're unfamiliar with their brand, read the Testimonial section for some first-person recommendations. Samples:

- Distance golf balls
- Graphite or steel drivers
- Steel putters
- Steel wedges

**Search:** No
**Photos:** Yes
**Ordering:** Online, Phone, Fax, Email
**Gift Wrap:** No
**Delivery:** Ground, 3rd Day

## Balata Bill's

http://www.balatabills.com

You'll find quality golf clubs and equipment at decent prices from this store. Familiar brand names like Titleist, Wilson, and King Cobra stock many of the virtual racks. Select the club you want and then choose the correct length. Balata Bill's stores are known at many country clubs around the world. Samples:

- Divot tool
- Fleece club covers
- Gloves
- Golf bags
- Iron, woods, putters, and wedges
- Men's, women's, and kid's golfing shoes

**Search:** No
**Photos:** Some
**Ordering:** Online, Phone, Fax
**Gift Wrap:** No
**Delivery:** Ground, 2nd Day

## Chipshot.com

http://www.chipshotgolf.com

As a member of the Harvard golf team, this student started selling clubs from his dorm room! He's expanded a bit. The store's claim to fame today (according to him, of course) is that they're the largest Internet retailers of custom-built golf clubs. And they do have a huge selection for men, women, and kids! Delivery takes 2-4 business days for custom-built clubs and 1–3 business days for in-stock items. Don't forget to check out their golfing tip of the day. Samples:

- Acer titanium custom drivers
- Back supports
- Ball retrievers
- Custom wedges, irons, and putters
- Elbow pads
- Golf-bag valet
- Golfing software
- Knee pads and wraps
- Magnetic elbow wrap
- Mini golf gym
- Rain sweater
- Sports caddy
- Swing trainer and exerciser
- Tees
- Training aids
- Umbrellas
- Videos of golf instruction
- Wrist bands

**Search:** Some
**Photos:** Yes
**Ordering:** Online, Phone
**Gift Wrap:** No
**Delivery:** Ground, 3rd Day

# Golf Circuit

http://www.golfcircuit.com

This place is incredible. It's a golfing store, yes, but it's so much more. A golfer could get lost here just looking at all of the information available—updates from Augusta from CNNSI, fantasy golf tours, info about golf cruises in the Caribbean, chat forums with other golfers, info on LPGA, PGA, and Senior Tours, and pro golfer statistics. Oh, and they also sell a lot of golfing products. You'll find all of the well-known brand names here, too. The available merchandise listed below is but a small sampling. Every item you see comes in many different sizes and colors. Nice plus: They offer a flat ground shipping fee of $7.95, no matter how much you order. Samples:

- Aluminum pull carts
- Foam-lined, dual golf bag straps
- Golf balls
- Irons, woods, putters, and wedges
- Leather golf bags
- Men's and women's golf shoes
- Metal and soft cleats
- Practice golf clubs
- Visors

**Search:** Yes
**Photos:** Yes
**Ordering:** Online, Phone, Fax
**Gift Wrap:** No
**Delivery:** Ground, 3rd Day, 2nd Day, Overnight

# Golf Club Exchange

http://
www.golfclubexchange.com

A golf store, swap, and auction site. But if you want a particular club, or would like to sell a bag full, come here. You can bid on used clubs, or just buy new stuff, and you get two days to try out the clubs before you are committed. They offer a blue book of prices based on sales over the last four months, so you can see what's normal. Their search lets you be specific about shaft type, shaft flex, year, manufacturer, gender, and handedness. Oh, and they do sell golf books, too.

Sample products:

- Ben Hogan practice tee collection
- Kangaroo golf glove
- New white bronze putter with trapezoidal insert
- Used 4-wood, gripless stiff shaft, right-handed men's club from 1997
- Used Arnold Palmer putter
- Used left-handed ladies' 4-iron from Hogan, 1994–1995, with bubble shaft, and ladies' flex
- USGA Rules of Golf video

**Search:** Yes
**Photos:** Some
**Ordering:** Online, Fax
**Gift Wrap:** No
**Delivery:** Ground, 3rd Day, 2nd Day, Overnight

# Golf.com

http://golf.com

Stay caught up on the world of golfing by plugging into NBC Sports via this store. Looking for a place to retire near a golf course, or maybe for that perfect golfing vacation? You'll find that info here. Their Pro Golf Shop carries everything you think it would, plus a nice section for kid golfers in the KIDZ golf section. Samples:

- Ball retrievers
- Cleaners
- Clothing and shoes for men and women
- Clubs for kids
- Golf software and screensavers
- Golfing artwork, photographs, and sculptures
- Instructional books and videos
- Motor caddies
- Practice items
- Pull carts
- Rebuilt irons
- Travel and real estate information
- Shag bags
- Wedges and woods

**Search:** Yes
**Photos:** Yes
**Ordering:** Online, Phone
**Gift Wrap:** No
**Delivery:** Ground

## GolfDiscount.com

http://www.golfdiscount.com

Over two decades of experience have taught the owners of this store that if they buy in huge quantities they can sell to their customers at a big discount. Today, they are selling at terrific prices to customers all around the world. Brand names such as Callaway, King Cobra, Orlimar, Taylor Made, Titleist, and Top-Flite supply this store with excellent golf clubs. If you have any golfing questions, you can either email or phone your questions to their professionals. Most of the time, their experts are available online, live! Samples:

- Golf bags
- Men's and ladies' waterproof golf shoes
- Padded travel covers with wheels
- Women's and men's carrying bags
- Woods, putters, irons, and wedges

**Search:** Yes
**Photos:** Some
**Ordering:** Online, Phone, Fax, Email
**Gift Wrap:** No
**Delivery:** Ground, 3rd Day, 2nd Day, Overnight

## Golf Furniture

http://www.golffurniture.com

You might be wondering why we're listing a furniture store in this chapter, but when you look at the items they have for sale, you'll realize that only golfers will appreciate the tables for sale here (and you really have to go to the store and look at the pictures). The selection is very small, but perfectly tailored to the folks who just love getting up at the crack of dawn on the weekends to beat the crowd. Samples:

- Cherry (or walnut or hunter-green) pottery-top golf table, complete with a little flag
- Golf pottery-top table with glazed finish

**Search:** No
**Photos:** Yes
**Ordering:** Online
**Gift Wrap:** No
**Delivery:** Ground

## Golf Gods

http://www.bestvaluegolf.com

Huge selection of golf equipment and accessories at dynamite prices. You'll find many of the top brand names for clubs and clothes. Samples:

- Ball retrievers
- Gift certificates
- Golfing equipment for kids
- Golfing furniture
- Irons, putters, and chippers
- Magnetic insoles for men and women
- Wearable magnets for low back pain

**Search:** Some
**Photos:** Yes
**Ordering:** Online, Phone
**Gift Wrap:** No
**Delivery:** Ground

## Golf Outlet

http://www.golfoutlet.com

There are over 1,500 products for sale here, so you should be able to find just the right putter or wedge to make your set complete. They carry a lot of favorite brand names like Callaway, King Cobra, Taylor Made, Titleist, and Mizuno. You'll find golf products for men, women, kids, seniors, and lefties. Luckily, they offer a number of different ways to search, such as by product, brand name, or category. If your golf bag is full, you might want to look at all of the other "necessities" they offer for sale at great prices. They also have different sales every week, so you may want to check back occasionally. The last time we visited, we found a Pure Spin Diamond Face wedge with steel shaft for $99. Samples:

- Apparel for everyone
- Auto hitting net
- Beryllium nickel wedges
- Golf course directory
- Golf memorabilia
- Golfing software and games
- Graphite irons
- Instructional videos

- Laser rangefinder
- Shag bags
- Titanium drivers

**Search:** Yes
**Photos:** Yes
**Ordering:** Online, Phone, Fax, Email
**Gift Wrap:** No
**Delivery:** Ground, 2nd Day, Overnight

# Golf Shop Online

http://www.catalog.com/
golfshop

This store has everything. Some stores carry a lot of clubs with a sprinkling of other accessories, but this place wants to be your one-stop shop and packs their inventory to prove it. They sell a lot of golf accessories with college logos on them. Prices are very good.
Samples:

- Bag tags
- Ball racks
- Books on golf
- Chipping mats
- College logo golf bags
- Electric motor caddy
- Electronic scorekeepers
- Gift certificates
- Golf apparel (with optional embroidery offered)
- Golf business-card holders
- Golf clubs
- Golfing software
- Indoor chippers
- Portable coolers
- Swing analyzers
- Training aids
- Travel cases
- Umbrellas
- Videos

**Search:** Yes
**Photos:** Yes
**Ordering:** Online, Phone
**Gift Wrap:** No
**Delivery:** Ground

# Golf Training Aids.com

http://
www.golftrainingaids.com

If you'd like to improve your game while you're off the course, this is the store for you. Lots of innovative products that will help you improve your swing, your stance, and your putting. Most of these items can be set up either in your backyard or in your office.
Samples:

- Balance rotator
- Chipping net
- Golfercise
- Half-circle trainers
- High-tech putting track
- Mini golf gym
- Putting mats and trainers
- Rangefinder
- Spin doctor
- Stance minder
- Starter kits for kids
- Swing trainers
- Swing vision mirror

**Search:** Yes
**Photos:** Yes
**Ordering:** Online
**Gift Wrap:** No
**Delivery:** Ground

# International Golf Outlet

http://www.igogolf.com

There's a nice selection of golfing clubs and accessories at this worldwide Internet store. (In fact, you can set the store to appear in either English, German, French, Spanish, or Japanese.) You'll find individual clubs, as well as club sets. There are also clubs for women, lefties, and even used quality clubs. Samples:

- Apparel for men, women, and kids
- Bags designed for men or women
- Cedar shoe trees
- Cleated and noncleated shoes for men and women
- Electronic carts
- Golf clubs

- Rain gear
- Rangefinder
- Shag bag
- Suede shoe bag
- Training aids
- Umbrella
- Youth-sized golf club sets

**Search**: Some
**Photos**: Yes
**Ordering**: Online, Fax, Email
**Gift Wrap**: No
**Delivery**: Ground, 2$^{nd}$ Day, Overnight

## Interested in other sports? Tee off for these chapters:

- Baseball & Softball
- Basketball
- Bicycles
- Boating & Sailing
- Bowling
- Skating
- Tennis

## Par Golf Supply, Inc.

http://www.pargolf.com

How about a store that sells custom-imprinted golf accessories? Great as a business calling card, or for personalized gifts, tournaments, or golf schools and teams. If you have a particular logo you'd like to have put on the items, just send it to them. They can imprint in dozens of colors. Rush orders OK. Sample items that can be personalized:

- Bag tags
- Business cards
- Divot repairers
- Golf balls and tees
- Golf combo packs
- Golf gift packs
- Golfing towels
- Matchbooks
- Putting cups
- Tournament gifts

**Search**: Some
**Photos**: Yes
**Ordering**: Online, Phone, Fax
**Gift Wrap**: No
**Delivery**: Ground, 3$^{rd}$ Day

# Hair Care

It used to be easy. You'd go to the grocery store and buy some shampoo, a crème rinse or conditioner, and possibly some hair spray. Now there are dozens of products made especially for your type of hair, including gels, mousses, reconstructing sprays, and hair revitalizers. Luckily, there are some terrific online stores that sell quality hair products, with nice specialty boutiques. The only thing missing from these virtual salons is the pile of outdated magazines.

## A Cut Above

http://www.acutabove.com

This Connecticut salon for men and women has added an online segment. You'll find products from well-known manufacturers like Nexxus, Matrix, and Redken. They also offer their own brand, "A Cut Above Collection." Samples:
- Alcohol-free mousse
- Controlling gels
- Curling irons
- Herbal shave crèmes
- Volumizing shampoo and conditioner

**Search:** No
**Photos:** Yes
**Ordering:** Online
**Gift Wrap:** No
**Delivery:** Ground

## African Formula Cosmetics

http://africanformula.com

A large selection of natural products for your hair, body, and skin can be found at this store. The hair treatments are said to "restore life and stimulate growth." Be sure to check out the special discounts offered on bulk orders. Don't have that much to order? Call some of your friends! Samples:
- African bee-pollen high-quality shampoo
- African shea-butter hot-oil treatment
- Botanical hair and scalp repair and rinse
- High-potency root conditioner
- Organic styling gel
- Shine 'n set spray
- Super-active hair tonic

**Search:** Yes
**Photos:** Yes
**Ordering:** Online, Phone
**Gift Wrap:** No
**Delivery:** Ground

## Ball Beauty Supply

http://ballbeauty.com

This company started out as a supplier of beauty supplies to the entertainment industry. They've spread out and now offer these products online. The store offers brand-name shampoos and conditioners, but it also sells hair dyes, brushes, curlers, dryers, makeup, and skin-care products. The atmosphere reminded us of the dressing rooms of fashion photographers, cluttered with hair spray, underwear, and spray bottles, with powder dusting the mirrors. We love their motto, "What we ain't got, you don't need." Samples:
- Gift certificates
- KMS
- Mason Pearson hairbrushes
- Sebastian
- Solis hair dryers
- Steam rollers
- Styling appliances

**Search:** Yes
**Photos:** Some
**Ordering:** Online, Phone, Fax
**Gift Wrap:** No wrap, but sends a card
**Delivery:** Ground, 2nd Day, 3rd Day, Overnight

# Beauty Boutique

http://www.beautenaturel.com

Large assortment of hard-to-find beauty, hair, and bath products from around the world. Nice touch: They offer free samples with each purchase. Keep an eye out for their occasional Blow-out Sales. Samples:

- Arnica and honey shampoo
- Avocado hair treatments
- Jojoba shampoo
- Panama wood shampoo

**Search**: Yes
**Photos**: Yes
**Ordering**: Online, Phone
**Gift Wrap**: Yes
**Delivery**: Ground, 2nd Day, Overnight

# Beauty Naturally

http://
www.beautynaturally.com

This 20-year-old company's philosophy is that "as human beings, we should live in harmony with nature and immerse ourselves in the beauty that surrounds us in life." Sounds good to us. Does that include a week in Hawaii? They have high ideals, though. Their skin-care and hair-care products strive to bring your skin up to its youthful potential by healing it and then keeping it healthy using all-natural ingredients. Samples:

- Dandruff shampoo
- Hair-lightener sets
- Leave-in conditioners with sunscreen
- Non-aerosol hair spray
- Nontoxic and organic perms and hair colors

**Search**: Some
**Photos**: No
**Ordering**: Online, Phone, Fax
**Gift Wrap**: No
**Delivery**: Ground, 2nd Day, 3rd Day

# Body Maintenance

http://
www.bodymaintenance.com

Started a decade ago, this Miami-based company has become well-known, at least among its upscale clientele, by providing the highest-quality products. They rely on fresh vegetable, plant and fruit extracts for all their products. Their motto says it best: "Keep it simple. Keep it natural." You won't find any animal by-products in any of these products, and, of course, none of their merchandise is tested on the little furry creatures. You might think that their merchandise is pricey, but everything is very reasonably priced. Samples:

- 100% cotton-plush terry towels
- Alcohol-free hair gel
- Hair travel kits
- Papaya mango conditioner
- Passion fruit shampoo
- Rosemary citrus shampoo
- Skin-care products

**Search**: Some
**Photos**: Yes
**Ordering**: Online, Fax, Phone
**Gift Wrap**: Yes
**Delivery**: 2nd Day

# Color by Robert Craig

http://www.robertcraig.com

Click on Robert's Interactive Color Selector to discover a hair-color formula for you. Whether you want to permanently change the color of your hair, hide the gray, or just add some temporary highlights, this informative site has everything you need. Before you take the plunge and change the color of your hair, you should read the informative articles and tips scattered through this shop. Robert Craig has also developed his own hair-care product line, uniquely created for different water types. Samples:

- Conditioners
- Leave-in conditioning spray
- Mousse

- Pomade
- Soft and hard water shampoo
- Spray gel

**Search:** Yes
**Photos:** Yes
**Ordering:** Online, Phone
**Gift Wrap:** No
**Delivery:** Ground

## Dearinger

http://www.dearinger.com

If you like Aveda products, this is the place to come to. Aveda has a beautiful Web site, but alas, they don't sell any of their products there. This La Jolla, California, salon got the bright idea to sell these organic hair products, plus some other items from online. We found the list of Aveda products to be quite complete. Samples:

- Chakra Absolutes
- Deep-Penetrating Hair Revitalizer
- Hair detoxifier
- Makeup
- Pure-Fume candles
- Shampure

**Search:** Yes
**Photos:** Some
**Ordering:** Online, Phone
**Gift Wrap:** No
**Delivery:** Ground

## Discount Beauty.com

http://www.discountbeauty.com

The first thing this store asks its customers to do is to identify their hair type (fine, oily, dry, dandruff, and so on), and then it suggests a whole range of products based on that. Of course, you don't have to take their recommendations, you can just shop the site as you would any other, except here you shop with their guarantee that they will beat any Internet price. The store sells several brands, such as Bain de Terre, Back to Basics, KMS, and

Wella. Samples:
- Finishing spray
- Leave-in conditioner
- Molding gel
- Ultra-body shampoo

**Search:** Yes
**Photos:** No
**Ordering:** Online
**Gift Wrap:** No
**Delivery:** Ground, 2nd Day, Overnight

## Hair Care for Less

http://www.haircareforless.com

Just as the name implies, this shop offers 10%–30% off brand-name products. You know those stores at the mall that have just about every brand at a discount? Well, this online store is just like the ones at the mall, except it delivers! You'll find hair-care products from Bain de Terre, Back to Basics, KMS, Nexxus, Paul Mitchell, Redken, and others. If you already have a favorite, and just want to get a good price on a few bottles, come here. Because they have so many different brands, you may also stumble on something you just feel like trying out, and, at these prices, you might as well experiment a little. Samples:

- Cleanse Phree Shampoo
- Dandarrest
- Finishing spritz
- Flaxseed style gel
- Gelato Gloss
- Ginseng hair revitalizer
- Karaphix

**Search:** Yes
**Photos:** No
**Ordering:** Online, Phone, Fax
**Gift Wrap:** No
**Delivery:** Ground

## Jean-Pierre Creations de Paris

`http://www.jean-pierre-creations.com`

What does Jean-Pierre create? Hairbrushes and other products for your hair. Despite the name, Jean-Pierre is a Canadian company with a branch in the U.S. These excellent brushes are made to "gently stimulate the scalp without producing static." There's a good section on how to care for your brushes and an unintentionally funny do's and don'ts section: don't machine-wash your brush or put it into the clothes dryer. Well, OK, if you say so, Jean-Pierre. Samples:

- Crystalline nylon hairbrushes
- Natural boar-bristle hairbrushes
- Purse-size hairbrushes

**Search:** No
**Photos:** Yes
**Ordering:** Online
**Gift Wrap:** Yes
**Delivery:** Ground

## The Natural Body Bar

`http://www.naturalbodybar.com`

One of the largest online selections of natural beauty products. This well-designed site carries just about everything in hair, skin, body, bath, and foot products. It even supplies a line of all-natural children's products. Samples:

- Baby banana shampoo
- Comfrey-root shampoo
- Gift baskets
- Hair-thinning products
- Keratin-protein shampoo
- Skin and bath products

**Search:** Yes
**Photos:** Some
**Ordering:** Online, Phone, Fax
**Gift Wrap:** Yes
**Delivery:** Ground, Overnight

## Having a bad hair day?

Split ends got you down? Maybe your fly-away strands are going into the stratosphere. Wish you knew a hair doctor you could go to? Well there is one on the Internet, and he's got a British accent to boot! Email your questions by going to this site: http://www.the-hair-doctor.com/

## Now that you've got your hair under control, you might want to comb through these chapters:

- Beauty & Cosmetics
- Beauty & Cosmetics—Going Natural
- Health Products
- Herbs

# Health Products

As we look back at the last millennium, we have all become more aware of the environmental dangers posed by the industrial revolution, and efforts to eliminate or reverse some of the damage inflicted on our planet and on our bodies. The companies described in this section have some wonderful products for anyone who prefers a healthy lifestyle. Allergy sufferers will find this section especially helpful. Some of the stores listed in this section offer medication for sale. However, if you're looking for a large selection of stores that sell and deliver prescription and non-prescription drugs on the Web, go to the chapters on Herbs, and Prescription & Over-the-Counter Drugs.

## All About Health

http://www.allabouthealth.com

First off, you should know that this is one of the best online stores available. Great pictures, advice, a terrific search divided into 22 categories, such as diabetes, weight control, allergies, ear health, workplace. This site looks good and makes shopping a breeze. All other online sites should study it. Samples:

- Body-fat analyzers
- Breast pumps
- Compact wrist blood-pressure monitors
- Ear thermometers
- HEPA air purifiers
- Insulin travel supplies
- Nutritional supplements
- Urea skin-care creams
- Water-filter systems

**Search:** Yes
**Photos:** Yes
**Ordering:** Online, Phone, Fax

**Gift Wrap:** No
**Delivery:** Ground

## Allergy Clean Environments

http://www.allergyclean.com

If you've been diagnosed with allergies, your doctor may have given you a catalog from this company. They sell a terrific selection of products specifically designed to eliminate or reduce those things that you are allergic to. You'll find their information helpful. There's also a good section on controlling common household irritants. They have some custom-size products available for special order, too. Samples:

- Anti-allergy cotton gloves
- Asthma educational books
- Box-spring and mattress protectors
- Compressor-driven nebulizers
- Disposable pillow and comforter encasings
- Dust and pollen masks
- Filters and filter systems
- HEPA air cleaners
- Humidity gauges
- Mattress encasings
- ULPA and HEPA vacuums and bags

**Search:** Yes
**Photos:** Some
**Ordering:** Online
**Gift Wrap:** No
**Delivery:** Ground, 3rd Day, 2nd Day, Overnight

## American Health and Comfort Online SuperStore

http://www.ahcp.com

This place truly lives up to its name of SuperStore. You'll find many products for allergy sufferers, plus comfort items for back pain, maternity, breathing problems, and so much more. Make sure you check out their "Close-Out" section. Samples:

- Adjustable beds
- Air cleaners

- Baby-activity gyms
- Dehumidifiers
- Lumbar supports
- Massage loungers
- Mattress encasings
- Nursing pillows

**Search**: Yes
**Photos**: Some
**Ordering**: Online, Phone, Fax
**Gift Wrap**: No
**Delivery**: Ground

# American Health Herbs

http://healthherbs.com

This could best be described as an herbal superstore. You can find a plethora of herbs plus herbal formulas for a slew of disorders, including acne, after-birth pains, allergies, arthritis, asthma, diabetes, hypoglycemia, insomnia, and much, much more. They offer a 2% discount for online orders. One minus of this site is that you can't just click on the name of the herb to automatically drop it into a shopping cart. Instead, you have to type all the products you want on an order form. Samples:

- Audiocassettes on ailments and cures
- Books on herbs, remedies
- Colloidal silver generators
- Herbal formulas
- Oils, liniments, and lotions
- Powders and poultices
- Videos about herbalism
- Vitamins
- Water-filtration systems
- Weight-loss tinctures

**Search**: Some
**Photos**: No
**Ordering**: Online, Phone, Fax
**Gift Wrap**: No
**Delivery**: Ground

# Breathfree.com

http://www.breathfree.com

If you have trouble breathing for any reason, you know how distressing it can be. This store is THE place for people suffering from allergies, asthma, chemical sensitivities, emphysema, and immune deficiencies. The guaranteed products sold here will purify the air of dust, pollen, toxic fumes, pet dander, mold, bacteria, and a lot more. Samples:

- FREE air-purifier video
- High-intensity negative-ion generator
- Home HEPA filters
- Low-cost humidifiers and water purifiers
- Portable air purifiers (great for cars)
- Room air purifiers

**Search**: Yes
**Photos**: Yes
**Ordering**: Online, Phone, Fax
**Gift Wrap**: No
**Delivery**: Ground

# Care4U—Aids for Daily Living

http://www.care4u.com

This focused online store carries just about every product made to assist you with a physical or health disability. Conveniently laid out in specific categories, such as Eating/Drinking, Hand Aids, Wheelchair Accessories, Grooming, Pediatric Aids, and much more, the store also carries a whole line of products to make life's little challenges easier for the elderly. It has a link to HealthBoards.com so you can connect with others going through the same experiences. Samples:

- Easi-grip scissors
- Elevated toilet seat
- Inflatable travel-shampoo tray
- Key turner
- Pill-splitter
- Remote toenail clipper
- TelePhone extension arms
- Wheelchair cup holder

**Search**: Yes
**Photos**: Yes

**Ordering:** Online
**Gift Wrap:** No
**Delivery:** Ground

## Carrington Laboratories

http://www.carringtonlabs.com

After looking through stores intent on grabbing our attention with their slick, bold graphics, we were pleasantly surprised to visit this tranquil site. They have spent millions on their medical research, and the site reflects that. So who or what are Carrington Labs? According to their site, they are a "research-based bio-pharmaceutical company currently developing therapeutics for ulcerative colitis and mucositis, nutraceutical raw materials, consumer products and wound-care products utilizing naturally occurring complex carbohydrates found in Aloe vera L and stabilized by Carrington's patented process." Translation: They have taken the aloe vera that is grown from their plantation in Costa Rica and made a host of beneficial products from it. Samples:

- Diabetic products
- Incontinence items
- Nutritional supplements
- Odor-control products
- Radiation skin-care creams
- Wound cleansers and dressings

**Search:** Yes
**Photos:** Yes
**Ordering:** Online, Phone, Fax
**Gift Wrap:** No
**Delivery:** Ground, 2nd Day, Overnight

## Comfort House

http://www.comforthouse.com

Started as a catalog company, the Comfort House has used that experience to design an easy-to-use, well-thought-out online store. This site bills itself as "the source for products that make your life easier." They certainly live up to that motto. This store has many products for the physically impaired, as well as items that when you use them you think, "This stuff should be available everywhere." Spoil yourself a little with the great products here and remember to check out their Close-Out and Special sections for some great bargains. Samples:

- Arthritis aids
- Full-spectrum lighting
- Heated cushions to relieve back pain
- Incontinence products
- Inversion chairs
- Orthopedic supports and wraps
- Reachers and grabbers
- Wheelchair ramps

**Search:** Yes
**Photos:** Yes
**Ordering:** Online, Phone, Fax
**Gift Wrap:** No
**Delivery:** Ground

## CRH International, Inc.

http://www.aloealoe.com

The juice of the aloe-vera plant has long been a folk remedy for soothing the skin of burns and in the relief of minor arthritis pain. This store specializes in products made from this succulent. If you have a little time, you can even get some custom-blended products. Samples:

- After-sun lotion
- Anti-wrinkle cream
- Arthritic body rub
- Facial mask
- Medicated gel
- Moisturizers
- Pure aloe-vera juice
- Whole-leaf aloe-vera capsules

**Search:** No
**Photos:** No
**Ordering:** Online, Phone
**Gift Wrap:** No
**Delivery:** Ground, 2nd Day, 3rd Day, Overnight

## MediStore

`http://www.mediconsult.com/home/store`

A wonderful supply of hard-to-locate products, especially medical supplements. This store offers a great search divided into 60 medical topics, taking the time out of finding that special product. You'll also find support groups and a drug reference section. Everything for sale at the site has a full, money-back guarantee. Samples:

- Adult life-care kit
- Antioxidants
- Carbo Edge energy drink
- Hip-replacement rehab video
- Home medical-assistance service
- Hormone-monitoring kit
- Medical software
- Vitamins and supplements

**Search:** Yes
**Photos:** Some
**Ordering:** Online
**Gift Wrap:** No
**Delivery:** Ground

## MotherNature.com

`http://www.mothernature.com`

From homeopathy to aromatherapy, this health store carries a long list of natural products to help keep you well and, if you are sick, to make you feel better. Shipping is free on orders over $50. Samples:

- Allergy and hay fever remedies
- Appetite suppressants
- Circulation formulas
- Health bars
- Herbal teas
- Vitamins and minerals

**Search:** Yes
**Photos:** Yes
**Ordering:** Online
**Gift Wrap:** No
**Delivery:** Ground, 2nd Day

## Planet Rx

`http://www.planetrx.com`

This is another well-thought-out drugstore that fills prescription drug orders and also sells a lot home-medical supplies. (They accept most insurance carriers.) You'll also find a Health Topic Library with lots of articles and information on more than 100 different medical conditions. If you want to find some herbal remedies, click on the Alternative Card Index which lists many treatment options for various ailments. But like all good drugstores, this one also carries lots of over-the-counter drugs, as well as beauty and skin products and fragrances. This is a nice store to visit if you want find something fast, or to just browse. Samples:

- Assisted-living devices
- Auto injectors and pumps
- Bedwetting alarms
- Blood-glucose test strips
- Blood pressure kits
- Canes and tips
- Carpal-tunnel braces
- Diabetic skin care
- First-aid kits
- Knee braces
- Lancets and lancing devices
- Lung-function test
- Ovulation predictors
- Pregnancy tests
- Thermometers
- Urine-ketone test

**Search:** Yes
**Photos:** Yes
**Ordering:** Online, Fax
**Gift Wrap:** No
**Delivery:** Ground, 2nd Day, Overnight

## Price's Power International

`http://www.prices-power.com`

This is a store that specializes in products, especially supplements, for people who are aggressively working out. They responsibly list the benefits and possible side effects of many of the items sold. They offer free shipping on orders over $100. Samples:

- Fat burners
- Health and fitness bulletin board
- Liquid Creatine
- Powerlifting gear
- Protein bars

**Search:** Some
**Photos:** Some
**Ordering:** Online, Phone, Fax
**Gift Wrap:** No
**Delivery:** Ground, 2nd Day

# Where do you spend most of your day?

If it's inside, you should consider that the EPA estimates that chemical levels are 70 times higher inside the home than outside.

# If you'd like to find other products that can make you feel good, you might examine these chapters:

- Beauty & Cosmetics—Going Natural
- Food—Organic & Special Diets
- Herbs
- Prescription & Over-the-Counter Drugs
- Vitamins & Supplements

# Herbs

When he was young, Jonathan visited one of his old cousins, who showed him her half-acre herb garden, so neatly laid out with signs, flowers, and carved wooden owls to keep rodents and birds away. How beautiful and practical that garden was! It yielded compresses, rubs, and teas whenever the doctor's pills seemed unable to grapple with a sprain, a rash, or a cough.

Almost eliminated by the march of science, despite the fact that herbal remedies have been used for thousands of years in folk and peasant cultures around the world, the power of herbs has only recently come back into general popularity. High-tech westerners, partly out of dissatisfaction with "modern" medicine, have started to investigate these so-called alternative approaches, because, besides making food taste better, herbs can gently cure some maladies, help our bodies stay healthy, and scent our rooms. Here are the best herb shops on the Web.

## 1001 Herbs

http://www.1001herbs.com

Yes, there are thousands of herbs and herbal combinations available at this store, but you'll also find cookbooks, articles, books, magazines, and even music and videos all related to healthy living. If you're not sure which product would be best for your ailment, go to the Symptoms section and then click the appropriate symptom (gum disease, hot flashes, bedwetting, circulation, and so on) to get a list of herbal remedies. This is one of the most sophisticated of all of the stores in this category, and one of the most informative,

because of all the reference materials they sell. Samples:

- Acne remedies
- Antioxidants
- Arthritis relief
- Collatrim capsules
- Cookbooks using herbs
- Essential oils
- New Age and ancient music
- Valerian root
- Weight-loss formulas

**Search:** Yes
**Photos:** Some
**Ordering:** Online, Phone, Fax
**Gift Wrap:** No
**Delivery:** Ground

## Abby's Herb Company

http://www.abbysherbs.com

This store offers a unique selection of handmade herbal creams and lotions, plus herb baths, tub "teas," insect repellents, herbal supplies, and a lot more. All of the products are made from Abby's own formula. A nice touch is the custom service offered where Abby will custom-blend a formula for you, or possibly for a very good friend. She uses all-natural ingredients. Like her products, this store is simple, pure, and easy to use. Samples:

- Bulk herbs
- Foot soaks
- Gift baskets
- Insect repellents
- Massage oils
- Regenerating skin cream
- Seeds
- Tub "teas"
- Varicose-vein lotion

**Search:** Yes
**Photos:** Yes
**Ordering:** Online, Fax, Mail
**Gift Wrap:** Yes
**Delivery:** Ground

## AllHerb.com

http://www.allherb.com

With a name like this you expect a store that sells herbs —and that this one does. What sets it apart from many other such stores is the depth of information available here. There are many helpful articles from herbalists and other health-food specialists. If you are tired of traditional Western medicine, you should examine the information offered here. Samples:
- Anti-aging multipacks
- Detox formulas
- Free health newsletter
- Gift sets
- Teas
- Vitamins
- Windowsill herbal "medicine chests"

**Search:** Yes
**Photos:** Some
**Ordering:** Online
**Gift Wrap:** No
**Delivery:** Ground

## American Health Herbs

http://healthherbs.com

This could best be described as an herbal superstore, with a plethora of herbs plus herbal formulas for a slew of disorders, including acne, after-birth pains, allergies, arthritis, asthma, diabetes, hypoglycemia, insomnia, and much, much more. They offer a 2% discount for online orders. Unfortunately, you can't just click on the name of the herb to automatically go into a shopping cart. You have to type in the products you want on an order form. Samples:
- Arthritis aids
- Bee pollen
- Books, videos, and cassettes
- Eucalyptus oil
- Herbal formulas
- Herbal kits
- Oils, liniments, and lotions
- Vitamins

- Weight-loss tincture

**Search:** Some
**Photos:** No
**Ordering:** Online, Phone, Fax
**Gift Wrap:** No
**Delivery:** Ground

## Better Botanicals

http:// www.betterbotanicals.com

This store offers a range of skin, hair, body, and bath products based on the ancient Indian healing system known as Ayurveda, which means "knowledge of life," which we have found extremely helpful with problems that Western medicine could not handle. According to the Ayurveda tradition, health is maintained when the three body energies (Kapha, Pitta, and Vata) are in balance. The products sold at this store are all made from various food-grade herbs and plant oils. They DO NOT contain synthetic color or fragrance. They are all blended to suit your individual constitution. You can fill out the online questionnaire to find out your type so you can determine which products are best suited for you. Samples:
- Amla Shine shampoo
- Aromatherapy
- Baby products
- Clarifying facial scrub
- Dead Sea bath salt therapy
- Herbal cleansers
- Massage oil
- Neem care shampoo
- Pure gloss conditioner
- Rose and tulsi toners
- Sandalwood moisturizer

**Search:** Yes
**Photos:** Yes
**Ordering:** Online, Phone, Fax
**Gift Wrap:** Yes
**Delivery:** Ground

## Botanics of California

http://
www.botanicscalifornia.com

Joan Griswold noticed big changes in her hair and skin after 30. Finding some of the traditional remedies her grandmother used, Griswold started her own organic garden and raised the plants, herbs, and flowers needed to keep her hair looking youthful. Several years later, she refined these "recipes" and started her own company. You won't find any fillers, additives, or chemicals in these reasonably priced skin, hair, and body products. Samples:

- Great list of herbs and their benefits
- Mallow massage lotion
- Meadowsweet clay masks
- Mint exfoliants
- Rose-geranium cleansers
- Rosemary toner
- Sampler kits

**Search:** No
**Photos:** Some
**Ordering:** Online, Phone
**Gift Wrap:** No
**Delivery:** Ground

## Crusoe Island

http://www.crusoeisland.com

Fresh-milled organic flours, grains, herbs, beans, seeds, and baking supplies are just some of the items available here. Everything has been grown free of any trace of agricultural chemicals or pesticides. Even the containers and bags are processed and packaged with no chemical additives or preservatives. The prices are extremely reasonable. Samples:

- All-purpose seasonings
- Dairy-free beverages
- Dash-o-dill
- Granulated garlic
- Oregano
- Raspberry hot mustard
- Sea vegetables

- Shiitake-and-sesame vinaigrette
- Soy products

**Search:** Yes
**Photos:** No
**Ordering:** Online, Fax, Phone
**Gift Wrap:** No
**Delivery:** Ground, 3rd Day, 2nd Day, Overnight

## Emelauren's

http://www.emelauren.com

Handcrafted, environmentally friendly, herbal bath and skin-care products are what you'll find in this store. The specialty of this Pennsylvania family-owned business is herbal soaps. (Emelauren is a blend of their daughters' names.) Samples:

- Aromatherapy essentials
- Bug spray and soap
- Herbal bath bags
- Herbal foot bath bags
- Jojoba lip butter
- Men's products
- Poison-ivy care
- Synthetic-free jojoba moisture lotion

**Search:** Minimal
**Photos:** Some
**Ordering:** Online
**Gift Wrap:** No
**Delivery:** Ground

## Foxhollow Herb Farm

http//www.foxhollowherbs.com

The herbs and herb-related products sold at this store are organically grown and then manufactured at a farm in Hollister, California. Everything is made in small batches to ensure quality. What do we mean by "quality"? Well, for example, they steep their herbs and flowers in "sun warmed oils for several weeks to extract their fragrance and active ingredients." Pretty good, huh? Samples:

- Baby powder

- Bath oils
- Facial steams
- Gift packages
- Herbal lotions and soaps
- Lip balms
- Natural deodorant
- Tea-tree foot powder
- Wedding favors

**Search:** Yes
**Photos:** Some
**Ordering:** Online, Phone
**Gift Wrap:** No
**Delivery:** Ground

## Green Tree

http://www.greentree.com

This store not only sells you vitamins, supplements, and herbal and homeopathic remedies, it also supplies you with mountains of research and informative articles. It offers a free nutritional analysis for either men or women. You answer some questions (which take about two minutes) and then they come up with a vitamin plan for you, based on your answers. You can also search for a particular vitamin and then find out everything there is to know about it, such as what it is good for. Samples:

- Allergy formulas
- Arthritis remedies
- Athlete's vitamins
- Boosting immune-system therapies
- B-Stress with Siberian ginseng
- Carbo vegetabilis
- Creatine fuel powder
- Energy formulas
- Gallbladder disorder remedies
- Individual vitamin plans
- Melatonin
- Multivitamins

**Search:** Yes
**Photos:** Some
**Ordering:** Online, Phone, Fax
**Gift Wrap:** No
**Delivery:** 2nd Day

## Karen's Health Store

http://
www.karenshealthfoods.com

This Texas-based store specializes in a small but good assortment of organic health items. A big emphasis is placed on the herbs and herbal combinations. Samples:

- Hair and Skin Care
- Herbal Actives Milk Thistle
- Herbal formulas for cancer, menopause, fluid retention, and high blood pressure
- Homeopathics
- Kava Kava Root Extract
- St. John's Wort Extract
- Weight-loss products
- Vitamins

**Search:** Yes
**Photos:** No
**Ordering:** Online
**Gift Wrap:** No
**Delivery:** Ground

## Natural Living Center

http://www.ncenter.com/
products.htm

Start by taking the online nutritional questionnaire specifically tailored for men or women. After that, you'll receive a custom formula just for you. There's other online help, such as a calorie-VS-exertion calculator. You also find a lot of information on diverse topics such as arthritis "cures" and the value of antioxidants. Oh, and there are lot of herbal remedies. Free shipping on orders over $50. Samples:

- Arctic root
- Aromatherapy
- Black Cohosh
- Diet and sports nutrition
- Dong quai
- Herbal liquids
- Herbal teas
- Homeopathic tinctures

**Search:** Yes
**Photos:** Some
**Ordering:** Online, Phone, Fax
**Gift Wrap:** No
**Delivery:** Ground, 2$^{nd}$ Day

# Now that you've ordered your herbal tinctures, teas, and creams, perhaps you'd like to taste these chapters as well:

- Beauty & Cosmetics—Going Natural
- Food—Organic & Special Diets
- Health Products
- Prescription & Over-the-Counter Drugs
- Vitamins & Supplements

# Hollywood Paraphernalia & Memorabilia

When we were young, there was a movie house in New York City that had stars shining on the ceiling when the lights were dimmed. We remember thinking that we were in heaven as the movie started to roll. Some people liken viewing certain movies to spiritual experiences. Of course, not all movies are like that. In fact, most of them aren't that way at all. But we keep going back, waiting for that special one, that puts everything together in a heavenly way.

Maybe that's why Hollywood memorabilia is so popular. Even though fifty years have passed since *Gone With the Wind, The Wizard of Oz, Casablanca,* and *Citizen Kane* were filmed, we still like looking at the original posters. In this chapter we found stores that sell products from yesterday's and today's movies and TV shows. If you're looking to buy or rent a video, please jump to the chapter on Movies & Videos.

## Autograph World

http://www.autographworld.com

All of the autographed pictures and posters sold at this online store are backed with a certificate of authenticity. They have over 3,000 available. You'll find autographed products from major TV and movie stars:

- Anne Bancroft black-and-white autographed portrait
- *Gone With the Wind* poster signed by Ann

Rutherford and Evelyn Keyes
- *It's a Wonderful Life* mat autographed by Frank Capra, Donna Reed, Ellen Corby, Sheldon Leonard, and James Stewart
- Large *The Ten Commandments* mat signed by Charlton Heston, Yvonne deCarlo, Vincent Price, John Derek, Yul Brynner, and Anne Baxter
- *Written on the Wind* publicity pose, autographed by Robert Stack and Lauren Bacall

**Search:** Yes
**Photos:** Yes
**Ordering:** Online, Email
**Gift Wrap:** No
**Delivery:** Ground, 3rd Day, 2nd Day

## Class Act Movie Posters

http://www.movieposters.net

You'll find lots of posters here, mostly advertising newer movies and TV shows. What's fun is that you can also get these same posters (depending upon the title) in Japanese, German, Italian, or French. You'll also be able to find posters of some of your favorite music artists and a few sports posters. If you're a collector, you might want to browse through their selection of lobby card sets. Samples:

- *2001 Space Odyssey* poster
- Italian poster of *Bladerunner*
- *Seven Samurai* poster
- *The Big Chill* 15th Anniversary poster
- *There's Something About Mary* lobby card set

**Search:** No
**Photos:** Yes
**Ordering:** Online, Phone, Email
**Gift Wrap:** No
**Delivery:** Ground

## eMerchandise

http://www1.emerchandise.com

There's a lot of TV and movie memorabilia at this store. There are, for instance, calendars, mugs, shirts, ties, neon art, action figures, even mouse pads. Most of the movie stuff is from movies made in the last 20 years, although they do have some items from classics like *Gone With the Wind* and *From Here to Eternity*. Lots of sci-fi stuff from the movies and TV. Don't forget to check out their Bargain Basement for some good deals. Samples:

- James Bond silk boxer shorts
- Life-size standup of Scarlett and Rhett from *Gone With the Wind*
- *Psycho* "Bates Motel" T-shirt
- Script from *The X-Files* episode "Fire Script"
- *Wizard of Oz* "I'm melting" tie

**Search:** Yes

**Photos:** Some

**Ordering:** Online

**Gift Wrap:** No

**Delivery:** Ground, 3rd Day, Overnight

## Entertainment Earth

http://
www.entertainmentearth.com

If you're looking for something tied in to your favorite recent science fiction movie or TV show, this is the place to shop. They have posters, action figures, clothing, and more. Terrific section on *Star Wars* memorabilia, with a definite emphasis on the science-fiction genre. Samples:

- Darth Vader watches
- Droid Fighter vehicles
- Life-size bust of Chewbacca
- Obi-Wan light saber
- *Planet of the Apes* action figures
- Velociraptor claw movie prop from *Jurassic Park*

**Search:** Yes

**Photos:** Yes

**Ordering:** Online, Phone, Fax

**Gift Wrap:** No

**Delivery:** Ground, 2nd Day

## E! Online.com

http://shop.eonline.com

If you want to get all of the latest juicy Hollywood gossip, then go to E! Online's address at www.eonline.com. But if you want to hook into a whole bunch of Hollywood

collectibles, go to their store at the URL listed above. You'll find T-shirts, posters, toys, games (for adults and kids) for television and Broadway shows. Samples:

- 35mm film cel from original *The X-Files*
- Authentic director's bullhorn
- *Casablanca* poster
- Foreign film posters
- *I Love Lucy* jigsaw puzzle
- Looney Toons Tazmanian Devil photograph frame
- Mickey Mouse clocks
- *Phantom of the Opera* stationery
- *Wizard of Oz* figurines

**Search:** Yes

**Photos:** Yes

**Ordering:** Online

**Gift Wrap:** No

**Delivery:** Ground, 2nd Day, Overnight

## The Hollywood Collection

http://
www.thehollywoodcollection.com

Have you ever admired the ruby-drop earrings Vivien Leigh wore in *Gone With the Wind*? How about the diamond-and-ruby ring Bogey donned in *Beat the Devil*? This store specializes in creating original reproductions of the jewelry worn in many classic Hollywood films. This site is a one-of-a-kind place. Prices are very reasonable. Samples:

- Audrey Hepburn's diamond-tear earrings from *Roman Holiday*
- Bette Davis' dark-blue sapphire ring from *Dark Victory*
- Betty Grable's aquamarine gold-and-sterling-silver ring from *Springtime in the Rockies*
- Marilyn Monroe's diamonds from *Gentlemen Prefer Blondes*

**Search:** Yes

**Photos:** Yes

**Ordering:** Online, phone

**Gift Wrap:** No

**Delivery:** Ground, 2nd Day

## Hollywood U.S.A.

`http://www.hollywood-usa1.com`

You'll find lots of mint-condition movie posters (mostly for $16). They don't have any (at least when we looked) that go back past the 1960s. They also carry a few posters of movies that haven't been released yet. Autographs, hats, calendars, and T-shirts are for sale, too. They also carry some TV and cartoon memorabilia. Samples:

- Autographed, framed picture of Clint Eastwood as Dirty Harry
- *Bladerunner* poster
- Bubba Fett T-shirt
- Clark Gable lithograph
- *Dr. No* poster
- Framed, autographed picture of Sean Connery as 007
- *Godfather* series posters
- James Dean lithograph
- Laurel and Hardy lithograph

**Search:** No
**Photos:** Yes
**Ordering:** Online
**Gift Wrap:** No
**Delivery:** Ground

## Movie Memories

`http://www.moviememories.com`

Ah, here's the real deal. How about a place that sells original movie posters from the Golden Era of the Silver Screen? Their posters come in all sizes, such as half sheets and full sheets, and they also carry a good supply of lobby cards and inserts. Prices vary widely, depending upon the condition of the poster. Samples:

- *Dark Passage* lobby cards
- Half-sheet poster of *Grand Hotel*
- Large poster of *North by Northwest*
- Lobby cards of 1945's *A Bell for Adano*
- Lobby poster of *Wells Fargo*
- Poster of 1933's *Jesse James*

**Search:** No
**Photos:** Some

**Ordering:** Online, Phone, Email
**Gift Wrap:** Card
**Delivery:** Ground

## New Line Cinema Studio Store

`http://www.newline.com`

Merchandise from the New Line and Fine Line film companies are for sale at this company store. You'll find the usual array of T-shirts, hats, posters, videos, and even soundtracks. The store is currently chock full of *Austin Powers* memorabilia, but they do have some other products, too. You won't find any oldies, but they do have some goodies. Samples:

- *Austin Powers* key chain and pin set
- *Lost in Space* robot
- *Rush Hour* T-shirts
- *Wedding Singer* nightshirt

**Search:** Yes
**Photos:** Yes
**Ordering:** Online, Phone, Fax
**Gift Wrap:** No
**Delivery:** Ground, 2nd Day

## Universal Studios

`http://store.universalstudios.com`

You can just imagine all of the stuff that's for sale here, including clothing, software, videos, DVDs, and tickets to their various theme parks. But what will interest you, since you came to this chapter, are their "Collectibles." Samples:

- Chucky doll
- *Dracula* Limited Edition cookie jar
- *Empire Strikes Back* LED print
- *Frankenstein* bronze bust
- *Frankenstein* puppet
- "Groovy" gifts from *Austin Powers*
- *Star Trek* Latinum Borg Queen figure
- *Star Trek* Picard figure
- *The Wolfman* cold-cast porcelain statue

**Search:** Yes

**Photos:** Yes
**Ordering:** Online
**Gift Wrap:** No
**Delivery:** Ground, 2nd Day

## Vintage Magazine Company

`http://www.vinmag.com`

There's a lot to browse through at this site, because it's more than a store. But when you do decide to get out your credit card, you'll be rewarded with a fine selection of true TV and movie memorabilia. It has one of the largest selections of movie posters available. Plus, as a nice added attraction, they have a lot of Italian movie posters. Want to see what the poster for *Citizen Kane* looked like in a cinema in Naples? You can see that and a lot more. They also have a good selection of recent stuff. Samples:

- Groucho Marx mouse pad
- *Man from UNCLE* T-shirt
- *Metropolis* robot statue
- *Nosferatu* poster in Italian
- Poster of *Plan 9 from Outer Space*
- Replicas of Academy Award statuettes
- Rudolph Valentino poster

**Search:** Yes
**Photos:** Yes
**Ordering:** Online, Phone, Fax
**Gift Wrap:** Card
**Delivery:** Ground, 2nd Day

## If you can't get enough movies, you might screen these chapters, too:

- Movies & Videos
- TV & Video Gear

## Hollywood Trivia Lovers Unite

Come to the place for information on any movie ever made at the Internet Movie Database at
http://www.imdb.com

# Home Office Supplies

When you work at home, you need the same kind of supplies as big companies do—but a lot less. Instead of a truckload of paper, you might settle for a box. And if you take your work on the road, you may have to stock up on batteries, cables, and enough gear to talk to clients from your phone, your hotel, your golf course. From 4-inch paper clips and yellow stickies to a new desk, Web stores compete to offer you specialty items, plus the regular stuff. And you don't have to haul that box of paper in from the car—let the FedEx or UPS people do that.

## 1-800-Batteries

http://www.1800batteries.com/

Have you ever run out of juice just when you were reaching a new level on the laptop computer game? Or lost a call because your cell phone batteries died? Keep this Web site address in your wallet, for every conceivable kind of battery, plus lots of attachments, cables, and gizmos to go with your mobile office. Samples:
- Aluminum attaché case for laptop
- Attachable numeric keypad for laptop computer
- Docking gear and port replicators
- Notebook computer luggage
- Retractable phone line in a cartridge
- Solar panels
- Video camcorders

**Search:** Yes
**Photos:** Yes
**Ordering:** Online
**Gift Wrap:** No
**Delivery:** Ground, 2nd Day, Overnight

## At Your Office

http://
www.atyouroffice.comdefault.asp

A very well-organized and helpful office store, with endless aisles of must-have products, as well as fun impulse items. You can browse from a detailed list, or search by keyword or catalog number. They have a special location for refills. Neat features: You can set up a regular shopping list, so you don't forget items you need to buy every time you visit, or you can ask the site to show you what you bought last time, as a reminder. They also keep you up to date on the contents of your shopping cart, so you don't overspend. They ship on the next business day, and there is no shipping charge for orders over $25. Samples:
- Business forms
- Digital audio recorder
- Label maker
- Laser pointer
- Paper shredder
- Personal copier
- Portable wireless public address system
- Toner and paper for your fax

**Search:** Yes
**Photos:** Yes
**Ordering:** Online
**Gift Wrap:** No
**Delivery:** Ground

## CDW

http://www.cdw.com/

An efficient and friendly site, with a focus on computer-related gear. They have some neat specials—for example, a light pen and software you can use to mark up a Windows document on your screen and print out your comments as if you'd scratched them on the paper copy. Bargain basement, rebates, and a hard-copy catalog, if you want it. They tell you when a product is in stock (no uncertainties!), and you can have them let you know when a product's price goes down, or when they receive a product that was out of stock. You can even email the product description to a friend, via a click of the envelope icon. Samples:

- Flatbed scanner
- Keyboard templates
- Manuals, documentation
- Network hubs, routers, cards
- Personal digital assistant
- Plotter pens
- Tape drive cleaners

**Search:** Yes
**Photos:** Yes
**Ordering:** Online
**Gift Wrap:** No
**Delivery:** Ground, 2$^{nd}$ Day, Overnight

## DayTimer

http://www.daytimer.com

Yes, these are the planner folks. You get the complete range of planners and accessories. Visit the Sales Annex for specials! They guarantee that once you've placed your order, they will get it out the door within two days, even if you've asked them to engrave a brass plate on the front of a binder. Sample products:

- Loose-leaf or wire-bound planners
- Organizer, calendar, and address book software
- Refill pages that have been personalized with your own special dates
- Your name or initials engraved on pens, pencils, or planners

**Search:** No
**Photos:** Yes
**Ordering:** Online
**Gift Wrap:** No
**Delivery:** Ground

## Franklin Covey

http://www.franklinquest.com

Yes, this is the store for highly effective people, or wannabes. It accompanies half a dozen online commu-

nities set up for people who are following Dr. Covey's advice at home or at work, or training others in the approach. Threads follow each of the habits he advocates, such as putting first things first. The site sells his books, tapes, and workshops, as well as classy office supplies. Samples:

- Ergonomic hole punch for binder or planner paper
- LCD clock for traveling (displays time, day, date, month, and temperature)
- Leather mouse pad with rubber backing
- Motivational posters based on *The Seven Habits of Highly Effective People*
- Palm-connected organizers
- Reflections on living

**Search:** No
**Photos:** Yes
**Ordering:** Online
**Gift Wrap:** No
**Delivery:** Ground, 2$^{nd}$ Day, Overnight

## iPrint

http://www6.iprint.com

You can order printing over the net. The fastest printing is on paper. For instance, standard business cards, letterhead, envelopes, announcements, invitations, labels, and rubber stamps take two to four days to print, depending on the color and number of inks used. Postcards, full-color business cards, Post-It notes, Memo pads, screen-printed magnets, and bumper stickers take seven to ten days to print. Because you are ordering real printing on golf balls, t-shirts, or mouse pads, there may be a seven- to ten-day wait before the results are shipped. Samples:

- Business cards
- Mouse pads with your images
- Mugs with pictures in them
- Photo puzzles with your image, text, and layout
- Rubber stamps
- Yellow sticky notes

**Search:** No
**Photos:** Yes
**Ordering:** Online

**Gift Wrap:** No
**Delivery:** Ground, Overnight

## Kinko's

`http://www.kinkos.com`

You can now have an electronic file printed and made into multiple copies at your local Kinko's copy center, placing your order online, and then sending the file over the Internet. Use this site to locate your local store, and check ahead of time which kind of files your local store can handle. Then fill out the form telling the staff what you want done with your file. You get to review a faxed proof of the printout before you OK the multiple copies. Sample services:

- Binding
- Collating
- Cutting
- Drilling
- Folding
- Printing
- Stapling

**Search:** No
**Photos:** No
**Ordering:** Online
**Gift Wrap:** No
**Delivery:** Local delivery, or 2nd Day, Overnight

## Mobile Office Outfitters

`http://www.mobilegear.com`

If you work out of your car, visit this site. They can put a desk in your front seat, so you can sort out your papers, organize your supplies, and avoid sitting on your invoices. They can help you keep track of your disks, computer, handheld personal digital assistant, as well as lunch. Sample products:

- Backseat organizer with many pockets
- CD organizer that fits in your visor
- Cigarette-lighter outlet extensions
- File organizers that fit in your trunk
- Inverters to convert from Direct Current to the

Alternating Current your computer needs
- Window-mounted holder for your Palm Pilot

**Search:** Yes
**Photos:** Yes
**Ordering:** Online
**Gift Wrap:** No
**Delivery:** Ground, 3rd Day, 2nd Day, Overnight

## Office Max

`http://www.officemax.com`

If you're near a metropolitan area, you probably know the glass-and-steel stores. They offer 20,000 products online, rebates, and low-price guarantees. If you have their paper catalog, you can use it to locate and order a product without having to browse. Caution: Deliveries come in their trucks, within their "trade area," which means you may not be served if you are way out in the country. Shipping is free for orders over $50. Samples:

- Banner paper
- Boxes of paper for ink-jet and laser printers
- Cards and labels for laser and ink-jet printers
- Decorative bulletin boards
- Drafting tables
- Legal pads and steno books
- Overhead projectors
- Paper rolls for fax, adding machines
- Plastic and hardwood clipboards

**Search:** Yes
**Photos:** Yes
**Ordering:** Online
**Gift Wrap:** No
**Delivery:** Overnight, except weekends

## Onsale

`http://www.onsale.com/depart-ments/homeoffice.htm`

Real-time fun during the day, if you like bargains and auctions. Along with low-priced computers, peripherals, and software, Onsale offers one-hour auctions on lots of refurbished or close-out high-tech gear for the home office. If your bid is accepted, you may get a big savings off the suggested retail price. Brands are well-known. Most items are available for immediate shipping, but some are in short supply (that's why they are on sale), and if you want a computer built to your specs, that may take three to five days. Sample products:

- Combination printer, fax, copier
- Cordless phones
- Digital cameras
- Digital color copier
- Drawing tablet with pressure pen
- Electric bench grinder
- Joysticks

**Search:** Yes
**Photos:** Yes
**Ordering:** Online
**Gift Wrap:** No
**Delivery:** Ground, 2nd Day, Overnight (but not Saturdays)

## Staples

http://www.staples.com

Right off, they offer to let you browse an aisle (a general product category), look at one type of product (a shelf), or go right for the one item you want. You can streamline your repeat shopping by making up a personal list of stuff you want to buy on every visit (after all, their name is *Staples*), and asking for an email reminder. Shipping is next day within 30 miles of a local Staples store; otherwise, it will take from three to five days, via Ground. (Furniture may take longer.) Shipping is free on orders over $50. Samples:

- Brass fasteners
- Bulldog clips
- Cash register
- Construction paper
- Giant paper clips
- Self-adhesive paper
- Tons of paper, pens, and ink

**Search:** Yes
**Photos:** Yes

**Ordering:** Online
**Gift Wrap:** No
**Delivery:** Ground, Overnight

## If you're still furnishing your office, you might put these chapters on your to-do list:

- Computers & Computer Gear
- Consumer Electronics
- Craft & Art Supplies
- Furnishings for Home & Office
- School Supplies
- Writing Tools

# Investment Planning & Research

These sites help you keep track of your own investment portfolio, explore possible buys, pick up breaking news, gossip, or prices, and chat with other folks interested in Wall Street markets, personal financial planning, or, well, anything to do with using your money to make even more money.

If you sign on with an online broker, you get access to some of this software, data, and research, but usually not as much as these sites provide. These sites don't sell stocks, they sell insight.

Some of these sites charge a subscription fee for advanced info, or sell you books and newsletters, but all offer a lot of free information, as long as you put up with their ads or visit their host. You get to nibble the smorgasbord so you can decide whether you really need a full plate.

For actual online stockbrokers, see our chapter Stocks & Bonds.

## American Association of Individual Investors

http://www.aaii.com

This nonprofit organization has 175,000 members, most of whom seem to have quite a bit of cash ready to invest, although the association does give advice to beginners, too. AAII offers stock screening, downloadable software such as a Warren Buffett Valuation Spreadsheet (much easier than making this up from scratch, we found), message boards, and portfolio quotes. Their online journal has how-to articles, with deep archives, and they offer lots of tips on using your computer to do a better job of investing. One typical article explores exactly how the different companies rank mutual funds, so you can decide which service fits your approach. No fluff here. You can download useful planning worksheets, pricing models, planners, and analysis tools. Some are free with your membership, others are shareware. You can buy subscriptions to their print journals, such as *Computerized Investing*, get a free trial membership, or sign up for the full membership. Samples:

- Computerized investing
- Dogs of the Dow table
- Downloadable reports and software
- Message boards
- Stock screening
- Technical analysis

**Search:** Yes
**Photos:** A few charts
**Ordering:** Online, Phone
**Gift Wrap:** No
**Delivery:** Online, Download, Ground

## Bloomberg

http://www.bloomberg.com

You want news, you got it! From reports on top financial and world events, you can dip to technology hits, movers on the market, rates, bonds, and currency stories. You can play Real Audio news about the hour's hottest stocks, companies in the news, international markets; and, if you really like listening to your computer, you can tune in for a one-hour newsmagazine every morning. Plus, there's video! The site seems alive because it offers so many tools you might, in the past, have only gotten with software on your home computer (or on a terminal hooked to a mainframe at a brokerage firm), and all this software is tied into live data over the Internet. The monitor, for instance, lets you track 10 stocks or indices, which get updated every few seconds; if you have questions about one of the items, you can jump to the most recent information, such as company profiles, key data, news, and performance. Even more fun are services such as Market Movers, showing good detail and charts on companies whose shares are trading at high volumes or soaring prices at the moment. Using slightly delayed prices, you can even build yourself a chart showing as many as four stocks and four indices, for comparisons on the fly. Naturally, you get a chance to subscribe to the Bloomberg's *Personal Finance* magazine, and get a customized Portfolio Tracker. Samples:

- Currency calculator
- IP Center
- Monitor (for current prices, averages)
- Most active futures
- Most active options
- Municipal bond yields
- U.S. Treasury rates

**Search**: Yes
**Photos**: Good charts
**Ordering**: Online
**Gift Wrap**: No
**Delivery**: Online

## Hoovers Online

http://www.hoovers.com

From the folks who created some of the classic library reference volumes about corporations, this site provides great news and background, and OK screening of potential investments. Visitors can explore company capsules, IPO news, the basic stock screener, lists of links, and plenty of advice. To get all of Hoovers' company profiles, industry studies, lists of officers, professional search tools, and up-to-the-minute SEC filings, you have to subscribe. In partnership with various vendors, the bookstore offers business and credit reports, magazines, reports, software, but with some of their own products, they prefer fax and email rather than online ordering. Sample services:

- Career Center
- IPO Central
- Lead Finder

- Power Tool to locate companies by industry, location, annual sales, company type, with links to job openings
- Stock Screener

**Search**: Yes
**Photos**: Charts
**Ordering**: Online, Fax, Email
**Gift Wrap**: No
**Delivery**: Online, Ground

## Ino

http://www.ino.com/

Feeling brave? If you are itching to make a killing in futures or options, this site offers lots of free samples, trial versions of other companies' newspapers, data, videos, links to brokers, plus current charts, quotes, news, and discussions, most focused on day trading, futures, and options. Typical books in their store: *Trade Like a Bookie* and *The Day Trader's Manual*. Samples:

- Discussion boards
- Foreign exchange
- Free trial subscriptions to data services
- Futures World News
- Press releases
- Stock quotes on extreme stocks

**Search**: Yes
**Photos**: A few
**Ordering**: Online, Phone, Fax
**Gift Wrap**: No
**Delivery**: Online, 3rd Day, 2nd Day

## Investor Map

http://www.investormap.com

If you need to find financial information somewhere on the Web, this site offers more than 3,000 links, sorted into 130 categories (such as advisories, day trading, gold, market timing, dividend reinvestment plans), so you can go well beyond general sites to find the particular niches you want. Their Daily Market page lists almost a hundred Web sources for news of the day, so you can go right to the latest items, skipping past the home pages, welcomes, and splash screens. They also post samples from investment newsletters (with the opportunity to subscribe). They recommend a lot of good books, many on sale via links to a good online bookstore called Traders Press. Sample resources:

- Daily Markets, a fast-loading one-page summary of news and analysis
- Financial Directory of links
- Newsletter samples and links

**Search:** Yes
**Photos:** No
**Ordering:** Online
**Gift Wrap:** No
**Delivery:** Online

## Market Guide

http://www.marketguide.com

You can do research on more than 12,000 companies with Market Guide's big but very sophisticated screening programs, one a Java application with 20 variables, the other a giant downloadable application, most meaningful if you have a detailed knowledge of investments. For total control, with 550 variables, and 12 pages on each company, you have to call or email for a subscription. (The cost is just under $4,000 a year for weekly updates, with a slight extra cost for overnight delivery). (What the heck, we say, splurge for the overnight delivery!) The site itself offers headlines, commentary, too, and link to Multex for more research. No portfolio tracking right now.

- Big Losers
- Hot Stocks
- Market reports
- Sector guides
- StockQuest® screening with 50 variables

**Search:** Yes
**Photos:** No
**Ordering:** Online
**Gift Wrap:** No
**Delivery:** Online, Download

## MSN Money Central Investor

http://www.investor.com

An excellent way to keep up-to-date with your portfolio as prices change during the day, and a fast, even slick way to search for new investments, decide what to drop from your list, and learn about new companies, sectors, opportunities. You download their free software in about five minutes, and it lets you track up to 5,000 securities (isn't that enough?) in several different portfolios, as well as stocks you're thinking about buying. You can import transactions from Quicken or Money, and download an account directly from a broker. The manager shows information such as a mutual fund's chart, basic facts, expenses, fees, and Morningstar rating. You have to subscribe to get the more detailed hundred-criteria searches, insider trading news, and in-depth reviews (we have looked at some of these on stocks we know well, and regularly found them very detailed and reassuring, if you want to know the complete nitty-gritty). If you volunteer for a trial subscription, you get 25 real-time quotes for NYSE and Nasdaq even after the trial period; and if you subscribe (for less than $10 a month), you get 100 free real-time quotes a day. Direct links to major online brokerages. Sample services:

- Charting
- Company earnings estimates
- Custom, or personal fund searching
- Insider trading news
- Investing models and strategies
- Investment matcher
- Market reports
- Portfolio tracking
- Predefined searches
- Quotes on international securities
- SEC Filings

**Search:** Yes, yes, yes
**Photos:** Good charts
**Ordering:** Online
**Gift Wrap:** No
**Delivery:** Online

# Morningstar

`http://www.morningstar.com/`

This is the big book on mutual funds, the mother lode of number-crunchy analysis of funds, stocks, and Internet plays. The site adds articles, commentaries, and the chance to discuss investment with 300,000 other investors. If you sign up for the free membership, you can find your next fund or stock with customized selectors, run a Portfolio X-Ray on your holdings, get 20-minute delayed quotes, and read feature articles. Subscribing (at less than $10 a month) gets you more analyst reviews, deeper data, stock-and-fund selection, breaking news. You can also get samples of their print packages, but you have to order their books and newsletters by phone. You can buy individual reports for a few bucks over the Web, and books on investing via Amazon. Sample services:

- Forums on investing
- Fund Selector
- Investing 101 tips
- Morningstar Ratings
- Portfolio
- Portfolio X-Ray
- Stock Selector

**Search:** Yes
**Photos:** Good charts
**Ordering:** Online, Phone
**Gift Wrap:** No
**Delivery:** Online, Ground

# Motley Fool

`http://www.motleyfool.com/`

How can you dislike a site that offers 13 steps to investing foolishly? The Motley Fool shows you the weaknesses, greed, and cliquishness behind conventional wisdom, which led the so-called professionals at 75% of the mutual funds to underperform the market's average. Contrarian, irreverent, casual, and funny, this site strips away the fakery of the old-line brokerages, showing you how to run your own investment

program. Amazing, to find a site that actually has a philosophy, written up in a book you can read online. You can track your portfolio here, get stock ideas, news, quotes, and lots of features. We particularly like the fact that ideas that come up in the discussions may be surfaced on the home page, so you can zip right to the thread. The discussions are well-organized, easy to navigate, and down-to-earth. In their pleasant store, you can subscribe to email newsletters, purchase investment tax guides, gift certificates, and software. Best buy: a hat identifying you simply as a Fool. Samples:

- Fool's School
- Foolish Portfolio Tracker spreadsheet for Excel, updatable when online
- Quotes
- Stock Ideas

**Search:** Yes
**Photos:** Yes
**Ordering:** Online, Phone, Fax
**Gift Wrap:** Gift certificates
**Delivery:** Online, Ground

# Multex

`http:www.multexinvestor.com`

The Multex Investor Network advertises itself as research for "serious investors," a place where you can pick up more than 250,000 investment research reports from more than 200 brokerage houses, investment banks, and other researchers. Not just the summaries, but the actual research. As a visitor, you can search the ticker, view headlines, and join the chat. If you register (for free) you can get advanced searches, pick up a few reports for free, and buy lots of others for about $5 each (the ones we looked at contained great statistics, analyst gossip, insider dope, and competitive analysis). The site is flush with news articles, too, so it's a good place to start investigating an industry or a company. Samples:

- Ace Consensus
- Highs and Lows
- New Buys
- Research from 200 firms
- Stock Snapshots

- Tech Beat
- What's Hot

**Search:** Yes
**Photos:** Charts
**Ordering:** Online
**Gift Wrap:** No
**Delivery:** Online

## Mutual Funds Interactive

http://
www.fundsinteractive.com

If you're concentrating on mutual funds, here's a chance to dip into the research from heavyweights like Lipper, Value Line, and Zack's. Solid content, well presented and easy to navigate, makes this a wonderful resource for beginners and experienced investors. We particularly like the fund screening software, and the visually delightful interactive charts for averages or stocks, with their attached news, analyst estimates, SEC filings, broker research, and company profiles. Books they recommend are available through Amazon. Samples:

- Columns
- Fund Talk
- Links to fund Web sites
- Profiles
- Screening and fund lookup

**Search:** Yes
**Photos:** Great graphics
**Ordering:** Online
**Gift Wrap:** No
**Delivery:** Online

## Quicken

http://www.quicken.com

We use their software, and like it, so we expected ease of use and a broad understanding of our needs at their site. In general, we found those qualities, with departments going beyond investments to cover banking, credit, insurance, mortgages, retirement, savings, small

business, and taxes. You sign up for free, and get to track and analyze your portfolio, if you want. Oddly, you can follow only your account balances, not transactions, for which you have to use a weird averaging wizard. You can jump from your portfolio to charts (from one week to five years), a Morningstar profile, an abbreviated Value Line Profile, discussion, and news. Screening offers fewer criteria than other info services, but good ability to compare companies, with some predefined searches for fast answers. Naturally, they communicate with Quicken and TurboTax software, and let you import account info from some brokers. If you want Quicken software, you can buy it from the next-door Intuit store, along with supplies like checks. You can download TurboTax, too. Samples:

- Alerts
- Charts
- College Planner
- Debt-Reduction Planner
- Market news
- Portfolio
- Quotes
- Retirement Planner
- Roth IRA Calculator

**Search:** Yes
**Photos:** Charts
**Ordering:** Online
**Gift Wrap:** No
**Delivery:** Online, Download, Ground, 3rd Day, 2nd Day, Overnight

## Silicon Investor

http://
www.siliconinvestor.com

If you live in Silicon Valley or want to invest in high-tech stocks and funds, this site offers a chance to listen in to another100,000 folks who are involved in the technology sector all day (and for a lifetime fee of $200 you can contribute). The other people on the boards are pretty much insiders, so their opinions matter more than those of Wall Street analysts, who are often a whole continent away from the action. Ten dollars a month gets you in. The site monitors messages to eject pitchmen, yank spam, cut down on cussing, and extinguish flames. Luckily, you can search by subject or stock, because there are more than 8 million messages on file already. Charts focusing on computers, software, communications, and semiconductors come with news, profiles, earnings, and forecasts. There are profiles for 1,000 technology companies. Samples:

- Charts
- Community chats
- Profiles of companies
- Quotes
- Stock talk

**Search:** Yes
**Photos:** Charts
**Ordering:** Online
**Gift Wrap:** No
**Delivery:** Online

## Smart Money

`http://www.smartmoney.com/`

Based on the popular magazine, this site is open, friendly, and good for beginners and intermediate investors. Their main focus is on the market, but they offer lots of advice on auto purchases, college planning, debt management, home ownership, insurance, mortgages, retirement and estate planning, and taxes. The Portfolio Management System lets you track 20 different portfolios, each with 20 securities, if you have that many, with stocks updated all day, and funds each morning. Their Chart Center software, which takes a while to download, is well worth the wait, because you can do far more than look at prices with it; you can compare funds or stocks over different time periods, for cumulative or periodic performance, and use various indices for a baseline. Tables offer cross-tabbed information on funds such as major holdings, operations, recent pricing, relative risk, volatility, and year-to-date return. Most amazing chart: their Map of the Market, which uses different-size blocks to stand for 600 companies with different market capitalizations, and a range of colors to indicate which ones went up, down, or stayed the same during the last 15 minutes, sector by sector. When you hover over a block that, say, went up by 6% in consumer staples, you see the

name of the stock, the increase, and a few details (you can click to get more). But the overview is wonderful, too, because you get to see which sectors were going up or down, as a whole, and how the market as a whole was moving. Yes, you can subscribe to the paper version, too, if you want. Samples:

- Asset allocator
- Broker ratings
- Dueling portfolios
- Hourly stock update
- Investor calendar
- News search
- Pundit watch
- Sector tracker

**Search:** Yes
**Photos:** Great diagrams and charts
**Ordering:** Online
**Gift Wrap:** No
**Delivery:** Online

## Stock Smart

`http://www.stocksmart.com`

With no ads, and a white-paper, almost bare-bones look, these folks pull together the research of many financial service firms analyzing some 20,000 stocks and 7,000 mutual funds in countries around the world. You can set up your own alert to get news when a particular event occurs, such as a price change or unusual volume. On the free welcome page, colorful charts show you the day in brief on major exchanges, indices, and industries, as well as trends in mutual funds over the last month, and the day's big losers and winners. You also get to look at industry rollups (how are auto parts doing today?), rankings of mutual funds, and the latest results in markets all around the world. Great for a quick overview of the finances of Earth. But for extra details, you need to subscribe at $13 a month, which is a little more than similar services but gives you an enormous amount of research. Then you can run your portfolio, get profit-and-loss statements, watching your net gain or loss, less commissions. If you wonder about a particular investment, you can tweak the content and format of charts of its annualized returns, relative performance compared to other investments, to explore the material from different perspectives. You also have access to all that research, which they claim to review, to remove pitches and assure quality. You can dial in from mobile devices, as well as your computer. And, believe it or not, they do respond to email. Sample services:

- Bonds
- Charting
- Corporate actions
- Earnings
- Industries
- Institutional holders
- IPOs
- Most active stocks
- Mutual funds screening
- Portfolio
- Quotes
- Stock screening
- Technical analysis
- World markets

**Search:** Yes
**Photos:** Color diagrams and charts
**Ordering:** Yes
**Gift Wrap:** No
**Delivery:** Online

## TheStreet.com

`http://www.thestreet.com`

A fascinating, purely online magazine with portfolio tracking and quotes. Basic information, market news, and discussion groups are free to a visitor. For $10 a month, you subscribe to get the insider commentary by columnists, published entirely online (no waiting for the print edition). For example, the hedge-fund expert James Cramer may post articles several times a day, as news breaks. The live ticker updates every five minutes, with time-delayed quotes. Amazing: A customer service phone number appears at the top of the pages! Samples:

- Basics of investing, with Investors' Bookshelf
- Charts on 24,000 stocks, funds, indices
- Commentary
- Community chats with their experts
- Funds

- International
- Markets
- Portfolio
- SEC filings
- Stock News
- Tools for analysis and research, with Lipper data

**Search:** Yes
**Photos:** Charts
**Ordering:** Online
**Gift Wrap:** No
**Delivery:** Online

## Thomas Register

`http://www.thomasregister.com`

Want to know how to get in touch with a company that makes a product you like? Need to find a service but don't know where to start? Or do you just want to learn how to reach a company you're thinking of working for? Thomas Register has a simple site that can lead you, fast, to detailed background on a company. Starting with their big book, Thomas has spun off its database, with info on more than 155,000 companies, 60,000 products or services, and 124,000 brand names, offering much of that information, bit by bit, for free, and plugging their line of information books and CD-ROMs. They also give you links to 5,500 online supplier catalogs, and faxed literature from 1,000 eager corporations. Neat extra: For products that can be drawn with computer-aided drafting, the site offers sample drawings from some companies, so you can see the front, side, top, and bottom (but first you have to download a 3MB plug-in). Samples:

- 34-volume *Thomas Register in Print*
- *Thomas Register* on CD-ROM
- *American Export Register*
- *The Thomas Food Industry Register*

**Search:** Yes
**Photos:** No
**Ordering:** Online, Phone
**Gift Wrap:** No
**Delivery:** Ground

# Thomson Investors Network

`http://www.thomsoninvest.net`

As a guest, you can track up to 10 securities in your portfolio here, but the real appeal is the depth and graphic display of the analysis of performance showing which investments are doing best and worst, and how your money pie is sliced up among them. The free tip sheet summarizes analyst ideas. The fund-selection tool works well. If you subscribe, you get 25 reports a month, earnings estimates, and holdings information. (You can buy some of these items as a guest, by paying per view or day.) With an additional log-in name and password, you can get real-time quotes from a subsidiary, with very useful tip sheets showing analysis consensus, performance charts, pricing momentum, and key measures comparing the company to its industry and the Standard & Poors 500. Sample services:

- Interactive Charting
- Portfolio with email updates
- Real-time quotes
- Searchable news from Reuters
- Shareholder News
- Stock Screening
- Tip of the Day

**Search:** Yes
**Photos:** Charts
**Ordering:** Online
**Gift Wrap:** No
**Delivery:** Online

# Wall Street Journal Interactive

`http://www.wsj.com`

Somewhat slower than TheStreet.com, but with great depth, this online version of the world's best-written financial newspaper includes more of their in-depth reporting than the print editions. You can find out a lot just by searching through the archives of the *Journal* and other top business publications here. For the searches, customized news folders, investment tracking portfolio, and briefing books, you need to subscribe, for $59 a year, discounted to half of that if you already

get the print edition of *Barron's* or *WSJ*. Sample services:

- 5 portfolios
- Briefing Books on background, performance, news, with charts
- Real-time quotes (50 a day)

**Search:** Yes
**Photos:** Charts
**Ordering:** Online
**Gift Wrap:** No
**Delivery:** Online

# Yahoo! Finance

`http://quote.yahoo.com`

Best for news, OK for its portfolio tracking, though not very sophisticated analysis. Great links to other Web sites and world finance locations on the Yahoo world. A broad focus, with useful info and tools on auto loans, credit reports, initial public offerings, insurance quotes, mortgage quotes, tax refunds. Useful news and advice imported from the Motley Fool and TheStreet.com, with company profiles from Market Guide. The 3D Stock Viewer is a large, downloadable Java application that lets you watch how a stock performs compared to your purchase price, picking various ways to search and compare items in your portfolio. The revolving flashing graphics will entertain you even on down days. The screening tools are good, though not fancy. For a fee, you can order up your own credit report. You can customize your welcome page with news about your investments, too, although you can't easily jump back and forth from a Yahoo member page to the Finance section, without re-entering the Web address. Samples:

- 3-D Portfolio Viewer
- Auto Loan Rates
- Finance Club
- Loan Center
- Mortgage Quotes
- Reuters stories
- SEC Filings
- Stock Chat
- Stock Screener
- Tax Refund Estimator

**Search:** Yes
**Photos:** Interactive charts
**Ordering:** Online
**Gift Wrap:** No
**Delivery:** Online

# ZD Inter@ctive Investor

http://www.zdii.com

Part of the gigantic Ziff-Davis Net, this site lets you
search through advisory comments, message boards,
news, research reports, and reviews. Lots of good
chunking of top stock news. You get full quotes, with
charts, estimates, filings, financials, product lists,
reviews, and stories about competitors and the
industry. More than 250,000 research reports can be
had for free, or a few bucks, through their Research-
on-Demand, powered by Multex. Sample resources:

- Earnings reports
- Economic news
- Industry indices
- IPO news
- Licensing news
- Market summary
- Mergers and acquisitions news
- Personnel announcements

**Search:** Yes
**Photos:** Charts
**Ordering:** Yes
**Gift Wrap:** No
**Delivery:** Online

# If you're ready to enter the market, you might invest in the chapter on Stocks & Bonds.

# Jewelry

Who would have thought that buying jewelry on the Web would work? After all, isn't jewelry one of those very personal items? Thanks to some detailed photos, great selections, unique items, and terrific discounts, jewelry has become a growing part of the Internet shopping community. Browse through these stores and find out why.

Also, you should know that we've listed only stores that specialize in jewelry in this chapter. There are a quite a few megastores that sell, as part of their massive inventory, jewelry. There's nothing wrong with those stores, but you will probably find shopping for jewelry a lot easier at the stores mentioned below, because there are fewer distractions, and more attention devoted to gems, pendants, settings, and karats.

## Alle Fine Jewelry

http://www.allejewelry.com

You'll find an ample selection of fine jewelry here. From pearls to watches, they carry a little of everything. In a hurry? Click on the Quick Gift icon for a sampling of earrings, bracelets, and necklaces. Samples:

- Gemstone bracelets, rings, and pendants
- Gray baroque pearl necklace
- Necklace of black cultured pearls and diamonds
- Platinum and gold wedding bands
- Ridged door-knocker earrings
- Seiko watches
- Sterling-silver bamboo bracelet

**Search:** Yes
**Photos:** Yes
**Ordering:** Online
**Gift Wrap:** Yes
**Delivery:** Ground, 2nd Day, Overnight

## David Morgan

http://www.davidmorgan.com

When you think of jewelry, the first thing you probably *don't* think of is Wales. But David Morgan has set up his Welsh store with an amazing collection of Celtic-inspired jewelry. Lots of interwoven bands, dragons, and other symbols. It doesn't really go with the rest of the store, but you'll also find jewelry from the Pacific Northwest. Go figure. Samples:

- Celtic diamond engagement and wedding rings
- Celtic knot cuff links
- Creyr earrings
- Gold Chi-Rho necklace
- Highbush cranberry pin
- Triskele rings
- Welsh brooches

**Search:** Yes
**Photos:** Yes
**Ordering:** Online, Phone, Fax
**Gift Wrap:** Card
**Delivery:** Ground, Phone, Fax

## Fortunoff

http://www.fortunoff.com

For three quarters of a century, this jewelry store has built its name on assuring customers that they are getting what they pay for. This tradition continues today. According to Fortunoff, "Every diamond, gemstone and cultured pearl is carefully inspected by our team of quality-control experts. Fourteen- and 18-karat gold and platinum are scientifically tested." From time to time they offer free shipping on ground orders. Gift wrapping is always free. Samples:

- Bridal gift registry
- Children's gold jewelry
- Cultured freshwater dyed pearl necklace
- Diamond and 14K white gold bow pin
- Diamond-accented charms
- Star of David with gemstones pendant
- Sterling-silver dog-tag necklace

**Search:** Yes
**Photos:** Yes
**Ordering:** Online

**Gift Wrap:** Yes
**Delivery:** Ground, 2nd Day, Overnight

## Gem of the Day

http://www.gemday.com

If you can't find the bauble you're looking for in the more traditional jewelry stores, surf over to this one. Unlike most jewelry stores on the Internet, this one *started* as a Web store. Knowing that people are sometimes a little skittish about buying jewelry on the Web, they offer a generous 30-day no-hassle return policy. They'll also custom-design jewelry for you. We really like the selection. They offer a lot of services for free, such as free delivery, gift wrapping, and ring sizing, and there's no sales tax to anywhere in the U.S. Samples:

- 14-karat gold-and-diamond bicycle brooch
- Automatic underwater watch
- Mother-and-child blue agate cameo
- Multi color tourmaline ring
- Pearl swirl earrings
- Ruby, diamond, and sapphire ring
- Terra-cotta cameo pin
- Yellow-and-black dial quartz chronograph
- Wedding Web sites

**Search:** Yes
**Photos:** Yes
**Ordering:** Online, Phone
**Gift Wrap:** Yes
**Delivery:** Ground, 2nd Day, Overnight

## Gems and Jewels.com

http://www.gemsandjewels.com

If you've every sat patiently watching the QVC Shopping channel on TV, waiting for just the right trinket, you'll love this store—because now you can shop without the wait. iQVC's Gems and Jewels.com is one of the largest, if not the largest, jewelry store on the Web. You'll find it all here, from gold and silver to gemstones. The selection is enormous. For example, click on the diamond jewelry section and you'll be given many choices as to stone choice, cut, karat weight, ring type, and metal for the band. Samples:

- 14-karat gold money clips
- African-garnet hoop earrings
- Bangle-style watches
- Diamond pendants
- Jewelry boxes
- Jewelry-cleaning systems
- Joan Rivers bee pin
- Marble Rosary beads
- Southwestern-style silver jewelry
- Waterford-crystal jewels
- Wedding and engagement rings

**Search:** Yes
**Photos:** Yes
**Ordering:** Online, Phone
**Gift Wrap:** Yes
**Delivery:** Ground, 3rd Day, 2nd Day, Overnight

## The Hollywood Collection

http://
www.thehollywoodcollection.com

Have you ever admired the ruby-drop earrings Vivien Leigh wore in *Gone With the Wind*? Or how about the diamond-and-ruby ring Bogey donned in *Beat the Devil*? This store specializes in creating original reproductions of the jewels worn in many classic Hollywood films. This site is a one-of-a-kind place. Prices are very reasonable. Samples:

- Audrey Hepburn's diamond-tear earrings from *Roman Holiday*
- Bette Davis' dark-blue sapphire ring from *Dark Victory*
- Betty Grable's aquamarine gold and sterling ring from *Springtime in the Rockies*
- Marilyn Monroe's diamonds from *Gentlemen Prefer Blondes*

**Search:** Yes
**Photos:** Yes
**Ordering:** Online, Phone
**Gift Wrap:** No
**Delivery:** Ground, 2nd Day

## JewelryWeb.com

http://www.jewelryweb.com

Fine jewelry at a 40%–60% savings off retail. Add good-quality photos and how can you miss? New items are added every month, so the inventory doesn't get stale. Don't forget to check out the weekly specials for additional savings. And jewelry with that month's birthstone is often on sale. Multi-pay, no-interest payment plans available. Samples:

- 14-karat Brazilian amethysts-and-diamond ring
- Platinum-and-gold cross necklace
- Platinum demi-hoop earrings
- Star enamel laser-cut heart pendant
- Sterling-silver bangle cuffs and bracelets
- Two-tone diamond ring

**Search:** Yes
**Photos:** Yes
**Ordering:** Online, Phone, Fax
**Gift Wrap:** Yes
**Delivery:** Ground, 2nd Day

## Jigowat

http://www.fabric8.com/
jigowat

Ringologist Jigowat travels the world looking for unusual rings for his Web store, which looks as if it was designed by someone motivated by some of the darker space movies. The rings are supposedly inspired by other-world inhabitants who evidently like lots of thick silver with colorful stones. Most of the rings can be custom-made with the stone of your choice. Samples:

- Blue, pink, white, and red opal
- Green adventurine
- Hermatite
- Onyx
- Rose quartz

**Search:** Some
**Photos:** Yes
**Ordering:** Online, Fax
**Gift Wrap:** No
**Delivery:** Ground

## New Watch

http://www.newwatches.com

Get out those credit cards. You'll be hard-pressed to find a better selection of high-quality watches at better prices anywhere, except maybe from that seedy-looking guy on the street with the box under his coat. Some watches were discounted 70% off retail. We really liked the theme of this store. You can search in all of the usual ways, but for fun, New Watch has search categories, such as Car Pool, Couch Potato, First Job, Mid-Life Crisis, Old and New Money . . . you get the idea. As if that weren't enough, they offer free shipping anywhere in the U.S. You'll have a good time shopping here. Samples:

- Accutron gold alpine
- Cindy Crawford Omega
- Gold and diamond Rotary
- Seiko two-tone
- Swiss Army calvary
- Tissot Ballade

**Search:** Yes
**Photos:** Yes
**Ordering:** Online, Phone
**Gift Wrap:** Yes
**Delivery:** Ground, 2nd Day, Overnight

## Simon and Co.

http://www.simonco.com

An exquisite selection of beautiful jewelry designed in Europe, Israel, Morocco, and the U.S. We like the way they display their jewelry. Instead of showing just one piece at a time, they reveal a lot on one page and you can click on the one(s) that you like, to see a bigger picture. Samples:

- Diamond engagement and wedding rings
- European crystal
- Old-gold filigree pendants
- Sapphire-and-emerald earrings
- Topaz, pearl, and onyx rings

**Search:** Yes
**Photos:** Yes
**Ordering:** Online, Phone, Fax

**Gift Wrap:** Yes
**Delivery:** Ground

## Zales

`http://www.zales.com`

This is definitely your online diamond store. They must travel to South Africa and fill hundreds of steamer trunks with the brilliant gems. Zales also carries an assortment of jewelry made from pearls and other gemstones, but diamonds are Zales' best friends. Samples:

- 14-karat gold-and-diamond hoop earrings
- Bridal sets
- Cultured pearls
- Diamond heart pendant
- Diamond wedding bands
- Semiprecious rings

**Search:** Yes
**Photos:** Yes
**Ordering:** Online, Phone
**Gift Wrap:** Yes
**Delivery:** Ground, 2nd Day

## Now that you have the ring, you might as well try this chapter on for size:

- Weddings

# Kitchenware & Cooking Equipment

If you like to cook, you'll love this chapter. Most cooks we know really enjoy browsing through cookware shops, looking at the neat little gadgets and hefting the heavy-duty pots and pans. We know we do. We were pleasantly surprised at the wide variety of stores in this category. From top-of-the-line, imported cookware to discount restaurant supplies, you can find just about anything you need or want to prepare that perfect meal. If you're looking for a housewarming present, this is a great chapter to read through. Just look for the stores that offer either gift wrapping or a gift card. If you'd like to find out more about gourmet food shops that deliver, please turn to the chapter on Food—Gourmet.

## A Cook's Gallery

http://www.cooksgallery.com

If you're tired of answering the question "What's for dinner tonight?" you'll enjoy this store. Not only does it have a full line of neat products for the chef, but it also has a bunch of delicious recipes up on its site for you to print out. You can also sample some of their culinary classes or ask their concierge service, if you have a question about a particular product. Shipping charges are 6% of your total order. Samples:

- Clear-glass sauce boat
- Cutlery
- Enamel kettles
- Fondue set
- French-press coffeemakers
- Garlic roaster
- Glass trifle bowl
- Herb grill
- Non-electric froth maker
- Nonstick baking pans and sheets
- Pedestal server
- Round French ovens
- Taco-pan set
- Thermal coffeemaker

**Search:** Yes
**Photos:** Yes
**Ordering:** Online, Phone, Fax
**Gift Wrap:** Yes
**Delivery:** Ground

## Chef's Catalog

http://www.ccddee.com

For 20 years, this store has specialized in providing professional restaurant equipment to the home chef. If you're looking for a gift, you can email their Gift Concierge, who will help you find just the perfect item. Choose from such well-known brands as Bodum, Calphalon, Cuisinart, Farberware, KitchenAid, Krups, Le Creuset, Weber, and many more. The prices are good, better than those at most department stores. Samples:

- Cappuccino maker
- Charcoal barbecues
- Clear breadbox
- Copper casserole dish
- Double boilers
- Electric buffet skillet
- Electric can openers
- Juicer
- Nonstick stainless steel omelet and fry pans
- Outdoor grilling woks
- Saucières

**Search:** Yes
**Photos:** Yes
**Ordering:** Online
**Gift Wrap:** Card
**Delivery:** Ground, 2nd Day

## The Chef's Store

`http://www.chefstore.com`

Here's yet another store that sells wonderful kitchen and cooking products at terrific prices. (Even better prices can be found at their Clearance Sale department.) This shop has one of the best searches of all the sites in this chapter, because they give several different ways to search. Have questions? Go to the Ask the Chef section and email what's on your mind. They often will grant free shipping on orders over $50. Samples:

- Bakers' blades
- Ceramic knives
- Coffee roasters
- Color spatulas
- Cookie press
- Copper bowls
- Dutch ovens
- Food digital thermometers
- Nonstick griddles
- Pressure cookers
- Strawberry hullers

**Search:** Yes
**Photos:** Yes
**Ordering:** Online, Phone, Fax
**Gift Wrap:** No
**Delivery:** Ground, 2nd Day

## Cooking.com

`http://www.cooking.com`

This is a terrific store for any cook. Why? Because they've put on their chefs' caps and thought about how a shopper would like to browse through any online store. The search is superb (you can look up an item by keyword, product, brand name, category, even by gift ideas). There's lots of white space so you can really appreciate the clear pictures of their inventory. This should be enough, but they also offer good prices, over 850 recipes for you to print out, advice from master chefs, and more. You'll find all the well-known brand names, such as All-Clad, Calphalon, Cuisinart, KitchenAid, Krups, Le Creuset, Magnalite, Waring,

and Zyliss, as well as some lesser-known and imported brands. We guarantee you'll love shopping here. Samples:

- Asparagus-prep tools
- Cordless hand blender
- Disposable doilies
- Flavor injector
- Folding stainless-steel dish rack
- Glass beer mugs
- Gourmet food items
- Hand-anodized nonstick omelet pan
- Heart-shaped waffle iron
- Ice-cream maker
- Knife sharpeners
- Mini food processor
- Natural-bristle vegetable brush
- Nonstick commercial-size roaster pan with rack
- Pizza or baking stone

**Search:** Yes
**Photos:** Yes
**Ordering:** Online
**Gift Wrap:** Yes
**Delivery:** Ground, 3rd Day, Next Day

## Cook's Nook

`http://www.cooksnook.com`

You'll find a good assortment of gourmet food here, but what this store specializes in is cooking appliances, gadgets, and accessories that will make your cooking experience a real treat. Unsure what to get? Let their staff answer your questions. Samples:

- Authentic 1940s ice bag
- Brass Turkish pepper mill
- Chinook roasting planks
- Cookbooks
- Endurance cocktail shaker
- Microwave hot plate
- Scanpan line of cookware
- Thermal/vacuum carafe

**Search:** Yes
**Photos:** Yes
**Ordering:** Online, Phone, Fax
**Gift Wrap:** No
**Delivery:** Ground, 2nd Day, Overnight

# Cooks World

http://www.cooksworld.com

This family-run store has over 3,000 gourmet kitchen items for sale. They pride themselves on carrying the best products in several categories. Samples:

- Belgian waffle maker
- Cast-iron muffin pan
- Clay cookers
- Electric stand mixer
- Electric teakettle
- Fluted quiche-and-brioche pan
- Jelly-roll pans
- Percolator
- Rice steamer
- Slicing knives
- Tinned-steel madeleine pan
- Toaster

**Search**: Yes
**Photos**: Yes
**Ordering**: Online
**Gift Wrap**: Yes
**Delivery**: Ground

# CT Creations

http://www.ctcreations.com

If you live by the water, or yearn to get back on your boat, you may enjoy this shop, which offers dishes and cookware all on a nautical theme, featuring images of fish, ships, and sails. Many of their dishes, towels, and other kitchen accessories are very brightly colored, and very pretty. They have other things for sale at this store besides kitchenware, so if you like the undersea creatures of this world, swim on over to this shop. Samples:

- Fish-with-swirls salad plates
- Fish-shaped trivets
- Fully equipped picnic baskets
- Mini-whale cutting board
- Nautical-patterned place mats
- Regatta cookie canister
- Sailboat and set-sail dish towels
- Seashell glass ornaments
- Seafood buffet dinnerware
- Sea-glass potpourri

**Search**: Yes
**Photos**: Yes
**Ordering**: Online, Phone
**Gift Wrap**: Yes
**Delivery**: Ground, 2nd Day

# Dean and Deluca

http://www.dean-deluca.com

An airy, light-filled store down in New York's SoHo district (south of Houston Street), D and D's has fed and supplied artists, gallery owners, tourists, and neighbors for more than 25 years. The owners, Joel Dean and Giorgio DeLuca, expanded their deli as New Yorkers discovered this gourmet mecca, and now the pair have taken the store onto the Web. You can't grab some smoked turkey and sourdough to go, but, without the crowds, you can now salivate at the wonderful offerings online, and browse through their intriguing selection of cookware, accessories, and gadgets. Samples:

- Aluminum multicooker
- Avocado skinner
- Cutting machine
- Garlic peeler
- German martini glass
- Hand-blown martini pitcher
- Hot-chocolate bowl
- Hungarian classic deco mouth-blown-crystal wine cooler
- Italian lead-crystal ice bucket
- Silver-plated cocktail shaker
- Tahitian vanilla beans
- Wine
- Wood with silver-leaf serving tray

**Search**: Yes
**Photos**: Yes
**Ordering**: Online
**Gift Wrap**: Card
**Delivery**: Ground, 2nd Day, Overnight

# Design Buy

http://www.designbuy.com

Designer-made cooking products, like what you might see in the Museum of Modern Art. If you are especially intrigued by something, you can learn more about the person who designed it. If you haven't figured it out yet, this isn't the place to shop if you're budgeting on a shoestring. Samples:

- Bread knife
- Carrot knife for paring
- Kettle with a bird-shaped whistle
- Potato-handled potato peeler
- Standing-person corkscrew

**Search:** No
**Photos:** Yes
**Ordering:** Online, Fax
**Gift Wrap:** Card
**Delivery:** Ground

# EZ Shop.com

http://www.ezshop.com

Besides finding lots of pots, pans, and appliances for your kitchen, you'll also find tons of furniture and accessories for your home at this store. You'll find many of the brand names that you are familiar with, such as DeLonghi, Hamilton Beach, Sharp, and Toastmaster. Excellent prices. Ground shipping to the continental U.S. is free. Samples:

- Bagel slicers
- Blenders
- Bread makers
- Coffee and espresso makers
- Bean 'n sauce pots
- Convection ovens
- Cookware sets
- Crock pots
- Deep fryers
- Food processors
- Heavy cast-aluminum baking pans
- Oval roasters
- Rice cookers
- Waffle makers

**Search:** Yes
**Photos:** Yes

**Ordering:** Online, Phone
**Gift Wrap:** No
**Delivery:** Ground

# GourmetMarket.com

http://www.gourmetmarket.com

This gourmet "general store" carries epicurean morsels from around the world and publishes a library full of articles about food and health, recipes, and wine reviews. They sell lots of neat cooking utensils and kitchenware. Samples:

- Barware
- Butcher blocks
- Coffeemakers
- Cutlery
- Kitchen linens
- Outdoor grills
- Pot racks
- Salt and pepper shakers
- Wine accessories

**Search:** Yes
**Photos:** Some
**Ordering:** Online, Phone, Fax
**Gift Wrap:** No
**Delivery:** 3rd Day

# The Internet Kitchen

http://www.your-kitchen.com

Great source for quality-brand kitchen products at good prices. Which brands are we talking about? How about Cuisinart, Farberware, Fiskars, KitchenAid, and Krups, to name just a few. They have individual items, cooking sets, and even some china sets. You'll also find those other items, so necessary in the kitchen, such as aprons, towels, and dredgers. Don't forget to check for open stock specials. This is a good place to shop if you're looking for a gift, because the gift wrapping is free. Samples:

- Breadmakers
- Chef's blue or white jacket

- Compact coffeemakers
- Electric cooking products
- Espresso makers
- Food processors
- Hand blenders
- Hand-anodized nonstick cookware sets
- Hardwood cutting tables
- Ice-cream makers
- Nonstick stainless-steel cookware sets
- Rice cookers
- Steamers
- Strainers and colanders
- Toasters
- Wafflemakers

**Search:** Yes
**Photos:** Yes
**Ordering:** Online, Phone, Fax
**Gift Wrap:** Yes
**Delivery:** Ground

## Kitchen and Company

http://
www.kitchenandcompany.com

Dishes by Mikasa, glassware and formal place settings by Lenox, knives by Chicago, and lots of other nice things to put on your table. They also carry a decent assortment of kitchen gadgets and cookware. The prices are excellent. This is a good place to go if you need to replenish a set. Samples:

- Coffeepots
- Crystal
- Demitasse with saucers
- Formal dinnerware
- Graters
- Juice extractors
- Maple-handle knives
- Serving bowls
- Silver-plated flatware
- Sterling flatware
- Toasters
- Whisks
- Wood and plastic cooking tools

**Search:** Some
**Photos:** Yes

**Ordering:** Online, Fax
**Gift Wrap:** Card
**Delivery:** Ground, 3rd Day

## Restaurant Wholesale Super Store

http://www.cutlery-store.com

How would you like to shop at a store that stocks over 450,000 different cooking (and eating) items that can be delivered to your door overnight? We found one on the Web. And don't let the "Restaurant" in the name fool you. This store has been providing high-end cooking equipment and cutlery for over 50 years. You can buy a lot or a little. You'll find brand names, such as AllClad, Cuisinart, Dexter-Russel, J. A. Henckels, KitchenAid, and Wusthof-Trident. Some of the items for sale come with free shipping. Samples:

- Baking products
- Blenders
- Bowls
- Bridal registry
- Buffetware
- Cutlery
- Disposable pastry bags
- Electric fryers
- Food pans
- Food processors
- Juicers
- Toasters
- Utensils

**Search:** Yes
**Photos:** Yes
**Ordering:** Online
**Gift Wrap:** No
**Delivery:** Ground, Overnight

## Worked up an appetite? Try a taste of these chapters:

- Coffee & Tea
- Food—Gourmet
- Food—Organic & Special Diets

# Maps & Atlases

Maps seem to put the world in our hand, as if we were astronauts looking down on a cloud-less landscape, with borders carefully drawn across the open plains, beaches dividing land precisely from sea, and volcanoes pluming. Whether we need to get across town or around a continent, we reach for maps to get our bearings, establish our context, plan our adventures. The love of maps brings us to-gether across all frontiers, and now that we can acquire and create digital maps as well as paper ones, we can be makers, or publishers, as well as users. If you are a map maven, or just need a good map, these sites will appeal to you.

## Blackwells

http://www.blackwell.co.uk

This old Oxford bookstore carries lots of atlases, available at a slow pace over the sea for Americans. If you are trying to track down a map of someplace outside the United States, you may find it here. Good textual detail, few images. We've found their service good, and they also offer a wonderful selection of books, old and new, in many languages, if you feel like studying up on some of the more obscure dots on the maps. Samples:

- Map of Wales
- Michelin *Environs de Paris* map
- Pathfinder map of Carmarthen
- Robinson Projection World Map

**Search:** Yes
**Photos:** No
**Ordering:** Online
**Gift Wrap:** No
**Delivery:** Ground

## DeLorme

http://www.delorme.com

A major publisher of maps, with a light touch. Their Yarmouth, Maine, store features a giant globe called Eartha, which won the Guinness award for biggest globe in the world. Samples:

- *Eartha World Travelog*, atlas with satellite imagery
- GPS Receiver
- Map sealant to waterproof a map
- Map tacks
- Solus maps for handheld computers
- Topo USA™ DVD, covers entire U.S. on one DVD

**Search:** Yes
**Photos:** Yes
**Ordering:** Online
**Gift Wrap:** No
**Delivery:** Ground, 2nd Day, Overnight

## Elstead Maps

http://www.elstead.co.uk

They offer more than 9,000 maps from their store out in Godalming, Surrey, England. Fortunately, they also provide a currency converter so you can figure out dollar amounts. British and European maps predomi-nate. Air shipments take about a week to get to U.S. street addresses, but you can pay more for faster delivery. (Some items require 24 hours to ship.) You earn bonus points to apply to any title you like. Samples:

- *Auto Route Express Europe 2000* CD-ROM, with 400,000 destinations in 45 countries from Ireland to the Urals, compatible with GPS systems
- *GPS Land Navigation*, by Michael Ferguson
- *Ordnance Survey Historical Map and Guide to Ancient Britain*

**Search:** No
**Photos:** A few
**Ordering:** Online, Phone, Fax
**Gift Wrap:** No
**Delivery:** Air, 3rd Day, 2nd Day

# Hammond Maps

http://www.hammondmap.com

The giant map company spins out every atlas, poster, and map from one gigantic database, so they can be up-to-date. Nice bonus: They offer a full world map or time-zone map (definitely the best we have ever seen) to download and use as wallpaper on your computer screen. Also, free flag images you can use for personal Web sites. They have a whole library of digital images, showing flags and physical and political layouts. Samples:

- Climate map of the world
- *Hammond Atlas of the World* CD-ROM
- Stereogram of Oahu

**Search:** No
**Photos:** Yes
**Ordering:** Online, Fax
**Gift Wrap:** No
**Delivery:** Ground

# Map and Travel Center

http://www.mapper.com

A retail store with 27,000 items in stock, this California store can ship items right away. You get to look at samples of most lines. Sample products:

- Argentina wall map
- Digital versions of USGS topographical maps on CD-ROM
- *Los Angeles City* CD-ROM, aerial photo street atlas, Mac or Windows

**Search:** Yes
**Photos:** Some
**Ordering:** Online
**Gift Wrap:** No
**Delivery:** Ground

# Map Art

http://www.map-art.com

Visually lush images of globes, world maps, regional maps, and right on down to city maps. You can download samples (with their logo across the image), then buy a digital version from Cartesia Software, the host. Orders that come in by 2:30 P.M. Eastern Time, go out that day. Samples:

- Image of globe showing North and South America, in GIF or JPEG
- *MapArt Geopolitical Deluxe World* collection of 600 maps in 12 styles, with international roads, ocean floor relief, in Adobe Illustrator format

**Search:** Yes
**Photos:** Yes
**Ordering:** Online, Phone, Fax
**Gift Wrap:** No
**Delivery:** Ground, 2nd Day, Overnight

# MapQuest

http://www.mapquest.com

Looking for an address, town, or ZIP code? You can get a brightly colored, well-labeled map here and print it out. Ditto for door-to-door driving directions. This company makes its money working with businesses who want to find a new location, add mapping services to their sites, or just create interactive maps. These interactive maps let you recenter the map, move around, identify icons, and zoom in. You can have the map show attractions, banks, restaurants, hotels, or schools, if you want. Looking at the map of our neighborhood, we discovered a lane we hadn't known was a real street (we thought it was a driveway). Samples:

- *London by the Underground* map, 18"x 26"
- *Nova Scotia Fishing Map*, 27"x 39"
- Reproduction of Blaeu's Map of Europe, from 1620
- Small, medium, large maps online
- Up to 25 free maps in GIF format to put up on your Web site

**Search:** Yes
**Photos:** Yes
**Ordering:** Online
**Gift Wrap:** No
**Delivery:** Online, Email, or Ground

## Maps Online

`http://www.mapsonline.co.uk`

An efficient British site, with a reasonable search mechanism. Samples:

* Brecon Beacons National Park, Eastern Area
* Hallwag map of Budapest

**Search:** Yes
**Photos:** Some
**Ordering:** Online, Phone, Fax
**Gift Wrap:** No
**Delivery:** Ground

## Mapsworld

`http://www.mapsworld.com`

A branch of the National Map Centre in London, this site sells digital maps online. You can download maps in Freehand, Illustrator, and GIF formats for both Windows and Mac computers. Layers let you turn borders, rivers, or roads on or off, and you can modify the fonts and colors, adding your own text. Samples:

* Robinson Projection world map from Magellan, GIF
* Year's subscription to the Explorers' Club, so you can order any of 800 maps online, without individual billing

**Search:** Yes
**Photos:** Yes
**Ordering:** Online
**Gift Wrap:** No
**Delivery:** Download

## USGS

`http://edcwww.cr.usgs.gov/`
`Webglis/glisbin/finder_main.`
`pl?dataset_name=MAPS_LARGE`

The United States Geological Survey offers wonderfully detailed maps and aerial photographs for non-professionals via the Global Land Information System (GLIS). You use their Map Finder, then order online (or go down to one of their local map dealers). You pay $4 per map, around $16 for a 9-inch color print (they come in sizes up to four feet wide), plus a handling fee of $3.50 for the entire order, no matter how many maps you get. You enter a place-name and a state, and the system shows a map; if you want to order, you click. You send your order in online, but you have to follow up with a phone call or fax, or mail in a check to complete it. You can get an index of maps of your state for free. Samples:

* *Bash Bish Falls* map, Connecticut
* Color aerial photo of Los Ranchos, New Mexico

**Search:** Yes
**Photos:** Yes
**Ordering:** Online, Fax
**Gift Wrap:** No
**Delivery:** Ground

## World of Maps

`http://www.worldofmaps.com`

An Ottawa store with all the Canadian government maps, plus topographic and aeronautical charts. You can click through a map to spot the precise location you want. Samples:

* Aeronautical charts of Ontario
* Map of Montreal South Shore

**Search:** Yes
**Photos:** Yes
**Ordering:** Online, Phone
**Gift Wrap:** No
**Delivery:** Ground

## Would you like to see every map site this side of Mars, with a few from mapmakers on imaginary planets?

Visit Oddens' Bookmarks. The geography faculty of Holland's University of Utrecht, coordinated by Odden, has put together a list of more than 6,000 map-related sites, at http://kartoserver.frw.ruu.nl/80

# Movies & Videos

DVD or not to DVD, that is the question. Don't know the answer? Then skip this section. For you movie buffs, whether to buy a DVD system is probably a question you've been grappling with for a while. (We say "go for it" 'cause we got one and absolutely love it.) Anyway, in this chapter you'll find out about places where you can buy or even rent videos (yes, you have to send them back). There are hundreds of stores on the Web that sell videos, but the stores listed in this chapter specialize in them, and try hard to make your shopping experience a pleasant one. From superstores that carry all the latest, to the small, out-of-the-way jewels, almost any movie is available. So go ahead and put the popcorn bag in the microwave and order a neat video, like *Casablanca*. Come on, you know how to order, don't you? Just put your fingers to the keyboard and blow, er, press.

## AMR Video

http://www.amr1.com

Ever see a good show on A&E, the Discovery Channel, or maybe the History Channel and later wish that you'd taped it? If your answer is yes, then head over to this store that comes to you from Alaska. They have over 12,000 titles, including lots of documentaries, how-to videos, and theatrical titles. DVD and laser disks are available, too. Samples:

- A&E's *Biography* series
- *A Gift for Life: Helping Your Child Stay Drug and Alcohol Free*
- *A Guide to Good Cooking* series
- *Baby Basics: The Complete Video Guide for New Parents*
- *Feeling Good Again: Coping with Breast Cancer*

- *Great Mansions of Europe*
- *Lonely Planet* series

**Search:** Yes
**Photos:** No
**Ordering:** Online, Phone, Fax
**Gift Wrap:** No
**Delivery:** Ground

## Artbeats

http://www.artbeats.com

If you really want to heat up your presentations, CD-ROMs, or Web site, you can get great video clips from this site. Each clip is 2 to 30 seconds long, within a collection that may span 6 to 15 minutes total. On the site, you get to see a sequence of stills taken from each clip in a collection, and if you want to see the actual moving images, you can run the short clips, using various viewers. The support information is extensive. These professionally done clips focus on backgrounds like sky effects, storm clouds, and time-lapse landscapes. No actors, as far as we can tell. The moving images of fire and storm clouds are astonishing. Samples:

- 10 seconds of a storm cloud roiling up, within the *Storm Clouds* collection
- 71 clips of dust, scratches, light leaks, burns, countdowns, averaging 2.66 seconds each, in *Film Clutter* collection
- 30 clips of full and partial-frame fire, fireworks, smoke, averaging 6 seconds each, called *ReelFire1*

**Search:** No
**Photos:** Yes, and movies, too
**Ordering:** Online, Fax, Phone
**Gift Wrap:** No
**Delivery:** 2nd Day, Overnight

## Best Buy

http://www.bestbuy.com

Despite all the amps, players, and speakers out in their retail stores, the online version of Best Buy currently sells only music and video CDs and DVDs. Lots of info about the DVDs; songlists with Real Audio track samples for the music CDs. Samples:

- DVD of *Practical Magic*, with subtitles and sound

in French and English, Dolby Digital, plus production notes, behind-the-scenes documentaries, feature-length audio commentaries by star, director, producer, and composer
• Julian Lennon, *Photograph Smile*, CD

**Search:** Yes
**Photos:** Yes
**Ordering:** Online
**Gift Wrap:** No
**Delivery:** Ground, 2nd Day, Overnight

## Best Video

http://www.bestvideo.com

For those of you who search out the small cinemas that show interesting movies around midnight, search no farther, because Best Video will bring those hard-to-find foreign, cult, and classic films to your VCR. This place is nice. It doesn't try to compete with the big guys. It has its own niche and milks it. They also offer DVD and laser discs as well as used versions, too. For fun, check out their movie poster section. They've scanned in the posters from each Academy Award winner since 1927! Samples:
• *Almodovar*
• Japanese animations
• *Jean de Florette*
• Joe Bob Briggs drive-in movies
• *On the Waterfront*
• *The Cabinet of Dr. Caligari*
• Windsor McKay cartoons

**Search:** Yes
**Photos:** No
**Ordering:** Online, Phone, Fax
**Gift Wrap:** No
**Delivery:** Ground, 3rd Day

## Big Star

http://www.bigstar.com

Big store, big selection, big sales, big chats, big contests—get the idea? They usually have a freebie order (you order $20 and get a free video; the day we checked in, the free

video was Disney's *101 Dalmations*). There's also lots of information on this site. Film buffs will love it. Click on *Moonstruck,* and you'll be able to get background info on the director, 11 cast members, the screenwriter, photography director, producers, music composer, and editor. A fantastic search helps you through their huge selection. Samples:
• DVDs
• Foreign films
• Gospel
• How-to videos
• Kids' videos
• Movie-star birthday finder
• Movie stills from most of the films offered
• Teaching aids
• Theatrical releases

**Search:** Yes
**Photos:** Yes
**Ordering:** Online, Fax
**Gift Wrap:** No
**Delivery:** Ground

## Blockbuster Entertainment

http://www.blockbuster.com/video

There's probably a glass-and-steel Blockbuster somewhere in your town. They seem to have sprung up all over, just like Jim Carrey movies. If you don't want to stand in line on a Friday night, or just prefer to browse from your home, visit the online store. Fill out a brief questionnaire, and Clair V, their movie mind-reader, will offer recommendations every time you visit. Get reminders on new releases, too, so you can be the first on your block to have the hottest movies. Did anyone say *The Phantom Menace*? Samples:
• Classic westerns
• DVDs
• Foreign films
• Music MTV-type videos
• QuickTime video clips
• Special-interest videos and how-tos
• Sweepstakes and other contests

**Search:** Yes
**Photos:** Some

**Ordering:** Online
**Gift Wrap:** Gift cards
**Delivery:** Ground

## Critic's Choice Video

http://www.ccvideo.com

This video store is a nice place to hang around; not very detailed, but somehow able to sell many films at 40% to 50% off. This isn't the largest video store on the Web, but it's got a good atmosphere. Samples:

- "B" movies
- Biographies of many Hollywood stars
- DVDs
- Exclusive titles just for CCVideo
- Movie books

**Search:** Yes
**Photos:** Yes
**Ordering:** Online
**Gift Wrap:** No
**Delivery:** Ground, 2nd Day, Overnight

## Festival Films

http://www.mdle.com/
ClassicFilms/featuredbideo/
festival.html

Hard-to-get, no, almost impossible-to-locate classic films are available here. To give you an idea how rare some of these gems are, they are offered only on 16mm! (If you are very young, what that means is film on a reel that goes through a projector and is shown on a screen, or just the living room wall.) Great selection of silents from the U.S. and abroad. These 16mm films are antiques and are priced accordingly; some go for more than $500. They also have "newer" films, from the '40s forward, on video and laser discs. Film historians will go nuts here. Samples:

- Busby Berkeley's *Footlight Parade*
- Cecil B. DeMille's *The Cheat* (1915)
- *Dr. Jekyll and Mr. Hyde* (1920 with John Barrymore)
- D.W. Griffith's *Intolerance* (1916)
- From 1910: *The Abyss* (Denmark)

- Laurel and Hardy's *Way Out West*
- Movie poster reproductions

**Search:** Yes
**Photos:** No
**Ordering:** Online, Phone, Fax
**Gift Wrap:** No
**Delivery:** Ground

## Good Movies

http://www.goodmovies.com

Many of the stores in this chapter will give you lots of information about the various videos you are considering. This store does that, but it also gives you the news and the gossip, Gen X style. Discover why Jack Nicholson says he'll never need Viagra or what Whoopi Goldberg thinks about rail-thin models. Pamela and Roz will give you their version of thumbs-up or thumbs-down on over 30,000 titles. Samples:

- Kid movies
- Letterbox videos
- New DVDs
- New releases
- Very detailed search

**Search:** Yes
**Photos:** Some
**Ordering:** Online, Phone, Fax
**Gift Wrap:** No
**Delivery:** Ground

## The Hollywood Collection

http://
www.thehollywoodcollection.com

OK, so this store doesn't "technically" belong in this chapter. But, hey, you love the movies; you'll love this store. Why? Well, have you ever admired the ruby-drop earrings Vivien Leigh wore in *Gone With the Wind*? Or how about the diamond-and-ruby ring Bogey donned in *Beat the Devil*? This store specializes is in creating original reproductions of the jewels worn in many classic Hollywood films. This site is a one-of-a-kind place. Prices are very reasonable. Samples:

- Audrey Hepburn's diamond-tear earrings from *Roman Holiday*
- Bette Davis' dark-blue sapphire ring from *Dark Victory*
- Betty Grable's aquamarine-gold and sterling-silver ring from *Springtime in the Rockies*
- Marilyn Monroe's diamonds from *Gentlemen Prefer Blondes*

**Search:** Yes
**Photos:** Yes
**Ordering:** Online, phone
**Gift Wrap:** No
**Delivery:** Ground, 2nd Day

# KidFlix.com

http://www.kidflix.com

You guessed it! This store sells only movies suitable for kids. Of course, *you* might also like some of their videos, too. There are two things that make this store so good for parents: One is that there are a lot of categories you can use to browse through, and two, the prices are low. Samples:

- *Anastasia*
- *Antz*
- *Barney's Alphabet Zoo*
- *Charlotte's Web*
- *Field of Dreams*
- *Free Willy*
- *Jumanji*
- *Mulan*
- *Quest for Camelot*
- *Rugrats Passover*

**Search:** Yes
**Photos:** Yes
**Ordering:** Online
**Gift Wrap:** No
**Delivery:** Ground, 2nd Day

# NetMarket

http://www.netmarket.com

In their Movies department, you'll find name-brand kids'

videos, plus VHS tapes, and DVD disks at genuinely low prices, if you join up. The site is easy to navigate, with a neat interface. You pick a category such as Foreign, they tell you how many items they have (27), and let you narrow your search by title, star, or director. When you do pick a product, you get a picture with a paragraph describing it, and a list of details. You have to spend a buck to become a member to get the best discounts for three months (then $70 per year). No gift wrapping, but they offer a Gift Finder wizard to help you locate an appropriate gift, or you can get a Personal Shopper to help (a human being who considers your description of the recipient, and gets back to you within two days with suggestions). Their low-price guarantee is outstanding: If you find a lower price at another authorized dealer, they will confirm it, then they will send you a check for the difference, plus 35% of the difference. There's a discount on the shipping charges for bulk orders. Samples:

- *Ah Kam*, Hong Kong action flick with English subtitles, Cantonese sound track, VHS
- *Antz*, 1998, from Dreamworks, in English, VHS
- *Blade*, in English, DVD

**Search:** Yes
**Photos:** Yes
**Ordering:** Online
**Gift Wrap:** No
**Delivery:** Ground

# Opera World

http://www.operaworld.com

Adam Sandler doesn't sing on these videos, but Pavarotti, Te Kanawa, and Domingo do. Most of these filmed operas are available on VHS, but there are some DVDs for sale, also. Samples:

- Bizet's *Carmen*
- Mozart's *The Magic Flute*
- Opera posters
- Puccini's *La Boheme*
- Verdi's *Rigoletto*

**Search:** Some
**Photos:** Some
**Ordering:** Online, Phone, Fax
**Gift Wrap:** No
**Delivery:** Ground, 2nd Day

# Reel.com

`http://www.reel.com`

With over 100,000 movies and 2,500 DVD titles available, this is *the* Web video superstore. Reel knows what they're doing when it comes to satisfying your video needs. You can buy new or used videos, and they've created a great search to make finding just that special film real easy. Laser discs are also available, many at 15% discount. So go ahead, make your day and order one. Samples:

- Gift sets
- Kids' videos
- Movie matches
- Oscar coverage
- Sale DVDs for $9.99
- Sale videos for $4.99

**Search:** Yes
**Photos:** Yes
**Ordering:** Online, Phone, Fax
**Gift Wrap:** No
**Delivery:** Ground

# Schoolroom.com

`http://www.schoolroom.com`

You'll find over 7,000 inspirational and instructional videos, as well as some software, at this store. Many of the videos serve as home-schooling tools (but there are some "entertaining" videos, as well). The videos aren't for educating kids alone, though. They also have a vast supply of instructional videos for all sorts of subjects adults want to know about. They also sell 1,500 Christian and educational books. The video prices are reasonable, but you should check the Today's Special section for some truly outstanding bargains. Sample video subjects:

- Boating and sailing
- Cooking
- English and verbal skills
- Gardening
- Math skills
- Native American history
- Nature and wildlife

- Theology
- War and military

**Search:** Yes
**Photos:** No
**Ordering:** Online, Phone
**Gift Wrap:** No
**Delivery:** Ground, 2nd Day

# Video Movie Wholesale

`http://www.usedmovies.com`

Started 10 years ago as a place that sold used videos (oops, we mean "previously viewed" movies) to retail stores, the business grew quickly and now they sell to anyone on the Web. You might worry about the quality of these tapes. According to VMW, they clean and electronically check each video for defects before shipping. However, if you aren't satisfied with the caliber of *your* video, send it back and they'll replace it. These videos cost about half what you'd pay for a new one. You can also buy new videos. To track down a title, use their Movie Finder email. Sample categories:

- Disney
- Foreign
- New releases

**Search:** Some
**Photos:** No
**Ordering:** Online, Phone, Fax
**Gift Wrap:** No
**Delivery:** Ground, 3rd Day, 2nd Day

# For more flicks, view:

- Hollywood Paraphernalia & Memorabilia
- TV & Video Gear

# Music CDs & Tapes

Music turns out to be one of the easiest items to order on the Web, and interestingly, one of the most international items. U.S. stores carry a wide selection of Caribbean, European, Mexican, and world-beat music, and they sell CDs, DVDs, music videos, T-shirts, and even 12" vinyl and laser discs to customers around the globe.

These days, you can often play samples of sound tracks so you can listen before you buy; on some sites, you can even order up a customized CD, or download one track at a time. The competition in this area is intense, so you can usually find a bargain on any fairly popular item, and, even when you can't get a deep discount, you can locate an obscure, independent, or import item in at least one of these sites.

## 101cd

http://194.205.125.30/oneprd/oone01.asp

Deep discounts on 450,000 titles, including British and European music, video, and video-game titles. This store operates from the U.K. but ships twice a week from U.S. locations so Americans get their orders within a week. You don't have to pay any of those extra customs or that nasty Value-Added Tax (VAT), as a European would. You get bigger discounts if you pre-order a title that's about to come out. You can search by artist, title, song title, label, or catalog number. Product descriptions are tiny, but some include reviews by customers. (If you know exactly what you want, this store will be fine.) Samples:

- Glenn Gould, *5 Beethoven Piano Concerti*, CD
- Worcester Cathedral Choir, Handel's *Messiah*

**Search:** Yes
**Photos:** No
**Ordering:** Online
**Gift Wrap:** Gift message
**Delivery:** Ground, 3rd Day

## All Independent Music

http://www.allindependentmusic.com

A site devoted to the indies, with explanations of what independent groups and producers contribute to the music scene, resources for independent bands, and a newsletter. Categories include alternative, blues, charity, Christmas, country, gospel, jazz, metal, modern, R and B, rap, rock, top 50. For each product, you get a brief description, total playing time, and sample Real Audio tracks to listen to. Perhaps because these albums are independently produced, their prices are quite low. Samples:

- Fast and Bulbous, *Memorial Barbecue, A Tribute to the Music of Frank Zappa*, CD
- Stradlatter, *Mariposa*, CD
- Sunrise Harmony, *It's All Right*, CD

**Search:** Yes
**Photos:** Yes
**Ordering:** Online, Phone
**Gift Wrap:** No
**Delivery:** Ground

## Amazon

http://www.amazon.com

Yes, the book folks now bring you music, too, and with the same attractive interface. You can browse by artist, chart toppers, media mentions, styles (alternative, blues, classical, so on), year, even Grammy Winners. They tell you when each item will ship, provide pictures of the album cover, list names of similar CDs that other customers also bought, list the tracks, include their own reviews, plus reviews by other customers (very revealing!), and usually offer you sample tracks to listen to. Discounts are good, with some around 30%. When you order more than one album, you can have Amazon ship the complete order when everything is ready, or ship as the items become available, which costs a bit more. We love this service, and use it too much for our own good. Samples:

- Chieftains, *Tears of Stone*, CD
- Lauryn Hill, *The Miseducation of Lauryn Hill*, CD
- Loreena McKennitt, *The Book of Secrets*, CD
- Van Morrison, *Back on Top*, CD

**Search:** Yes
**Photos:** Yes
**Ordering:** Online
**Gift Wrap:** Yes
**Delivery:** Ground, 2nd Day, Overnight

## Best Buy

http://www.bestbuy.com

This online store provides song lists and some Real Audio sample tracks from music CDs. They offer 30% off on the top soundtrack albums. Get your order in before 10:40 A.M. Central Time if you want 2nd Day or Overnight shipping, or by 1:40 P.M. Central Time to have it shipped the next business day. Samples:

- Blondie, *No Exit*, CD or cassette
- Julian Lennon, *Photograph Smile*, CD
- Sound track from *Varsity Blues*, CD or cassette

**Search:** Yes
**Photos:** Yes
**Ordering:** Online
**Gift Wrap:** No
**Delivery:** Ground, 2nd Day, Overnight.

## BestPrices

http://www.bestprices.com

The Music department of this superstore has some good bargains in cassettes and CDs, particularly in the classical area. Search by artist, genre, or title. Little information about the albums, except part numbers and occasional track lists. On the CDs we investigated, there were no samples to play. Shipping and handling seem a bit stiff. Samples:

- Chumbawamba, *Tubthumping*, CD
- McNair, Harnoncourt, *Pergolesi Stabat Mater, Vivaldi Stabat*, CD
- *Titanic Soundtrack*, CD or cassette

**Search:** Yes
**Photos:** Some
**Ordering:** Online, Phone, Fax
**Gift Wrap:** No
**Delivery:** Ground

## Camelot Music

http://www.camelotmusic.com

This 500-store chain offers a bright and colorful site, with interesting departments that go beyond the conventional list of genres. For instance, the Cutting Edge area features bands such as Barenaked Ladies and Garbage, and praises Rammstein as "the intersection of gothic and industrial music while the guttural German lyrics run over the top, Du, Du, Hast, Du Hast Mich." Each album description features a discography for the artist and a track list with some samples to play. Prices are near the bottom of the market, with special deals on box sets. The search is a bit quirky; looking for Bach turns up Burt Bacharach and Bachman-Turner Overdrive as well as that guy who wrote the *Toccata and Fugue in D Minor*. Sample products:

- Fear Factory, *Obsolete*, CD
- Pablo Casals, *Bach Cello Suites*, CD
- Rhino, *Beg Scream and Shout, 60s Soul*, 6-CD box

**Search:** Yes
**Photos:** Yes
**Ordering:** Online, Phone
**Gift Wrap:** No, but gift advice online
**Delivery:** Ground

## Cash for CDs

http://207.71.196.181/
cashforcds.asp

Here's a twist. This place will pay you for your used CDs, as long as they have front covers that are still in excellent condition. Maybe you've outgrown the music, never played the disks, don't have room for them, or just need cash. You use their AutoQuote™ to enter four or more CDs that you want to sell. You find an entry for the CD you want to sell by entering the group name, artist's last name, or first few letters of the title. (Of course, they may not be in the market for your more obscure CDs.) When you pick the CD from their list, you tell them what condition it's in (*excellent*, for no marks, with mirror finish; *good*, with a few scuffs; *fair*, with many light marks; or regardless of the condition, *missing the back cover*, which means you get less money for it). In about five seconds they get back to you with a quote. If you agree, you tell them your mailing address, and they send you a free, postage-paid mailing kit so you can send the CDs to them. Once they get the CDs, they inspect them to make sure they are in good condition, with the front cover (missing back covers mean a reduced rate, but you **must** have the front cover). If all is OK, they send you a check. Sample quote:

- Quote on two excellent CDs by the Beatles and Blondie, two good-condition CDs by the Ramones
- Quote on four good-condition CDs of folk songs sung by African choirs

**Search:** Yes
**Photos:** No
**Ordering:** By listing the CDs you want to sell
**Gift Wrap:** No
**Delivery:** Free, postage-paid mailer sent to you

# CD Connection

http://www.cdconnection.com

Home of the Golden Ears, a society that rates the music for you. You guessed it. Those golden earlobes belong to a quarter-million customers, and as soon as you set up an account, you can vote, too. These ratings help get you past the items that are popular today. Album descriptions vary enormously, from the basics (artist, title, release date, part number, price, and availability) to liner notes, track lists, ratings, reviews from the All-Music Guide, and suggestions about other albums you might like, because other customers who were interested in this album bought those ones, too. Only one shipping charge per order, at flat rate; free on

U.S. orders over $100. Samples:

- Aerosmith, *Get Your Wings/Toys*, 3 albums in one, CD
- Blur, *Blur*, CD
- Smashing Pumpkins, *Adore*, CD

**Search:** Yes
**Photos:** Some
**Ordering:** Online
**Gift Wrap:** No
**Delivery:** Ground, 3rd Day, 2nd Day

# CD Now

http://www.cdnow.com

For most music stores, CD Now is the site to beat, because it's big (300,000 music-related items, including T-shirts), good, and well-established, with alliances to major portals around the Web, and their prices include many discounts. Undecided? Their Album Advisor may point you toward music you'll like. Or turn to *Billboard* charts, the MTV CD Lounge, or the VH1 Music Shop. They provide many downloadable samples in Real Audio. You can make up your own CD. If you can't afford everything you want, put items on a wish list, so you can buy them later. If friends visit, put your dream albums into a Gift Registry, too. Shipping options vary depending on the amount and merchandise you order and your address, but the order form tells you how fast you'll get your music. Samples:

- Beth Orton, *Central Reservation*, CD
- Joey Ramone, "1969," track to add to a do-it-yourself CD
- Selena, *All My Hits, Todos Mis Exitos*, cassette, CD

**Search:** Yes
**Photos:** Yes
**Ordering:** Online
**Gift Wrap:** Yes
**Delivery:** Ground, 2nd Day, Overnight

# CD Quest

http://www.cdquest.com

An attractive, well-organized site with low prices on 225,000 items, where you can make your own CD, preview upcoming releases, find out what's just come out. Search by artist, song, sound track, or title. Or follow a quest; the Quest Pages list all available recorded works by a particular artist, identifying what the artist contributed. Individual album descriptions include the label, issue date, formats, cover, and occasionally a track list. Sample items:

- Afro-Cuban All Stars, *A Toda Cuba le Gusta*, CD
- Bruce Springsteen, *Tracks*, 4-cassette, 4-CD box sets
- David Lee Roth, *Crazy from the Heat*, cassette, CD
- Jay-Z, *Hard Knock Life, Volume 2, Explicit Version*, cassette, CD

**Search:** Yes
**Photos:** Yes
**Ordering:** Online, Email
**Gift Wrap:** No
**Delivery:** Ground, 3rd Day, 2nd Day

## CDshop

http://www.cdshop.com

First you pick a country, because these U.K. folks mail albums around the world, and their prices include shipping. You pick a category, such as Rock, then a letter of the alphabet, and they show you a list of everyone whose name begins with that letter. Good place to come for British and Euro releases. They sell only albums, no singles, and no vinyl (because it's hard to ship safely). Their product descriptions are nil, with prices in pounds (approximately $1.62 U.S.). Given the fact that they include packaging and shipping costs in each price, their prices, particularly on U.K. items, are competitive with other sites. They claim to ship within 4 to 30 days of your order, and U.S. and Canadian addresses then take another week or so after that. Samples:

- David Bowie, *Black Tie White Noise*, CD or cassette
- Robbie Williams, *I've Been Expecting You*, CD, cassette, MiniDisc
- Royal Scots Dragoon Guard, *In the Finest Tradition*, CD

**Search:** Yes
**Photos:** Yes
**Ordering:** Online

**Gift Wrap:** No
**Delivery:** Ground

## CD Source

http://www.cdsource.com

Offers 320,000 items, ten times what an average physical store can offer. That total includes 2 million song titles, hundreds of thousands of audio clips, 20,000 imports and music videos. Good search mechanism, by artist, album, song, style, or label. Good detail on each CD, with list of participants, tracks (with some audio clips), timings, and a chance to give a detailed review. (Reviews in French, German, Italian, Portuguese, Spanish.) Excellent prices, below all but the deepest discounters. You get different delivery times and depending on what you order (imports take longer, some items have to be back-ordered). Samples:

- Dixie Chicks, *Wide Open Spaces*, CD or cassette
- Phil Collins, *Hits*, CD

**Search:** Yes
**Photos:** Yes
**Ordering:** Online
**Gift Wrap:** Gift certificates
**Delivery:** Ground, 3rd Day, 2nd Day, Overnight

## CD Universe

http://www.cduniverse.com

More than 200,000 items to choose from, including 4,000 imports, compact discs, cassettes, CDs, and VHS music videos. Prices are among the lowest on the Web. With this many items, you need a good search system, which they have. For instance, in the classical department, you can search by composer, ensemble, conductor, performer, title, label. Descriptions are good, with stock status, running time, label, number of disks, detailed track info. You can save shipping charges by having the store wait for back-ordered items to show up. Samples:

- Collective Soul, *Dosage*, CD
- Ricky Martin, *Vuelve*, CD
- Wilco, *Summer Teeth*, CD
- Yo-Yo Ma, Ton Koopman, Amsterdam Baroque,

*Simply Baroque,* CD
**Search:** Yes
**Photos:** Yes
**Ordering:** Online, Phone, Fax
**Gift Wrap:** No
**Delivery:** Ground, 3rd Day, Overnight

## CD World

http://www.cdworld.com

The music department lives at the core of this site, surrounded by stores selling comic books, software, movies, games and puzzles, sheet music, and video games (475,000 items all told). Much discounting goes on here, because they comparison-shop to ensure they are offering the lowest prices. Descriptions include release date, list price, CD World price, and availability. They have some 2 million tracks, of which almost 300,000 can be sampled in Real Audio. The most popular albums get audio reviews as well, so you can listen as you browse. Neat service: Sign up to have a song sung to someone on the phone, for a birthday, anniversary, or special event. Samples:

- Leonard Bernstein, New York Philharmonic, *Bernstein Conducts Bernstein,* CD
- Nuclear Rabbit, *Intestinal Fortitude,* CD

**Search:** Yes
**Photos:** Small and large
**Ordering:** Online, Phone
**Gift Wrap:** No
**Delivery:** Ground

## E Music

http://www.emusic.com

With more than 140,000 albums and 40,000 videos, this store focuses on low prices and fast delivery. You can search for most music by artist, label, media (12" vinyl, 12" laser disc, cassette, compact disc, DVD, MiniDisc), song, style, title. They offer separate searches for classical music, hot sellers, essential collections, new releases, hot deals, and bargains. You can get free music, buy individual tracks by downloading them, play samples, listen to e-radio. Album

descriptions may include release date, price, labels, availability, track listings, and, sometimes, liner notes and customer reviews, if any; downloadable albums offer samples in MP3 stereo or mono, or wav files. Samples:

- Alfred Apaka, *My Isle of Golden Dreams,* CD
- Guns N Roses, *Spaghetti Incident?,* CD
- Mozart, "Komm, Lieber Mai," downloadable track from Boys Choir of Vienna Woods, *Romantic Vienna*

**Search:** Yes
**Photos:** Yes
**Ordering:** Online
**Gift Wrap:** Just a message
**Delivery:** Ground, 3rd Day, 2nd Day

## ERock

http://www.erock.net

A site that offers classified-ad auctions for rock 'n roll music and paraphernalia such as concert tour books, guitar picks, handbills, instruments, posters, and stage passes and tickets. They link to rock group sites, host a chat room, and accept your wish lists. Good deals are possible. Remember, though, you are dealing with individuals. Most are honorable, but a few might try to stiff you. But you and the sellers have to register, which means you get an email address, phone number, and snail mail address. Erock claims that most buyers and sellers complete the transaction happily. Samples:

- 2 pair of size 2B neon-colored drumsticks
- Beach Boys, *The Greatest Single of All Time CD,* 5-track CD issued in UK by *Mojo* magazine to celebrate "Good Vibrations" winning first place in a survey
- Elvis Presley, memorial pins (set of 2)
- *John Fogerty Blue Moon Swamp Tour at the Fillmore Poster,* 19" x 13", matted and framed

**Search:** Yes
**Photos:** Some
**Ordering:** Online bidding
**Gift Wrap:** No
**Delivery:** Shipping costs and methods are often listed, but otherwise must be negotiated with seller by email

## Harmony House

http://www.harmonyhouse.com

Twenty percent off all CDs all the time sounds lovely, even though this store tends to limit its inventory to new releases and hot items in each category (alternative, classical, country, easy listening, electronic, jazz, blues, rap, rock, shows, world). They show the *Billboard* top singles. Harmony TV also brings you video and audio shows in Real Audio and Real Video formats; these alone are worth the visit. You can win a free CD by answering trivia questions. Samples:

- Joe Arroyo, *Cruzando el Milenio*, CD
- Latin Playboys, *Dose*, CD set
- Victoria De Los Angeles, *Songs of Spain*, CD set

**Search:** Yes
**Photos:** No
**Ordering:** Online
**Gift Wrap:** No, but they have gift certificates
**Delivery:** Ground, 2nd Day, Overnight

## His Music Place

http://www.hismusicplace.com

Quoting *Ephesians*, their slogan is "Sing and make music in your hearts to the Lord!" This store carries thousands of independent Christian artists. You can search by artist, album, or song, browse by categories (accompaniment, alternative and ska, children's, choral and instrumental, country and folk, gospel, international, pop, praise, rap and hip-hop, techno praise, and dance), and they have a bargain basement. "We welcome all types because we believe the Lord can use ALL types of music to further His kingdom." Product descriptions sometimes include Real Audio samples. Sample products:

- Brenda Lowe, *Waiting*, CD and cassette
- Maranatha Praise Band, *Jesus Mighty God*, CD or cassette

**Search:** Yes
**Photos:** Some
**Ordering:** Online
**Gift Wrap:** No
**Delivery:** Ground

## Italian Music

http://www.italian-music.com/index_uk.htm

This Italian site speaks English (and Italian), and offers 25% discounts on new Italian releases, plus free shipping worldwide if you buy five CDs. Prices are in lira or Euros (a little over a buck, depending on the exchange rate). Samples:

- Marina Rei, *Anime belle*, CD
- Pino Daniele, *Un gelato all'Equatore*, CD
- Tenori, *40 Grandissimi degli ultimi 40 anni*, Double CD

**Search:** No
**Photos:** No
**Ordering:** Online
**Gift Wrap:** No
**Delivery:** International air (may be up to two weeks)

## Music Boulevard

http://www.musicblvd.com

Available in English, French, German, Japanese, Portuguese, and Spanish, this site offers lots of categories to browse (including Disney Music and Vinyl), charts, T-shirts (extra-large and large only), and prizes such as Lava Lites, frequent flyer miles, and a chance to put together your own CD or download individual songs in Liquid Audio from a short list of popular artists. Descriptions include pricing, shipping time, label, release date, tracks, links to lists of other items by the same artist, and occasional song samples in Liquid Audio, MPEG, or Real Audio. Want to catch up on the critics? Check out the newsstand, with excerpts from a dozen music magazines. If you feel like concentrating on rock, jazz, or classics, you can jump to Music Boulevard sites devoted to those areas, with plenty of inside information. Most orders go out within a day or two, on weekdays. Samples:

- Mieczyslaw Horszowski, *Bach Recital*, CD
- Shakira, *Donde Estan Los Ladrones*, CD
- T. S. Monk, "Crepuscule with Nellie," downloadable track from *Monk on Monk*

**Search:** Yes
**Photos:** Yes

**Ordering**: Online
**Gift Wrap**: Yes
**Delivery**: Ground, 2nd Day, Overnight

## Music Favorites

http://www.musicfavorites.com

Brought to you by K Mart, this pleasant site offers 100,000 titles in alternative, blues, classical, country, jazz, pop, rock, and urban genres. Descriptions include price, release date, availability, a little information about the production, and sometimes track lists with Real Audio clips. Orders received by 1 P.M. Eastern Time, weekdays, get shipped that day; later orders go on next business day. Sample products:

- Astrid Hadad Y Los Tarzanes, *Ay!*, CD
- Charles Lloyd, *Voice in the Night*, CD
- Orpheus Chamber, *A Set of Pieces, Music by Charles Ives*, CD

**Search**: Yes
**Photos**: Yes
**Ordering**: Online
**Gift Wrap**: No
**Delivery**: Ground, 3rd Day, 2nd Day

## Musicforce

http://www.musicforce.com

A Christian music store with the slogan "If Heaven had a music store!" Browse by artist or category (alternative, children, Christmas, contemporary, country, dance, folk, hip-hop, inspirational, instrumental, jazz, rock, ska, Southern Gospel, Urban Gospel). They offer track lists, with some clips you can try out over the Web. They also give news of music, online events, tours, and concerts. Samples:

- Acappella, *Act of God*, CD
- Jars of Clay, *Drummer Boy*, CD
- Newsboys, *Step up the Microphone*, CD

**Search**: Yes
**Photos**: Yes, sometimes showing front, above, back, inside, and CD
**Ordering**: Online
**Gift Wrap**: No

**Delivery**: Ground, 3rd Day, Overnight

## MusicHQ

http://www.musichq.com/cdhq

With 250,000 music titles, you'll probably find something you like. Search by album title, artist, charts, or style (avant-garde, bluegrass, blues, Cajun, classical, comedy, country, easy, environmental, exercise, folk, gay, gospel, holiday, Latin pop, march, rap, reggae, rock, spoken, vocal, women's, world). Within each style you may find three dozen subcategories to pick from. Product descriptions list tracks, show the album cover, and specify the genre, length, and label. For some titles you get reviews from 200 experienced music critics, via the All-Music Guide. You can have the site make up your own CD, with 70 minutes of songs. You can also pre-order a title, and it will be shipped the Monday before the official release date. They ship only on weekdays. Orders that come in by 12 noon Eastern Time go out that day. They charge a single flat fee for shipping, no matter how many CDs or shipments are needed. Samples:

- Barenaked Ladies, *Stunt*, CD
- Chubby Carrier, *Dance All Night*, CD
- Gaelic Storm, *Gaelic Storm*, CD
- Phil Collins, *Hits*, CD

**Search**: Excellent
**Photos**: Yes
**Ordering**: Online, Phone, Fax
**Gift Wrap**: No, but you can send gifts
**Delivery**: Ground, 2nd Day, Overnight

## NetMarket

http://www.netmarket.com

In their Music department, you'll find name-brand cassettes and CDs at genuinely low prices, if you join up. The site is easy to navigate, with a neat interface. You pick a category such as Classical, they show you their chart-toppers, and you get to browse by options such as composer, title, work, catalog, conductor, orchestra, or performer. Entering "Bach" or "Beethoven" broke the bank with more than a million matches (probably the number of records in the database), but entering Boston as the orchestra found 548 matches. When you do pick a product, you get a picture with a paragraph describing the CD or cassette, a list of the tracks, and sometimes a few sample Real Audio passages you can listen to with a Real Player. You have to spend a buck to become a member to get the best discounts for three months (then $70 per year). Their low-price guarantee is outstanding. If you find a lower price at another authorized dealer, they will confirm it, then they will send you a check for the difference, plus 35%). No gift wrapping, but they offer a Gift Finder wizard to help you find an appropriate gift, or you can get a Personal Shopper to help (a human being who considers your description of the recipient, and gets back to you within two days with suggestions). Samples:

- Boston Museum Trio, *Bach Sonatas,* CD
- Madonna, *Erotica,* CD
- Rob Zombie, *Hellbilly Deluxe,* CD or cassette

**Search:** Yes
**Photos:** Yes
**Ordering:** Online
**Gift Wrap:** No
**Delivery:** Ground

# Real Net

http://www.real.com/
index.html

Hosted by the company that makes the Real Audio player, the software that lets you listen to some samples of music on the Web, this site also offers utilities for speeding up downloads of music and video, and creating and editing digital audio or video. (You can also download the free RealPlayer, and buy a souped-up version if you want.) The site offers sample audio bytes from specialists in music, show business, sports, science, culture, and money, as well as talk-show outtakes from the likes of Dr. Laura, Dr. Ruth, and Rolling Stone Radio. If you like sound, you'll bookmark this site. Sample products:

- *AudioTrack* by Waves, software for digital equaliza-

tion, compression, and gating (box or download)
- *IQfx 3D Audio* from Qsound Labs, turns mono or stereo streams into 3-D RealAudio, controls width of stereo expansion, expands bass range
- *Mixman Studio Pro,* software to create royalty-free RealAudio music and sound effects, for Windows
- *TweakDUN* software for speeding up downloads, Windows

**Search:** No
**Photos:** Small
**Ordering:** Online
**Gift Wrap:** No
**Delivery:** Download, Ground, 2nd Day, Overnight

# Think CD/Video

http://www.goldpaint.net/cgi-
bin/nph-tame.cgi/thinkcd/
index.tam

They offer 350,000 CDs, 30,000 movies and videos on VHS, DVD and laser discs, 10,000 imports, and, yes, T-shirts. Selection, then, is the big plus here. Minimal information about each product, and the prices are not low. No shipping on weekends or holidays. Samples:

- Aerosmith, T-shirt
- Blondie, *No Exit,* CD
- Faith Evans, *Keep the Faith,* CD

**Search:** Yes
**Photos:** No
**Ordering:** Online, Phone, Fax
**Gift Wrap:** No, but gift suggestions
**Delivery:** Ground, 3rd Day, 2nd Day

# Total E

http://www.totale.com

One of the lowest-priced music sites, Total E features 150,000 albums, including newly released music, 1,500 DVDs, 35,000 videos, and do-it-yourself custom 5-track CDs. During one sale, everything was 30% off. Good site for classical music. Even though it is owned by Columbia House, this site turns out to be a separate business, so you can't get Columbia House bonuses, and you can't use their Dividend Dollars here.

Shipping methods vary, depending on whether you
want your stuff fast or cheap. Samples:
- Eric Clapton, *24 Nights*, DVD Music video
- Janet Jackson, *Velvet Rope Tour Live Concert*, VHS
- Meade "Lux" Lewis, "Boogie Woogie Prayer,"
  performed by Albert Ammons, from *The Boogie
  Woogie Trio, Volume 1*, track for custom CD

**Search:** Yes
**Photos:** Yes
**Ordering:** Online
**Gift Wrap:** No
**Delivery:** Ground, 2nd Day, Overnight

# If you'd like more electronic entertainment, play these chapters:

- Movies & Videos
- TV & Video Gear
- Video & Computer Games

# Party Supplies

Having a party? Oh, you've got lots to do, then. Invite the guests, plan the food, cook the food, buy the decorations, put up the decorations, and last, but not least, don't forget to clean the house. Parties are lots of fun to attend, but they can be extremely time-consuming to give. We've found some cheerful stores on the Web that will help you every step of the way. Some sell complete party packages; others help you set the proper mood. We've included a gourmet food store that delivers mouthwatering morsels. (If you'd like a larger selection to choose from, please go to the chapters on Food—Gourmet, or Food—Organic & Special Diets.

## BalloonTyme, Inc.

http://www.balloontyme.com

We've seen a lot on the Web. And just when we thought we had seen it all, BalloonTyme proved us wrong. By the name of this store, you've already assumed you know what they sell. But here's the great part. Their latex balloons are *biodegradable*. These balloons are delivered to your door with disposable helium tanks, if you want. Besides collecting oodles of balloons, you can also order party theme kits (invitations, utensils, table covers, cups, blowups, hats, stickers). Themes include lots of kid birthday-types (Hot Wheels, Barbie, Star Wars, Dr. Seuss) and other themed parties (St. Patrick's Day, football, baseball, St. Valentine's Day). You can order anything separately, but the best buys come when you purchase the packages. Samples:

- Aisle runners
- Balloon animal kits
- Balloon weights
- Curling ribbon
- Hawaiian leis
- "It's a boy" or "It's a girl" balloons
- Jewel, pearlized, and metallic balloons
- Mini top hats
- Special-occasion balloons
- Star Confetti
- Wedding bubbles

**Search:** Yes
**Photos:** Yes
**Ordering:** Online
**Gift Wrap:** No
**Delivery:** Ground

## Birthday USA

http://www.birthdayusa.com

Originally started as a source for busy parents who lovingly wanted to give their children a fantastic birthday party, this store has now expanded to help anyone put together a great themed party. If you have to plan baby showers, end-of-the-season sport parties, luaus, or even fiestas, you will find a wide assortment of party supplies. We found it incredible all the things you can easily get here — even forks, spoons, and party favors. Depending on which party set you order, you'll get balloons, cups, candles, plates, napkins, thank-you notes, streamers, a tablecloth, and more. The box sets come for eight guests. You also can order what they call a la carte items, such as extra themed party-favor bags, invitations, and hats. If you're not too fussy on what theme you want for your party, check out the Clearance Sale Items for some great discounts. Sample party themes:

- Barney
- Blues Clues
- Football
- Little Mermaid
- New Baby
- Rugrats
- Sesame Street
- Soccer
- Star Wars

**Search:** Yes
**Photos:** Yes
**Ordering:** Online, Phone, Fax
**Gift Wrap:** No
**Delivery:** Ground, 3rd Day

## Caesar's Palate

http://www.caesarspalate.com

The selection at this store is incredible. If you want to have a taste of the good life (or are entertaining and want to make an indelible impression on your guests), shop here. The food isn't cheap, but you won't feel cheated, either. Samples:
- Gift baskets
- Goose foie gras with truffles
- Gourmet fruit mixes
- Russian Beluga caviar
- Smoked, sliced turbot
- Wild-boar tenderloin

**Search:** Yes
**Photos:** Yes
**Ordering:** Online
**Gift Wrap:** Card
**Delivery:** 2nd Day

## Chocolate Gallery

http://
www.chocolategallery.com

With more than 300 solid-chocolate novelties, this shop's the place to go for chocolate tailored to someone's hobby, pet, or interests. They make wonderful party favors. Personalize a box with the recipient's name or send a personalized chocolate "telegram." Samples:
- Baby-bottle chocolate
- Ballerina chocolate
- Bingo-card chocolate
- Cat-and-kitty chocolate
- Complete chocoholic home-repair kit
- Cowboy-hat chocolate
- Frog chocolate
- Gold coins for birthday, anniversary, Christmas, Hanukkah, or birth announcements
- MacSNACK or PCSNACK solid chocolate 3.5" disks

**Search:** No
**Photos:** Drawings

**Ordering:** Online, Phone, Fax
**Gift Wrap:** Yes
**Delivery:** Ground

## Cool Stuff Cheap

http://coolstuffcheap.com

What party would be complete without the proper sound or lighting? You might not want to spend a lot on this, but since it can make a big difference between a good party and a *great* one, we looked all over the place for a store where you could spend a little to get a lot. We found one. Samples:
- Calming, soothing bubbles
- Disco-ball package (includes ball, motor, and spotlight)
- Fog machine
- Geometric-motion lamps
- Lava lamps
- Retro metal signs
- South Park doormats
- Strobe lights

**Search:** Some
**Photos:** Yes
**Ordering:** Online
**Gift Wrap:** No
**Delivery:** Ground

## Party Makers

http://www.partymakers.com

This is an all-purpose party store that goes the extra mile to supply you with resources (such as a party planner and a place to share ideas with other parents) and some themed kits not available at the other stores. They'll help you plan your party by your child's age or interest. This is strictly a child's birthday-party supply store. Samples:
- Balloon bouquets
- Chocolate or vanilla birthday cakes
- Dinosaur theme kits
- Gymnast theme kit
- Personalized balloons

**Search:** Yes
**Photos:** Some
**Ordering:** Online
**Gift Wrap:** No
**Delivery:** Ground

# Terror by Design

`http://www.btprod.com`

We used to set up a haunted house every year on Halloween. We bought acres of gauze and stretched it around our basement. Before the kids entered, we blindfolded them and made them put one hand in a bucket of eyeballs and the other in a bucket of brains (they were just grapes and cooked spaghetti, but you know how great the imagination is). We wish we had known about this store back then. It not only has every conceivable item you could want to set up a haunted house, it also has a haunted house how-to video for sale. Samples:

- Fog machine and fluid
- Ghost scanners
- Glow paints and pigments
- Programmable lighting and thunder sounds
- Props
- Strobe lights
- Web shooter

**Search:** Some
**Photos:** Some
**Ordering:** Online, Phone, Fax
**Gift Wrap:** No
**Delivery:** Ground

# True Legends

`http://www.truelengends.com/index.htm`

This is the place to come for grown-up party supplies. Oh, it's not X-Rated (we aren't including X-Rated stuff in this book, anyway), it's just that the themes they have available wouldn't mean very much to our kids, but are a kick to us. The best theme for a party is Betty Boop, in terms of paper goods, but who could resist a Marilyn

Monroe switch plate at a party? Sample themes:

- Betty Boop
- Elvis
- I Love Lucy
- James Dean
- The Beatles

**Search:** Yes
**Photos:** Some
**Ordering:** Online, Phone, Fax
**Gift Wrap:** No
**Delivery:** Ground

# Need a little help in the recipe department?

Pillsbury has a Web site full of recipes for every occasion, including Children's Birthday Parties. Go to http://www.pillsbury.com and click the Gatherings tab. You'll find recipes for:

- Crescent Dogs
- Corn-on-the-Cob
- Kids' Favorite Fruit Salad
- Mini Mouse Party Cupcakes

# If you want to throw the party of parties, you might open these chapters:

- Flowers
- Food—Gourmet
- Gifts
- Weddings

# Phones, Pagers, & Beepers

Shopping for a phone or pager at the mall or in a giant electronics store is a little confusing, with the salespeople coming and going, loud TVs blaring, and hard-to-compare units, all of which look so shiny they must be good. We've found that buying online lets you be a little more thoughtful about what you really need. Also, you'll definitely get some better deals than you would find in a retail store, and sometimes you can even beat the warehouse stores, as well. But what kind of phone is best for you?

Of course, some of us still use gear designed 50 years ago for what the technicians call POTS (Plain Old Telephone Service). But going digital lets you break away from your wall jack. If you decide to buy a digital cell phone, you'll find various strengths, from a bit shaky reception to powerful ear-blasters that work well even in an enclosed parking garage.

Plus, if you are roaming around, you may want to get a pager that alerts you to a phone number, a brief text, or, best of all, voice mail. Of course, to make purchasing more complicated, services force you to navigate through various complex agreements, covering your town, state, region, or the whole country. But the best sites walk you through the choices one at a time, using wizards, so you don't have to stare at all those numbers at once.

## 5-Star Advantage

http://www.aaaaadvantage.com/

Yes, that's five a's in a row, aaaaah!. If you want a lot of choices, try here. For instance, just for cell phones, they have equipment from AudioVox, Bosch, Ericsson, Mitsubishi, Mobile Access, Motorola, Nextel, Nokia, and PanaVise. They offer live online support. Prices are mid-range. Samples:

- Desktop charger with two slots for overnight charging of cell phone batteries
- Nokia 2160 cell phone with authentication, call forwarding, caller ID, call waiting, selective call acceptance, short message service, voice privacy
- Windshield-mounted phone holder for cell phone

**Search:** No
**Photos:** Yes
**Ordering:** Online
**Gift Wrap:** No
**Delivery:** Ground

## Ahern

http://www.aherncorp.com/ahern.html

Aimed at small business, this site offers some of the more obscure phone items you might want at home, such as headsets, conference phones, line simulators, and music on hold. But they have many major vendors, and a lot of products in each category, so even if you just want a cell phone, you'll find several good possibilities here. Samples:

- Adapter to bring phone signal into headsets, with mute button
- Alcohol-free phone wipes for cleaning headsets, PC screens, phones
- Headset that rests on the head or on the ear, for hands-free phone conversations
- Opentech Miracle Phone, with DirectVibe™ Pulsator, to transmit sounds via bones
- Sony 900 MHz cordless phone with caller ID, digital answering system, for wandering around the house without losing the signal

**Search:** No

**Photos:** Yes
**Ordering:** Online, Phone, Fax
**Gift Wrap:** No
**Delivery:** Ground, 2ⁿᵈ Day

**Photos:** Yes
**Ordering:** Online
**Gift Wrap:** No
**Delivery:** Ground, Overnight

## Arch

`http://www.arch.com`

Billing themselves as "a more personal paging company," Arch sells you pagers from several different vendors, along with the services you need. First you decide whether you want local or national paging, and whether you want numbers or numbers and text, then you dip down into a list of pagers for your area, add accessories, and go. Good descriptions, with warranties. If you have questions, they claim they will call you within five minutes of an email. Samples:

- Motorola WORDline, text pager, one-line of text, 16 message slots, selective erase, with annual or quarterly billing for the nationwide text paging service and voice mail
- Regional paging service

**Search:** Yes
**Photos:** Yes
**Ordering:** Online
**Gift Wrap:** No
**Delivery:** Ground

## BestBeep

`http://www.bestbeep.com`

Metroplex beepers and pagers unite! You can buy pagers, service, and even maps of your area (from Boston to Washington). They post the pager manuals and detailed maps of the coverage areas, which is great. Prices are discounted, though not enormously. Order early. If you get your order in before 9 A.M. Eastern Time, it will go out within 48 hours. Samples:

- Free pager in New York area, for Pager Maintenance Plan of $1 a month, plus monthly service and Voice Mail
- PalmPilot PagerCard

**Search:** No

## Cellular Experience

`http://www.icatmall.com/cellx`

A small shop focused on cell phones, but because the store is small, the owners emphasize that they care. Samples:

- AirTouch 60 monthly service
- Nextel menu-driven speakerphone with caller ID, monthly access plan
- Nokia digital phone with rapid travel charger, 37 hours standby

**Search:** No
**Photos:** A few
**Ordering:** Online
**Gift Wrap:** No
**Delivery:** Ground

## Consumer Direct

`http://www.consumer-direct.com`

On this big site, one area is devoted to a few dozen telephones, with good descriptions, and prices that are hard to beat, because the site gets big discounts to begin with, and sometimes they limit their charges to whatever they paid for the items. You get to see your shipping costs on the same page as the product description, so you can decide how fast you really need to get it. All items except overstocks are new.

- Toshiba 25-channel cordless phone with caller ID and call waiting
- Uniden EX1960 900 MHz digital cordless phone with caller ID

**Search:** No
**Photos:** Yes
**Ordering:** Online, Phone
**Gift Wrap:** No
**Delivery:** Ground, 2ⁿᵈ Day, Overnight

# Electronics.Net

`http://electronics.net/`
`Homepage.htm`

From the home page go to Telephones. In categories such as 2.4 GHz phones, 25-channel cordless, 900 MHz cordless, corded, designer, integrated, and multiple line phones, they offer a handful of products (from two or three to a dozen) from a few manufacturers, at substantial discounts from retail. "We will not be undersold!" If you discover a listed competitor offering a lower price within 10 days of purchase, they will beat that price by 10%, match the competitor's price, or refund your money. For each product, they offer a photo (or two), a table of features (not always completely filled in), and specs. For orders placed by 3 P.M. New Jersey time, you can get various versions of rapid delivery (except large, bulky items). Samples:

- Panasonic 2.4 GHz/900 MHz dual-transmission phone, with dual antennas, dual keypads, hands-free speakerphone, 32 channels
- Uniden 900 MHz phone with speakerphone, dual keypad

**Search:** Excellent
**Photos:** Small and big
**Ordering:** Online, Phone
**Gift Wrap:** No
**Delivery:** 2nd Day, Overnight

# Global Mart

`http://www.globe-mart.com`

These folks must like to talk on the phone. Their communications section of this large site offers a handful of phones in categories such as 900 MHz, 2.4 GHz, decorator, 25-channel cordless, and corded telephone systems, plus video phones, cellular and PCS accessories, 2-way radios, and headsets. Very thorough descriptions. Samples:

- Betty Boop Novelty Phone
- Lucent 7630 25-Channel Cordless Phone with Digital Answering Machine
- Magellan WorldPhone, for use with satellite communication for voice, fax, and data; 5 pounds

- Siemens Gigaset 2420 2.4 GHz Cordless Phone System, two lines, speed dial, speakerphone, call log, no need for external phone jack

**Search:** No
**Photos:** Yes
**Ordering:** Online, Phone
**Gift Wrap:** No
**Delivery:** Ground, 2nd Day, Overnight

# NCT

`http://www.nct-active.com/`
`store2.htm`

If you have trouble hearing on your wireless phone when you are in heavy traffic or at the airport, you might want to get a headset that attaches to the cell phone. Give NCT about a day to pick and ship an order. For faster delivery, use their 800 number. Samples:

- Noisebuster headset, extension cable
- ProActive 3000 Earmuff headset

**Search:** No
**Photos:** Yes
**Ordering:** Online
**Gift Wrap:** No
**Delivery:** Ground

# Pager1

`http://www.netaxs.com/people/`
`pagers/`

This site shows paging coverage areas throughout the U.S. You can scan through Motorola pagers, comparing airtime plans, then choose alphanumeric or numeric service for one or two regions, or the whole country. You get the pager via FedEx or UPS. You order online, and because these plans can get complicated, they phone you to confirm the details, so there are no mistakes. Samples:

- Advisor Gold Flex Alphanumeric Pager, 4-line display for text and numbers, personal notebook, message alarm
- Nationwide coverage in over 1,000 cities and

suburbs, with one pager, for frequent travelers
- PocketTalk pocket answering machine for store-and-forward voice mail, no activation fee

**Search:** No
**Photos:** Yes
**Ordering:** Online, Phone, Fax, Email
**Gift Wrap:** No
**Delivery:** Ground, Overnight

## Phone Guys

http://www.cordless-guys.com

They're also the Cordless Guys, and the Radio Guys, depending on what products you want. Good descriptions. Samples:
- Lucent analog cordless phone with jack for optional headset
- Uniden 25-channel cordless phone with voice scrambling, digital answering system, speaker phone, and caller ID
- Uniden 900 MHz phone with two lines, dual keypad, speakerphone, caller ID
- Uniden EP 100 Axis Internet e-Mail Phone, digital home information center, caller ID, email

**Search:** No
**Photos:** Yes
**Ordering:** Online, Phone, Fax
**Gift Wrap:** No
**Delivery:** Ground, Overnight

## ProBeep

https://wwwprobeep.com

Although located in New York, these folks claim they can provide coverage of 90% of the country with their pagers. Samples:
- Motorola Renegade, and national service
- OmniRoam service
- QuoteExpress, personal investment monitoring system, alerting you to changes in your investments, real time, works with pager or PCS phone
- Regional service
- Talkabout Radios using the new frequency band

for Family Radio Service
**Search:** No
**Photos:** Yes
**Ordering:** Online
**Gift Wrap:** No
**Delivery:** Ground

## Service Merchandise

http://
www.servicemerchandise.com

Under Electronics, this store has two or three items in each of about ten categories of phones, prepaid phone cards, and caller ID gear. Since the firm sells brand-name items, you can probably get a popular item here, at good discounts. Their prices are in the low end. Samples:
- Barbie Telephone Answering Machine
- Long Distance Prepaid Phone Card
- Lucent Big Button Plus Phone

**Search:** No
**Photos:** Small
**Ordering:** Online, Phone
**Gift Wrap:** No
**Delivery:** Ground, 2nd Day

## Shopping.com

http://www.shopping.com/

The Consumer Electronics department has phones at discount, some at the bottom range of their pricing. The categories are many (25-channel, 2.4 GHz, 900 MHz, answering machines, caller ID, corded phones, headsets, Internet phones, multiple line, novelty, and video phones), but within each category you won't find more than a few products. So it's a crapshoot. Good deals, if you find products that you want. On the product page you see how much you are saving, how much shipping will cost, and, if you want, you can get the warranty, too. They also eagerly show you how much you are saving when compared with brick-and-mortar competitors like Circuit City. Shipping fees are fixed quite low. Sample phones:
- 60-Name and number caller ID unit, black

- Panasonic 2.4 GHz phone with speaker and answering machine

**Search:** Yes
**Photos:** Yes
**Ordering:** Online
**Gift Wrap:** Certificates
**Delivery:** Ground

## SutterTel

http://dish.suttertel.com

With regular and cordless phones from vendors such as Casio, Panasonic, Sony, and Toshiba, Rick Sutter slashes the prices, so you can buy these items at or near wholesale. Then he offers free shipping, too. As a result, in each category, this site offers great bargains on several dozen phones that are normally expensive, or at least mid-range in prices. We found the write-ups and illustrations useful. Meanwhile, Sutter stresses that his phone lines are answered by real human beings, and fast.

- 2-line deluxe speakerphone with LCD display, 32-number memory, busy redial
- Discount international phone service calling Moscow (24 cents a minute, no surcharges)
- Uniden 2-line dual keypad 900 MHz cordless phone with speakerphone, 20-number speed dial

**Search:** No
**Photos:** Yes
**Ordering:** Online, Phone
**Gift Wrap:** No
**Delivery:** Ground

## TeleDynamics

http://www.teledynamics.com

You can focus on whatever features matter most to you, in this substantial range of products (two dozen cordless phones, for instance). Need an accessory, or answering machine? Here are several, along with decorative phones, headsets, mobile communications, and security systems. Descriptions are good, if short. Sample items:

- Mirafone DirectVibe Pulsator phone for hearing-impaired folks to hear through the bone (also works as conventional phone)
- Panasonic cordless phone with speakerphone, caller ID, 900 MHz, 20-channel memory
- Tiffany cow phone (Close-Out)

**Search:** Yes
**Photos:** Yes
**Ordering:** Online
**Gift Wrap:** No
**Delivery:** Ground, 2nd Day, Overnight

## If you'd like more electronic gadgets, press the button for these chapters:

- Computers & Computer Gear
- Consumer Electronics
- TV & Video Gear
- Video & Computer Games

# Photography

We've had a great time using traditional 35mm point-and-shoot cameras to take pictures on vacations, but playing with a digital camera has meant we can tweak the picture's brightness, adjust the contrast, and crop out annoying intruders (such as other tourists) before we print. When we make up brochures, we also turn to clip art photos and stock photos, because they make us look, well, more professional than we really are. A lot of the traditional camera stores have put brochures up on the Web, without going whole hog and allowing online ordering. The manufacturers, in general, just point the way to their dealers, or, if they sell anything online, do so at the exaggeratedly high MSRP (manufacturer's suggested retail price), which no one else charges. We've bypassed all those, and found the best (and the least expensive) online stores for cameras of all types, film, and photographs.

## Access Discount Camera and Video

http://www.accesscamera.com

With more than 10,000 items, and lowest prices guaranteed, this might be a first stop if you are looking for a particular camera or accessory. Good prices, even though they claim that all products are authorized, factory fresh, not gray market. (Gray-market items are products not authorized for sale in the U.S., so they may not have a U.S. warranty, or accessories in the box.) Some sale items are one quarter of the list price. Great detail on cameras and lenses. Samples:

- Hasselblad Quick Release Flash Adapter
- Nikonos V underwater camera body, orange
- Perfect Picture Kit to accompany any new camera,

including batteries, film, book on photography, lens-care kit, and photo album
**Search:** Yes
**Photos:** Yes
**Ordering:** Online
**Gift Wrap:** No
**Delivery:** Ground, 2nd Day, Overnight

## Agfa Direct

http://www.agfadirect.com

Even though this site is hosted by a company that made its name in film and printing, one department brings together thousands of royalty-free images you can use for your personal or business documents. Samples:

- 60 images of dancers, masks, and feathers in photos from John Foxx's *Carnival in Rio* CD-ROM
- Background images created by the artist Fischer Bessi, on a CD called *Syberia*
- *Classic Televisions and Gadgets*, including rabbit ears, a CD-ROM of photos with clipping paths, so they stand out from your backgrounds
**Search:** No
**Photos:** Yes
**Ordering:** Online
**Gift Wrap:** No
**Delivery:** Ground, 2nd Day, Overnight

## B and H

http://www.bhphotovideo.com

A huge inventory of point-and-shoot, 35mm, digital, medium-format, large-format, and panorama cameras, filters, light boxes, light meters, loupes, and supports. Samples:

- Arca-Swiss Discover 4 x 5 System, precision micro-gear focusing, yaw-free movements, built-in tripod sockets
- Agfa ePHOTO 780 digital camera, 1024 x 768 resolution, 2 MB smart memory card, 1.8" LCD

screen, auto flash, video out
**Search:** Yes
**Photos:** Yes
**Ordering:** Online, Phone
**Gift Wrap:** No
**Delivery:** Ground, 2nd Day, Overnight

## Camera Shop

https://www.camerashopinc.com

A well-designed, easy-to-tour site with a fair sampling of products at different price levels in each category, such as single-lens reflex cameras, underwater cameras, video camcorders. They also offer services like putting pictures on a mug, and a few products they talk about only on the phone (such as albums). Samples:

- Kodak Max Sport, for one-time-use, waterproof camera, rubberized, good down to 14 feet
- Ricoh RDC-300 Zoom Digital Camera, 640 x 480 pixel resolution, auto focus, color LCD display, 2 MB memory card

**Search:** Yes
**Photos:** Yes
**Ordering:** Online, Phone
**Gift Wrap:** No
**Delivery:** Ground

## Camera World

http://www.cameraworld.com

Regular and digital cameras make up the majority of products on this site, but it also offers video and audio gear. Hundreds of cameras from major manufacturers, at substantial discounts off the manufacturer's suggested retail price (sometimes almost half off). Descriptions often include features or specs, related accessories, and a picture of the product. Samples:

- Canon Photo Sure Shot A-1 Pack, waterproof camera, good to depths of 16.4 feet, with wide-angle lens, auto focus
- Hasselblad single-lens reflex 202FA medium format black body
- UV Haze filter, absorbs ultraviolet light, good for

landscapes
**Search:** Yes
**Photos:** Some
**Ordering:** Online, Phone
**Gift Wrap:** No
**Delivery:** Ground

## Corbis Images

http://www.corbisimages.com

An enormous collection: 1.4 million digital images ready to be licensed for business projects (for which you have to get a password), and 20,000 royalty-free images for personal use (no password needed). You can download a "comp" version to test out before buying. Prices start low and go up as you get more resolution. Samples:

- 2-disc CD-ROM set with photos of models of buildings and monuments, with the background removed, so you can drop them into another picture, or a Web page
- Mission Operations Control Center, NASA, news photo in color
- Woman screaming because she has overcooked a bunch of cookies (color photo)

**Search:** Yes, very detailed, with good suggestions for refining your search
**Photos:** Yes
**Ordering:** Online, Phone
**Gift Wrap:** No
**Delivery:** Download, Ground

## EyeWire

http://www.adobestudios.com

This slick Adobe-sponsored site offers professional fonts and digital photos. They sell individual images, whole CD-ROMs of photos, and almost any font you might want. Samples:

- *Antique Toys*, such as a rocking horse, ball, and block, on a CD-ROM
- Color photo of swimmer, shot from underwater,

in the *Exercise and Wellness* collection
- Color photo of woman on horseback against the setting sun, in the *Outdoor Adventures* collection
- Wiesbaden Swing Dingbats, font from Linotype-Hell AG

**Search:** Yes
**Photos:** Yes
**Ordering:** Online, Phone, Fax, Email
**Gift Wrap:** No
**Delivery:** 2nd Day, Overnight, Saturday

## Global Mart

http://www.globe-mart.com

Very clean, quick site, with regular, digital, and video cameras, and photo-publishing tools. Good range of major vendors, though not all are represented here. Moderate pricing. Samples:
- Case Logic Point-and-Shoot Camera Bag
- Digital color dye-sublimation thermal transfer printer, with roll paper, high resolution, Windows or Mac
- Fuji MX-700 Digital Camera

**Search:** No
**Photos:** Yes
**Ordering:** Online, Phone
**Gift Wrap:** No
**Delivery:** Ground, 2nd Day, Overnight

## Hungry Eye

http://www.leicasource.com

Leicas, Leicas, and nothing but Leicas. Used or new, reflex, range-finder cameras, binoculars, and scopes, but little info about each camera or lens, so you need to know exactly what you want before you visit. An official franchisee. They stress that they really ship when they say they are going to ship. "No bunk, no bull, no runaround." They also tell you about any available rebates. In-stock items are shipped immediately, and on back orders, they "keep you apprised." Samples:
- Leica M6 Titanium Rangefinder camera

- Leica R105-280/4.0 APO reflex lens
- Leica R8 Silver camera with lenses

**Search:** Yes
**Photos:** Some
**Ordering:** Online, Phone
**Gift Wrap:** No
**Delivery:** Ground

## Insight

http://www.insight.com

If you've had a hard time finding a particular digital camera, come to this so-called discount center for computer hardware and software, because it has a good selection of digital cameras listed under Input devices. Prices do not seem particularly low. But this site lists a lot of products from each of the major vendors, and the site also tells you how many units are in stock, so you know whether you can get the product right away, or have to wait for the store to order it from the manufacturer. Some products come with specs, but many have just names and numbers. Sample products:
- Kodak Digital Science DC 260 Zoom camera
- Toshiba Digital Camera PDR-5, with 2.5" LCD, fixed-focus lens, multiple-shot screen review

**Search:** Yes
**Photos:** Some
**Ordering:** Online
**Gift Wrap:** No
**Delivery:** Ground, 2nd Day, Overnight

## Norman Camera

http://www.normancamera.com

With the top few products from the leading vendors in areas such as digital cameras, film scanners, and single-lens reflex cameras, this site helps you decide which product will be best for you. They have extensive tips and hints. They also offer a table comparing features of digital cameras, and another side-by-side comparison of pictures taken by digital cameras (showing a wide variation even within a single manufacturer's line, from blue tint to orange). Nice service: They post new drivers for digital cameras, so you can update without going to the original vendor! They also display some customers' shots in their Shooters' Gallery. Samples:

- Mamiya 645 SVX Pack, medium format, camera body with 80mm f/2.8 lens with SV Power Grip for continuous firing at 1 frame per second
- Mousepad that displays your 4"x 6" print
- Nikon Pronea S Kit with 30-60mm lens

**Search:** Yes
**Photos:** Yes
**Ordering:** Online, Phone
**Gift Wrap:** No
**Delivery:** Ground, 3rd Day, 2nd Day, Overnight

## PhotoCollect

http://photocollect.com

Here's a wonderful gallery of excellent fine art photographs from the 19th and 20th centuries. Amazingly, they post prices. Ordering is a bit unusual. You email the gallery with an expression of interest, and they call you, on their dime, to work out details. You get to view the photograph on your own wall for a week, before you have to decide whether to keep it. The gallery will also do framing. Samples:

- Karl Blossfeldt, *Untitled* photogravure, print, 1936
- Billings and Matthews, *Apparatus for Taking Composite Photographs of Skulls, No. 5*, photo lithograph, print, 1885
- Brassaï, *Ballet School, Paris, Feet up on Piano*, vintage gelatin silver print, 11"x 7.5", 1953

**Search:** No
**Photos:** Small and large
**Ordering:** Email
**Gift Wrap:** No
**Delivery:** By arrangement

## Photofilm

http://www.photofilm.com

Just film and batteries, in a very clean site built around their database. No information about the products, no pictures. You just pick an item and see the price, then set the quantity you want, and add it to your order. They stock almost the entire line of Agfa, Fuji, Kodak, and Polaroid films, as well as Duracell, Panasonic, and camera batteries. Samples:

- Agfa Color Print Film, HDC 135-36
- Fujicolor Superia film 135-12

**Search:** Yes
**Photos:** No
**Ordering:** Online
**Gift Wrap:** No
**Delivery:** Ground

## PhotoNet

http://photo.net

If you love photography, visit Phil Greenspun's site. He teaches at MIT, and he has set up this site as a model of the way an Internet community should be set up. You can find discussions of almost any photographic subject you want to learn about, post classifieds, browse exhibits, learn how to publish a database-backed site like this, read reviews of equipment by readers and experts. A photographer himself, Phil "sells" a few gorgeous color C and Ilfochrome prints, but with a difference. You send a check made out to the Angell Memorial Animal Hospital, where he set up a fund after the death of his dog George, or the SARA Sanctuary No-Kill Shelter. A company called Portland Photographics makes the prints for free, and he chips in shipping out of his pocket. Your whole check goes to charity. Your picture is shipped anywhere from next day to several weeks, depending on where Phil is when you order. Samples:

- *Moeraki Boulders (New Zealand) Seascape*, by Phil Greenspun
- *Travels with Samantha*, travel pictures and text by Phil Greenspun (gets 10,000 hits a day)

**Search:** No
**Photos:** Spectacular, rich, professional
**Ordering:** Online, or send check by mail
**Gift Wrap:** No
**Delivery:** Ground

## Samy's Camera

http://www.samys.com/

A spin-off of a huge photo store, with studios, rental equipment, and 200 suppliers. "We don't play games with gray-market goods." Bags, cases, consumer, collectible, digital, and professional cameras, darkroom supplies, lighting gear. Examples:
- Beseler Print and Film Developing Starter Kit
- JOBO Nova Academy II archival 16" x 20" print washer
- Kodak DC-120 digital camera, with 120 x 960 pixel picture resolution, 2 MB internal storage

**Search:** No
**Photos:** Some
**Ordering:** Online, Phone
**Gift Wrap:** No, but they have gift suggestions
**Delivery:** Ground

## Slickrock Gallery

http://www.boulderutah.com/
slickrock/index.html

Beautiful images of the Southwest, direct from the artist, Kipp Greene. All images printed on archival material, 100% cotton museum board, hand signed by artist, ready for framing. Prices, which are quite reasonable, show up when you pick the photo from the dropdown list in the order form. Full refund if you are not satisfied. Samples:
- *Anasazi Ruins, Colorado Plateau*
- *Coyote Gulch, Escalante Wilderness*
- *Lenticular Clouds, along the Book Cliffs*

**Search:** No
**Photos:** Yes
**Ordering:** Online
**Gift Wrap:** No
**Delivery:** To be arranged

## Tech Store

http://www.techstore.com

Within the vast high-tech warehouse, go to the Digital Cameras department (over in Hardware) for long lists of products from major vendors. The site provides well-displayed technical specs for almost every product, along with shipping costs, and availability. Samples:
- Nikon Coolpix 700 Digital Camera with Nikkor lens for photographic image quality at print sizes up to 11" x 14"; 4-step digital zoom, high-speed continuous shooting up to 2 frames per second, auto focus, flash, metering, and white balance
- Sony DSC-D700 Professional Digital Still Camera with 5X zoom

**Search:** Yes
**Photos:** No
**Ordering:** Online
**Gift Wrap:** No
**Delivery:** Ground, 3rd Day, 2nd Day, Overnight

## The F STOPS Here

http://www.thefstop.com

New and used large and medium format cameras and equipment. Visit their gallery of striking images by large-format artists, with prices for mounted prints, and links to the artists' sites. "If you are new to large format and lack the knowledge to make an intelligent buying decision, please call." Product pages come with multiple photos of the cameras and specs. The site also offers a bulletin board for people using large-format cameras, a newsletter, workshops, and links to related sites. Equipment shipped within 24 hours of order. Samples:
- Richard Schwarzchild's hillside view, *Tuscany*, 16" x 24" matted to 22" x 28"
- Toyo 4" x 5" AX all-metal camera, 5.8 pounds
- Used Mamiya 6 medium-format camera
- Wisner 4" x 5" Pocket Expedition, geared front axis tilt, geared front rise

**Search:** No
**Photos:** Yes
**Ordering:** Online, Phone
**Gift Wrap:** No
**Delivery:** Ground, 2nd Day

## Wolf Camera

`http://www.wolfcamera.com`

These folks are taking over the photo-developing booths and stores at the malls, and now their slick online store offers lots of cameras, film, processing, as well as camcorders, books, and accessories. They handle almost all the top brands at average street prices. Orders placed by 3 P.M, Eastern Standard Time are shipped that day, except holidays and weekends. Samples:

- Kodak DC260 Pro digital camera with 2X digital zoom, 1536 x1024 pixels resolution, with two 16 MB Picture Cards
- Polaroid 600 Single Pack
- Wolfpro film processing of color 35mm film, 12 exposures, making large, glossy 4" x 6" prints

**Search:** Yes
**Photos:** Yes
**Ordering:** Online, Phone
**Gift Wrap:** No
**Delivery:** Ground, 2nd Day, Overnight (if you phone)

## Want even more imaging gear? Put these chapters in your viewfinder:

- Computers & Computer Gear
- Consumer Electronics
- Surveillance Gear

# Prescription & Over-the-Counter Drugs

Have you ever waited on a long line to get your prescription filled? Have you ever called in to renew a prescription, driven to the drugstore, only to find out that the pharmacist couldn't reach your doctor? If you have, then you'll love this wonderful aspect of shopping on the Web. We've found stores that will take your new prescription or transfer an existing one and then mail your medicine to your door. Many of these stores offer other helpful items for sale, such as over-the-counter drugs, home health-care items and large medical equipment. Some give you free shipping, and others will automatically refill long-term prescriptions, so you never run out. Most of them handle insurance for you and some will even give you free prescriptions by charging only the insurance company and forgetting about your copayment or deductible. Not all remedies come out of a pharmacist's shelf, though. We also have discovered stores that sell homeopathic and herbal remedies. There are even some stores that do both.

If you are looking for large health products, such as humidifiers, HEPA air purifiers, and water-filter systems, you should also read the Health Products chapter. You might also want to read the Herbs chapter for a listing of stores that specialize in nothing but herbal remedies. And, if you're looking strictly for vitamins, please turn to the chapter on Vitamins & Supplements.

## ABee Well Pharmacy

http://www.abeewell.com

Deep discounts are the reason you'll want to shop at this drugstore. Have a prescription? Mail or fax it in to them. Or you can have them call your doctor (this goes for renewals, too). Just like the drugstore on the corner, they'll keep records on you to check for possible drug interactions and will send you a leaflet regarding your medication. You can ask for child-proof caps or non-child-proof caps. All of their prescriptions are sent via 2–3-day mail, but if you're in a hurry, you can ask for Overnight delivery for an addition $10 to $15, depending on the weight of your order. They also offer a nice selection of links, such as one to the informative Virtual Hospital and another to a site describing medical software. Samples:
- Prescription drugs
- Vitamins

**Search:** No
**Photos:** No
**Ordering:** Online, Phone, Fax
**Gift Wrap:** No
**Delivery:** 3rd Day, 2nd Day, Overnight

## American Health Herbs

http://healthherbs.com

This could best be described as an herbal superstore. You can find a plethora of herbs plus herbal formulas for a slew of disorders including acne, after-birth pains, allergies, arthritis, asthma, diabetes, hypoglycemia, insomnia, and much, much more. They offer a 2% discount for online orders. One minus of this online site is that you can't just click on the name of the herb to automatically drop it into a shopping cart. You have to type the products you want on an order form. Samples:
- Books, videos, and cassettes
- Colloidal silver generators
- Herbal formulas
- Oils, liniments, and lotions
- Powders and poultices
- Vitamins

- Water-filtration systems
- Weight-loss tinctures

**Search:** Some
**Photos:** No
**Ordering:** Online, Phone, Fax
**Gift Wrap:** No
**Delivery:** Ground

## Chemist Net

http://www.chemistnet.com

This New York–based pharmacy has been in business over 50 years. They have several walk-in stores sprinkled throughout the New York City area. They offer over-the-counter drugs, but they also stock a large assortment of homeopathic and herbal remedies for a number of ailments, including diabetes and hypertension. Got a question? Email their chemist. Shipping within the continental U.S. is a flat $6. Samples:

- Clinical nutrients for diabetes
- Cosamin DS
- Herbal V (Viagra alternative)
- Sinus and allergy formulas

**Search:** Yes
**Photos:** No
**Ordering:** Online, Fax
**Gift Wrap:** Card
**Delivery:** Ground

## Community Prescription

http://www.prescript.com

This Web store is probably the only national prescription service owned and operated by HIV-positive folks. Besides offering prescription services (new or transferable, then refills), they give the HIV+ person a lot of medical information, such as detailed descriptions of the latest medicines and treatments. There is also an in-depth section for women who are HIV+ and many links. To use their prescription service, you must first enroll, stating whether you want to pay by cash or credit card for the entire order (discounts apply) and whether you have an active insurance policy. You can

also opt for an automatic refill program, so you don't have to email your order in every month. Samples:

- Combivir
- Delavirdine
- Fortovase
- Steroids for wasting syndrome
- Zerit

**Search:** Some
**Photos:** No
**Ordering:** Online, Phone
**Gift Wrap:** No
**Delivery:** Ground, 2nd Day

## CRH International, Inc.

http://www.aloealoe.com

The juice of the aloe-vera plant has long been a folk remedy for soothing the skin of burns and relieving minor arthritis pain. Now science is proving what many have known for a long time, that aloe vera really heals. This store specializes in products made from this succulent. If you have a little time, you can even get some custom-blended products. Samples:

- After-sun lotion
- Anti-wrinkle cream
- Arthritic body rub
- Medicated gel
- Moisturizers
- Pure aloe-vera juice
- Whole-leaf aloe-vera capsules

**Search:** No
**Photos:** No
**Ordering:** Online, Phone
**Gift Wrap:** No
**Delivery:** Ground, 2nd Day, 3rd Day, Overnight

## Cyberspace Telemedical Office

http://www.telemedical.com

This place has it all: medications, hearing aids, skin care, first-aid supplies, and a lot more. Click on the Nutraceuticals button and you'll be taken to the Cyberspace Health Food Store, where you can buy whole foods, vitamins, supplements, and herbal remedies. If you want to use their mall for prescription drugs, click on the Prescription Ordering System, and you can choose one of ten national pharmacy chains, such as Walgreens, Rite Aid, or Longs Drugs. This mall also offers lot of articles and links to health-related sites and they help you shop for health and dental insurance. Samples:

- Baby products
- Eye care
- Fitness equipment
- Home health care products
- Nutritional formulas
- Prescriptions
- Senior care products
- Vitamins

**Search:** Yes
**Photos:** Some
**Ordering:** Online
**Delivery:** Ground

# Drug Emporium

http://www.drugemporium.com

If you have a Drug Emporium store in your town, then you know exactly what you can buy on this site. If you don't have one locally, then let us tell you that if you close your eyes and imagine walking into *your* local drugstore, then you'll know what this place sells. You can get the everyday items, such as toothpaste or aspirin, and larger electronic ones, such as AM/FM cassette radios and cameras. They will fill new prescriptions or you can have your old one transferred. Samples:

- Band Aids
- Cosmetics
- Cough drops
- Hair-care products
- Mouthwash
- Nose spray
- Pregnancy/ovulation tests
- Prescriptions

**Search:** Yes
**Photos:** Some

**Ordering:** Online
**Gift Wrap:** No
**Delivery:** Ground, 2nd Day

# Drugs by Mail

http://www.drugsbymail.com

This store really wants your business. So much so, in fact, that they created the Rational Relief program. This program gives you your Rx at no cost beyond what your insurance pays (assuming that your insurance pays 80% or more). And even better, they do all the insurance paperwork. Mail your prescription to them or have your doctor call it in. Samples:

- All prescription drugs
- Cosamin DS
- Viagra

**Search:** No
**Photos:** No
**Ordering:** Online, Phone
**Gift Wrap:** No
**Delivery:** 2nd Day, Overnight

# Drugstore.com

http://www.drugstore.com

This is a drug megastore. You name it, they got it. Over-the-counter drugs, cosmetics, oral care products, just about everything you could want from a drugstore and more. They also have an extensive prescription drug department. Give them your prescription and they'll set up a patient profile for each member of your family. If you have insurance, give them that information, too. You can ask their pharmacist questions and you can look up the prices of their prescription drugs by clicking the Drug Index section. They also offer affordable prices on some medications that your insurance may not cover, such as birth control pills or estrogen replacement, or Retin-A therapies. Samples:

- Allergy medication
- Baby care products
- Blood pressure kits

- Cleansers, soaps, and moisturizers
- Feminine care
- Herbal remedies
- Over-the-counter drugs
- Prescription drugs
- Rogaine
- Thermometers
- Vitamins and minerals
- Wellness formulas

**Search:** Yes
**Photos:** Yes
**Ordering:** Online, Phone
**Gift Wrap:** No
**Delivery:** Ground, 3rd Day, 2nd Day, Overnight

## Green Tree

http://www.greentree.com

This store not only sells you vitamins, supplements, and herbal and homeopathic remedies, it also supplies you with mountains of research and informative articles. They also offer a free nutritional analysis for either men or women. You answer some questions (in about two minutes) and then they come up with a vitamin plan for you based on your answers. You can also search for a particular vitamin and find out everything there is to know about it, such as what it is good for. Samples:

- Allergy formulas
- Arthritis remedies
- Athlete's vitamins
- Boosting immune system therapies
- B-Stress with Siberian ginseng
- Carbo vegetabilis
- Creatine fuel powder
- Energy formulas
- Gallbladder disorders
- Individual vitamin plans
- Melatonin
- Multivitamins

**Search:** Yes
**Photos:** No
**Ordering:** Online, Phone, Fax
**Gift Wrap:** No
**Delivery:** 2nd Day

## Home Pharmacy

http://www.homepharmacy.com

This is another one of those Internet drugstores that carry just about everything, with a slight emphasis on home-health products. Have questions? Ask one of their pharmacists. But you won't have to ask too many questions, as they offer a detailed description of each product they have for sale. When this book went to press they did not have their online pharmacy up and running, but it should be operational by the time you read this. By the looks of their store, and the amount of information they've supplied on each and every product, we suspect that this pharmacy is going to be one of the best for online shoppers. Samples:

- Cholesterol tests for the home
- Diabetes care
- Hemorrhoid relief
- Home HIV test
- Incontinence products
- NicoDerm CQ
- Ostomy products
- Over-the-counter medications
- Rogaine
- Vitamins

**Search:** Yes
**Photos:** Yes
**Ordering:** Online, Phone, Fax
**Gift Wrap:** No
**Delivery:** Ground, 2nd Day, Overnight

## Home Shopping Pharmacy

http://
www.homeshoppingpharmacy.com

The specialty of this Internet drugstore is prescriptions. They strive to fill your prescriptions in a jiffy and get them to you the next day. They also carry some over-the-counter medications plus some alternative medicine remedies. They take most insurance plans and you don't have to pay up front, if you have one. If you need to, you can consult with one of their pharmacists. Samples:

- Customized PMS pills

- Menopause formulas
- Prescriptions
- Weight-loss remedies

**Search:** Yes
**Photos:** No
**Ordering:** Online
**Gift Wrap:** No
**Delivery:** Overnight

## IPS

http://www.ipsrx.com

The IPS stands for Immediate Pharmaceutical Services, Inc. (which is a subsidiary of Discount Drug Mart, Inc.). Their online store specializes in vitamins, supplements, and herbal extracts and teas. (You can re-fill prescriptions that you've previously had filled with one of their brick-and-mortar stores.) They have a Remedy Search section where you click on an ailment, such as arthritis pain, headache, or stress, and it will suggest vitamin or herbal remedies tailored for that condition. Samples:

- Acidophilus capsules
- Beta-carotene soft gels
- Echinacea
- Feverfew
- Folic acid tablets
- Herbal energizer
- Melatonin
- Multivitamins
- Saw palmetto extract
- Slimming tea-orange spice

**Search:** Yes
**Photos:** Yes
**Ordering:** Online, Phone, Fax
**Gift Wrap:** No
**Delivery:** Ground

## MediQuest Pharmacy

http://
www.mediquestpharmacy.com

You'll find some specialized services here, such as

hormone replacement and life-enhancing drugs. Looking for a Hormone Replacement Specialist? Type in your ZIP code, and MediQuest will locate one for you. Samples:

- 5-HTP
- Alpha-hydroxy gel
- Cartilade
- Creatine monohydrate
- Exfoliating net sponge
- Hormone replacement therapy
- Hormone therapy
- Kava-kava
- Nondairy superdophilus
- Rejuvamin
- Siberian ginseng
- Viagra
- Vitamins and antioxidants
- Weight-loss formulas

**Search:** Yes
**Photos:** Yes
**Ordering:** Online, Phone, Fax
**Gift Wrap:** No
**Delivery:** Ground, 2nd Day, Overnight

## MediStore

http://www.mediconsult.com/
home/store

A wonderful supply of hard-to-locate products, especially medical supplements. A great search, divided into 60 medical topics, takes the time out of finding that special product. You'll also find support groups and a drug reference section. Everything for sale at the site has a full, money-back guarantee. Samples:

- Adult life-care kit
- Antioxidants
- Carbo Edge energy drink
- Health-related reference books
- Hip-replacement rehab video
- Home medical-assistance service
- Hormone-monitoring kit
- Medical software
- Vitamins and supplements

**Search:** Yes
**Photos:** Some

**Ordering:** Online
**Gift Wrap:** No
**Delivery:** Ground

## MotherNature.com

`http://www.mothernature.com`

From homeopathy to aromatherapy, this health store carries a long list of natural products to help keep you well and also help when you're sick. Shipping is free on orders over $50. Samples:

- Allergy and hay-fever remedies
- Appetite suppressants
- Circulation formulas
- Health bars
- Herbal teas
- Vitamins and minerals

**Search:** Yes
**Photos:** Yes
**Ordering:** Online
**Gift Wrap:** No
**Delivery:** Ground, 2nd Day

## Natural Living Center

`http://www.ncenter.com/`
`products.htm`

A friendly site that's like having a friend who brews up herbal teas for you. Start by taking the online nutritional questionnaire specifically tailored for men or women. After that, you'll receive a custom formula just for you. There's other online help, such as a calorie counter vs. exertion calculator. You also find a lot of information on diverse topics, such as arthritis "cures" and the value of antioxidants. Free shipping on orders over $50. Samples:

- Arctic root
- Black Cohosh
- Diet and sports nutrition
- Dong quai
- Herbal liquids
- Herbal teas
- Homeopathy

**Search:** Yes
**Photos:** Some
**Ordering:** Online, Phone, Fax
**Gift Wrap:** No
**Delivery:** Ground, 2nd Day

## Planet Rx

`http://www.planetrx.com`

This is another well-thought-out drugstore. They offer a prescription drug service where you can search out any drug and find out what it is, what benefit it is to your system, and what, if any, side effects you may encounter when taking it. You'll also be able to quickly see how much the drug costs. They accept most medical plans. You'll also find a Health Topic Library with lots of articles and information on more than 100 different medical conditions. If you want to find some herbal remedies, click on the Alternative Card Index, which lists many treatment options for various ailments. But like all good drugstores, this one also carries lots of over-the-counter drugs, as well as beauty and skin products, fragrances, and other medical supplies. This is a nice store if you want to find something fast, or if you just want to browse. Free Ground shipping in the continental U.S. for just prescriptions. Samples:

- Arthritic-pain relief
- Athlete's foot cure
- Bed-wetting alarms
- Blood-glucose monitors
- Diabetic skin-care products
- First-aid products
- Home HIV/AIDS test
- Lice treatments
- Moisturizers and cleansers
- Nasal sprays
- Ovulation predictors
- Vitamins and nutrition bars
- Weight-control drugs

**Search:** Yes
**Photos:** Yes
**Ordering:** Online, Fax
**Gift Wrap:** No
**Delivery:** Ground, 2nd Day, Overnight

# Pro Mark Pharmacies

`http://www.pro-mark-pharmacies.com`

You'll find a nice blending of traditional drugstore supplies combined with durable medical equipment here. They will also fill new or transfer old prescriptions and have them delivered to your home. You can complete and email their price quote form if you are looking to price-shop on prescriptions you use often. This company sells worldwide and you can have their online store information translated into German, French, Italian, Portuguese, or Spanish. Medicare assignment and insurance billing is accepted. Samples:

- AIDS medication
- Apnea monitors
- Breast prosthesis
- Foley catheters
- Home health care
- Infusion services
- Movable beds
- Nebulizers and inhalation medication
- Wheelchairs

**Search:** Yes
**Photos:** Some
**Ordering:** Online, Phone
**Gift Wrap:** No
**Delivery:** Ground

# TrinityRX

`http://www.drugplace.com`

This is a natural-remedy pharmacy. You'll find natural products formulated to help with a number of maladies. You'll find products that will help you lose weight, stop smoking, and help boost your immune system. Samples:

- Antioxidants
- Cellular Forte with IP6
- Citrithin
- Esberitox
- Green tea extract
- Hydroxytryptophan
- HyperiMed

- Inflamzyme
- Ivy extract
- Kidsoothe–St. John's Wort complex
- Meta-sitosterol
- Ultravitamins for men and women

**Search:** No
**Photos:** No
**Ordering:** Online, Phone
**Gift Wrap:** No
**Delivery:** Ground

# Wal-Mart Pharmacy

`http://www.wal-mart.com/pharmacy`

Now you can order your prescriptions (or have them transferred from another drugstore or refill them), then go shopping in the other Wal-Mart departments. Their drugstore offers an automatic refill option. Samples:

- Department store items
- Over-the-counter drugs
- Prescription drugs

**Search:** Yes
**Photos:** Some
**Ordering:** Online, Phone
**Gift Wrap:** No
**Delivery:** Ground

# School Supplies

We're going to show our advanced age here by saying that we actually remember going to school when all you had to bring was a notebook (with paper and dividers), a pencil, a pen, a ruler, and an assignment pad. Today, kids come home from school with huge lists of stuff to bring, some for our kid, but some for the classroom and bathroom, because the school board can't afford items such as crayons, binders, tissues, and even, in some cases, soap. If you've ever gone to your local store to pick up these supplies, you know what a zoo it can be—empty shelves, frantic parents, and hyped-up kids. This year, take the list and browse the virtual aisles of these stores, with your child sitting right next to you. Of course, you'll have to come back several times during the year, so you'll want a store that carries everything. We also found some stores that go beyond the basic pen and pencils and sell wonderful educational supplies, such as maps, workbooks, felt posters, and graphing mats. If you are homeschooling your children, you won't have to worry about preprinted shopping lists—you'll make up your own. Some of these stores offer full-curriculum programs. Many of the stores in this chapter sell books and software. But if you want to find stores that specialize in those areas, please read the chapters on Books and Software.

## A+ Teaching Materials

http://www.aplusteaching.com

Quality educational materials for parents, teachers, and students. The emphasis is on the developmental needs of your child. Samples:

- Art paper
- Arts and crafts idea booklet for parents and teachers
- Challenging literature-based lesson plans
- Civil-rights photo history
- Early readers
- Educational software
- Internet Resource books
- Lego-top play table
- Pre-algebra worksheets
- Science-based lesson sets
- U.S.A. reference pack

**Search:** Yes
**Photos:** Yes
**Ordering:** Online
**Gift Wrap:** No
**Delivery:** Ground

## Altai Corporation

http://www.edumart.com/altai

You'll find a huge assortment of educational supplies for the home or for the classroom here. They also sell a good assortment of audiovisual and computer equipment. You'll find supplies for kids all through their school years. Samples:

- Algebra resource books
- Alphabet bulletin board sets
- Audiovisual equipment and carts
- Calculators
- Children's books and software
- Curriculum and classroom management aids
- Finger puppets
- Giant floor puzzles
- Probability and graphing supplies
- Science experiments for chemistry and physics
- Sign language workbook
- Slide projectors

**Search:** Yes
**Photos:** Yes
**Ordering:** Online, Phone, Fax, Email
**Gift Wrap:** No
**Delivery:** Ground

# Bender-Burkot

http://www.bender-burkot.com

There's a lot to shop for at this store. They carry all of the usual educational supplies, but they also have an excellent selection of playground equipment. Some of this equipment is really best suited for small schools or preschools, but some of it may wind up in *your* backyard. They also carry some products for the gifted child, including a book, *What to Do with the Gifted Child*. Samples:

- Beanbag toss
- Commercial play centers
- Daily language test forms
- Fun thinkers, reading and math activities for gifted children
- Geometry-block sets
- Grammar and punctuation charts
- Language fundamental homework sheets
- Shape dominoes
- Soft tunnel climber
- Teacher resources
- Three-dimensional rubber stamps
- Wall-hung easel

**Search**: Yes
**Photos**: Yes
**Ordering**: Online, Phone, Fax
**Gift Wrap**: No
**Delivery**: Ground

# Bookmark's Fun Station

http://www.edumart.com/
bookmark

This family-owned shop has been around for 20 years. They started out as a bookstore and gradually added other educational supplies and accessories along the way. They also carry a nice selection of musical instruments and cassettes. They offer a 10% discount for online orders. Minimum order is $20. Samples:

- African-American chart set
- Author-studies materials
- Award ribbons and rosettes
- Beads and lacing boards

- Bulletin boards
- Cots and mats
- Educational software
- Health-and-safety curriculum
- Interactive math activities
- Internet-resource books
- Pretend-and-play supermarket checkout

**Search**: Yes
**Photos**: Some
**Ordering**: Online, Phone, Fax, Email
**Gift Wrap**: No
**Delivery**: Ground

# Carolina School and College Products

http://www.edumart.com/
carolina

There are over 30,000 school and office supplies for sale at this store. A nice plus is that they have materials for college students, too. You can also order custom-imprinted spiral books, portfolios, ring binders, pencils, and rubber stamps. They offer a number of different ways to search so you can go through their vast supply fairly easily. This is a good place to come when you've got a long list of supplies to purchase. Samples:

- Art and drafting supplies
- Book covers
- Computer disks
- Erasers
- File folders
- Glue sticks
- Loose-leaf paper
- Report covers
- Teacher's notebooks
- Tissues
- U.S. flags
- Washable crayons

**Search**: Yes
**Photos**: Yes
**Ordering**: Online, Phone, Fax
**Gift Wrap**: No
**Delivery**: Ground

# GW School Supply

`http://www.gwschool.com`

There are over 15,000 different items for sale here. You'll find just about everything you need for your student and for yourself, whether you are a teacher or a parent. You can search by name, by grade, or, if you want to just browse through their immense inventory, you can do that, too.

- Alphabet and number activities
- Artwaxers
- Bingo games
- Blank awards and diplomas
- Cardboard puzzles
- Children's books
- Classroom furniture
- Fabric human-body kit
- Flannel boards
- Flash cards
- Geometric wooden forms
- Graphing mat
- Pattern-and-shape games
- Peg boards

**Search:** Yes
**Photos:** Yes
**Ordering:** Online, Phone, Fax, Email
**Gift Wrap:** No
**Delivery:** Ground

# Kaplan

`http://catalog.kaplanco.com`

This is a wonderful store that carries a multitude of neat products that are fun for your child to use while he or she is learning. You'll find a terrific selection for the very youngest child in preschool, through products suitable for kids at the end of elementary school. They also carry some items for children with Special Needs, as well some materials in Spanish. Samples:

- Addition-and-subtraction number line
- Alphabet hand puppets
- Create-a-word super mat
- Deluxe chalkboards
- Discovery kits

- Flannel boards
- Lego sets
- Manipulative sets
- Multicultural career puppets
- Play tray-sorting games
- Puzzle blocks
- Ready-to-read phonics
- Tactile letter-and-number blocks
- Tempera paint
- Ten-counter abacus

**Search:** Yes
**Photos:** Yes
**Ordering:** Online, Phone
**Gift Wrap:** No
**Delivery:** Ground, 2nd Day

# Office Depot

`http://www.officedepot.com`

Don't let the name fool you. They carry a large inventory of top-quality school supplies. The range is terrific. You'll find crayons for your first-grader and slide rulers for your high school student. Delivery is free on orders over $50 in the continental U.S. Samples:

- Binders with pockets
- Calendars
- Desk accessories
- Dividers
- Educational software
- Markers
- Maps
- Paper
- Pencils and pens
- Reference books
- Rulers
- Spiral notebooks
- Three-ring binders

**Search:** Yes
**Photos:** Yes
**Ordering:** Online, Fax
**Gift Wrap:** No
**Delivery:** Ground, 2nd Day, Overnight

## The School Connection

`http://www.edumart.com/`
`classmate`

The emphasis of this store is to "offer innovative, superior and trusted educational materials . . . to prepare students for tomorrow." Their selection is quite imaginative. Teachers: Check the Teacher's Forum for free projects. Samples:

- Creative-writing aids
- Crepe puzzles
- Flannel boards
- Internet lesson plans for teachers
- Kid-size career hats and costumes
- Math flip-overs
- Mid-school science mind stretchers
- Musical instruments
- Pre-algebra worksheets
- Timed math drills

**Search**: Yes
**Photos**: Yes
**Ordering**: Online, Phone, Fax, Email
**Gift Wrap**: No
**Delivery**: Ground

## Stretch Text Book Covers

`http://www.stretchtext.com`

After looking at all the stores listed in this chapter selling every single school supply under the sun, we thought we'd show you a store that specializes in one thing only—book covers. If you're laughing, it's either because your kids are very young and you've never spent the first night of school cutting brown paper bags into various shapes to fit six or seven books. Then again, you might be laughing because you've been there, done that. Either way, bookmark this store. They sell a bunch of "cool" covers, according to our kids, whom we asked to take a look at these covers. We've come to rely on their cool-o-meters at times like this. The covers actually stretch and you can get them on very easily. So save those grocery bags for taking out the garbage. Samples:

- Stretchable book covers

**Search**: No

**Photos**: Yes
**Ordering**: Online, Phone, Email
**Gift Wrap**: No
**Delivery**: Ground

## Wal-Mart

`http://www.wal-mart.com`

You're probably well aware of the things you can buy at this superstore. In fact, in previous years, you've probably shopped their store, school supply list in hand. This year, how about shopping here without the crowds? Samples:

- Binders and portfolios
- Cliff's Notes
- Computers and printers
- Educational software
- Home-schooling notebooks
- Memo pads
- Merriam-Webster's *Notebook Dictionary*
- Paper
- Pencil pouches
- Planners and diaries
- Teaching workbooks

**Search**: Yes
**Photos**: Yes
**Ordering**: Online, Phone
**Gift Wrap**: No
**Delivery**: Ground

## Does the cost of those supplies got you down? How about trading them in?

Go to the Curriculum Swap at http://theswap.com for some great deals.

## Need more supplies? Turn to:

- Home Office Supplies

# Sculpture & Art

The art world is slow to computerize. Most galleries, if they display any artwork on the Web, resist offering originals for online sale. Of course, you can use these virtual galleries to decide which real ones to visit. But remember: The dealers prefer to make their pitch in person, because when you can touch the actual sculpture or smell the oil paint, you are more likely to listen as they explain why you ought to pay more. Few individual artists have done more than post slides, hoping you will call. That leaves galleries created just for the Web, plus museum shops, which offer lots of posters, prints, postcards, and books, plus beautiful objects based loosely on original artworks in the collections. Having been designed by artists and refined by marketeers, these objects are almost always appealing, and many are simply gorgeous.

## AAA Art Gallery

http://aaa.artselect.com

Also known as Art Select, this site looks at first like the kind of gallery that would put four A's in its name so it could show up first in search lists. But the posters and prints are a lot better than those sold in black-velvet discount stores in side streets of tourist towns. You can put together the art and one of the frames they have specially chosen for that particular print, then have both shipped for free. They claim to offer a discount of 40% to 50% on the total cost of print, mat, frame, glass, and mounting fees, compared to walk-in frame shops. But you have to get the whole package; they do not sell unframed prints, and they do not frame prints you might send them. They offer three levels of print quality: standard, gallery, and a special canvas texture with gloss finish that is supposed to look like a real painting. Nice touch: You can have them magnify the image, and show it inside the frame you have chosen, so you can imagine what it will really look like on your wall. The framed art is ready to ship within five business days, but certain frames may take as many as 10 days to be ready for shipping. Ground shipping is free. Samples:

- Claude Monet, *Haystacks 1889*, with 2" wood frame with gold paint and beading (picking up the color in the hay), and snow-white mat.
- Diego Rivera, *Nude with Calla Lilies*, with umber mat (redwood edge), and 2" wood frame painted gold
- Hervé Fenouil, *Harbour Side*, with ivory linen mat with midnight-blue edge, inside 1" wood frame, painted matte black

**Search:** Yes
**Photos:** Full-color
**Ordering:** Online, Phone
**Gift Wrap:** No, but they offer gift certificates
**Delivery:** Ground

## Above Average Pencil Portraits

http://www.zianet.com/aa-portraits

The modest title is correct. These portraits are well done, better than those of your average street artist, and at least as good as many indoor commercial drawings. You might have a baby picture done here for the grandparents. You send Jason LaDere your photo, wait three weeks, and get the finished portrait back along with your original photo. If you don't like what he's done, you can return it and get your money back. Pricing seems reasonable. Samples:

- 9" x12" pencil portrait from photo
- 11" x14" pencil portrait from photo

**Search:** No
**Photos:** Samples of pencil drawings
**Ordering:** Online and by mail
**Gift Wrap:** No
**Delivery:** Ground

# Almost Originals

http://
www.almostoriginals.com

These folks take almost any print you can think of and turn it into a canvas painting. You buy a paper print, and they lift the ink off the paper and apply it to the canvas, adding a protective coating, and brush strokes in a clear acrylic gel. Of course, this used to be called counterfeiting, but they do it on the up-and-up. For a few hundred dollars, you can have, well, an almost original artwork. The original artworks they promote tend to favor the highly skilled no-name artisans painting sentimental subjects very realistically, but the team will duplicate classics as well. Shipping is free for retail orders. Samples:

- Frank Weston Benson, *Summer*, 30 ¾" x 36" with frame
- Ned Young, *White Door*, framed, 23 7/8" x 29 ½"

**Search:** No
**Photos:** Some
**Ordering:** Online, Phone
**Gift Wrap:** No
**Delivery:** Ground

# Art.com

http://www.art.com

More than 100,000 prints, posters, and frames, they boast, and this site looks like it, with searches by artist, title, color, subject, and free items (you get one print free for joining their club, called ArtClique). The famous artists are enormously outnumbered here, but the cost for individual prints is low. Unframed prints come rolled up in a tube. What costs money is the exquisite framing. Unframed art ships within two weeks; framed art goes out within three weeks. Samples:

- Andrea Palladio, *Temple at San Pietro*, 12" x 15.5"
- *Cycles Gladiator* poster with frosted gold wood frame, and Plexiglas

- Egon Schiele, *Weiblicher Akt mit langem Haar*, drawing, 16" x 12"

**Search:** Yes, very good
**Photos:** Excellent
**Ordering:** Online
**Gift Wrap:** No, but they offer gift certificates
**Delivery:** Ground

# Artnet

http://www.artnet.com

The Big Momma of art sites, with links to galleries, museums, individual artists, and dealers. You can use this site as a central clearinghouse for a wide variety of antiques, paintings, prints, and exhibitions, even though many individual artists and galleries do not sell online. Because the fine arts world is so secretive about prices, many galleries want to talk to you personally about their major works, but you can find prints priced for sale. This site carries an auction database recording prices from more than 1.8 million lots sold at 500-plus auction houses. Artnet itself sells books, and plans a print store and online auctions. Sample items:

- Carved Chippendale bonnet-top chest on chest
- *Cornell/Duchamp in Resonance*, by Ecke Bonk, available from Artnet
- *So Help Me Hannah (Snatch Shot with Ray Guns) from a set of 40,* by Hannah Wilke, from Ronald Feldman Fine Arts

**Search:** Yes
**Photos:** Yes
**Ordering:** Online for books, some prints
**Gift Wrap:** No
**Delivery:** Ground, 2nd Day, Overnight

# Artville

http://www.artville.com

Delicately designed site with royalty-free sketches and photographs you can use in presentations, brochures, and Web pages. The drawings are much more detailed than cartoons, with the kind of shading and coloring you might get from watercolors, or those 96-color pencil sets. Each group of electronic files has the feeling of an individual artist's personality, so if you like the style, you can use a series of images from the same group to work together. You can download an image directly, or order a CD-ROM with a whole collection. Images come in various resolutions (or dots per inch), so you only have to pay for the dots you want. You can download a comp image, with "Artville" stamped all over it, to see if it works in your document, before you buy the real thing, which, of course, does not contain their logo. And once you register, you get to use "light boxes," places you can store sets of images you are thinking about buying, while you ponder the issue (up to a month). Samples:

- David Wasserman, *Open Window*, architectural detail in full-color photo, at 72 dots per inch
- Picture of a giant penny, with Abe Lincoln, illustrating the metaphor that a penny saved is a penny earned

**Search:** By subject, concept, metaphor, number, type of art, orientation, medium used, artist, CD title, or keyword
**Photos:** Thumbnail, large size
**Ordering:** Online
**Gift Wrap:** No
**Delivery:** 2nd Day, Overnight

## Global Gallery Curator

http://www.globalgallery.net

A colorful and efficient site with a great range of prints, original silk screens, and posters, by skilled but not-so-famous artists, as well as the famous ones. You can find information about the famous artists. The site-meisters will also track down an art print for you, as long as it is still being published. You can search by artist, genre, subject, size, color, or keyword. They don't do framing, so you get your art in a tube. Samples:

- Deborah Allwright, *Classical Labyrinth I* (Gold Foil Embossed), 27.5" x 39"
- Leonardo da Vinci, *Human Proportions*, 27.5" x 19.5"

- Yellow-ochre communication art example 3, Jules Cheret's poster for the *Folies-Bergère, La Loie Fuller*, 28.5" x 22.5".

**Search:** Excellent
**Photos:** Bright
**Ordering:** Online, Fax
**Gift Wrap:** No
**Delivery:** Ground, 3rd Day, 2nd Day, Overnight

## Island Arts of Whidbey Island

http://www.islandarts.com

Picking up glass on the beach on this island in Puget Sound so that her daughter wouldn't cut her feet, Linda Richmond got the idea of making votive glasses, plates, and mugs from the sand-washed glass fragments. Each glass object is hand produced. If you want colors you don't see on the site, you can email her and get a special object in those colors. Soft, translucent, personal, each design is unique. Orders are shipped after two or three weeks. Samples:

- Aqua/amber-tweed design votive, 4" high, with tea candle
- Confetti-design decorative plate, 10" in diameter

**Search:** No
**Photos:** Yes
**Ordering:** Online, Fax, or Email
**Gift Wrap:** No
**Delivery:** Ground

## Louvre

http://mistral.culture.fr/
louvre/louvrea.htm

Available in English, French, and Spanish, the Louvre's museum site, which used to be limited to announcing new exhibits, has recently been beefed up to include a virtual tour, guided virtual visits, workshops, and databases, as well as (any moment now) a book shop and gift shop. The site is still stingy with artwork from the permanent collection, showing just some "major works," but you can buy tickets to the next shows online, avoiding the long, long lines in front of the glass pyramid.

- Tickets to exhibitions through Ticketweb, in U.S. and Canada

**Search:** No
**Photos:** Yes
**Ordering:** Via Ticketweb
**Gift Wrap:** Non!
**Delivery:** Via Ticketweb, Ground

# Metropolitan Museum of Art

`http://www.metmuseum.org`

This site gives you a good feeling for the premiere American museum of art. Featuring jewelry, gifts, and adaptations of objects of art from the museum and around the world, the store also claims to be the largest art bookstore in America. Separate annex: the Mezzanine, which sells real art, but only via fax or mail. Samples:

- Blue earthenware sculpture of a hippopotamus, based on sculpture from 12th Dynasty Egypt
- *Horn*, 1993, Aquatint on Somerset paper by Joe Andoe
- *The Jackson Pollock Sketchbooks,* facsimile edition in three spiral-bound volumes, with booklet

**Search:** Yes
**Photos:** Yes, lovely
**Ordering:** Online, Phone, Fax, Mail
**Gift Wrap:** No
**Delivery:** Ground

# Museum of Bad Art

`http://www.glyphs.com/moba`

The MOBA store supports a collection of the worst of amateur art, arranged in shows such as "Bright Colors, Dark Emotions." Their slogan is "Art too bad to be ignored!" You can protect your brain with their logo hat and other "branded" products:

- Eileen T-shirts, described as "hideously handpainted," with "a crude version of MOBA's stolen masterpiece"
- Museum of Bad Art Greeting Card set, perfect for a death in the family
- Refrigerator magnets featuring miniatures of paintings from the permanent collection
- T-shirt featuring the masterpiece, *Sunday on the Poet with George* (a pointillist fat guy in his underwear)

**Search:** No
**Photos:** Yes
**Ordering:** Phone, Fax, Email
**Gift Wrap:** No
**Delivery:** Ground

# Museum of Modern Art

`http://www.moma.org`

The most spectacular museum store in the U.S. goes online, with more pizzazz for its products than the museum's site gives to the pictures in its collection. (In the store, for instance, you can zoom in close to see a product, in color.) The site does offer plenty of info about the exhibitions, programs, library, publications, and the progress of their new construction, but, alas, the site shows very little of the collection, and even those pictures need better lighting. Also, MOMA publications are not yet available online. The store focuses on objets d'art, or, at least, well-designed and expensive consumer items. Items coming from international manufacturers may not be shipped for several weeks. Samples from the store:

- 5-piece place setting of stainless-steel flatware (very flat) made in Japan from design by Takenobu Igarashi
- Jacquard silk tie based on confetti design by Charles Eames
- Small round travel alarm in chrome-plated brass
- Three-wheeled trolley for serving drinks and hors d'oeuvres, made of glass, aluminum, and steel in Italy

**Search:** Yes
**Photos:** Yes

**Ordering:** Online
**Gift Wrap:** No
**Delivery:** Ground, 3rd Day

## National Gallery of Art

http://www.nga.gov

A quiet store in a great museum, selling books, posters, reproductions of art, stationery, scarves, and jewelry, plus special items for kids, and materials relating to current exhibitions. Samples:

- Art lotto
- CD-ROM with lives and works by 600 artists exhibited in the museum
- Journal illustrated with drawings from the museum
- Metal tray of flexible magnets in geometric shapes
- National Gallery of Art Screen Saver
- Nontoxic basswood art blocks with Monet's haystacks, water lilies, and landscapes
- Poster of Pierre Bonnard's *Stairs in the Artist's Garden*
- Van Gogh floral note cards

**Search:** No
**Photos:** Yes
**Ordering:** Online, Fax, Phone
**Gift Wrap:** Gift message only
**Delivery:** Ground

## National Museum of American Art

http://nmaa-ryder.si.edu

Dedicated to the collection, education, and study programs, this site offers a few hard-to-find-elsewhere items of Americana through the Museum Shop. Samples:

- National Museum of American Art CD-ROM
- Paperbound book: *American Wicker: Woven Furniture from 1850 to 1930*
- Postcard book: *Harlem, The 30s: Photographs by*

*Aaron Siskind.*
**Search:** No
**Photos:** Yes
**Ordering:** Online, Fax
**Gift Wrap:** No
**Delivery:** Ground, 2nd Day

## Noguchi Museum

https://www.noguchi.org

Here's a whole museum devoted to artworks by one artist, but what an artist! His sculptures are at once heavy and light, thick and transparent, granite and paper. This is a site for Noguchi's fans, and anyone who wants to get a taste of his work. Samples:

- Black cotton T-shirt with shapes from Noguchi's Worksheet for Sculpture
- *Isamu Noguchi: Space of Akari and Stone*, exhibition catalog
- Water Table Image of granite sculpture

**Search:** No
**Photos:** Some
**Ordering:** Online
**Gift Wrap:** No
**Delivery:** Ground

## Seattle Art Museum

http://www.seattleartmuseum.org

Yes, they have exhibition catalogs and wearables bearing their logo. But this museum store also offers some African, Asian, Egyptian, and Native American merchandise, as well as glass and jewelry. Not much in each category, mind you. But what's available is neat. Samples:

- Book called *Leonardo's ABC's*
- Hand-crafted Korean lantern
- Seattle Art Museum Camel Pin made out of pewter, based on 15th century Chinese sculptures weighing 15,000 pounds each

**Search:** No
**Photos:** Yes
**Ordering:** Online
**Gift Wrap:** No
**Delivery:** Ground, 2nd Day, Overnight

# World Wide Art

`http://www.world-wide-art.com/art/index.html`

A glorified frame shop (you can become a frequent framer), with posters and prints from contemporary artists and Disney classics. Shipments are insured, and free for orders over $500. Samples:
- Alex Katz, aquatint *Maria I*, signed and numbered, with certificate of authentication
- Conservation framing
- *Duck Daze—Donald Duck with Flowers* (framed original production cel)
- Realistic images of nostalgic American scenes

**Search:** Yes
**Photos:** Yes
**Ordering:** Online, Phone, Fax, Email, Mail
**Gift Wrap:** No
**Delivery:** Ground

# Want to make your own art and crafts? View this chapter:

- Crafts & Art Supplies

# Skating

One of us grew up in the icy wastes of New England, where skating was the way you spent your winters. Jonathan skated across Lake Wononscopomuc, played hockey at the open-air rinks, and even skated down a hill that was covered with deep snow that had frozen into a thick crust. He has a hard time understanding going around and around in an oval, at city rinks, when he remembers gliding over black ice, looking down at the frozen weeds and rocks below, and watching the birch trees zip by on shore. This chapter takes a broader perspective: it covers figure skating, in-line skating, ice-skating, and hockey. Whether your hero is Nancy Kwan or Wayne Gretzky, you'll find what you're looking for in these stores, from custom-designed skates to premade ones, plus protective gear and even sequined outfits. If you're a coach, you'll find a lot of stores that sell team outfits and offer discounts or free shipping on large orders.

## 1-888-Wwinline

http://www.1888wwinline.com

This site gets the award for the best name, because it includes its phone number and Web address! Besides being wizards of PR, they also happen to be one of the largest dealers in the world for in-line skates and accessories. They stock kids', men's, and women's skates and let you search by price range, among other categories. (If you're new to this sport, you might want to check out their supply of $49 to $99 skates.) Their prices are very good, as is the selection. There's a small area for clothes, too. They have lots of free information and expert advice. Samples:

- Grind plates
- Helmets
- Off-road, fitness, hockey, and aggressive in-line skates
- Protective gear
- Skate tote bags and backpacks
- Wheels and bearings

**Search:** Yes
**Photos:** Yes
**Ordering:** Online, Phone, Fax
**Gift Wrap:** No
**Delivery:** Ground

## Great Skate

http://www.greatskate.com

Ice hockey skaters will find this store to be their home away from home. You name it, this store carries it. The site gives you several ways to search, which is very helpful with all the stuff. Most of the clothes are available in sizes Medium to XXL. There is a good supply of in-line skates. Free ground shipping in the continental U.S. Samples:

- Authentic team jerseys
- Bauer skates for adults and youths
- Elbow pads
- Goalie equipment
- Heavy-duty hockey gloves
- In-line skates
- Padding
- Practice jerseys
- Sticks

**Search:** Yes
**Photos:** Yes
**Ordering:** Online
**Gift Wrap:** No
**Delivery:** Ground, 2nd Day

## Hockey2

http://www.hockey2.com

Excellent prices and a huge inventory make this a wonderful place to shop for hockey skates and equipment as well as in-line skates and accessories. We really like how you can scroll to the bottom of the home page and see pictures that represent each category, just in case you're a little fuzzy on what the categories contain. Free shipping on orders over $300 in the continental U.S. Samples:

- Discount referee supplies
- Goalie equipment and accessories
- Helmets and masks
- Hockey bags
- Hockey sticks and pucks
- Hockey tape
- Lycra pants
- Metal goals with nets
- Neck protectors
- Shin-guard strap
- Skate guards
- Team first-aid kit

**Search:** Yes
**Photos:** Some
**Ordering:** Online, Phone, Fax
**Gift Wrap:** No
**Delivery:** Ground

# In-line Skate Store

http://www.in-lineskatestore.com

In-line skates are a hefty investment. If a part breaks, it's usually much cheaper to replace it than to buy new skates. That's what this store specializes in: parts, parts, and more parts. This is also an excellent store to shop if you want to upgrade or customize your skates. The prices are terrific. They also offer further discounts to teams and skate clubs. Samples:

- Aluminum-bearing spacers
- Axle kits
- Bearings
- Decorated wheels
- Outdoor and indoor wheels
- Team jerseys

**Search:** No
**Photos:** Yes
**Ordering:** Online, Phone, Fax
**Gift Wrap:** No
**Delivery:** Ground

# NetSkate

http://www.netskate.com

Sometimes skaters can find paradise on the Web. We don't just mean in-line skaters, or roller skaters, hockey players, or even skateboarders, we mean just about all skaters (except regular ice skaters, who'll just have to find another heavenly store). Whether you're a beginner or a pro, you'll be able to find just the skate or part you need at this family-owned store. They carry premade skates and also make custom-made skates, built to your specifications. Samples:

- Bearings
- Helmets
- Hockey boots
- In-line skates
- Protective gear
- Quad skates (roller skates)
- Rollometer
- Skate bags and backpacks
- Skateboards
- Stunt gloves

**Search:** No
**Photos:** Some
**Ordering:** Online, Phone
**Gift Wrap:** No
**Delivery:** Ground, 2nd Day, Overnight

# Rupp's

http://www.rupps.com

Lots of skates for men, women, and children (in-line, figure, and ice hockey) and a terrific selection of hockey clothes from practice outfits to authentic NHL apparel. This is a good place to go shopping if you're looking to outfit your kids, because they carry a lot of equipment and clothes in youth sizes. With all of the stuff they offer online, you can call Rupp's an online super skating store. Samples:

- Adjustable (4 sizes) Rollerblades for kids
- Customized jerseys
- Goal equipment and nets
- Hockey gel
- Mini goal net (for backyards)

- Referee equipment
- Sticks
- Wheels and bearings

**Search:** Yes
**Photos:** Yes
**Ordering:** Online, Phone
**Gift Wrap:** No
**Delivery:** Ground, 3rd Day, 2nd Day, Overnight

## Skates Away

http://www.skatepro.com/
catalog

This online shop is a combination of two California skate stores, Skate Pro Sports and Gui 'N Da Hood (say it quickly, you'll get it). They sell lots of skates and accessories, like many of the stores in this chapter, but they also offer you their honest evaluation of each of the products, which is good when the selection is so vast. When shopping here, always make sure you scroll down to the bottom of the page and check out their sales. Samples:

- Aggressive skates
- Cleaners
- Helmets
- Men's and women's in-line, hockey, and ice skates
- Protective gear
- Skate bags
- Wheels and bearings
- Youth-sized adjustable Rollerblades

**Search:** Some
**Photos:** Some
**Ordering:** Online, Phone
**Gift Wrap:** No
**Delivery:** Ground, 3rd Day, 2nd Day, Overnight

## Sports and Athletics On Line

http://www.das-mall.com/
sportsandathletics/hockey.htm

Hockey players, pick up your sticks (not too high, though) and swoosh on over to this store. They have a huge selection and great prices on just about everything you'll need to smack that puck around the ice

rink. When we shopped here, we saw that the store will be adding the same service for other sports in the near future. Samples:

- Face protectors
- Goalie equipment
- Hockey skates
- In-line skate equipment
- Neck protectors
- Pants and jerseys
- Shin guards
- Shoulder pads
- Sticks

**Search:** No
**Photos:** No
**Ordering:** Online
**Gift Wrap:** No
**Delivery:** Ground, 2nd Day, Overnight

## Syosset Sport Center

http://
www.syossetsportcenter.com

This is one of those stores where you have to sign in to begin browsing, which we don't really like, but a nice plus is that they ask you what kind of music you like, and will play that type of music for you as you resume your shopping. This store specializes in basketball, lacrosse, and, more to the point of this chapter, ice and roller hockey. They have the best selection of hockey clothes out of all the stores listed. They have an excellent search that lets you look at the pictures, or search by text. Samples:

- Goaltending equipment
- Jerseys
- Protective gear for men and women
- Skates
- Skating apparel
- Sticks for women

**Search:** Yes
**Photos:** Yes
**Ordering:** Online, Phone, Fax
**Gift Wrap:** No
**Delivery:** Ground

## Toe Picks to Toe Shoes

```
http://www.www.aimin.com/
eoi/index.htm
```

Sounds like a ballet supply store, right? Well, it is. So, what's it doing in this category? We're not exactly sure. But the fact is that this store also sells ice skates and some other neat stuff for women skaters. If you're a little leery of buying ice skates on the Web, go to their Custom Boot Fitting room for step-by-step instructions on how to order the correct size. You can also order size 13 and up for an additional $30. This is also a nice place to come when you're looking for a gift for your favorite skater. Samples:

- Blade soakers
- Blades by Mitchell-King and Wilson
- Boots by Klingbeil (foam imprint is extra)
- Gift certificates
- Knee pads
- Pro-Filers
- Sequined competition dresses
- Skate guards
- Skating tights
- Spin trainer
- Wrist guards

**Search:** Some
**Photos:** No
**Ordering:** Online, Phone
**Gift Wrap:** Yes
**Delivery:** Ground, Overnight

## Interested in other sports?
## Push off for these chapters:

- Baseball & Softball
- Basketball
- Bicycles
- Boating & Sailing
- Bowling
- Golf
- Tennis

# Soccer

If there's a worldwide sport, then soccer must be it. Popular around the world during the twentieth century, it's making big inroads into the United States as we enter the new millennium. Will it ever be as popular a sport in the U.S. as baseball, basketball, or football?

For all you hard-headed fans, here are some soccer supply stores that can ship anything you need to your house before the next game. Most of these stores carry a huge amount of equipment and clothes.

## Athletic Team Uniforms Direct

http://
www.ateamuniformsdirect.com

One-stop shopping for all your team uniforms. This place specializes in outfitting your individual team or your whole league. There is a $100 minimum order requirement. All colors are available. Sizes come in small to XXL for adults; small to large youth sizes. Goalie unforms are also for sale. The more you buy, the greater your discount. Shipping is $10 on orders under $200 and $15 on orders over $200. Samples:

- Jerico jerseys
- Jerico RT soccer shorts
- Soccer socks
- Union Jacks Capital jerseys (fade-out graphics)
- Union Jacks Europa and Durango soccer shorts
- Union Jacks Potomac soccer and Windsor shorts
- Union Jacks Vienna soccer jerseys
- Warm-up suits

**Search:** Some
**Photos:** Yes
**Ordering:** Online, Phone, Fax
**Gift Wrap:** No
**Delivery:** Ground

## Big Toe Sports

http://www.bigtoesports.com

No, this isn't a sporting goods store for people with big feet, but it's a wonderful place to shop if anyone in your family is into soccer. You'll find everything you need for either kids or adults, from clothing to equipment. It's an especially good store to visit if you are coaching a soccer team. If soccer is your life, don't forget to click on the Web-related links provided on the front page. Samples:

- Balls, bags, and shin guards
- Coaching gear
- Goalkeeping jerseys and equipment
- Jerseys
- Jewelry
- Screw-in cleat shoes
- Team kits
- Turf shoes

**Search:** Yes
**Photos:** Yes
**Ordering:** Online, Phone, Fax
**Gift Wrap:** No
**Delivery:** Ground, 2nd Day

## Eurosport

http://www.soccer.com

There's a lot to browse through at this international shop, including equipment and clothes for men, women, and kids. You'll also be able to read interviews with various World Cup soccer stars as well as tap into a wide world of soccer links. If you'd like to talk to other soccer fans, go to their chat area. If you think you'd like to shop here often, you'll probably want to join their Goal Club ($24.95 for a one-time membership fee) and save 10% on all purchases. Samples:

- Ankle supports
- Authentic team jerseys
- Coaches First Aid kit
- Equipment bags
- Fluorescent linesman flags
- Goalkeeping gear
- Molded and turf shoes
- Referee uniforms

- Soccer air freshener balls
- Soccer software
- Training goals
- Wristbands

**Search**: Some
**Photos**: Yes
**Ordering**: Online, Phone
**Gift Wrap**: No
**Delivery**: Ground, Overnight

# Fogdog Sports

http://www.fogdog.com

What kind of a name is this for a sporting goods store? We asked and found out that one definition of fog dog is the "arc or ray of light sometimes seen burning through the fog." Well, soccer players will surely see the light after shopping here. This Web store is huge—it has it all, not just soccer stuff (but they do have a special soccer store that is superb). If after all this you still can't find what you're looking for, contact the Fogdog Search Squad and they'll personally find it and buy it for you. Samples:

- Cushioning soles
- Full-coverage bra tops
- Molded cleats
- Practice training equipment
- Sports medicine
- Team gear and equipment
- Turf shoes
- Warm-up sets

**Search**: Yes
**Photos**: Yes
**Ordering**: Online, Phone
**Gift Wrap**: No
**Delivery**: Ground

# Soccer 4 All

http://www.soccer4all.com

Love soccer? You'll love this store. Clothes (many in sizes up to XXL), equipment, accessories for men, women, and kids are all here. And they don't just carry one item in a category; they carry lots and lots of stuff in each category. Click on the footwear category. You'll be amazed. If you can't find what you're looking for here, go to Mars. There also some deals available for team sales. Samples:

- Balls
- Goalkeeper equipment
- Referee clothes
- Reflex gloves
- Shinguards
- Soccer afghans
- Soccer shorts, socks, jackets, and jerseys
- Team bags
- Turf shoes
- Youth suede shoes

**Search**: Yes
**Photos**: Yes
**Ordering**: Online, Phone, Fax
**Gift Wrap**: No
**Delivery**: Ground

# Soccer Mania

http://www.soccermania.com

You can buy individual soccer items and clothes here, but they're really interested in supplying teams. Youth teams (clothes start at Youth Small) to Adults (sizes to XXL). Free shipping on team uniform sales over $100 and on equipment orders over $200. Samples:

- Backyard goals
- Corner flags
- Field paint
- Rebounder net
- Soccer shorts, socks, and jerseys
- Striping machine
- Uniforms
- Warm-up sets

**Search**: Yes
**Photos**: Yes
**Ordering**: Online, Phone, Fax
**Gift Wrap**: No
**Delivery**: Ground

# Software

The Web is just software in action, so buying software online was one of the first ways people shopped the Net. You can get almost any program quickly from online dealers, and if you can't wait for a delivery by truck, you can download some 100,000 commercial programs, as well as more than 300,000 shareware programs (try one and pay, usually by check, only if you decide to keep it). Some sites offer only hot items, others list everything; some concentrate on a special category such as software for handheld or notebook computers. Sites also differ on the amount of information they provide, which can make a big difference if you haven't quite made up your mind which product to buy. We decided not to list software manufacturers' sites because, although they are worth visiting for the latest information, tutorials, plug-ins, technical support, and inspiring white papers, these sites usually keep their prices unrealistically high, so that their dealers and resellers can offer fabulous "street" discounts.

## 1st Stop Software

http://www.1stopsoft.com

They claim to offer 100,000 programs for immediate downloading! Because the products are in electronic form, they are never out of stock, and because software vendors don't have to pay for a box, you get a little discount. You can locate your orders by email address, check whether the order has been shipped (if you are having it delivered the old-fashioned way), and you can view your invoice online. Best, you can get them to retransmit, if the phone company interrupts the download. Sample items:

- *Ad Café Pro* from InfoHiway
- *NetObjects Fusion* for Macintosh Upgrade
- *PaperMaster*, an electronic filing cabinet

**Search:** Yes
**Photos:** Yes
**Ordering:** Online
**Gift Wrap:** No
**Delivery:** Downloadable, Ground

## AsiaSoft

http://www.asiasoft.com

A cybershop for Japanese, Chinese, and Korean software. Not just American software in translation, either. For instance, AsiaSoft carries ATOK 12, a kana-kanji conversion system used by most computer folks in Japan. These products handle the special challenges of Asian fonts, too. For instance, one bundle includes *Illustrator Chinese* for the Mac and *DynaFonts 38 Traditional Chinese True Type Fonts*, so you can turn Chinese text into graphics whenever you want. Sample items:

- *Dynafont 85 Japanese True Type Fonts* for the Mac
- *FileMaker Pro 3.0 Korean* for the Mac

**Search:** Yes
**Photos:** Yes
**Ordering:** Online, Fax, Phone
**Gift Wrap:** No
**Delivery:** Ground, 2nd Day, Overnight

## Beyond.com

http://www.beyond.com

Starting in a room over a barbershop in Menlo Park, California, Beyond.com has expanded to much bigger quarters in Cupertino, handling more than 39,000 titles, of which 5,600 are available for download. They also serve as a software provider for famous partners, such as America Online, Excite, and Microsoft. These folks even undertake to download the textbooks for Ziff-Davis University courses, a process that worked fine for us. You can even cancel a downloaded order by using their Letter of Destruction (LOD), swearing you have destroyed the download. Our only hesitation with this site is that they skimp on information about the products, so you can't always compare items intelligently without going elsewhere to look up reviews, or to get complete specs. Great feature: Some software turns out to be free, when you send in the rebate. Samples:

- *JumpStart Pre-Kindergarten*
- *Ultimate Family Tree Deluxe*
- *Universal Translator*, to translate text in 25 different languages

**Search:** Yes
**Photos:** Some
**Ordering:** Online, Fax, Phone
**Gift Wrap:** No
**Delivery:** Ground, 2nd Day, Overnight

## Bookmark Software

http://
www.bookmarksoftware.com

Founded by a computer scientist and his wife, this store is well-organized and efficient. Even though they sell Unix, Netware, and mini-computer products, they focus on a home store, home office shop, and gift shop (which has suggestions for gifts for boys and girls, men and women, and gamesters). Minimal info about each of their 12,000 products from 500 vendors. Free shipping on orders over $100. Samples:

- Electronic Arts' *NHL 99*
- Metrowerks *CodeWarrior for Novell Netware 5*
- *Powerquest Partition Magic*
- SoftQuad's *HoTMetal PRO*
- *Turok: Dinosaur Hunter*

**Search:** Yes
**Photos:** Yes
**Ordering:** Online, Fax, Phone
**Gift Wrap:** No
**Delivery:** Ground, 2nd Day, Overnight

## Buyonet

http://www.buyonet.com

If you're looking to download one of those hard-to-find products from small, international publishers, with a

sprinkling of American giants, this Swedish-American site is the place. In general, you download, then pay, but sometimes you have to pay first. We love the Bag-O-Salad concept, so naturally we had to visit this buy-on-the-net site, even if it does sound like a bayonet. We also like that you earn Buy-O-Bonuses in the form of Buy-O-Coins for each purchase of downloadable software. This site speaks English, French, German, Spanish, and Swedish, and if you make a mistake clicking, you may end up with the product description in another language; the products, too, are ones that have international appeal. Samples:

- *Cloudragon I Ching for the Apple Newton*
- *Key Into French,* bilingual and bidirectional dictionary, English-French, French-English, with 40,000 entries
- *Lotus 1-2-3 in Finnish for Win 95*
- *Nisus Writer* in English for the Mac
- *Vorton Financial Tools* in English, for Windows

**Search:** No
**Photos:** Few
**Ordering:** Online
**Gift Wrap:** No
**Delivery:** Download

## BuySoft

http://www.buy.com/bc/
noframes/software.asp

A major shop within the Buy.com mall, offering lowest prices guaranteed. If you find a lower price within seven days of your invoice date, from an authorized reseller, BuySoft refunds the difference, and gives you a dollar. You can have products listed by category, manufacturer, or keyword. Special deals appear at the top of the list. Blurbs about software products tend to be short, so figure out what you want before you come here. They focus on business and professional products, with almost no shareware. Samples:

- AltaVista Search Intranet Extension for NT, capable of searching 1,000 pages of information, to create up-to-date index
- Apple Web Page Construction Kit for the Mac
- Linux utilities for desktop publishing, graphics, dynamic HTML, personal finance, plus reference

material, from SSI
- Metrowerks *Code Warrior* for Playstation

**Search:** Good
**Photos:** A few
**Ordering:** Online, Phone
**Gift Wrap:** No
**Delivery:** Ground, 2nd Day, Overnight

## BuySoftware Network

http://www.buysoftware.com

This dealer specializes in close-outs and overstocks. You'll also find fun, inexpensive items that are only a little dusty. The site ships everywhere, but not to post office boxes. Interestingly, you may end up here on the BuySoftware Network when you thought you were dialing into another site; evidently, they have a variety of store fronts for use by different physical stores around the country. Caution: If you start buying software at a BuySoftware store, and innocently click a button leading to one of the ShopNow stores they advertise at the bottom of their pages, you lose whatever was in your shopping cart, because, despite appearances, ShopNow is a different company, a kind of host of hosts. Sample products:
- *Peachtree Complete Accounting Plus Time and Billing*
- *The Interior Design Collection for Lightwave\Inspire*, with real-world scaled 3D objects for planning home scenes
- *X-Portal Searching Software* for conducting multiple Internet searches at the same time

**Search:** Yes
**Photos:** Some
**Ordering:** Online
**Gift Wrap:** No
**Delivery:** Ground, 2nd Day, Overnight

## CDW

http://www.cdw.com

A major hardware reseller, CDW tries to be a complete one-stop shop, so they sell software to go with your latest computer. Info is often skimpy, but with popular products CDW shows you reviews from Ziff-Davis publications, such as *PC Magazine,* so you can see what the critics think. When several products occupy a niche, CDW offers you a table of competing products; you check the ones you are interested in, and CDW provides a comparison chart. If there's a rebate or coupon offered by the manufacturer, you can find out about that, too. Before rebate, the prices here are low, although not rock bottom. If you register, you can get buyer's alerts on products whose prices you want to track. Samples:
- *FileMaker Home Page* for Mac or Windows
- *Intelliquis Web Site Traffic Builder*
- *Macromedia Flash* for fast vector graphics and animations without programming

**Search:** Yes
**Photos:** Some
**Ordering:** Online
**Gift Wrap:** No
**Delivery:** Ground

## Common Sense

http://www.cdromcsc.com

This dealer specializes in close-outs, overstocks, adult software, hybrid Mac/PC CD-ROMs, Mpeg movies, DVDs, new and used VHS videotapes, and CD-ROMs of every kind. They carry ancient children's titles, get-rich-quick CDs, French porn, and limited edition and underground collections of Japanese animes. Most of the movies are actually on the Reel.com site, which this one jumps to. Samples:
- *Live Sex Shows of Paris* DVD
- *Man in the Iron Mask* DVD
- *Manga Mania,* with 12,500 anime images
- *Official Red Hat Linux for i386, Alpha, and SPARC*
- *The City Mouse and the Country Mouse,* with crayons and cassette tape

**Search:** Yes
**Photos:** Crude
**Ordering:** Online, Email
**Gift Wrap:** No
**Delivery:** 3rd Day

## CompUSA Direct

http://www.compusa.com

In addition to hardware, they offer truckloads of software, famous and obscure, in boxes and downloads, with special clearance sections; an Apple Store (and showcases for other manufacturers, if you want to shop by brand); a special area for IBM employees; and a very thorough search mechanism. The download area carries plenty of popular items, as well as cheap and innovative programs from small companies; evidently, this process is being outsourced, because the interface and routines seem to be those of a company called Digital River, whose customer service info was not working on four of our visits. Good news: If a download fails, you can do it again. Samples:

- DeLorme Earthmate GPS Receiver and Mapping Software
- Downloadable version of *Adage webAnalyst Suite*
- *FlashBack*, software for recovering earlier versions of a file

**Search:** Yes
**Photos:** Yes
**Ordering:** Online, Phone
**Gift Wrap:** No
**Delivery:** Ground, 3rd Day, 2nd Day, Overnight, Immediate download

## Egghead

http://www.egghead.com

Remember their local store, down at the mall? These folks closed down all their physical stores and took the whole business online. They sell books, small business software, and home programs, but they also handle development tools and utilities. Some very good prices, even on brand-new products. Software downloads appear in boutiques devoted to solutions (the tax center) or vendors (IBM, Symantec); you can try before you buy, with some products. High point: the liquidation center with bargains on surplus products, and the auction center. Cheapest products: occasional freebies. Sample items for sale:

- Adobe *Acrobat 3* for the Mac

- *Barbie Magic Hair Styler*
- *Corel Office Pro 7*
- Micrografx *Picture Publisher*, on liquidation
- NetObjects *Bean Builder*

**Search:** Yes, once you enter a department
**Photos:** Some
**Ordering:** Online purchase or bid, Fax, Phone
**Gift Wrap:** No
**Delivery:** Download, Group 1, 2nd Day, Overnight

## HyperDrive

http://www.hyperdrive.com

A thoughtful, fully realized site with an interesting focus. These folks concentrate on CD-ROMs rather than business software, so they have a lot of home, educational, and entertainment titles, including some from small, international publishers. They provide full reviews, lists of contents, and large screenshots. Samples:

- *Encyclopaedia Britannica CD-99*
- *Flemish and Dutch Painters,* 5 Windows/Mac CD-ROM set
- *Keeping Fit During Pregnancy, En Forma en el Embarazo,* Windows/Mac CD-ROM
- *StarCraft,* guaranteed best price on Web
- *Up to the Himalayas, Kingdoms in the Clouds,* Teachers' Edition, with lab pack

**Search:** Yes
**Photos:** Large
**Ordering:** Online, Fax, Phone
**Gift Wrap:** No
**Delivery:** Ground, Overnight

## J and R Music World, Computer World

http://www.jandr.com

For more than a quarter century, this store has sold electronic gear in New York City. They've won awards as Retailer of the Year, and one of New York's 100 Best Little Places to Shop. So software is just one sliver of this online business, but they have earned the respect of Excite, which steers some software customers their way. Some very popular products appear at almost a third of what the competition advertises. Other prices are good, but not absolute bottom, and sometimes manufacturers insist that no price be displayed. Samples:

- *Alien Skin Eye Candy* for the Mac (PhotoShop filters)
- Broderbund *Kid Pix Studio Deluxe*
- NeoPost *Simply Postage*
- Nova *Web Animation Explosion*

**Search:** Yes
**Photos:** Rare
**Ordering:** Online, Phone
**Gift Wrap:** No
**Delivery:** 2nd Day, Overnight

## Jumbo

http://www.jumbo.com

The elephant among shareware and freeware sites, with more than 300,000 programs ranging from the amateur to the highly polished; the shareware prices are not always visible, but range from a buck or two to several hundred dollars. Look here for games, hobby software, screensavers, wallpaper, antivirus utilities, and hundreds of original fonts. There's usually not much describing the program, so you have to download and test it to see if it's anything like what you are after. We find we only keep one of four shareware programs. But the ones we like are very useful, in areas that the bigger programs ignore or do badly. Remember that if you end up adopting a shareware program, you're morally committed to paying up eventually, even if the program doesn't keep urging you to register. Samples:

- *Ablaze Pro Automatic Web Promotion*
- *Bit Morph* for special effects
- *Chess Ballet* screensaver
- *Lauryn Hill* wallpaper
- *SiteSweeper* for cleaning up your Web site
- *Verve TrueType* font

**Search:** Yes
**Photos:** No
**Ordering:** Click the icon to download; pay if you decide to keep the shareware, send good vibes to the makers of

freeware
**Gift Wrap:** No
**Delivery:** Download

## Microwarehouse

http://www.warehouse.com

Fast—that's the word for these folks. We've bought software from them, and found them speedy and reliable. This gigantic site offers software for Mac and PC. For many products, they suggest extras or accessories you might want to add, such as boxes of checks for personal finance software, or related programs. Their Download Warehouse is run by Digital River, with 90,000 items available. They also link to British, Canadian, Dutch, French, German, and Swedish Microwarehouse stores with local currency and Euro pricing. The French site, for instance, reviews Microsoft's *Monster Truck Madness* as "complètement fou." Sample American products:

- Adobe *Graphic Studio Bundle* for the Mac
- Clearance sale on out-of-date version of Deneba's *Canvas* software for Mac and PowerMac
- *Microsoft Project 98* for Windows 95 or NT

**Search:** Yes
**Photos:** Some
**Ordering:** Online, Phone
**Gift Wrap:** No
**Delivery:** Ground, Overnight

## Playback Shopping

http://www.playback.com

If you want real bargains in Nintendo, Sony, and computer games, as well as some regular software, you might consider buying used software. That's what makes this site unique. They let you know the condition of the used software's cardboard box, jewel case, instructions, and inserts, if any survive. Average prices fall between $10 and $15, and they offer additional discounts if you can find a better price elsewhere. Some packages are only a few months old, but many are two or three years old. These older "pre-owned" disks might be a way to try out a program to see if you really want to buy the current version. You can even trade in your own programs. Samples:

- *101 Dog Breeds*
- *1999 World Book*
- *NBA 1996*
- *Steel Panthers III: Brigade Command, 1939–1999*

**Search**: Yes
**Photos**: No
**Ordering**: Online, Fax, Phone
**Gift Wrap**: No
**Delivery**: 3rd Day

# RKS Software Store

`http://www.rks-software.com`

In English, French, German, Italian, Portuguese, and Spanish, this site lets you download software, try it out, and then, if you like it, buy a serial number to convert the trial version into a fully registered version. So this software is a form of shareware, or test-before-you-buy, a way for independent programmers to market their work without creating a real company. Quality varies from excellent to mediocre, so you do need to try stuff out. The site offers software for fax, mailing, labels, calendars, business cards, diaries, envelopes, alarms, and projects. For each program, the site offers a description, screenshots, version history, and instructions on downloading or ordering.

- *Calendar Builder*
- *It's Personal, Personal Diary Software*
- *Visual Business Cards*

**Search**: Yes
**Photos**: Screenshots
**Ordering**: Online
**Gift Wrap**: No
**Delivery**: Download

# Screen Savers a2z

`http://www.sirius.com/`
`~ratloaf`

Fun new screensavers, and tools for making and tracking screensavers or wallpaper. Most programs are shareware (try before you buy), but some are freeware (free to use, but copyrighted by the authors), and a few have been put into the public domain (the author has given up all rights, and no one else can copyright the program). This site provides you with a link to the download site, which is usually at the original author's site. Because the a2z site gets little or no money for these products, it seems to depend on advertising, or love, for its survival. Caution: Because you don't know where these files come from, you might want to drop them on a separate floppy when downloading, and examine them with an up-to-date virus checker before running them for the first time. Samples:

- *Aquarium* screensaver, with guppies, seahorses, and angelfish
- *Loch Ness Monster* screensaver
- *Psychedelic* screensaver if you like art or "just have a history of mental illness"
- *Virtual Slideshow Screen Saver* kit for making your own screen saver or wallpaper

**Search**: No
**Photos**: No
**Ordering**: Download and find out whether the program is shareware or not; then, if it is, and you want to keep it, send the author some dough.
**Gift Wrap**: No
**Delivery**: Download

# Software2Buy

`http://www.software2buy.com`

Thousands of titles, many at wholesale prices, in educational, entertainment, and game areas as well as business, utilities, and programming. Some software is downloadable. Information on most titles resembles the copy on the box, without screenshots. Samples:

- *Clickart 200,000 Image Pack* from Broderbund
- *Equilibrium Debabelizer Pro* for one user
- *Golf 1999 Edition*

**Search**: Good, if you guess which category the program might be in
**Photos**: A few
**Ordering**: Online, Fax, Phone

**Gift Wrap:** No
**Delivery:** Ground

## Software Street

http://
www.softwarestreet.com

Ecologists, listen up! One percent of this company's profit goes to the National Forest Foundation, to plant trees in a U.S. National Forest. Plus, they save more trees by not making up a paper catalog. They argue that because they have no expensive retail locations, they can offer "the lowest discounted prices to be found anywhere," a claim we would debate on particular products. Still, the prices do show up in the low end of PriceScan's surveys. They sell consumer, developer, and big business software, as well as books. Info on each product is ugly box copy, enough to confirm that this is the product you read about in a magazine, barely enough to make an informed comparison. Helpful gesture: They show you the shipping costs on any product, as you look at the details. Samples:
- DeLorme Mapping, *AAA Map N Go DVD Deluxe*
- Microsoft *Exchange Server 5.5*
- Microsoft *Publisher Deluxe 98 for Windows*

**Search:** Yes
**Photos:** No
**Ordering:** Online, Phone
**Gift Wrap:** No
**Delivery:** Ground, 2nd Day, Overnight

## TigerDirect

http://www.tigerdirect.com

Along with selected hardware, Tiger offers some of the most popular programs, at good prices. They guarantee that they will match prices appearing in national mass-circulation print media (magazines and newspapers), not counting promotions. If you spot a lower price there, you get a Tiger credit. If you want something most people have heard of, come here. If the product is obscure, well, Tiger may not carry it. We've used their

software store with pleasure, and have always been satisfied with their phone people, too. Samples:
- *Corel WordPerfect Suite 8* Standard Upgrade
- MIPS *VersaCheck Web Commerce*
- Perseus' *Survey Solution for the Web*

**Search:** Yes
**Photos:** Some
**Ordering:** Online
**Gift Wrap:** No
**Delivery:** Ground, 2nd Day, Overnight

## Unboxed Software

http://www.unboxed.com

Their motto is: "Download software and get everything but the box. Save a tree." Who knew that downloading was so ecological? Everything they sell is downloaded, along with software that lets you send them your order and get back an unlocking password. Mac, Newton, Pilot, Palmtop, and Windows software, with the focus on handhelds.
- *Intellisync for PalmPilot Connected Organizers*
- *Now Synchronize* for Pilot, Windows or Mac
- *Zachary's Wheel 2.8* for Newton

**Search:** Yes
**Photos:** No
**Ordering:** Online
**Gift Wrap:** No
**Delivery:** Download

## Virtual Software Store

http://
www.virtualsoftware.com

Downloadable software from a few commercial software developers, and a lot of shareware from authors and hobbyists. Here you pay before you download. You get one paragraph about each product, with icons indicating the operating system. On our visit, most software was no-name, but many programs looked useful, or interesting. Samples:
- *BrowseGate Web Proxy Server*
- *Image AXS* graphic organizer

- *Imágenes para los Tiempos Litúrgicos*
- *ImageStream 97* graphic import filters for Microsoft Office

**Search**: Yes
**Photos**: No
**Ordering**: Online
**Gift Wrap**: No
**Delivery**: Download

# WebShopper

`http://www.webshopper.com`

Hosted by the International Data Group (IDG), this site offers you tons of reviews, award lists, buying advice, and product roundups from their many publications, and the ability to order the products through other companies, known as resellers. As "an objective consumer advocate," the site does not endorse any particular product or reseller, but at the moment it only has a few resellers, and they don't carry a full range of programs, either. With popular products, you get to choose between the resellers, who compete on price and service. One caution: When you get email confirmation of your order from the reseller, make sure the price is what you expected, because the resellers may have changed it before WebShopper got the news. Sample items:

- Bungie *Myth II: Soulblighter for Windows*
- *FileMaker Pro 4.1* Mac
- Microsoft *Combat Flight Simulator*

**Search**: Yes
**Photos**: Some
**Ordering**: Online, Phone
**Gift Wrap**: No
**Delivery**: Overnight

Good product info. Samples:

- Downloadable version of *Lotus FastSite*
- Learning Company, *Carmen Sandiego Math Detective*
- *Norton Utilities 4* for the Mac

**Search**: Yes
**Photos**: Yes
**Ordering**: Online purchase or bid, lease; Phone
**Gift Wrap**: No
**Delivery**: Ground, 3$^{rd}$ Day, Overnight

# You may also want to check out the next chapter:

- Software for Kids

# Zones.com

`http://www.zones.com`

These are the mail-order folks who have gone online with software in boxes or downloads. They have a short list of manufacturers, focused on the most popular items. If you've already had a good experience with their mail-order operation, as we have, you may feel at home here.

# Software for Kids

You might be wondering why we included a separate chapter for kids' software. It's because the computer needs of your children are often very different from your own. Children's software basically falls into two categories, educational software and games. The very best titles do both — hence the name "edutainment." Most sites that sell children's software exclusively will help you decide what are the best titles for your kids. In the site descriptions, we'll go into more depth, so you can find the perfect store for your family. Because we've been involved in the family software industry for the past 17 years (mostly as reviewers), we'll share our expertise, when appropriate.

## Andromeda Software, Inc.

http://
www.andromedasoftware.com

Like gazing at the stars?  In recent years, there have been some truly heavenly computer programs devoted to our galaxy. Alas, many of them are quite expensive. This company has traveled through Earth's atmosphere gathering up the best, the brightest, and the cheapest. They also have a blue-ribbon selection of science software.  Sample titles:

- *Astro 2001:  The Wonders of the Universe*
- *Beyond Planet Earth and Beyond*
- *Color Digital Photographs of Space*
- *Comet Explorer*
- *Earth Image Atlas*
- *Explore the Planets*

**Search:** Yes
**Photos:** Yes
**Ordering:** Online, Fax, Email
**Gift Wrap:** No
**Delivery:** Ground

## The Disney Store

http://store.disney.go.com

Disney has quickly become one of the largest children's software manufacturers by creating titles starring characters from their hit movies. Some of these are so-so, but others are terrific. (Our personal favorites are *My Disney Kitchen* and *Disney's Magic Artist 2*.) They're a tad skimpy on the descriptions, so if you shop here, you should do a little research ahead of time. From their front page, click the CD-ROM button or search by character name. You can also shop for other Disney items at this store, because it's like their shop in the Mall. Samples:

- *Aladdin*
- *Hercules*
- *The Lion King*

**Search:** Yes
**Photos:** Yes
**Ordering:** Online
**Gift Wrap:** Gift box available on some items
**Delivery:** Ground, 4th Day

## Edmark

http://www.edmark.com

Edmark is one of the premier educational software companies, probably in the world. The only reason they aren't better known, we think, is they create only original programs, not "recycled" ones from popular movies or TV shows. The head of Edmark is actually a teacher, with umpteen years experience, not a marketing whiz who's just looking to make a buck. Their *Mighty Math* and *Thinkin' Things* series are classics. But what makes this site even more special is the extensive information offered in categories with topics, such as Special Needs, Girls and Computers, Gifted Children, and Homeschooling. Sample titles:

- *Astro Algebra*
- *Bailey's Book House*
- *Calculating Crew*
- *Fripple Town*
- *Let's Go Read!*
- *Millie's Math House*

- *Sammy's Science House*
- *Sky Island Mysteries*
- *Zap!*

**Search:** Yes
**Photos:** Yes
**Ordering:** Online
**Gift Wrap:** No
**Delivery:** Ground, 2$^{nd}$ Day, Overnight

## The Edutainment Catalog

`http://www.edutainco.com`

They've taken their printed catalog version and put it on the Web. They carry a decent assortment of children's titles, including some older, hard-to-find ones. You'll find out a lot about any software title because they also reprint reviews by the Children's Software Review Company. Samples:

- Children's books
- Gift Guide
- Toys
- Videos for kids

**Search:** Yes
**Photos:** Yes
**Ordering:** Online, Phone, Fax
**Gift Wrap:** Yes
**Delivery:** Ground, 2$^{nd}$ Day

## ESI Online

`http://www.edsoft.com`

This is a good site, especially for teachers or homeschooling parents, because they sell over 8,000 K–12 educational titles from 350 different publishers. They've conveniently given you two ways to search their huge inventory: You can use their searchable (by several categories) Educational Software Catalog or you can browse their table of contents. The ordering information is a little complicated (it is set up primarily for teachers), so if you're just looking for one or two titles for your kids, we'd recommend going elsewhere, but if you're looking for curriculum material, this is a fine place to look. Samples:

- Books
- Cross-curricular series
- Special Needs software
- Subject software
- Teacher utilities
- Test-preparation materials

**Search:** Yes
**Photos:** No
**Ordering:** Online, Phone, Fax
**Gift Wrap:** No
**Delivery:** Ground

## eToys

`http://www.etoys.com`

As the name implies, eToys' forte is its toy collection. So when you get to the first page, make sure you click the Software tab. Then you'll be brought to their software page, which gives you a number of ways to search. They offer a one-paragraph product description, no reviews, of the software. A fun feature is their Wish List. Have some child you know sign up, and he or she can type in their favorites. Great for sending birthday or holiday gifts. Samples:

- Best software sellers
- Children's audiotapes
- Children's videos
- Computerized toys

**Search:** Yes
**Photos:** Yes
**Ordering:** Online, Phone
**Gift Wrap:** Yes
**Delivery:** Ground, 3$^{rd}$ Day, 2$^{nd}$ Day

## Humongous Entertainment

`http://www.humongous.com`

Humongous started a software revolution with the cute little car character Putt-Putt and added other characters, such as Freddi Fish, Pajama Sam, and Spy Fox. They hit the brass ring when they created the software for Blue of the fabulously popular TV show *Blue's Clues*. Humongous titles are consistently top rated, especially for preschoolers. You can buy their software at their Web site and your kids will have fun there, too, playing the easy games. Sample titles:

- *Big Thinkers Kindergarten*
- *Blue's Birthday Adventure*
- *Freddi Fish: Case of the Stolen Conch Shell*
- *Pajama Sam 2*
- *Putt-Putt Enters the Race*

**Search:** Yes
**Photos:** Yes
**Ordering:** Online, Phone, Fax
**Gift Wrap:** No
**Delivery:** Ground, 3rd Day

## KBkids.com

`http://www.kbkids.com`

KB Toys merged with BrainPlay.com this year to form KBkids.com. This store has the most information about kid's software titles out of all the Web stores. They offer in-depth reviews by software experts, articles by child development specialists and teachers, and also give you the entire product description. They also have a terrific collection of articles about children with special needs. If you are looking for a gift, you can check what their experts recommend for a certain age group or interest. You'll find just about every kid's title imaginable. At various times of the year, the staff goes completely crazy and offers a blow-out 99 cent sale on POPULAR titles. Samples:

- Children's videos and musical instruments
- Free software demos
- Parent software reviews
- Some productivity software
- Top software choices by age
- Toys
- Video games

**Search:** No
**Photos:** Yes
**Ordering:** Online, Phone
**Gift Wrap:** No
**Delivery:** Ground, 2nd Day, Overnight

## Knowledge Adventure

`http:// www.knowledgeadventure.com`

This has become one big software company. You've probably heard their name, because they are the creators of the very successful JumpStart series. But they've also added the Blaster series, Dr. Brain, Sierra, Fisher-Price, and the new Teletubbies to their line of software for the whole family. The site has activities for kids to play around with, and there's always some useful information for parents, too. Sample titles:

- *3D Dinosaur Adventure*
- *Captain Kangaroo's Life's First Lessons*
- *Grammar Games*
- *Sabrina the Teenage Witch*
- *Spanish for the Real World*
- Test-preparation software

**Search:** Yes
**Photos:** Yes
**Ordering:** Online, Phone
**Gift Wrap:** No
**Delivery:** Ground, 2nd Day

## The Learning Company

`http://www.learningco.com`

This is another one of those mega-software companies that has, over the past two years, bought out other software companies and then added them to their inventory. Their most recent acquisition was Broderbund. They now host some of the most recognizable software series names in the business. Their site sells everything, but it also has a really helpful Learning Center for parents who want to find out more about what their kids are learning in school. Click on a grade and you'll be brought to a large chart. Of course, TLC will suggest software appropriate for that subject, but this is a store, after all. If you joint their TLC Adv@ntage club, you'll get 5% off every order. Sample titles:

- Carmen Sandiego series
- *Geo Bee Challenge*
- *Kid Pix*

- *Logical Journey of the Zoombinis*
- Madeline series
- Reader Rabbit series
- Schoolhouse Rock series

**Search**: Yes
**Photos**: Yes
**Ordering**: Online, Phone
**Gift Wrap**: No
**Delivery**: Ground, 3$^{rd}$ Day

# Schoolroom.com

`http://www.schoolroom.com`

There's a lot to discover here, including software. Even though this site has a fantastic supply of videos (over 7,000 hard-to-find inspirational and instructional videos), it also has a good supply of CD-ROMs, too. Many of the titles serve as homeschooling tools (but there are some "entertaining" programs, as well). They also sell 1,500 Christian and educational books. You should check the Today's Special section for some truly outstanding bargains. Sample software subjects:

- Activity and art
- Bible reference
- Bible storybooks
- Children's Bibles
- History and geography
- Music
- SAT prep
- Science

**Search**: Yes
**Photos**: No
**Ordering**: Online, Phone
**Gift Wrap**: No
**Delivery**: Ground, 2$^{nd}$ Day

# Tom Snyder Productions

`http://www.teachtsp.com`

Twenty years ago teacher Tom Synder (not the late-night TV guy) started using computers to help teach his students. Seeing that there was a terrible lack of products, he started creating his own software and other teaching materials. His products are geared toward teachers, but any parent, whether they are homeschooling or not, will appreciate them. They also offer free demos so you can try before you buy. Sample titles:

- Africa Inspirer
- Choices, Choices series
- Decisions, Decisions series
- Fizz and Martina Adventure series
- Inner Body Works Jr.
- Science Court series

**Search**: Some
**Photos**: Some
**Ordering**: Online, Phone
**Gift Wrap**: No
**Delivery**: Ground

# You may also want to click through to these chapters:

- School Supplies
- Software
- Toys

# Sporting Goods

Big sporting goods stores are fun for a number of reasons. You can browse through them and marvel at all the neat stuff available for a particular sport and you can discover new equipment to help make that sport more enjoyable. Most of the stores in this chapter are mega sporting stores, meaning that they sell a lot stuff for a lot of different sports.

We've also included a few stores that equip a particular sport that didn't get its own chapter, such as archery and volleyball.

## Bingham Projects, Inc.

http://www.
binghamprojects.com

The Recurve bow was created by ElMont Bingham in his high school industrial arts class. Out of the many items he made for his classes, the Recurve bow was the most popular. Today, you can purchase a kit to reconstruct ElMont's original design, as well as several other kits. The kids include the building materials and a blueprint. Samples:
- Long bow kit
- Recurve bow kit
- Take-down bow kit
- Youth take-down bow kit
- Instructional videos

**Search:** No
**Photos:** Some
**Ordering:** Online, Phone, Fax
**Gift Wrap:** No
**Delivery:** Ground, 2nd Day

## BowMan's Archery Solutions

http://www.thebowman.com

This is a nifty store for all you archers out there. It's stocked with high-quality archery gear and also serves as a good resource where you can get many of your questions answered. Unusual for a Web store, they offer a layaway plan! You might also want to click the Sweepstakes button and see what's on there. Samples:
- Bow cases
- Bow package deals
- Bow sights
- Bows for the physically challenged
- Crossbows
- Custom-made bowstrings
- Target curves

**Search:** No
**Photos:** Some
**Ordering:** Online, Phone
**Gift Wrap:** No
**Delivery:** Ground

## Fogdog Sports

http://www.fogdog.com

What kind of a name is this for a sporting goods store? We asked and found out that one definition of fog dog is the "arc or ray of light sometimes seen burning through the fog." Well, athletes of any sort will surely see the light after shopping here. This Web store is huge, it has it all. If after all this you still can't find what you're looking for, contact the Fogdog Search Squad and they'll personally find it and buy it for you. Samples:
- Adult sport clothing and shoes
- Camping equipment
- Children's shoes
- Fitness equipment
- Portable basketball hoops
- Soccer, baseball, and football equipment
- Sport memorabilia
- Team uniforms

**Search:** Yes
**Photos:** Yes

**Ordering:** Online, Phone
**Gift Wrap:** No
**Delivery:** Ground

# Gear.com

`http://www.gear.com`

This is one big sporting goods store. They have a section for just about every sport you can think of. Don't believe us? How about climbing, kayaking, snowboarding, and wakeboarding. There are clothes for men and women to go with all of these sports, too. Everything in this store is heavily discounted. Samples:

- Antifog goggles
- Backpacks
- Baseball, basketball, and soccer equipment
- Down jackets
- ErgoPedic air bed
- Folding motorized treadmill
- Pool cue
- Racquetball racquets
- Water boots
- Wet suits
- Wilderness survival kit

**Search:** Yes
**Photos:** Yes
**Ordering:** Online, Phone, Fax
**Gift Wrap:** No
**Delivery:** Ground, 2nd Day

# Online Sports.com

`http://www.onlinesports.com`

This store is a sports mega complex. It has a little for just about every sport, from Alpine skiing to water polo. You'll find a lot of generic supplies good for many different sports, as well as items specifically tailored to your favorites. They also have a terrific sports memorabilia section. Samples:

- Aerobic clothing
- Al Unser autographed color photo
- Babe Ruth Yankee jersey
- Bart Starr autographed football and display case
- Billie Jean King autographed tennis ball
- Cave exploration gear

- Elbow wraps
- Horse and stable equipment
- Instructional books and videos
- Joe DiMaggio autographed baseball and jersey
- Joe Montana "3-time Super Bowl MVP" card
- Kites
- Locker organizer
- Mark McGwire Cardinals jersey
- Scuba diving equipment
- Trampolines
- Various football autographed helmets
- Wilson tennis racquets
- Y.A. Tittle autographed 8 x 10 color photo

**Search:** Yes
**Photos:** Some
**Ordering:** Online, Phone, Fax
**Gift Wrap:** No
**Delivery:** Ground, 3rd Day, 2nd Day

# REI

`http://www.rei.com`

When our kids were tiny tots, their favorite activity was to go to our local REI store with us and "sample" all of the tents. Our kids have good taste. Now REI is also on the Web, so you can shop here anytime, no matter where you live. This is a terrific store, especially if you are looking for camping gear, but they also have a fine selection of gear for snow sports, cycling, and hiking. All of their products are first rate. Samples:

- Child carriers
- Climbing gear
- External frame packs
- Family camping bags
- Hydration packs
- Self-inflating pads
- Snow sports gear and clothes
- Survival gear
- Thermal underwear for kids and adults
- Winter/mountaineering tents

**Search:** Yes
**Photos:** Yes
**Ordering:** Online, Phone, Mail
**Gift Wrap:** No
**Delivery:** Ground, 3rd Day, Overnight

## Spike Nashbar

http://www.spikenashbar.com

A great store for the volleyball athlete. You'll find a complete line of sporting equipment, clothes, and accessories. This is the only sport they cater to, so it's very easy to find what you're looking for or to just browse the "aisles." Lots of clothes for both men and women. Stop by their Close-Outs department for some good bargains. Samples:

- Game accessories
- Net systems
- Power bars
- Protective wear
- Sunglasses
- Teamwear
- Volleyball shoes
- Warm-up suits

**Search:** Yes
**Photos:** Some
**Ordering:** Online
**Gift Wrap:** Card
**Delivery:** Ground, 2$^{nd}$ Day, Overnight

## World Wide Sports

http://1888wwsports.com

If you think of sporting equipment that makes you go fast (and mostly for your feet), you'll be able to picture this store. The prices are about what you'd pay in any store, but check the Clearance Department for some out-of-sight sales. We found a pair of $300 in-line skates for $99. Samples:

- Bicycles
- Clothing
- Ice skates
- In-line skates
- Roller skates
- Skateboards
- Skis
- Snowboards

**Search:** Some
**Photos:** Yes
**Ordering:** Online, Phone, Fax

**Gift Wrap:** No
**Delivery:** Ground

## You may also want to jog over to these other active chapters:

- Baseball & Softball
- Basketball
- Bicycles
- Boating & Sailing
- Bowling
- Camping & Hiking
- Golf
- Skating
- Soccer
- Tennis

# Stargazing

We're far enough away from the city lights to see the stars revolving overhead, and we like picking out the constellations in the early evening, wandering around our chile patch to see past the elms and cottonwoods, but what we are most interested in is space. We really follow space flights, and get a thrill out of even the more routine missions, like the ones designed to fix the plumbing on Mir.

If your imagination goes up with the astronauts' latest launch, you will find tools, images, charts, and software to help you get closer to the stars, through a bunch of Web sites set up especially for space aficionados and astronomers, from amateur to pro. Here are the star sites we think offer the best products, services, and wow.

## Astromart

`http://www.astromart.com`

Here's a techie site for star watchers, best if you know what you are doing. They host people's classified ads and personal auctions of astrographs, binoculars, eyepieces, filters, finders, mounts, parts, telescopes. They also have an astronomy bookstore, and science auctions. Samples:

- 8" Starhopper Dob reflector telescope, 25mm eyepiece
- Takahashi E-160 Astrograph with 7 x 50 finder, tube holder, and camera adaptor for Olympus camera, less than a year old

**Search:** Yes
**Photos:** Sometimes
**Ordering:** Email with seller
**Gift Wrap:** No
**Delivery:** Negotiated with seller

## Cutler of New England

`http://www.cutlerofnewengland.com`

Hand-crafted replicas of telescopes from the 18th and 19th centuries. You can have an engraved plate attached to one, if you want to put it in your living room. Samples:

- Octagon Star Telescope, 24" barrel made out of mahogany, refractor telescope on tripod
- Octagonal Sundial pen holder

**Search:** No
**Photos:** Yes
**Ordering:** Online, Phone, Fax
**Gift Wrap:** No
**Delivery:** Ground

## EarthRISE

`http://earthrise.sdsc.edu/earthrise`

A great site for 100,000 public domain (free) pictures of Earth from outer space, a lot easier to use than NASA, which took most of the images in the first place. You can search using a form, a map, or a list of political entities. They also feature highlights, and pictures recommended or sent in by customers. You can probably get a space view of your backyard here. For hard copy prints, you have to write to the Johnson Space Center. Samples:

- *Albuquerque Rio Grande, with 65% Cloud Cover,* color image in JPEG
- *Greece, Thessaloniki, Lakes,* color image in JPEG format
- *Moonrise over Earth,* color image in JPEG format

**Search:** Yes
**Photos:** Yes
**Ordering:** Online for free
**Gift Wrap:** No
**Delivery:** Download

# NSSDC Photo Gallery

`http://nssdc.gsfc.nasa.gov/photo_gallery`

The National Space Science Data Center offers many spectacular photos of planets, nebulae, galaxies, globular clusters, stars, and "exotic objects," as well as the sun and spacecraft. You get information about the object, processing involved, and additional captions. On the site you get thumbnails and downloadable JPEG format images. NASA also offers 44 different CD sets, containing 890 individual volumes, with some combination of full-resolution images, browsable subsamples, and compressed versions of the full resolution. Prices for these fantastic images are incredibly cheap. In some cases, you may need to get one of the freeware browsers they provide links for. Samples:

- *ROSAT Images, Complete Set*, 8-CD Set, with all high-resolution images of X rays in space, taken January 1993 through October 1997, as FITS and GIF images
- *Voyager to the Outer Planets, Jupiter*, with compressed and uncompressed images, 3 CDs
- *Welcome to the Planets*, CD-ROM, Mac or PC

**Search:** No
**Photos:** Yes
**Ordering:** Online, Phone, Fax
**Gift Wrap:** No
**Delivery:** Ground

# Sky and Telescope

`http://store.skypub.com`

This online store hosted by the publication *Sky and Telescope* offers atlases, celestial software, getting started books, globes, planispheres, plus info about taking images of stars and making and using telescopes. Low prices, with an additional discount if your astronomy club subscribes to their magazine. Samples:

- *Complete Space and Astronomy*, 5-CD-ROM set
- *Deep-Sky Imaging Using a CCD Camera*, CD
- *Deep-Sky Planner 3.0*, software so you can plan the best time to view any of 100,000 objects, planetary ephemeredes, and events

- *Eagle Nebula Close-Up*, Hubble Space Telescope Spotlight Print, 16" x 20" on high-quality Kodak paper
- Ernest H. Cherrington, Jr., *Exploring the Moon through Binoculars and Small Telescopes*, 229 pages
- John Dobson, *Telescope Building*, VHS tape
- *Poster-size Skygazer's Almanac Wall Chart*, showing which planets will be visible, when the moon rises, when twilight ends, for observers near latitude 40° N

**Search:** Yes
**Photos:** Yes
**Ordering:** Online
**Gift Wrap:** No
**Delivery:** 2ⁿᵈ Day

# Space Movie Archive

`http://graffiti.u-bordeaux.fr/MAPBX/roussel/anim-ewf.html`

Courtesy of the University of Bordeaux, France, Frank Roussel has put together this collection of more than 2,500 downloadable animations and movies of solar eclipses, shuttle missions, Voyager flybys, available in various formats, including MPEG, QuickTime, and Avi, mostly compressed with gzip (suffix .gz). The site also offers animation players for every platform. Samples:

- *Apollo 13 Launch*, Avi format, 1.5 MB
- *Flyby of an atom, spinning electrons*, MPEG, 402K
- *STS-71 1ˢᵗ Shuttle Mir Docking Atlantis Mission, Day 1*, with crew walkouts, MPEG, 887K

**Search:** Yes
**Photos:** No
**Ordering:** Free
**Gift Wrap:** No
**Delivery:** Download

# Scope out these chapters, too:

- Photography
- Weather Gear

# Stocks & Bonds

Trading online lets you move a little faster, with more information, less gab on the phone with brokers, and a lot less commission than when you use a regular street broker. You tend to feel more in charge of your investments, and, depending on the day and the site, you are. What you have to watch is the time when your order is actually executed. Because you are online, you can see what the price is at the moment, but even if you buy or sell right away, the trade may not go through immediately, and you could get stuck with a very different price if the market is volatile. You should look for ways to put a limit on your order, such as specifying the threshold prices for buying or selling, so the brokerage firm can't just take whatever the markets offer when it gets around to your request. Also, if you get caught up in a rush and network traffic slows down, you might not even get through, or your order could come in late; in such circumstances, you need a company with excellent customer support to straighten things out.

Recently, online brokers have begun adding a lot of research to persuade you to use their sites. This data looks good, but it isn't yet as extensive as that found on some of the sites that focus on reporting and analyzing financial information, with or without a fee. You may want to browse some of the news, analysis, discussion, and screening sites we've listed in the chapter on Investment Planning & Research, to find a supplement to your online broker.

One other note: There are plenty of scams out there from bogus companies with fake, dead, or illegal stock ventures. We recommend sticking to these established brokers and their exchanges, and if you feel tempted, checking the info sites for their opinions before jumping to a hot unknown.

## AmeriTrade

http://www.ameritrade.com

A good-looking site with slick, colorful buttons, but if you are at home, the graphics-heavy display may slow down access. You can use the Web, a Touch Tone connection, or a Sharp® Zaurus personal digital assistant and a regular modem to connect. If you don't want to know too much, their research includes key company profiles, earnings estimates, financial ratios, four-year historical data, news items, pricing, ownership, recent earnings, and results. You can use StockQuest™ to screen 10,000 companies trading on the NYSE, AMEX, Nasdaq, and OTC exchanges, using more than 50 criteria. Trades run just a little slower than Datek and SureTrade, its main competitors for the day trader audience. They charge 30% more than Datek for Limit Orders, but 20% less on Market Orders, without a limit on volume. You can even pay less than other services charge when you need the help of a live broker. You get 100 free real-time quotes when you sign up, and 100 more for every Internet order filled. They charge for outgoing domestic or foreign wire transfers, but less than most of the other brokers. Samples:

- Bonds
- Mutual funds
- Options
- Real-time portfolio of your account
- Stocks

**Search:** Yes
**Photos:** Charts
**Ordering:** Online, Phone
**Gift Wrap:** No
**Delivery:** Online

## Datek

`http://www.datek.com`

Great if you are a day trader, or just like zipping in and out on the fast lane, so you need low commissions. Rated #1 by a survey of online investors by The Street.com, Datek scored high on reliability, execution, commissions, speed, and ease of use. You start by putting $2,000 into an IRA, joint, corporate, or custodial account (or you send them the equivalent in fully paid stock). Once you have done that, you can borrow funds from Datek at a low rate, hovering near what good mortgages are going for. Datek's commissions for Limit Orders on the NYSE, AMEX, and Nasdaq are 20% less than their nearest competitor in our group of brokers, and all of their commissions are 50% less than DLJ Direct and E*Trade. Also, Datek sets one flat fee for Limit Orders, Market Orders, through Nasdaq, NYSE, or AMEX for the first 5,000 shares, and for each additional 5,000 shares. Datek moves fast, too. They claim to execute marketable orders within ten seconds, and promise to waive your commission if the order takes longer than 60 seconds. Another neat aspect of Datek: They offer free real-time quotes, without limits. You can review your daily activity, open orders, and messages at any time. Free outgoing domestic or foreign wire transfers. The service provides some charting and investment software, such as a utility that lets you download your current account information into Quicken, links to market data, advice on trading and investing, stock tips, databases, and books you can buy through Amazon.com. Sample services:

- Bonds
- Market orders
- Mutual funds
- Real-time portfolio of your account
- Stocks

**Search:** Yes
**Photos:** Charts
**Ordering:** Online
**Gift Wrap:** No
**Delivery:** Online

## DLJ Direct

`http://www.dljdirect.com`

If you already have an account with DLJ, you might want to switch to their online site, which carries all the original stock research done by DLJ's regular Equity Research Department. If new to DLJ, you can open an account with no minimum amount. To get real-time quotes, after the 100 you get free for opening an account, you have to execute an order, or pay a fee. On the first 1,000 shares, they charge more than twice as much as day-trader brokers like Datek and SureTrade for Limit Orders and Market Orders, and the commission goes to 2 cents a share above that (even more for dubious stocks selling under a buck apiece). DLJ offers a Touch-Tone phone transfer service so you can place money in your account overnight for next-day purchases (or you can mail in a personal check, or bank check for more than $10,000). You cannot pay with a credit card, credit card check, bank check under $10,000, money order, or cash. You get an up-to-the-night-before personal portfolio, with alerts on any developments on securities you hold or monitor, and 120 days of account transaction history, Samples:

- Bonds
- Mutual funds
- Options
- Precious metals
- Stocks

**Search:** Yes
**Photos:** Charts
**Ordering:** Online, Phone, Broker
**Gift Wrap:** No
**Delivery:** Online

## E*Trade

`http://www.etrade.com`

For ease and comfort, E*Trade stands out, particularly with their clean menus and pop-up advice, and good customer service. They make the information you need visible, but you pay something for the special attention, and you may have to wait a while for these graphic pages to load during market hours. You can connect with E*Trade from AOL, CompuServe, Prodigy, WebTV, direct cable modem, and their own speech-recognition phone investing system, if you want. You can open almost any imaginable kind of account for as little as $1,000, and get a margin account for $2,000. For Limit Orders on your first 5,000 shares on the NYSE, AMEX, and Nasdaq, as well as Market Orders on Nasdaq, they charge as hefty a commission as DLJ Direct, beating them only on Market Orders for the NYSE and AMEX. They do not reduce their commission if the trade takes too long to go through. For an additional 5,000 shares, the commission gets multiplied by 5. Real-time quotes are now free to members if you sign a series of agreements with the original exchanges supplying the info; otherwise, you can get them free if you make 30 trades a quarter, or you can just pay a fee. From the quote itself, you can get financials such as annual and quarterly balance sheets, annual cash flow, and key ratios. Additional research includes charts, company info, indexes, ratings and analyst recommendations, stories from newsletters and newspapers, and sector ratings. Also, there's a good Learning Center on the basics of investing. Market orders, they claim, are executed within a few seconds. Neat extra: Join Initial Public Offerings, through their IPO Center. They charge you bank rates for outgoing domestic or foreign wire transfers. Samples:

- Bonds
- DRIPs
- Initial Public Offerings
- Mutual funds
- Options
- Real-time portfolio of your account
- Stocks

**Search:** Yes
**Photos:** Charts
**Ordering:** Online
**Gift Wrap:** No
**Delivery:** Online

# Fidelity

http://www311.fidelity.com

If you're already part of the enormous Fidelity family of mutual funds, you might just want to make them your

online broker, particularly if you are more interested in long-term growth than in-and-out profits. We like a site that starts off with Peter Lynch talking to us about investing, even if what he says is already in his books. Plus, there's a mutual fund search, detailed descriptions of their funds, and specific information for personal investing, with info on news, in-depth studies, retirement advice, and planning tips. To get started, you have to deposit $5,000 in assets (actual stock certificates, check, mutual funds, transfer of stocks, wire transfer).Once you are accepted, you can buy, sell, and hold a lot more than mutual funds here! By keeping pages lean, Fidelity loads data fast, and their trades are usually completed in less than 60 seconds. Commissions are mid-range, more than twice as high as Datek for Market Orders. They don't handle futures, currency, or commodities. Samples:

- Annuities
- Bonds, corporate and municipal
- Certificates of deposit
- Employee stock options
- Foreign securities
- Initial Public Offerings
- Life insurance
- Mutual funds
- Previous metals
- Stocks
- Treasury securities

**Search:** Yes
**Photos:** Peter Lynch and charts
**Ordering:** Online
**Gift Wrap:** No
**Delivery:** Online

# Schwab

http://www.schwab.com

Here's another site where you may already have some stocks in the firm, as we do, and going online with them may simplify your life. As one of the first and already the largest online brokers, Charles Schwab has grown fast, and learned a lot, creating a site that seems best if you plan to buy and hold, rather than do a lot of trading, because of their relatively high commissions and constraints on trade in hot Net crazes. The interface is friendly. They even offer Chinese, French, and Spanish versions. We found their phone support clear, friendly, and fast. Unfortunately for beginners, the minimum deposit to open a new account is $2,500, with an annual fee, although the fee can be waived if you deposit $100 a month, keep a big balance, make two trades a year, or sign up for special services. You get 100 real-time quotes for free, and another 100 for each trade, then pay a minute-by-minute fee for more. You receive a lot of good research, with analyst comments, fund performances, market news, mutual fund and stock screening, as well as advice on planning. If you are interested in playing high-tech stocks fast, you may want to go elsewhere, though, because some Initial Public Offerings are removed from the electronic trading system when Schwab expects super-fast market conditions when these offerings begin trading (for these stocks, use a human broker). Similarly, Schwab raises the amount of money you have to have in your account to buy certain high-flyers and low-dippers on margin, that is, with money you borrow from Schwab. For the first 5,000 shares, their commission is high, being three times that of Datek or SureTrade, and they don't let up for the next 5,000 either. They charge as much as a bank for wire transfers. Still, we like the account information, showing positions, portfolio performance (although you may have to spend a while setting this up accurately), transaction history, transfers, and payments. Samples:

- Bonds
- Foreign stocks
- Life insurance
- Money markets and CDs
- Mutual funds
- Options
- Treasuries

**Search:** Yes
**Photos:** Charts
**Ordering:** Online, Phone
**Gift Wrap:** No
**Delivery:** Online

## SureTrade

http://www.suretrade.com

A Fleet financial company, which *Fortune* called "the ultimate in no-frills, bare-bones online trading," this site

is the arch rival of Datek for day trading, beating them by 20% on Market, and matching them on Limit Orders. You have to pay higher fees for penny stocks (those selling for less than $2 a share). You can dial in with Touch-Tone, for a little more money, and place a phone order with a broker for less than what Schwab charges for a Web buy. You get real-time quotes, some good information on the trading page, including constant updates of the current trading, so you can decide whether to get in or stay out, or put in a Limit Order, if the stock is hopping around. Also, their help material seems detailed, and thoughtful. No, you can't buy into an Initial Public Offering here. Timing on execution varies, sometimes slowing to several minutes. Samples:

- Bonds
- No-load and load mutual funds
- Options
- Penny stocks
- Stocks
- Treasury bills, notes, and bonds

**Search:** Yes
**Photos:** Charts
**Ordering:** Online, Phone
**Gift Wrap:** No
**Delivery:** Online

## Waterhouse Web Broker

http://www.waterhouse.com

Founded 20 years ago with 150 branch offices around the country, Waterhouse has won *Smart Money*'s award as Best Discount Broker, with "the best mix of price, product, service, and reputation." An excellent brokerage with a human touch, midway in pricing between day-trading sites like Datek, and bigger, more expensive firms like Schwab and Fidelity. You can start a retirement account with no minimum balance, or a regular account with $1,000. When you sign up, you are assigned to a real live broker somewhere in your area, so you actually have a human to talk to if you have questions. You can get free 15-minute delayed quotes at any time. To get 100 real-time quotes, open an account. After that, you have to execute a trade, or pay a small fee. Other research available includes many charts, compilations of research from 3,000 analysts at 240 firms, put together by Zacks. You can use the Morningstar mutual fund screening data. Internet stock trades on Limit Orders and Market Orders go through quickly. Commissions on these are low, but still hover about 20% above Datek and Sure Trade for 1 to 5,000 shares, then go to 1 cent per share for any order that totals more than 5,000 shares. (Commissions on Touch-Tone telephone and personal trades through your Account Officer go up by a factor of 3 or 4.) Buying one of a thousand no-load and low-load mutual funds incurs a flat fee, no matter what the size; trades of another 7,000 load funds are not charged, because the funds pay Waterhouse a fee for the business. You can have money transferred from your bank account once a month, or once a quarter, or through direct deposit. Your portfolio can track up to 10 stocks. Samples:

- Bonds
- Mutual funds
- Options
- Stocks

**Search:** Yes
**Photos:** Charts
**Ordering:** Online, Phone
**Gift Wrap:** No
**Delivery:** Online

## Web Street Securities

`http://` `webstreetsecurities.com`

If you want to trade hot Internet stocks, you may want to steer away from Schwab and Waterhouse, because they impose caution and restrictions on this incredibly volatile action, with an eye toward saving your skin. But Web Street Securities encourages day trading, with free commissions on 1,000 or more shares of Nasdaq stock (which is what most Net start-ups issue). You don't have to put in a minimum balance to get started, either. Research includes free Baseline company profiles, free real-time quotes, and a glossary. And, if you are trading fast, you can place an order on one side of the screen, while watching your Order Status frame show the results of an earlier trade. You can have up to 10 watch lists going at one time, too, with live updating for a fee. Execution averages less than 10 seconds, and the

confirmation pops up on your screen. They charge medium-range commissions on any trades other than 1,000 or more Nasdaq stocks, at about half of what Schwab demands. Your portfolio is kept up to date as prices change while you are online, and as transactions occur. If you think you might need customer service, anticipate longish waits on the phone, compared with places like Schwab. Samples:

- Bonds
- Equity and index options
- Mutual funds
- Stocks

**Search:** Yes
**Photos:** Charts
**Ordering:** Online, Phone
**Gift Wrap:** No
**Delivery:** Online

## A few tips on electronic trading:

1. Don't place the same order twice. When the market goes into overdrive, heavy trading makes prices bounce around, and slows down confirmation of your order. If you have received a tracking number for your order, count on it being executed. Resist issuing a duplicate. Canceling is hard to do. When the market is bubbling away, the trade goes through before you can stop a Market Order. If the market is boiling, you may not be able to get through to cancel a Limit Order, either.

2. "Real time" is almost. Even real-time quotes depend on someone sending them out, and when the market gets crazy, the quotes are not perfectly up to date.

3. When a stock is hot, its price changes more often and more quickly than you could ever imagine when you read the newspaper.

# SEC Chair, Arthur Levitt, cautions:

"Investing in the stock market—however you do it and however easy it may be—will always entail risk. I would be very concerned if investors allowed the ease with which they can make trades to shortcut or bypass the three golden rules for all investors:

(1) Know what you are buying;

(2) Know the ground rules under which you buy and sell a stock or bond;

(3) Know the level of risk you are undertaking.

On-line investors should remember that it is just as easy, if not more, to lose money through the click of a button as it is to make it."

# You may also want to invest in this chapter:

* Investment Planning & Research

# Surveillance Gear

Here's where the spies shop. Some of these places emphasize protecting your home from invasions of your privacy by hackers, phone tap artists, and long-distance microphones. Other stores include items that allow you to monitor distant locations to make sure all is well there, hunt or work in the dark with night-vision goggles, and hide your valuables where no one can find them. Some shops also help you listen in, snap pictures, and track vehicles, just like real snoops, whether official or criminal. Most of these stores walk both sides of the street, selling to any consumers who want to protect themselves, or experiment on the edge of spycraft.

## BRD Security

http://www.spybase.com

From Buy Right Distributors, running under the name of Spybase, this store offers listening devices, and mobile surveillance. This gear is for both pros and amateurs who like wearing facial disguises and sneaking around. Most orders are shipped within 24 hours, with as much as 5 days delay for out-of-stock items. Of course, some items like pepper spray can't be shipped by air. Samples:
* Lincoln beard, ash blond
* Modern Edition Book Safe
* Oscor OSC-5000 Omni Spectral Correlator, which monitors and detects threats 24 hours a day, automatically
* Spy Sunglasses with rearview vision
* XR900 Wireless Video Transmitter, 900 MHZ video up to 1400 feet, world's smallest video transmitter

**Search:** No
**Photos:** Yes
**Ordering:** Online, Phone
**Gift Wrap:** No
**Delivery:** Ground

## Global Mart

http://www.globe-mart.com

In the Electronics section of this bright site, you can find night-vision optics, metal detectors, and security gear. Samples:
* Philips RT-24A video recorder with 24-hour real-time, or 96 hours with time-lapse video
* Remington High-Tech audio/video security camera
* Remington Simulated Security Camera

**Search:** No
**Photos:** Yes
**Ordering:** Online, Phone
**Gift Wrap:** No
**Delivery:** Ground, 2nd Day, Overnight

## Imall

http://www.imall.com

If you want to set up a video camera a few hundred feet away from an observer, to monitor a door, swimming pool, or parking lot, you might want to get a wireless video transmitter and receiver from this store's electronics department. Some shipping and handling is free; orders go by air Sample items:
* CCC Complete Digital Color Camera, with cigarette lighter adapter for auto, rechargeable battery pack, and 4" color LCD monitor for security, surveillance, mobile video coverage, or viewing hazardous processes
* WVR, Wireless Video Receiver
* WVT High Performance Wireless Video Transmitter

**Search:** Yes
**Photos:** Yes
**Ordering:** Online
**Gift Wrap:** Card
**Delivery:** 3rd Day

# LAN Optics

http://www.tiac.net/users/
lanint

Good prices on Russian optical gear, such as night-vision binoculars, goggles, and scopes. These products are heavily ruggedized, with a full one-year warranty, the latest modifications, and presale inspection and adjustment. Shipping varies depending on the product's price and weight, and your address. Samples:

- Compact Night Vision Goggles designed for pilots and night builders, with built-in infrared illuminator to see and read in absolute darkness
- Night Vision Telescope 4 x 48, 600 yards viewing range, 12" field of vision, 1.5 pounds

**Search:** No
**Photos:** Yes
**Ordering:** Online
**Gift Wrap:** No
**Delivery:** Ground, 3rd Day

# MicroSurveillance

http://
www.microelec.force9.co.uk

The shop for James Bond, 007, supplying Her Majesty's Government with surveillance and counter-surveillance equipment. Prices in pounds or dollars. They ship fast or slow to the U.S. Samples:

- Bug detector, with range of 3MHZ to 3.5GHZ, with audio confirmation so you can hear the bug and spot its location
- Matchstick-size microphone, with miniature amplifier, picks up whispers 40 feet away
- Miniature pinhole camera
- Pen transmitter
- Phone tap detector, defeats tapping, recording, transmitting of calls

**Search:** No
**Photos:** Some
**Ordering:** Online, Phone, Fax, Email
**Gift Wrap:** No
**Delivery:** Ground, 3rd Day

# Spy Company

http://www.spycompany.com

Set up by the Goldman Computers Online company, this store has a great slogan: "Your privacy is none of their business . . . It's ours." They offer bug detectors, locksmithing tools, telephone monitoring, vehicle tracking, video surveillance, wireless video. Same-day shipping, worldwide. Samples:

- Electric Pick Gun, battery-powered lock picker
- Nanny cam with wireless video
- Secure Phone with Automatic Line Guard
- Sony Infrared camera

**Search:** No
**Photos:** Yes
**Ordering:** Online
**Gift Wrap:** No
**Delivery:** Ground, 2nd Day, Overnight

# SpyMart

http://www.spymart.com

Sherlock Holmes is their icon, puffing his pipe at the top of the screen. Sponsored by Thrift Marty Discount, the site has a good range of products. Orders over $2,000 must be paid for with a cashier's check or wire transfer. Most items go out within 48 hours, unless they are special orders. Samples:

- Alarmed Briefcase, for transporting valuable items, with siren and 26,000 volts of shock triggered by your remote control
- Comsec Wire Tap Detector, to detect computer hackers, government agencies, and the phone company listening on your line
- Night Vision Binoculars, with infrared illuminator, 4X magnification, 12-degree field of view, rubberized body

**Search:** No
**Photos:** Yes
**Ordering:** Online, Phone, Fax
**Gift Wrap:** No
**Delivery:** Ground

# Spy Products

http://www.spyproducts.com

A spy store with covert cameras, listening probes, microphones, motion detectors, night-vision gear, tracking systems, and wireless surveillance equipment. Allow up to four weeks for delivery. Call for faster shipping. Samples:

- Extension Monitor, to listen in on calls without clicks, volume decreases, or voltage drops
- Home Security Motion Alarm, 2,000 square foot area
- Ninja Throwing Stars, 4.25" with carrying case
- Pencil-eraser size microphone picks up normal conversation at distances of 25 feet

**Search:** No
**Photos:** Yes
**Ordering:** Online, Fax
**Gift Wrap:** No
**Delivery:** Ground

# The Spy Store

http://www.thespystore.com

Surveillance and countersurveillance gear, books, videos, and links. Samples:

- Audio transmitter detector
- Key Mold Kit
- Tactical Assault Rappelling Gloves
- Tom Larsen, *Bench-Tested Circuits for Surveillance and Counter-surveillance Technicians*

**Search:** No
**Photos:** Yes
**Ordering:** Online, Phone, Fax, Email
**Gift Wrap:** No
**Delivery:** Ground, 2nd Day, Overnight

# Spy Supply

http://www.spysupply.com

Good detail about a relatively small collection of unusual or hot items for surveillance and counter-

measures, personal protection, weapons detection, and electronic vehicle tracking. Samples:

- ActionEar™ Sport stereo amplifier with hearing protection, to locate direction of sounds picked up by stereo microphones
- MicroAlert RF/Microwave Bug Detector
- The "X" Phone, calls you whenever it picks up sounds in the area, so you can tell if there are intruders

**Search:** No
**Photos:** Yes
**Ordering:** Online
**Gift Wrap:** No
**Delivery:** Ground

# Spy Tech Agency

http://www.spytechagency.com

With more than 2,000 products, this online store is a spinoff of a private investigative agency. They rent and sell gear for countermeasures, detection, encryption, locksmithing, night vision, optics, security, tracking and video. Samples:

- Global Positioning System Digital Tracking System, with targets, GPS receiver, cellular phone, and base station showing target on electronic map
- Video Camera Detector, to determine if hidden surveillance cameras are being used in a room
- Voice Changing Phone, to switch voice from male to female, adult to child, or back

**Search:** No
**Photos:** Some
**Ordering:** Online, Phone, Fax, Email
**Gift Wrap:** No
**Delivery:** Ground

# You may also want to check out these chapters:

- Consumer Electronics
- Photography
- TV & Video Gear

# Tennis

Tennis used to be the sport of the rich, but no longer. There are tennis courts in public parks all around the country. Little boys and girls can watch endless hours of tennis on TV, whether it be from England during Wimbledon or from New York for the U.S. Open. Tennis is truly an international sport—no language barrier or different rules for different countries. We actually thought we'd find a lot of online stores that met our tough criteria for inclusion in this book, but we were surprised that there really weren't a lot. What we did find, though, were a few wonderful stores that will be able to sell you what you need, except we couldn't find one that offered a cure for tennis elbow.

## Online Sports.com

http://www.onlinesports.com/
pages/top,sprt,tenn.html

Tennis is just one section of this large online sports megacomplex. But they sell so much tennis equipment, clothes, and accessories, we thought to include it in this chapter. If you're into memorabilia, click that button. On the day we browsed through this department we found autographed tennis balls by such greats as Chris Evert, Ivan Lendl, Pete Sampras, and Jimmy Connors. Samples:

- Elbow wraps
- Instructional books and videos
- Locker organizer
- Nets
- Tennis balls
- Wilson tennis racquets

**Search:** Yes

**Photos:** Some
**Ordering:** Online, Phone, Fax
**Gift Wrap:** No
**Delivery:** Ground, 3rd Day, 2nd Day, Overnight

## The Tennis Co.

http://www.tenniscompany.com

You'll find lots of new tennis stuff here, but a nice twist is that you can also buy used tennis equipment at a terrific price. Great if you're just trying out the sport or are looking for some slightly used (or broken in) quality merchandise. Not sure what to buy? Check out their ample reviews written by tennis pros. They also list a big selection of helpful information, such as selecting the correct racquets if you suffer from tennis elbow or how to choose the right string for your racquet. Don't forget to scroll to the bottom of the front page for some terrific bargains. On the day we shopped, we found a $250 Head Big Bang Tennis Racquet going for $90. Samples:

- Air cast elbow brace
- Bags
- Balle de Match clothing for kids
- Competivision sunglasses
- Elbow shock absorber
- Graphite and titanium racquets
- Nike tennis clothes for men and women
- Strings and grips
- Tennis shoes for men and women
- Visors

**Search:** Some
**Photos:** Some
**Ordering:** Online, Phone, Fax
**Gift Wrap:** No
**Delivery:** Ground, 3rd Day, 2nd Day, Overnight

## Tennis Menace

http://www.tennismenace.com

From the state of Georgia comes this Internet pro shop. Some of the items for sale are Tennis Menace exclusives; others are brand-name products that you're very familiar with. They are especially proud of their "Gummi Grip," which is made of surgical-grade silicone rubber. They say it has the most "tacki" surface of any grip available. Racquets are custom strung at no additional charge. Has a great selection of tennis-type gifts, such as tennis key chains and greeting cards. Samples:

- Clothing for men and women
- Cross string protectors
- Custom-strung racquets
- Dry grip and Gummi grip
- Head tape
- New and used ball machines
- Oakley sunglasses
- Sport gels shoe insert
- Tennis bags

**Search:** Some
**Photos:** Some
**Ordering:** Online, Phone, Fax
**Gift Wrap:** No
**Delivery:** Ground, 3rd Day, Overnight

## Tennis Warehouse

http://www.tennis-warehouse.com

A discount tennis store with lots of equipment, clothes, and some accessories. You can also custom-order your racquets by selecting the product, then choosing the grip/head size, string type, and tension. There's a big variety of quality brand names here at rock-bottom prices. If you're looking to save even more money, go to their Bargains and Close-Out section. Samples:

- Grips
- Grommets and bumpers
- Head tape
- Men's and women's shoes and clothing
- Shoulder tote tennis bags
- Titanium racquets
- Vibration dampeners

**Search:** Yes
**Photos:** Yes
**Ordering:** Online, Phone
**Gift Wrap:** No
**Delivery:** Ground, 2nd Day, Overnight

## If you enjoy other sports, you may also want to jump the net to explore these other active chapters:

- Baseball &Softball
- Basketball
- Bicycles
- Boating & Sailing
- Bowling
- Camping & Hiking
- Golf
- Skating
- Soccer
- Sporting Goods

# Toys

This was one of the most enjoyable chapters to write, for obvious reasons. There are many, many online toy stores. You'll be familiar with some of the names, and others will probably be new to you. Read this chapter carefully. We found some real gems that you may never have heard of. There are the mega toy stores that sell a lot of the popular brands, and others that look for those uniquely special toys. We found some that are zany and others that will fire your child's imagination.

Not sure what toy to buy? Why not get advice from the expert—Dr. Toy? Dr. Stevanne Auerbach, better known to millions as Dr. Toy, has graciously allowed us to reprint from her wonderful Web site (www.drtoy.com) the checklist she suggests parents use before buying a toy. You'll find the checklist at the end of this chapter. If you have a baby, you should also check the Baby Stuff chapter. If you're looking to send a present, check to see that they offer gift wrapping.

## A2Z Toys.com

http://www.a2ztoys.com

One of the older of the Web toy stores (it's four years old!) this store carries all of the good stuff, like Brio, Lionel Trains, Playmobil, and offers them for sale at a discount. Now, the emphasis at this toy store is definitely on toy trains and train tracks, but you will find some other items. If your kids (or you) like laying out train tracks, check out their free expansion ideas. Samples:
- Beanie Buddies
- Busytown Brio train vehicles
- Lionel Trains

- Playmobile sets
- Teletubbies

**Search:** Yes
**Photos:** Yes
**Ordering:** Online, Phone, Mail
**Gift Wrap:** No
**Delivery:** Ground, 2nd Day, Overnight

## Access Quality Toys

http://www.accessqualitytoys.com

This toy store is run by parents, toy specialists, and health professionals. They take a special interest in toys that will encourage healthy development in your child. The toys are all sturdy and well-made. They have a wonderful service called Help Me Choose, where you give them your child's age and sex and answer some brief questions and they will bring your question to the appropriate person for an answer. They have a language pathologist and physical therapist on call to answer your questions about helpful toys for children with special needs. Samples:
- Alphabet blocks
- Infant carrier play center
- Knotty dolls
- Magnetic marbles
- My First Clock
- Puzzle Pals
- Soft toddler bolster chair

**Search:** Yes
**Photos:** Yes
**Ordering:** Online, Phone
**Gift Wrap:** Yes
**Delivery:** Ground, 2nd Day, Overnight

## Charlie's Toys

http://mall6.register.com/ontexusa/charlielow.htm

Most of the toys from this store come from China via

Hong Kong. The toys are cute and all are geared toward some sort of development for your child. Most of these toys are not readily available any other place on the Web. Samples:

- Clever math twist
- Electronic matching game
- Farm jingle play musical mat
- Funny animal piano
- Melody sound block
- Musical soft play panel for cribs

**Search:** Yes
**Photos:** Yes
**Ordering:** Online, Phone, Fax
**Gift Wrap:** No
**Delivery:** Ground, 2nd Day, Overnight

## Child's Play

http://www.toysntrains.com

If your kids like trains, this is a great place to shop. Oh, they have some other goodies, but you can tell that the owner has a special fondness for trains. They even offer coloring-book-type drawings of trains that you can print out and give to your child to color. Free shipping on orders over $25. Samples:

- FELTkids
- GeoSafari globe
- Lionel trains
- Brio trains
- Thomas trains
- Playmobile theme playsets
- Robotix starter, core, and motorized sets
- Beanie Babies

**Search:** Yes
**Photos:** Yes
**Ordering:** Online
**Gift Wrap:** No
**Delivery:** Ground, 2nd Day, Overnight

## Cool Toy Shop

http://www.cooltoys.com

Bet you never thought you'd find a store that carries

McDonald's Happy Meal toys, did you? Just another useful service of this book. This place must make its living by buying up batches of cool toys once they've become a little warm. (OK, some of the stuff is real current, but the fun stuff has a touch of nostalgia to it.) If your kids "discovered" *Star Wars* this summer, be sure to check out the extensive section of toys related to this epic serial. Samples:

- Action figures
- Barbie dolls
- Beanie Babies
- Cabbage Patch dolls
- California Raisins
- Character drinking glasses
- Pez dispensers
- Smurfs

**Search:** Yes
**Photos:** Some
**Ordering:** Online, Mail
**Gift Wrap:** No
**Delivery:** 3rd Day, 2nd Day, Overnight

## Copernicus

http://www.1q.com/copernicus

Their motto is "toys and gifts for the imagination," and they really mean it. They also carry a few musical instruments designed for small hands. They send a free gift with every order and there's free shipping on orders over $250. Samples:

- Root beer-making kit
- Finger puppets
- Backward clock
- Notre Dame puzzle
- Solar kit
- Laser pointers
- Small guitar

**Search:** Some
**Photos:** Yes
**Ordering:** Online, phone
**Gift Wrap:** No
**Delivery:** Ground, Overnight

## The Disney Store

`http://store.disney.go.com`

You've probably had to drag your kid out of Disney's brick-and-mortar store in the mall. Now you can browse their aisles in peace. Just about everything you find at their mall store is available on the Web. As an added extra attraction, you can also book your next visit to Disney World from this site. You know the stuff, but we'll give you some samples anyway. Samples:

- Bucket of Bugs
- Classic doll collection
- Disney's Giga Pets
- Little Mermaid felt kit
- Mickey and Minnie plush sleeping bags
- Minnie's 50-piece kitchen play set
- Pooh and Tigger baby boat
- Princess nail kit

**Search:** Yes
**Photos:** Yes
**Ordering:** Online
**Gift Wrap:** Gift box available on some items
**Delivery:** Ground, 4th Day

## eToys

`http://www.etoys.com`

Looking for a toy? How about a store that carries over 500 brand-name playthings? That's eToys, and they have just about every toy you could imagine. Usually when a store offers so much, it takes forever to find just what you're looking for, but eToys has devised several ways for you to search (by brand name, toy category, toy name, etc.) They also carry children's software and video games, but toys are the main attraction. Samples:

- Barbie dolls
- Beanie Babies
- Fisher-Price Briarberry Collection
- Legos
- Playmobile theme sets
- Tiffany-style stained-glass kits
- Victorian doll houses

**Search:** Yes
**Photos:** Yes
**Ordering:** Online, Phone
**Gift Wrap:** Yes
**Delivery:** Ground, 3rd Day, 2nd Day

## FAO Schwarz

`http://st2.yahoo.com/ faoschwarz`

The first thing you'll notice is that this shop has the prettiest home page of all the toy stores, which doesn't surprise us, because their store in New York City always has the most innovative front window of any toy store around. This is the store where Tom Hanks and Robert Loggia danced on a giant keyboard in *Big*. Known for their creative and wondrous toys, this online store won't disappoint you (or your kids, either)! You'll find things here you won't be able to find anyplace else. The prices can be exorbitant (we found a music box for $7,000) for some of their classics. Samples:

- 1929 Santa ornament
- Bank teller
- Blue Ribbon rocking horse
- Dream cuisine kitchen
- Lead soldier collection
- Patsy doll
- Super machine workshop

**Search:** Yes
**Photos:** Yes
**Ordering:** Online
**Gift Wrap:** No
**Delivery:** Ground, 3rd Day

## The Handmade, Homemade Toy Shop

`http://www.crafttoys.com`

Searching for something special? Look no further. This is the place of sturdy, handcrafted toys. Solid wood, porcelain, special fabrics all made by skilled artisans. These toys will still be in use when you become a grandparent. Because each toy is handmade after you place your order, most of them are easy to personalize. Samples:

- Luxurious Victorian doll houses
- Name puzzles
- Ride-on toys
- Rocking Dory boats
- Sailboats
- Wooden trains, planes, and cars

**Search:** Yes
**Photos:** Some
**Ordering:** Online, Phone, Fax
**Gift Wrap:** Yes
**Delivery:** Ground

## KBkids.com

http://www.KBkids.com

A friendly site that is consistently named as one of the best stores for shopping on the Web. Besides all the toys, you'll also be able to pick up video games, musical instruments, and lots of children's software. And don't forget to read their articles by child development experts—something that makes this site stand out. Samples:

- Activity Kids
- Baby Animal Puzzles
- Barbie dolls
- Collectibles
- Pound N Play
- Star Wars–type toys
- Toy trains

**Search:** Yes
**Photos:** Yes
**Ordering:** Online, Phone
**Gift Wrap:** No
**Delivery:** Ground, 2nd Day, Overnight

## National Parenting Center

http://www.tnpc.com

Founded as a parenting information service 10 years ago, this organization has grown steadily to give advice to parents about all sorts of products for children from newborns to elementary-school age kids. All of their products are reviewed by other parents. If you see it for sale, you'll know the item received a "thumbs-up!" They have a nice selection of products for kids and lots of useful information for parents. Samples:

- Audiotapes
- Block toys
- Board games
- Books
- Children's videos
- Educational software
- Electronic games
- Math games and toys

**Search:** Some
**Photos:** Yes
**Ordering:** Online, Mail
**Gift Wrap:** No
**Delivery:** Ground

## Nightmare Factory

http://
www.nightmarefactory.com

You know those stores that pop up around September in the mall that have a ton of Halloween costumes, masks, makeup, and other assorted creepy stuff? Now you don't have to wait for fall. You can shop at this Halloween superstore all year round. Besides all the things you can buy, they also give you tips on setting up a haunted house. Now, we don't want to give you the impression that Halloween costumes are all they offer. You can also get all sorts of other costumes, like an Easter bunny and various biblical costumes. Samples:

- Adult and children *Star Wars* costumes
- Batman and Robin costumes and masks
- Fangs and teeth

- Talosian latex bust
- Various body parts

**Search:** Yes
**Photos:** Yes
**Ordering:** Online, Fax, Phone
**Gift Wrap:** No
**Delivery:** Ground

## Noodle Kidoodle

http://www.noodlekidoodle.com

This is the most colorful toy store on the Web. The artist should win an award for creativity, which fits the site well because this store sells toys that will ignite your child's imagination. Samples:

- Alphabet puzzle mat
- Animal trail
- Barney foam puzzle
- Battery engine train set
- Blue's Clues Playscenes
- Medical kit
- Newborn Noah's Ark
- Sawmill with dumping depot
- Wooden rocking horse

**Search:** Yes
**Photos:** Yes
**Ordering:** Online
**Gift Wrap:** Yes
**Delivery:** Ground, 3rd Day

## Plato's Toybox

http://www.platostoybox.com

What a delightful find! The philosophy of the owners of Plato's Toybox is that it's important to "give your child a fundamental knowledge of the Arts and Humanities and to encourage them to pursue their individual interests." Sound a little different from many toy stores? Well, this one is in a class by itself. Just by looking at the toy categories (Ancient, Build It, Egypt, Knights, Native American, China, Mythology, and many more), you'll see that this store wants to encourage your child to play in a number of innovative

ways. This store also offers teachers and homeschoolers a 10% discount on all their products. Samples:

- American Indian Moccasin kit
- Artwork Lantern
- Clay Bead Jewelry
- Fine Art Game
- Leonardo Construction Company
- Mummy Rummy card game
- Stamp a Story

**Search:** Yes
**Photos:** Yes
**Ordering:** Online, Phone, Fax
**Gift Wrap:** Yes
**Delivery:** Ground

## Red Rocket

http://www.redrocket.com

Easy to find toys because of a wonderful search that lets you look for toys by many different categories, including IQ-building products, toys you wish you had as a kid, and kids' favorites. You'll find many of the popular toys alongside the less well-known, creative ones. Red Rocket also serves as a distributor for Nickelodeon toys (a.k.a. Rugrats). Samples:

- Jewelry making kits
- Phonics bus
- Brain-O-Matic
- Gooey Anatomy
- Crazy Bones starter kit
- Metal detector
- Yo-yos

**Search:** Yes
**Photos:** Yes
**Ordering:** Online, Phone, Fax
**Gift Wrap:** Yes
**Delivery:** Ground, 2nd Day, Overnight

## Top Hat Toys

http://www.tophattoys.com

Oh, wow, did we find the store to supply you with all of your April Fool's Day needs. Can't wait that long?

No problem, if you have a practical joker or magician wannabe in the house. This store is one of those little gems on the Web. Just take a look at some of the items this crazy store sells. Samples:

- Bug guns
- Fake desert tarantula
- Fake puke
- Fake tattoos
- Gooey eyeballs
- Magic Chinese rings
- Magic sets
- Stink bomb
- X-ray glasses

**Search:** Yes
**Photos:** Detailed drawings
**Ordering:** Online, Fax, Mail
**Gift Wrap:** No
**Delivery:** Ground

# Toysmart.com

www.toysmart.net

You might remember Holt Educational Outlet. Well, Holt didn't like that name for the Web and changed it this year to Toysmart.com. They still sell the same reliable toys for your children. If you're looking for more info about the toys that you're thinking of purchasing, read their articles. Don't forget to click the "Free" button. Sometimes you can get lucky and get something really good. One day when we shopped here they were offering a free gift from K'NEX. Samples:

- Flower garden starter set
- Playmobile police helicopter
- Rokenbok basic start/power chutes
- Software
- Solar-power model set
- Stuffed animals

**Search:** Yes
**Photos:** Yes
**Ordering:** Online
**Gift Wrap:** No
**Delivery:** Ground, 2nd Day, Overnight

# Toys R Us

http://toysrus.com

Remember when you first saw their store many years ago.? Didn't you think that someone should have told them that the "R" was on backward? They took that backward "R" and turned it into a toy empire. Today, many of the toys you can find in their superstores are available on the Web. Their search, unfortunately, is surprisingly limited. Samples:

- Action figures
- Baby registry
- Barbie dolls
- Blues Clues notebook
- Bubble mower
- Ride-on toys
- Video games

**Search:** Yes
**Photos:** Yes
**Ordering:** Online, Phone
**Gift Wrap:** Yes
**Delivery:** Ground, 3rd Day, 2nd Day

# Ask Dr. Toy!

Dr. Stevanne Auerbach, better known as Dr. Toy, is the founder of the innovative San Francisco International Toy Museum. As a child psychologist and former teacher, she lectures about play, gives parenting workshops, and is a consultant. Author of 14 books and syndicated King Features columnist, her latest book, *Dr. Toy's Smart Play: How to Raise a Child with a High P.Q. (Play Quotient),* is from St. Martin's Press. Dr. Toy is no stranger to Web shopping. Her Web site was first on the Web to review toy products. Dr. Toy is interviewed frequently in newspapers, on TV, and on radio shows. She's also been the toy expert on The Home Shopping Network. Dr. Toy says, "Shopping on the Web is a wonderful and convenient way to locate that perfect toy. Look over my list to discover how to select a good toy or product for your child." If you'd like to get more pearls of wisdom from Dr. Toy, go to her Web site at http://www.drtoy.com, which is where this list is reprinted from, and check out the more than 1,000 products she has reviewed.

## How to pick a good toy or product for your child

As you examine any potential children's product, before you purchase it, ask yourself the following questions:

1. **Is the product appropriate now?** Does the product fit the child's age, skills, and abilities? Will it hold the child's interests?

2. **Is the toy /product well-designed?** Is it safe? Are there any potential hazards such as sharp edges, parts that can be swallowed, or loose ties? Is it nontoxic? Does it meet Consumer Product Safety Standards? How durable is it? Will it take rough treatment? Is there a guarantee on the product?

3. **Is the toy or product appealing?** Is it something the child will enjoy using for a long time? Does it have long-lasting play value? Does it have versatility?

4. **Does the toy offer an opportunity to stimulate creativity?** The right products in arts, crafts, hobbies, language, reading, music, movement, and drama can help to expand the child's imagination, thinking, and comprehension.

5. **Does the toy match the package and the package match the toy?** If the toy does not match ads or package it can be disappointing. Is age grading clear?

6. **Will the product teach?** Does it help expand positive self-esteem, values, understanding, cultural awareness? Does it help encourage the growth of self-esteem, values, or cultural values and offer practice in skills, eye-hand coordination, or fine and large motor skills? Does the product help teach communication skills? Does it expand understanding of the environment, the community and world? Does it teach or practice computer skills?

7. **Is the toy affordable?** Does the price match the value received?

8. **Will the product frustrate or challenge the child?** Does the product offer an opportunity to think, learn something new, practice or try something that will be beneficial? Or will it be too difficult for the child to use? However, the product may be perfect for doing an activity, a construction project, a craft, a hobby, or for playing a game.

Having fun together as a family is an important part of the child's play experiences.

9. **Will the toy help to nurture childhood?** Can children use the product by themselves? Will it help them gain independent skills? Does the product help the child express emotions, experience care and concern for others, practice positive social interaction? Is there any violence, sexism, or negative aspect to the product?

10. **Is the toy fun?** Most important, will the child enjoy using the product? Will it make him or her laugh? Relax? Feel good? Play is after all a time to have fun. Learning is a lot easier and is more enduring if it's fun!

—Dr. Stevanne Auerbach

# You may also want to play with these chapters:

- Party Supplies
- School Supplies
- Software for Kids

# Travel Adventures

Adventures take you beyond the tourist sites, buses, and must-see cathedrals. You get to chat with a farmer, swim in a back-jungle pool, herd some reindeer. If you've already done the one-weekend tour thing, or covered ten countries in ten days, perhaps you'd like to try getting closer to the scenery, with a tour set up to take you walking, snorkeling, or horseback riding through some of the most amazing mountains, fields, and islands on earth, as well as the back alleys of ancient towns. Having a guide means you don't waste time on detours, get lost, or end up hurt in a ditch, but on these trips, the guide is a participant and buddy, not just a voice at the front of the bus. Perhaps because of their history of setting up individual tours, many companies that set up adventure trips content themselves with putting up brochures on the Web, because, if you want to take one of their trips, they prefer to talk to you on the phone. But if you really want to book an adventure over the Web, here are the best places to get you trekking immediately.

## Backroads

http://www.backroads.com

You can't just take off. First you have to plan and make reservations. That said, this site gives you plenty of choices for your next adventure journey, bicycling, hiking, walking, or playing various sports in 35 countries. You can stay at an inn or sleep out under the stars, sip wine or stare at the beach, travel solo, with companions, or with your whole family. You even get to set some limits on the physical effort involved. Each trip starts in a town accessible by plane, train, or bus, and you can book van or bus transfers from these spots

to the meeting place for the trip. You receive a detailed packet in the mail, describing your trip. Discounts for kids. They also offer a Travelgrams Gallery, with luscious photos of destinations you might want to persuade someone else to visit with you; you just email them with the picture. Sample adventures:

- Biking in Bali, staying in luxury inns
- Canoeing, snorkeling, swimming, and hiking through the Belize rain forest and beaches, staying in local cottages among pine trees and orchids
- Easy walking tour of Victoria Falls and Okavango Delta, with luxury hotels and rooms formed from cave walls and thatched roofs
- Hiking through Katmandu and the Himalayan mountains, staying in tents and the Yak and Yeti Hotel, an 18th century palace

**Search:** Yes
**Photos:** Yes
**Ordering:** Online, Phone
**Gift Wrap:** No
**Delivery:** Ground

## Calypso

http://www.calypsotours.com

If you've ever wanted to visit Costa Rica with its 36 microclimates, waterfalls, mountains, hot springs, volcanoes, and rain forests, this company can help you. They offer a virtual reality tour to tempt you, showing Tortuga Island, the jungle, and the Panama islands. You can ride horseback, do mountain biking, go golfing. The site helps you book the tour, hotel, and car. Lots of great background on Costa Rica's history, art, geography, too. Samples:

- Astronomy cruise, in phosphorescent Pacific Ocean waters in the Gulf of Nicoya, stargazing from giant trampolines between the bows of the yacht
- Cruise to Punta Coral Private Reserve, a dry tropical forest with a beach, walking nature trails, exploring with sea kayak or just swimming
- Survival School run by U.S. Special Forces vets, with wilderness first aid, water operations, rope management
- Tour through the forest canopy, literally swinging

from tree to tree, platform to platform, on pulleys and cables

**Search:** No
**Photos:** Yes
**Ordering:** Online, Phone
**Gift Wrap:** No
**Delivery:** Ground

## Country Walkers

http://www.countrywalkers.com

If you like soaking up a place, step by step, up close, you may want to take advantage of the walking tours organized by this Vermont company. With 20 years' experience in preparing walking tours in Asia, Africa, Canada, Central and South America, Europe, the South Pacific, and the U.S., these folks seem sensitive to people's needs, probing, gently, to find out, really, how far you can walk on level ground, or hills, what your allergies are, what physical limitations you face, and what size T-shirt you wear. Nicely detailed descriptions of what you will see and do. The schedule shows you when the tours are available. They introduce you to some of the guides, report stories from other participants, and bring you news about, well, walking. Samples:

- 6-day tour of Bryce Canyon and Zion National Park
- 8-day walking tour of Granada, visiting the palaces of the Alhambra, the fortifications of the Alcazaba, and the gardens of the Generalife, as well as surrounding villages for a swim and a glass of local wine with tapas, a snack made out of olives, almonds, and ham
- 11-day trek through New Zealand's South Island, staying at wilderness lodges, lake- and glacier-side hotels, with lunches at vineyards

**Search:** No
**Photos:** Yes
**Ordering:** Online, Phone
**Gift Wrap:** No
**Delivery:** Ground

## Equitour

http://www.ridingtours.com

If you want to go back to the basics, riding horseback through new scenery, this company has put together more than 100 riding adventures, from cattle round-ups in the Rockies to jumping instruction in England and dressage training in Portugal. To make sure the adventure fits your experience, they ask questions about the number of trail rides you take each month, what instruction you regularly get in jumping, dressage, flatwork, hunting, or Western, and ask you to rate your ability from beginner to advanced ("An independent seat, soft hand, and capable of handling a spirited horse"). Samples:

- 6-day ride through farmland and lava fields in Iceland, bathing at hot water pools, nights in huts
- 8-day ride across Wales, starting at Cwmfforest Farm, going across the Black Mountains to the coast, then along the River Wye, and back
- 10-day Egyptian ride on Arabians between the Nile and the desert, past the pyramids, temples, and the Sphinx, staying in Bedouin camps
- 19-day tour of Mongolia, riding Mongolian ponies six or seven hours a day at a moderate to fast pace with the reindeer tribes, visiting nomads, fishing, birding, and walking

**Search:** No
**Photos:** Yes
**Ordering:** Online, Phone
**Gift Wrap:** No
**Delivery:** Ground

## Europe Express

http://www.europeexpress.com

If you want to get out of the tour bus, these folks will help you walk, bike, or barge across Europe. Many of the barge tours are expensive, but they offer inexpensive biking and walking tours, as well as car rental, hotel reservations, and more conventional sightseeing tours, with or without airfare. Samples:

- Half-day sightseeing tour of Copenhagen, visiting canals, gardens, museums

- 6–night cruise on 6-passenger barge with outdoor heated pool, with shore excursions in private minivan, visiting Paris, Chantilly, and Monet's home in Giverny
- 6 nights on the Chanterelles, a 24-passenger hotel barge cruising along canals paralleling the Loire, through castles, vineyards, and medieval towns, 3 nights in Paris
- 8-day guided biking tour along the Danube, visiting Austria, the Czech Republic, Hungary, and Slovakia, traveling 6–8 hours a day, in daily distances of 28 to 40 miles

**Search:** Yes
**Photos:** Yes
**Ordering:** Online, Fax
**Gift Wrap:** No
**Delivery:** Ground

# Grand European Tours

http://www.getours.com

They emphasize leisure here. You start with a table full of tours, showing the days and prices. Generally, they take care of your round-trip airfare, first-class hotels, and meals, including tips, baggage handling, and a tour director. The prices are very reasonable for most of these tours, and they offer additional discounts based on date of departure. Samples:

- 10-day cruise through Greek islands, outside cabin, visiting Athens, Mycenae, Epidaurus, Patmos, Rhodes, Mykonos, Santorini, and Heraklion
- 14-day river cruise from Heidelberg through Luxembourg to Belgium and Holland
- 16-day grand tour of France by motor coach, visiting Notre Dame, Versailles, Papal Palace at Avignon, Roman aqueduct at Pont du Gard, Nimes, French Riviera, medieval Carcassonne, Loire vineyards, Mont St. Michel, Normandy beaches, Chartres Cathedral

**Search:** Yes
**Photos:** Yes
**Ordering:** Online, Phone
**Gift Wrap:** No
**Delivery:** Ground

# Hawaii Helicopters

http://hawaiiheli.com

Want to fly through a rainbow or over a volcano? Wearing Bose noise-canceling headsets, you can tour the Big Island, Kauai, or Maui. If booked more than a week in advance, you get a 15% discount. Samples:

- Tour of Hawaii
- Tour of Kauai
- Tour of Maui

**Search:** No
**Photos:** Yes
**Ordering:** Online, Phone, Fax
**Gift Wrap:** No
**Delivery:** Online

# You may also want to explore these chapters:

- Travel Planning & Reservations
- Travel Supplies & Luggage

# Travel Planning & Reservations

If you have a favorite airline, car rental agency, or hotel chain, you can usually use their Web site to make reservations. But if you would like help putting together air, car, cruise, and hotel reservations to make a trip, particularly to a destination you've never visited before, you may want to visit sites that allow you to explore all kinds of places, pick a particular kind of travel, develop a complete itinerary, then make all the reservations. These full-reservation sites act the way a travel agent does, but a lot faster. Of course, not being human, they can't give you personal tips, but they often load you up with travel articles, books, maps, weather guides, and pictures. You'll also get a direct path to discounts, on many sites, whereas a regular airline, hotel chain, or car rental agency tends to downplay or hide such bargains.

## 1Travel

http://www.1travel.com

A full reservation system that lets you zero in on exactly the kind of travel you like. For instance, right off, you can pick a specific type of travel you are interested in (Alaska cruises, car rentals, discount cruises, discount air, escorted tours, Europe cruises, first-class travel, luxury cruises, river cruises, small ships, theme cruises, train, tropical cruises). You can similarly pinpoint choices for lodging, destinations, and sports vacations. But our favorite menu offers ads and links for specialty trips (archaeology, casinos, conferences, couples, culture, discount, Disney, family vacations, gay travel, group travel, historical tours, honeymoons, language study, millennium, nature,

New Age, retreats, senior citizens, singles, student, theater, weddings, wineries, women, yachting, and youth camps). We like their airline savings tool kit, with tips about using alternate airports because of their low-fare airlines ("Drive a Little"). They work with so-called consolidators, who pull together low airfares, discount hotel listings, and other bargains. Plus, they have comedy cards you can send someone, for no particular reason. Phone support is available during business hours in Central Time. Samples:

- Currency exchange
- Full reservations for air, car, cruise, hotel, and tour, with electronic tickets where available
- Travel protection
- Weather news

**Search:** Yes
**Photos:** Yes
**Ordering:** Online, Phone
**Gift Wrap:** No
**Delivery:** 2nd Day, Overnight

## 10,000 Vacation Rentals

http://www.10kvacationrentals.com

If you would like to go somewhere and settle into an apartment, cottage, studio, or villa so you can get to know a locale in depth, this site lets you search through a ton of listings. You can't make reservations here. You get a description, phone number, fax number, and email address. Prices vary with luxury, but most are better than any nearby hotels. Sometimes there is a link to the owner's Web page. Depending on the owner, you may get confirmation of your reservation by mail, phone, fax, or email. Samples:

- 10th-floor Rio de Janeiro condo with two bedrooms, two baths, views of the water, near Copacabana Strip, with daily maid service, ceiling fans
- 300 farmhouses, cottages, manor houses, and villas throughout France
- Modern, refurbished apartment in downtown Budapest for short- or long-term stay

**Search:** No
**Photos:** Some

**Ordering**: Phone, Email
**Gift Wrap**: No
**Delivery**: Varies depending on owner

## Air Travel Manager

`http://www.airtm.com`

If you're really serious about getting into the data, this downloadable software goes out over the Internet to gather as many as 80 flights on one screen, so you can book a typical round trip in less than five minutes. You can also reserve rental cars and hotels via this program. Because AirTM is not owned by an airline, you see all competing airlines, even Southwest (blacked out by other airlines' systems), with prices matched to individual flights, so you have more control than in some systems that just show a total price tag. Searches take about a minute, depending on your connection. You can sort the results of your searches in several ways at once (price, total time, airline). The system also points out where the flights stop en route, so you can avoid bad connections and surprises. You can manage as many as five legs on a trip, with up to 20 different flights. You can also query and reserve rooms at about 28,000 individual hotels, with 100 hotels on a screen at a time, if you want. Samples:

- Booking of air, car, and hotel
- Complex searches on airfares
- Electronic tickets where available

**Search**: Yes
**Photos**: No
**Ordering**: Online
**Gift Wrap**: No
**Delivery**: Download

## Best Fares

`http://www.bestfares.com`

So you just want to get a bargain and go right away? Built around Tom Parson's magazine on discount travel, this site displays a great collection of bargains, many of which are immediately available, which is great if you want to take off in the next few days. We

like their offer to collect complaints about the airlines, and their bulldog approach to passenger rights. For many of the bargains, you have to become a member (for a $60 subscription to the magazine), but you certainly save that on the first ticket you order. Samples:

- 50% off hotel rooms in 2,100 hotels
- $125 discount on round trip tickets around the world
- *Best Fares Discount Travel Magazine*

**Search**: Yes
**Photos**: No
**Ordering**: Online, Phone
**Gift Wrap**: No
**Delivery**: Online, Ground

## Biztravel

`http://www.biztravel.com`

Set up with business travelers in mind, this site is so neat and efficient you may want to use it for vacations and family visits, too. Completing the profile lets you take advantage of their ability to book you into hotels, airlines, cars, and events that give you frequent-flyer miles, bonuses, or automatic upgrades. They're set up to help you plan everything for a trip, but you can skip the airplane, car, or hotel, if you wish. You can pick seats, or they will help you get the kind of seat you said you like when you completed your profile. If you complete your ticket purchase before 6 P.M. on a business day, your tickets should arrive the next business day; after 6 P.M. they'll take another day; weekends, then the tickets arrive Tuesday. They notify you when you get a chance to upgrade, they send you flight status updates on your pager, and they keep track of your points and miles (at least the ones booked through them), so you know how close you are getting to a free flight, or stay, somewhere. Their magazine offers technical and tactical tips, lost baggage solutions, and sleep strategies. Through partners, they let you set up tours, cruises, and do-it-yourself vacations. Good detail even on foreign hotels. For some major cities, you can get info on hotels, restaurants, airports (with diagrams), business services, weather, and driving directions, as well as comments from other users. But the amount of info varies enormously. For instance, from their description of Honolulu, you might think the city extends from one side of Oahu to the other, lacks hotels and restaurants, and offers no way to drive from City Hall to the airport. (Amsterdam, on the other hand, has lush detail.) Sample services:

- Complete travel planning and reservations
- Electronic airline tickets on selected airlines and routes
- Tracking frequent-flyer miles

**Search:** Yes
**Photos:** Yes
**Ordering:** Online
**Gift Wrap:** No
**Delivery:** 2nd Day, Overnight

# Carnival

http://www.carnival.com

"Every evening's a guaranteed good time!" (They include a real guarantee on their site.) So now the biggest cruise line is also the first to offer its own online booking over the Web. You can pick a cruise by port of call, ship, day of the week. For each cruise you get a paragraph blurb, a photo of the destinations, and a dreamy image of the ship itself. The site also spells out all the fun, fun, fun things you can do (family fun, fun ship weddings, fun dining, parties, shows, spas, and so on). Having been on several cruises on other lines, we found these descriptions somewhat fluffy, but what the heck. They do show diagrams of the ships. You can make the reservation yourself, and credit your local travel agent, if you want some human backup. Samples:

- One-week cruise from New Orleans to Jamaica, Grand Cayman, and the Yucatán
- 5-day cruise from New York to Nova Scotia and St. John

**Search:** Yes
**Photos:** Yes
**Ordering:** Online, Phone
**Gift Wrap:** No
**Delivery:** Ground

# Cheap Tickets

http://www.cheaptickets.com

Nice focus: discount air tickets on regularly scheduled flights out of major airports on major airlines. Visit the Specials page for a preview of the discounts. Yes, you have to build your profile and credit card information ahead of time, but once you do, you get free access, so you can look through the database for discount fares, then book the flights. Nice touch: Next to the form you can see a calendar right on screen. You see a list of fares, with a button taking you to the specific regulations that apply, and a chance to check on availability. The best discounts were definitely hundreds of dollars below the fares we found elsewhere, although the complete list of suggested fares also included a lot of fares that don't qualify as discounts in our view. (Just skip the last items on the list.) Tickets may take five business days to arrive. Samples:

- Discount airfares
- Discount hotels

**Search:** Yes
**Photos:** No
**Ordering:** Online, Phone
**Gift Wrap:** No
**Delivery:** Ground

# Expedia

http://expedia.msn.com

Microsoft's entry into the travel-planning world works well. You can book a flight, reserve a room, rent a car, pick vacation and cruise packages, explore resorts, look for travel that caters to a sport or activity you like, even pick out casinos. The site offers rich pictures of destinations, with postcards you can make up (using half a million pictures in the Corbis Picture Experience, another Microsoft store), best places, and tours. The depth of information about some destinations is ten times what you find elsewhere, and so well-organized you don't feel overwhelmed. We discovered new attractions in places we know well, using these city guides. Nice touch: You can move the map around to see more. There's a whole section of deals, with more items than in most online agencies. Interactive maps help you find a famous site, or just an address, and figure out how to drive there. In addition to the prepared material, the site offers very carefully organized chat sessions, so you can focus on a particular destination or issue (what is it like to tour with seniors?). Sample services:

- Complete reservation services
- Fare Compare, to find lowest published fares, with the airlines' own rules for each one
- Saved Itineraries, from previously purchased, reserved, or planned trips
- Travel news
- Up-to-the-minute flight info on arrivals and departures

**Search**: Yes
**Photos**: Yes
**Ordering**: Online
**Gift Wrap**: No
**Delivery**: Ground

## Hotel Discounts

http://www.hoteldiscounts.com

Just hotels, and just discounts, but the deals are excellent, with some going as low as a third of regular rates. The Hotel Reservations Network buys up hundreds of thousands of rooms every year, in 16 major cities in the U.S., and 11 more around the world, so you may be able to find a room through this service, even when the hotels are saying they are sold out. For each hotel with discounted rooms on the dates you want, you get information, a good map, and a button that lets you book immediately. As soon as you make the reservation, you are charged, which means you freeze the discount in but pay ahead of time. At checkout, you owe the hotel only for incidental room charges, and you have saved a lot. You do not have to pay the site any membership fee, and there are no minimum-night stays required. Samples:

- Free Hot Deals newsletter
- Frequent flyer miles for a stay of at least three nights
- Rooms for shopping weekends, Jazzfest in New Orleans, Cherry Blossom Festival in Washington

**Search**: Yes
**Photos**: Yes
**Ordering**: Online, Phone
**Gift Wrap**: No
**Delivery**: Ground

## Intellicast

http://www.intellicast.com

If you're traveling to one of hundreds of cities around the world, or just going out to the country for a day, this site gives you the weather forecast and travel tips. If you just want to get ski reports, golf course news, sailing forecasts, or tropical temperatures, you can get a whole bunch of information all collected for quick comparison. We particularly like the maps; for instance, the SKIcast shows forecasted snowfall, windchill, 24-hour temperature changes, snowstorm tracking, snow cover, and areas of sun and clouds, where you may need your sunglasses or lights. Their shops offer survival tools, weather instruments, books, and videos. Samples:

- Desktop weather radio, to keep you informed if there is a severe weather alert in your area
- Hurricane tracking charts
- Kestral Hand-Held Anemometer
- Sunlit World Globe, with lightbulb inside, showing which part of the world is in sunlight, mounted on oak stand, motorized to rotate

**Search**: No
**Photos**: Yes
**Ordering**: Online
**Gift Wrap**: Card
**Delivery**: Ground, 2nd Day

## Internet Travel Network

http://www.itn.com

This is a network of 3,000 travel agencies, so you can make complete travel reservations here, or with one of those partners. The first time you use their service, you fill out a profile, which takes 10minutes or so, but then you can rely on their having the information in the future, to help decide what kind of seats you like on an airplane, whether you want a nonsmoking room in a hotel, or which rental car company you like best. You can book flights, cars, hotels, and some complete vacations (just name a destination, and they list a handful of medium-priced packages handled by a few major airlines), including cruises. Our first searches for round trips often came up with expensive, out-of-the-way routes, but when we pressed for more, the system settled down and handed us much more reasonable routes and fares. The layout is clear, and you can easily pick the trips you like. The Great Deals area puts you in touch with hotel discounts (pretty good, in the areas we are familiar with), classified ads, and the Amazon travel bookstore. For info on 4,000 possible destinations, you can read material from the Rough Guide series, with quick takes on dining, lodging, museums, tickets, and the scene. Sample services:

- Electronic tickets to airlines
- Email alerting you about low fares
- Hotel Discounts in 18 major cities, with maps and information
- Low Fare Ticker (Java applet that shows you the lowest fares from your hometown to just about everywhere)
- World Clock, to find out what time it is anywhere on the planet

**Search:** Yes
**Photos:** Yes
**Ordering:** Online, Phone
**Gift Wrap:** No
**Delivery:** Online, Ground, 3rd Day

## Preview

http://
previewtravel.lycos.com

A good service for making reservations, and learning about your destination. Their Farefinder gives you a summary of the lowest fares to major cities. Carfinder spots low car rental rates at world airports. For best service, you fill out a detailed form spelling out your preferences (you have 10 airplane meal choices, for instance). Once you fill out this long form, you can have Preview help you plan an itinerary, reserving

airline seats, hotel rooms, and car rentals. (Southwest Airlines, which is the low-fare leader in our area, refuses to participate in the database behind most of these online travel agencies, so we ended up with higher fares than necessary, on the recommended air itineraries.) If you ask for more possibilities, you get quite a variety, some of which are very indirect (flying east for a thousand miles in order to go back three thousand miles to the west), but the layout is clear, and attractive, and you can choose easily. Interesting extra: You get to see the flight's on-time statistics, some of which can be downright discouraging. Destination guides (based on Fodor's guides) make planning your visit a lot of fun with pictures, maps, videos, and advice about arriving (where is the taxi stand at the airport?) and departing, converting currency, and attractions to take in. There's lot of news about specials, discounts, and possible strikes, too. Sample services:

- Airplane reservations
- Car reservations
- Destination planning
- Hotel reservations
- Travel news wire

**Search:** Yes
**Photos:** Yes
**Ordering:** Online, Phone
**Gift Wrap:** No
**Delivery:** Online, Ground, 3rd Day

## The Trip

http://www.thetrip.com

If you don't want to be distracted by attractive pictures, deals, and tidbits of information, this rather austere site can help you look up prices, book air, car, and hotel reservations, and get news and advice about traveling. The reservation system works very quickly, and we liked the tips on angling for lower fares. Because an average day sees more than 100,000 price changes go into the Apollo system, which lies behind The Trip, you may want to try again later, perhaps using different criteria, if you don't like your first set of fares. For major cities and countries, you get reasonable guidebook info, dealing with sightseeing, shopping, transportation, and weather, as well as eating out. The basics are here, without photos or flare. Their magazine, though, has interesting, personal stories about common problems like heaving laptops onto airplanes, taking advantage of frequent-flyer programs, and getting bumped. Chat sessions follow the themes of the magazine, and postings collect travelers' tales, tips, and cautions about particular cities. Samples:

- Car Planner
- *Complete Traveler* magazine
- Flight Planner, with electronic tickets where possible
- Flight tracking
- Hotel Planner
- Trip Planner

**Search:** Yes
**Photos:** No
**Ordering:** Online
**Gift Wrap:** No
**Delivery:** Ground, 2$^{nd}$ Day

## Travel Now

http://www.travelnow.com

In four years, this online site claims to have served more than 6 million travelers making air, car, and hotel reservations through some 30,000 hotels in 5,000 cities and 140 countries. They offer discounts up to 65% on more than 700 hotels in most cities, and up to 40% on more than 7,000 hotels around the world. (Look for the red star, indicating a discounted hotel.) In looking up airfare, you get to choose among several possible itineraries, and then they run off to see if they can do better. They always do. The rates are within a few dollars of other low fares on other sites. Because Travel Now receives commissions from the car rental agencies, hotels, and airlines, you do not have to pay any of their overhead. On business days, you can always deal with a live agent if you wish. Samples:

- Air travel booking
- Car rental
- Hotel reservations

**Search:** Yes
**Photos:** Few
**Ordering:** Online

**Gift Wrap:** No
**Delivery:** Overnight

## Travelocity

http://www.travelocity.com

A full reservation system for air, car, cruise, and hotel, with news, destination descriptions, and special deals. Their layout emphasizes speed. Using the Sabre reservation system, they help you make plans and purchase trips online, but you can pick up tickets from your local travel agency if it is part of Sabre. If you depart more than two weeks from the day you make the reservation, you get tickets by mail; if you depart sooner, you get them by FedEx overnight. Samples:

- Access to discounted fares through outside consolidators at Cheap Tickets
- Currency converter
- Fare Watcher emails
- Flight paging (with updates on your pager)
- Full reservation of cars, cruises, hotels, with electronic tickets where available
- Newsletter subscription
- Travel agency locator
- Travel books

**Search:** Yes
**Photos:** A few
**Ordering:** Online, Phone
**Gift Wrap:** No
**Delivery:** Ground, Overnight

## TravelWeb

http://www.travelweb.com

A friendly, well-organized site with an informal feel because of the hand-drawn sketches they use for menu items. They pull together links from all over the Web. The hotel search lets you limit the results to hotels that take online reservations. For each hotel you get the blurb and the photo, a local map (pretty good), a pop-up weather forecast from Weather.com, and a chance to make reservations (which are usually confirmed within 10 seconds). Airline booking goes through

Microsoft's Expedia. Samples:
- Discount hotels
- Hotel reservations
- Links to Expedia for air reservations

**Search:** Yes
**Photos:** Yes
**Ordering:** Online, Phone
**Gift Wrap:** No
**Delivery:** Ground

## Uniglobe

http://www.uniglobe.com

Built on more than 1,000 retail travel agencies around the world, Uniglobe lets you order online, while giving credit to the local agent, if you wish, so they are not stepping on any toes. You can plan your trip, and book reservations for air, cruise, hotel, cars, using their reservation system, which you can fine-tune using the optional profile of your preferences. Their database comes up with a good range of reasonable fares for complex trips. They work with a lot of partners, featured in their Travel Mall, so there are lots of outgoing links to extra services. They carry some news on savings, tips about cruises, and the latest bargains. If you want to find out a lot about a destination, though, you'll need to go elsewhere; Uniglobe includes marketing stuff about their hotel packages, but they cover only a dozen destinations, with text and photos from veteran travel writer Lee Foster. Hey, if you want books, they list some you can buy at Amazon. Sample services:
- Cruise planning by season
- Currency converter
- Driving directions
- Getaway suggestions at off-season resorts
- Planning and reservations for air, car, hotel, and cruise
- Weather around the world

**Search:** Yes
**Photos:** Yes
**Ordering:** Online, Phone
**Gift Wrap:** No
**Delivery:** Online, Ground

## Weather Channel

http://www.weather.com

The cable-TV channel helps you predict driving conditions for major cities and interstates. You click a road and get forecasts for your trip. Wonder if you'll be hitting fog, wind, or storms? They have maps of your route, showing 18-hour and 36-hour forecasts. For every spot in the U.S., the site gives you the day's weather, with maps showing radar, rain, snow, and thunderstorms, plus forecasts morning, noon, and night. They help you predict weather wherever you are traveling, going to the country, a big sports event, or the seashore. They will deliver your personalized weather info to your PCS phone or pager. And when you are on the road, you can call them for current conditions, severe storm reports, forecasts for boat and beaches, and driving (at 95 cents a minute). Their store offers amusing gear with some vague relationship to weather. Samples:
- Battery-Heated Gloves
- Lightning Tie
- Parkway Car Thermometer
- Storm Chaser Cap
- Traveler Overshoes, with high-traction soles, waterproof fabric, Velcro closure

**Search:** No
**Photos:** Yes
**Ordering:** Online
**Gift Wrap:** Yes
**Delivery:** Ground, 3rd Day

## For even more preparation for traveling, take a tour of these chapters:

- Travel Adventures
- Travel Supplies & Luggage

# Travel Supplies & Luggage

The more we travel, the more attention we pay to what we pack. Lightweight, washable clothes begin to seem more attractive; we become interested in extra pockets; we wonder how to keep our belongings from sliding together into a jumble at the bottom of a duffel bag. We long for neat, tight organizers, luggage without hassles, and little kits crammed with tiny versions of necessities like scissors and tweezers. In that mood, we recommend the best Web shops specializing in travel supplies.

## Easy Going

http://www.easygoing.com

A wonderful store we used to visit in Berkeley, California, now online. They have neat stuff to make your trip easier, books, and links to useful sites with information about passports, currency, and advice. The staff votes certain products the Flying Suitcase Award, and emails you with advice on particular electric adapters you have questions about. Sample products:

- EarPlanes, ear plugs that regulate air pressure to fend off pain while flying
- Flexi-Flask, insulated, collapsible water bottle for wine, coffee, or water, can be boiled or frozen
- Passport carrier, strap, steel cable
- Shortwave radio with antenna, world time for 24 international cities, alarm, headphones, pouch
- *The Packing Book,* by co-founder of the store, Judy Gilford

**Search:** Yes
**Photos:** Yes
**Ordering:** Online, Phone
**Gift Wrap:** Yes
**Delivery:** Ground

## Luggage Express

http://www1.luggagexpress.com

Fine new luggage at a discount, with free shipping and handling. This is an Internet-only store reselling lots of models from American Tourister, Lark, and Samsonite luggage, so they have no warehousing costs. Prices are excellent. Orders go out within a week; you pay for shipping only if you want a fast delivery. Samples:

- American Tourister 500 Series, Cadence 2 attachable carry-on in navy nylon, zipper, four wheels
- Samsonite 550 Series Ultralite 3 hardside carry-on upright suit bag in black, with wheels

**Search:** No
**Photos:** Yes
**Ordering:** Online
**Gift Wrap:** No
**Delivery:** Ground, 2nd Day, Overnight

## Magellan's

http://www.magellans.com

A wonderful source of travel supplies, including lots you never knew you had to have. To judge from the elegance and practicality of these items, the store owners have done a lot of traveling on their own. One example: They help you figure out what voltage your destination country uses, and therefore which telephone and electric adaptors you need. They ship within 24 hours of your order. Order before 2 P.M. Pacific Time to get fast delivery. Samples:

- 230-volt water distiller
- Complete medical kit for traveler (not just a backpacker)
- Glowpoint pen, supplies its own light
- Lightweight, wrinkle-resistant, machine-washable, two-sided jacket with numerous pockets, including a hidden zippered security pocket inside another pocket
- Mosquito hat
- Nongrounding plug for adapting polarized plug to nonpolarized socket in Central Pacific

- Pack Mate to compress bulky items like sweaters, by squeezing them into a special laminated plastic bag, then sucking the excess air out (not so good for clothes that wrinkle easily)

**Search:** Yes
**Photos:** Yes
**Ordering:** Online, Phone, Fax
**Gift Wrap:** No
**Delivery:** Ground, 2$^{nd}$ Day, Overnight

- Laptop computer case with built-in bumpers, aluminum frame, foam insert, factory direct
- Light-weight garment bags with central zipper, nylon fabric, two pockets, navy

**Search:** No
**Photos:** Yes
**Ordering:** Online, Phone, Fax, Email
**Gift Wrap:** No
**Delivery:** Ground, 3$^{rd}$ Day, 2$^{nd}$ Day, Overnight

## Medport

http://www.medportinc.com

If you have to take medicine along with you, this site will help you pack it safely, so you don't end up at midnight in a strange city wondering how to get a refill. Samples:

- Diabetic's wallet, insulated, rigid case carrying four predrawn syringes, monitor, refreezable ice pack, fits in pocketbook
- Fold-away CarryPak to hang on walker or wheelchair during travel, with pockets for glasses, beverages, personal items
- Inhaler case with clip to attach to belt
- Medicine reminder, contains pills, beeps when you need to take them
- Medtraveler, a kit for organizing and carrying temperature-sensitive medicines, with waterproof compartment, clear zippered pocket, and open storage area, forest-green

**Search:** Yes
**Photos:** Yes
**Ordering:** Online, Phone, Fax, Email
**Gift Wrap:** No
**Delivery:** Ground

## SunFun

http://www.sunfun.com

They emphasize their second syllable, with bright icons, nice pictures, and gear for traveling out in the sun. When you land here, you even get a new cursor, a bright orange sun that moves around the screen. Samples:

- Acupressure wrist band for prevention of motion sickness, focusing on the nai-kan point in the wrist
- SafeSun, an electronic device that picks up ultraviolet rays, and beeps you when you should head for the shade (size of a tiny cell phone), discounted for members of the National Association of Albinism and Hypo-Pigmentation (NOAH)
- Travel organizer with 36 see-through zippered pockets, brass hanger to store on door or closet

**Search:** No
**Photos:** Yes
**Ordering:** Online, Phone
**Gift Wrap:** No
**Delivery:** Ground

## Santa Maria Discount Luggage

http://www.luggageman.com

Here's where Columbus bought his luggage before coming to the New World. You can get discounts on luggage from a dozen major vendors. They rate their items on durability. Samples:

## Travel Smith

http://www.travelsmith.com

A wonderfully graphic catalog with traveling clothes for men and women, luggage, and accessories. They focus on wrinkle-free fabric, waterproof and easy-to-pack items from Petite to Extra, Extra Large. And they supplement their products with neat features, such as suggested packing lists; tips for different kinds of trips; suggestions of unusual journeys; and weather (what's the temperature like this month in Tokyo?) and travel info (do we need any vaccinations?). Sample products:

- Men's featherweight trench coat
- Packable panama hat
- Pack-It cubes, nylon organizers to hold dress shirts, blouses, or trousers, even neckties, or small items like socks, underwear, and T-shirts
- Petite size indispensable black dress
- Photojournalist's vest
- Security neck pouch, made of lightweight, water-resistant nylon, with compartments for airline tickets, currency, passports, designed to be hidden under clothing

**Search:** Yes
**Photos:** Yes, small and large
**Ordering:** Online, Phone, Fax
**Gift Wrap:** No
**Delivery:** Ground, 2nd Day, Overnight

# Walkabout Travel Gear

http://
www.walkabouttravelgear.com

It's a long address, but appropriate for a store named after the aborigine ritual of wandering around for spiritual cleansing. As experienced trekkers, they organize their travel gear around the challenges: bugs, electricity, health, safety, sleep, and water. Sprinkled throughout the site are tips from fellow travelers. (We learned that you should take a pair of pliers with you to India for exchanging money, because large wads of Indian currency come stapled together, and you have to pry the metal loose without damaging the bills, because taxi wallahs do not accept damaged bills.) They ship most orders within 24 hours. Order by 3 P.M. Mountain Time to get faster deliveries. Samples:

- Multipurpose pocketknife with two blades, bottle and can opener, plus detachable fork and spoon
- SleepScreen, a net tent that hangs on fiberglass poles over your bed or sleeping bag, to keep out bugs
- Water purifier with filter, carrying case, filter-cleaning brush, soft water bottle for removing

99.9% of Giardia, bacteria, viruses
- Zelco Lock-Up, to lock your door, pick-proof, with quick-release lever for fast emergency exit, carrying pouch

**Search:** No
**Photos:** Yes
**Ordering:** Online
**Gift Wrap:** Certificates
**Delivery:** Ground, 3rd Day, 2nd Day, Overnight

# World Traveler

http://www.worldtraveler.com

A well-organized, quick site with a wide range of classy luggage and travel goods, with guaranteed lowest prices. You can shop by brand (Eagle Creek, Hartmann, JanSport, Kenneth Cole, Ricardo, Samsonite, ZERO Halliburton) or by product. They have a lot of items from each manufacturer, so you won't have to settle. They even offer a few dozen special bargains at more than two-thirds off the list price, plus promotional items, and specials such as free shipping on certain products. They emphasize customer service, going so far as to put their 800 number on the home page. Samples:

- Atlantic® Professional Cosmetic Tote, constructed of ballistic nylon, with padded honeycomb frame, fully lined cases, retractable handle, in-line skate wheels, corner guards
- Eagle Creek All-Terrain Money Belt, with zipper
- Impuls® Targa 14" Personal Bag, with front pocket, cushioned handles, shoulder strap, mesh pocket, bottle loops
- Samsonite® 725/DLX Expandable Medium EZ Cart Suiter, with 4 wheels, push-button handle, and compartments
- Tilley khaki safari hat in green

**Search:** Yes
**Photos:** Yes
**Ordering:** Online, Phone, Email
**Gift Wrap:** No
**Delivery:** 3rd Day, 2nd Day, Overnight

# TV & Video Gear

We were TV deprived as kids, so now we can't watch enough. We even spent six months sitting in darkened rooms at ad agencies watching TV commercials for a book called *The Best Thing on TV*. We made video art and broadcast TV, but now we just watch. The bigger the screen, the better. The higher the resolution, the more we ooh and aah.

So we've had fun browsing for the latest and the best in video and TV gear for the home. In general, we dismiss manufacturers' sites because their prices are so much higher than street prices, and we also leave out a lot of "gift" sites that offer only a few TVs, at middling or high prices.

## Brandsmall

`http:// catalog.brandsmall.com/eshop`

Occasionally, this site's Electronic Expo posts the lowest prices on the Web, or nearly so (depends on which bot we use). They don't sell lots of brands, but they have TVs arranged by screen size, VCRs by the number and kind of recording heads, and DVD players. Not every item is a super bargain, though. Samples:

- JVC 36" Stereo Color TV with two tuners
- RCA 9" color TV with FM radio
- Pioneer DV 414 DVD/CD/Video CD Player

**Search:** Yes
**Photos:** Yes
**Ordering:** Online
**Gift Wrap:** No
**Delivery:** Ground (for most products), 3rd day

## Code-Free DVD

`http://www.codefreedvd.com`

Most DVD players come with a lock that prevents you from viewing movies sold outside of your part of the world. If you are bothered by "region-locking," because you want to see movies from other countries or intend to move around a lot, this company has tweaked the locks so that their DVD players will accept and play movies from anywhere. The company is located in the United Kingdom, but promises fast delivery around the world. Also, they swear they never advertise items that are out of stock. They give good explanations of this weird international agreement to carve up the world into sales regions; also, they use icons to give key details about each product, such as Dolby Digital sound, laser disc compatibility, and 96 KHz audio. Samples:

- Pioneer DVL-909, code free, capable of playing PAL or NTSC discs from regions 1–6 now and in the future, also laser discs
- Sony wide-screen TV with Dolby Pro Logic, S-Video, for connection with DVD equipment (discounted when purchased with DVD player)

**Search:** No
**Photos:** Yes
**Ordering:** Online, Phone, Fax
**Gift Wrap:** No
**Delivery:** Overnight in Europe, 2–5 days worldwide

## Consumer Direct

`http://www.consumer-direct.com`

By buying in bulk direct from factories, this company gets large discounts, so they can offer prices that beat most mail-order companies. All items except overstocks are brand new. Each product description includes a good feature list and shipping costs. Samples:

- DirecPC® do-it-yourself installation kit for digital satellite system (dish and PC card, as well as Internet service plans, sold separately)
- Sony WebTV™ wireless keyboard
- Wavecom™ Jr. Wireless audio-video transmitting

device, to distribute video or stereo audio signals throughout your house without putting in new wires

**Search:** Yes
**Photos:** Yes
**Ordering:** Online
**Gift Wrap:** No
**Delivery:** Ground, 2ⁿᵈ Day, overnight

# DVD City

`http://www.dvdcity.com`

A large selection of name-brand DVD players, receivers, speakers, and even cables. They ship most orders the same day the order comes in! They organize their offerings by price tag, so you can start within your budget, and see what's available at each price point up to the very best products on the market. Substantial discounts on the manufacturer's suggested retail prices, too. Samples:

- JVC XB501BK DVD player with 10-bit, 24 MHz sampling, component video, composite video, S-video outputs, virtual surround-sound, joystick
- Pioneer DV-09 Elite DVD player with Digital Theater sound, jog-and-shuttle remote control, graphic menu system, component video output (a fantastic machine, at the top of the line, based on our own experience)

**Search:** Yes
**Photos:** Yes
**Ordering:** Online, Phone
**Gift Wrap:** No
**Delivery:** Ground, 2ⁿᵈ Day, overnight

# eBay

`http://pages.ebay.com/`
`electronics`

The electronics department of this auction house carries more than 4,000 pieces of video and DVD equipment being put up for auction in new or used state by individuals. Unfortunately, the giant list is not alphabetical; in fact, it is not organized, so you have to skim a lot of items to find one you like. (Searching with specifics works better.) Each item carries info about the current high bidder, first bid, bid history, reserve price (price that must be met), and the seller's description. Remember: When the seller is an individual, they do not have a store's incentive to keep you happy, for repeat business, so be careful out there. Sample items offered for bid:

- New Sony Trinitron VEGA Flat Screen 32" TV
- Philips 42" Flat-TV Color TV, plasma display, twin-tuner split-screen, 4.5" deep, Dolby Pro Logic Surround Sound
- New RCA DVD and Divx player, with universal remote, original box

**Search:** Yes
**Photos:** Sometimes
**Ordering:** By online bidding
**Gift Wrap:** No
**Delivery:** Negotiated with seller

# Electronics.Net

`http://electronics.net`

"The biggest electronics store everywhere!" TVs are one of their hot buttons, arranged according to screen sizes, each with anywhere from two to 12 sets from a few manufacturers, at substantial discounts off retail. "We will not be undersold!" Within 10 days of purchase, they beat a lower price from a listed competitor by 10%, match another competitor's price, or refund your money. Some categories that we expected, such as DVD players, were not represented when we visited. For each product, they offer a photo (or two), a table of features (not always completely filled in), and specs. Samples:

- JVC 20" stereo TV with universal remote
- ProScan 20" MTS TV set with S-video input, expanded stereo
- RCA 46" Home Theatre Projection with digital focus, picture-in-picture, dual S-video inputs, and glow-in-the-dark remote
- RCA digital satellite system, with 8-event scheduler, 32-bit processor, digital optical output
- Sharp 3 Viewcam, 64X zoom, stabilized, with 3" color LCD screen

**Search:** Excellent
**Photos:** Yes
**Ordering:** Online, Phone
**Gift Wrap:** No
**Delivery:** Ground, 2nd Day, Overnight

## NetMarket

http://www.netmarket.com

In their Electronics department, you'll find name brand TVs, DVD players, VCRs, and satellite hookups at genuinely low prices, if you join up. The site is easy to navigate, with a neat interface. You pick a category such as Projection TVs, and they tell you how many models they have (27), and let you narrow your search by price range, features (9 options), or manufacturer (Magnavox, Mitsubishi, Panasonic, Proscan, Sony, Toshiba, Zenith). When you do pick a product, you get a picture with a paragraph describing it, and news of any options. You have to spend a buck to become a member to get the best discounts for three months (then $70 per year). Their low-price guarantee is outstanding: If you find a lower price at another authorized dealer, they will confirm it, then they will send you a check for the difference, plus 35% of the difference. Very large TVs may take three or four weeks to arrive. Samples:

- Dish Network Echo 5000 Digital Satellite System, with MTS stereo for local programs, caller ID, event timer for VCR, V-chip for parental control
- Sony DVP-C600D DVD/5-CD Carousel Changer with built-in Dolby Digital, 96KHz/24-bit audio

**Search:** Yes
**Photos:** Yes
**Ordering:** Online
**Gift Wrap:** No
**Delivery:** Ground

## One Call

http://www.onecall.com

An electronics retailer who went online to combat the big stores, and got high marks from consumers, One Call offers audio, phones, photography, TV, and video.

Some items are available only in their local area, up in the state of Washington. They provide an absolute minimum of information about each product, so you might come here only after you've read the magazines for product reviews. They claim to offer 90% of all the DVD players built, with more than 400 DVD movies in stock at all times. Samples:

- Panasonic 900MHz cordless phone
- Toshiba 6-head VCR

**Search:** No
**Photos:** No
**Ordering:** Online, Phone
**Gift Wrap:** No
**Delivery:** Ground

## Roxy

http://www.roxy.com

Taking a cue from the old Roxy theaters, this site features good deals on one or two selected items in key categories, such as digital satellite television, home theater systems, audio and video, including DVD. Lengthy explanations of new technology. Sample items:

- Home Theater sound system with 100-watt surround sound, 5 speakers, subwoofer, remote
- Value bundle of satellite dish, receiver, surge protector, installation kit, and three months of programming

**Search:** No
**Photos:** Yes
**Ordering:** Online
**Gift Wrap:** No
**Delivery:** 3rd Day

## Samy's Camera

http://www.samys.com

This photo store carries top-level video cameras with full specs. You can order online, but it's clear this store prefers personal contact, so you have to call for some prices, and they offer a personal adviser to put together complex systems.

- Canon XL-1 Digital Video Camcorder, with

interchangeable lenses, battery pack, wireless controller, video cables, digital videocassette
- Fuji DS Digital Card Camera 560 compatible with Nikon lenses, continuous 3 frames per second, ISO 800 or higher, 1280 x 1000 pixel files
- Olympus D-600L digital camera, 1280 x 1024 or 640 x 512 pixel resolution, 3X zoom, LCD screen

**Search:** No
**Photos:** Yes
**Ordering:** Online, Phone
**Gift Wrap:** No
**Delivery:** Ground

# Tek Discount Warehouse

http://www.tekgallery.com

Within a larger Yahoo store, there is a good department devoted to consumer and low-end professional video, TV, and DVD. Reassuring variety of major brands, with pretty good prices. Samples:
- 4-head VCR with wireless remote, digital auto tracking, multilanguage on-screen display, high-speed search, auto repeat, playback, and rewind
- Handheld travel TV with 2.5" active-matrix color LCD screen, headphone output, and external rod antenna
- Sima Video Editmaster, Video Editor, and Sound Mixer, with fade to black, color detail and brightness controls, split screen, compatible with S-VHS and Hi-8

**Search:** Yes
**Photos:** Yes
**Ordering:** Online, Phone
**Gift Wrap:** No
**Delivery:** Ground

# You may also want to channel-surf over to these chapters:

- Consumer Electronics
- Movies & Videos
- Photography

# Video & Computer Games

Our son Noah likes to go online to pick up cheat codes for video and computer games. Suddenly he's zipping from level to level, and taking over the world. We've followed him to sites that sell these games and the joysticks, memory cards, and gizmos that make the action go even faster. We've found that the gigantic stores can offer good discounts, probably because of their volume, but you may prefer some of the smaller shops, because they obviously love the games, and load their sites with tips, news, and, yes, free cheat codes.

## Access Micro

http://www.accessmicro.com

Big site, with 45,000 computer products. If you want speed, choose Text Only at their welcome screen. When you investigate a particular game (in the software area), you learn little more than price, availability, manufacturer, and shipping charges. Prices are OK. Samples:

- Activision, *MechWarrior 2: Mercenaries 3D FX Edition*
- Sierra On-Line, *King's Quest 8 Mask of Eternity*
- Softkey, *Tomb Raider*
- Virgin, *The 11ᵗʰ Hour: The Sequel to 7ᵗʰ Guest* by Triolobyte

**Search:** Yes
**Photos:** No
**Ordering:** Online, Phone, Fax
**Gift Wrap:** No
**Delivery:** Ground, 3ʳᵈ Day, 2ⁿᵈ Day, Overnight

## BuyGames

http://www2.buy.com/game

Another niche in the empire of Buy This and Buy That. Nicely organized around game types (Game Boy, Super Nintendo, Nintendo 64, Sega CD, Sega 32, Sega Saturn, Sega Genesis, Sony PlayStation). Lots of products, including items that have recently been canceled, and some used titles from video stores. One caution: They forgot to ship our order, even though the item was in stock, and when we tried to use their order tracking, the system refused to accept the log-in and password we had created (and they had confirmed by email). The woman on the phone was able to get the shipment started, but had no idea what to do about the lockout. Hmmm. Samples:

- Interplay, *Caesar's Palace for Gameboy*
- Sega, *Golf Magazine 36 Holes*, for Sega 32
- Sony, *Xena Warrior Princess* for Sony PlayStation

**Search:** Yes
**Photos:** No
**Ordering:** Online
**Gift Wrap:** No
**Delivery:** Ground, 2ⁿᵈ Day, Overnight

## BuyRight Videogames

http://www.buyrite1.com

Some of the cheapest prices around on games, accessories, and systems. They claim to destroy the competition with their unbeatable low price guarantee. When you turn to the product description, you get a slide show of screen shots, so you see what the graphics are like. Samples:

- Final Fantasy 8 wall scrolls
- Neo Pocket Color
- *Panzer Dragoon Saga*, for Sega Saturn
- Puru Puru Vibration Pack for any home console
- Sega Dreamcast system

**Search:** No
**Photos:** Yes
**Ordering:** Online, Phone, Fax
**Gift Wrap:** No
**Delivery:** Ground, 2ⁿᵈ Day, Overnight

## Computers4Sure

http://www.computers4sure.com

The site looks like a box of index cards, with a bunch of tabs poking up for just about anything electronic. Under Software, when you pick Games and Entertainment from the dropdown list, you see table after table listing major products from most major vendors (hundreds of products). To go to a particular product or vendor, you'll do better to use the search. They often have excellent bargains, sometimes the lowest prices on the Web. This site is not for browsing, though. You get the product name, number in stock, and a Buy button. If you want to order a product that hasn't yet been released, you can have Computers4Sure send you a Shopping Alert by email the day the product becomes available. Order by 4 P.M. Eastern Time to get your package shipped the next business day. They offer online tracking of your order. Samples:

- Activision, *Extreme Rodeo*
- Ocean of America, *Total Air War*

**Search:** Yes
**Photos:** No
**Ordering:** Online, Phone
**Gift Wrap:** No
**Delivery:** Ground, 2nd Day, Overnight

## Game Cellar

http://www.gamecellar.com

Focused on games, this Yahoo store sells hardware and games for Sega Dreamcast and Linux as well as Game Boy, Nintendo, PlayStation, and Windows. Descriptions are one paragraph long, with a snapshot of the jewel box. A few good deals, but some of the discounts are, well, ho-hum. Samples:

- Activision, *Civilization: Call to Power,* for Linux
- Game Boy Color Solid Purple

**Search:** Yes
**Photos:** Yes
**Ordering:** Online
**Gift Wrap:** No
**Delivery:** Ground, Overnight

## GamEscapes

http://www.gamelovers.com

If you have a bunch of old video games, this site will help you sell or trade them. You can then stock up on new or used games and hardware, if you want. To sell or trade, you mail or fax them a description of each game (Does it have a box? Manual?). They get back to you offering a quote. Sample products:

- *Bomberman 64 Player's Guide*, Prima, Used
- New *Jurassic Park* for 3DO
- Used Nintendo 64 core system with one controller

**Search:** Yes
**Photos:** No
**Ordering:** Online, Email
**Gift Wrap:** No
**Delivery:** Ground, 2nd Day, Overnight

## Game Max

http://www.gamemax.com

If you are just wondering what kind of games are available, use this site to browse, using the good descriptions, large illustrations (front and back of the box, plus images from the games), and lots of hints. For instance, if you look at a card-game product, they offer lists of related titles from the same vendor, other card games, multiplayer games, Internet card games, and educational programs that might be related. For each product, they offer several screenshots you can enlarge, and they tell you the minimum hardware requirements, as well as recommended ones. Samples:

- Expert, *Bicycle Rummy*, Windows
- Interactive Magic, *Apache*, for Macintosh
- Mindscape, *Ardennes Offensive*, Windows

**Search:** Yes
**Photos:** Yes
**Ordering:** Online
**Gift Wrap:** No
**Delivery:** Ground

## Interact!

`http://www.interactcd.com`

Obsessed with interactive CD-ROMs for your computer, this site lets you look up games for the Mac or PC, investigate new releases or used games. Flat rate shipping per order, not per title, up to 10 titles. Samples:

- 989 Studios, *Everquest*, Windows
- Disney, *101 Dalmatians Animated Storybook*, Windows or Mac
- New World, *Heroes of Might and Magic III*, Windows

**Search:** Yes
**Photos:** Yes
**Ordering:** Online, Phone
**Gift Wrap:** Yes
**Delivery:** Ground, 2nd Day, Overnight

## Lazarus Games

`http://www.lazarusgames.com/sellmain.html`

Yes, right there on the main page is the tomb from which this site's owner seems to have risen. Focused on Nintendo 64, Sony PlayStation, and Sega Saturn, this site also lets you offer to swap something you have for one of their games. Prices look good. If you long for a game they don't carry, you can consult their Game Detective, telling him how much money you are willing to pay for the game, or what you would trade for it. The detective tracks down a copy of the game, and, if you agree with the terms, the deal is made. Their Magazine Rack offers links to Web sites of game publishers, video game magazine, and user groups. Samples:

- Nintendo 64 *Blast Corps*
- Sega Saturn *F1 Challenge*
- *Sony PlayStation Alien Trilogy*

**Search:** No
**Photos:** No
**Ordering:** Online, Trade
**Gift Wrap:** No
**Delivery:** Ground

## McGlen

`http://www.mcglen.com`

A computer site with more than 800 computer games. Product descriptions are minimal, so you need to know exactly what you want before you search, but at least they show you what the shipping costs will be for each product. Samples:

- Eidos, *Thief: The Dark Project*, Windows
- Segasoft, *Web Vengeance*, Windows
- Softkey, *High Heat Baseball*, Windows

**Search:** Yes
**Photos:** No
**Ordering:** Online
**Gift Wrap:** No
**Delivery:** Ground, 2nd Day, Overnight

## Microwarehouse

`http://www.warehouse.com`

You may have seen their paper catalogs for computer hardware and software, with blurbs for same day shipping for overnight delivery (not always available everywhere). We've bought software from them, and found them fast and reliable. This site offers computer games sorted into PC and Mac categories, and within those you get subcategories such as action, classic, kids-simulation, sports, strategy, and trivia, as well as best sellers. You get a pretty good range of products, with details on the game, requirements, and sometimes screenshots. Most games are shipped the day you order them. Samples:

- *Murder She Wrote Mystery Jigsaw Puzzles,* for Mac
- *Riven, The Sequel to Myst*, for Mac or PC
- *Star Wars: Dark Forces*, for Mac

**Search:** Yes
**Photos:** Some
**Ordering:** Online, Phone
**Gift Wrap:** No
**Delivery:** Ground, Overnight

# NECX

http://necxdirect.necx.com

Started as a global swap site for more than 200 million electronic, computer, and network products, NECX has branched into an online store focusing on office and personal high-tech, with a large section devoted to gaming software for the personal computer. They cover the waterfront as far as manufacturers go, but they stock only a few titles from each, which is fine if the title you want is popular. Prices are very low. They also offer side-by-side comparisons, rebates and coupons, and specs on many products. To speed up delivery, they ship from one of 34 warehouses around the country. For Saturday delivery, call on Friday. Samples:

- 20th Century Fox Entertainment, *X-Files Unrestricted Access*, Mac, Windows
- Hasbro, *Frogger*, Windows
- Interplay, *Carmeggeddon II: Carpocalypse Now*, Windows

**Search:** Yes
**Photos:** Small
**Ordering:** Online, Phone
**Gift Wrap:** No
**Delivery:** Ground, 2nd Day, Overnight

# Outpost

http://www.outpost.com

A colorful computer store with auctions, steals, and deals. Their Game Outpost helps you focus in on Windows, Mac, DOS, Nintendo, and PlayStation games, as well as some hardware to make your gaming go better. They claim to be able to ship within 24 hours most of the time. They run specials on shipping, too. Samples:

- 4 MB expansion pack for Nintendo 64 game console
- Expert, *100 Amazing Kids' Games*, Windows
- Konami, *Metal Gear Solid*, for Sony PlayStation
- Trackball with four buttons

**Search:** Yes
**Photos:** Yes
**Ordering:** Online, Phone

**Gift Wrap:** No
**Delivery:** Ground, Overnight

# PreBookGames

http://www.prebookgames.com

This bright site distinguishes itself by offering free shipping and handling. They love games, it seems, offering their own ratings, tips, and tricks, as well as player guides. And, yes, they offer a ton of cheat codes for free. Sample products:

- Brady, *Darkstalkers 3 Official Strategy Guide*
- Konami, *Silent Hill*, for Sony PlayStation
- Nintendo 64 Alpha64 Controller from Nyko

**Search:** Yes
**Photos:** Yes
**Ordering:** Online
**Gift Wrap:** No
**Delivery:** 3rd Day, 2nd Day, Overnight

# Shopping.com

http://www.shopping.com/store

One of their power stores is devoted to video games for Game Boy, Nintendo, PlayStation, Sega, and others. You can see tables comparing prices, and get short descriptions and pictures for each product. Very detailed help system. You will get good prices here, and because this site is connected to so many other stores in the Shopping environment, you can zip to all the other items on your shopping list, after you pick up the games you want. Samples:

- Game Boy Camera, blue
- *MarioKart* for Nintendo 64
- *Syphon Filter* for PlayStation

**Search:** Yes
**Photos:** Yes
**Ordering:** Online
**Gift Wrap:** Certificates
**Delivery:** Ground

## Tronix

http://www.tronixweb.com

Here's a chatty site with a lot of imports, and gossip about upcoming games. For instance, you can get games for the Japanese version of the Sony PlayStation here. They also let you sign up in advance for games that are going to be "heavily allocated," that is, in short supply as soon as they are released. (Tronix also provides you with links to the newsgroups who are spreading rumors and news.) When they get down to the very last box, they post it on the Specials board, with even deeper discounts. If you can get your order in by 4 P.M. Eastern Time, in-stock items go out that day. Samples:

- 3DO, Army Men 3D for American Sony PlayStation
- Monster Race, Japanese PDA version
- Pokemon Snap for Japanese Nintendo 64

**Search:** No
**Photos:** A few
**Ordering:** Online
**Gift Wrap:** No
**Delivery:** Ground, 3rd Day, 2nd Day, Overnight

## Zones

http://www.zones.com

Originally a mail-order operation, this software-and-hardware store divides its site up into zones (Mac, PC, education, business, auction), but, alas, games do not yet rank a zone of their own. So you have to look in the Mac or PC Zone first, then explore Software, and dip into Entertainment, or search by manufacturer. Descriptions vary from a paragraph to breakouts of key features, requirements, and possible add-ons, plus a box shot, the price, and manufacturer. If you get your order in by 8 P.M. Eastern Time, the Zones will ship it that day. Nice touch: They advertise their phone and email for customer service and tech support. Samples:

- Activision, *Dark Reign: The Future of War*, Windows
- Davidson, *Diablo*, Mac
- Hasbro, *Mr. Potato Head Activity Pack*, Mac

**Search:** Yes
**Photos:** Yes
**Ordering:** Online, Phone
**Gift Wrap:** No
**Delivery:** Ground, 3rd Day, Overnight

## Game Week

If you wonder what the game business looks like from the inside, you might be interested in Game Daily, a site set up by the publishers of a trade journal called *GameWEEK*. Along with the day's breaking news, you can read interviews with the people who create and sell the games, check out product release schedules, and review industry-wide data on sales. Our kids have been angling to invest in two or three of these game companies, and they like the financial news section, with game-maker gainers, losers, and most active stocks, all at http://www.gamedaily.com/

## Ready for more hardware and software to go with those games? Plug into these chapters:

- Batteries
- Computers & Computer Gear
- Consumer Electronics
- Movies & Videos
- Software
- Software for Kids
- TV & Video Gear

# Vitamins & Supplements

This is another one of those burgeoning sectors of Web shopping. There are lots of stores that want to sell you vitamins. Some are kind of funky, others are definitely high tech. Most of them offer lower prices than you'd get by shopping with your feet instead of your mouse. In fact, many of these stores offer lots of information that you, perhaps, wouldn't get when browsing the aisles of a brick-and-mortar store. While many of the stores mentioned in this chapter sell more than vitamins and supplements, there are some other chapters you might want to read. For example, if you have questions about health care products, such as those for allergy control, diabetes, or arthritis, look at the Herbs and Health Products chapters. If you are looking for stores that can fill your prescriptions or sell over-the-counter drugs, read Prescription & Over-the-Counter Drugs.

## eNutrition

http://www.enutrition.com

This large, easy-to-use store has been designed for the Web shopper. Each section (such as the weight-loss, allergies, germs, bodybuilding, cancer, and AIDS areas) is loaded with facts and helpful articles, many of them reprinted from national health magazines. Besides vitamins, there are a lot of homeopathic and herbal remedies and many formulas for various ailments. Once you've ordered here, you can sign up for quick checkout (in other words, no more filling in name, credit card numbers, etc.) for subsequent orders. Samples:

- Amino acids

- Anxiety-alleviating snack bars
- Belladonna
- Enzymes (digestive aids)
- Healthy shake powders
- Kali Bichromicum
- Liquid predigested protein powders
- Phytonutrients
- Power bars
- Sports nutritional products
- Vitamin E complexes

**Search:** Yes
**Photos:** Some
**Ordering:** Online
**Gift Wrap:** No
**Delivery:** 3rd Day, 2nd Day, Overnight

## Green Tree

http://www.greentree.com

This store not only sells you vitamins, supplements, herbal and homeopathic remedies, it also supplies you with mountains of research and informative articles. They also offer a free nutritional analysis for either men or women. You answer some questions (takes about two minutes), and then they come up with a vitamin plan for you based on your answers. You can also search for a particular vitamin and then find out everything there is to know about it, such as what it is good for. Samples:

- Allergy formulas
- Arthritis remedies
- Athlete's vitamins
- Boosting immune-system therapies
- B-Stress with Siberian ginseng
- Carbo vegetabilis
- Diet fuel caps (Ma Huang Free)
- Energy formulas
- Ginseng
- Zinc
- Vitamin E
- Individual vitamin plans
- Melatonin
- Multivitamins

**Search:** Yes
**Photos:** Some

**Ordering**: Online, Phone, Fax
**Gift Wrap**: No
**Delivery**: Ground, 2nd Day, Overnight

## HealthShop.com

`http://www.healthshop.com`

This shop believes in helping to promote a healthy lifestyle. One of the things they've created is a health planner. You answer a bunch of questions and they will suggest which vitamins and minerals to take based on your answers. A nice plus is that they also *explain* the answers, you're not just fed a list of vitamins to take. Samples:

- Antioxidant formulas
- Bioflavonoids
- Carotenes
- Digestive enzymes
- Essential fatty acids
- Ginkgo biloba concentrate
- Kava Kava
- Lactobacillus acidophilus
- Men's and women's multivitamins
- Multiminerals
- Primrose oil
- Selenium
- Soy concentrates
- Vitamin E

**Search**: Yes
**Photos**: Yes
**Ordering**: Online
**Gift Wrap**: No
**Delivery**: Ground, 2nd Day, Overnight

## IPS

`http://www.ipsrx.com`

The IPS stands for Immediate Pharmaceutical Services, Inc. (which is a subsidiary of Discount Drug Mart, Inc.). Their online store specializes in vitamins, supplements, and herbal extracts and teas. They have a Remedy Search section where you click on an ailment, such as arthritis pain, headache, or stress, and it will

suggest a vitamin or herbal remedy tailored for that condition. Samples:

- Acidophilus capsules
- Beta-carotene soft gels
- Echinacea
- Feverfew
- Folic acid tablets
- Herbal energizer
- Melatonin
- Multivitamins
- Saw palmetto extract
- Slimming tea-orange spice

**Search**: Yes
**Photos**: Yes
**Ordering**: Online, Phone, Fax
**Gift Wrap**: No
**Delivery**: Ground

## MediStore

`http://www.mediconsult.com`

A wonderful supply of hard-to-locate products, especially medical supplements, is available here. A great search divided into 60 medical topics takes the time out of finding that special product. There is a lot of information about each vitamin or supplement that they sell. You'll also find support groups and a drug reference section. Everything for sale at the site has a full, money-back guarantee. Samples:

- Adult life care kit
- Antioxidants
- Ascorbic acid
- Carbo Edge energy drink
- Choline caps
- Health-related reference books, tapes, and videos
- Medical software
- Methyl caps
- Vitamin B-3

**Search**: Yes
**Photos**: Some
**Ordering**: Online
**Gift Wrap**: No
**Delivery**: Ground

# MotherNature.com

`http://www.mothernature.com`

From homeopathy to aromatherapy, this health store carries a long list of natural products to help keep you well and also help when you're sick. You can search in a number of unique ways for the item you are looking for, such as product name, lifestyle, what ails you, etc. When we browsed they had a nice article on traditional Ayurveda massage. Shipping is free on orders over $50. Samples:

- Allergy and hay-fever remedies
- Anxiety solutions
- Appetite suppressants
- Ayurvedic products
- Beta-carotene
- Biotin
- Children's vitamins
- Circulation formulas
- Folic acid
- Health bars
- Herbal teas
- Vitamin A and D soft gel capsules

**Search:** Yes
**Photos:** Yes
**Ordering:** Online
**Gift Wrap:** No
**Delivery:** Ground, 2nd Day

# Nutrasource

`http://www.nutrasource.com`

This place sells vitamins and supplements—lots of them. They also sell vitamin formulas to help alleviate various ailments. If you want to know more, go to their Nutrition Library for some healthy reading. Shipping is free when you order seven or more products. Also, when you see the "Buy two get one free" note, the second item really is free, meaning they don't charge shipping for that item. Samples:

- A and D vitamins
- Amino acids
- Beta-carotene plus A and D
- Bilberry

- Bromeliad
- B-vitamins
- Echinacea/golden-seal
- Lactobacillus acidophilus
- Milk enzymes
- Multivitamins
- Niacin nonflush
- Odorless garlic tabs

**Search:** Yes
**Photos:** Some
**Ordering:** Online, Fax, Email
**Gift Wrap:** No
**Delivery:** Ground

# Price's Power International

`http://www.prices-power.com`

First of all, there's no relation between the authors and this store, although we think our bodybuilding teenage son wishes there were. This is a store that specializes in products, especially supplements, for people who are aggressively working out. They also responsibly list the pros and possible side effects of many of the items sold. They offer free shipping on orders over $100. Samples:

- Androstenedione
- Beta Boost
- Health and fitness bulletin board
- Creatine monohydrate
- Supplements
- Ionic Whey
- Chrysin
- Protein bars

**Search:** Some
**Photos:** Some
**Ordering:** Online, Phone, Fax
**Gift Wrap:** No
**Delivery:** Ground, 2nd Day

# Vitamins.com

`http://www.vitamins.com`

Fantastic selection of vitamins and supplements with great prices. There's also a lot of herbal remedies for sale. You'll find a few articles and some expert advice. Check out their FAQ section for some answers to everyday nutritional questions. Shipping in the U.S. is only $1 per order. The store is updated daily. Samples:

- Animal shapes plus iron children's multivitamins
- Antioxidant tablets
- B-complex vitamins
- Brewer's yeast
- Calcium pyruvate
- DHEA
- Melatonin
- Shark fin cartilage
- St. John's Wort
- Weight-loss supplements

**Search:** Yes
**Photos:** Yes
**Ordering:** Online
**Gift Wrap:** No
**Delivery:** Ground

# VitaminShoppe.com

http://www.vitaminshoppe.com

You'll find vitamins made from many of the national brands, such as Twin Lab, Nature's Way, and Nature Balance. They also have lots of herbal and homeopathic products, plus books and bodybuilding items. Most of their vitamins are 30% off retail, making their prices one of the most competitve on the Web. They also offer lots of information about all of the products they sell. Samples:

- Actisyn
- Bee pollen
- Gift certificates
- Green tea
- Kudzu powder
- Multiminerals with boron
- Royal jelly
- Weight-gain formulas
- Wheat germ oil

**Search:** Yes
**Photos:** Yes
**Ordering:** Online, Phone
**Gift Wrap:** No
**Delivery:** Ground, 2nd Day, Overnight

# Vitamins Network

http://www.vitamins.net

It had to happen, and it has. This store is part of a vitamin meganetwork. You'll get a ton of information on so many related topics. Want to know about homeopathic products, esoteric arts?  Go to their Spirit Store. Want to talk to other folks interested in keeping their bodies in good working order?  Sign in at the chat rooms. Rather stay anonymous?  Go to the message boards. There're always several articles about vitamins. The day we browsed we saw two just on reasons to take carnitine. They also have a lot of alternative medicine–type formulas, as well as formulas for bodybuilders. Samples:

- Acidophilus wafers
- Bone meal plus
- Chelated minerals
- Chewable aloe-vera tablets
- Children's multivitamins
- Fibersol
- Herbal diuretic tablets
- Lecithin granules
- Migraine-free Ayurvedic formula
- Multivitamins
- Oat bran plus
- Ultra nail formula
- Ultrapotency multiple vitamin

**Search:** Yes
**Photos:** Yes
**Ordering:** Online
**Gift Wrap:** No
**Delivery:** Ground

# Weather Gear

Where we live, in the high desert, we can feel the moisture leeching out of the soil during droughts, watch dust storms blowing across the mesa by day, and see clouds bearing down on the cliffs at the far side of town whenever a storm drifts out of the Pacific, across Baja California, or down from the north.

We relish our binoculars, rain gauges, and weather-watching products, perhaps because we are a mile high, and feel as if we are already inside the weather. So we've enjoyed picking the best sites offering skygazing gear, plus maps, images, and tables you can use to make sense out of all the data you acquire.

## AccuWeather

http://www.accuweather.com

No matter where you are, you can get a five-day forecast here, including local radar pictures, and animations of the national or regional weather and temperature changes (the animations are fantastic but take a while to download). They also offer in-depth research on radar, rain, satellites, temperature, and weather facts. Want to see what the beach is like? Their Recreation section summarizes wave heights, surf temperature, and the tanning index for each area. You can get their weather by email, which we do, so even if you don't look outside, you know whether it's raining or snowing. Better yet, if you want warning of approaching tornadoes, flash floods, or snow, you can get an alert on your pager, for a fee. If you subscribe (for a little more than a dime a day), you can get 10-day and hourly forecasts, severe weather watches, the very latest local, regional, and national radar. Their online store offers posters, instruments, and software. Samples:

- AccuWeather Forecast Center, a portable and wipable bulletin board showing examples of satellites, Doppler radar, and weather images
- Davis Complete Weather Station in a box, monitoring wind, barometric pressure, temperature, humidity, with optional rain collector, external temperature and humidity sensors, and software for computer analysis
- Tracking maps for Atlantic and East Pacific storms in Acrobat format
- Weather Pager Service, to alert you to changes in the weather, severe storms, travel warnings
- Weather Wizard III, to monitor and store data about temperature, wind direction, wind speed, and windchill

**Search:** Yes
**Photos:** Great animations, diagrams, and maps
**Ordering:** Online
**Gift Wrap:** No
**Delivery:** Download, Ground

## EarthWatch® Weather on Demand

http://www.earthwatch.com

Watch the weather move in, with clouds drifting across the world. This company provides professional weather software to TV stations and meteorologists, but you can get a custom image of the weather in any part of the world, in radar or 3-D views. (The views of U.S. weather are sometimes less than 20 minutes old.) The clouds seem to pile up like mountains, above the raised mountain ridges and boundary lines below. You can capture the images using your browser, or print them out. Samples:

- *3-D View of Weather for Southwest U.S.*, full color
- *Storm Watch*, Radar View, U.S.

**Search:** No
**Photos:** Yes
**Ordering:** Free, Online
**Gift Wrap:** No
**Delivery:** Download

# Global Mart

`http://www.globe-mart.com/`
`outdoors`

In the Ourdoors section of this bright site, you can find sports optics, along with their outdoor tools, tents, backpacks, and sleeping bags. Some large discounts are available. Samples:

- Bushnell Yardage Pro 800 Laser Rangefinder, 6X magnification, to measure distance within one yard, water- and shock-resistant, lightweight, rubber-armored
- Olympus EXPS Pathfinder Binoculars 8 x 42, for bird watching, hunting, sports, astronomy

**Search:** No
**Photos:** Yes
**Ordering:** Online, Phone
**Gift Wrap:** No
**Delivery:** Ground, 2$^{nd}$ Day, Overnight

# Intellicast

`http://www.intellicast.com`

A colorful site, with lots of neat pictures and plenty of information about the weather, tailored for your particular interests. For instance, if you just want to get ski reports, golf course news, outdoor activity weather, sailing forecasts, or tropical temperatures, you can get a whole bunch of information all collected for quick comparison. We particularly like the maps; for instance, the Atlantic Tropical Visible Image proved that there were no hurricanes emerging, and the Tropical Winds Analysis showed Florida with only light breezes. Their shops offer survival tools, weather instruments, books, and videos. Samples:

- *Audubon Guide to the Night Sky*
- Desktop weather radio, to keep you informed if there is a severe weather alert in your area
- Hurricane-tracking charts
- Kestral Hand-Held Anemometer
- *Old Farmer's Almanac, Book of Weather and Natural Disasters*
- Patio thermometer
- Weather One Radio with three weather channels

**Search:** No
**Photos:** Yes
**Ordering:** Online
**Gift Wrap:** Card
**Delivery:** Ground, 2$^{nd}$ Day

# LAN Optics

`http://www.tiac.net/users/`
`lanint`

Just what you didn't know you needed. Surplus Russian optical gear at good prices. Ruggedized, with full one-year warranty, latest modifications, presale inspection, and adjustment. Shipping varies depending on the product's price and weight, and your address. Samples:

- Giant Binoculars, central focus, 20x60 magnification, for boat, night sky, with strong depth perception at extreme ranges
- Maksutov Telescope, Heavy Duty, for photography, astronomy, with universal or Pentax camera attachment, 1000mm focal length, 8 meters minimum focus range, retractable shade, dew shield, tripod, 4.5 pounds
- Military Scope and Rangefinder, 10X magnification, two parts, collapsible pocket size, focus from 15 yards, 12mm eye relief

**Search:** No
**Photos:** Yes
**Ordering:** Online
**Gift Wrap:** No
**Delivery:** Ground, 3$^{rd}$ Day

# Scientific Sales

`http://`
`www.scientificsales.com`

Come here for instruments for anything to do with weather, such as wireless weather stations, meteorological balloons, and gear for monitoring barometric pressure, humidity, lightning, rain, snow, temperature, and wind. Samples:

- Digital barometer with pressure range from 26.50 to 32.50 inches of mercury, at 8-second intervals,

35-day memory
- Hand-Held Lightning Detector picks up electrical activity up to 40 miles away, warning of storm approach with audible tone, and display of distance
- Maestro Set Wind Speed and Direction Set (Silver)
- Plastic Rain Gauge (up to 11")
- Pocket Wind Meter

**Search:** No
**Photos:** Yes
**Ordering:** Online
**Gift Wrap:** No
**Delivery:** Ground

# Weather Channel

http://www.weather.com

The cable-TV channel brings you the day's weather, with maps showing radar, rain, snow, and thunderstorms, plus forecasts morning, noon, and night. They help you predict weather wherever you are traveling, going to the country, a big sports even, or the seashore. They will deliver your personalized weather info to your PCS phone or pager. The store ships within one business day. Samples:
- Desktop Weather Valet, with remote sensors, alarm clock, barometric forecast, temperature readings for three locations
- Glynne Sundial, replica of 18th century original
- Polished brass rain gauge
- Singing Bird Clock Weather Station, showing indoor temperature and humidity
- The Weather Channel umbrella
- Wireless indoor-outdoor thermometer

**Search:** No
**Photos:** Yes
**Ordering:** Online, Phone, Fax
**Gift Wrap:** Yes
**Delivery:** Ground, 3rd Day

# Weather Graphics Technologies

http://www.weathergraphics.com

Great tools for the serious weather researcher, including free and shareware software, available on disk or by download, maps, and poster-size charts. Samples:
- *Digital Atmosphere*, downloaded
- *Digital Chart of the World*, 1.7 GB of map data in resolutions of less than a mile, on 4 CD-ROMs, covering every spot on earth
- *Global Tracks, Hurricane and Typhoon Tracking Software*, with historical database going back to late 1800s for the Atlantic, mid-1900s for other oceans (downloadable)
- *Weathergraph*, two-sided, laminated 11" x 17" reference chart on all facets of weather observation and forecasting

**Search:** No
**Photos:** Yes
**Ordering:** Online, or download
**Gift Wrap:** No
**Delivery:** 3rd Day, 2nd Day, Overnight

# Weather Research Center

http://www.wxresearch.com

An elaborate nonprofit site with its own camp and a ton of images, maps, and data about tides, lightning, local weather outlooks, rainfall, seasonal heating and cooling, surface wind directions, temperatures, tides, and ultraviolet exposure. The bulk of this info is free, but they offer some services for which you have to sign up, and pay a fee for each click (hurricane, severe damage, coastal services). Samples:
- NOAA Satellite Images of U.S. weather
- Severe Weather Summary, U.S., last two days
- World Lightning Strike Summary, a color-coded map from NASA, organized by year and month

**Search:** No
**Photos:** Yes
**Ordering:** Free, or pay-by-click for special services
**Gift Wrap:** No
**Delivery:** Download

## Weather Simulator

http://members.aol.com/
eburger/wxsim.html

Use this shareware program on a Windows computer to predict temperatures in your area, depending on the season and sky conditions such as dew, fog, frost, or wind speed, or, just in case, solar eclipses. The author says he's been a weather nut since he was twelve and spent lots of his youth forecasting temperature changes. Product:

- Weather Simulator, Version 5.2

**Search:** No
**Photos:** No
**Ordering:** Online
**Gift Wrap:** No
**Delivery:** Downloadable

## What in the World

http://www.whatintheworld.com

A cheerful site encouraging you to get outdoors to watch the stars, the weather, or the waves. (They sell kayaks, too.) Binoculars, microscopes, and telescopes, used and new, along with sky software and news of current celestial events. ("Vast stellar disks set stage for planet birth in new Hubble images.") For fast delivery, phone them. Samples:

- Canon 12 x 36 Image Stabilized Binoculars
- Celestron, *The Sky Level 1*, CD-ROM
- Meade Starfinder 6"
- Takahashi 160mm F/3.3 Epsilon Astrograph

**Search:** Yes
**Photos:** Yes
**Ordering:** Online, Phone, Fax
**Gift Wrap:** No
**Delivery:** Ground

## Wild Birds Forever

http://www.birdsforever.com/
binoc.html

Binoculars and spotting scopes that are perfect for birding, sports, or weather-watching. Advice on how to pick the best optics for your situation. Product descriptions are very detailed, with some customer testimonials. They process orders within 48 hours, but some items are sent directly from the manufacturer, within 72 hours. Samples:

- Bausch and Lomb Binoculars, 19mm, 8 x 36 magnification, field of view 341 feet at 1,000 yards, close focus 10 feet, weather resistant, OK with sunglasses and eyeglasses
- Bushnell Birder Binoculars, 12mm, 8 x 40 magnification, field of view 356 feet at 1,000 yards
- Bushnell Natureview Spotting Scope, 60mm objective lens, field of view 150 feet at 1,000 yards

**Search:** No
**Photos:** Yes
**Ordering:** Online, Fax
**Gift Wrap:** No
**Delivery:** Ground

## You may also want to set your binoculars on these chapters:

- Maps & Atlases
- Photography
- Stargazing

# Weddings

Who would have thought that the Web could be an engaged couple's bonanza? For the busy couple with not a lot of time on their hands, or the frugal couple who want the day to be special, without costing a fortune, these shops are terrific.

We've mostly included stores that cater to your big day by offering gowns or tuxedos, accessories, and advice. But we've also sprinkled in a few jewelry stores (for a complete listing of jewelry stores, go to the Jewelry chapter) and some shops that offer unique wedding gifts and favors.

## Alle Fine Jewelry

http://www.allejewelry.com

Finding just the right engagement ring or wedding band, and at the right price, too, can be difficult. At this store, you'll find a huge selection, all discounted below retail prices. Large photos, many showing different angles, make the selection process a little easier. Samples:
- 14K comfort fit wedding bands
- 14K Marquise diamond solitaire ring
- Gold channel set diamond wrap rings
- Matching 10K gold diamond cut chevron wedding bands
- Platinum and gold wedding bands
- Polished gold 14K diamond wedding sets
- Two-tone diamond bands

**Search:** Yes
**Photos:** Yes
**Ordering:** Online
**Gift Wrap:** Yes
**Delivery:** Ground, 2nd Day, Overnight

## August Veils

http://www.augustveils.com

Whenever you look through catalogs of veils, they always show how those veils look closed. This store goes out of its way to design and manufacture veils that look gorgeous after you lift them. Customize your headpiece and veil by selecting the length, style, pearls or sequins, types of edges, and colors. Shipping costs are $10 per veil. Samples:
- Custom designed headpieces and veils

**Search:** No
**Photos:** Yes
**Ordering:** Online, Phone, Fax
**Gift Wrap:** No
**Delivery:** Ground

## A Victorian Elegance

http://www.gator.net/~designs

If you'd like to walk down the aisle with a Victorian flare, stop by this store, where you'll find antique wedding gowns, jewelry, and accessories. The pictures are good and a great deal of information about the dresses (all measurement sizes, for example) is given. The selection varies depending on what they've found. Samples:
- Beaded purse
- Fans
- Hair combs
- Hats from the old days
- Shoe clips
- Parasols
- Traditional perfumes
- Victorian lace gown
- Vintage shoes
- Wedding dress worn around the time of the Grant administration

**Search:** Some
**Photos:** Yes
**Ordering:** Online, Phone, Email
**Gift Wrap:** No
**Delivery:** Ground

## Brides R Us

http://www.brides-r-us.com

This is a good place to shop if you want to save a bundle on your wedding gown, bridesmaid dresses, the groom's tux, or many different accessories for the big day. They carry over 100 different wedding gown styles with over 200 matching veil styles. Most gowns are available from size 4 to size 20. Beautiful, full-length pictures with complete descriptions will help you make your decision. If the gown you want is in stock, it will be shipped to you within a week. If you're planning to elope tomorrow, you can have the gown rushed to you for $40; otherwise shipping is about $15 per gown. They ship worldwide. Samples:

- Back pieces
- Bridesmaid dresses
- Bun Rings
- Crowns
- Floral bands
- Floral wreaths
- Flower girl dresses
- Hats, caps, and caplets
- Headbands
- Men's formalwear
- Tiaras
- V-bands
- Wedding gowns

**Search:** Yes
**Photos:** Yes
**Ordering:** Online, Phone
**Gift Wrap:** No
**Delivery:** Ground, 2nd Day

## Chocolate Arts

http://www2.cybernex.net/
~mhourin

If you're looking for a unique wedding favor or centerpiece, give this place a lick, er, we mean a try. They have many objects made from delicious chocolate, or you can custom-order something (engraving is OK) and they will make a mold just for you. They can also make your gift up using sugar-free chocolate. If

you want something custom-ordered, make sure to phone ahead early. They ship noncustom orders within two weeks; favors take six weeks. They ship with a cold pack in hot weather or to warm climates. Samples:

- Chocolate roses
- Chocolate swans
- Chocolate flower pats with roses, daisies, or tulips
- Truffles
- Chocolate pretzels

**Search:** No
**Photos:** Yes
**Ordering:** Online, Phone, Fax, Email
**Gift Wrap:** Card
**Delivery:** 2nd Day, Overnight

## David Morgan

http://www.davidmorgan.com

The Celtic patterns of interwoven lines have a special pertinence to wedding rings—two intertwined ribbons signify two intertwined lives. The terminal figure for the ribbons is the heron, Creyr in Welsh, meaning Creator. The Celtic wedding rings created at this store are offered in three widths. Each width shows the pattern in a distinctive way. Sample wedding rings:

- 14K gold with lighter ribbons
- Celtic diamond engagement rings
- Heavy ribbons with a bold pattern
- Thin heavy ribbons
- Trinity wedding rings

**Search:** Yes
**Photos:** Yes
**Ordering:** Online, Phone, Fax
**Gift Wrap:** Card
**Delivery:** Ground

## eTuxedo

http://www.etuxedo.com

If you're thinking of buying a tux instead of renting one, check this store out. They have great prices on quality tuxedos and accessories. (Tuxedos start at $169.) You'll find many different styles and sizes (36R to 50L, with extra-large sizes available) to choose from. If you're still not sure, they offer a full refund on any unaltered garments returned within 30 days. Samples:

- Classic 100% pure worsted wool cutaway
- Double-breasted wool tuxedos
- One-button, shawl-collar white dinner jacket
- Pure cotton and cotton blend wing-tip formal shirts
- Single-breasted tailcoat
- Tuxedo separates
- White double-breasted tailcoat

**Search:** Yes
**Photos:** Yes
**Ordering:** Online, Phone, Fax
**Gift Wrap:** No
**Delivery:** Ground, 2nd Day, Overnight

# Foxhollow Herb Farm

http://www.foxhollowherbs.com

The herb-related products sold at this store are organically grown and then manufactured from a farm in Hollister, California. Everything is made in small batches to ensure quality. One of the unique items they make is heart-shaped herbal soap wedding favors. The soaps are wrapped in white or off-white netting, tied with a ribbon and dried flowers (call and give them the colors of your wedding, so everything is coordinated). You can add a heart-shaped note indicating what the herbs used in each soap stands for. (Rosemary for remembrance, mint for virtue, etc.) Also included are the bride and groom's name and date of wedding. Samples:

- Geranium rose
- Lavender
- Lemongrass
- Oatmeal and lavender
- Rosemary and mint

**Search:** Yes
**Photos:** Some
**Ordering:** Online, Phone
**Gift Wrap:** No
**Delivery:** Ground

# Gem of the Day

http://www.gemday.com

This is one of the most unusual jewelry stores on the Internet. Have you ever walked in the mall going from jewelry store to jewelry store only to find that each one basically had the same stuff? Then, all of a sudden, you enter one and *everything* looks good? Well, this store is like that. Unlike most jewelry stores on the Internet, this one *started* as a Web store. Not following any traditional wedding criteria, this store will make your proposal very new millenniumish. Gem of the Day will create a custom-designed Web site, complete with your picture, your intended's picture, your engagement ring, and anything else you'd like. They're not cheap, but they do offer a lot of services for free, such as free delivery, gift wrapping, and ring sizing, and there's no sales tax to anywhere in the U.S. Samples:

- 14K gold and diamond bicycle brooch
- Anniversary rings
- Classic diamond engagement rings
- Matching diamond baguette wedding rings
- Men's nugget diamond ring
- Multicolor tourmaline ring
- Oil well ring
- Pearl swirl earrings
- Ruby, diamond, and sapphire ring
- 7-marquise diamond band

**Search:** Yes
**Photos:** Yes
**Ordering:** Online, Phone
**Gift Wrap:** Yes
**Delivery:** Ground, 2nd Day, Overnight

# Gowns Online.com

http://www.gownsonline.com

This is a great place to shop if you're real busy and don't have the time to go from bridal shop to bridal shop. You browse through their online catalog or you can ask them for a gown you saw in a magazine. In fact, Gowns Online offers discount subscription prices on some bridal magazines. Some of the designers are

Eve of Milady, Jim Hjelm, Mon Cheri, and Illisa Bridals. Samples:

- Bridesmaid dresses
- Headpieces
- Wedding gowns

**Search:** Yes
**Photos:** Yes
**Ordering:** Online
**Gift Wrap:** No
**Delivery:** Ground

## Next Step Bridal Shoes

http://www.bridalshoes.com

Great selection of formal shoes at this shop. You'll find everything from classic pumps to Victorian-style ankle boots. They also carry lots of accessories and appliqués for your shoes. They have a great search, especially if you know exactly what you want and don't need to browse. If, in the case of bridesmaid or mother-of-the-bride dresses, you'd like to have the shoes custom-tinted, just send them a fabric swatch. Sizes vary according to shoe style, but most of them come in a narrow width. They have a large selection of children's sizes, too. They also sell a few neat little items for the wedding, such as table cameras. The prices are terrific. Samples:

- Bridal boots
- Coordinated handbags
- Handbag and shoe appliqués
- Satin wedding shoes in many styles

**Search:** Yes
**Photos:** Yes
**Ordering:** Online, Fax, Email
**Gift Wrap:** No
**Delivery:** Ground

## Romantic Headlines

http://
www.romanticheadlines.com

This is a wonderful place to shop for bridal veils, headpieces, tiaras, hats, and other accessories. Once you've picked out the headpiece you want, they'll give you matching veil selections to choose from. Samples:

- Bridal lingerie
- Cake servers
- Cake tops
- Engraved gifts for the groomsmen
- Flower girl headpieces and veils
- Headpieces, tiaras, veils, and hats
- Lace garters
- Unity candles
- Wedding bubbles
- Wedding gloves in various lengths

**Search:** Yes
**Photos:** Yes
**Ordering:** Online, Phone, Fax
**Gift Wrap:** No
**Delivery:** Ground, 2nd Day, Overnight

## Unique Wedding Internet Bridal Shop

http://www.angelfire.com/biz/
uniquewedding

Wholesale prices for the bride and groom at this store will leave you some money for your honeymoon. They sell some new and used wedding gowns (some for only $99), but what they specialize in are the accessories. (We saw some lovely veil and headpiece sets for only $39.) Shipping is just $5 per order for Ground and $20 for Overnight (that includes everything in your order, no matter what the weight!). Samples:

- Bun wraps
- Headbands
- Headpieces
- Necklaces with matching earring sets made out of rhinestones and pearls
- Princess Diana tiara replicas
- Veil hats
- Veils

**Search:** No
**Photos:** Yes
**Ordering:** Online, Mail
**Gift Wrap:** No
**Delivery:** Ground, Overnight

## The Wedding Channel

`http://www.vintagewedding.com`

This store has lots of things for sale for the big day, as well as offering lots of services to help you through the maze and save you some time. They give the traditional advice, such as bride and groom checklists, etiquette do's and don'ts, but they also publish some unusual ones, like skin-care advice, learning how to select the right tux for one's body type, and a financial planner. They also have a neat honeymoon planner (via the Internet Travel Network) where you can browse through romantic locations, and if you want, make your reservations. Need a wedding planner? They'll help you find one, too. If you're looking to buy your wedding gown online, click on their advanced search, which gives you 12 categories to fill in so you don't waste time browsing. Samples:

- Bridal gowns
- Bridal registry
- Bridesmaids' and groomsmen's and children's gifts
- Cake accessories
- Garters
- Money bags
- Mother-of-the-bride dresses
- Reflection goblets
- Ring pillow
- Shoes
- Veils
- Wedding favors

**Search:** Yes
**Photos:** Yes
**Ordering:** Online, Phone, Fax
**Gift Wrap:** Card
**Delivery:** Ground

## Wedding Expressions

`http://weddingexpressions.com`

This is a wonderful, one-stop store for everything you'll need for a beautiful wedding. And, to top it off, they offer 30%–50% off of retail prices. Loved the selection of wedding favors. If you've ever been in the dressing room just before a wedding, you'll appreciate the Wedding Day Emergency Kit. It comes with those little things that can lead to catastrophes if you forget them, such as sewing needle, nail file, hair pins, aspirin, pearl buttons, safety pins, Band-Aids, and even pierced earring backs. If you know someone who is getting married, a nice gift might be a gift certificate to this place. Samples:

- Boutonniere
- Bridal bouquet gift set
- Bridal gown storage bag
- Cowboy-inspired wedding favors
- Eco-safe wedding bubbles
- Garters
- Ring bearer's tux
- Satin roses
- Wedding gowns
- Wedding luminaries
- Wedding time capsule and planner

**Search:** No
**Photos:** Yes
**Ordering:** Online, Phone
**Gift Wrap:** No
**Delivery:** Ground, 2nd Day, Overnight

## Leah Ingram suggests Way Cool Weddings

"My favorite wedding-related site isn't a store per se, although it may become more commercial in the near future. It's called Way Cool Weddings at http://www.waycoolweddings.com, which features fun and funky Web sites about weddings. Each week a new Web site is featured. It was started by a husband and wife who were way ahead of their time and created a Web site for their wedding five years ago. The response they got was so enthusiastic that they decided to seek out other personal wedding Web sites to see what others were doing. When they found way cool ones, they created a link from their own page. Now it's sort of a status thing for cyberbrides and grooms to create a Web page and submit it to Way Cool Weddings for consideration. What I think is wonderful about the site is it lets you look at the Web sites for tons of other weddings, from which you can get great ideas for your own wedding."

Leah Ingram is the author of *The Bridal Registry Book* (Contemporary Books, 1995), *The Portable Wedding Consultant* (Contemporary Books, 1997), and the forthcoming *Your Wedding Your Way* (Contemporary Books, 2000).

## You may also want to check out these chapters:

- Clothes—Men
- Clothes—Women
- Flowers
- Food—Gourmet
- Jewelry
- Party Supplies
- Photography
- TV & Video Gear
- Wine

# Wine

This is another growing area on the Web that surprised us for its depth. There are stores selling $10,000 bottles of wine and others that comb the world looking for inexpensive, small wineries that sell their wine for a song. Most of the stores in this chapter specialize in wine, but a few also sell other alcoholic beverages. You might be wondering how that works with 21 being the legal age to drink in most places. This is how: When they mail your order to you, they give instructions to the delivery service that the order must be signed for and proof of age must be given to by the person signing for the package. If you think this may be a problem, you may want to have your package delivered to your office. Depending upon the state you live in, you may or may not be able to have wine delivered to your door.

## 1-800 Wine Shop

http://www.1800wineshop.com

Wine from this northern California company comes boxed in elegant packaging, making it a perfect place to shop when you want to send a bottle or a few bottles of wine as a gift. They offer gift baskets, and you can also have your company's logo or special message etched on the packaging. Of course, you can also send some *your* way, too. If you join their Cellar Select Wine Club (a kind of wine of the month club), you'll get two bottles from nearby wineries that will entitle you to discounts on their gift baskets. Don't forget to check their specials. Samples:

- Cellar Wine Club
- Chocolate truffles and wine gift baskets
- Cigar and wine gift baskets
- Domaine Montreaux sparkling wine 3-bottle set
- Magnum and triple magnum bottles
- Wine samplers (all white, all red, or mixed)

**Search:** No
**Photos:** Yes
**Ordering:** Online, Phone
**Gift Wrap:** Yes
**Delivery:** Ground, 2nd Day, Overnight

## A Wine Store on the Internet

http://www.awinestore.com

This store gets the award as the most bland yet descriptive name on the Web. They sell a good selection of premium California wines. Each bottle has a full description, which is good, because let's say you want a bottle of Cabernet Sauvignon—this store sells 11 different labels. Minimum order is three bottles or $45. They are set up to ship their wine internationally. Samples:

- 3-bottle gift packs
- Chardonnay
- Fumé Blanc
- Merlot
- Pinor Noir
- Zinfandel

**Search:** Yes
**Photos:** No
**Ordering:** Online, Phone, Fax
**Gift Wrap:** Card
**Delivery:** Ground, 2nd Day

## California Wine

http://www.calwine.com

Searching for your favorite bottle of wine is easy from this store. You can search by winery, variety, price, or region. Not sure what vintage to get? Ask their pros. Like so many of the California shops, they offer a Wine Club, which sends you a two-bottle sample every month. If you are looking for a gift or wine for a wedding, you may want to try their custom label service, where you supply the graphic and they make up the labels. The wine here isn't cheap; in fact, it's expensive. But besides getting premium wine, you'll also get a full description, including the composition,

alcohol, sugar, acidity, and pH levels. Samples:
- Books about wine
- Chateau Potelle Cabernet Sauvignon
- Gift certificates
- Iron Horse sparkling wines
- Napa Valley sampler
- RSV Reserve Merlot
- Storybook Mt. Zinfandel
- Swanson Chardonnay
- Truchard Pinot Noir

**Search:** Yes
**Photos:** Yes
**Ordering:** Online, Phone, Fax
**Gift Wrap:** No
**Delivery:** Ground, 2nd Day, Overnight

## City Wine

http://www.citiwine.com

The goal of this store is simple: They want to provide you with the most inexpensive fine wines. They are their own wine testers and are always on the lookout for a small but delicious new label. And that's what they sell to you. Their wines come from California, New Mexico, France, Italy, Chile, Germany, and Australia. Always make sure to check their featured wines, which are discounted by 15% individually and 20% by the case. Samples:
- Chateau Leoville Varton Bordeax
- Colin-Deleger Bourgogne Burgundy
- Domaine Tremont Chenas Beaujolais
- Gruet Blance de Noirs Brut
- Karly Zinfandel
- L'Orval Chardonnay
- La Playa Merlot
- Sample cases of red and white wines

**Search:** No
**Photos:** No
**Ordering:** Online, Phone, Fax
**Gift Wrap:** No
**Delivery:** Ground

## Grand Cru Wine Cellar

http://www.grandcru-winecellar.com

Looking for a big, bold Cabernet Sauvignon from Chile or a supple, robust Shiraz from Australia? Yes? Then shop here. You'll also be able to sample wines from Petits Chateaux in France and vineyards in California. Besides selling fine wine, you can also purchase other spirits as well as a cigar and glassware. You'll receive a 5% discount when you order six or more bottles and 10% discount on order of over 12 bottles. Samples:
- 15-year-old single malt Scotch whiskey
- Chateau Ferriere, Margaux
- Chateau Fontenil, Fronsac
- Chateau Mouton Rothschild
- Custom home wine cellar and racking systems
- Les Fortes de Latour, Pauillac
- Riedel glassware
- Trefetham Reserve, Cabernet Sauvignon

**Search:** Yes
**Photos:** No
**Ordering:** Online
**Gift Wrap:** No
**Delivery:** Ground, 2nd Day, Overnight

## Liquor by Wire

http://lbw.com

This store specializes in sending wine, champagne, and gift baskets to anywhere around the world. They can also send customized orders. There are over 1,000 different alcohol beverage gifts to choose from, so you should be able to find something you like and that fits your budget. They also have a good selection of old and rare wines and other liquor. Samples:
- Aberlour 18-year-old malt Scotch
- Beers of the World gift box
- Bombay Gin
- Far Niente Chardonnay
- Gift baskets
- Herraduras Seleccion Suprema tequila
- Kendal Jackson Merlot

- Louis Jadot Pinot Noir
- Moët and Chandon Brut
- Opus One Cabernet Sauvignon
- Wild Turkey Rare Breed bourbon

**Search:** Yes
**Photos:** Yes
**Ordering:** Online, Fax
**Gift Wrap:** Yes
**Delivery:** 3rd Day, 2nd Day, Overnight

## Tinamou Wine Company

http://www.tinamou.com

A tinamou is a small bird found in South America and South Africa. Some people think it's one of those missing links due to its reptilian characteristics. But it's one of the oldest species in the world and is revered as a symbol of versatility and endurance—just like many of the French wines and English ports (some going back to 1900) for sale from this store. Samples:

- 1900 Chateau Lafite Rothschild
- 1900 Chateau Latour
- 1937 Colheitas tawny port
- 1943 Sandeman port
- 1948 Cockburn port
- 1974 St. Julien Beychevelle
- French dessert wines
- Petits Chateaux
- Regional French wines

**Search:** Yes
**Photos:** Some
**Ordering:** Online, Email
**Gift Wrap:** No
**Delivery:** Ground, 2nd Day

## Virtual Vineyards

http://www.virtualvin.com

This is a lovely store that not only sells wine but also sells some tasty delectables to go with it. You'll find a lot of the more common wines, as well as some bottles from smaller, lesser-known vineyards. They offer gift certificates, and you can also order samplers that have a few bottles of wine in one box. And, of course, there's a monthly wine program available, too. You'll love the vast search engine that lets you find what you are looking for in a variety of different ways. Samples:

- Black olive pâté
- Cardboard tote of wine, coffee, chocolate, and cookies
- Chocolate ribbon sticks
- Corteaux de L'Aubance Chenin Blanc
- De Medici truffle oil
- Dried Porcini mushrooms
- Mas Grand Plagniol Rouge
- Monte Volpe Moscato
- Per Sempre Estate Cabernet Sauvignon engraved bottle
- Whitehall Lane "Bommarito" Merlot

**Search:** Yes
**Photos:** Yes
**Ordering:** Online, Phone, Fax
**Gift Wrap:** Yes
**Delivery:** Ground, 2nd Day

## The Wine Broker, Inc.

http://www.thewinebrokers.com

This store may not be for everyone, and we'll tell you why. They are wine brokers. With their inventory of over 100,000 bottles of wine (and some port), they sell primarily to restaurants. However, they will also sell to wine enthusiasts, like you. If you are looking for rare wine, they have a section of newly acquired "cellar jewels," as they call them. These go quickly, so check back often. They sell wines from just about every wine-growing region in the world. Their wine club offers two bottles a month with a 5% discount on all wine orders for joining the club. The prices are very good here, and the selection is fantastic, but they won't hold your hand as much as some of the other stores. Samples:

- Deloach Barbieri Zinfandel
- Dom Dopll Riesling
- Piper-Heidsieck Brut
- Rabbit Ridge Sauvignon Blanc
- Rainwater Madeira

- Schlumberger Pinot Blanc

**Search:** Yes
**Photos:** No
**Ordering:** Online
**Gift Wrap:** No
**Delivery:** Ground, 2nd Day

# Cool idea

Wine doesn't taste real good when it's been heated, so it's best to get the fastest shipping possible. And if you think you may not be home when it is delivered, instead of having the wine sit on your doorstep for a few hours, how about having it delivered to your office?

# Can I have wine delivered from out of state?

Some states have laws preventing you from receiving wine shipped from out-of-state addresses. To find out if your state is one of them, go to the Wine Law site at http://www.winelaw.org

# You may also want to taste these chapters:

- Chocolate
- Cigars
- Food—Gourmet

# Writing Tools

Writers get personal with their pens, pencils, papers, books, and even keyboards. If you like to sharpen a few pencils before you write a report, or if you love filling an elegant fountain pen, these stores will appeal to you. Whether you're writing a diary or a screenplay, these stores seem to understand the intensely personal process, and make it a pleasure.

## America's Pen Collection

http://penonline.com/store/
commerce.cgi

Fancy pens galore! Pens with solid gold nibs. Pens in elegant boxes. Gorgeous sets in gold, silver, and platinum. Pens inspired by Fabergé Imperial Easter Eggs. Oh, and they have plenty of organizers, too. Samples:
- Filofax supplies, including notepaper and maps
- Gold-plated fountain pens with platinum inlays
- Leather pen pouches
- Sterling silver pen sets
- Travel pens for slightly less than $1,000

**Search:** Yes
**Photos:** Yes
**Ordering:** Online, Phone, Fax
**Gift Wrap:** No
**Delivery:** Ground

## Artlite Office Supply

http://www.artlite.net/pens

If you want a discount on a slightly used demonstration model from the retail store, or a discontinued item, you can get more than half off at this site. They also sell a dozen major brands of fine pens. Samples:

- Falcon black fountain pen
- Stationery with raised print lettering
- Townsend Sterling Silver fountain pen
- Vanishing Point fountain pen with retractable tip

**Search:** Yes
**Photos:** Yes
**Ordering:** Online
**Gift Wrap:** Box
**Delivery:** 3rd Day, 2nd Day, Overnight

## B and D Woodworking

http://www.digisys.net/
bdpens/order.html

These folks craft magnifying glasses, pens and pencils for you using exotic woods such as cedar, Honduras rosewood, maple, myrtlewood, orange, purpleheart, tulipwood, and zebra wood, with titanium gold plating if you wish. If you have a deer antler, they can make a pen out of it. No plastics are ever used, they swear. Samples:
- Box Elder Burlwood ballpoint pen with 10K gold-plated components
- Oak pen holder
- Rosewood pen
- Ruby Dymondwood pen and pencil
- Tulipwood ballpoint pen

**Search:** No
**Photos:** Yes
**Ordering:** Online, Fax
**Gift Wrap:** Gift box or velvet pouch
**Delivery:** Ground

## Diary House USA

http://www.diaryhouseusa.com

If you love writing a journal, here are some wonderful diary books to fill. You can have your name or initials placed on the cover. Samples:
- Desk diary with gilt edge, sections for year planning, expenses, and addresses

- Executive writing portfolio with hand-stitched padded cover
- Leather-bound time planner with gold corners and international maps
- Letts of London slim diary with year planner, expense, and address sections
- Pocket-size diary with gilt edges and ribbon

**Search:** No
**Photos:** Some
**Ordering:** Online
**Gift Wrap:** No
**Delivery:** Ground

## English Channel

http://www.e-channel.com/rf/
calligraphy.html

A choice selection of gifts, with some neat pen-and-paper sets. Despite the focus on English products, this site sells through Yahoo, and delivers within a week, anywhere in the world. Samples:
- Brass wax seal with your initials
- Calligraphy pen with gold ink and star seal
- Correspondence sets with sealing wax
- Inkslinger pen-and-ink set

**Search:** Yes
**Photos:** Yes
**Ordering:** Online
**Gift Wrap:** Yes
**Delivery:** Ground

## Fine Pens Online

http://www.finepensonline.com

Magnificent pens from all over the world, with pictures that make you want to reach out and write. Typical manufacturers represented: Aurora, Bexley, Cross, Delta, Élysée, Fabergé, Lamy, Michel Perchin, Montblanc, Namiki, OMAS, Otis, Parker, Pelikan, Sensa, Sheaffer, S.T. DuPont, Stipula, Tibaldi, Waterford, and Waterman. Begun as a department

within an art store, this online store is now partnered with a member of the Pen Collectors of America, which inspects for quality. Lots of background on how each pen is manufactured and used. Samples:
- 12-sided fountain pen with gold band
- Celluloid pens
- Genesis of the Olympics pen from Pelikan with differential piston refill mechanism
- Pens with engraved silver barrels covered with enamel
- Rare special edition pens celebrating the 650th anniversary of the University of Pisa

**Search:** No
**Photos:** Yes
**Ordering:** Online, Phone, Fax
**Gift Wrap:** Yes
**Delivery:** 3rd Day, 2nd Day, Overnight

## Franz Schmidt Pens

http://www.southwind.net/
market/woodpens

Gary Franz likes making pens by hand, with 24-karat gold on the outside. Choose a wood for the barrel, and a style, and he assembles the pen for you. Samples:
- 1920-style ballpoint
- Maple burlwood slimline ballpoint pen
- Tulipwood rollerball pen

**Search:** No
**Photos:** Yes
**Ordering:** Online, Email
**Gift Wrap:** Maplewood case
**Delivery:** Ground

## Levenger

http://levenger.com

A luxurious store for readers and writers, with special lamps, bookholders, and writing tools, such as their Ergoraser, a specially designed eraser that fits into your hand like a plastic spoon, with a thick end for big swaths of erasing, and a thin end for pinpoint erasure. The Leveens started their company by supplying halogen reading lights for "serious readers," then branched out as their customers kept asking for more products. Generally, they take a few days to assemble an order, but you should receive your order within two weeks—faster if you insist. Samples:

- Box of pencils with sharpeners attached
- Ergorasers
- Leatherbound pencil sharpeners with two sizes of sharpening hole, in red, black, blue, or tan
- Pair of eraser stones
- Second Chance Inkwell, made of acrylic, with tiny transparent rubber feet
- Spiral inkwell

**Search:** Yes
**Photos:** Yes
**Ordering:** Online
**Gift Wrap:** Boxes
**Delivery:** Ground, 4th Day, 2nd Day, Overnight

## Merriam Webster

`http://www.m-w.com/home.htm`

The dictionary people bring you the word of the day, word games, and an online bookstore for anyone who loves words. You never knew there could be so many ways to package a dictionary! Look words up online, read the scripts of the radio broadcast Word for the Wise, and explore the lighter side of language. Ordering is through Amazon.com or Barnes and Noble, so you use this site to pick a book, then click a button to have a superstore take your order. Sample books:

- Audio dictionaries on CD-ROM
- Bilingual dictionaries of English and Spanish or English and Japanese
- Biographical dictionaries
- College-level, compact, desk, or pocket dictionaries
- Crossword dictionaries
- Dictionaries on CD-ROM
- Geographical dictionaries
- Thesauruses
- Word-game software

**Search:** No
**Photos:** Some
**Ordering:** Online, via Amazon.com or Barnes and Noble
**Gift Wrap:** Yes
**Delivery:** Ground, 2nd Day, Overnight

## World Pen

`http://www.worldpen.com/index.html`

A friendly, even chatty site for an international selection of pens, including specials and rarities. For newbies, they provide answers to frequently asked questions about pens, links to pen collector sites such as the Pen Museum, pen stores around the world, and manufacturers. They offer ink, books about pens, and refills, and do repairs. Samples:

- Celluloid resin fountain pen with gold nib
- Ink stain remover
- Solid brass ballpoint pen in colored lacquers
- Stainless-steel ballpoint pen with lacquer image of computer

**Search:** No
**Photos:** Blurry
**Ordering:** Online
**Gift Wrap:** Occasional boxes
**Delivery:** Ground, 3rd Day, Overnight

## Writer's Computer Store

`http://www.writerscomputer.com`

A big catalog aimed at playwrights, sit-com writers, and Hollywood wannabes as well as the pros. Sample goodies:

- Audio books about writing
- Automated contracts
- Dictionaries, word hoards, reference books
- Film production, management, and budgeting software

- Flip-top manuscript boxes
- Outliners and brainstorming software
- Script covers and fasteners
- Software for formatting plays and films
- Software to help you develop plots and characters
- Videos on screenwriting

**Search:** No
**Photos:** Yes
**Ordering:** Online, Phone, Fax
**Gift Wrap:** No
**Delivery:** Ground, 2nd Day, Overnight

## Writer's Digest

http://www.writersdigest.com

The well-organized home of *Writer's Market*, the bible of writers who want to find magazines or book publishers for their latest novel, poem, or article. The site offers samples from their magazines, plus electronic versions of the guidelines from more than a thousand magazines—helpful if you're not sure how to format or send your submission. You'll hear about upcoming contests, and courses at the Writer's Digest School (but, alas, these are not offered online). The Market of the Day alerts you to new publications, or old ones you may not have considered.

- 200 books on writing
- Enrollment in their book club
- Subscriptions to *Writer's Digest*
- *Writer's Market* on paper or CD-ROM or both

**Search:** Yes
**Photos:** Some
**Ordering:** Online, Phone, Fax
**Gift Wrap:** No
**Delivery:** Ground, Phone for overnight

## Writer's Edge

http://www.thewritersedge.com

Next time you go into space, take one of these pens with you. Built for NASA, the Fisher Space Pens can't leak, even if you write upside down floating in zero gravity. The manufacturer claims the ink will stay fluid for a hundred years. You can get commemorative coins with some pens. The store does laser or silkscreen engraving, and hot-stamps your name or logo on some pens. Samples:

- All-chrome pen on 30" silver necklace
- Astronaut model pens
- Laser key chains that project smiley faces as well as dots
- Pen with built-in light (red, green, white)
- Pens coated with titanium nitride to look like bullets
- Retractable rubber-coated space pens
- Star Trek pens

**Search:** No
**Photos:** Yes
**Ordering:** Online
**Gift Wrap:** Boxes
**Delivery:** Ground, 2nd Day

## If you're in a writing mood, you may also want to browse these chapters:

- Books
- Home Office Supplies

# Addresses

Here's an alphabetical list of the stores and sites mentioned in this book—with their Web addresses. To locate descriptions of these sites, please look in the index.

| Store or Site | Web Address |
| --- | --- |
| 10,000 Vacation Rentals | http://www.10Kvacationrentals.com |
| 1001 Herbs | http://www.1001herbs.com |
| 101 Furniture | http://www.101 furniture.com |
| 101CD | http://www.194.205.125.30/oneprd/oone01.asp |
| 1-800-Flowers | http://www.1800flowers.com |
| 1-800-Batteries | http://www.1800batteries.com |
| 1-800-Birthday | http://www.1800birthday.com |
| 1-800 Wine Shop | http://www.1800wineshope.com |
| 1-888-Wwinline | http://www.1888wwinline.com |
| 1st in Flowers | http://www.1stinflowers.com |
| 1st Stop Software | http://www.1ststopsoft.com |
| 1 Travel | http://www.1travel.com |
| 2BuyPC | http://www.2buypc.com/shop |
| 3 Friends in Kona | http://www.aloha.net/~chee/3friends.html |
| 5-Star Advantage | http://www.aaaaadvantage.com |
| 800.com | http://www.800.com |
| 888 Live Flowers | http://www.liveflowers.com |
| 911 Gifts | http://www.911 gifts.com |
| A+ Teaching Materials | http://www.aplusteaching.com |
| A-1 Cheap Golf | http://www.cartserver.com |
| A2Z Toys.com | http://www.a2ztoys.com |
| AAA Art Gallery | http://aaa.artselect.com |
| AAA Spectra Discount Golf | http://www.discount-golf.com |
| Aardvark Batteries | http://www.aardvarkbat.com |
| Aardvark Pet | http://www.aardvarkpet.com |
| Abby's Herb Company | http://www.abbysherbs.com/index.html |
| ABee Well Pharmacy | http://www.abeewell.com |
| About.com | http://www.about.com |
| Above Average Pencil Portraits | http://www.zianet.com/aa-portraits |
| ABS – Alternative Book Shop | http://web-star.com/alternative/books.html |
| Acadian Rain | http://www.acadianrain.com/index.html |
| Access Batteries | http://www.accessbattery.com |

| | |
|---|---|
| Access Discount Camera | http://www.accesscamera.com |
| Access Micro | http://www.accessmicro.com |
| Access Quality Toys | http://www.accessqualitytoys.com |
| AccuWeather | http://www.accuweather.com |
| A Cook's Gallery | http://www.cooksgallery.com |
| Action Direct | http://www.action-direct.com |
| A Cut Above | http://www.acutabove.com |
| Advanced Custom Golf | http://www.tylan.com |
| Advanced Recording Products | http://www.tapeweb.com |
| Advantage Products | http://www.advantageproducts.com |
| Adventure Gear | http://www.ewalker.com |
| AFE Cosmetics and Skincare | http://www.cosmetics.com |
| African Formula Cosmetics | http://www.africanformula.com |
| Agfa Direct | http://www.agfadirect.com |
| A Happy Camper | http://www.ahappycamper.com |
| Ahern | http://www.aherncorp.com/ahern.html |
| Air Animal | http://www.airanimal.com |
| Air Travel Manager | http://www.airtm.com |
| All About Health | http://www.allabouthealth.com |
| Alle Fine Jewelry | http://www.allejewelry.com |
| Allergy Clean Environments | http://www.allergyclean.com |
| Allherb.com | http://www.allherb.com/consumer |
| All Independent Music | http://www.allindependentmusic.com |
| All Internet Shopping Directory | http://www.all-internet.com |
| All Seasons Spas & Accessories | http://www.allseasonsspas.com |
| Almost Originals | http://www.almostoriginals.com |
| Altai Corporation | http://www.edumart.com/altai |
| Amazon.com | http://www.amazon.com |
| Ambrose Gardens | http://www.ambrosegardesn.com/index.cfml |
| America's Pen Collection | http://www.penonline.com/store/commerce.cgi |
| American Assc. of Ind. Investor | http://www.aaii.com |
| American Digital | http://www.am-dig.com |
| American Foods | http://www.americanfoods.com |
| American Health & Comfort | http://www.ahcp.com |
| American Health Herbs | http://www.healthherbs.com |
| America Offprice | http://www.amoffprice.com |
| AmeriTrade | http://www.ameritrade.com |

| | |
|---|---|
| AMR Video | http://www.amr1.com |
| Andromeda Software | http://www.andromedasoftware.com |
| Angler's Express | http://www.anglers-express.com/index.htm |
| Anna Cris Maternity | http://www.annacris.com |
| Ann Hemyng Candy's | http://www.mmink.com/mmink/dossiers/choco.html |
| Anything PC | http://www.anythingpc.com |
| Appointments | http://www.appointments.com |
| Appybean | http://www.appybean.com |
| April Cornell | http://www.aprilcornel.com |
| Arbonne International | http://www.personalskincare.com |
| Arcata Pet Online | http://www.arcatapet-online.com |
| Arch | http://www.arch.com |
| Arnold's Men's Online Store | http://www.arnoldsmensstore.com |
| Aroma Borealis | http://www.tgx.com/coffee |
| Art & Woodcrafter Supply | http://www.artwoodcrafter.com |
| Artbeats | http://www.artbeats.com |
| Art.com | http://www.art.com |
| Artlite Office Supply | http://www.artlite.net/pens |
| Artnet | http://www.artnet.com |
| Artville | http://www.artville.com |
| Asia Soft | http://www.asiasoft.com |
| As Seen on TV | http://www.asontv.com |
| Astromart | http://www.astromart.com |
| Athletic Team Uniforms | http://www.ateamuniformsdirect.com |
| At Your Office | http://www.atyouroffice.com/default.asp |
| Auction Gate | http://www.auctiongate.com |
| Auction Max | http://www.auctionmax.com |
| Auction Universe | http://www.auctionuniverse.com |
| Audradella's | http://www.audradella.com |
| August Veils | http://www.augustveils.com |
| Autobytel | http://www.autobytel.com |
| AutoConnect | http://autoconnect.com |
| Autograph World | http://www.autographworld.com |
| Autoweb.com | http://www.autoweb.com |
| Avalon | http://www.emporium.net/avalon |
| Avalon Garden.com | http://www.avalongarden.com |
| Avalon Intimates | http://www.emporium.net/avalon |

| | |
|---|---|
| A Victorian Elegance | http://www.gator.net/~designs |
| Avon | http://www.avon.com |
| A Wine Shop on the Internet | http://www.awinestore.com |
| Azazz | http://www.azazz.com |
| B & D Woodworking | http://www.digisys.net/bdpens/order.html |
| B and H | http://www.bhphotovideo.com |
| Babies 'N Bells | http://www.babiesnbells.com |
| Baby Bag Boutique | http://www.babybag.com |
| Baby Becoming | http://www.babybecoming.com |
| Baby Best Buy | http://www.babybestbuy.com |
| Baby Connect | http://www.babyconnect.com |
| Baby Cyberstore | http://www.babycyberstore.com |
| Baby Grams | http://www.babygrams.com |
| Baby Lane | http://thebabylane.com |
| Backcountry Store | http://www.bcstore.com |
| Backpack Computing | http://www.shopbuilder.com/backpack |
| Backroads | http://www.backroads.com |
| Balata Bill's | http://www.balatabills.com |
| Balducci's | http://www.balducci.com |
| Ball Beauty Supply | http://ballbeauty.com |
| BalloonTyme, Inc. | http://www.balloontyme.com |
| Banker's Collection | http://www.bankers-collection.com |
| Barnes and Noble | http://www.barnesandnoble.com |
| Barrington | http://www.barrington-ltd.com |
| Bart's Water Sports | http://www.barswatersports.com |
| Baseball Express | http://www.baseballexp.com |
| BasketPatterns | http://www.basketpatterns.com |
| Bass Pro Shops | http://www.basspro-shops.com |
| Batter's Choice | http://www.batterschoice.com |
| Battery Outlet | http://www.batteryoutlet.com |
| Battery Terminal at Wholesale | http://www.wholesaleadvantage.com/ battery_index.htm |
| Beach Bowl Pro Shop | http://www.beachbowlproshop.com |
| Beanie Furniture | http://www.beaniefurniture.com |
| Bearing Alert | http://www.bearingalert.com |
| Beauty Boutique | http://www.beautenaturel.com |
| Beauty Naturally | http://www.beautynaturally.com |

| | |
|---|---|
| BedandBath.com | http://www.bedandbath.com |
| Beehive Botanicals | http://www.beehive-botanicals.com |
| Beer and Wine-making Supplies | http://www.aardvarkbrewing.com |
| Beer, Beer and More Beer | http://www.morebeer.com |
| Belgian Chocolate Online | http://www.chocolat.com |
| Belgian Chocolate Shop | http://www.giftex.com/belgian |
| Bender-Burkot | http://www.bender-burkot.com |
| BestBeep | http://www.bestbeep.com |
| Best Buy | http://www.bestbuy.com |
| Best by Mail | http://www.bestbymail.com |
| Best Fares | http://www.bestfares.com |
| BestPrices | http://www.bestprices.com |
| Best Video | http://www.bestvideo.com |
| Better Batter | http://www.betterbatter.com |
| Better Botanicals | http://www.betterbotanicals.com |
| Better Business Bureau | http://www.bbbonline.org |
| Beyond.com | http://www.beyond.com |
| Bid Find | http://www.bidfind.com |
| BigBowling.com | http://www.bigbowling.com |
| Big Horn Quilts | http://www.bighornquilts.com |
| BigMen, TallMen, StoutMen's | http://www.bigmen.com |
| Big Star | http://www.bigstar.com |
| Big Toe Sports | http://bigtoesports.com |
| Bike Nashbar | http://www.bikenashbar.com |
| Bill's Khakis | http://www.billskhakis.com |
| Bingham Projects, Inc. | http://www.binghamprojects.com |
| BioDerm | http://www.bioderm.com |
| Birkenstocks | http://www.birkenstockexpress.com |
| Birthday U.S.A. | http://www.birthdayusa.com |
| BizTravel | http://www.biztravel.com |
| BK Puff and Stuff | http://www.bkpuffnstuff.com/baby.htm |
| Blackwells | http://www.blackwell.co.uk |
| Blockbuster Entertainment | http://www.blockbuster.com/video |
| Bloomberg | http://www.bloomberg.org |
| Bloomingdale's | http://www.bloomingdales.com |
| Boat Show | http://www.boatshow.com |
| Body Maintenance | http://www.bodymaintenance.com |

| | |
|---|---|
| Body Trends | http://www.bodytrends.com |
| Bone to Be Wild | http://www.io.com/life/pets |
| Bookmark Software | http://www.bookmarksoftware.com |
| Bookmark's Fun Station | http://www.edumart.com/bookmart |
| Books.com | http://www.books.com |
| Borders | http://www.borders.com |
| Botanics of California | http://www.botanicscalifornia.com |
| Bottom Dollar | http://www.bottomdollar.com |
| Bowler's Depot | http://www.bowlersdepot.com |
| Bowl USA | http://www.bowlusa.com |
| BowMan's Archery Solutions | http://www.thebowman.com |
| Brandsmall | http://catalog.brandsmall.com/eshop |
| Brauns | http://www.brauns.com |
| BRD Security | http://www.spybase.com |
| Breathfree.com | http://www.breathfree.com |
| Brew Your Own Beverages | http://www.onlinesu.com/byob |
| Brides R Us | http://www.brides-r-us.com |
| Brigittine Monks Gourmet | http://greatbend.com/brentw/fidge.htm |
| Bron Shoe Company | http://www.bronshoe.com |
| Brooks Brothers | http://www.brooksbrothers.com |
| Burpee | http://www.burpee.com |
| Business & Computer Bkstr. | http://www.bcb.com |
| Buycomp | http://www.buy.com |
| Buyer's Index | http://www.buyersindex.com |
| BuyFlowers.net | http://www.buyflowers.net |
| BuyGames | http://www2.buy.com |
| BuyItOnTheWeb.com | http://www.buyitontheweb.com |
| Buyonet | http://www.buyonet.com |
| BuyRight Videogames | http://www.buyrite1.com |
| BuySoft | http://www.buy.com/bc/noframes/software.asp |
| BuySoftware Network | http://www.buysoftware.com |
| Caesar's Palate | http://www.caesarspalate.com |
| Calculated Industries | http://www.calculated.com |
| California Wine | http://www.calwine.com |
| Calypso | http://www.calypsotours.com |
| Camelot Music | http://www.camelotmusic.com |
| Camera Shop | http://www.camerashopinc.com |

| | |
|---|---|
| Camera World | http://www.cameraworld.com |
| Camping World Online | http://www.campingworld.com |
| Camp Store | http://www.shopforcamp.com |
| Canterbury Farms | http://www.spiritone.com/~canfarms |
| Cap'n | http://www.thecapn.com |
| Capsized | http://www.capsized.com |
| Car Point | http://www.carpoint.msn.com |
| Care4U—Aids for Daily Living | http://www.care4u.com |
| Care-a-lot Pet Supply | http://www.carealot.org |
| Carnival | http://www.carnival.com |
| Carolina School Products | http://www.edumart.com/carolina |
| Carpenters Lace, Inc. | http://www.carpenterslace.com |
| Car Point | http://www.carpoint.msn.com |
| Carrington Laboratories | http://www.carringtonlabs.com |
| Cars.com | http://www.cars.com |
| Carushka | http://www.caruska.com |
| Casa de Fruta | http://www.casadefruta.com |
| Cash for CDs | http://www.207.71.196.181/casgforcds.asp |
| CashmereClub.com | http://www.millionchasmere.com |
| Cassette House | http://www.tape.com |
| Cat Tracker | http://www.cattracker.com |
| CD Connection | http://www.cdconnection.com |
| CD Now | http://www.cdnow.com |
| CD Quest | http://www.cdquest.com |
| CDshop | http://www.cdshop.com |
| CD Source | http://www.cdsource.com |
| CD Universe | http://www.cduniverse.com |
| CDW | http://www.cdw.com |
| CD World | http://www.cdworld.com |
| Celestaire | http://www.celestaire.com |
| Cellular Experience | http://www.icatmall.com/cellx |
| ChairNet | http://www.chairnet.com |
| Charlie's Toys | http://www.mall6.register.com/ontexusa/ charlielow.htm |
| Charm Woven Labels | http://www.charmwoven.com |
| Cheap Tickets | http://www.cheaptickets.com |
| Chef's Catalog | http://www.ccddee.com |

| | |
|---|---|
| Chemist Net | http://www.chemistnet.com |
| Cherry Tree Hill Yarn | http://www.cherryyarn.com |
| Chic Paris | http://www.inetbiz.com/chic |
| Children's Wear Digest | http://xoom.freeshop.com/pg00523.htm |
| Child's Play | http://www.toysntrains.com |
| Chin Chin | http://www.chinchin.com |
| Chipshot.com | http://www.chipshotgolf.com |
| Chocoholic | http://www.chocoholic.com |
| Chocolate Arts | http://www2.cybernex.net/~mhourin |
| Chocolate Gallery | http://www.chocolategallery.com |
| Chocolate Rampage | http://www.fishnet.net/~chocolate |
| Chocolates, Etc. | http://www.leisurelan.com/connections/shops/ chocetc |
| Christina Shops | http://www.christinaschoice.com.market.html |
| Chronicle Books | http://www.chronbooks.com |
| CIBO's | http://www.greatfood.com |
| Cigar International | http://www.cigarintl.com |
| City Wine | http://www.citywine.com |
| Class Act Movie Posters | http://www.movieposters.net |
| Classy Kids | http://www.classykids.com/home.htm |
| Clean Kids Naturally | http://www.kidprices.com |
| Click for Flowers | http://www.clickforflowers.com |
| Clinique | http://www.clinique.com |
| Cloud Nine | http://www.cloudninehi.com |
| Code-Free DVD | http://www.codefreedvd.com |
| Color by Robert Craig | http://www.robertcraig.com |
| Colorado Cyclist | http://www.coloradocyclist.com |
| Comfort House | http://www.comforthouse.com |
| Common Sense | http://www.cdromcsc.com |
| Community Prescription | http://www.prescript.com |
| Compaq Computer | http://www.compaq.com |
| Compare Net | http://comparenet.com |
| CompUSA Direct | http://www.compusa.com |
| ComputerLiteracy.com | http://www.clbooks.com/home.htm |
| Computers4Sure | http://www.computers4sure.com |
| Computer World | http://www..jandr.com |
| Connoisseurs Cigar Company | http://www.ccigar.com/ordering/index.html |

| | |
|---|---|
| Consumer Action | http://www.consumer-action.org |
| Consumer Direct | http://www.consumer-direct.com |
| Consumer Information Center | http://www.pueblo.gsa.org |
| Consumer Reports | http://www.consumerreports.org |
| Consumer World | http://www.consumerworld.org |
| Cooking.com | http://www.cooking.com |
| Cook's Nook | http://www.cooksnook.com |
| Cook's Thesaurus | http://www.switcheroo.com/Equipment.html |
| Cooks World | http://www.cooksworld.com |
| Cool Stuff Cheap | http://www.coolstuffcheap.com |
| Cool Toy Shop | http://www.cooltoys.com |
| Copernicus | http://www.lq.com/copernicus |
| Corbis Images | http://www.corbisimages.com |
| Corsair Ties | http://www.couchpotato.net/~corsair |
| Cosmetic Mall | http://www.cosmeticmall.com |
| Cosmetics Counter | http://www.cosmeticcounter.com |
| CosmopolitanHome.com | http://www.cosmopolitanhome.com |
| Cotton Cordell | http://www.cottoncordell.com |
| Country Walkers | http://www.countrywalkers.com |
| CPA Web Trust | http://www.aicpa.org |
| Crabtree and Evelyn, Ltd. | http://www.crabtree-evelyn.com |
| Cranberry Lane | http://www.cranberrylane.com |
| CRH International, Inc. | http://www.aloealoe.com |
| Critic's Choice Video | http://www.ccvideo.com |
| Crooks Clothing | http://www.crooksclothing.com |
| Cross Stitches | http://xstitches.com |
| Crusoe Island | http://www.crusoeisland.com |
| CT Creations | http://www.ctcreations.com |
| Curriculum Swap | http://www.theswap.com |
| Cute as a Bug | http://www.cuteasabug.com |
| Cutler of New England | http://www.cutlerofnewengland.com |
| CyberCash | http://www.cybercash.com |
| CyberPet | http://www.cyberpet.com/cyberdog/breed |
| Cyberspace Telemedical | http://www.telemedical.com |
| Dan Howard Maternity Outlet | http://www.momshop.com |
| Dan's Garden Shop | http://dansgardenshop.com |
| Daskalides Chocolatier | http://www.daskalides.com |

| | |
|---|---|
| Datek | http://www.datek.com |
| David Morgan | http://www.davidmorgan.com |
| Dawn Software | http://www.dawnsoft.com |
| DayTimer | http://www.daytimer.com |
| DealerNet | http://www.dealernet.com |
| Dean and Deluca | http://www.dean-deluca.com |
| Dearinger | http://www.dearinger.com/welcome.htm |
| Delia's Clothing | http://www.delias.com |
| Dell Computer | http://www.dell.com |
| DeLorme | http://www.delorme.com |
| Denali | http://www.denalil.com |
| Denim Blues | http://21stcenturyplaza.com/blues/jeans.html |
| Design Buy | http://www.designbuy.com |
| Designer Deals | http://www.designerdeals.com |
| Desperate.com | http://www.desperate.com |
| Diane's Designs | http://www.host.fptdoday.com/dianes |
| Diary House USA | http://www.diaryhouseusa.com |
| Dinner Direct | http://www.dinnerdirect.com |
| Dionis | http://www.dionissoap.com |
| Direct Sports | http://www.directsports.com |
| Discount Art Supplies | http://www.discountart.com |
| Discount Beauty.com | http://www.discountbeauty.com |
| Discount Lingerie Rack | http://www.lingerierack.com |
| Disney Store | http://store.disney.go.com/shopping |
| Dixie Diner Club | http://www.dixiediner.com |
| Dixie's Gifts | http://www.dixiesgifts.com |
| DLJ Direct | http://www.dljdirect.com |
| Doggie Diamonds | http://www.doggiediamonds.com |
| Dogtoys.com | http://www.dogtoys.com |
| Domino Video Company | http://www.dvcnet.com |
| Dr. Goodpet | http://www.goodpet.com |
| Dr. Toy | http://www.drtoy.com |
| Drug Emporium | http://www.drugemporium.com |
| Drugs by Mail | http://www.drugsbymail.com |
| Drugstore.com | http://www.drugstore.com |
| Drum & Spear | http://www.drumandspear.com |
| DVD City | http://www.dvdcity.com |

| | |
|---|---|
| EarthDream | http://www.earthdream.com |
| Earthly Delights | http://www.earthy.com |
| EarthRISE | http://earthrise.sdsc.edu/earthrise |
| EarthWatch Weather | http://www.earthwatch.com |
| Easy Going | http://www.easygoing.com |
| E-Battery | http://www.e-battery.com |
| eBay | http://www.ebay.com |
| Ecobaby | http://www.ecobaby.com |
| Eddie Bauer | http://www.eddiebauer.com/home/home.html |
| Edmark | http://www.edmark.com |
| Edmund's Roses | http://www.edmundsroses.com |
| Edutainment Catalog | http://www.edutainco.com |
| Egghead | http://www.egghead.com |
| EGift | http://www.egift.com |
| Electronic Marketplace | http://www.emrkt.com |
| Electronics.Net | http://electronics.net/Homepage.htm |
| ElectroWeb | http://www.electroweb.com |
| Elstead Maps | http://www.elstead.co.uk |
| Emelauren's | http://www.emelauren.com |
| eMerchandise | http://www1.emerchandise.com |
| E Music | http://www.emusic.com |
| Encore Auction | http://www.encoreacution.com |
| English Channel | http://www.e-channel.com/rf/calligraphy.html |
| Entertainment Earth | http://www.entertainmentearth.com |
| eNutrition | http://www.enutrition.com |
| E! Online | http://shop.eonline.com |
| Epic Menswear | http://www.epicmenswear.com |
| Equitour | http://www.ridingtours.com |
| ERIC Clearinghouse | http://www.ericae.net/bstore |
| ERock | http://www.erock.com |
| ESI Online | http://www.edsoft.com |
| Especially for You | http://www.kids-store.com |
| eToys | http://www.etoys.com |
| E*Trade | http://www.etrade.com |
| eTuxedo | http://www.etuxedo.com |
| Europe Express | http://www.europeexpress.com |
| Eurosport | http://www.soccer.com |

| | |
|---|---|
| Everybody's Store | http://www.nas.com/~goodbuy |
| Everything But The Baby | http://www.everythingbutthebaby.com |
| Excite Classifieds and Auctions | http://www.excite.com/collectibles |
| Excite Shopping | http://www.excite.com/shopping |
| Expedia | http://expedia.msn.com |
| Expedition Leader | http://www.expedition-leader.com |
| Extreme Lengths | http://www.extremelengths.com |
| Eye Wire | http://www.adobestudios.com |
| EZ Shop.com | http://www.ezshop.com |
| Fair Trade Naturals | http://www.algomaya.com |
| Fancy Foods Gourmet Club | http://www.ffgc.com |
| FAO Schwarz | http://www.st2.yahoo.com/faoschwarz |
| Farmacopia | http://www.farmacopia.com |
| Fascinating Folds | http://www.fascinating-folds.com |
| Fashion Mall | http://www.fashionmall.com |
| Federal Trade Commission | http://www.ftc.gov |
| Festival Films | http://www.mdle.com/ClassicFilms/FeaturedVideo/festival.htm |
| Fidelity | http://www311.fidelity.com |
| Fine Pens Online | http://www.finepensonline.com |
| First Auction | http://www.firstauction.com |
| Fishing Mall | http://www.fishingmall.com |
| Fitness Zone | http://www.fitnesszone.com |
| Fit-Net Health Clubs | http://www.fit-net.com |
| Fleurs Per Mail | http://www.fleurspermail.com |
| Florist.com | http://www.florist.com |
| Flowernet | http://www.flowernet.com |
| Flowers Direct | http://www.flowersdirect.com |
| Fogdog Sports | http://www.fogdog.com |
| Foodstuffs | http://www.foodstuffs.com |
| Fortunoff | http://www.fortunoff.com |
| Foxhollow Herb Farm | http://www.foxhollowherbs.com |
| Fragrance Net | http://www.ordermill.com/~fragrance |
| Frame U.S.A. | http://www.frameusa.com |
| Franklin Covey | http://www.franklinquest.com |
| Franz Schmidt Pens | http://www.southwind.net/market/woodpens |
| Fruit of the Hands | http://www.fruit-of-the-hands.com |

| | |
|---|---|
| FTD | http://www.ftd.com |
| Furniture.com | http://www.furniture.com |
| FurnitureFind.com | http://www.furniturefind.com |
| FurnitureOnline.com | http://www.furnitureonline.com |
| Future Fantasy Bookstore | http://www.futfan.com/home.html |
| Game Cellar | http://www.gamecellar.com |
| Game Daily | http://www.gamedaily.com |
| Game Max | http://www.gamemax.com |
| GamEscapes | http://www.gamelovers.com |
| Gap, Gap Kids & Baby Gap | http://gap.com/onlinestore/gap |
| Garden Botanika | http://www.gardenbotanika.com |
| Garden.com | http://www.garden.com |
| Garden Talk | http://gardentalk.com |
| Gardener's Supply Company | http://www.gardeners.com |
| Gary's Island | http://www.garysisland.com |
| Gateway Computer | http://www.gw2k.com |
| Gear.com | http://www.gear.com |
| Gem of the Day | http://www.gemday.com |
| Gems and Jewels.com | http://www.gemsandjewels.com |
| Giftopia | http://www.giftopia.com |
| Gift Tree | http://www.gifttree.com |
| Gigabuys | http://www.gigabuys.us.dell.com |
| Girl Shop | http://girlshop.com |
| Global Gallery Curator | http://www.globalgallery.net |
| Global Mart | http://www.globe-mart.com |
| Go Babies | http://www.gobabies.com |
| Godiva Chocolatier | http://www.godiva.com |
| Golf Circuit | http://www.golfcircuit.com |
| Golf Club Exchange | http://www.golfexchange.com |
| Golf.com | http://www.golf.com |
| Golf Discount.com | http://www.golfdiscount.com |
| Golf Furniture | http://www.golffurniture.com |
| Golf Gods | http://www.bestvaluegolf.com |
| Golf Outlet | http://www.golfoutlet.com |
| Golf Shop Online | http://www.catalog.com/golfshop |
| Golf Training Aids.com | http://www.golftrainingaids.com |
| Good Eats | http://www.goodeats.com |

| | |
|---|---|
| Good Movies | http://www.goodmovies.com |
| Go To | http://www.goto.com |
| Gottschalks | http://www.gotts.com |
| GourmetMarket.com | http://www.gourmetmarket.com |
| Gourmet Trader | http://www.gourmettrader.com |
| Gowns Online.com | http://www.gownsonline.com |
| Grand Cru Wine Cellar | http://www.grandcru-winecellars.com |
| Grand European Tours | http://www.getours.com |
| Great Flowers | http://www.greatflowers.com |
| GreatFood.com | http://www.greatfood.com |
| Great Skate | http://www.greatskate.com |
| Green Drop Ink | http://206.216.201.175 |
| Greenhouse Express.com | http://www.greenhouseexpress.com |
| Green Tree | http://www.greentree.com |
| GW School Supply | http://www.gwschool.com |
| Gymboree | http://www.gymboree.com |
| Hair Care for Less | http://www.haircareforless.com |
| Hair Doctor | http://www.the-hair-doctor.com |
| Hammacher Schlemmer | http://www.hammacher.com |
| Hammond Maps | http://www.hammondmap.com |
| Handmade, Homemade Toys | http://www.crafttoys.com |
| Hanna Andersson | http://www.hannaandersson.com |
| Hanover Clothing Co. | http://www.bigandtall.com |
| Hard Candy Cosmetics | http://www.hardcandy.com |
| Harmon Discount | http://www.harmondiscount.com |
| Harmony House | http://www.harmonyhouse.com |
| Harolds | http://harolds.net |
| Harry and David | http://www.harryanddavid.com |
| Hatfields & McCoys Brew | http://www.hatfields-mccoys.com |
| Hawaii Helicopters | http://hawaiiheli.com |
| Health Check Systems, Inc. | http://www.healthchecksystems.com |
| HealthShop.com | http://www.healthshop.com |
| Healthy Trader | http://www.healthytrader.com |
| Heirloom Shoppe | http://www.spinneret.com/heirloom |
| Hern Marine | http://www.hernmarine.com |
| Hiking Shack | http://www.hikingshack.com |
| His Music Place | http://www.his musicplace.com |

| | |
|---|---|
| Hitchcock Shoes | http://www.wideshoes.com |
| Hobby Builders Supply | http://www.minatures.com |
| Hockey2 | http://www.hockey2.com |
| Hollywood Collection | http://www.thehollywoodcollection.com |
| Hollywood U.S.A. | http://www.hollywood-usa.com |
| Homebrew Experience | http://www.brewguys.com |
| Home Harvest Garden Supply | http://www.homeharvest.com |
| Home Office Direct | http://www.homeofficedirect.com |
| Home Pharmacy | http://www.homepharmacy.com/hp |
| HomeRuns | http://www.homeruns.com |
| Home Shopping Pharmacy | http://www.homeshoppingpharmacy.com |
| Honeycomb Mittens | http://www.altnews.com.au/mittens |
| Hoovers Online | http://www.hoovers.com |
| HotBot Shopping Director | http://www.hotbot.com/shop |
| Hotel Discounts | http://www.hoteldiscounts.com |
| Hot Mamas | http://www.hot-mamas.com |
| House of Batteries | http://houseofbatteries.com |
| HugeStore.com | http://www.hugestore.com |
| Humongous Entertainment | http://www.humongous.com |
| Hungry Eye | http://www.leicasource.com |
| HyperDrive | http://www.hyperdrive.com |
| iBaby.com | http://www4.ibaby.com |
| IC London | http://www.iclondon.com |
| imall | http://www.imall.com |
| Indian River Gift Fruit | http://www.giftfruit.com |
| Infinite Auction | http://www.sweetdeal.com |
| Inksite | http://www.inksite.com |
| In-line Skate Store | http://www.in-lineskatestore.com |
| Ino | http://www.ino.com |
| Insight | http://www.insight.com |
| Intellicast | http://www.intellicast.com |
| Interact! | http://www.interactcd.com |
| InterCenter | http://www.Intercenter.com |
| International Coffee House | http://www.21stcentury plaza.com/stor101/ stor101.htm |
| International Golf Outlet | http://www.igogolf.com |
| International Gourmet | http://www.intlgourmet.com |

| | |
|---|---|
| Internet Kitchen | http://www.your-kitchen.com |
| Internet Mall | http://www.shopnow.com |
| Internet Movie Database | http://www.imbd.com |
| Internet Travel Network | http://www.itn.com |
| Investor Map | http://www.investormap.com |
| iPrint | http://www6.iprint.com |
| IPS | http://www.ipsrx.com/secure/index.htm |
| iQVCNetwork | http://www.iqvc.com |
| Iron Viking | http://www.ironviking.com |
| Island Arts of Whidbey Island | http://www.islandarts.com |
| Island Gifts Direct | http://www.oldhawaii.com/igd |
| Istanbul Express | http://www.istanbulexpress.com |
| Italian Music | http://www.italian-music.com/index._uk.htm |
| J & R Music World | http://www.jandr.com |
| Jackson and Perkins | http://www.jacksonandperkins.com |
| Jaggar Maternity | http://www.maternityclothes.com |
| Japanese Weekend | http://www.japaneseweekend.com |
| J. Crew | http://www.www.jcrew.com/cgi-bin/index.cig |
| JC Penney | http://www.jcpenney.com |
| JC Wunderlich & Co. | http://www.jcwunderlich.com |
| Jean-Pierre Creations de Paris | http://www.jean-pierre-creations.com |
| JewelryWeb.com | http://www.jewelryweb.com |
| Jigowat | http://www.fabric8.com/jigowat |
| Jumbo | http://www.jumbo.com |
| Kamyra in Print | http://www.partyinvitations.com |
| Kaplan | http://www.catalog.kaplanco.com |
| Karen's Health Store | http://www.karneshealthfoods.com |
| KBkids.com | http://www.kbkids.com |
| Kelley Blue Book | http://www.kbb.com |
| Kelly Bike.com | http://www.kellybike.com |
| Kerrits | http://www.kerrits.com |
| KidFlix.com | http://www.kidflix.com |
| Kids' Camps | http://www.kidscamps.com |
| Kid's Clothing Outlet | http://www.kidclothing.com |
| Killer App | http://www.killerapp.com |
| Kinko's | http://www.kinkos.com |
| Kinnikinnick Foods | http://www.kinnikinnick.com/kinnik/welcome.vs |

| | |
|---|---|
| Kitchen and Company | http://www.kitchenandcompany.com |
| Knowledge Adventure | http://www.knowledgeadventure.com |
| Lafeber's Critter Products | http://www.lafeber.com |
| Lamp Fashions | http://www.lamp-fashions.com |
| LAN Optics | http://www.tiac.net/users/lanint |
| Landscape USA | http://www.landscapeusa.com |
| Lands' End | http://www.landsend.com |
| La Patisserie | http://www.patisserie.com |
| Laptop-Battery | http://www.laptop-battery.com |
| Latin American Nexus | http://www.lanexus.com |
| Lazarus Games | http://www.lazarusgames.com |
| LBIC | http://www.lbic.com |
| L-Bow Mittens | http://www.lbow.com |
| Learning Company | http://www.learning.co.com |
| Levenger | http://levenger.com/shop/PenInk |
| Limbo Bros. Cigar Company | http://www.cigar98.com |
| Liquor by Wire | http://www.lbw.com |
| Lite Cosmetics | http://www.litecosmetics.com |
| Little Koala | http://www.littlekoala.com |
| Little Prince and Princess | http://www.royalbaby.com |
| L.L. Bean | http://www.llbean.com |
| Loon Lake Outfitters | http://www.loonlake.com |
| Louvre | http://www.mistral.culture.fr/louvre/louvrea.htm |
| Luggage Express | http://www.luggageexpress.com |
| Lycos Shopping | http://www.lycos.com |
| Mac Mall | http://www.cc-inc.com |
| MacWorks | http://www.macworks.com |
| Macy's | http://www.macys.com |
| Madazz Enterprises, Ltd. | http://www.madazz.co.nz |
| Madison Avenue Salons | http://www.madison-avenue.com |
| Magellan's | http://www.magellans.com |
| Major League Baseball | http://www.majorleaguebaseball.com |
| Making It Big | http://www.bigwomen.com |
| Map and Travel Center | http://www.mapper.com |
| Map Art | http://www.map-art.com |
| MapQuest | http://www.mapquest.com |
| Maps Online | http://www.mapsonline.co.uk |

| | |
|---|---|
| Mapsworld | http://www.mapsworld.com |
| Marine Scene | http://www.marinescenemall.com |
| Maritech Marine Electronics | http://www.maritech.com |
| Market Guide | http://www.marketguide.com |
| Maternity Mall.com | http://www.maternitymall.com |
| Maui Coffee Store | http://www.maui.net/~jstark/mauicofe.html |
| McGlen | http://www.mcglen.com |
| Me Body and Bath | http://www.mebodyandbath.com |
| MediQuest Pharmacy | http://www.mediquestpharmacy.com |
| MediStore | http://www.mediconsult.com |
| Medport | http://www.medportinc.com |
| Meissner Winches | http://www.meissner-winches.com |
| Melrose Place Fashion | http://www.www.ibcnet.com/dir/fashion/melrose |
| Mendocino Chocolate | http://www.mendocino-chocolate.com |
| Merriam Webster | http://www.m-w.com/home.htm |
| Merrick Pet Delicatessen | http://www.merrick-deli.com |
| Metropolitan Museum of Art | http://www.metmuseum.org |
| MicroSurveillance | http://www.microelec.force9.co.uk |
| Microwarehouse | http://www.warehouse.com |
| Mobile Office Outfitters | http://www.mobilegear.com |
| Mori Nu Tofu | http://www.morinu.com |
| Morningstar | http://www.morningstar.com |
| MotherNature.com | http://www.mothernature.com |
| Motley Fool | http://www.motleyfool.com |
| Mountain Gear | http://www.mgea.com |
| Movie Memories | http://www.moviememories.com |
| MSN Money Central Investor | http://www.investor.com |
| Multex | http://www.multexinvestor.com |
| Museum of Bad Art | http://www.glyphs.com/moba |
| Museum of Modern Art | http://www.moma.org |
| Museum Shop | http://www.www.museumshop.com |
| Music Boulevard | http://www.musicblvd.com |
| Music Favorites | http://www.musicfavorites.com |
| Musicforce | http://www.musicforce.com |
| Music HQ | http://www.musichq.com/cdhq |
| Mutual Funds Interactive | http://www.fundsinteractive.com |
| My Basics.com | http://www.mybasics.com |

| | |
|---|---|
| My Simon | http://www.mysimon.com |
| Nat'l Basketball Assc. Stor | http://www.store.nba.com |
| Nat'l Fraud Information | http://www.fraud.org |
| Nat'l Gallery of Art | http://www.nga.gov |
| Nat'l Museum of American Art | http://www.nmaa-ryder.si.edu |
| Nat'l Parenting Center | http://www.tnpc.com |
| Natural Body Bar | http://www.bodybar.com |
| Natural Living Center | http://www.ncenter.com/products.htm |
| Natural Luxury Home Style | http://www.widerview.com |
| Nature's Pet Marketplace | http://www.nautrespet.com |
| Nautilus Arts & Crafts | http://www.nautilus-crafts.com |
| Navstation | http://www.maritech.com |
| NC Buy Book Store | http://www.ncbuy.com/books |
| NCT | http://www.nct-active.com/store2.htm |
| NECX | http://www.necxdirect.necx.com |
| NetCheck | http://www.netcheck.com |
| Net Grocer | http://www.netgrocer.com |
| Net Market | http://www.netmarket.com |
| Netropolitan Plaza | http://netropolitanplaza.com |
| NetSkate | http://www.netskate.com |
| New Line Cinema Studio Store | http://www.newline.com |
| New Watch | http://www.newwatches.com |
| Next Step Bridal Shoes | http://www.bridalshoes.com |
| Niche Gardens | http://www.nichegdn.com |
| Nightmare Factory | http://www.nightmarefactory.com |
| Noah's Pet Supplies | http://noahspets.com |
| Noguchi Museum | http://www.noguchi.org |
| Noodle Kidoodle | http://www.noodlekidoodle.com |
| Nordstrom | http://www.nordstrom.com |
| Norman Camera | http://www.normancamera.com |
| Northend Cigars | http://www.necigars.com |
| North Sails One Design | http://www.northsailsod.com |
| Notebook Superstore | http://www.notebooksuperstore.com |
| NPC Activeware | http://www.npcwear.com |
| NSSDC Photo Gallery | http://nssdc.gsfc.nasa.gov/photo_gallery |
| Nutrasource | http://www.nutrasource.com |
| O'Neil's | http://www.oneils.com |

| | |
|---|---|
| O'Sullivan | http://www.furnituredirect.com |
| Oddens' Bookmarks | http:kartoserver.frw.ruu.nl/80 |
| Office Depot | http://www.officedepot.com |
| Office Furniture Concepts | http://www.ofconcepts.com |
| Office Max | http://www.officemax.com |
| Oleda | http://www.oleda.com |
| Omaha Steaks | http://www.omahasteaks.com |
| One Call | http://www.onecall.com |
| Online Sports.com | http://www.onlinesports.com |
| Only Gourmet.com | http://www.onlygourmet.com |
| Onsale | http://www.onsale.com/departments/homeoffice.htm |
| Onsale at Auction | http://www.onsale.com |
| On the Fringe | http://www.onthefringe.com |
| Opera World | http://www.operaworld.com |
| Orvis | http://www.orvis.com |
| Outdoor.com | http://www.theoutdoor.com |
| Outdoor Woman | http://www.theoutdoorwoman.com |
| Outpost | http://www.outpost.com |
| Pacific Pedestal | http://www.carmelnet/PacificPedestal |
| Pager1 | http://www.netaxs.com/people/pagers |
| Paper Paradise | http://www.khs.com |
| Paper Studio | http://www.paperstudio.com |
| Parenting Concepts | http://www.parentingconcepts.com |
| Par Golf Supply, Inc. | http://www.pargolf.com |
| Party Makers | http://www.partymakers.com |
| Patchworks | http://www.reproductionfabrics.com |
| PC Connection | http://www.pcconnection.com |
| PC Flowers and Gifts | http://www.pcflowers.com |
| PC Mall | http://www.cc-inc.com |
| Peapod | http://www.peapod.com |
| Pearsall's Garden Center | http://www.pearsalls.com |
| Peet's Coffee and Tea | http://www.peets.com |
| Pennsylvania Avenue Mall | http://www.amishfurniture.com |
| Perfect Present Picker | http://presentpicker.com/ppp |
| Personal Solar | http://www.yessolar.com |
| Pet Expo | http://www.pet-expo.com/petspets.htm |
| PetHouse, Inc. | http://www.netusa.com/pethouse.html |

| | |
|---|---|
| PetPro | http://www.petpro.com |
| Pets.com | http://www2.pets.com |
| Phone Guys | http://www.cordless-guys.com |
| Photo Collect | http://photocollect.com/home.htm |
| Photofilm | http://www.photofilm.com |
| PhotoNet | http://photo.net/photo/index.html |
| Pillsbury | http://www.pillsbury.com |
| Planet Rx | http://www.planetrx.com |
| Plato's Toybox | http://www.platostoybox.com |
| Playback Shopping | http://www.playback.com |
| Powell's Books | http://powells.com |
| PowerPalace | http://www.powerpalace.com |
| PreBook Games | http://www.prebookgames.com |
| Premier Formal Wear | http://www.magibox.net/~premier |
| Preview | http://www.previewtravel.lycos.com |
| PricePoint | http://www.pricepoint.com |
| PriceSCAN | http://www.pricescan.com |
| Price Search | http://pricesearch.net |
| Price's Power International | http://www.prices-power.com |
| Price Watch | http://www.pricewatch.com |
| ProBeep | http://www5.web201.com/probeep/wwwfp/products/cellular/index.html |
| Prof. Bowling Instruction Site | http://www.pbiin.com |
| ProFlowers | http://www.proflowers.com |
| ProMark Pharmacies | http://www.pro-mark-pharmacies.com |
| Quicken | http://www.quicken.com |
| "R" Dreams | http://www.rdreams.com |
| Rabid Home | http://www.rabidhome.com |
| Radio Fence | http://www.radiofence.com |
| RainBee | http://www.rainbee.com |
| R.C. Steele Co. | http://www.rcsteele.com |
| Real Net | http://www.real.com/index.html |
| Red Rocket | http://www.redrocket.com |
| Reel.com | http://www.reel.com |
| REI | http://www.rei.com |
| Restaurant Wholesale Store | http://www.cutlery-store.com |
| Rex Art | http://www.rexart.com |

| | |
|---|---|
| Ricardo's Cigar Shop | http://www.ricardoscigar.com |
| RJTech | http://www.rjtech.com |
| RKS Software Store | http://www.rks-softwware.com |
| Romantic Headlines | http://www.romanticheadlines.com |
| Roxy | http://www.roxy.com |
| Rubber Neckties | http://www.rubber-neckties.com |
| Rupp's | http://www.rupps.com |
| Sailor's Choice | http://www.sailorschoice.com |
| Samy's Camera | http://www.samys.com |
| Santa Cruz Bicycles | http://www.santacruzmtb.com |
| Santa Maria Discount Luggage | http://www.luggageman.com |
| Sarris Candies | http://www.nb.net/~bsarris/index.html |
| Scent Warehouse | http://www.scentwarehouse.com |
| School Connection | http://www.edumart.com/classmate |
| Schoolroom.com | http://www.schoolroom.com |
| Schwab | http://www.schwab.com |
| Schwinn | http://www.schwinn.com |
| Scientific Sales | http://www.scientificsales.com |
| Scrapbooks 'n More | http://www.scrapbooksmore.com/catalog.html |
| Screen Savers a2z | http://www.sirius.com/~ratloaf |
| Sculpture.Org | http://www.sculptor.org |
| Sears | http://www.sears.com |
| Seattle Art Museum | http://www.seattleartmuseum.org |
| Serenity Shop | http://www.serenityshop.com |
| Service Merchandise | http://www.servicemerchandise.com |
| Seuss Wear | http://www.seusswear.com |
| Sharper Image | http://www.sharperimage.com |
| Shepherd's Garden Seeds | http://www.sheperdseeds.com |
| Sherpa Products | http://www.sherpapet.com |
| She Sails | http://www.aztec.com/shesails |
| ShipStore.com | http://www.shipstore.com |
| Shop Find | http://www.shopfind.com |
| Shopping.com | http://www.shopping.com |
| Short Sizes, Inc. | http://www.shortsizesinc.com |
| Sierra Enterprises | http://www.sierra-enterprises.com |
| Silicon Investor | http://www.siliconinvestor.com |
| Simon and Co. | http://www.simonco.com/index.shtml |
| Sinopia | http://www.sinopia.com |
| Skates Away | http://www.skatepro.com/catalog |

| | |
|---|---|
| Skin Life Products | http://www.skinlife.com |
| Sky and Telescope | http://www.store.skypub.com |
| Slickrock Gallery | http://www.boulderutah.com/slickrock/index.htm |
| Smart Home | http://www.smarthome.com |
| Smart Money | http://www.smartmoney.com |
| Smith Sports | http://www.netsportstore.com |
| Smokey's Cigar Shop | http://www.smokeyscigars.com |
| Smoking Place | http://w3.sistelcom.com/smoking-place |
| Snap | http://www.snap.com |
| Soccer 4 All | http://www.soccer4all.com |
| Soccer Mania | http://soccermania.com |
| Software2Buy | http://www.software2buy.com/shop |
| Software Street | http://www.softwarestreet.com |
| South Eastern Gifts | http://www.southeasterngifts.com |
| Southwest Shopping Mall | http://www.swshopmall.com |
| Space Movie Archive | http://graffiti.u-bordeaux.fr/MAPBX/roussel/animewf.html |
| Speak to Me! | http://www.clickshop.com/speak |
| Spider Gear | http://www.spidergear.com |
| Spike Nashbar | http://www.spikenashbar |
| Sports and Athletics Online | http://www.das-mall.com/sportsandathletics/iskates.htm |
| Sports Fan | http://www.sports-fans.com |
| Spy Company | http://www.spycompany.com |
| SpyMart | http://www.spymart.com |
| Spy Products | http://www.spyproducts.com |
| Spy Store | http://www.thespystore.com |
| Spy Supply | http://www.spysupply.com |
| Spy Tech Agency | http://www.spytechagency.com |
| Staples | http://www.staples.com/st/home.asp |
| Starbucks | http://www.starbucks.com |
| State Line Tack | http://www.statelinetack.com |
| Stock Smart | http://www.stocksmart.com |
| Stoie's Stogies | http://www.astogie4u.com |
| Stones and Bones | http://www.stonesbones.com |
| Storyteller Audio Bookstore | http://audio-books.com/index.html |
| Stretch Text Book Covers | http://www.stretchtext.com |
| Suit Source | http://www.suitsource.com |

| | |
|---|---|
| SunFun | http://www.sunfun.com |
| Sunland Imports | http://www.sunlandimports.com |
| SureTrade | http://www.suretrade.com |
| SutterTel | http://www.suttertel.com |
| Syosset Sport Center | http://www.syossetsportcenter.com |
| Tackle Outlet, Inc. | http://www.hooklineandsinker.com |
| Tech Store | http://www.techstore.com |
| Tek Discount Warehouse | http://www.tekgallery.com/tekgallery |
| TeleDynamics | http://www.teledynamics.com |
| Tennis Company | http://www.tenniscompany.com |
| Tennis Menace | http://www.tennismenace.com |
| Tennis Warehouse | http://www.tennis-warehouse.com |
| Terror by Design | http://www.btprod.com |
| Teuscher Chocolate | http://www.2nite.com |
| The Baby Lane | http://thebabylane.com |
| The Beauty Cafe | http://www.beautycafe.com |
| The Cap'n | http://www.thecapn.com |
| The Chef's Store | http://www.chefstore.com |
| The F STOPS Here | http://www.thefstop.com |
| The Gap | http://www.gap.com/onlinestore/gap |
| The Gift | http://www.thegift.com |
| The Internet Mall | http://www.shopnow.com |
| The Learning Company | http://www.learningco.com |
| The Natural Place | http://www.naturalplace.com |
| TheStreet.com | http://www.thestreet.com |
| The Territory Ahead | http://www.territoryahead.com |
| The Trip | http://www.thetrip.com |
| The View | http://www.the-view.com |
| The Wine Broker, Inc. | http://www.thewinebrokers.com |
| Think CD/Video | http://www.goldpaint.net/cgi-bin/nph-tame.cgi/ thinkcd/index.tam |
| Thomas Register | http://www.thomasregister.com |
| Thomson Investors Network | http://www.thomsonivest.net |
| Tiger Direct | http://www.tigerdirect.com |
| Tinamou Wine Company | http://www.tinamou.com |
| TNT Cigars | http://tntcigars.com |
| Toe Picks to Toe Shoes | http://www.aiminc.com/eoi/eoimain.htm |
| Tom Snyder Productions | http://www.teachtsp.com |

| | |
|---|---|
| Tomtom Cigars | http://www.tomtom.co.uk |
| Top Drawer | http://www.k9design.com |
| Top Hat Toys | http://www.tophattoys.com |
| Total E | http://www.totale.com |
| Totally Outdoors | http://www.totallyoutdoors.com |
| Total Mart | http://www.totalmart.com |
| Toysmart.com | http://www.toysmart.net |
| Toys R Us | http://www.toysrus.com |
| Track Town Smoke Shop | http://www.tracktownsmokeshop.com |
| Travel Now | http://www.travelnow.com |
| Travelocity | http://www.travelocity.com |
| Travel Smith | http://www.travelsmith.com |
| TravelWeb | http://www.travelweb.com |
| Trinity Rx | http://www.drugplace.com |
| Tronix | http://www.tronixweb.com |
| Tropic Traders | http://www.tropicgifts.com |
| True Legends | http://www.truelengends.com/index.htm |
| Ulla Popken | http://www.ullapopken.com |
| Unboxed Software | http://www.unboxed.com |
| Uniglobe | http://www.uniglobe.com |
| Unique Wedding | http://www.angelfire.com/biz/uniquewedding |
| Universal Studios | http://www.store.universalstudios.com |
| Up4Sale | http://up4sale.com |
| Uptown Baskets | http://giftsforyou.com |
| Uptown Cigar Company | http://www.uptowncigar.com |
| Urban Decay | http://www.urbandecay.com |
| U.S. Consumer Gateway | http://www.consumer.gov |
| U.S. Geological Survey | http://edcwww.cr.usgs.gov/Webglis/glisbin/ finder_main.pl?dataset_name=MAPS_LARGE |
| Utrecht | http://www.utrechtart.com |
| Varsity Books | http://varsitybooks.com |
| Vegas Today | http://www.vegastoday.com |
| Video Movie Wholesale | http://www.usedmovies.com |
| Vintage Magazine Company | http://www.vinmg.com |
| Virtual Software Store | http://www.virtualsoftware.com |
| Virtual Vineyards | http://www.virtualvin.com |
| Vis Seafood | http://www.visseafoods.com |
| Vitamins.com | http://www.vitamins.com |

| | |
|---|---|
| VitaminShoppe.com | http://www.vitaminshoppe.com |
| Vitamins Network | http://www.vitamins.net |
| Voltex | http://www.voltexcomputers.com |
| Walkabout Travel Gear | http://www.walkabouttravelgear.com |
| Wall Street Journal Interactive | http://www.wsj.com |
| Wal-Mart | http://www.wal-mart.com |
| Wal-Mart Pharmacy | http://www.wal-mart.com/pharmacy |
| Waterhouse Web Broker | http://www.waterhouse.com |
| Way Cool Weddings | http://www.waycoolweddings.com |
| Weather Channel | nttp://www.weather.com |
| Weather Graphics | http://www.weathergraphics.com |
| Weather Research Center | http://www.wxresearch.com/~wrc/wrc.htm |
| Weather Simulator | http://www.members.aol.com/eburger/wxsim.html |
| Webauction | http://www.webauction.com |
| Web Shopper | http://www.webshopper.com |
| Web Street Securities | http://www.webstreetsecurities.com |
| Wedding Channel | http://www.vintagewedding.com |
| Wedding Expressions | http://www.weddingexpressions.com |
| West Point Market | http://www.westpoint-market.com |
| What in the World | http://www.whatintheworld.com |
| Whole Foods | http://www.wholefoods.com |
| Wholesale Fitness Products | http://www.shopsite.com/whfp |
| Wholesell.com | http://www.wholesell.com |
| Wholy Smokes | http://www.wholysmokes.com |
| Wide West Imports | http://www.big-mountain.com/widewestimports |
| Wild Alaska Smoked Salmon | http://www.smoked-fish.com |
| Wild Birds Forever | http://www.birdsforever.com/binoc.html |
| Wild Oats | http://www.wildoats.com |
| Wine Broker | http://www.thewinebrokers.com |
| Wine Law | http://www.winelaw.org |
| Wolf Camera | http://www.wolfcamera.com/wolfhome.html |
| Wolff Fishing Products | http://www.wolffishing.com |
| Wood N Crafts | http://www.wood-n-crafts.com |
| World Class Cigars | http://www.wccigars.com |
| World of Maps | http://www.worldofmaps.com |
| World Pen | http://www.worldpen.com/index.htm |
| World Traveler | http://www.worldtraveler.com |
| World Wide Art | http://www.world-wide-art.com/art/index.html |

| | |
|---|---|
| World Wide Sports | http://www.1888wwsports.com |
| Writer's Computer Store | http://www.writerscomputer.com |
| Writer's Digest | http://www.writersdigest.com |
| Writer's Edge | http://www.thewritersedge.com |
| Yacht Saver | http://www.yachtsaver.com |
| Yahoo! Auctions | http://auctions.yahoo.com |
| Yahoo! Finance | http://quote.yahoo.com |
| Yahoo! Shopping | http://shopping.yahoo.com |
| Zales | http://www.zales.com |
| ZD Inter@ctive Investor | http://www.zdii.com |
| Ziff-Davis Shareware | http://www.zdnet.com/swlib |
| Zones.com | http://www.zones.com |
| ZZZap | http://www.zzzap.com |

# Index

# About the Authors

Lisa and Jonathan Price are award-winning authors who have been writing about computers, software, and online technology for over a decade. They are the authors of more than a dozen books, including *Fun with Digital Imaging* (IDG Books), *The Dummies' Guide to Windows '95 for Kids and Parents* (IDG Books), *Discover Microsoft Home Essentials* (IDG Books), and *The Trail Guide to America Online* (Addison-Wesley). Their articles regularly appear in national magazines such as *Family Fun, Family PC, Reader's Digest, MacWorld, Harper's,* and *Cooking Light.*

Lisa is the Features Editor for KBkids.com (formerly BrainPlay.com), an online store that sells products for children. She has been active in e-commerce since its inception. Jonathan consults with teams developing online information systems, from CD-ROMs and Help systems to Web sites, at companies such as Apple, Canon, Nikon, Oracle, Pioneer, and Sony. He recently was elected an Associate Fellow of the Society for Technical Communication (STC). His book, *The Virtual Macintosh Playhouse,* won the top prize for a book, at the International STC annual convention.

Lisa and Jonathan regularly speak on the air and at conventions about e-commerce, online information, and writing for the Web. Their Web site is at http://www.theprices.com and they can be reached at ThePrices@swcp.com

And, yes, their last name really is Price.